ATHLETICS RANKINGS

and

RESULTS 2018

In Historical Perpective

Ton van Vuuren

CONTENTS

PREFACE

Content

This book is a comprehensive collection of results for events held at athletics meetings in 2017. Publication of these results is by no means original. Data and statistics can be found all over the web; www.iaaf.org, trackinsun.blogspot.com and www.tilastopaja.eu are particularly useful sites to consult if you are interested in athletics results of the highest level.

The added value this book offers compared with viewing single results of events of an individual athletic meeting is found in the compilation it provides. By amassing the most significant results in 2018 per event as well as results in major championships and world rankings in the past 5 years (or past 6 years), in addition to the highest world rankings of all time at the end of 2018, it is easier to compare results and rankings of the athletes, and to rate their strengths in a historical perspective as well. Of all the outdoor track events, the most important results in 2018 of the individual events are shown in just a few pages. This enables the reader to make an assessment of the athletes' performances during the year, and to rate the development of these performances. How consistent were these performances? Did they consist of many highs or lows?

The 2018 World Rankings are included on the same page as the results of the 2018 European Championships of the event concerned, enabling the reader to easily compare both.

In the pages that follow per event, the results of the World Indoor Championships, held in Birmingham, United Kingdom, 1-4 March 2018 (if applicable) are included, as well as the World Indoor Rankings of 2018.

Recorded next are the most important results (aside from the European Championships) of outdoor meetings of the *track* event concerned in the year 2018. Keep in mind, the results were not collected in this book of outdoor *field* events other than the European Championships in the year 2018, or of indoor track and field events (aside from the World Championships).

The next pages of each track and field event consist of what have been titled:

- 'OVERVIEW WORLDWIDE OUTDOOR CHAMPIONSHIP FINALISTS OF THE PAST 6 YEARS
- 'OVERVIEW WORLDWIDE INDOOR CHAMPIONSHIP FINALISTS OF THE PAST 5 YEARS
- 'OVERVIEW TOP 10 WORLD OUTDOOR RANKINGS OF THE PAST 5 YEARS
- 'OVERVIEW TOP 10 WORLD INDOOR RANKINGS OF THE PAST 5 YEARS

These pages allow the reader to compare:

a. the rankings and results of the athletes in finals of major outdoor and indoor championships worldwide (i.e. World Championships or Olympic Games) held between 2013 (outdoor) respectively 2014 (indoor) and 2018

b. the outdoor and indoor World Rankings between 2014 and 2018

c. the performances in Worldwide Championships of the athletes between 2013 (outdoor) respectively 2014 (indoor) and 2018 (a) with their standings in the world rankings between 2014 and 2018 (b).

By making these comparisons, the strengths of the athlete may be rated in their event in recent history. Please note that many athletes tend to repeat their participation in worldwide finals and Top 10 world rankings. Naturally these repetitions contribute to their status as a top athlete, and it is therefore easier to attribute a kind of 'hero'-status to them.

The information of each event ends with the all-time world rankings in that event by December 31st, 2018. If the times, distances or heights achieved in the past five years are compared with the all-time rankings, a deeper historical perspective can be drawn. Athletic heroes of the past may also be recalled when looking at these all-time rankings. Some of them are still found in the Top 45 of all-time rankings, despite several new technical and scientific developments which have taken place, and subsequently led to better times, distances and heights for other athletes since the end of these heroes' careers.

Analysis

When overseeing the results, what is striking is that the results highly depend on the manner in which they are observed. There is no analysis per event made in the book, but this is left up to the reader, as each analysis can be rather personal. Making such a personal 'discovery', when analysing the different data, gives a satisfaction to the reader of which he/she would be deprived if the analysis was made for him/her.

How to read the various rankings, as compiled below

When brackets are used, this indicates that the enclosed result shows the outcome of a previous round in the same meeting which was valuable to collect.

When brackets are used after the World Rankings for 2018, the abbreviation of a meeting is indicated. The abbreviations are explained in the pages with the name 'Venue Meetings', except for the abbreviations of marathon results.

The underscore sign beneath an athlete's name implies that the athlete beneath the sign did not advance to the round that the athlete above the sign did. Therefore, the sign divides the finalists from the semi-finalists, and the semi-finalists from athletes who did not qualify for the semi-finals.

Subjective choices

A collection of statistical data begins with making choices which have subjective elements, this one being no exception.

Some of the choices made are the following:

1. Only included are athletes in world rankings for the year 2018 who have attained certain minimum achievements. These minimum performances represent special feats which necessarily qualify as being 'historically significant'. The required minimum accomplishments, outdoor as well as

indoor, can be found in the page titled 'Required Minimum Achievements'.

2. Included are normally a maximum of 45 athletes per discipline in rankings, based on the conviction that the top level of the world's athletes reaches its limit around 45 athletes per discipline.

3. Not included are abbreviations of venue meetings in the world rankings if the event in which the athlete achieved the result that is part of these world rankings did not consist of sufficient athletes belonging to the top of the world class.

4. Not collected are results of field events meetings, with the exception of the World and European Championships. This is due to the author's personal preference, which is aimed more toward outdoor track events than field events. Accordingly, no results of indoor meetings have been collected, save World or European Championships.

5. Included are results of the 60m indoor Hurdles event in the paragraphs of the 100m and 110m outdoor Hurdles results. In these disciplines many of the same athletes compete. The Men's Heptathlon indoor results are included in the Decathlon outdoor results for the same reason. The Women's Pentathlon indoor results are included in the Heptathlon outdoor results for the same reason.

OUTDOOR VENUE MEETINGS 2018

Abbreviation:	Venue Meeting	date
Ass	African Championships, Assaba (NGR)	1/5-8-2018
Aub	Auburn (USA)	21-4-2018
Aus	Austin (USA)	31-3-2018; 14-4-2018
Azu	Azusa (USA)	20-4-2018
Bel	Bellinzona (SUI)	18-7-2018
Ber	Berlin (GER)	2-9-2018
Bir	Birmingham (GBR)	18-8-2018
BL	Bad Langensalza (GER)	30-6-2018
BM	Baie Mahault (FRA)	12-5-2018
BR	Baton Rouge (USA)	7-4-2018; 5-5-2018
Bri	Brisbane (AUS)	4-2-2018; 28-3-2018
Bru	Brussels (BEL)	31-8-2018
Car	Carquefou (FRA)	16-6-2018
CG	Coral Gables (USA)	7-4-2018; 14-4-2018
Cho	Chorzow (POL)	8-6-2018; 22-8-2018
Cle	Clermont (USA)	28-4-2018; 12-5-2018
Col	Columbia (USA)	21-4-2018
CON	Continental Cup, Ostrava (CZE)	8/9-9-2018
CV	Chula Vista (USA)	9-6-2018
Des	Dessau (GER)	8-6-2018
DM	Des Moines (USA)	28-4-2018
Do	Doha (QAT)	4-5-2018
Ebe	Eberstadt (GER)	26-8-2018
ECh	European Championships, Berlin (GER)	6/12-8-2018
Eug	Eugene (USA)	25/26-5-2018
Fay	Fayetteville (USA)	27-4-2018
Fuk	Fukagawa (JPN)	11-7-2018
Gai	Gainesville (USA)	30-3-2018; 13-4-2018
GC	Gold Coast (AUS), Commonwealth Games	8/15-4-2018
Göt	Göteborg (SWE)	18-8-2018
Gre	Greensboro (USA)	13-4-2018
Gtz	Götzis (GER)	26/27-5-2018
Hen	Hengelo (NED)	3-6-2018
Heu	Heusden-Zolder (BEL)	21-7-2018
Hue	Huelva (ESP)	8-6-2018
JAC	Jamaican Championships, Kingston (JAM)	21/24-6-2018

Abbreviation:	Venue Meeting	date
Jak	Asian Games, Jakarta (INA)	25/30-8-2018
KeT	Kenyan Trials, Nairobi (KEN)	21/23-6-2018
Kin	Kingston (JAM)	19-5-2018; 9-6-2018
Kno	Knoxville (USA)	12/13-5-2018
Lau	Lausanne (SUI)	4/5-7-2018
LCF	La Chaux-de-Fonds (SUI)	1-7-2018
Lev	Leverkusen (GER)	16-6-2018
Lon	London (GBR)	21/22-7-2018
Lub	Lubbock (USA)	27-4-2018
Luz	Luzern (SUI)	9-7-2018
Mad	Madrid (ESP)	22-6-2018
Mel	Melbourne (AUS)	13-12-2018
Mnt	Montreuil (FRA)	19-6-2018
Mon	Monaco (Mon)	20-7-2018
Mtv	Montverde (USA)	9-6-2018
NAC	NACAC Championships, Toronto (CAN)	8/12/-8-2018
Nai	Nairobi (KEN)	17-2-2018
Nan	Nancy (FRA)	27-6-2018
NCA	NCAA Championships, Eugene (USA)	6/9-6-2018
Osa	Osaka (JPN)	20-5-2018
Osl	Oslo (NOR)	7-6-2018
Ost	Ostrava (CZE)	12/13-6-2018
PA	Palo Alto (USA)	31-3-2018; 3-5-2018; 12/13-5-2018
Paa	Paarl (RSA)	22-3-2018
Pad	Padua (ITA)	2-9-2018
Par	Paris (FRA)	30-6-2018
Per	Perth (AUS)	20-1-2018
Pra	Prague (CZE)	4-6-2018
Pre	Pretoria (RSA)	10-2-2018; 8-3-2018; 16/17-3-2018
Rab	Rabat (MAR)	13-7-2018
Ral	Raleigh (USA)	3-8-2018
Rat	Ratingen (GER)	16/17-6-2018
Rom	Rome (ITA)	31-5-2018
Rov	Rovereto (ITA)	23-8-2018
Sac	Sacramento (USA)	25-5-2018
Sha	Shanghai (CHN)	12-5-2018
Sto	Stockholm (SWE)	10-6-2018
Sze	Székesfehervar (HUN)	1/2-7-2018
Tal	Talence (FRA)	15/16-9-2018
Tam	Tampa (USA)	25-5-2018

Abbreviation:	Venue Meeting	date
Tem	Tempe (USA)	6/7-4-2018
Tmp	Tampere (FIN)	13-7-2018
Tor	Torrance (USA)	21-4-2018
Tub	Tübingen (GER)	16-6-2018
Tuc	Tucson (USA)	28-4-2018
Tur	Turku (FIN)	5-6-2018
USC	US Championships, Des Moines (USA)	21/24-6-2018
Wac	Waco (USA)	21-4-2018; 13-5-2018
WC	World Cup, London (GBR)	15-7-2018
Yam	Yamaguchi (JPN)	8-12-2018
Yok	Yokohama (JPN)	20-10-2018; 10-11-2018
Zag	Zagreb (CRO)	3/4-9-2018
Zhu	Zhukovskiy (RUS)	13-6-2018; 23-6-2018; 30-6-2018; 1-7-2018
Zü	Zürich (SUI)	29/30-8-2018

Required Minimal Achievements

Event	Men Outdoor	Men Indoor	Women Outdoor	Women Indoor
60m		6.60		7.20
100m	10.05		11.15	
200m	20.30	21.00	22.70	23.20
400m	45.30	46.50	51.20	52.20
800m	1.45.50	1.47.30	2.00.00	2.02.00
1.500m	3.35.30	3.41.00	4.05.50	4.12.50
Mile	3.54.00	3.57.00	4.30.00	4.34.00
3.000m	7.43.00	7.46.00	9.00.00	9.00.00
5.000m	13.16.00		15.09.00	
10.000m	27.40.00		32.00.00	
60m hurdles		7.63		8.00
100m hurdles			12.90	
110m hurdles	13.45			
400m hurdles	49.30		56.00	
300m steeplechase	8.22.50		9.36.00	
High jump	≥ 2.30	≥ 2.30	≥ 1.94	≥ 1.94
Pole vault	≥ 5.70	≥ 5.70	≥ 4.50	≥ 4.50
Long jump	≥ 8.08	≥ 8.08	≥ 6.70	≥ 6.70
Triple jump	≥ 17.00	≥ 17.00	≥ 14.00	≥ 14.00
Javelin Throw	≥ 81.50		≥ 62.00	
Discus Throw	≥ 64.00		≥ 63.00	
Hammer Throw	≥ 77.00		≥ 70.00	
Shot Put	≥ 20.30	≥ 20.10	≥ 18.70	≥ 18.35
Pentathlon				≥ 4480 pts
Heptathlon		≥ 5900 pts	≥ 6260 pts	
Decathlon	≥ 8160 pts			
4 x 100m relay	39.15		44.00	
4 x 400m relay	3.04.00	3.09.00	3.30.00	3.32.00
Marathon	2.12.00			2.32.00

100 m Men Outdoor / 60 m Men Indoor

EUROPEAN CHAMPIONSHIPS 2018: 7-8-2018:

1.	Zharnel Hughes (GBR)	(10.01)	9.95
2.	Reece Prescod (GBR)	(10.10)	9.96
3.	Jak Ali Harvey (TUR)	(10.09)	10.01
4.	Chijindu Ujah (GBR)	(10.14)	10.06
5.	Filippo Tortu (ITA)	(10.12)	10.08
6.	Churandy Martina (NED)	(10.18)	10.16
7.	Emre Zafer Barnes (TUR)	(10.21)	10.29
	Jimmy Vicaut (FRA)	(9.97)	dns

9.	Yazaldes Nascimento (POR)		10.22
10.	Alex Wilson (SUI)		10.22
11.	Lamont Marcell Jacobs (ITA)		10.28
12.	Dominik Kopec (POL)		10.29
13.	Ján Volko (SVK)		10.31
14.	Carlos Nascimento (POR)		10.31
15.	Christopher Garia (NED)		10.31
16.	Lucas Jakubczyk (GER)		10.32
17.	Zdenek Stromsik (CZE)		10.37
18.	Julian Reus (GER)		10.37
19.	Hensley Paulina (NED)	(10.34)	10.38
20.	Federico Cattaneo (ITA)		10.39
21.	José Lopes (POR)	(10.38)	10.40
22.	Jonathan Quarcoo (NOR)	(10.37)	10.45
23.	Silvan Wicki (SUI)	(10.28)	10.49
24.	Amaury Golitin (FRA)		10.55

25.	Yigitcan Hekimoglu (TUR)	10.40
26.	Kevin Kranz (GER)	10.41

WORLD RANKING 2017:

1.	Christian Coleman (USA)	9.79(Bru)
2.	Ronnie Baker (USA)	9.87(Cho)
3.	Noah Lyles (USA)	9.88(USC)
4.	Michael Rodgers (USA)	9.88(USC)
5.	Zharnel Hughes (GBR)	9.91(Kin)
	Su Bingtian (CHN)	9.91(Mad)
	Jimmy Vicaut (FRA)	9.91(Par)
8.	Isiah Young (USA)	9.92(Mtv)
9.	Cameron Burrell (USA)	9.93(USC)
	Akani Simbine (RSA)	9.93(Lon)
11.	Arthur Cissé (CIV)	9.94(Lev)
	Reece Prescod (GBR)	9.94(Bir)
	Yohan Blake (JAM)	9.94(Bru)
14.	Tyquendo Tracey (JAM)	9.96(Lon)
15.	Jaylen Bacon (USA)	9.97(Sac)
	Xie Zhenye (CHN)	9.97(Mnt)
	Barakat Al Harthi (OMA)	9.97
18.	Andre Ewers (JAM)	9.98(Tam)
19.	Kendal Williams (USA)	9.99(Kno)
	Filippo Tortu (ITA)	9.99(Mad)
	Jak Ali Harvey (TUR)	9.99(Bel)
22.	Cejhae Greene (ANT)	10.00
	Tosi Ogunode (QAT)	10.00(Jak)
	Ryota Yamagata (JPN)	10.00(Jak)
25.	Gavin Smellie (CAN)	10.01
	Bryce Robinson (USA)	10.01
	Alonso Edward (PAN)	10.01
	Emile Erasmus (RSA)	10.01
29.	Jeff Demps (USA)	10.02(USC)
	Paulo Camilo de Oliveira (BRA)	10.02
31.	Justin Gatlin (USA)	10.03(Ost)
	Abdullah Abkar Mohammed (KSA)	10.03(Par)
	Hassan Taftian (IRI)	10.03(Par)
	Mario Burke (BAR)	10.03
35.	Ojie Edoburun (GBR)	10.04(Pra)
36.	Jason Rodgers (SKN)	10.05

WORLD INDOOR CHAMPIONSHIPS: 3-3-2018:

1. Christian Coleman (USA)   (6.45)   6.37
2. Su Bingtian (CHN)   (6.52)   6.42
3. Ronnie Baker (USA)   (6.52)   6.44
4. Xie Zhenye (CHN)   (6.57)   6.52
5. Hassan Taftian (IRI)   (6.57)   6.53
6. Ján Volko (SVK)   (6.58)   6.59
7. Sean Safo-Antwi (GHA)   (6.59)   6.60
8. Emre Zafer Barnes (TUR)   (6.58)   6.64
----
9. Arthur Cissé (CIV)   6.59
   Ben Youssef Meité (CIV)   6.59
11. Everton Clarke (JAM)   6.63
   Abd. Abkar Mohammed (KSA)(6.62) 6.63
   Andrew Robertson (GBR)   6.63
14. Kimmari Roach (JAM)   6.65
   Remigiusz Olszewski (POL)   6.65
16. Warren Fraser (BAH)   6.66
17. Ángel David Rodríguez (ESP)   6.67
   Dominik Záleský (CZE)   6.67
19. Michael Pohl (GER)   6.71
20. Odain Rose (SWE)   6.74
21. Tosin Ogunode (QAT)   (6.72)   6.77
22. Jean-Yann de Grace (MRI)   (6.78)   6.83
   Chijindu Ujah (GBR)   (6.59)   dsq
   Kim Collins (SKN)   (6.77)   dns
----
25. Peter Emelieze (GER)   6.77
26. Keston Bledman (TTO)   6.79
27. Emmanuel Callender (TTO)   6.80

WORLD INDOOR RANKING 2018:

1. Christian Coleman (USA)   6.34
2. Ronnie Baker (USA)   6.40
3. Su Bingtian (CHN)   6.42
4. Michael Rodgers (USA)   6.50
5. Hassan Taftian (IRI)   6.51
   Bryce Robinson (USA)   6.51
7. Andre Ewers (JAM)   6.52
   Yunier Pérez (ESP)   6.52
   Blake Smith (USA)   6.52
   Xie Zhenye (CHN)   6.52
   Elijah Hall-Thompson (USA)   6.52
12. Chijindu Ujah (GBR)   6.53
   Raheem Chambers (JAM)   6.53
14. Everton Clarke (JAM)   6.54
   Kirk Wilson (USA)   6.54
   Brandon Carnes (USA)   6.54
   Jeff Demps (USA)   6.54
18. Jeryl Brazil (USA)   6.55
   Ben Youssef Meité (CIV)   6.55
   Emre Zafer Barnes (TUR)   6.55
   Demek Kemp (USA)   6.55
22. Ojie Edoburun (GBR)   6.56
23. Tevin Hester (USA)   6.57
   Arthur Cissé (CIV)   6.57
   Christophe Lemaitre (FRA)   6.57
   Noah Lyles (USA)   6.57
   Ján Volko (SVK)   6.57
28. Ejowvokoghene Oduduru (NGR)   6.58
29. Kenzo Cotton (USA)   6.59
   Kimmari Roach (JAM)   6.59
   Andrew Fisher (BRN)   6.59
   Adam Gemili (GBR)   6.59
   Sean Safo-Antwi (GHA)   6.59
   Jaylen Mitchell (USA)   6.59
   Anthony Schwartz (USA)   6.59
36. John Otugade (GBR); Tré James (USA) 6.60
   Kim Collins (SKN); Jaylen Bacon (USA) 6.60
   Jalen Miller (USA)   6.60
   Julian Reus (GER)   6.60
   Abdullah Abkar Mohammed (KSA)   6.60
   Emelio Ferguson (JAM)   6.60
   Zdenek Stromsik (CZE)   6.60
   Desmond Lawrence (USA)   6.60
   John Teeters (USA)   6.60
   Derrius Rodgers (USA)   6.60
   Mobolade Ajomale (CAN)   6.60

Shanghai, 12-5-2018:
1.	Reece Prescod (GBR)	10.04
2.	Su Bingtian (CHN)	10.05
3.	Xie Zhenye (CHN)	10.17
4.	Chijindu Ujah (GBR)	10.18
5.	Isiah Young (USA)	10.18
6.	Ramil Guliyev (TUR)	10.20
7.	Justin Gatlin (USA)	10.20
8.	Andre de Grasse (CAN)	10.25

Eugene, 26-5-2018: + 2.4 m/s:
1.	Ronnie Baker (USA)	9.78
2.	Christian Coleman (USA)	9.84
3.	Reece Prescod (GBR)	9.88
4.	Su Bingtian (CHN)	9.90
5.	Isiah Young (USA)	9.94
6.	Chijindu Ujah (GBR)	10.12
7.	Ben Youssef Meité (CIV)	10.13
8.	Gavin Smellie (CAN)	10.16

Rome, 31-5-2018:
1.	Ronnie Baker (USA)	9.93
2.	Jimmy Vicaut (FRA)	10.02
3.	Filippo Tortu (ITA)	10.04
4.	Christian Coleman (USA)	10.06
5.	Akani Simbine (RSA)	10.13
6.	Michael Rodgers (USA)	10.13

Eugene, NCAA, 9-6-2018:
1.	Cameron Burrell (USA)	(10.07)	10.13
2.	Elijah Hall-Thompson (USA)	(10.10)	10.17
3.	Andre Ewers (JAM)	(10.00+)	10.19
4.	Cravon Gillespie (USA)	(10.02+)	10.27
5.	Raheem Chambers (JAM)	(10.05+)	10.33
6.	McKinley West (USA)	(10.10)	10.36
7.	Cejhae Greene (ANT)	(10.05+)	10.37
8.	Mario Burke (BAR)	(10.10)	10.41

9.	Waheem Williams (JAM)		10.06+
10.	Kenzo Cotton (USA)	(10.07)	10.09
11.	Jaylen Bacon (USA)		10.10
12.	Divine Oduduru (NGR)		10.12
13.	TJ Brock (USA)		10.13+
14.	Riak Reese (USA)		10.14+
15.	Darryl Haraway (USA)		10.15
16.	Kendal Williams (USA)		10.16

Kingston, 9-6-2018:
1.	Zharnel Hughes (GBR)	9.91
2.	Noah Lyles (USA)	9.93
3.	Yohan Blake (JAM)	10.00

Ostrava, 13-6-2018:
1.	Justin Gatlin (USA)	10.03
2.	Akani Simbine (RSA)	10.13
3.	Michael Rodgers (USA)	10.15

Montreuil, 19-6-2018:
1.	Xie Zhenye (CHN)	9.97
2.	Akane Simbine (RSA)	10.04
3.	Paulo Camilo de Oliveira (BRA)	10.10

Madrid, 22-6-2018:
1.	Su Bingtian (CHN)	(10.04)	9.91
2.	Filippo Tortu (ITA)	(10.04)	9.99
3.	Akane Simbine (RSA)	(9.98)	10.01
4.	Paulo Camilo de Oliveira (BRA)		10.06
5.	Henricho Bruintjes (RSA)	(10.11)	10.13

JAM CHAMPIONSHIPS, Kingston, 22-6-2018:
1.	Tyquendo Tracey		10.07
2.	Kenroy Anderson	(10.11)	10.24
3.	Nesta Carter	(10.19)	10.30
4.	Javon Tucker		10.33
5.	Kimmari Roach		10.34
6.	Romario Williams		10.39
7.	Julian Forte	(10.11)	19.80

Yohan Blake	(10.11)	dns

US CHAMPIONSHIPS, Des Moines, 22-6-2018:

1.	Noah Lyles	(9.89)	9.88
2.	Ronnie Baker	(9.94)	9.90
3.	Kendal Williams	(10.02)	10.00
4.	Isiah Young	(9.93)	10.00
5.	Cameron Burrell	(9.93)	10.04
6.	Jeff Demps	(10.02)	10.13
7.	Bryce Robinson	(10.10)	10.55
8.	Jaylen Bacon	(10.09)	dns
9.	Kenzo Cotton	(10.13)	10.14
10.	Cordero Gray	(10.13)	10.18
11.	Cravon Gillespie	(10.13)	10.23
12.	Ryan Clark		10.26
13.	Riak Reese	(10.14)	10.27
14.	Remontay McClain	(10.13)	10.28
15.	Chris Jefferson	(10.12)	10.37
	Michael Rodgers	(9.89)	dns
17.	Demek Kemp		10.19
18.	McKinley West		10.22
19.	Tevin Hester		10.23
20.	Jarrion Lawson		10.23

Paris, 30-6-2018:

1.	Ronnie Baker (USA)	9.88
2.	Jimmy Vicaut (FRA)	9.91
3.	Su Bingtian (CHN)	9.91
4.	Akane Simbine (RSA)	9.94
5.	Yohan Blake (JAM)	10.03
6.	Michael Rodgers (USA)	10.10
7.	Arthur Cissé (CIV)	10.15
8.	Jeff Demps (USA)	10.23

Rabat, 13-7-2018:

1.	Christian Coleman (USA)	9.98
2.	Ronnie Baker (USA)	9.98
3.	Noah Lyles (USA)	9.99
4.	Michael Rodgers (USA)	10.01
5.	Reece Prescod (GBR)	10.09
6.	Chijindu Ujah (GBR)	10.19

London, 21-7-2018:

1.	Ronnie Baker (USA)	(9.96)	9.90
2.	Zharnel Hughes (GBR)	(9.97)	9.93
3.	Akane Simbine (RSA)	(9.93)	9.94
4.	Yohan Blake (JAM)	(9.99)	9.95
5.	Michael Rodgers (USA)	(9.96)	9.98
6.	Tyquendo Tracey (JAM)	(9.96)	9.98
7.	Isiah Young (USA)		10.01
8.	Xie Zhenye (CHN)	(10.01)	10.01
9.	Cameron Burrell (USA)		10.07
10.	Ojie Edoburun (GBR)		10.10
	Jeff Demps (USA)		10.10
12.	Hassan Taftian (IRI)		10.15
13.	Brandon Carnes (USA)		10.16
14.	Harry Aikines-Aryeetey (GBR)		10.18

AFR CHAMPIONSHIPS, Assaba (NGR), 2-8-2018:

1.	Akane Simbine (RSA)		10.25
2.	Arthur Cissé (CIV)	(10.29)	10.33
3.	Simon Magakwe (RSA)		10.35
4.	Ben Youssef Meité (CIV)		10.36

NACAC CHAMPIONSHIPS, Toronto, 11-8-2018:

1.	Tyquendo Tracey (JAM)		10.03
2.	Kendal Williams (USA)		10.11
3.	Cameron Burrell (USA)		10.12
4.	Bismark Boateng (CAN)		10.16
5.	Gavin Smellie (CAN)	(10.15)	10.21
6.	Warren Fraser (BAH)	(10.20)	10.26
	Kenroy Anderson (JAM)		dnf

Birmingham, 18-8-2018:

1.	Christian Coleman (USA)	(10.01)	9.94
2.	Reece Prescod (GBR)		9.94
3.	Noah Lyles (USA)		9.98
4.	Yohan Blake (JAM)	(10.03)	9.99
5.	Zharnel Hughes (GBR)		10.05
6.	Akane Simbine (RSA)	(10.07)	10.09
7.	Tyquendo Tracey (JAM)		10.15
8.	Chijindu Ujah (GBR)	(10.13)	10.17
9.	Michael Rodgers (USA)		10.22

Jakarta, 26-8-2018:

1.	Su Bingtian (CHN)	9.92
2.	Femi Ogunode (QAT)	10.00
3.	Ryota Yamagata (JPN)	10.00

Brussels, 31-8-2018:
1. Christian Coleman (USA)   9.79
2. Ronnie Baker (USA)   9.93
3. Yohan Blake (JAM)   9.94
4. Reece Prescod (GBR)   9.99
5. Akane Simbine (RSA)   10.03
6. Michael Rodgers (USA)   10.16
7. Chijindu Ajah (GBR)   10.17
8. Isiah Young (USA)   10.26

CONTINENTAL CUP, Ostrava, 9-9-2018:
1. Noah Lyles (AME)   10.01
2. Su Bingtian (ASI)   10.03
3. Akane Simbine (AFR)   10.11
4. Jak Ali Harvey (EUR)   10.19
5. Arthur Cissé (AFR)   10.23

OVERVIEW WORLDWIDE OUTDOOR CHAMPIONSHIP FINALISTS OF PAST 6 YEARS

	Wch 17	OG 16	Wch 15	Wch 13
Justin Gatlin (USA)	9.92 (1)	9.89 (2)	9.80 (2)	9.85 (2)
Christian Coleman (USA)	9.94 (2)			
Usain Bolt (JAM)	9.95 (3)	9.81 (1)	9.79 (1)	9.77 (1)
Yohan Blake (JAM)	9.99 (4)	9.93 (4)		
Akani Simbine (RSA)	10.01 (5)	9.94 (5)		
Jimmy Vicaut (FRA)	10.08 (6)	10.04 (7)	10.00 (8)	
Reece Prescod (GBR)	10.17 (7)			
Su Bingtian (CHN)	10.27 (8)		10.06 (9)	
Andre de Grasse (CAN)		9.91 (3)	9.92 (3)	
Ben Youssef Meité (CIV)		9.96 (6)		
Trayvon Bromell (USA)		10.06 (8)	9.92 (3)	
Mike Rodgers (USA)			9.94 (5)	10.04 (6)
Tyson Gay (USA)			10.00 (6)	
Asafa Powell (JAM)			10.00 (7)	
Nesta Carter (JAM)				9.95 (3)
Kemar Bailey-Cole (JAM)				9.98 (4)
Christophe Lemaitre (FRA)				10.06 (7)
James Dasaolu (GBR)				10.21 (8)

OVERVIEW WORLDWIDE INDOOR CHAMPIONSHIP FINALISTS OF PAST 5 YEARS

	Wch 18	Wch 16	Wch 14
Christian Coleman (USA)	6.37 (1)		
Su Bingtian (CHN)	6.42 (2)	6.54 (5)	6.52 (4)
Ronnie Baker (USA)	6.44 (3)		
Xie Zhenye (CHN)	6.52 (4)	6.53 (4)	
Hassan Taftian (IRI)	6.53 (5)		
Ján Volko (SVK)	6.59 (6)		
Sean Safo-Antwi (GHA)	6.60 (7)		
Emre Zafer Barnes (TUR)	6.64 (8)		
Trayvon Bromell (USA)		6.47 (1)	
Asafa Powell (JAM)		6.50 (2)	
Ramon Gittens (BAR)		6.51 (3)	
Mike Rodgers (USA)		6.54 (6)	
Marvin Bracy (USA)		6.56 (7)	6.51 (2)
Kim Collins (SKN)		6.56 (8)	
Richard Kilty (GBR)			6.49 (1)
Femi Ogunode (QAT)			6.52 (3)
Gerald Phiri (ZAM)			6.52 (5)
Dwain Chambers (GBR)			6.53 (6)
Nesta Carter (JAM)			6.57 (7)
Kimmari Roach (JAM)			6.58 (8)

OVERVIEW TOP 10 WORLD OUTDOOR RANKINGS OF PAST 5 YEARS

	2018	**2017**	**2016**	**2015**	**2014**
Christian Coleman (USA)	9.79 (1)	9.82 (1)			
Ronnie Baker (USA)	9.87 (2)				
Noah Lyles (USA)	9.88 (3)				
Michael Rodgers (USA)	9.89 (4)			9.86 (5)	9.91 (4)
Zharnel Hughes (GBR)	9.91 (5)				
Su Bingtian (CHN)	9.91 (5)				
Jimmy Vicaut (FRA)	9.91 (5)		9.86 (4)	9.86 (5)	9.95 (8)
Isiah Young (USA)	9.92 (8)				
Cameron Burrell (USA)	9.93 (9)	9.93 (6)			
Akani Simbine (RSA)	9.93 (9)	9.92 (4)	9.89 (5)		
Yohan Blake (JAM)		9.90 (2)	9.93 (10)		
Julian Forte (JAM)		9.91 (3)			
Justin Gatlin (USA)		9.92 (4)	9.80 (1)	9.74 (1)	9.77 (1)
Christopher Belcher (USA)		9.93 (6)			
Wayde van Niekerk (RSA)		9.94 (8)			
Thando Roto (RSA)		9.95 (9)			
Usain Bolt (JAM)		9.95 (9)	9.81 (2)	9.79 (2)	
Trayvon Bromell (USA)			9.84 (3)	9.84 (4)	
Femi Ogunode (QAT)			9.91 (6)	9.91 (9)	9.93 (5)
Andre de Grasse (CAN)			9.91 (6)		
Jak Ali Harvey (TUR)			9.92 (8)		
Asafa Powell (JAM)			9.92 (9)	9.81 (3)	9.87 (3)
Kim Collins (SKN)			9.93 (10)		9.96 (9)
Keston Bledman (TTO)				9.86 (5)	
Tyson Gay (USA)				9.87 (8)	9.93 (5)
Nickel Ashmeade (JAM)				9.91 (9)	
Richard Thompson (TTO)					9.82 (2)
Kemarley Brown (JAM)					9.93 (5)
Chijindu Ujah (GBR)					9.96 (9)
Nesta Carter (JAM)					9.96 (9)
Kemar Bailey-Cole (JAM)					9.96 (9)

OVERVIEW TOP 10 WORLD INDOOR RANKINGS OF PAST 5 YEARS

	2018	**2017**	**2016**	**2015**	**2014**
Christian Coleman (USA)	6.34 (1)	6.45 (1)			
Ronnie Baker (USA)	6.40 (2)	6.45 (1)	6.47 (2)	6.52 (6)	
Su Bingtian (CHN)	6.42 (3)		6.50 (6)		
Michael Rodgers (USA)	6.50 (4)		6.51 (8)	6.52 (6)	6.51 (10)
Hassan Taftian (IRI)	6.51 (5)				
Bryce Robinson (USA)	6.51 (5)				
Andre Ewers (JAM)	6.52 (7)				
Yunier Pérez (CUB)	6.52 (7)	6.53 (5)			6.49 (4)
Blake Smith (USA)	6.52 (7)				
Xie Zhenye (CHN)	6.52 (7)				
Elijah Hall-Thompson (USA)	6.52 (7)				
Kendal Williams (USA)		6.51 (3)			
Kim Collins (SKN)		6.52 (4)	6.49 (5)	6.47 (1)	6.49 (4)
Cameron Burrell (USA)		6.53 (5)	6.48 (4)		
Richard Kilty (GBR)		6.54 (7)	6.50 (6)	6.51 (3)	6.49 (4)
Leshon Collins (USA)		6.54 (7)			
Chijindu Ujah (GBR)		6.56 (9)			
Sean Safo-Antwi (GHA)		6.56 (9)			
Jaylen Bacon (USA)		6.56 (9)			
Ryan Shields (JAM)		6.56 (9)			
Asafa Powell (JAM)			6.44 (1)	6.52 (6)	
Trayvon Bromell (USA)			6.47 (2)		
Marvin Bracy (USA)			6.51 (8)		6.48 (2)
Ramon Gittens (BAR)			6.51 (8)		
Ryan Bailey (USA)				6.50 (2)	
Akeem Haynes (CAN)				6.51 (3)	
Trell Kimmons (USA)				6.51 (3)	6.49 (4)
James Dasaolu (GBR)				6.52 (6)	6.47 (1)
John Teeters (USA)				6.52 (6)	
Jimmy Vicaut (FRA)					6.48 (2)
Tosin Ogunode (QAT)					6.50 (8)
Nesta Carter (JAM)					6.50 (8)
Femi Ogunode (QAT)					6.51 (10)

WORLD RANKING ALL TIME:

1.	Usain Bolt (JAM)	9.58 (2009)
2.	Tyson Gay (USA)	9.69 (2009)
	Yohan Blake (JAM)	9.69 (2012)
4.	Asafa Powell (JAM)	9.72 (2008)
5.	Justin Gatlin (USA)	9.74 (2015)
6.	Nesta Carter (JAM)	9.78 (2010)
7.	Maurice Greene (USA)	9.79 (1999)
	Christian Coleman (USA)	9.79 (2018)
9.	Steve Mullings (JAM)	9.80 (2011)
10.	Richard Thompson (TTO)	9.82 (2014)
11.	Donovan Bailey (CAN)	9.84 (1996)
	Bruny Surin (CAN)	9.84 (1999)
	Trayvon Bromell (USA)	9.84 (2015)
14.	Leroy Burrell (USA)	9.85 (1994)
	Olusoji Fasuba (NGR)	9.85 (2006)
	Michael Rodgers (USA)	9.85 (2011)
17.	Carl Lewis (USA)	9.86 (1991)
	Frank Fredericks (NAM)	9.86 (1996)
	Ato Boldon (TTO)	9.86 (1998)
	Francis Obikwelu (POR)	9.86 (2004)
	Keston Bledman (TTO)	9.86 (2012)
	Jimmy Vicaut (FRA)	9.86 (2015)
23.	Linford Christie (GBR)	9.87 (1993)
	Obadele Thompson (BAR)	9.87 (1998)
	Ronnie Baker (USA)	9.87 (2018)
26.	Shawn Crawford (USA)	9.88 (2004)
	Walter Dix (USA)	9.88 (2010)
	Ryan Bailey (USA)	9.88 (2010)
	Michael Frater (JAM)	9.88 (2011)
	Noah Lyles (USA)	9.88 (2018)
31.	Travis Padgett (USA)	9.89 (2008)
	Darvis Patton (USA)	9.89 (2008)
	Ngonidzashe Makusha (ZIM)	9.89 (2011)
	Akani Simbine (RSA)	9.89 (2016)
35.	Nickel Ashmeade (JAM)	9.90 (2013)
36.	Dennis Mitchell (USA)	9.91 (1996)
	Leonard Scott (USA)	9.91 (2006)
	Derrick Atkins (BAH)	9.91 (2007)
	Daniel Bailey (ANT)	9.91 (2009)
	Churandy Martina (NED)	9.91 (2012)
	James Dasaolu (GBR)	9.91 (2013)
	Femi Ogunode (QAT)	9.91 (2015)
	Andre de Grasse (CAN)	9.91 (2016)
	Julian Forte (JAM)	9.91 (2017)
	Zharnel Hughes (GBR)	9.91 (2018)
	Su Bingtian (CHN)	9.91 (2018)

WORLD RANKING ALL TIME INDOOR (60m):

1.	Christian Coleman (USA)	6.34 (2018)
2.	Maurice Greene (USA)	6.39 (1998)
3.	Ronnie Baker (USA)	6.40 (2018)
4.	Andre Cason (USA)	6.41 (1992)
5.	Dwain Chambers (GBR)	6.42 (2009)
	Su Bingtian (CHN)	6.42 (2018)
7.	Tim Harden (USA)	6.43 (1999)
8.	Asafa Powell (JAM)	6.44 (2016)
9.	Bruny Surin (CAN)	6.45 (1993)
	Leonard Myles-Mills (GHA)	6.45 (1999)
	Terrence Trammell (USA)	6.45 (2001)
	Justin Gatlin (USA)	6.45 (2003)
	Ronald Pognon (FRA)	6.45 (2005)
	Trell Kimmons (USA)	6.45 (2012)
15.	Jon Drummond (USA)	6.46 (1998)
	Marcus Brunson (USA)	6.46 (1999)
	Jason Gardener (GBR)	6.46 (1999)
	Tim Montgomery (USA)	6.46 (2001)
	Leonard Scott (USA)	6.46 (2005)
20.	Linford Christie (GBR)	6.47 (1995)
	Shawn Crawford (USA)	6.47 (2004)
	Dwight Phillips (USA)	6.47 (2005)
	Lerone Clarke (JAM)	6.47 (2012)
	James Dasaolu (GBR)	6.47 (2014)
	Kim Collins (SKN)	6.47 (2015)
	Trayvon Bromell (CAN)	6.47 (2016)
27.	Leroy Burrell (USA)	6.48 (1991)
	Deji Aliu (NGR)	6.48 (1999)
	Morne Nagel (RSA)	6.48 (2002)
	John Capel (USA)	6.48 (2003)
	Michael Rodgers (USA)	6.48 (2011)
	Jimmy Vicaut (FRA)	6.48 (2013)
	Marvin Bracy (USA)	6.48 (2014)
	Cameron Burrell (USA)	6.48 (2016)
35.	Mark McKoy (CAN)	6.49 (1993)
	Colin Jackson (GBR)	6.49 (1994)
	Michael Green (JAM)	6.49 (1997)
	Ato Boldon (TTO)	6.49 (1997)
	Randall Evans (USA)	6.49 (1997)
	Freddy Mayola (CUB)	6.49 (2000)
	Coby Miller (USA)	6.49 (2003)
	Olusoji Fasuba (NGR)	6.49 (2007)
	Nesta Carter (JAM)	6.49 (2012)
	D'Angelo Cherry (USA)	6.49 (2013)
	Yunier Pérez (CUB)	6.49 (2014)
	Richard Kilty (GBR)	6.49 (2014)

200 m Men

EUROPEAN CHAMPIONSHIPS 2018: 9-8-2018:

1.	Ramil Guliyev (TUR)	(20.33)	19.76
2.	Nethaneel Mitchell-Blake (GBR)	(20.35)	20.04
3.	Alex Wilson (SUI)	(20.16)	20.04
4.	Bruno Hortelano (ESP)	(20.29)	20.05
5.	Adam Gemili (GBR)	(20.46)	20.10
6.	Eseosa Desalu (ITA)	(20.35)	20.13
7.	Leon Reid (IRL)	(20.38)	20.37
8.	Solomon Bockarie (NED)	(20.41)	20.39

9.	Mickael-Méba Zeze (FRA)		20.49
10.	Churandy Martina (NED)		20.51
11.	Likoúrgos Tsákonas (GRE)	(20.49)	20.54
12.	Serhiy Smelyk (UKR)		20.54
13.	Ján Volko (SVK)		20.58
14.	Robin Vanderbemden (BEL)	(20.50)	20.62
15.	Steven Müller (GER)		20.76
16.	Daniel Rodríguez (ESP)		20.77
17.	Andrew Howe (ITA)	(20.60)	20.78
18.	Robin Erewa (GER)	(20.69)	20.79
19.	Davide Manenti (ITA)	(20.70)	20.81
20.	Aleixo Platini Menga (GER)		20.83
21.	Taymir Burnet (NED)	(20.67)	20.84
22.	Jonathan Quarcoo (NOR)	(20.77)	21.07
	Stuart Dutamby (FRA)	(20.64)	dns

24.	Marcus Lawler (IRL)	20.80
25.	Delano Williams (GBR)	20.89

WORLD RANKING 2018:

1.	Noah Lyles (USA)	19.65(Mon)
2.	Clarence Munyai (RSA)	19.69(Pre)
3.	Steven Gardiner (BAH)	19.75(CG)
4.	Ramil Guliyev (TUR)	19.76(ECh)
5.	Akeem Bloomfield (JAM)	19.81(Lon)
6.	Michael Norman (USA)	19.84(Par)
7.	Alonso Edward (PAN)	19.90(Luz)
8.	Alex Quiñónez (ECU)	19.93
	Isiah Young (USA)	19.93(Mtv)
10.	Isaac Makwala (BOT)	19.96(Osa)
11.	Kyle Greaux (TTO)	19.97
12.	Aaron Brown (CAN)	19.98(Osl)
13.	Jereem Richards (TTO)	19.99(Do)
	Rai Benjamin (USA)	19.99(Par)
15.	Ncincilili Titi (RSA)	20.00
	Bernardo Baloyes (COL)	20.00
17.	Luxolo Adams (RSA)	20.01
18.	Bruno Hortelano-Roig (ESP)	20.04
	Nethaneel Mitchell-Blake (GBR)	20.04(ECh)
	Alex Wilson (SUI)	20.04(ECh)
21.	Anaso Jobodwana (RSA)	20.07
22.	Adam Gemili (GBR)	20.10(ECh)
23.	Elijah Hall-Thompson (USA)	20.11(Aus)
24.	Ejowvokoghene Odururu (NGR)	20.13(Wac)
	Ameer Webb (USA)	20.13(USC)
	Eseosa Desalu (ITA)	20.13(ECh)
27.	Kendal Williams (USA)	20.15(Kno)
28.	Xie Zhenye (CHN)	20.16(Osa)
29.	Sydney Siame (ZAM)	20.18
30.	Christophe Lemaitre (FRA)	20.19(Ost)
	Rasheed Dwyer (JAM)	20.19
32.	Vitor Silva (BRA)	20.21
	Jahnoy Thompson (JAM)	20.21
34.	John Lundy (USA)	20.22
35.	Zharnel Hughes (GBR)	20.23(Bri)
	Derick De Souza (BRA)	20.23(Aub)
	Mustaqeem Williams (USA)	20.23(NCA)
	Aldemir Da Silva (BRA)	20.23
	Yuki Koike (JPN)	20.23(Jak)
	Chun-Han Yang (TPE)	20.23(Jak)
41.	Ján Volko (SVK)	20.24
42.	Jaylen Bacon (USA)	20.25
43.	Rodney Rowe (USA)	20.26 et al.

WORLD INDOOR RANKING 2018:

1.	Elijah Hall-Thompson (USA)	20.02
2.	Ejowvokoghene Oduduru (NGR)	20.18
3.	Rai Benjamin (USA)	20.34
4.	Andrew Hudson (USA)	20.42
5.	Ncincilili Titi (RSA)	20.45
6.	Jereem Richards (TTO)	20.52
7.	Christophe Lemaitre (FRA)	20.53
8.	Mustaqeem Williams (USA)	20.55
	Jaron Flournoy (USA)	20.55
10.	Andre Ewers (JAM)	20.60
11.	Kenzo Cotton (USA)	20.61
12.	Marqueze Washington (USA)	20.64
	Karol Zalewski (POL)	20.64
14.	Mickael-Meba Zeze (FRA)	20.65
	Khance Meyers (USA)	20.65
16.	Mobolade Ajomale (CAN)	20.67
17.	Fred Kerley (USA)	20.68
	Óscar Husillos (ESP)	20.68
19.	Obi Igbokwe (USA)	20.69
20.	Correion Mosby (USA)	20.70
21.	Dwight St. Hillaire (TTO)	20.73
22.	Rodney Rowe (USA)	20.74
	Cordell Lamb (USA)	20.74
24.	Winston George (GUY)	20.76
	Omar McLeod (JAM)	20.76
26.	Antonio Infantino (ITA)	20.77
27.	Terrance Laird (USA)	20.79
	Jeremy Dodson (SAM)	20.79
	Martin Owusu Antwi (GHA)	20.79
30.	Dedric Dukes (USA)	20.80
31.	Terrell Smith (USA)	20.81
32.	Nick Gray (USA)	20.82
33.	Micaiah Harris (USA)	20.83
	Joseph Amoah (GHA)	20.83
35.	Chris Jefferson (USA)	20.85
	McKinley West (USA)	20.85
37.	Keitavious Walter (USA)	20.86
38.	Dylan Peebles (USA)	20.87
	Kasaun James (USA)	20.87
40.	Steven Champlin (USA)	20.89
	Roy Ejiakuekwu (GBR)	20.89
	Julius Morris (MNT)	20.89
43.	Darrion Flowers (USA)	20.90
	Pavel Maslák (CZE)	20.90
45.	Teray Smith (BAH)	20.92

Doha, 4-5-2018:

1.	Noah Lyles (USA)	19.83
2.	Jereem Richards (TTO)	19.99
3.	Ramil Guliyev (TUR)	20.11
4.	Aaron Brown (CAN)	20.18
5.	Nethaneel Mitchell-Blake (GBR)	20.37
6.	Andre de Grasse (CAN)	20.46

Osaka, 20-5-2018:

1.	Isaac Makwala (BOT)	19.96
2.	Xie Zhenye (CHN)	20.16
3.	Dedric Dukes (USA)	20.32

Eugene, 26-5-2018:

1.	Noah Lyles (USA)	19.69
2.	Jereem Richards (TTO)	20.05
3.	Aaron Brown (CAN)	20.07
4.	Anaso Jobodwana (RSA)	20.42
5.	Nethaneel Mitchell-Blake (GBR)	20.51
6.	Ameer Webb (USA)	20.56
7.	Ramil Guliyev (TUR)	20.57

Oslo, 7-6-2018:

1.	Ramil Guliyev (TUR)	19.90
2.	Aaron Brown (CAN)	19.98
3.	Jereem Richards (TTO)	20.19
4.	Adam Gemili (GBR)	20.21
5.	Ameer Webb (USA)	20.45

Eugene, NCAA, 9-6-2018:

1.	Divine Odururu (NGR)	(20.33)	20.28
2.	Andre Ewers (USA)	(20.31)	20.29
3.	Kendal Williams (USA)	(20.23)	20.32
4.	Jaron Flournoy (USA)	(20.26)	20.43
5.	Rodney Rowe (USA)	(20.49)	20.52
6.	Mustaqeem Williams (USA)	(20.23)	20.62
7.	Kenzo Cotton (USA)	(20.38)	20.73
8.	McKinley West (USA)	(20.54)	20.84

Stockholm, 10-6-2018:

1.	Ramil Guliyev (TUR)	19.92
2.	Aaron Brown (CAN)	20.07
3.	Luxolo Adams (RSA)	20.36
4.	Ameer Webb (USA)	20.41
5.	Nethaneel Mitchell-Blake (GBR)	20.47

Ostrava, 13-6-2018:

1.	Aaron Brown (CAN)	20.05
2.	Jereem Richards (TTO)	20.09
3.	Ramil Guliyev (TUR)	20.09
4.	Christophe Lemaitre (FRA)	20.19
5.	Jan Volko (SVK)	20.36
6.	Anaso Jobodwana (RSA)	20.48
7.	Likourgos-Stefanos Tsakonas (GRE)	20.48

US CHAMPIONSHIPS, Des Moines, 24-6-2018:

1.	Ameer Webb	(20.13)	20.47
2.	Terrell Smith	(20.44)	20.74
3.	Andrew Hudson	(20.38)	20.80
4.	Justin Walker	(20.53)	20.80
5.	Kenzo Cotton	(20.72)	20.82
6.	Amir James		20.82
7.	Marqueze Washington	(20.47)	24.67
	Michael Norman	(20.35)	dns
9.	Bryce Robinson		20.53
10.	Tevin Hester		20.59
11.	John Lundy	(20.63)	20.83
12.	Brandon Carnes		20.89
13.	Kyree King		20.90
14.	Jason Crow		20.90
15.	Curtis King		21.28
	Dedric Dukes		dnf

JAM CHAMPIONSHIPS, Kingston, 24-6-2018:

1.	Jahnoy Thompson		20.21
2.	Nigel Ellis		20.37
3.	Tyquendo Tracey		20.51
4.	Rasheed Dwyer		20.55
5.	Romario Williams	(20.70)	20.79
6.	Oshane Bailey	(20.83)	20.84
7.	Daniel Jamieson		20.92
8.	Renard Howell	(20.77)	22.77

Paris, 30-6-2018:

1.	Michael Norman (USA)	19.84
2.	Rai Benjamin (ANT)	19.99
3.	Alex Quinonez (ECU)	20.08
4.	Luxolo Adams (RSA)	20.21
5.	Bruno Hortelano (ESP)	20.30

Lausanne, 5-7-2018:

1.	Noah Lyles (USA)	19.69
2.	Michael Norman (USA)	19.88
3.	Alex Quinonez (ECU)	20.08
4.	Rai Benjamin (ANT)	20.16
5.	Paulo Camilo de Oliveira (BRA)	20.33
6.	Isiah Young (USA)	20.43

Luzern, 9-7-2018:

1.	Alonso Edward (PAN)	19.90
2.	Akeem Bloomfield (JAM)	20.00
3.	Sydney Siame (ZAM)	20.35
4.	Leon Reid (GBR)	20.40
5.	Yuki Koike (JPN)	20.44
6.	Shota Iizuka (JPN)	20.47

Monaco, 20-7-2018:

1.	Noah Lyles (USA)	19.65
2.	Ramil Guliyev (TUR)	19.99
3.	Alex Quinonez (ECU)	20.03
4.	Alonso Edward (PAN)	20.15
5.	Jereem Richards (TTO)	20.16
6.	Aaron Brown (CAN)	20.17

London, 22-7-2018:

1.	Akeem Bloomfield (JAM)	19.81
2.	Alonso Edward (PAN)	20.01
3.	Alex Quinonez (ECU)	20.13
4.	Nethaneel Mitchell-Blake (GBR)	20.21
5.	Adam Gemili (GBR)	20.30
6.	Churandy Martina (NED)	20.32
7.	Ncincilili Titi (RSA)	20.44

Zürich, 30-8-2018:

1.	Noah Lyles (USA)	19.67
2.	Ramil Guliyev (TUR)	19.98
3.	Jereem Richards (TTO)	20.04
4.	Aaron Brown (CAN)	20.14
5.	Alex Quinonez (ECU)	20.34
6.	Alex Wilson (SUI)	20.40
7.	Luxolo Adams (RSA)	20.51
8.	Nethaneel Mitchell-Blake (GBR)	20.53

Zagreb, 4-9-2018:

1.	Alonso Edward (PAN)	20.17
2.	Aaron Brown (CAN)	20.23
3.	Ncincilili Titi (RSA)	20.48

CONTINENTAL CUP, Ostrava, 8-9-2018:

1.	Alonso Edward (AME)	20.19
2.	Ramil Guliyev (EUR)	20.28
3.	Alex Quinonez (AME)	20.36
4.	Yuki Koike (ASI)	20.57
5.	Churandy Martina (EUR)	20.68
6.	Ncincilili Titi (AFR)	20.78
7.	Baboloki Thebe (RSA)	20.79

OVERVIEW WORLDWIDE OUTDOOR CHAMPIONSHIP FINALISTS OF PAST 6 YEARS

	Wch 17	OG 16	Wch 15	Wch 13
Ramil Guliyev (TUR)	20.09 (1)	20.43 (8)	20.11 (6)	
Wayde van Niekerk (RSA)	20.11 (2)			
Jereem Richards (TTO)	20.11 (3)			
Nethaneel Mitchell-Blake (GBR)	20.24 (4)			
Ameer Webb (USA)	20.26 (5)			
Isaac Makwala (BOT)	20.44 (6)			
Abdul Hakim Sani Brown (JPN)	20.63 (7)			
Isiah Young (USA)	20.64 (8)			
Usain Bolt (JAM)		19.78 (1)	19.55 (1)	19.66 (1)
Andre de Grasse (CAN)		20.02 (2)		
Christophe Lemaitre (FRA)		20.12 (3)		
Adam Gemili (GBR)		20.12 (4)		20.08 (5)
Churandy Martina (NED)		20.13 (5)		20.35 (7)
Lashawn Merritt (USA)		20.19 (6)		
Alonso Edward (PAN)		20.23 (7)	19.87 (4)	
Justin Gatlin (USA)			19.74 (2)	
Anaso Jobodwana (RSA)			19.87 (3)	20.14 (6)
Zharnel Hughes (GBR)			20.02 (5)	
Femi Ogunode (QAT)			20.27 (7)	
Nickel Ashmeade (JAM)			20.33 (8)	20.05 (4)
Warren Weir (JAM)				19.79 (2)
Curtis Mitchell (USA)				20.04 (3)
Jaysuma Saidy Ndure (NOR)				20.37 (8)

OVERVIEW TOP 10 WORLD OUTDOOR RANKINGS OF PAST 5 YEARS

	2018	2017	2016	2015	2014
Noah Lyles (USA)	19.65 (1)	19.90 (4)			
Clarence Munyai (RSA)	19.69 (2)				
Steven Gardiner (BAH)	19.75 (3)				
Ramil Guliyev (TUR)	19.76 (4)			19.88 (6)	
Akeem Bloomfield (JAM)	19.81 (5)				
Michael Norman (USA)	19.84 (6)				
Alonso Edward (PAN)	19.90 (7)		19.92 (8)	19.87 (4)	19.84 (3)
Alex Quiñónez (ECU)	19.93 (8)				
Isiah Young (USA)	19.93 (8)			19.93 (8)	
Isaac Makwala (BOT)	19.96 (10)	19.77 (1)			19.96 (5)
Wayde van Niekerk (RSA)		19.84 (2)		19.94 (9)	
Christian Coleman (USA)		19.85 (3)			
Akani Simbine (RSA)		19.95 (5)			
Jereem Richards (TTO)		19.97 (6)			
Yohan Blake (JAM)		19.97 (6)			
Christopher Belcher (USA)		20.01 (8)			
Andre de Grasse (CAN)		20.01 (8)	19.80 (4)	19.88 (6)	
Ameer Webb (USA)		20.01 (8)	19.85 (6)		
Lashawn Merritt (USA)			19.74 (1)		
Justin Gatlin (USA)			19.75 (2)	19.57 (2)	19.68 (1)
Usain Bolt (JAM)			19.78 (3)	19.55 (1)	
Churandy Martina (NED)			19.81 (5)		
Miguel Francis (ANT)			19.88 (7)		
Nethaneel Mitchell-Blake (GBR)			19.95 (9)		
Brendon Rodney (CAN)			19.96 (10)		
Rasheed Dwyer (JAM)				19.80 (3)	19.98 (7)
Anaso Jobodwana (RSA)				19.87 (4)	
Femi Ogunode (QAT)				19.97 (10)	20.06 (9)
Warren Weir (JAM)					19.82 (2)
Nickel Ashmeade (JAM)					19.95 (4)
Dedric Dukes (USA)					19.97 (6)
Adam Gemili (GBR)					19.98 (7)
Antoine Adams (SKN)					20.08 (10)
Christophe Lemaitre (FRA)					20.08 (10)

OVERVIEW TOP 10 WORLD INDOOR RANKINGS OF PAST 5 YEARS

	2018	2017	2016	2015	2014
Elijah Hall-Thompson (USA)	20.02 (1)				
Ejowvokoghene Oduduru (NGR)	20.18 (2)				
Rai Benjamin (USA)	20.34 (3)				
Andrew Hudson (USA)	20.42 (4)				
Ncincilili Titi (RSA)	20.45 (5)				
Jereem Richards (TTO)	20.52 (6)	20.31 (2)			
Christophe Lemaitre (FRA)	20.53 (7)		20.43 (1)		20.58 (10)
Mustaqeem Williams (USA)	20.55 (8)				
Jaron Flournoy (USA)	20.55 (8)				
Andre Ewers (JAM)	20.60 (10)				
Christian Coleman (USA)		20.11 (1)	20.54 (4)		
Just'n Thymes (USA)		20.36 (3)			
Omar McLeod (JAM)		20.48 (4)			
Lalonde Gordon (TTO)		20.49 (5)		20.71 (10)	
Nethaneel Mitchell-Blake (GBR)		20.49 (5)	20.51 (3)		
Rondel Sorrillo (TTO)		20.49 (5)			
Robin Erewa (GER)		20.52 (8)		20.70 (8)	20.56 (8)
Marqueze Washington (USA)		20.56 (9)			
Cameron Williams (USA)		20.57 (10)	20.58 (8)		
Pavel Maslák (CZE)		20.57 (10)			20.52 (4)
Brendon Rodney (CAN)			20.46 (2)	20.69 (6)	
Mickael-Meba Zeze (FRA)			20.54 (4)		
Arman Hall (USA)			20.55 (6)		20.55 (7)
Julian Reus (GER)			20.55 (6)		
Devin Jenkins (USA)			20.58 (8)		
Ronnie Baker (USA)			20.60 (10)		
Sam Watts (GBR)			20.60 (10)	20.69 (6)	
Trayvon Bromell (USA)				20.19 (1)	
Andre de Grasse (CAN)				20.26 (2)	
Shavez Hart (BAH)				20.57 (3)	
Aaron Ernest (USA)				20.66 (4)	
Karol Zalewski (POL)				20.66 (4)	
Bryce Robinson (USA)				20.70 (8)	
Deondre Batson (USA)					20.32 (1)
Dedric Dukes (USA)					20.34 (2)
Wallace Spearmon (USA)					20.51 (3)
Calvin Nkanata (KEN)					20.52 (4)
Aaron Brown (CAN)					20.53 (6)
Tyreek Hill (USA)					20.57 (9)

WORLD RANKING ALL TIME:

1.	Usain Bolt (JAM)	19.19 (2009)
2.	Yohan Blake (JAM)	19.26 (2011)
3.	Michael Johnson (USA)	19.32 (1996)
4.	Walter Dix (USA)	19.53 (2011)
5.	Justin Gatlin (USA)	19.57 (2015)
6.	Tyson Gay (USA)	19.58 (2009)
7.	Xavier Carter (USA)	19.63 (2006)
8.	Wallace Spearmon (USA)	19.65 (2006)
	Noah Lyles (USA)	19.65 (2018)
10.	Frank Fredericks (NAM)	19.68 (1996)
11.	Clarence Munyai (RSA)	19.69 (2018)
12.	Pietro Mennea (ITA)	19.72 (1979)
13.	Michael Marsh (USA)	19.73 (1992)
14.	LaShawn Merritt (USA)	19.74 (2016)
15.	Carl Lewis (USA)	19.75 (1983)
	Joe Deloach (USA)	19.75 (1988)
	Steven Gardiner (BAH)	19.75 (2018)
18.	Ramil Guliyev (TUR)	19.76 (2018)
19.	Ato Boldon (TTO)	19.77 (1997)
	Isaac Makwala (BOT)	19.77 (2017)
21.	Shawn Crawford (USA)	19.79 (2004)
	Warren Weir (JAM)	19.79 (2013)
23.	Christophe Lemaitre (FRA)	19.80 (2011)
	Rasheed Dwyer (JAM)	19.80 (2015)
	Andre de Grasse (CAN)	19.80 (2016)
26.	Alonso Edward (PAN)	19.81 (2009)
	Churandy Martina (NED)	19.81 (2016)
	Akeem Bloomfield (JAM)	19.81 (2018)
29.	Tommie Smith (USA)	19.83 (1968)
30.	Francis Obikwelu (NGR)	19.84 (1999)
	Wayde van Niekerk (RSA)	19.84 (2017)
	Michael Norman (USA)	19.84 (2018)
33.	John Capel (USA)	19.85 (2000)
	Konstantinos Kenteris (GRE)	19.85 (2002)
	Nickel Ashmeade (JAM)	19.85 (2012)
	Ameer Webb (USA)	19.85 (2016)
	Christian Coleman (USA)	19.85 (2017)
38.	Don Quarrie (JAM)	19.86 (1971)
	Maurice Greene (USA)	19.86 (1997)
	Jason Young (USA)	19.86 (2012)
	Isiah Young (USA)	19.86 (2013)
42.	Lorenzo Daniel (USA)	19.87 (1988)
	John Regis (GBR)	19.87 (1994)
	Jeff Williams (USA)	19.87 (1996)
	Anaso Jobodwana (RSA)	19.87 (2015)

WORLD RANKING ALL TIME INDOOR:

1.	Frank Fredericks (NAM)	19.92 (1996)
2.	Elijah Hall-Thompson (USA)	20.02 (2018)
3.	Wallace Spearmon (USA)	20.10 (2005)
4.	Christian Coleman (USA)	20.11 (2017)
5.	Ejowvokoghene Odururu (NGR)	20.18 (2018)
6.	Trayvon Bromell (USA)	20.19 (2015)
7.	Linford Christie (GBR)	20.25 (1995)
8.	Obadele Thompson (BAR)	20.26 (1999)
	John Capel (USA)	20.26 (2000)
	Shawn Crawford (USA)	20.26 (2000)
	Andre de Grasse (CAN)	20.26 (2015)
12.	Walter Dix (USA)	20.27 (2006)
13.	Xavier Carter (USA)	20.30 (2006)
14.	Coby Miller (USA)	20.31 (2001)
	Jereem Richards (TTO)	20.31 (2017)
16.	Rohsaan Griffin (USA)	20.32 (1999)
	Kevin Little (USA)	20.32 (1999)
	Diondre Batson (USA)	20.32 (2014)
19.	Dedric Dukes (USA)	20.34 (2014)
	Rai Benjamin (USA)	20.34 (2018)
21.	Ato Boldon (TTO)	20.35 (1997)
22.	Bruno Marie-Rose (FRA)	20.36 (1987)
	Derrick Thompson (USA)	20.36 (1996)
	Rubin Williams (USA)	20.36 (2008)
	Just'n Thymes (USA)	20.36 (2017)
26.	Ameer Webb (USA)	20.37 (2013)
27.	Rodney Martin (USA)	20.38 (2005)
	Curtis Mitchell (USA)	20.38 (2010)
29.	Rakieem Salaam (USA)	20.39 (2011)
30.	Jeff Williams (USA)	20.40 (1996)
	Sergiy Osovich (UKR)	20.40 (1998)
	LaShawn Merritt (USA)	20.40 (2005)
	Kerron Clement (USA)	20.40 (2005)
34.	Nikolay Antonov (BUL)	20.41 (1992)
	Maurice Mitchell (USA)	20.41 (2011)
36.	Ramon Clay (USA)	20.42 (1998)
	Leo Bookman (USA)	20.42 (2004)
	Milton Campbell (USA)	20.42 (2006)
	Sebastian Ernst (GER)	20.42 (2011)
	Andrew Hudson (USA)	20.42 (2018)
41.	Domenik Peterson (USA)	20.43 (2005)
	Christophe Lemaitre (FRA)	20.43 (2016)

400 m Men

EUROPEAN CHAMPIONSHIPS 2018: 10-8-2018: | **WORLD RANKING 2018:**

1. Matthew Hudson-Smith (GBR)	(44.76)	44.78
2. Kevin Borlée (BEL)	(45.07)	45.13
3. Jonathan Borlée (BEL)	(44.87)	45.19
4. Karol Zalewski (POL)	(45.11)	45.34
5. Luka Janezic (SLO)	(44.93)	45.43
6. Óscar Husillos (ESP)	(45.17)	45.61
7. Ricardo dos Santos (POR)	(45.14)	45.78
8. Karsten Warholm (NOR)	(44.91)	46.68

----

9. Matteo Galvan (ITA)		45.17
10. Rabah Yousif (GBR)		45.30
11. Liemarvin Bonevacia (NED)		45.39
12. Dwayne Cowan (GBR)		45.45
13. Lucas Bua (ESP)		45.48
14. Davide Re (ITA)		45.53
15. Janis Leitis (LAT)		45.53
16. Pavel Maslák (CZE)		45.59
17. Dylan Borlée (BEL)		45.63
18. Donald Blair-Sanford (ISR)		45.68
19. Martyn Rooney (GBR)		45.73
20. Lukasz Krawczuk (POL)		45.78
21. Samuel García (ESP)	(45.63)	45.87
22. Vitaliy Butrym (UKR)	(45.82)	46.01
23. Robert Parge (ROM)	(45.99)	46.07
24. Patrick Schneider (GER)	(46.15)	46.58

----

25. Dariusz Kowaluk (POL)		46.18
26. Oleksiy Pozdnyakov (UKR)		46.47

WORLD RANKING 2018:

1. Michael Norman (USA)	43.61(NCA)
2. Steven Gardiner (BAH)	43.87(Do)
3. Akeem Bloomfield (JAM)	43.94(NCA)
4. Abdalelah Haroun (QAT)	44.07(Lon)
5. Nathon Allen (JAM)	44.13(NCA)
6. Emmanuel Kipkurui Korir (KEN)	44.21(KeT)
7. Isaac Makwala (BOT)	44.23(Sha)
8. Fred Kerley (USA)	44.33(Rom)
9. Nathan Strother (USA)	44.34(Kno)
10. Kirani James (GRN)	44.35(Kin)
11. Paul Dedewo (USA)	44.43(Lon)
12. Baboloki Thebe (BOT)	44.54(Lon)
13. Dwight St. Hillaire (TTO)	44.55(Tam)
14. Kahmari Montgomery (USA)	44.58(USC)
15. Luguelín Santos (DOM)	44.59
16. Quincy Hall (USA)	44.60(Tem)
17. Abderrahman Samba (QAT)	44.62(Lon)
18. Matthew Hudson-Smith (GBR)	44.63(Lon)
19. Bralon Taplin (USA)	44.67
20. Bruno Hortelano-Roig (ESP)	44.69(Mad)
21. Tyrell Richard (USA)	44.70(NCA)
22. Wilbert London (USA)	44.73(Wac)
Óscar Husillos (ESP)	44.73(Mad)
24. Rai Benjamin (USA)	44.74(Tor)
25. Deon Lendore (TTO)	44.81(Mtv)
26. Michael Cherry (USA)	44.85(USC)
27. Alejandro Jhon Perlaza (COL)	44.86
28. Jonathan Borlée (BEL)	44.87(ECh)
29. Christopher Taylor (JAM)	44.88(JaC)
30. Karsten Warholm (NOR)	44.91(ECh)
31. Luka Janezic (SLO)	44.93(ECh)
32. Mar'Yea Harris (USA)	44.94(NCA)
Obi Igbokwe (USA)	44.94(NCA)
34. Nery Brenes (CRC)	45.00(Mad)
35. Derick Mokaleng (RSA)	45.02(Wac)
36. Liemarvin Bonevacia (NED)	45.03(LCF)
Jonathan Sacoor (BEL)	45.03
38. Christian Taylor (USA)	45.07(Hen)
Kevin Borlée (BEL)	45.07(ECh)
40. Demish Gaye (JAM)	45.08(Kin)
41. Dashawn Morris (JAM)	45.09
Josephus Lyles (USA)	45.09(Cle)
43. Javon Francis (JAM)	45.11(GC)
Karol Zalewski (POL)	45.11(ECh)

WORLD INDOOR CHAMPIONSHIP8: 3-3-2018:

1.	Pavel Maslák (CZE)		45.47
2.	Michael Cherry (USA)	(45.73)	45.84
3.	Deon Lendore (TTO)	(46.33)	46.37
4.	Aldrich Bailey Jr (USA)	(46.33)	46.44
	Óscar Husillos (ESP)	(45.69)	dsq
	Luguelín Santos (DOM)	(46.31)	dsq

7.	Luka Janezic (SLO)		46.37
8.	Rafal Omelko (POL)		46.39
9.	Jakub Krzewina (POL)	(46.57)	46.69
10.	Javon Francis (JAM)		46.73
11.	Juander Santos (DOM)		46.83
12.	Asa Guevara (TTO)		46.91
13.	Patrik Sorm (CZE)	(46.99)	47.04
14.	Lee Thompson (GBR)	(46.81)	47.14
15.	Lucas Búa (ESP)	(46.96)	47.14
16.	Mikhail Litvin (KAZ)	(47.16)	47.94
17.	Chidi Okezie (NGR)	(46.91)	48.53
18.	Yousef Karam (KUW)	(46.86)	dnf

19.	Vitalii Butrym (UKR)		47.45
	Steven Gayle (JAM)		dsq
	Abdalleleh Haroun (QAT)		dsq
	Bralon Taplin (GRN)		dsq
	Nery Brenes (CRC)		dsq

WORLD INDOOR RANKING 2018:

1.	Michael Norman (USA)	44.52
2.	Akeem Bloomfield (JAM)	44.86
3.	Bralon Taplin (GRN)	44.88
4.	Mylik Kerley (USA)	45.16
5.	Fred Kerley (USA)	45.18
6.	Marqueze Washington (USA)	45.24
	Kahmari Montgomery (USA)	45.24
8.	Nathon Allen (JAM)	45.27
9.	Obi Igbokwe (USA)	45.38
10.	Steven Solomon (AUS)	45.44
11.	Pavel Maslák (CZE)	45.47
12.	Dontavious Wright (USA)	45.50
13.	Michael Cherry (USA)	45.53
14.	Nathan Strother (USA)	45.56
15.	Vernon Norwood (USA)	45.58
16.	Karsten Warholm (NOR)	45.59
	Aldrich Bailey Jr (USA)	45.59
18.	Paul Dedewo (USA)	45.61
19.	Derick Mokaleng (RSA)	45.68
20.	Óscar Husillos (ESP)	45.69
21.	Gil Roberts (USA)	45.80
22.	Zachary Shinnick (USA)	45.81
23.	Jeffrey Green (USA)	45.82
24.	Robert Grant (USA)	45.84
25.	Deon Lendore (TTO)	45.85
26.	Brycen Spratling (USA)	45.91
27.	Wilbert London (USA)	45.95
28.	Steven Champlin (USA)	45.97
	Javon Francis (JAM)	45.97
30.	Luka Janezic (SLO)	46.02
31.	Cordell Lamb (USA)	46.04
32.	Rhayko Schwartz (USA)	46.08
	Sean Bailey (JAM)	46.08
34.	Benjamin Lobo Vedel (DEN)	46.14
	Ricky Morgan (USA)	46.14
	Alejandro Jhon Perlaza (COL)	46.14
37.	Jakub Krzewina (POL)	46.15
	Kemar Mowatt (JAM)	46.15
39.	Mar'Yea Harris (USA)	46.17
40.	Kunle Fasasi (NGR)	46.18
41.	Karol Zalewski (POL)	46.20
42.	Lee Thompson (GBR)	46.23
43.	James Burnett (USA)	46.25
44.	Dan Chisena (USA)	46.27
45.	Luguelín Santos (DOM)	46.31
	Brian Herron (USA)	46.31

Tempe, 7-4-2018:
1. Quincy Hall (USA) — 44.60
2. Paul Dedewo (USA) — 44.62
3. Derrick Motaleng (RSA) — 45.17

Gold Coast (Commonwealth Games), 10-4-2018:
1. Isaac Makwala (BOT) — 44.35
2. Baboloki Thebe (BOT) — 45.09
3. Javon Francis (JAM) — 45.11
4. Mohammed Yahiya (IND) — 45.31
5. Bralon Taplin (USA) — 45.38

Torrance, 21-4-2018:
1. Michael Norman (USA) — 44.53
2. Rai Benjamin (USA) — 44.74
3. Paul Dedewo (USA) — 44.78
4. Kahmari Montgomery (USA) — 44.91
5. Patrick Blake Leeper (USA) — 45.05

Doha, 4-5-2018:
1. Steven Gardiner (BAH) — 43.87
2. Abdalelah Haroun (QAT) — 44.50
3. Isaac Makwala (BOT) — 44.92
4. Gil Roberts (USA) — 45.22
5. Baboloki Thebe (BOT) — 45.58

Shanghai, 12-5-2018:
1. Steven Gardiner (BAH) — 43.99
2. Isaac Makwala (BOT) — 44.23
3. Abdalelah Haroun (QAT) — 44.51
4. Fred Kerley (USA) — 44.71
5. Christian Taylor (USA) — 45.24
6. Michael Cherry (USA) — 45.60

Knoxville, 13-5-2018:
1. Nathon Allen (JAM) — 44.28
2. Nathan Strother (USA) — 44.34
3. Dwight St. Hillaire (TTO) — 45.05

Rome, 31-5-2018:
1. Fred Kerley (USA) — 44.33
2. Abdalelah Haroun (QAT) — 44.37
3. Paul Dedewo (USA) — 44.58
4. Michael Cherry (USA) — 44.97
5. Gil Roberts (USA) — 45.22
6. Davide Re (ITA) — 45.49

Hengelo, 3-6-2018:
1. Abdalelah Haroun (QAT) — 44.35
2. Paul Dedewo (USA) — 44.50
3. Michael Cherry (USA) — 44.90
4. Christian Taylor (USA) — 45.07

Eugene, NCAA, 8-6-2018:
1. Michael Norman (USA) — (44.66) 43.61
2. Akeem Bloomfield (JAM) — (44.72) 43.94
3. Nathon Allen (JAM) — (44.83) 44.13
4. Mar'Yea Harris (USA) — (44.94) 45.00
5. Tyrell Richard (USA) — (44.70) 45.10
6. Obi Igbokwe (USA) — (44.94) 45.16
7. Kahmari Montgomery (USA) — (44.92) 45.75
8. Wilbert London (USA) — (44.98) 46.20
----
9. Steven Solomon (AUS) — 45.30
10. Trevor Stewart (USA) — 45.35

Chorzow, 8-6-2018:
1. Paul Dedewo (USA) — 44.56
2. Luguelín Santos (DOM) — 44.75
3. Karol Zalewski (POL) — 45.15

Kingston, 9-6-2018:
1. Kirani James (GRN) — 44.35
2. Fred Kerley (USA) — 44.36
3. Bralon Taplin (USA) — 45.11

Madrid, 22-6-2018:
1. Luguelín Santos (DOM) — 44.66
2. Bruno Hortelano (ESP) — 44.69
3. Óscar Husillos (ESP) — 44.73
4. Nery Brenes (CRC) — 45.00
5. Baboloki Thebe (RSA) — 45.00
6. Emmanuel Bamidele (NGR) — 45.36

Mohamed Nasir Abbas (QAT) — 45.15

US CHAMPIONSHIPS, Des Moines, 23-6-2018:
1. Kahmari Montgomery — 44.58
2. Paul Dedewo — 44.64
3. Michael Cherry — 44.85
4. Nathan Strother — 44.89
5. Obi Igbokwe — (45.21) 45.23
6. Josephus Lyles — 45.31
7. Wilbert London III — (45.35) 45.57
8. Myles Pringle — (45.38) 45.92

JAM CHAMPIONSHIPS, Kingston, 24-6-2018:
1.	Christopher Taylor	44.88
2.	Demish Gaye	45.23
3.	Fitzroy Dunkley	45.77
4.	Rusheen McDonald	46.47
5.	Steven Gayle	46.50

Rabat, 13-7-2018:
1.	Akeem Bloomfield (JAM)	44.33
2.	Abdalelah Haroun (QAT)	44.69
3.	Matthew Hudson-Smith (GBR)	44.79
4.	Luguelín Santos (DOM)	44.80
5.	Paul Dedewo (USA)	44.82
6.	Michael Cherry (USA)	45.40

London, 21-7-2018:
1.	Abdalelah Haroun (QAT)	44.07
2.	Paul Dedewo (USA)	44.43
3.	Kirani James (GRN)	44.50
4.	Baboloki Thebe (BOT)	44.54
5.	Abderrahman Samba (QAT)	44.62
6.	Matthew Hudson-Smith (GBR)	44.63
7.	Nathon Allen (JAM)	44.72
8.	Nathan Strother (USA)	45.17

Chorzow, 22-8-2018:
1.	Steven Gardiner (BAH)	44.43
2.	Karol Zalewski (POL)	45.32
3.	Christian Taylor (USA)	45.34

Zürich, 30-8-2018:
1.	Fred Kerley (USA)	44.80
2.	Nathan Strother (USA)	44.93
3.	Matthew Hudson-Smith (GBR)	44.95
4.	Paul Dedewo (USA)	45.18
5.	Baboloki Thebe (BOT)	45.41

CONTINENTAL CUP, Ostrava, 9-9-2018:
1.	Abdalelah Haroun (ASI)	44.72
2.	Baboloki Thebe (AFR)	45.10
3.	Nathan Strother (AME)	45.28
4.	Matthew Hudson-Smith (EUR)	45.72
5.	Mohammed Yahiya (ASI)	45.72
6.	Luguelín Santos (AME)	45.81
7.	Kevin Borlée (EUR)	46.26

OVERVIEW WORLDWIDE OUTDOOR CHAMPIONSHIP FINALISTS OF PAST 6 YEARS

	Wch 17	OG 16	Wch 15	Wch 13
Wayde van Niekerk (RSA)	43.98 (1)	43.03 (1)	43.48 (1)	
Steven Gardiner (BAH)	44.41 (2)			
Abdalelah Haroun (QAT)	44.48 (3)			
Baboloki Thebe (BOT)	44.66 (4)			
Nathon Allen (JAM)	44.88 (5)			
Demish Gaye (JAM)	45.04 (6)			
Fred Kerley (USA)	45.23 (7)			
Isaac Makwala (BOT)	dns (8)		44.63 (5)	
Kirani James (GRN)		43.76 (2)	43.78 (3)	44.99 (7)
Lashawn Merritt (USA)		43.85 (3)	43.65 (2)	43.74 (1)
Machel Cedenio (TTO)		44.01 (4)	45.06 (7)	
Karabo Sibanda (BOT)		44.25 (5)		
Ali Khamis Khamis (BRN)		44.36 (6)		
Bralon Taplin (GRN)		44.45 (7)		
Matthew Hudson-Smith (GBR)		44.61 (8)		
Luguelin Santos (DOM)			44.11 (4)	44.52 (3)
Rabah Yousif (GBR)			44.68 (6)	
Yousef Ahmed Masrahi (KSA)			45.15 (8)	44.97 (6)
Tony McQuay (USA)				44.40 (2)
Jonathan Borlée (BEL)				44.54 (4)
Pavel Maslák (CZE)				44.91 (5)
Anderson Henriques (BRA)				45.03 (8)

OVERVIEW WORLDWIDE INDOOR CHAMPIONSHIP FINALISTS OF 5 PAST YEARS

	Wch 18	Wch 16	Wch 14
Pavel Maslák (CZE)	45.47 (1)	45.44 (1)	45.24 (1)
Michael Cherry (USA)	45.84 (2)		
Deon Lendore (TTO)	46.37 (3)	46.17 (3)	
Aldrich Bailey Jr (USA)	46.44 (4)		
Oscar Husillos (ESP)	dsq		
Luguelín Santos (DOM)	dsq		
Abdalelah Haroun (QAT)		45.59 (2)	
Bralon Taplin (GRN)		46.56 (4)	
Boniface Mweresa (KEN)		46.86 (5)	
Lalonde Gordon (TTO)		47.62 (6)	46.39 (5)
Chris Brown (BAH)			45.58 (2)
Kyle Clemons (USA)			45.74 (3)
David Verburg (USA)			46.21 (4)
Nery Brenes (CRC)			47.32 (6)

OVERVIEW TOP 10 WORLD OUTDOOR RANKINGS OF PAST 5 YEARS

	2018	2017	2016	2015	2014
Michael Norman (USA	43.61 (1)				
Steven Gardiner (BAH)	43.87 (2)	43.89 (4)	44.46 (10)	44.27 (8)	
Akeem Bloomfield (JAM)	43.94 (3)				
Abdalelah Haroun (QAT)	44.07 (4)	44.48 (10)		44.27 (8)	
Nathon Allen (JAM)	44.13 (5)	44.19 (6)			
Emmanuel Kipkurui Korir (KEN)	44.21 (6)				
Isaac Makwala (BOT)	44.23 (7)	43.84 (3)		43.72 (3)	44.01 (3)
Fred Kerley (USA)	44.33 (8)	43.70 (2)			
Nathan Strother (USA)	44.34 (9)				
Kirani James (GRN)	44.35 (10)		43.76 (2)	43.78 (4)	43.74 (1)
Wayde van Niekerk (RSA)		43.62 (1)	43.03 (1)	43.48 (1)	44.38 (5)
Baboloki Thebe (BOT)		44.02 (5)	44.22 (5)		
Gil Roberts (USA)		44.22 (7)			44.53 (7)
Wilbert London III (USA)		44.47 (8)			
Vernon Norwood (USA)		44.47 (8)			
Lashawn Merritt (USA)			43.85 (3)	43.65 (2)	43.92 (2)
Machel Cedenio (TTO)			44.01 (4)	44.36 (10)	
Tony McQuay (USA)			44.24 (6)		
Karabo Sibanda (BOT)			44.25 (7)		
Ali Khamis Khamis (BRN)			44.36 (8)		
Bralon Taplin (GRN)			44.38 (9)		
Yousef Ahmed Masrahi (KSA)				43.93 (5)	44.43 (6)
Rusheen McDonald (JAM)				43.93 (5)	
Luguelin Santos (DOM)				44.11 (7)	44.53 (7)
Deon Lendore (TTO)					44.36 (4)
Chris Brown (BAH)					44.59 (9)
Martyn Rooney (GBR)					44.71 (10)

OVERVIEW TOP 10 WORLD INDOOR RANKINGS OF PAST 5 YEARS

	2018	2017	2016	2015	2014
Michael Norman (USA)	44.52 (1)				
Akeem Bloomfield (JAM)	44.86 (2)				
Bralon Taplin (GRN)	44.88 (3)	45.19 (2)	45.20 (1)	45.39 (5)	
Mylik Kerley (USA)	45.16 (4)	45.68 (6)			
Marqueze Washington (USA)	45.24 (6)	45.63 (4)	45.72 (7)		
Kahmari Montgomery (USA)	45.24 (6)		45.78 (8)		
Nathon Allen (JAM)	45.27 (8)				
Obi Igbokwe (USA)	45.38 (9)				
Steven Solomon (AUS)	45.44 (10)				
Fred Kerley (USA)		44.85 (1)			
Adekunle Rilwan Fasasi (NGR)		45.57 (3)			
Michael Cherry (USA)		45.64 (5)	45.61 (6)		
Pavel Maslák (CZE)		45.77 (7)	45.44 (2)	45.27 (1)	45.24 (3)
Luguelin Santos (DOM)		45.80 (8)			
Óscar Husillos (ESP)		45.92 (9)			
Karsten Warholm (NOR)		45.96 (10)			
Lalonde Gordon (TTO)			45.51 (3)		45.17 (2)
Deon Lendore (TTO)			45.56 (4)	45.38 (4)	45.03 (1)
Abdalelah Haroun (QAT)			45.59 (5)	45.39 (5)	
Arman Hall (USA)			45.79 (9)		45.28 (4)
Vernon Norwood (USA)			45.80 (10)	45.31 (2)	45.39 (5)
Najee Glass (USA)				45.34 (3)	
Clayton Parros (USA)				45.75 (7)	
Aldrich Bailey (USA)				45.96 (8)	
Christopher Giesting (USA)				45.98 (9)	
Hugh Graham Jr (USA)				45.98 (9)	
Zack Bilderback (USA)				45.98 (9)	
Chris Brown (BAH)					45.58 (6)
Kyle Clemons (USA)					45.60 (7)
David Verburg (USA)					45.62 (8)
Michael Berry (USA)					45.64 (9)
Nigel Levine (GBR)					45.71 (10)

WORLD RANKING ALL TIME:

1.	Wayde van Niekerk (RSA)	43.03 (2016)
2.	Michael Johnson (USA)	43.18 (1999)
3.	Butch Reynolds (USA)	43.29 (1988)
4.	Jeremy Wariner (USA)	43.45 (2007)
5.	Quincy Watts (USA)	43.50 (1992)
6.	Michael Norman (USA)	43.61 (2018)
7.	LaShawn Merritt (USA)	43.65 (2015)
8.	Fred Kerley (USA)	43.70 (2017)
9.	Isaac Makwala (BOT)	43.72 (2015)
10.	Kirani James (GRN)	43.74 (2014)
11.	Danny Everett (USA)	43.81 (1992)
12.	Lee Evans (USA)	43.86 (1968)
13.	Steve Lewis (USA)	43.87 (1988)
	Steven Gardiner (BAH)	43.87 (2018)
15.	Youssef Ahmed Masrahi (KSA)	43.93 (2015)
	Rusheen McDonald (JAM)	43.93 (2015)
17.	Akeem Bloomfield (JAM)	43.94 (2018)
18.	Larry James (USA)	43.97 (1968)
19.	Machel Cedenio (TTO)	44.01 (2016)
20.	Baboloki Thebe (BOT)	44.02 (2017)
21.	Angelo Taylor (USA)	44.05 (2007)
22.	Abdalelah Haroun (QAT)	44.07 (2018)
23.	Alvin Harrison (USA)	44.09 (1996)
	Jerome Young (USA)	44.09 (1998)
25.	Gary Kikaya (COD)	44.10 (2006)
26.	Luguelín Santos (DOM)	44.11 (2015)
27.	Derek Mills (USA)	44.13 (1995)
	Nathon Allen (JAM)	44.13 (2018)
29.	Roberto Hernández (CUB)	44.14 (1990)
30.	Anthuan Maybank (USA)	44.15 (1996)
31.	Otis Harris (USA)	44.16 (2004)
32.	Innocent Egbunike (NGR)	44.17 (1987)
33.	Samson Kitur (KEN)	44.18 (1992)
34.	Charles Gitonga (KEN)	44.20 (1996)
35.	Ian Morris (TTO)	44.21 (1992)
	Emmanuel Kipkurui Korir (KEN)	44.21 (2018)
37.	Gil Roberts (USA)	44.22 (2017)
38.	Tony McQuay (USA)	44.24 (2016)
39.	Karabo Sibanda (BOT)	44.25 (2016)
40.	Alberto Juantorena (CUB)	44.26 (1976)
41.	Alonzo Babers (USA)	44.27 (1984)
	Antonio Pettigrew (USA)	44.27 (1989)
	Darold Williamson (USA)	44.27 (2005)
44.	Andrew Valmon (USA)	44.28 (1993)
	Tyree Washington (USA)	44.28 (2001)

WORLD RANKING ALL TIME INDOOR:

1.	Michael Norman (USA)	44.52 (2018)
2.	Kerron Clement (USA)	44.57 (2005)
3.	Michael Johnson (USA)	44.63 (1995)
4.	Kirani James (GRN)	44.80 (2011)
5.	Fred Kerley (USA)	44.85 (2017)
6.	Akeem Bloomfield (JAM)	44.86 (2018)
7.	Bralon Taplin (USA)	44.88 (2018)
8.	LaShawn Merritt (USA)	44.93 (2005)
9.	Danny Everett (USA)	45.02 (1992)
10.	Torrin Lawrence (USA)	45.03 (2010)
	Deon Lendore (TTO)	45.03 (2014)
12.	Thomas Schönlebe (GER)	45.05 (1988)
	Alvin Harrison (USA)	45.05 (1998)
14.	Nery Brenes (CRC)	45.11 (2012)
15.	Mylik Kerley (USA)	45.16 (2018)
16.	Lalonde Gordon (TTO)	45.17 (2014)
17.	Calvin Harrison (USA)	45.18 (1998)
18.	Tony McQuay (USA)	45.21 (2011)
19.	Pavel Maslák (CZE)	45.24 (2014)
	Marqueze Washington (USA)	45.24 (2018)
	Kahmari Montgomery (USA)	45.24 (2018)
22.	Butch Reynolds (USA)	45.26 (1993)
23.	Nathon Allen (JAM)	45.27 (2018)
24.	Xavier Carter (USA)	45.28 (2006)
	Arman Geno Hall (USA)	45.28 (2014)
26.	Terry Gatson (USA)	45.29 (2005)
27.	Vernon Norwood (USA)	45.31 (2015)
28.	Demetrius Pinder (BAH)	45.33 (2011)
29.	Tyree Washington (USA)	45.34 (2003)
	Najee Glass (USA)	45.34 (2015)
31.	Alleyne Francique (GRN)	45.35 (2002)
32.	Pete Ashbourne Coley (JAM)	45.37 (2002)
33.	Obi Igbokwe (USA)	45.38 (2018)
34.	Jamie Baulch (GBR)	45.39 (1997)
	Marek Plawgo (POL)	45.39 (2002)
	Jeremy Wariner (USA)	45.39 (2004)
	Gil Roberts (USA)	45.39 (2012)
	Abdalelah Haroun (QAT)	45.39 (2015)
39.	Kelly Willie (USA)	45.41 (2005)
	Bershawn Jackson (USA)	45.41 (2010)
41.	Daniel Caines (GBR)	45.43 (2003)
42.	Mark Everett (USA)	45.44 (1991)
	Steven Solomon (AUS)	45.44 (2018)
44.	Andrew Pierce (USA)	45.46 (2001)
45.	Angelo Taylor (USA)	45.50 (1999)
	Dontavious Wright (USA)	45.50 (2018)

800 m Men

EUROPEAN CHAMPIONSHIPS 2018: 11-8-2018:

1.	Adam Kszczot (POL)	(1.46.11)	1.44.59
2.	Andreas Kramer (SWE)	(1.46.14)	1.45.03
3.	Pierre-A. Bosse (FRA)	(1.46.21)	1.45.30
4.	Michal Rozmys (POL)	(1.46.17)	1.45.32
5.	Mateusz Borkowski (POL)	(1.46.41)	1.45.42
6.	Andreas Bube (DEN)	(1.46.40)	1.45.92
7.	Álvaro de Arriba (ESP)	(1.46.43)	1.46.41
8.	Lukas Hodbod (CZE)	(1.46.50)	1.46.60

9.	Thomas Roth (NOR)		1.46.60
10.	Saul Ordóñez (ESP)		1.46.82
11.	Guy Learmonth (GBR)	(1.46.75)	1.46.83
12.	Daniel Rowden (GBR)	(1.46.59)	1.46.98
13.	Amel Tuka (BIH)	(1.46.47)	1.47.24
14.	Yevhen Hutsol (UKR)	(1.46.97)	1.47.29
15.	Elliot Giles (GBR)		1.47.40
16.	Daniel Andújar (ESP)	(1.46.99)	1.48.10

17.	Gabriel Tual (FRA)		1.47.26
18.	Elliott Crestan (BEL)		1.47.35
19.	Sven Cepus (SLO)		1.47.56
20.	Christoph Kessler (GER)		1.48.13

WORLD RANKING 2018:

1.	Emmanuel Kipkurui Korir (KEN)	1.42.05(Lon)
2.	Nijel Amos (BOT)	1.42.14(Mon)
3.	Clayton Murphy (USA)	1.43.12(Lon)
	Wyclife Kinyamal (KEN)	1.43.12(Lon)
5.	Brandon McBride (CAN)	1.43.20(Mon)
6.	Michael Saruni (KEN)	1.43.25(Tuc)
7.	Jonathan Kitlitit (KEN)	1.43.46(KeT)
8.	Saúl Ordóñez (ESP)	1.43.65(Mon)
9.	Ferguson Cheruiyot Rotich (KEN)	1.43.73(Par)
10.	Cornelius Tuwei (KEN)	1.43.82(Mon)
11.	Elijah Motonei Manangoi (KEN)	1.44.15(Bir)
12.	Pierre-Ambroise Boss (FRA)	1.44.20(Mon)
13.	Joseph Deng (AUS)	1.44.21(Mon)
14.	Alfred Kipketer (KEN)	1.44.28
15.	Marcin Lewandowski (POL)	1.44.32(Mon)
16.	Isaiah Harris (USA)	1.44.42(Par)
17.	Peter Bol (AUS)	1.44.56(Sto)
18.	Adam Kszczot (POL)	1.44.59(ECh)
19.	Jake Wightman (GBR)	1.44.61(Lon)
20.	Jackson Mumbwa Kivuva (KEN)	1.44.73(KeT)
	Guy Learmonth (GBR)	1.44.73(Lon)
22.	Mostafa Smaili (MAR)	1.44.90(Zag)
23.	Daniel Rowden (GBR)	1.44.97(Lon)
24.	Álvaro de Arriba (ESP)	1.44.99(Hue)
25.	Andreas Kramer (SWE)	1.45.03
26.	Jesus Tonatiu Lopez (MEX)	1.45.04
	Elliot Giles (GBR)	1.45.04(Lon)
28.	Erik Sowinski (USA)	1.45.07(Hen)
29.	Andrew Osagie (GBR)	1.45.09(Hen)
30.	Thiago Andre (BRA)	1.45.10(Hen)
31.	Antoine Gakeme (BDI)	1.45.14
32.	Rynhardt van Rensburg (RSA)	1.45.15(Hen)
33.	Kyle Langford (GBR)	1.45.16(GC)
34.	Nicholas Kiplangat Kipkoech (KEN)	1.45.20
35.	Boaz Kiprugut (KEN)	1.45.22(KeT)
36.	Marco Arop (CAN)	1.45.25(NCA)
37.	Michal Rozmys (POL)	1.45.32(ECh)
38.	Marc Reuther (GER)	1.45.42(Hen)
	Mateusz Borkowski (POL)	1.45.42(ECh)

WORLD INDOOR CHAMPIONSHIPS: 3-3-2018:

1. Adam Kszczot (POL)   (1.47.02)   1.47.47
2. Drew Windle (USA)   (1.45.52)   1.47.99
3. Saúl Ordóñez (ESP)   (1.47.11)   1.48.01
4. Elliot Giles (GBR)   (1.45.46)   1.48.22
5. Álvaro de Arriba (ESP) (1.45.44)   1.48.51
6. Mostafa Smaili (MAR)   (1.47.08)   1.48.75

----

7. Andreas Kramer (SWE)   1.47.21
8. Hamada Mohamed (EGY)   1.47.65
9. Antoine Gakeme (BDI)   1.49.66
   Donavan Brazier (USA)   dsq

WORLD INDOOR RANKING 2018:

1. Emmanuel Kipkurui Korir (KEN)   1.44.21
2. Donavan Brazier (USA)   1.45.10
3. Michael Saruni (KEN)   1.45.15
4. Álvaro de Arriba (ESP)   1.45.43
5. Elliot Giles (GBR)   1.45.46
6. Drew Windle (USA)   1.45.52
7. Mostafa Smaili (MAR)   1.45.96
8. Isaiah Harris (USA)   1.46.08
9. Amel Tuka (BIH)   1.46.33
10. Kyle Langford (GBR)   1.46.43
11. Adam Kszczot (POL)   1.46.47
12. Samuel Ellison (USA)   1.46.49
13. Marc Reuther (GER)   1.46.51
14. Nicholas Kiplangat Kipkoech (KEN)   1.46.52
15. Wycliffe Kinyamal (KEN)   1.46.54
16. Erik Sowinski (USA)   1.46.57
17. Clayton Murphy (USA)   1.46.61
18. Christian Harrison (USA)   1.46.83
19. Andreas Kramer (SWE)   1.46.87
20. Robert Heppenstall (CAN)   1.46.88
21. Marcin Lewandowski (POL)   1.46.90
22. Saúl Ordóñez (ESP)   1.46.96
23. Russell Dinkins (USA)   1.46.99
24. Andrew Osagie (GBR)   1.47.02
25. Neil Gourley (GBR)   1.47.04
26. John Lewis (USA)   1.47.14

Nairobi, 17-2-2018:
1.	Jonathan Kitilit (KEN)	1.44.64
2.	Wycliffe Kinyamal (KEN)	1.44.72
3.	Cornelius Tuwei (KEN)	1.44.91

Gold Coast, Commonwealth Games, 12-4-2018:
1.	Wycliffe Kinyamal (KEN)	1.45.11
2.	Kyle Langford (GBR)	1.45.16
3.	Luke Marshall (AUS)	1.45.60

Doha, 4-5-2018:
1.	Emmanuel Kipkurui Korir (KEN)	1.45.21
2.	Elijah Motonei Manangoi (KEN)	1.45.60
3.	Nicholas Kiplangat Kipkoech (KEN)	1.46.51
4.	Adam Kszczot (POL)	1.46.70
5.	Ferguson Cheruiyot Rotich (KEN)	1.46.76
6.	Clayton Murphy (USA)	1.47.22
7.	Antoine Gakeme (BDI)	1.47.25

Shanghai, 12-5-2018:
1.	Wycliffe Kinyamal (KEN)	1.43.91
2.	Jonathan Kitilit (KEN)	1.43.95
3.	Marcin Lewandowski (POL)	1.45.41

Eugene, 25-5-2018:
1.	Emmanuel Kipkurui Korir (KEN)	1.45.16
2.	Nijel Amos (BOT)	1.45.51
3.	Wycliffe Kinyamal (KEN)	1.46.14
4.	Kipyegon Bett (KEN)	1.46.46
5.	Kyle Langford (GBR)	1.46.53
6.	Adam Kszczot (POL)	1.46.64
7.	Ferguson Cheruiyot Rotich (KEN)	1.46.90
8.	Erik Sowinski (POL)	1.46.91

Rome, 31-5-2018:
1.	Wycliffe Kinyamal (KEN)	1.44.65
2.	Ferguson Cheruiyot Rotich (KEN)	1.44.74
3.	Jonathan Kitilit (KEN)	1.44.78
4.	Brandon McBride (CAN)	1.44.99
5.	Amel Tuka (BIH)	1.45.68

Hengelo, 3-6-2018:
1.	Jonathan Kitilit (KEN)	1.43.77
2.	Joseph Deng (AUS)	1.44.97
3.	Erik Sowinski (USA)	1.45.07
4.	Andrew Osagie (GBR)	1.45.09
5.	Thiago Andre (BRA)	1.45.10
6.	Rynhardt van Rensburg (RSA)	1.45.15
7.	Andreas Kramer (SWE)	1.45.38
8.	Marc Reuther (GER)	1.45.42

Stockholm, 10-6-2018:
1.	Peter Bol (AUS)	1.44.56
2.	Joseph Deng (AUS)	1.44.61
3.	Rynhardt van Rensburg (RSA)	1.45.73

KEN Trials, Nairobi, 23-6-2018:
1.	Jonathan Kitilit		1.43.46
2.	Ferguson Cheruiyot Rotich		1.44.26
3.	Jackson Mumbwa Kivuva		1.44.73
4.	Boaz Kiprugut		1.45.22
5.	Cornelius Tuwei		1.45.28
6.	Moses Kipkemboi Kibet		1.45.62
7.	Nicholas Kiplangat Kipkoech		1.46.03
8.	Edwin Kiplagat Melly	(1.45.89)	1.48.45

US CHAMPIONSHIPS, Des Moines, 24-6-2018:
1.	Clayton Murphy	1.46.50
2.	Isaiah Harris	1.47.11
3.	Erik Sowinski	1.47.76

Nancy, 27-6-2018:
1.	Alfred Kipketer (KEN)	1.44.28
2.	Nicholas Kiplangat Kipkoech (KEN)	1.45.20
3.	Cornelius Tuwei (KEN)	1.45.34
4.	Peter Bol (AUS)	1.45.35
5.	Filip Snejdr (CZE)	1.45.56
6.	Job Kinyor (KEN)	1.45.84

Paris, 30-6-2018:
1.	Ferguson Cheruiyot Rotich (KEN)	1.43.73
2.	Jonatan Kitilit (KEN)	1.43.83
3.	Saúl Órdoñez (ESP)	1.44.36
4.	Isaiah Harris (USA)	1.44.42
5.	Alfred Kipketer (KEN)	1.44.62
6.	Joseph Deng (AUS)	1.44.67
7.	Pierre-Ambroise Bosse (FRA)	1.45.19
8.	Erik Sowinski (USA)	1.45.34

Szekesfehervar, 2-7-2018:
1. Ferguson Cheruiyot Rotich (KEN)   1.44.08
2. Nijel Amos (BOT)   1.44.18
3. Alfred Kipketer (KEN)   1.44.64
4. Clayton Murphy (USA)   1.44.69
5. Andreas Kramer (SWE)   1.45.34
6. Adam Kszczot (POL)   1.45.60
7. Erik Sowinski (USA)   1.45.90

Monaco, 20-7-2018:
1. Nijel Amos (BOT)   1.42.14
2. Brandon McBride (CAN)   1.43.20
3. Saúl Órdoñez (ESP)   1.43.65
4. Cornelius Tuwei (KEN)   1.43.82
5. Jonathan Kitilit (KEN)   1.43.91
6. Pierre-Ambroise Bosse (FRA)   1.44.20
7. Joseph Deng (AUS)   1.44.21
8. Marcin Lewandowski (POL)   1.44.32

London, 22-7-2018:
1. Emmanuel Kipkurui Korir (KEN)   1.42.05
2. Clayton Murphy (USA)   1.43.12
3. Wycliffe Kinyamal (KEN)   1.43.12
4. Nijel Amos (BOT)   1.43.29
5. Jake Wightman (GBR)   1.44.61
6. Adam Kszczot (POL)   1.44.72
7. Guy Learmonth (GBR)   1.44.73
8. Daniel Rowden (GBR)   1.44.97
9. Elliot Giles (GBR)   1.45.04
10. Andrew Osagie (GBR)   1.45.25

AFR CHAMPIONSHIPS, Assaba, 3-8-2018:
1. Nijel Amos (BOT)   1.45.20
2. Emmanuel Kipkurui Korir (KEN)   1.45.65
3. Mostafa Smaili (MAR)   1.45.90
4. Antoine Gakeme (BDI)   1.45.91
5. Ferguson Cheruiyot Rotich (KEN)   1.46.33
6. Jonathan Kitilit (KEN)   1.46.88

Birmingham, 18-8-2018:
1. Emmanuel Kipkurui Korir (KEN)   1.42.79
2. Jonathan Kitilit (KEN)   1.43.53
3. Elijah Motonei Manangoi (KEN)   1.44.15
4. Ferguson Cheruiyot Rotich (KEN)   1.44.44
5. Marcin Lewandowski (POL)   1.44.75
6. Adam Kszczot (POL)   1.44.97
7. Jake Wightman (GBR)   1.45.00

Brussels, 31-8-2018:
1. Emmanuel Kipkurui Korir (KEN)   1.44.72
2. Marcin Lewandowski (POL)   1.45.21
3. Ferguson Cheruiyot Rotich (KEN)   1.45.28
4. Jake Wightman (GBR)   1.45.96
5. Clayton Murphy (USA)   1.45.97
6. Wycliffe Kinyamal (KEN)   1.46.02

Zagreb, 4-9-2018:
1. Nijel Amos (BOT)   1.44.08
2. Marcin Lewandowski (POL)   1.44.43
3. Jonathan Kitilit (KEN)   1.44.50
4. Cornelius Tuwei (KEN)   1.44.66
5. Mostafa Smaili (MAR)   1.44.90
6. Clayton Murphy (USA)   1.45.79

CONTINENTAL CUP, Ostrava, 8-9-2018:
1. Emmanuel Kipkurui Korir (AFR)   1.46.50
2. Clayton Murphy (AME)   1.46.77
3. Nijel Amos (BOT)   1.46.77

OVERVIEW WORLDWIDE OUTDOOR CHAMPIONSHIP FINALISTS OF PAST 6 YEARS

	Wch 17	OG 16	Wch 15	Wch 13
Pierre-Ambroise Bosse (FRA)	1.44.67 (1)	1.43.41 (4)	1.46.63 (5)	1.44.79 (7)
Adam Kszczot (POL)	1.44.95 (2)		1.46.08 (2)	
Kipyegon Bett (KEN)	1.45.21 (3)			
Kyle Langford (GBR)	1.45.25 (4)			
Nijel Amos (BOT)	1.45.83 (5)			
Mohammed Aman (ETH)	1.46.06 (6)			1.43.31 (1)
Thiago André (BRA)	1.46.30 (7)			
Brandon McBride (CAN)	1.47.09 (8)			
David Lekuta Rudisha (KEN)		1.42.15 (1)	1.45.84 (1)	
Taoufik Makhloufi (ALG)		1.42.61 (2)		
Clayton Murphy (USA)		1.42.93 (3)		
Ferguson Cheruiyot Rotich (KEN)		1.43.55 (5)	1.46.35 (4)	
Marcin Lewandowski (POL)		1.44.20 (6)		1.44.08 (4)
Alfred Kipketer (KEN)		1.46.02 (7)	1.47.66 (8)	
Boris Berian (USA)		1.46.15 (8)		
Amel Tuka (BIH)			1.46.30 (3)	
Musaeb Abdulrahman Balla (QAT)			1.47.01 (6)	
Nader Belhanbel (MAR)			1.47.09 (7)	
Nick Symmonds (USA)				1.43.55 (2)
Ayanleh Souleiman (DJI)				1.43.76 (3)
Andrew Osagie (GBR)				1.44.36 (5)
Duane Solomon (USA)				1.44.42 (6)
Abdulaziz Mohammed (KSA)				1.46.57 (8)

OVERVIEW WORLDWIDE INDOOR CHAMPIONSHIP FINALISTS OF 5 PAST YEARS

	Wch 18	Wch 16	Wch 14
Adam Kszczot (POL)	1.47.47 (1)		1.46.76 (2)
Drew Windle (USA)	1.47.99 (2)		
Saúl Ordóñez (ESP)	1.48.01 (3)		
Elliot Giles (GBR)	1.48.22 (4)		
Álvaro de Arriba (ESP)	1.48.51 (5)		
Mostafa Smaili (MAR)	1.48.75 (6)	1.52.32 (6)	
Boris Berian (USA)		1.45.83 (1)	
Antoine Gakeme (BDI)		1.46.65 (2)	
Erik Sowinski (USA)		1.47.22 (3)	
Mohammed Aman (ETH)		1.47.97 (4)	1.46.40 (1)
Musaeb Abdulrahman Balla (QAT)		1.48.31 (5)	
Andrew Osagie (GBR)			1.47.10 (3)
André Olivier (RSA)			1.47.31 (4)
Thijmen Kupers (NED)			1.47.74 (5)
Marcin Lewandowski (POL)			dsq (6)

OVERVIEW TOP 10 WORLD OUTDOOR RANKINGS OF PAST 5 YEARS

	2018	2017	2016	2015	2014
Emmanuel Kipkirui Korir (KEN)	1.42.05 (1)	1.43.10 (1)			1.42.53 (2)
Nijel Amos (BOT)	1.42.14 (2)	1.43.18 (2)		1.42.66 (2)	1.42.45 (1)
Clayton Murphy (USA)	1.43.12 (3)	1.43.60 (3)	1.42.93 (4)		
Wycliffe Kinyamal (KEN)	1.43.12 (3)	1.43.94 (4)			
Brandon McBride (CAN)	1.43.20 (5)	1.44.41 (8)			
Michael Saruni (KEN)	1.43.25 (6)				
Jonathan Kiprotich Kitilit (KEN)	1.43.46 (7)		1.43.05 (5)		
Saúl Órdoñez (ESP)	1.43.65 (8)				
Ferguson Cheruiyot Rotich (KEN)	1.43.73 (9)	1.44.37 (7)	1.43.43 (8)	1.43.60 (9)	1.42.84 (4)
Cornelius Tuwei (KEN)	1.43.82 (10)				
Donovan Brazier (USA)		1.43.95 (5)	1.43.55 (10)		
Kipyegon Bett (KEN)		1.44.04 (6)			
Asbel Kiprop (KEN)		1.44.43 (9)			1.43.34 (6)
Antoine Gakeme (BDI)		1.44.44 (10)			
David Lekuta Rudisha (KEN)			1.42.15 (1)	1.43.58 (8)	1.42.98 (5)
Taoufik Makhloufi (ALG)			1.42.61 (2)		1.43.53 (7)
Alfred Kipketer (KEN)			1.42.87 (3)		
Nicholas Kiplangat Kipkoech (KEN)			1.43.37 (6)		
Pierre-Ambroise Bosse (FRA)			1.43.41 (7)		
Ayanleh Souleiman (DJI)			1.43.52 (9)	1.42.97 (3)	1.43.69 (9)
Amel Tuka (BIH)				1.42.51 (1)	
Boris Berian (USA)				1.43.34 (4)	
Adam Kszczot (POL)				1.43.45 (5)	
Mohamed Aman (ETH)				1.43.56 (6)	1.42.83 (3)
Robert Kiptoo Biwott (KEN)				1.43.56 (6)	
Marcin Lewandowski (POL)				1.43.72 (10)	
Timothy Kitum (KEN)					1.43.65 (8)
Yeimer López (CUB)					1.43.71 (10)

OVERVIEW TOP 10 WORLD INDOOR RANKINGS OF PAST 5 YEARS

	2018	2017	2016	2015	2014
Emmanuel Kipkirui Korir (KEN)	1.44.21 (1)	1.46.75 (6)			
Donavan Brazier (USA)	1.45.10 (2)		1.45.93 (3)		
Michael Saruni (KEN)	1.45.15 (3)	1.46.90 (10)			
Álvaro de Arriba (ESP)	1.45.43 (4)				
Elliot Giles (GBR)	1.45.46 (5)				
Drew Windle (USA)	1.45.52 (6)				
Mostafa Smaili (MAR)	1.45.96 (7)		1.46.50 (10)		
Isaiah Harris (USA)	1.46.08 (8)				
Amel Tuka (BIH)	1.46.33 (9)	1.46.59 (5)			
Kyle Langford (GBR)	1.46.43 (10)	1.46.79 (7)			
Casimir Loxsom (USA)		1.46.13 (1)			
Adam Kszczot (POL)		1.46.17 (2)	1.45.63 (1)	1.45.77 (2)	1.45.19 (3)
Nicholas Kiplangat Kipkoech (KEN)		1.46.34 (3)			
Kevin López (ESP)		1.46.58 (4)	1.46.26 (8)		1.45.69 (6)
Erik Sowinski (USA)		1.46.80 (8)		1.46.92 (10)	
Andreas Kramer (SWE)		1.46.86 (9)			
Boris Berian (USA)			1.45.83 (2)		
Musaeb Abdulrahman Balla (QAT)			1.45.93 (3)	1.45.48 (1)	
Andrés Arroyo (PUR)			1.46.20 (5)		
Thijmen Kupers (NED)			1.46.21 (6)		1.46.55 (9)
Pierre-Ambroise Bosse (FRA)			1.46.25 (7)		
Hector Hernandez (USA)			1.46.32 (9)		
Marcin Lewandowski (POL)				1.45.78 (3)	1.45.56 (5)
Jeremiah Kipkorir Mutai (KEN)				1.45.93 (4)	
André Olivier (RSA)				1.46.04 (5)	1.44.99 (2)
Edward Kibet Kemboi (KEN)				1.46.05 (6)	
Timothy Kitum (KEN)				1.46.55 (7)	
Andreas Almgren (SWE)				1.46.56 (8)	
Dylan Capwell (USA)				1.46.70 (9)	
Mohammed Aman (ETH)					1.44.52 (1)
Andrew Osagie (GBR)					1.45.22 (4)
Abraham Kipchirchir Rotich (KEN)					1.46.30 (7)
Stepan Poistogov (RUS)					1.46.53 (8)
Michael Rutt (USA)					1.46.71 (10)

WORLD RANKING ALL TIME:

1.	David Rudisha (KEN)	1.40.91 (2012)
2.	Wilson Kipketer (DEN)	1.41.11 (1997)
3.	Sebastian Coe (GBR)	1.41.73 (1981)
	Nijel Amos (BOT)	1.41.73 (2012)
5.	Joaquim Cruz (BRA)	1.41.77 (1984)
6.	Emmanuel Kipkurui Korir (KEN)	1.42.05 (2018)
7.	Abubaker Kaki (SUD)	1.42.23 (2010)
8.	Sammy Koskei (KEN)	1.42.28 (1984)
9.	Wilfred Bungei (KEN)	1.42.34 (2002)
10.	Mohammed Aman (ETH)	1.42.37 (2010)
11.	Yuriy Borzakovskiy (RUS)	1.42.47 (2001)
12.	Amel Tuka (BIH)	1.42.51 (2015)
13.	Timothy Kitum (KEN)	1.42.53 (2012)
	Pierre-Ambroise Bosse (FRA)	1.42.53 (2014)
15.	André Bücher (SUI)	1.42.55 (2001)
16.	Vebjörn Rodal (NOR)	1.42.58 (1996)
17.	Johnny Gray (USA)	1.42.60 (1985)
18.	Taoufik Makhloufi (ALG)	1.42.61 (2016)
19.	Patrick Ndururi (KEN)	1.42.62 (1997)
20.	Alfred Kirwa Yego (KEN)	1.42.67 (2009)
21.	Japheth Kimutai (KEN)	1.42.69 (1999)
	Hezekiel Sepeng (RSA)	1.42.69 (1999)
23.	Fred Onyancha (KEN)	1.42.79 (1996)
	Yusuf Saad Kamel (BRN)	1.42.79 (2008)
25.	Jean-Patrick Nduwimana (BDI)	1.42.81 (2001)
26.	Duane Solomon (USA)	1.42.82 (2012)
27.	Ferguson Cheruiyot Rotich (KEN)	1.42.84 (2014)
28.	Norberto Téllez (CUB)	1.42.85 (1996)
29.	Mbulaeni Mulaudzi (RSA)	1.42.86 (2009)
30.	Alfred Kipketer (KEN)	1.42.87 (2016)
31.	Steve Cram (GBR)	1.42.88 (1985)
32.	William Yiampoy (KEN)	1.42.91 (2002)
33.	Clayton Murphy (USA)	1.42.93 (2016)
34.	Boaz Kiplagat Lalang (KEN)	1.42.95 (2010)
	Nick Symmonds (USA)	1.42.95 (2012)
36.	Peter Elliott (GBR)	1.42.97 (1990)
	Ayanleh Souleiman (DJI)	1.42.97 (2015)
38.	Patrick Konchellah (KEN)	1.42.98 (1997)
39.	Kennedy Kimwetich (KEN)	1.43.03 (1998)
40.	Jonathan Kitilit (KEN)	1.43.05 (2016)
41.	Billy Konchellah (KEN)	1.43.06 (1987)
42.	Yeimer López (CUB)	1.43.07 (2008)
43.	José Luis Barbosa (BRA)	1.43.08 (1991)
44.	Djabir Said-Guerni (ALG)	1.43.09 (1999)
45.	Wycliffe Kinyamal (KEN)	1.43.12 (2018)

WORLD RANKING ALL TIME INDOOR:

1.	Wilson Kipketer (DEN)	1.42.67 (1997)
2.	Yuriy Borzakovskiy (RUS)	1.44.15 (2001)
3.	Emmanuel Kipkurui Korir (KEN)	1.44.21 (2018)
4.	Mohammed Aman (ETH)	1.44.52 (2014)
5.	Adam Kszczot (POL)	1.44.57 (2012)
6.	Joseph Mwengi Mutua (KEN)	1.44.71 (2004)
7.	Ismail Ahmed Ismail (SUD)	1.44.75 (2009)
8.	Pawel Czapiewski (POL)	1.44.78 (2002)
9.	Abubaker Kaki (SUD)	1.44.81 (2008)
10.	Mehdi Baala (FRA)	1.44.82 (2003)
11.	Paul Ereng (KEN)	1.44.84 (1989)
12.	Nico Motchebon (GER)	1.44.88 (1995)
13.	Sebastian Coe (GBR)	1.44.91 (1983)
	Mbulaeni Mulaudzi (RSA)	1.44.91 (2008)
15.	André Bücher (SUI)	1.44.93 (2002)
16.	Wilfred Bungei (KEN)	1.44.97 (2003)
17.	André Olivier (RSA)	1.44.99 (2014)
18.	Johnny Gray (USA)	1.45.00 (1992)
19.	Donovan Brazier (USA)	1.45.10 (2018)
20.	Hezekiel Sepeng (RSA)	1.45.12 (2003)
21.	Boaz Kiplagat Lalang (KEN)	1.45.15 (2009)
	Michael Saruni (KEN)	1.45.15 (2018)
23.	Andrew Osagie (GBR)	1.45.22 (2014)
24.	Antonio Manuel Reina (ESP)	1.45.25 (2002)
25.	Yusuf Saad Kamel (BRN)	1.45.26 (2008)
26.	Jean-Patrick Nduwimana (BDI)	1.45.33 (2001)
27.	Marcin Lewandowski (POL)	1.45.41 (2012)
28.	José Luis Barbosa (BRA)	1.45.43 (1989)
	Álvaro de Arriba (ESP)	1.45.43 (2018)
30.	Giuseppe D'Urso (ITA)	1.45.44 (1993)
31.	Johan Botha (RSA)	1.45.45 (1999)
32.	Elliot Giles (GBR)	1.45.46 (2018)
33.	Musaeb Abdulrahman Balla (QAT)	1.45.48 (2015)
34.	Drew Windle (USA)	1.45.52 (2018)
35.	Nils Schumann (GER)	1.45.57 (2003)
36.	David Lelei (KEN)	1.45.65 (2001)
37.	David Krummenacker (USA)	1.45.69 (2003)
	Kevin López (ESP)	1.45.69 (2014)
39.	Anthony Morrell (GBR)	1.45.72 (1988)
	Dmitrijs Milkevics (LAT)	1.45.72 (2008)
41.	El-Mahjoub Haida (MAR)	1.45.76 (1997)
	Dmitriy Bogdanov (RUS)	1.45.76 (2008)
43.	Einars Tupuritis (LAT)	1.45.80 (1996)
	William Yiampoy (KEN)	1.45.80 (2004)
45.	Boris Berian (USA)	1.45.83 (2016)

1500 m Men

EUROPEAN CHAMPIONSHIPS 2018: 10-8-2018:		WORLD RANKING 2018:	
1. Jakob Ingebrigtsen (NOR)	3.38.10	1. Timothy Cheruiyot (KEN)	3.28.41(Mon)
2. Marcin Lewandowski (POL)	3.38.14	2. Elijah Motonei Manangoi (KEN)	3.29.64(Mon)
3. Jake Wightman (GBR)	3.38.25	3. Filip Ingebrigtsen (NOR)	3.30.01(Mon)
4. Henrik Ingebrigtsen (NOR)	3.38.50	4. Jakob Ingebrigtsen (NOR)	3.31.18(Mon)
5. Charlie Da'Vall Grice (GBR)	3.38.65	5. Ayanleh Souleiman (QAT)	3.31.19(Mon)
6. Simas Bertasius (LTU)	3.39.04	6. Abdelaati Iguider (MAR)	3.31.59(Zü)
7. Timo Benitz (GER)	3.39.28	7. Brahim Kaazouzi (MAR)	3.31.62(Mon)
8. Ismael Debjani (BEL)	3.39.48	8. Samuel Tefera (ETH)	3.31.63(Sha)
9. Chris O'Hare (GBR)	3.39.53	9. Matthew Centrowitz (USA)	3.31.77(Mon)
10. Sheikh Ali Mohad Abdikadar (ITA)	3.39.95	10. Aman Wote (ETH)	3.31.90(Mon)
11. Joao Bussotti Neves Jr (ITA)(3.40.87)	3.41.31	11. Chris O'Hare (GBR)	3.32.11(Mon)
12. Filip Ingebrigtsen (NOR) (3.40.88)	3.41.66	12. Jakub Holusa (CZE)	3.32.49(Mon)
13. Homiyu Tesfaye (GER)	3.47.83	13. Yomif Kejelcha (ETH)	3.32.59(Zag)
--		14. Charles Cheboi Simotwo (KEN)	3.32.61(Par)
14. Kalle Berglund (SWE)	3.41.25	15. Ferguson Cheruiyot Rotich (KEN)	3.33.21(Ber)
15. Simon Denissel (FRA)	3.41.67	16. Jake Wightman (GBR)	3.33.96(Mon)
16. Elmar Engholm (SWE)	3.42.01	17. Charlie Da'Vall Grice (GBR)	3.34.20(Rab)
17. Marius Probst (GER)	3.42.37	18. Bethwell Birgen (KEN)	3.34.27(Par)
18. Isaac Kimeli (BEL)	3.42.77	19. Justus Soget (KEN)	3.34.33(Sha)
19. Jan Hochstrasser (SUI)	3.42.80	20. Ryan Gregson (AUS)	3.34.38(Rab)
20. Adrian Ben (ESP)	3.42.81	21. Ismael Debjani (BEL)	3.34.40(Ber)
21. Tamás Kazi (HUN)	3.42.98	22. Sadik Mikhou (BRN)	3.34.55(Par)
22. Amine Khadiri (CYP)	3.45.97	23. Stewart McSweyn (AUS)	3.34.82
23. Johan Rogestedt (SWE)	3.49.73	24. Josh Kerr (GBR)	3.35.01
24. Jakub Holusa (CZE)	3.49.82	25. Marcin Lewandowski (POL)	3.35.06(Rab)
		26. Taresa Tolosa (ETH)	3.35.07(Do)
		27. Nick Willis (NZL)	3.35.25(Ber)

WORLD INDOOR CHAMPIONSHIPS: 4-3-2018:

1.	Samuel Tefera (ETH)	(3.44.00)	3.58.19
2.	Marcin Lewandowski (POL)	(3.40.78)	3.58.39
3.	Abdelaati Iguider (MAR)	(3.40.13)	3.58.43
4.	Aman Wote (ETH)	(3.40.20)	3.58.64
5.	Ben Blankenship (USA)	(3.40.23)	3.58.89
6.	Jake Wightman (GBR)	(3.47.23)	3.58.91
7.	Craig Engels (USA)	(3.47.55)	3.58.92
8.	Chris O'Hare (GBR)	(3.42.46)	4.00.65
9.	Vincent Kibet (KEN)	(3.44.26)	4.02.32

10.	Ryan Gregson (AUS)	3.44.44
11.	Marc Alcalá (ESP)	3.45.49
12.	Jakub Holusa (CZE)	3.45.84
13.	Kalle Berglund (SWE)	3.46.61
14.	Brahim Kaazouzi (MAR)	3.47.65
15.	Musa Hajdari (KOS)	3.47.68

WORLD INDOOR RANKING 2018:

1.	Edward Cheserek (KEN)	3.33.76
2.	Ayanleh Souleiman (DJI)	3.35.39
3.	Abdelaati Iguider (MAR)	3.35.79
4.	Samuel Tefera (ETH)	3.36.05
5.	Vincent Kibet (KEN)	3.36.86
6.	Brahim Kaazouzi (MAR)	3.36.95
7.	Chris O'Hare (GBR)	3.37.03
8.	Taresa Tolosa (ETH)	3.37.41
9.	Jake Wightman (GBR)	3.37.43
10.	Marcin Lewandowski (POL)	3.37.67
11.	Bethwell Birgen (KEN)	3.37.76
12.	Jakub Holusa (CZE)	3.37.91
13.	Ryan Gregson (AUS)	3.38.00
14.	Aman Wote (ETH)	3.38.35
15.	Justus Soget (KEN)	3.38.47
16.	Sadik Mikhou (BRN)	3.38.48
17.	Craig Engels (USA)	3.38.53
18.	Charlie Da'Vall Grice (GBR)	3.39.05
19.	Brannon Kidder (USA)	3.39.17
20.	Ben Blankenship (USA)	3.39.19
21.	Valentin Smirnov (ANA)	3.39.27
22.	Marc Alcala (ESP)	3.39.45
23.	Vladimir Nikitin (RUS)	3.39.52
24.	Kalle Berglund (SWE)	3.39.55
25.	Josh Kerr (GBR)	3.39.58
26.	Kevin López (ESP)	3.39.86
27.	Mohammed Ayoub Tiouali (BRN)	3.39.91
28.	Julian Oakley (NZL)	3.39.92
29.	Filip Sasinek (CZE)	3.39.98
30.	Samir Dahmani (FRA)	3.40.23
31.	Jakob Ingebrigtsen (NOR)	3.40.31
32.	Grzegorz Kalinowski (POL)	3.40.42
33.	Tarik Moukrime (BEL)	3.40.73
34.	Benjamin Kigen (KEN)	3.40.92

Nairobi, 17-2-2018:
1. Timothy Cheruiyot (KEN)   3.34.84
2. Elijah Motonei Manangoi (KEN)   3.35.42
3. Kumari Taki (KEN)   3.35.83

Gold Coast, Commonwealth Games, 14-4-2018:
1. Elijah Motonei Manangoi (KEN)   3.34.78
2. Timothy Cheruiyot (KEN)   3.35.17
3. Jake Wightman (GBR)   3.35.97

Doha, 4-5-2018:
1. Taresa Tolosa (ETH)   3.35.07
2. Elijah Motonei Manangoi (KEN)   3.35.53
3. Justus Soget Kiplagat (KEN)   3.35.71
4. Charles Simotwo (KEN)   3.36.40
5. Bethwell Birgen (KEN)   3.36.54
6. Abdelaati Iguider (MAR)   3.36.59
7. Ryan Gregson (AUS)   3.37.00
8. Collins Cheboi (KEN)   3.37.83
9. Vincent Kibet (KEN)   3.38.11

Shanghai, 12-5-2018:
1. Timothy Cheruiyot (KEN)   3.31.48
2. Samuel Tefera (ETH)   3.31.63
3. Abdelaati Iguider (MAR)   3.32.72
4. Charles Simotwo (KEN)   3.33.54
5. Justus Soget Kiplagat (KEN)   3.34.33
6. Aman Wote (ETH)   3.34.43
7. Thiago Andre (BRA)   3.35.40
8. Bethwell Birgen (KEN)   3.35.95
9. Vincent Kibet (KEN)   3.36.44
10. Ryan Gregson (AUS)   3.36.94

Rome, 31-5-2018:
1. Timothy Cheruiyot (KEN)   3.31.22
2. Elijah Motonei Manangoi (KEN)   3.33.79
3. Samuel Tefera (ETH)   3.34.84
4. Ayanleh Souleiman (DJI)   3.34.87
5. Charles Simotwo (KEN)   3.35.03
6. Charles Da'Vall Grice (GBR)   3.35.72
7. Taresa Tolosa (ETH)   3.36.22
8. Aman Wote (ETH)   3.36.30

KEN Trials, Nairobi, 23-6-2018:
1. Timothy Cheruiyot   3.34.82
2. Charles Simotwo   3.36.86
3. Jeromiah Kiptanui   3.36.98
4. Laban Kiplimo   3.37.37
5. Lawi Komen   3.38.28
6. Collins Cheboi   3.39.23

Paris, 30-6-2018:
1. Timothy Cheruiyot (KEN)   3.29.71
2. Ayanleh Souleiman (DJI)   3.31.77
3. Charles Simotwo (KEN)   3.32.61
4. Aman Wote (ETH)   3.32.81
5. Jakub Holosa (CZE)   3.32.85
6. Filip Ingebrigtsen (NOR)   3.32.87
7. Bethwell Birgen (KEN)   3.34.27
8. Sadik Mikhou (BRN)   3.34.55
9. Ismael Debjani (BEL)   3.35.71
10. Nick Willis (NZL)   3.36.26

Rabat, 13-7-2018:
1. Brahim Kaazouzi (MAR)   3.33.22
2. Filip Ingebrigtsen (NOR)   3.33.40
3. Ayenleh Souleiman (DJI)   3.33.42
4. Jakub Holosa (CZE)   3.33.80
5. Charles Da'Vall Grice (GBR)   3.34.20
6. Ryan Gregson (AUS)   3.34.38
7. Aman Wote (ETH)   3.34.39
8. Charles Simotwo (KEN)   3.34.75
9. Marcin Lewandowski (POL)   3.35.06
10. Matthew Centrowitz (USA)   3.35.17
11. Hicham Ouldha (MAR)   3.35.35

Monaco, 20-7-2018:
1. Timothy Cheruiyot (KEN)   3.28.41
2. Elijah Motonei Manangoi (KEN)   3.29.64
3. Filip Ingebrigtsen (NOR)   3.30.01
4. Jakob Ingebrigtsen (NOR)   3.31.18
5. Ayanleh Souleiman (DJI)   3.31.19
6. Brahim Kaazouzi (MAR)   3.31.62
7. Matt Centrowitz (USA)   3.31.77
8. Aman Wote (ETH)   3.31.90
9. Chris O'Hare (GBR)   3.32.11
10. Jakub Holusa (CZE)   3.32.49
11. Charles Simotwo (KEN)   3.32.77
12. Jake Wightman (GBR)   3.33.96
13. Ferguson Cheruiyot Rotich (KEN) 3.35.26

London, 22-7-2018:

1. Matthew Centrowitz (USA)   3.35.22
2. Ryan Gregson (AUS)   3.35.35
3. Justus Soget Kiplagat (KEN)   3.35.56
4. Henrik Ingebrigtsen (NOR)   3.35.61
5. Youssouf Hiss Bachir (DJI)   3.35.74
6. Nick Willis (NZL)   3.35.77
7. Andrew Hunter (USA)   3.35.90
8. Neil Gourley (GBR)   3.35.98
9. Vincent Kibet (KEN)   3.36.12
10. Jordan Williamsz (AUS)   3.36.78

Zürich, 30-8-2018:

1. Timothy Cheruiyot (KEN)   3.32.37
2. Ferguson Cheruiyot Rotich (KEN)   3.33.21
3. Ismael Debjani (BEL)   3.34.40
4. Bethwell Birgen (KEN)   3.34.60
5. Ryan Gregson (AUS)   3.34.89
6. Abdelaati Iguider (MAR)   3.35.12
7. Nick Willis (NZL)   3.35.25
8. Cornelius Tuwei (KEN)   3.35.72
9. Aman Wote (ETH)   3.36.84

Zagreb, 4-9-2018:

1. Elijah Motonei Manangoi (KEN)   3.32.52
2. Yomif Kejelcha (ETH)   3.32.59
3. Ayanleh Souleiman (DJI)   3.33.93
4. Abdelaati Iguider (MAR)   3.34.21
5. Bethwell Birgen (KEN)   3.34.57
6. Filip Ingebrigtsen (NOR)   3.35.66
7. Brahim Kaazouzi (MAR)   3.35.72
8. Nick Willis (NZL)   3.36.10
9. Henrik Ingebrigtsen (NOR)   3.36.46

CONTINENTAL CUP, Ostrava, 9-9-2018:

1. Elijah Motonei Manangoi (AFR)   3.40.00
2. Marcin Lewandowski (EUR)   3.40.42
3. Jakob Ingebrigtsen (EUR)   3.40.80
4. Charles Philibert-Thiboutot (AME)   3.40.90
5. Ryan Gregson (ASI)   3.40.91

OVERVIEW WORLDWIDE OUTDOOR CHAMPIONSHIP FINALISTS OF PAST 6 YEARS

	Wch 17	OG 16	Wch 15	Wch 13
Elijah Motonei Manangoi (KEN)	3.33.61 (1)		3.34.63 (2)	
Timothy Cheruiyot (KEN)	3.33.99 (2)		3.36.05 (7)	
Filip Ingebrigtsen (NOR)	3.34.53 (3)			
Adel Mechaal (ESP)	3.34.71 (4)			
Jakub Holusa (CZE)	3.34.89 (5)			
Sadik Mikhou (BRN)	3.35.81 (6)			
Marcin Lewandowski (POL)	3.36.02 (7)			
Nicholas Willis (NZL)	3.36.82 (8)	3.50.24 (3)	3.35.46 (6)	
Asbel Kiprop (KEN)	3.37.24 (9)	3.50.87 (6)	3.34.40 (1)	3.36.28 (1)
John Gregorek (USA)	3.37.56 (10)			
Fouad Elkaam (MAR)	3.37.72 (11)			
Chris O'Hare (GBR)	3.38.28 (12)			3.46.04 (12)
Matthew Centrowitz (USA)		3.50.00 (1)	3.36.13 (8)	3.36.78 (2)
Taoufik Makhloufi (ALG)		3.50.11 (2)	3.34.76 (4)	
Ayanleh Souleiman (DJI)		3.50.29 (4)		
Abdalaati Iguider (MAR)		3.50.58 (5)	3.34.67 (3)	
David Bustos (ESP)		3.51.06 (7)		
Ben Blankenship (USA)		3.51.09 (8)		
Ryan Gregson (AUS)		3.51.39 (9)		
Nathan Brannen (CAN)		3.51.45 (10)		3.38.09 (10)
Ronald Musagala (UGA)		3.51.68 (11)		
Charlie Grice (GBR)		3.51.73 (12)	3.36.21 (9)	
Ronald Kwemoi (KEN)		3.56.76 (13)		
Silas Kiplagat (KEN)			3.34.81 (5)	3.37.11 (6)
Leonel Manzano (USA)			3.37.26 (10)	
Robby Andrews (USA)			3.38.29 (11)	
Aman Wote (ETH)			dnf (12)	
Johan Cronje (RSA)				3.36.83 (3)
Nixon Kiplimo Chepseba (KEN)				3.36.87 (4)
Homiyu Tesfaye (GER)				3.37.03 (5)
Mekonnen Gebremedhin (ETH)				3.37.21 (7)
Henrik Ingebrigtsen (NOR)				3.37.52 (8)
Mohamed Moustaoui (MAR)				3.38.08 (9)
Florian Carvalho (FRA)				3.39.17 (11)

OVERVIEW WORLDWIDE INDOOR CHAMPIONSHIP FINALISTS OF 5 PAST YEARS

	Wch 18	Wch 16	Wch 14
Samuel Tefera (ETH)	3.58.19 (1)		
Marcin Lewandowski (POL)	3.58.39 (2)		
Abdelaati Iguider (MAR)	3.58.43 (3)		3.58.21 (3)
Aman Wote (ETH)	3.58.64 (4)	3.44.86 (6)	3.38.08 (2)
Ben Blankenship (USA)	3.58.89 (5)		
Jake Wightman (GBR)	3.58.91 (6)		
Craig Engels (USA)	3.58.92 (7)		
Chris O'Hare (GBR)	4.00.65 (8)	3.46.50 (8)	
Vincent Kibet (KEN)	4.02.32 (9)	3.45.17 (7)	
Matthew Centrowitz (USA)		3.44.22 (1)	
Jakub Holusa (CZE)		3.44.30 (2)	3.39.23 (5)
Nicholas Willis (NZL)		3.44.37 (3)	dsq (9)
Robby Andrews (USA)		3.44.77 (4)	
Dawit Wolde (ETH)		3.44.81 (5)	
Ayanleh Souleiman (DJI)		3.53.69 (9)	3.37.52 (1)
Ilham Tanui Özbilen (TUR)			3.39.10 (4)
Will Leer (USA)			3.39.60 (6)
Homiyu Tesfaye (GER)			3.39.90 (7)
Bethwell Birgen (KEN)			3.40.66 (8)

OVERVIEW TOP 10 WORLD OUTDOOR RANKINGS OF PAST 5 YEARS

	2018	2017	2016	2015	2014
Timothy Cheruiyot (KEN)	3.28.41 (1)	3.29.10 (2)	3.31.34 (4)		
Elijah Motonei Manangoi (KEN)	3.29.64 (2)	3.28.80 (1)	3.31.19 (3)	3.29.67 (6)	
Filip Ingebrigtsen (NOR)	3.30.01 (3)	3.32.48 (8)			
Jakob Ingebrigtsen (NOR)	3.31.18 (4)				
Ayanleh Souleiman (DJI)	3.31.19 (5)		3.31.68 (7)	3.30.17 (9)	3.29.58 (4)
Abdalaati Iguider (MAR)	3.31.59 (6)		3.31.40 (6)	3.28.79 (3)	3.29.83 (5)
Brahim Kaazouzi (MAR)	3.31.62 (7)				
Samuel Tefera (ETH)	3.31.63 (8)				
Matthew Centrowitz (USA)	3.31.77 (9)				
Aman Wote (ETH)	3.31.90 (10)	3.31.63 (5)		3.30.29 (10)	3.29.91 (6)
Ronald Kwemoi (KEN)		3.30.89 (3)	3.30.49 (2)		3.28.81 (3)
Sadik Mikhou (BRN)		3.31.34 (4)	3.32.30 (10)		
Silas Kiplagat (KEN)		3.32.23 (6)		3.30.12 (8)	3.27.64 (1)
Bethwell Birgen (KEN)		3.32.27 (7)			
Charles Simotwo (KEN)		3.32.59 (9)			
Vincent Kibet (KEN)		3.32.66 (10)			
Asbel Kiprop (KEN)		3.29.33 (1)	3.26.69 (1)	3.28.45 (2)	
Taoufik Makhloufi (ALG)			3.31.35 (5)	3.28.75 (2)	3.30.40 (8)
Mohamed Farah (GBR)			3.31.74 (8)	3.28.93 (4)	
Ryan Gregson (AUS)			3.32.13 (9)		
Nicholas Willis (NZL)				3.29.66 (5)	3.29.91 (6)
Robert Kiptoo Biwott (KEN)				3.30.10 (7)	
James Kiplagat Magut (KEN)					3.30.61 (9)
Leonel Manzano (USA)					3.30.98 (10)

OVERVIEW TOP 10 WORLD INDOOR RANKINGS OF PAST 5 YEARS

	2018	2017	2016	2015	2014
Edward Cheserek (KEN)	3.33.76 (1)				
Ayanleh Souleiman (QAT)	3.35.39 (2)		3.36.30 (4)		3.35.2 (2)
Abdelaati Iguider (MAR)	3.35.79 (3)		3.34.94 (1)		
Samuel Tefera (ETH)	3.36.05 (4)				
Vincent Kibet (KEN)	3.36.86 (5)		3.37.55 (9)	3.34.91 (3)	
Brahim Kaazouzi (MAR)	3.36.95 (6)				
Chris O'Hare (GBR)	3.37.03 (7)				
Taresa Tolosa (ETH)	3.37.41 (8)				
Jake Wightman (GBR)	3.37.43 (9)				
Marcin Lewandowski (POL)	3.37.67 (10)				
Ben Blankenship (USA)		3.36.42 (1)		3.35.28 (5)	
Ryan Gregson (AUS)		3.36.50 (2)			
Edward Cheserek (KEN)		3.37.01 (3)			
Bethwell Kiprotich Birgen (KEN)		3.37.32 (4)	3.37.55 (9)	3.34.62 (2)	3.35.3 (3)
Andrew Butchart (GBR)		3.37.58 (5)			
Elijah Motonei Manangoi (KEN)		3.37.62 (6)			
Kalle Berglund (SWE)		3.37.69 (7)			
John Gregorek (USA)		3.37.76 (8)			
Kyle Merber (USA)		3.37.83 (9)			
Ford Palmer (USA)		3.38.04 (10)			
Matthew Centrowitz (USA)			3.35.91 (2)	3.36.73 (9)	
Nicholas Willis (NZL)			3.36.12 (3)	3.36.73 (9)	
Mohamed Al-Garni (QAT)			3.36.35 (5)		
Benson Kiplagat Seurei (BRN)			3.37.08 (6)		
Said Aden Said (QAT)			3.37.29 (7)		
Musaab Adam Ali (QAT)			3.37.30 (8)		
Homiyu Tesfaye (GER)				3.34.13 (1)	3.37.35 (10)
Hillary Cheruiyot Ngetich (KEN)				3.35.26 (4)	
Nixon Kiplimo Chepseba (KEN)				3.35.28 (5)	3.37.02 (8)
Lee Emanuel (GBR)				3.35.66 (7)	
Collins Cheboi (KEN)				3.35.90 (8)	3.36.41 (6)
Mohamed Moustaoui (MAR)					3.35.0 (1)
Silas Kiplagat (KEN)					3.35.85 (4)
Aman Wote (ETH)					3.36.4 (5)
Caleb Mwangangi Ndiku (KEN)					3.36.8 (7)
Fouad Elkaam (MAR)					3.37.3 (9)

WORLD RANKING ALL TIME:

1.	Hicham El Guerrouj (MAR)	3.26.00 (1998)
2.	Bernard Lagat (USA)	3.26.34 (2001)
3.	Asbel Kiprop (KEN)	3.26.69 (2015)
4.	Noureddine Morceli (ALG)	3.27.37 (1995)
5.	Silas Kiplagat (KEN)	3.27.64 (2014)
6.	Noah Ngeny (KEN)	3.28.12 (2000)
7.	Timothy Cheruiyot (KEN)	3.28.41 (2018)
8.	Taoufik Makhloufi (ALG)	3.28.75 (2015)
9.	Abdelaati Iguider (MAR)	3.28.79 (2015)
10.	Elijah Motonei Manangoi (KEN)	3.28.80 (2017)
11.	Mo Farah (GBR)	3.28.81 (2013)
	Ronald Kwemoi (KEN)	3.28.81 (2014)
13.	Fermin Cacho (ESP)	3.28.95 (1997)
14.	Mehdi Baala (FRA)	3.28.98 (2003)
15.	Daniel Kipchirchir Komen (KEN)	3.29.02 (2006)
16.	Rashid Ramzi (BRN)	3.29.14 (2006)
17.	Vénuste Niyongabo (BDI)	3.29.18 (1997)
18.	William Chirchir (KEN)	3.29.29 (2001)
19.	Said Aouita (MAR)	3.29.46 (1985)
	Daniel Komen (KEN)	3.29.46 (1997)
21.	Augustine Kiprono Choge (KEN)	3.29.47 (2009)
22.	Caleb Mwangangi Ndiku (KEN)	3.29.50 (2013)
23.	Ali Saidi-Sief (ALG)	3.29.51 (2001)
24.	Amine Laalou (MAR)	3.29.53 (2010)
25.	Ayanleh Souleiman (DJI)	3.29.58 (2014)
26.	Nick Willis (NZL)	3.29.66 (2015)
27.	Steve Cram (GBR)	3.29.67 (1985)
28.	Sydney Maree (USA)	3.29.77 (1985)
	Sebastian Coe (GBR)	3.29.77 (1986)
	Nixon Kiplimo Chepseba (KEN)	3.29.77 (2012)
31.	Laban Rotich (KEN)	3.29.91 (1998)
	Aman Wote (ETH)	3.29.91 (2014)
33.	Filip Ingebrigtsen (NOR)	3.30.01 (2018)
34.	Timothy Kiptanui (KEN)	3.30.04 (2004)
35.	Rui Silva (POR)	3.30.07 (2002)
36.	Robert Biwott (KEN)	3.30.10 (2015)
37.	John Kemboi Kibowen (KEN)	3.30.18 (1998)
38.	Haron Keitany (KEN)	3.30.20 (2009)
39.	Cornelius Chirchir (KEN)	3.30.24 (2002)
40.	Ivan Heshko (UKR)	3.30.33 (2004)
41.	Collins Cheboi (KEN)	3.30.34 (2015)
42.	Matthew Centrowitz (USA)	3.30.40 (2015)
43.	Alex Kipchirchir (KEN)	3.30.46 (2004)
44.	Alan Webb (USA)	3.30.54 (2007)
45.	Abdi Bile (SOM)	3.30.55 (1989)

WORLD RANKING ALL TIME INDOOR:

1.	Hicham El Guerrouj (MAR)	3.31.18 (1997)
2.	Haile Gebrselassie (ETH)	3.31.76 (1998)
3.	Laban Rotich (KEN)	3.32.11 (1998)
4.	Daniel Kipchirchir Komen (KEN)	3.33.08 (2005)
5.	Deresse Mekonnen (ETH)	3.33.10 (2010)
6.	Vénuste Niyongabo (BDI)	3.33.17 (1998)
7.	Augustine Kiprono Choge (KEN)	3.33.23 (2011)
8.	Andrés Diaz (ESP)	3.33.32 (1999)
9.	Bernard Lagat (USA)	3.33.34 (2005)
10.	Edward Cheserek (KEN)	3.33.76 (2018)
11.	Haron Keitany (KEN)	3.33.96 (2009)
12.	Ivan Heshko (UKR)	3.33.99 (2005)
13.	Abdalaati Iguider (MAR)	3.34.10 (2012)
14.	Ismael Kipngetich Kombich (KEN)	3.34.13 (2011)
	Homiyu Tesfaye (GER)	3.34.13 (2015)
16.	Noureddine Morceli (ALG)	3.34.16 (1991)
17.	Peter Elliott (GBR)	3.34.20 (1990)
18.	Bethwell Birgen (KEN)	3.34.62 (2015)
19.	Nixon Kiplimo Chepseba (KEN)	3.34.63 (2011)
20.	Roberto Parra (ESP)	3.34.66 (2003)
21.	Mehdi Baala (FRA)	3.34.71 (2009)
22.	Ilham Tanui Özbilen (TUR)	3.34.76 (2012)
23.	William Tanui (KEN)	3.34.77 (1999)
24.	Cornelius Chirchir (KEN)	3.34.85 (2003)
25.	Mekonnen Gebremedhin (ETH)	3.34.89 (2012)
26.	Vincent Kibet (KEN)	3.34.91 (2015)
27.	Rui Silva (POR)	3.34.99 (1999)
28.	Mohamned Moustaoui (MAR)	3.35.0 (2014)
29.	Shadrack Korir (KEN)	3.35.03 (2007)
30.	Ayanleh Souleiman (DJI)	3.35.2 (2014)
31.	Suleiman Kipses Simotwo (KEN)	3.35.24 (2006)
32.	Silas Kiplagat (KEN)	3.35.26 (2012)
	Hillary Cheruiyot Ngetich (KEN)	3.35.26 (2015)
34.	Ben Blankenship (USA)	3.35.28 (2015)
35.	Fermin Cacho (ESP)	3.35.29 (1991)
36.	Aman Wote (ETH)	3.35.31 (2013)
37.	Gideon Gathimba (KEN)	3.35.40 (2010)
38.	Hailu Mekonnen (ETH)	3.35.58 (2000)
39.	Lee Emanuel (GBR)	3.35.66 (2015)
40.	Nick Willis (NZL)	3.35.80 (2010)
41.	Álvaro Fernández (ESP)	3.35.83 (2003)
42.	Collins Cheboi (KEN)	3.35.90 (2015)
43.	Ali Saidi-Sief (ALG)	3.36.02 (2004)
44.	José Luis González (ESP)	3.36.03 (1986)
45.	Samuel Tefera (ETH)	3.36.05 (2018)

Mile Men

WORLD RANKING OUTDOOR 2018:

1.	Timothy Cheruiyot (KEN)	3.49.87(Eug)
2.	Samuel Tefera (ETH)	3.51.26(Eug)
3.	Elijah Motonei Manangoi (KEN)	3.52.18(Eug)
4.	Jakob Ingebrigtsen (NOR)	3.52.28(Eug)
5.	Clayton Murphy (USA)	3.53.40(Eug)
6.	Matthew Centrowitz (USA)	3.53.61(Eug)
7.	Lopez Lomong (USA)	3.53.86(Ral)
8.	John Gregorek (USA)	3.54.539Ral)
9.	Bethwell Birgen (KEN)	3.54.60(Eug)
	Stewart McSweyn (AUS)	3.54.60(Bir)

WORLD RANKING INDOOR 2018:

1.	Edward Cheserek (KEN)	3.49.44
2.	Izaic Yorks (USA)	3.53.40
3.	Craig Engels (USA)	3.53.93
4.	Chris O'Hare (GBR)	3.54.14
5.	Josh Kerr (GBR)	3.54.72
6.	Ben Blankenship (USA)	3.54.77
7.	Julian Oakley (NZL)	3.55.10
8.	Henry Wynne (USA)	3.55.23
9.	Shadrack Kipchirchir (USA)	3.55.52
10.	Peter Callahan (BEL)	3.55.77
11.	Justyn Knight (CAN)	3.55.82
12.	Valentin Smirnov (ANA)	3.56.06
	Brannon Kidder (USA)	3.56.06
14.	Vladimir Nikitin (RUS)	3.56.44
15.	Charlie Da'Vall Grice (GBR)	3.56.47

Eugene, 26-5-2018:

1.	Timothy Cheruiyot (KEN)	3.49.87
2.	Samuel Tefera (ETH)	3.51.26
3.	Elijah Motonei Manangoi (KEN)	3.52.18
4.	Jakob Ingebrigtsen (NOR)	3.52.28
5.	Clayton Murphy (USA)	3.53.40
6.	Matthew Centrowitz (USA)	3.53.61
7.	Bethwell Birgen (KEN)	3.54.60
8.	Ayanleh Souleiman (QAT)	3.55.87
9.	Thiago Andre (BRA)	3.56.03
10.	Aman Wote (ETH)	3.56.49
11.	Ben Blankenship (USA)	3.56.67

Oslo, 7-6-2018:

1.	Elijah Motonei Manangoi (KEN)	3.56.95
2.	Sadik Mikhou (BRN)	3.57.10
3.	Taresa Tolosa (ETH)	3.57.92
4.	Filip Ingebrigtsen (NOR)	3.57.97
5.	Youness Essalhi (MAR)	3.58.00
6.	Henrik Ingebrigtsen (NOR)	3.58.46
7.	Ryan Gregson (AUS)	3.58.47
8.	Bethwell Birgen (KEN)	3.59.10
9.	Jake Wightman (GBR)	3.59.15
10.	Kumari Taki (KEN)	3.59.20
11.	Thiago Andre (BRA)	3.59.87

OVERVIEW TOP 10 WORLD OUTDOOR RANKINGS OF PAST 5 YEARS

	2018	2017	2016	2015	2014
Timothy Cheruiyot (KEN)	3.49.87 (1)	3.49.64 (3)	3.53.17 (10)		
Samuel Tefera (ETH)	3.51.26 (2)				
Elijah Motonei Manangoi (KEN)	3.52.18 (3)	3.49.08 (2)	3.52.04 (3)		
Jakob Ingebrigtsen (NOR)	3.52.28 (4)				
Clayton Murphy (USA)	3.53.40 (5)	3.51.99 (5)			
Matthew Centrowitz (USA)	3.53.61 (6)			3.51.20 (2)	3.50.53 (10)
Lopez Lomong (USA)	3.53.86 (7)				
John Gregorek (USA)	3.54.53 (8)				
Bethwell Birgen (KEN)	3.54.60 (9)				
Stewart McSweyn (AUS)	3.54.60 (9)				
Ronald Kwemoi (KEN)		3.49.04 (1)		3.52.57 (7)	
Vincent Kibet (KEN)		3.51.17 (4)	3.52.71 (8)		
Thiago André (BRA)		3.51.99 (5)			
Abdalaati Iguider (MAR)		3.52.77 (7)	3.51.96 (2)	3.53.21 (10)	3.49.09 (4)
Ben Blankenship (USA)		3.53.04 (8)			
David Torrence (PER)		3.53.21 (9)			
Filip Ingebrigtsen (NOR)		3.53.23 (10)			
Asbel Kiprop (KEN			3.51.48 (1)	3.51.25 (3)	3.50.26 (9)
Taoufik Makhloufi (ALG)			3.52.24 (4)		
Nicholas Willis (NZL)			3.52.26 (5)		3.49.83 (7)
Ryan Gregson (AUS)			3.52.59 (6)		
Charlie Grice (GBR)			3.52.64 (7)		
Silas Kiplagat (KEN)			3.53.04 (9)	3.51.72 (4)	3.47.88 (2)
Ayanleh Souleiman (DJI)				3.51.10 (1)	3.47.32 (1)
Pieter-Jan Hannes (BEL)				3.51.84 (5)	
James Kiplagat Magut (KEN)				3.52.33 (6)	3.49.43 (5)
Collins Cheboi (KEN)				3.52.63 (8)	3.49.56 (6)
Johan Cronje (RSA)				3.53.02 (9)	
Aman Wote (ETH)					3.48.60 (3)
Homiyu Tesfaye (GER)					3.49.86 (8)

WORLD RANKING OUTDOOR ALL TIME:

1.	Hicham El Guerrouj (MAR)	3.43.13 (1999)
2.	Noah Ngeny (KEN)	3.43.40 (1999)
3.	Noureddine Morceli (ALG)	3.44.39 (1993)
4.	Steve Cram (GBR)	3.46.32 (1985)
5.	Daniel Komen (KEN)	3.46.38 (1997)
6.	Vénuste Niyongabo (BDI)	3.46.70 (1997)
7.	Said Aouita (MAR)	3.46.76 (1987)
8.	Alan Webb (USA)	3.46.91 (2007)
9.	Bernard Lagat (USA)	3.47.28 (2001)
10.	Ayanleh Souleiman (DJI)	3.47.32 (2014)
11.	Sebastian Coe (GBR)	3.47.33 (1981)
12.	Laban Rotich (KEN)	3.47.65 (1997)
13.	Steve Scott (USA)	3.47.69 (1982)
14.	José Luis González (ESP)	3.47.79 (1985)
15.	John Kemboi Kibowen (KEN)	3.47.88 (1997)
	Silas Kiplagat (KEN)	3.47.88 (2014)
17.	William Chirchir (KEN)	3.47.94 (2000)
18.	Daham Najim Bashir (QAT)	3.47.97 (2005)
19.	Paul Korir (KEN)	3.48.17 (2003)
20.	Ali Saidi-Sief (ALG)	3.48.23 (2001)
21.	Daniel Kipchirchir Komen (KEN)	3.48.28 (2007)
22.	Andrés Diaz (ESP)	3.48.38 (2001)
23.	Steve Ovett (GBR)	3.48.40 (1981)
	William Kemei (KEN)	3.48.40 (1992)
25.	Asbel Kiprop (KEN)	3.48.50 (2009)
26.	Aman Wote (ETH)	3.48.60 (2014)
27.	Haron Keitany (KEN)	3.48.78 (2009)
28.	Sydney Maree (USA)	3.48.83 (1981)
29.	Deresse Mekonnen (ETH)	3.48.95 (2009)
30.	Craig Mottram (AUS)	3.48.98 (2005)
31.	Ronald Kwemoi (KEN)	3.49.04 (2017)
32.	John Walker (NZL)	3.49.08 (1982)
	Elijah Motonei Manangoi (KEN)	3.49.08 (2017)
34.	Abdelaati Iguider (MAR)	3.49.09 (2014)
35.	Peter Elliott (GBR)	3.49.20 (1988)
36.	Jens-Peter Herold (GDR)	3.49.22 (1988)
37.	Ilham Tanui Özbilen (KEN)	3.49.29 (2009)
38.	Joe Falcon (USA)	3.49.31 (1990)
39.	David Moorcroft (GBR)	3.49.34 (1982)
	Benjamin Kipkurui (KEN)	3.49.34 (2000)
41.	Andrew Baddeley (GBR)	3.49.38 (2008)
42.	Abdi Bile (SOM)	3.49.40 (1988)
43.	James Kiplagat Magut (KEN)	3.49.43 (2014)
44.	Mike Boit (KEN)	3.49.45 (1981)
45.	Rui Silva (POR)	3.49.50 (2002)

WORLD RANKING INDOOR ALL TIME:

1.	Hicham El Guerrouj (MAR)	3.48.45 (1997)
2.	Edward Cheserek (KEN)	3.49.44 (2018)
3.	Eamonn Coghlan (IRL)	3.49.78 (1983)
4.	Bernard Lagat (USA)	3.49.89 (2005)
5.	Matthew Centrowitz (USA)	3.50.63 (2016)
6.	Noureddine Morceli (ALG)	3.50.70 (1993)
7.	Galen Rupp (USA)	3.50.92 (2013)
8.	Marcus O'Sullivan (IRL)	3.50.94 (1988)
9.	Nick Willis (NZL)	3.51.06 (2016)
10.	Ray Flynn (IRL)	3.51.20 (1983)
11.	Lopez Lomong (USA)	3.51.21 (2013)
12.	Steve Scott (USA)	3.51.8 (1981)
13.	Peter Elliott (GBR)	3.52.02 (1990)
14.	Ciaran O'Lionaird (IRL)	3.52.10 (2013)
15.	Rui Silva (POR)	3.52.18 (2001)
16.	Kyle Merber (USA)	3.52.22 (2017)
17.	Frank O'Mara (IRL)	3.52.30 (1986)
18.	Sydney Maree (USA)	3.52.40 (1985)
19.	Will Leer (USA)	3.52.47 (2014)
20.	Mehdi Baala (FRA)	3.52.51 (2009)
21.	José Manuel Abascal (ESP)	3.52.56 (1983)
22.	Silas Kiplagat (KEN)	3.52.63 (2012)
23.	Caleb Mwangangi Ndiku (KEN)	3.52.66 (2012)
24.	John Walker (NZL)	3.52.8 (1981)
25.	Lawi Lalang (KEN)	3.52.88 (2014)
26.	Chris O'Hare (GBR)	3.52.91 (2016)
27.	Ben Blankenship (USA)	3.53.13 (2015)
28.	John Gregorek (USA)	3.53.15 (2017)
29.	Robby Andrews (USA)	3.53.16 (2016)
30.	Laban Rotich (KEN)	3.53.18 (2005)
31.	Eric Jenkins (USA)	3.53.23 (2017)
32.	Paul Korir (KEN)	3.53.26 (2004)
33.	Noah Ngeny (KEN)	3.53.31 (2001)
34.	Izaic Yorks (USA)	3.53.40 (2018)
35.	Reyes Estévez (ESP)	3.53.49 (2001)
36.	Tom Byers (USA)	3.53.6 (1982)
37.	Jens-Peter Herold (GER)	3.53.74 (1994)
38.	Cory Leslie (USA)	3.53.87 (2016)
39.	Daniel Kipchirchir Komen (KEN)	3.53.93 (2012)
	Craig Engels (USA)	3.53.93 (2018)
41.	Dawit Wolde (ETH)	3.54.02 (2016)
42.	Russell Brown (USA)	3.54.08 (2012)
43.	Deresse Mekonnen (ETH)	3.54.11 (2009)
44.	Christoph Impens (BEL)	3.54.13 (1997)
45.	Eric Dubus (FRA)	3.54.16 (1994)

3000 m Men

WORLD RANKING 2018:

1.	Yomif Kejelcha (ETH)	7.28.00 (Göt)
2.	Birhanu Balew (BRN)	7.34.26 (Rab)
3.	Stewart McSweyn (AUS)	7.34.79 (Rab)
4.	Paul Chelimo (USA)	7.34.83 (Rab)
5.	Muktar Edris (ETH)	7.36.13 (Rab)
6.	Hagos Gebrhiwet (ETH)	7.36.49 (Rab)
7.	Ryan Hill (USA)	7.36.81 (Rab)
8.	Selemon Barega (ETH)	7.37.53 (Ost)
9.	Eric Jenkins (USA)	7.38.19 (Rab)
10.	Telahun Haile Bekele (ETH)	7.38.55 (Ost)
11.	Chala Regasa (ETH)	7.38.78 (Ost)
12.	Abadi Hadis (ETH)	7.39.10 (Ost)
13.	Soufiyan Bouqantar (MAR)	7.39.42 (Rab)
14.	Thierry Ndikumwenayo (BDI)	7.41.04 (Ost)
15.	Ben True (USA)	7.41.86 (Ost)
16.	Berihu Aregawi (ETH)	7.42.12 (Göt)
17.	Cyrus Rutto (KEN)	7.42.53 (Rab)
18.	Bethwell Birgen (KEN)	7.42.72 (Rab)
	Henrik Ingebrigtsen (NOR)	7.42.72

WORLD INDOOR CHAMPIONSHIPS: 4-3-2018:

1. Yomif Kejelcha (ETH)   (7.42.83)   8.14.41
2. Selemon Barega (ETH)   (7.48.14)   8.15.59
3. Bethwell Birgen (KEN)   (7.45.06)   8.15.70
4. Hagos Gebrhiwet (ETH)   (7.43.55)   8.15.76
5. Adel Mechaal (ESP)   (7.43.83)   8.16.13
6. Younéss Essalhi (MAR)   (7.45.07)   8.16.63
7. Davis Kiplangat (KEN)   (7.48.26)   8.18.03
8. Clemens Bleistein (GER) (7.49.01)   8.18.24
9. Julian Oakley (NZL)   (7.55.92)   8.18.60
10. Birhanu Balew (BRN)   (7.44.03)   8.18.89
11. Yassin Bouih (ITA)   (7.50.65)   8.20.84
    Shadrack Kipchirchir (USA)(7.57.08) dsq

----

13. Federico Bruno (ARG)   7.58.98
    Paul Chelimo (USA)   dsq
    Richard Ringer (GER)   dsq

WORLD INDOOR RANKING 2018:

1. Selemon Barega (ETH)   7.36.64
2. Hagos Gebrhiwet (ETH)   7.37.91
3. Yomif Kejelcha (ETH)   7.38.67
4. Edward Cheserek (KEN)   7.38.74
5. Justus Soget (KEN)   7.39.09
6. Paul Chelimo (USA)   7.39.10
7. Abdelaati Iguider (MAR)   7.39.92
8. Davis Kiplangat (KEN)   7.40.12
9. Adel Mechaal (ESP)   7.40.14
10. Bethwell Birgen (KEN)   7.40.56
11. Muktar Edris (ETH)   7.40.69
12. Sadik Mikhou (BRN)   7.41.39
13. Soufiane El Bakkali (MAR)   7.41.88
14. Paul Kipsiele Koech (KEN)   7.41.97
15. Edwin Cheruiyot Soi (KEN)   7.42.02
16. Gemechu Dida (ETH)   7.42.14
17. Albert Rop (KEN)   7.42.34
18. Shadrack Kipchirchir (USA)   7.42.71
19. Dejen Gebremeskel (ETH)   7.42.78
20. Vladimir Nikitin (RUS)   7.42.82
21. Birhanu Balew (BRN)   7.44.03
22. Julian Oakley (NZL)   7.44.34
23. Mohammed Ayoub Tiouali (BRN)   7.44.58
24. Benjamin Kigen (KEN)   7.44.77
25. Emmanuel Bor (USA)   7.44.93
26. Younéss Essalhi (MAR)   7.45.07
27. Telahun Haile Bekele (ETH)   7.45.34
28. Justyn Knight (CAN)   7.45.86
29. Djamal Abdi Direh (DJI)   7.45.96

Ostrava, 13-6-2018:
1. Selemon Barega (ETH)   7.37.53
2. Birhanu Balew (BRN)   7.38.25
3. Telahun Haile Bekele (ETH)   7.38.55
4. Chala Regasa (ETH)   7.38.78
5. Abadi Hadis (ETH)   7.39.10
6. Thierry Ndikumwenayo (BDI)   7.41.04
7. Soufiyan Bouqantar (MAR)   7.41.04
8. Ben True (USA)   7.41.86
9. Yemaneberhan Crippa (ITA)   7.43.30
10. Haymanot Alewe (ETH)   7.43.36
11. Davis Kiplangat (KEN)   7.43.98
12. Melesse Birhan (ETH)   7.44.66
13. Ronald Musagala (UGA)   7.44.78
14. Charles Philibert-Thiboutot (CAN) 7.45.03
15. Abe Gashahun (ETH)   7.45.91
16. Ryan Gregson (AUS)   7.46.28

Rabat, 13-7-2018:
1. Yomif Kejelcha (ETH)   7.32.93
2. Birhanu Balew (BRN)   7.34.26
3. Stewart McSweyn (AUS)   7.34.79
4. Paul Chelimo (USA)   7.34.83
5. Muktar Edris (ETH)   7.36.13
6. Hagos Gebrhiwet (ETH)   7.36.49
7. Ryan Hill (USA)   7.36.81
8. Eric Jenkins (USA)   7.38.19
9. Soufiyan Bouqantar (MAR)   7.39.42
10. Cyrus Rutto (KEN)   7.42.53
11. Bethwell Birgen (KEN)   7.42.72
12. Abadi Hadis (ETH)   7.42.83

CONTINENTAL CUP, Ostrava, 9-9-2018:
1. Paul Chelimo (AME)   7.57.13
2. Mohammed Ahmed (AME)   7.57.99
3. Henrik Ingebrigtsen (EUR)   7.58.85

OVERVIEW WORLDWIDE INDOOR CHAMPIONSHIP FINALISTS OF PAST 5 YEARS

	Wch 18	Wch 16	Wch 14
Yomif Kejelcha (ETH)	8.14.41 (1)	7.57.21 (1)	
Selemon Barega (ETH)	8.15.59 (2)		
Bethwell Birgen (KEN)	8.15.70 (3)		
Hagos Gebrhiwet (ETH)	8.15.76 (4)		7.56.34 (5)
Adel Mechaal (ESP)	8.16.13 (5)		
Younéss Essalhi (MAR)	8.16.63 (6)		
Davis Kiplangat (KEN)	8.18.03 (7)		
Clemens Bleistein (GER)	8.18.24 (8)		
Julian Oakley (NZL)	8.18.60 (9)		
Birhanu Balew (BRN)	8.18.89 (10)		
Yassin Bouih (ITA)	8.20.84 (11)		
Shadrack Kipchirchir (USA)	dsq (12)		
Ryan Hill (USA)		7.57.39 (2)	
Augustine Choge (KEN)		7.57.43 (3)	7.57.46 (9)
Abdalaati Iguider (MAR)		7.58.04 (4)	
Caleb Mwangangi Ndiku (KEN)		7.58.81 (5)	7.54.94 (1)
Lee Emanuel (GBR)		8.00.70 (6)	
Paul Chelimo (USA)		8.00.76 (7)	
Isiah Kiplangat Koech (KEN)		8.01.70 (8)	
Mohammed Ahmed (CAN)		8.07.96 (9)	
Youssouf Hiss Bachir (DJI)		8.08.87 (10)	
Brett Robinson (AUS)		8.11.11 (11)	
Yenew Alamirew (ETH)		8.12.54 (12)	
Bernard Lagat (USA)			7.55.22 (2)
Dejen Gebremeskel (ETH)			7.55.39 (3)
Galen Rupp (USA)			7.55.84 (4)
Hayle Ibrahimov (AZE)			7.56.37 (6)
Elroy Gelant (RSA)			7.57.31 (7)
Cameron Levins (CAN)			7.57.37 (8)
Collis Birmingham (AUS)			7.57.55 (10)
Andrew Vernon (GBR)			7.58.25 (11)
Zane Robertson (NZL)			8.01.81 (12)

OVERVIEW TOP 10 WORLD OUTDOOR RANKINGS OF PAST 5 YEARS

	2018	2017	2016	2015	2014
Yomif Kejelcha (ETH)	7.28.00 (1)	7.32.27 (3)	7.28.19 (1)		7.36.28 (4)
Birhanu Balew (BRN)	7.34.26 (2)				
Stewart McSweyn (AUS)	7.34.79 (3)				
Paul Chelimo (USA)	7.34.83 (4)	7.31.57 (2)	7.37.98 (10)		
Muktar Edris (ETH)	7.36.13 (5)	7.32.31 (4)	7.33.28 (8)		
Hagos Gebrhiwet (ETH)	7.36.49 (6)		7.30.45 (3)	7.38.08 (9)	
Ryan Hill (USA)	7.36.81 (7)		7.30.93 (4)		7.38.64 (9)
Selemon Barega (ETH)	7.37.53 (8)				
Eric Jenkins (USA)	7.38.19 (9)				
Telahun Haile Bekele (ETH)	7.38.55 (10)				
Ronald Kwemoi (KEN)		7.28.73 (1)			
Caleb Mwangangi Ndiku (KEN)		7.33.36 (5)		7.35.13 (2)	7.31.66 (1)
Joshua Kiprui Cheptegei (UGA)		7.34.96 (6)			
Mohamed Farah (GBR)		7.35.15 (7)	7.32.62 (7)	7.34.66 (1)	7.36.8 (6)
Adel Mechaal (ESP)		7.35.28 (8)			
Ben True (USA)		7.35.53 (9)			
Andrew Butchart (GBR)		7.37.56 (10)			
Abdalaati Iguider (MAR)			7.30.09 (2)		7.34.99 (2)
Albert Kibichii Rop (BRN)/(KEN)			7.32.02 (5)		
Bethwell Kiprotich Birgen (KEN)			7.32.48 (6)		
Hayle Ibrahimov (AZE)			7.37.76 (9)		
Yenew Alamirew (ETH)				7.36.39 (3)	
Othmane El Goumri (MAR)				7.36.71 (4)	
Emmanuel Kiprono Kipsang (KEN)				7.37.05 (5)	
Isiah Kiplangat Koech (KEN)				7.37.16 (6)	
Edwin Cheruiyot Soi (KEN)				7.37.85 (7)	
Garrett Heath (USA)				7.37.97 (8)	
Ben Blankenship (USA)				7.38.08 (9)	
Thomas Pkemei Longosiwa (KEN)					7.35.28 (3)
Lawi Lalang (KEN)					7.36.44 (5)
Nicholas Willis (NZL)					7.36.91 (7)
Bernard Lagat (USA)					7.38.30 (8)
John Kipkoech (KEN)					7.38.97 (10)

OVERVIEW TOP 10 WORLD INDOOR RANKINGS OF PAST 5 YEARS

	2018	2017	2016	2015	2014
Selemon Barega (ETH)	7.36.64 (1)				
Hagos Gebrhiwet (ETH)	7.37.91 (2)	7.43.04 (6)			7.34.13 (1)
Yomif Kejelcha (ETH)	7.38.67 (3)		7.39.11 (6)		
Edward Cheserek (KEN)	7.38.74 (4)				
Justus Soget (KEN)	7.39.09 (5)				
Paul Kipkemoi Chelimo (USA)	7.39.10 (6)	7.42.39 (5)	7.39.00 (4)		
Abdelaati Iguider (MAR)	7.39.92 (7)		7.39.04 (5)		
Davis Kiplangat (KEN)	7.40.12 (8)				
Adel Mechaal (ESP)	7.40.14 (9)				
Bethwell Birgen (KEN)	7.40.56 (10)			7.43.77 (6)	7.37.17 (8)
Ryan Hill (USA)		7.40.80 (1)	7.38.60 (2)		7.34.87 (4)
Ben True (USA)		7.40.96 (2)			
Andrew Butchart (GBR)		7.41.05 (3)			
Mohammed Ahmed (CAN)		7.41.13 (4)			
Eric Jenkins (USA)		7.44.26 (7)	7.39.43 (9)	7.44.91 (8)	
Morhad Amdouni (FRA)		7.44.55 (8)			
Hillary Cheruiyot Ngetich (KEN)		7.44.73 (9)			
Mekonnen Gebremedhin (ETH)		7.44.95 (10)			
Dejen Gebremeskel (ETH)			7.38.03 (1)		7.34.70 (3)
Hassan Mead (USA)			7.38.85 (3)		
Augustine Kiprono Choge (KEN)			7.39.23 (7)		7.37.11 (7)
Mohamad Al-Garni (QAT)			7.39.23 (7)		
Mohamed Farah (GBR)			7.39.55 (10)	7.33.1 (1)	
Bernard Lagat (USA)				7.37.92 (2)	
Ali Kaya (TUR)				7.38.42 (3)	
Paul Kipsiele Koech (KEN)				7.39.68 (4)	7.37.22 (9)
Nixon Kiplimo Chepseba (KEN)				7.42.65 (5)	
Lee Emanuel (GBR)				7.44.48 (7)	
Galen Rupp (USA)				7.44.97 (9)	7.34.68 (2)
Cameron Levins (CAN)				7.45.21 (10)	
Caleb Mwangangi Ndiku (KEN)					7.36.27 (5)
Yenew Alamirew (ETH)					7.37.10 (6)
Garret Heath (USA)					7.37.40 (10)

WORLD RANKING ALL TIME OUTDOOR:

1.	Daniel Komen (KEN)	7.20.67 (1996)
2.	Hicham El Guerrouj (MAR)	7.23.09 (1999)
3.	Ali Saidi-Sief (ALG)	7.25.02 (2000)
4.	Haile Gebrselassie (ETH)	7.25.09 (1998)
5.	Noureddine Morceli (ALG)	7.25.11 (1994)
6.	Kenenisa Bekele (ETH)	7.25.79 (2007)
7.	Mohammed Mourhit (BEL)	7.26.62 (2000)
8.	Moses Kiptanui (KEN)	7.27.18 (1995)
9.	Yenew Alamirew (ETH)	7.27.26 (2011)
10.	Edwin Cheruiyot Soi (KEN)	7.27.55 (2011)
11.	Luke Kipkosgei (KEN)	7.27.59 (1998)
12.	Eliud Kipchoge (KEN)	7.27.66 (2011)
13.	Tom Nyariki (KEN)	7.27.75 (1996)
14.	Yomif Kejelcha (ETH)	7.28.00 (2018)
15.	James Kwalia C'Kurui (KEN)	7.28.28 (2004)
16.	Paul Bitok (KEN)	7.28.41 (1996)
17.	Assefa Mezgebu (ETH)	7.28.45 (1998)
18.	Benjamin Limo (KEN)	7.28.67 (1999)
19.	Paul Tergat (KEN)	7.28.70 (1996)
	Tariku Bekele (ETH)	7.28.70 (2010)
21.	Isaac Kiprono Songok (KEN)	7.28.72 (2006)
22.	Ronald Kwemoi (KEN)	7.28.73 (2017)
23.	Augustine Kiprono Choge (KEN)	7.28.76 (2011)
24.	Salah Hissou (MAR)	7.28.93 (1999)
25.	Brahim Lahlafi (MAR)	7.28.94 (1999)
26.	Bernard Lagat (USA)	7.29.00 (2010)
27.	John Kemboi Kibowen (KEN)	7.29.09 (1998)
28.	Isaac Viciosa (ESP)	7.29.34 (1998)
29.	Said Aouita (MAR)	7.29.45 (1989)
30.	Sileshi Sihine (ETH)	7.29.92 (2005)
31.	Ismail Sghyr (MAR)	7.30.09 (1995)
	Thomas Pkemei Longosiwa (KEN)	7.30.09 (2009)
	Abdelaati Iguider (MAR)	7.30.09 (2016)
34.	Vincent Kiprop Chepkok (KEN)	7.30.15 (2011)
35.	Mark Carroll (IRL)	7.30.36 (1999)
	Hagos Gebrhiwet (ETH)	7.30.36 (2013)
37.	Isiah Kiplangat Koech (KEN)	7.30.43 (2012)
38.	Dieter Baumann (GER)	7.30.50 (1998)
39.	El Hassan Lahssini (MAR)	7.30.53 (1996)
	Hailu Mekonnen (ETH)	7.30.53 (2001)
41.	Boniface Kiprotich Songok (KEN)	7.30.62 (2004)
42.	Jamal Bilal Salem (QAT)	7.30.76 (2005)
43.	Mustapha Essaid (FRA)	7.30.78 (1998)
44.	Bob Kennedy (USA)	7.30.84 (1998)
45.	Ryan Hill (USA)	7.30.93 (2016)

WORLD RANKING ALL TIME INDOOR:

1.	Daniel Komen (KEN)	7.24.90 (1998)
2.	Haile Gebrselassie (ETH)	7.26.15 (1998)
3.	Yenew Alamirew (ETH)	7.27.80 (2011)
4.	Augustine Kiprono Choge (KEN)	7.28.00 (2011)
5.	Eliud Kipchoge (KEN)	7.29.37 (2011)
6.	Edwin Cheruiyot Soi (KEN)	7.29.94 (2012)
7.	Galen Rupp (USA)	7.30.16 (2013)
8.	Kenenisa Bekele (ETH)	7.30.51 (2007)
9.	Tariku Bekele (ETH)	7.31.09 (2008)
10.	Caleb Mwangangi Ndiku (KEN)	7.31.66 (2013)
11.	Sammy Mutahi (KEN)	7.32.02 (2010)
12.	Sergio Sánchez (ESP)	7.32.41 (2010)
13.	Bernard Lagat (USA)	7.32.43 (2007)
14.	Markos Geneti (ETH)	7.32.69 (2007)
15.	Paul Kipsiele Koech (KEN)	7.32.78 (2010)
16.	Hagos Gebrhiwet (ETH)	7.32.87 (2013)
17.	Isiah Kiplangat Koech (KEN)	7.32.89 (2012)
18.	Alberto García (ESP)	7.32.98 (2003)
19.	Hicham El Guerrouj (MAR)	7.33.73 (2003)
	Bouabdellah Tahri (FRA)	7.33.73 (2010)
21.	Abraham Feleke (ETH)	7.34.05 (2009)
22.	Dejen Gebremeskel (ETH)	7.34.14 (2012)
23.	Mo Farah (GBR)	7.34.47 (2009)
24.	Craig Mottram (AUS)	7.34.50 (2008)
25.	Thomas Pkemei Longosiwa (KEN)	7.34.81 (2012)
26.	Ryan Hill (USA)	7.34.87 (2014)
27.	Abdalaati Iguider (MAR)	7.34.92 (2013)
28.	Moses Kiptanui (KEN)	7.35.15 (1995)
29.	Boaz Cheboiywo (KEN)	7.35.65 (2006)
30.	Million Wolde (ETH)	7.35.84 (2000)
31.	Shadrack Korir (KEN)	7.35.98 (2009)
32.	Ali Saidi-Sief (ALG)	7.36.25 (2000)
33.	Fermin Cacho (ESP)	7.36.61 (1996)
34.	Selemon Barega (ETH)	7.36.64 (2018)
35.	Garrett Heath (USA)	7.37.40 (2014)
36.	Mushir Salim Jawher (KEN)	7.37.46 (2002)
37.	Daniel Kipchirchir Komen (KEN)	7.37.47 (2007)
38.	Dieter Baumann (GER)	7.37.51 (1995)
39.	Andrew Bumbalough (USA)	7.37.62 (2014)
40.	Nixon Kiplimo Chepseba (KEN)	7.37.64 (2011)
41.	Vénuste Niyongabo (BDI)	7.37.82 (1995)
42.	Vincent Rono (KEN)	7.37.87 (2011)
43.	Ismail Sghyr (MAR)	7.37.93 (1997)
44.	Arne Gabius (GER)	7.38.13 (2012)
45.	Ali Kaya (TUR)	7.38.42 (2015)

5000 m Men

EUROPEAN CHAMPIONSHIPS 2018: 11-8-2018:

1. Jakob Ingebrigtsen (NOR) — 13.17.06
2. Henrik Ingebrigtsen (NOR) — 13.18.75
3. Morhad Amdouni (FRA) — 13.19.14
4. Yemaneberhan Crippa (ITA) — 13.19.85
5. Marc Scott (GBR) — 13.23.14
6. Polat Kemboi Arikan (TUR) — 13.23.42
7. Rinas Akhmadiyev (ANA) — 13.24.43
8. Julien Wanders (SUI) — 13.24.79
9. Chris Thompson (GBR) — 13.25.11
10. Soufiane Bouchikhi (BEL) — 13.25.22
11. Ben Connor (GBR) — 13.25.31
12. Florian Carvalho (FRA) — 13.28.08
13. Antonio Abadía (ESP) — 13.34.25
14. Kaan Kigen Özbilen (TUR) — 13.35.31
15. Robin Hendrix (BEL) — 13.36.15
16. Juan Pérez (ESP) — 13.37.07
17. Florian Orth (GER) — 13.37.46
18. Marcel Fehr (GER) — 13.37.66
19. Andreas Vojta (AUT) — 13.42.75
20. Benjamin de Haan (NED) — 13.42.95
    Adel Mechaal (ESP) — dnf

WORLD RANKING 2018:

1. Selemon Barega (ETH) — 12.43.02(Bru)
2. Hagos Gebrhiwet (ETH) — 12.45.82(Bru)
3. Yomif Kejelcha (ETH) — 12.46.79(Bru)
4. Muktar Edris (ETH) — 12.55.18(Bru)
5. Abadi Hadis (ETH) — 12.56.27(Bru)
6. Paul Chelimo (USA) — 12.57.55(Bru)
7. Richard Yator (KEN) — 12.59.44(Bru)
8. Getaneh Molla (ETH) — 12.59.58(Bru)
9. Birhanu Balew (BRN) — 13.01.09(Lau)
10. Mohammed Ahmed (CAN) — 13.03.08(Bru)
11. Ben True (USA) — 13.04.11(Bru)
12. Telahun Haile Bekele (ETH) — 13.04.63(Hue)
13. Bashir Abdi (BEL) — 13.04.91(Bru)
14. Stewart McSweyn (AUS) — 13.05.23(Bru)
15. Chala Regasa (ETH) — 13.06.98(Heu)
16. Nibret Melak (ETH) — 13.07.27(Heu)
17. Aron Kifle (ERI) — 13.07.59(Lau)
18. Stanley Waithaka Mburu (KEN) — 13.10.14(Sha)
19. Dawit Wolde (ETH) — 13.10.65(Heu)
20. Cyrus Rutto (KEN) — 13.10.79(Sha)
21. Stephen Kissa (UGA) — 13.10.93(Lau)
22. Albert Rop (BRN) — 13.11.84(Mnt)
23. Japhet Kipyegon Korir (KEN) — 13.11.86(Heu)
24. Yeneblo Biyazen (ETH) — 13.13.36(Car)
25. Davis Kiplangat (KEN) — 13.13.55(Sha)
26. Getnet Wale (ETH) — 13.13.87(Car)
27. Berihu Aregawi (ETH) — 13.15.44(Rov)
28. Rabia Doukhana (MAR) — 13.15.59(Car)
29. Brett Robinson (AUS) — 13.15.91(Heu)

Commonwealth Games, Gold Coast, 8-4-2018:
1. Joshua Kiprui Cheptegei (UGA)   13.50.83
2. Mohammed Ahmed (CAN)   13.52.78
3. Edward Pingua Zakayo (KEN)   13.54.06
4. Thomas Ayeko (UGA)   13.54.78
5. Stewart McSweyn (AUS)   13.58.96
6. Phillip Kipyeko (UGA)   13.59.59

Shanghai, 12-5-2018:
1. Birhanu Balew (BRN)   13.09.64
2. Paul Chelimo (USA)   13.09.66
3. Stanley Waithaka Mburu (KEN)   13.10.14
4. Cyrus Rutto (KEN)   13.10.79
5. Muktar Edris (ETH)   13.10.98
6. Nibret Melak (ETH)   13.10.99
7. Abadi Hadis (ETH)   13.11.04
8. Albert Rop (KEN)   13.12.72
9. Davis Kiplangat (KEN)   13.13.55

Stockholm, 10-6-2018:
1. Selemon Barega (ETH)   13.04.05
2. Birhanu Balew (BRN)   13.04.25
3. Abadi Hadis (ETH)   13.06.76
4. Mohammed Ahmed (CAN)   13.14.88
5. Ben True (USA)   13.16.48
6. Jacob Kiplimo (UGA)   13.19.66
7. Morhad Amdouni (FRA)   13.19.93

KEN Trials, Nairobi, 23-6-2018:
1. Ronald Kwemoi   13.38.27
2. Cyrus Rutto   13.38.81
3. Peter Ndegwa   13.39.35
4. Richard Kimunyan   13.39.86
5. Vidic Cheruiyot   13.41.94
6. Douglas Kipserem   13.42.61
7. Davis Kiplangat   13.43.31
8. Franklin Ngelel   13.43.65
9. Julius Tanki   13.44.40
10. Edwin Koech   13.46.91

Lausanne, 5-7-2018:
1. Birhanu Balew (BRN)   13.01.09
2. Selemon Barega (ETH)   13.02.67
3. Abadi Hadis (ETH)   13.03.62
4. Getaneh Molla (ETH)   13.04.04
5. Richard Yator (KEN)   13.04.97
6. Muktar Edris (ETH)   13.06.24
7. Telahun Haile Bekele (ETH)   13.07.02
8. Aron Kifle (ERI)   13.07.59
9. Stephen Kissa (UGA)   13.10.93
10. Davis Kiplangat (KEN)   13.13.57

London, 21-7-2018:
1. Paul Chelimo (USA)   13.14.01
2. Muktar Edris (ETH)   13.14.35
3. Yomif Kejelcha (ETH)   13.14.39
4. Birhanu Balew (BRN)   13.16.04
5. Hagos Gebrhiwet (ETH)   13.16.39
6. Cyrus Rutto (KEN)   13.16.49
7. Mohammed Ahmed (CAN)   13.16.82
8. Richard Yator (KEN)   13.17.98
9. Hassan Mead (USA)   13.19.81
10. Ben True (USA)   13.19.95
11. Bethwell Birgen (KEN)   13.20.08
12. Stewart McSweyn (AUS)   13.20.21
13. Shadrack Kipchirchir (UGA)   13.20.28
14. Emmanuel Bor (USA)   13.20.66

Heusden, 21-7-2018:
1. Chala Regasa (ETH)   13.06.98
2. Nibret Melak (ETH)   13.07.27
3. Dawit Wolde (ETH)   13.10.65
4. Japhet Kipyegon Korir (KEN)   13.11.86
5. Albert Rop (BRN)   13.13.96
6. Davis Kiplangat (KEN)   13.15.73
7. Brett Robinson (AUS)   13.15.91

AFR CHAMPIONSHIPS, Assaba, 5-8-2018:
1. Edward Zakayo (KEN)   13.48.58
2. Getaneh Molla (ETH)   13.49.06
3. Yemane Haileselassie (ERI)   13.49.58
4. Selemon Barega (ETH)   13.52.27
5. Cyrus Rutto (KEN)   13.53.78
6. Soufiyan Bouqantar (MAR)   13.53.99
7. Younes Essalhi (MAR)   13.58.64
8. Stephen Kissa (UGA)   13.59.90

Brussels, 31-8-2018:

1.	Selemon Barega (ETH)	12.43.02
2.	Hagos Gebrhiwet (ETH)	12.45.82
3.	Yomif Kejelcha (ETH)	12.46.79
4.	Muktar Edris (ETH)	12.55.18
5.	Abadi Hadis (ETH)	12.56.27
6.	Paul Chelimo (USA)	12.57.55
7.	Richard Yator (KEN)	12.59.44
8.	Getaneh Molla (ETH)	12.59.58
9.	Mohammed Ahmed (CAN)	13.03.08
10.	Ben True (USA)	13.04.11
11.	Bashir Abdi (BEL)	13.04.91
12.	Stewart McSweyn (AUS)	13.05.23

OVERVIEW WORLDWIDE OUTDOOR CHAMPIONSHIP FINALISTS OF PAST 6 YEARS

	Wch 17	OG 16	Wch 15	Wch 13
Muktar Edris (ETH)	13.32.79 (1)	dsq		13.29.56 (7)
Mohamed Farah (GBR)	13.33.22 (2)	13.03.30 (1)	13.50.38 (1)	13.26.98 (1)
Paul Kipkemoi Chelimo (USA)	13.33.30 (3)	13.03.90 (2)		
Yomif Kejelcha (ETH)	13.33.51 (4)		13.52.43 (4)	
Selemon Barega (ETH)	13.35.34 (5)			
Mohammed Ahmed (CAN)	13.35.43 (6)	13.05.94 (4)	14.00.38 (12)	
Aron Kifle (ERI)	13.36.91 (7)			
Andrew Butchart (GBR)	13.38.73 (8)	13.08.61 (6)		
Justyn Knight (CAN)	13.39.15 (9)			
Kemoy Campbell (JAM)	13.39.74 (10)			
Patrick Tiernan (AUS)	13.40.01 (11)			
Birhanu Balew (BRN)	13.43.25 (12)	13.09.26 (9)		
Cyrus Rutto (KEN)	13.48.64 (13)			
Awet Habte (ERI)	13.58.68 (14)			
Ryan Hill (USA)	dns (15)		13.55.10 (7)	13.32.69 (10)
Hagos Gebrhiwet (ETH)		13.04.35 (3)	13.51.86 (3)	13.27.26 (2)
Bernard Lagat (USA)		13.06.78 (5)		13.29.24 (6)
Albert Kibichii Rop (BRN)		13.08.79 (7)	14.00.12 (11)	
Joshua Kiprui Cheptegei (UGA)		13.09.17 (8)		
Abrar Osman (ERI)		13.09.56 (10)		
Hassan Mead (USA)		13.09.81 (11)		
Dejen Gebremeskel (ETH)		13.15.91 (12)		
Elroy Gelant (RSA)		13.17.47 (13)		13.43.58 (12)
Brett Robinson (AUS)		13.32.30 (14)		14.03.77 (15)
David Torrence (PER)		13.43.12 (15)		
Caleb Mwangangi Ndiku (KEN)			13.51.75 (2)	
Galen Rupp (USA)			13.53.90 (5)	13.29.87 (8)
Ben True (USA)			13.54.07 (6)	
Isiah Kiplangat Koech (KEN)			13.55.98 (8)	13.27.26 (3)
Ali Kaya (TUR)			13.56.51 (9)	
Edwin Cheruiyot Soi (KEN)			13.59.02 (10)	13.29.01 (5)
Imane Merga (ETH)			14.01.60 (13)	
Richard Ringer (GER)			14.03.72 (14)	
Tom Farrell (GBR)			14.08.87 (15)	
Thomas Pkemei Longosiwa (KEN)				13.27.67 (4)
Yenew Alamirew (ETH)				13.31.27 (9)
Dejene Regassa (BRN)				13.34.54 (11)
Sindre Buraas (NOR)				13.45.67 (13)
Zane Robertson (NZL)				13.46.55 (14)

OVERVIEW TOP 10 WORLD OUTDOOR RANKINGS OF PAST 5 YEARS

	2018	2017	2016	2015	2014
Selemon Barega (ETH)	12.43.02 (1)	12.55.58 (2)			
Hagos Gebrhiwet (ETH)	12.45.82 (2)		13.00.20 (5)	12.54.70 (2)	
Yomif Kejelcha (ETH)	12.46.79 (3)	13.01.21 (5)		12.53.98 (1)	
Muktar Edris (ETH)	12.55.18 (4)	12.55.23 (1)	12.59.43 (2)	13.00.30 (7)	12.54.83 (1)
Abadi Hadis (ETH)	12.56.27 (5)		13.02.49 (9)		
Paul Chelimo (USA)	12.57.55 (6)				
Richard Yator (KEN)	12.59.44 (7)				
Getaneh Molla (ETH)	12.59.58 (8)				
Birhanu Balew (BRN)	13.01.09 (9)				
Mohammed Ahmed (CAN)	13.03.08 (10)	13.08.16 (10)	13.01.74 (8)		
Joshua Kiprui Cheptegei (UGA)		12.59.83 (3)	13.00.60 (6)		
Mohamed Farah (GBR)		13.00.70 (4)	12.59.29 (1)		
Geoffrey Kipsang Kamworor (KEN)		13.01.35 (6)	12.59.98 (4)		
Cyrus Rutto (KEN)		13.03.44 (7)			
Albert Kibichii Rop (BRN)(KEN)		13.04.82 (8)			
Yenew Alamirew (ETH)		13.06.81 (9)			13.00.21 (5)
Dejen Gebremeskel (ETH)			12.59.89 (3)	13.00.49 (9)	
Thomas Pkemei Longosiwa (KEN)			13.01.69 (7)	12.59.72 (6)	12.56.16 (2)
Ibrahim Jeilan (ETH)			13.03.22 (10)		
Paul Kipngetich Tanui (KEN)				12.58.69 (3)	13.00.53 (6)
Imane Merga (ETH)				12.59.04 (4)	
Abdalaati Iguider (MAR)				12.59.25 (5)	
Ali Kaya (TUR)				13.00.31 (8)	
Caleb Mwangangi Ndiku (KEN)				13.05.40 (10)	12.59.17 (3)
Edwin Cheruiyot Soi (KEN)					12.59.82 (4)
Galen Rupp (USA)					13.00.99 (7)
Ben True (USA)					13.02.74 (8)
Hassan Mead (USA)					13.02.80 (9)
Lawi Lalang (KEN)					13.03.85 (10)

WORLD RANKING ALL TIME:

1.	Kenenisa Bekele (ETH)	12.37.35 (2004)
2.	Haile Gebrselassie (ETH)	12.39.36 (1998)
3.	Daniel Komen (KEN)	12.39.74 (1997)
4.	Selemon Barega (ETH)	12.43.02 (2018)
5.	Hagos Gebrhiwet (ETH)	12.45.82 (2018)
6.	Eliud Kipchoge (KEN)	12.46.53 (2004)
7.	Yomif Kejelcha (ETH)	12.46.79 (2018)
8.	Dejen Gebremeskel (ETH)	12.46.81 (2012)
9.	Sileshi Sihine (ETH)	12.47.04 (2004)
10.	Isiah Kiplangat Koech (KEN)	12.48.64 (2012)
11.	Isaac Kiprono Songok (KEN)	12.48.66 (2006)
12.	Yenew Alamirew (ETH)	12.48.77 (2012)
13.	Saif Saaeed Shaheen (KEN)	12.48.81 (2003)
14.	Thomas Pkemei Longosiwa (KEN)	12.49.04 (2012)
15.	Brahim Lahlafi (MAR)	12.49.28 (2000)
16.	John Kipkoech (KEN)	12.49.50 (2012)
17.	Mohammed Mourhit (BEL)	12.49.71 (2000)
18.	Paul Tergat (KEN)	12.49.87 (1997)
19.	Hicham El Guerrouj (MAR)	12.50.24 (2003)
20.	Abderrahim Goumri (MAR)	12.50.25 (2005)
21.	Moses Ndiema Masai (KEN)	12.50.55 (2008)
22.	Moses Ndiema Kipsiro (UGA)	12.50.72 (2007)
23.	Salah Hissou (MAR)	12.50.80 (1996)
24.	Ali Saidi-Sief (ALG)	12.50.86 (2000)
25.	Joseph Ebuya (KEN)	12.51.00 (2007)
26.	Edwin Cheruiyot Soi (KEN)	12.51.34 (2013)
27.	Vincent Kiprop Chepkok (KEN)	12.51.45 (2010)
28.	Albert Rop (BRN)	12.51.96 (2013)
29.	Sammy Kipketer (KEN)	12.52.33 (2003)
30.	Tariku Bekele (ETH)	12.52.45 (2008)
31.	Gebregziabher Gebremariam (ETH)	12.52.80 (2005)
32.	Abraham Chebii (KEN)	12.52.99 (2003)
33.	Mo Farah (GBR)	12.53.11 (2011)
34.	Khalid Boulami (MAR)	12.53.41 (1997)
35.	Mark Kosgei Kiptoo (KEN)	12.53.46 (2010)
36.	Imane Merga (ETH)	12.53.58 (2010)
37.	Bernard Lagat (USA)	12.53.60 (2011)
38.	Augustine Kiprono Choge (KEN)	12.53.66 (2005)
39.	Philip Mosima (KEN)	12.53.72 (1996)
40.	Assefa Mezgebu (ETH)	12.53.84 (1998)
41.	John Kemboi Kibowen (KEN)	12.54.07 (2003)
42.	Dejene Birhanu (ETH)	12.54.15 (2004)
43.	Abraham Cherkos Feleke (ETH)	12.54.19 (2006)
44.	Moses Mosop (KEN)	12.54.46 (2006)
45.	James Kwalia C'Kurui (KEN)	12.54.58 (2003)

10.000 m Men

EUROPEAN CHAMPIONSHIPS 2018: 7-8-2018:

1. Morhad Amdouni (FRA) — 28.11.22
2. Bashir Abdi (BEL) — 28.11.76
3. Yemaneberhan Crippa (ITA) — 28.12.15
4. Adel Mechaal (ESP) — 28.13.78
5. Andy Vernon (GBR) — 28.16.90
6. Soufiane Bouchikhi (BEL) — 28.19.04
7. Julien Wanders (SUI) — 28.22.02
8. Florian Carvalho (FRA) — 28.29.78
9. Juan Pérez (ESP) — 28.31.31
10. Kaan Kigen Özbilen (TUR) — 28.32.93
11. Chris Thompson (GBR) — 28.33.12
12. Daniel Mateo (ESP) — 28.44.43
13. Lorenzo Dini (ITA) — 28.45.04
14. Alexander Yee (GBR) — 28.58.86
15. Simon Debognies (BEL) — 29.00.98
16. Amanal Petros (GER) — 29.01.19
17. Vasyl Koval (UKR) — 29.07.23
18. Arttu Vattulainen (FIN) — 29.12.02
19. Nicolae Soare (ROM) — 29.13.82
20. Yevgeniy Rybakov (ANA) — 29.15.30
21. Dmytro Siruk (UKR) — 29.19.55
    Richard Ringer (GER) — dnf
    Aras Kaya (TUR) — dnf
    Polat Kemboi Arikan (TUR) — dnf

WORLD RANKING 2018:

1. Stanley Waithaka Mburu (KEN) — 27.13.01(Yok)
2. Richard Yator (KEN) — 27.14.70(Yok)
3. Joshua Cheptegei (UGA) — 27.19.62(GC)
4. Mohammed Ahmed (CAN) — 27.20.56(GC)
5. Rhonex Kipruto (KEN) — 27.21.08
6. Jonathan Muia Ndiku (KEN) — 27.28.27(Yok)
7. Rodgers Chumo (KEN) — 27.28.66(GC)
8. Jacob Kiplimo (UGA) — 27.30.25(GC)
9. Jake Robertson (NZL) — 27.30.90(GC)
10. Richard Ringer (GER) — 27.36.52(Lon)
11. Morhad Amdouni (FRA) — 27.36.80(Lon)
12. Hassan Chani (BRN) — 27.38.16
13. Shadrack Kipchirchir (USA) — 27.39.65(PA)

Commonwealth Games, Gold Coast, 13-4-2018:
1. Joshua Cheptegei (UGA)   27.19.62
2. Mohammed Ahmed (CAN)   27.20.56
3. Rodgers Chumo (KEN)   27.28.66
4. Jacob Kiplimo (UGA)   27.30.25
5. Jake Robertson (NZL)   27.30.90
6. Stephen Mokoka (RSA)   27.44.58
7. Timothy Toroitich (UGA)   27.47.35
8. Jonathan Muia Ndiku (KEN)   27.56.24

KEN Trials, Nairobi, 21-6-2018:
1. Vincent Rono   28.17.24
2. Josephat Bett   28.24.85
3. Kipsang Temoi   28.27.55
4. Stephen Arita   28.30.79
5. Peter Kiprotich   28.32.95
6. Kennedy Kimengwa   28.36.77
7. Wilfred Kimitei   28.38.73
8. Dominic Kiptarus   28.47.62
9. Nicholas Kosimbei   28.48.96
10. Noah Kipkemboi   28.52.26

AFR CHAMPIONSHIPS, Assaba, 1-8-2018:
1. Jemal Yimer (ETH)   29.08.01
2. Andamlak Belihu (ETH)   29.11.09
3. Timothy Toroitich (UGA)   29.11.87
4. Vincent Kipsang (KEN)   29.14.52
5. Kipsang Temoi (KEN)   29.25.54

OVERVIEW WORLDWIDE OUTDOOR CHAMPIONSHIP FINALISTS OF PAST 6 YEARS

	Wch 17	OG 16	Wch 15	Wch 13
Mohamed Farah (GBR)	26.49.51 (1)	27.05.17 (1)	27.01.13 (1)	27.21.71 (1)
Joshua Kiprui Cheptegei (UGA)	26.49.94 (2)	27.10.06 (6)	27.48.89 (9)	
Paul Kipngetich Tanui (KEN)	26.50.60 (3)	27.05.64 (2)	27.02.83 (3)	27.22.61 (3)
Bedan Karoki Muchiri (KEN)	26.52.12 (4)	27.22.93 (7)	27.04.77 (4)	27.27.17 (6)
Jemal Yimer (ETH)	26.56.11 (5)			
Geoffrey Kipsang Kamworor (KEN)	26.57.77 (6)	27.31.94 (11)	27.01.76 (2)	
Abadi Hadis (ETH)	26.59.19 (7)	27.36.34 (15)		
Mohammed Ahmed (CAN)	27.02.35 (8)			27.35.76 (9)
Shadrack Kipchirchir (USA)	27.07.55 (9)		28.16.30 (16)	
Andamlak Belihu (ETH)	27.08.94 (10)			
Aron Kifle (ERI)	27.09.92 (11)			
Abraham Naibei Cheroben (BRN)	27.11.08 (12)	27.31.86 (10)		
Leonard Essau Korir (USA)	27.20.18 (13)	27.35.65 (14)		
Timothy Toroitich (UGA)	27.21.09 (14)		27.44.90 (8)	
Hassan Mead (USA)	27.32.49 (15)		28.16.30 (15)	
Tamirat Tola (ETH)		27.06.26 (3)		
Yigrem Demelash (ETH)		27.06.27 (4)		
Galen Rupp (USA)		27.08.92 (5)	27.08.91 (5)	27.24.39 (4)
Zersenay Tadese (ERI)		27.23.86 (8)		
Nguse Amlosom (ERI)		27.30.79 (9)	28.14.72 (13)	27.29.21 (8)
Zane Robertson (NZL)		27.33.67 (12)		
Polat Kemboi Arikan (TUR)		27.35.50 (13)		
Abrar Osman (ERI)			27.43.21 (6)	
Ali Kaya (TUR)			27.43.69 (7)	
Muktar Edris (ETH)			27.54.47 (10)	
Mosinet Geremew (ETH)			28.07.50 (11)	
El Hassan Elabbassi (BRN)			28.12.57 (12)	
Cameron Levins (CAN)			28.15.19 (14)	27.47.89 (14)
Ibrahim Jeilan (ETH)				27.22.23 (2)
Abera Kuma (ETH)				27.25.27 (5)
Kenneth Kiprop Kipkemoi (KEN)				27.28.50 (7)
Dathan Ritzenhein (USA)				27.37.90 (10)
Thomas Ayeko (UGA)				27.40.96 (11)
Imane Merga (ETH)				27.42.02 (12)
Moses Ndiema Kipsiro (UGA)				27.44.53 (13)
Tsuyoshi Ugachi (JPN)				27.50.79 (15)

OVERVIEW TOP 10 WORLD OUTDOOR RANKINGS OF PAST 5 YEARS

	2018	2017	2016	2015	2014
Stanley Waithaka Mburu (KEN)	27.13.01 (1)				
Richard Yator (KEN)	27.14.70 (2)				
Joshua Kirui Cheptegei (UGA)	27.19.62 (3)	26.49.94 (2)			
Mohammed Ahmed (CAN)	27.20.56 (4)	27.02.35 (8)			
Rhonex Kipruto (KEN)	27.21.08 (5)				
Jonathan Muia Ndiku (KEN)	27.28.27 (6)				
Rodgers Chumo (KEN)	27.28.66 (7)				
Jacob Kiplimo (UGA)	27.30.25 (8)				
Jake Robertson (NZL)	27.30.90 (9)				
Richard Ringer (GER)	27.36.52 (10)				
Mohamed Farah (GBR)		26.49.51 (1)	26.53.71 (2)	26.50.97 (1)	
Paul Kipngetich Tanui (KEN)		26.50.60 (3)	27.05.64 (10)	26.51.86 (2)	26.49.41 (2)
Bedan Karoki Muchiri (KEN)		26.52.12 (4)		27.04.77 (4)	26.52.36 (3)
Jemal Yimer (ETH)		26.56.11 (5)			
Geoffrey Kipsang Kamworor (KEN)		26.57.17 (6)		26.52.65 (3)	
Abadi Hadis (ETH)		26.59.19 (7)	26.57.88 (5)		
Shadrack Kipchirchir (USA)		27.07.55 (9)			
Andamlak Belihu (ETH)		27.08.94 (10)			
Yigrem Demelash (ETH)			26.51.11 (1)		
William Malel Sitonik (KEN)			26.54.66 (3)		27.25.56 (8)
Tamirat Tola (ETH)			26.57.33 (4)		
Stephen Sambu (KEN)			26.58.25 (6)		26.54.61 (4)
Ibrahim Jeilan (ETH)			26.58.75 (7)		
Zersenay Tadese (ERI)			27.00.66 (8)		
Nicholas Mboroto Kosimbei (KEN)			27.02.59 (9)		
Cameron Levins (CAN)				27.07.51 (5)	
Galen Rupp (USA)				27.08.91 (6)	26.44.36 (1)
Muktar Edris (ETH)				27.17.18 (7)	
Imane Merga (ETH)				27.17.63 (8)	
Geoffrey Kipkorir Kirui (KEN)				27.17.91 (9)	
Mosinet Geremew (ETH)				27.18.86 (10)	
Leonard Barsoton (KEN)					27.20.74 (5)
Emmanuel Kipkemei Bett (KEN)					27.21.61 (6)
James Mwangi (KEN)					27.23.66 (7)
Edward Waweru (KEN)					27.26.92 (9)
Karemi Jeremiah Thuku (KEN)					27.28.27 (10)

WORLD RANKING ALL TIME:

1.	Kenenisa Bekele (ETH)	26.17.53 (2005)
2.	Haile Gebrselassie (ETH)	26.22.75 (1998)
3.	Paul Tergat (KEN)	26.27.85 (1997)
4.	Nicholas Kemboi (KEN)	26.30.03 (2003)
5.	Abebe Dinkesa Negera (ETH)	26.30.74 (2005)
6.	Micah Kemboi Kogo (KEN)	26.35.63 (2006)
7.	Paul Koech (KEN)	26.36.26 (1997)
8.	Zersenay Tadese (ERI)	26.37.25 (2006)
9.	Salah Hissou (MAR)	26.38.08 (1996)
10.	Ahmad Hassan Abdullah (QAT)	26.38.76 (2003)
11.	Sileshi Sihine (ETH)	26.39.69 (2004)
12.	Boniface Kiprop (UGA)	26.39.77 (2005)
13.	Samuel Kamau Wanjiru (KEN)	26.41.75 (2005)
14.	Lucas Kimeli Rotich (KEN)	26.43.98 (2011)
15.	Galen Rupp (USA)	26.44.36 (2014)
16.	Mo Farah (GBR)	26.46.57 (2011)
17.	Imane Merga (ETH)	26.48.35 (2011)
18.	Josphat Kipkoech Bett (KEN)	26.48.99 (2011)
19.	Eliud Kipchoge (KEN)	26.49.02 (2007)
20.	Moses Ndiema Masai (KEN)	26.49.20 (2007)
21.	Sammy Kipketer (KEN)	26.49.38 (2002)
22.	Paul Kipngetich Tanui (KEN)	26.49.41 (2014)
23.	Moses Mosop (KEN)	26.49.55 (2007)
24.	Assefa Mezgebu (ETH)	26.49.90 (2002)
25.	Joshua Cheptegei (UGA)	26.49.94 (2017)
26.	Richard Limo (KEN)	26.50.20 (2002)
27.	Dejen Gebremeskel (ETH)	26.51.02 (2013)
28.	Yigrem Demelash (ETH)	26.51.11 (2016)
29.	Emmanuel Kipkemei Bett (KEN)	26.51.16 (2012)
30.	Charles Waweru Kamathi (KEN)	26.51.49 (1999)
31.	Vincent Kiprop Chepkok (KEN)	26.51.68 (2012)
32.	Bitan Karoki (KEN)	26.52.12 (2017)
33.	William Sigei (KEN)	26.52.33 (1994)
34.	Mohammed Mourhit (BEL)	26.52.30 (1999)
35.	Gebregziabher Gebremariam (ETH)	26.52.33 (2007)
36.	Kenneth Kiprop Kipkemoi (KEN)	26.52.65 (2012)
	Geoffrey Kamworor (KEN)	26.52.65 (2015)
38.	Abera Kuma (ETH)	26.52.85 (2013)
39.	John Cheruiyot Korir (KEN)	26.52.87 (2002)
40.	Mark Kipkinyor Bett (KEN)	26.52.93 (2005)
41.	Matthew Kipkoech Kisorio (KEN)	26.54.25 (2011)
42.	Stephen Sambu (KEN)	26.54.61 (2014)
43.	Mark Kosgei Kiptoo (KEN)	26.54.64 (2011)
44.	William Malel Sitonik (KEN)	26.54.66 (2016)
45.	Leonard Patrick Komon (KEN)	26.55.29 (2011)

110 m Hurdles Men Outdoor / 60 m Hurdles Men Indoor

EUROPEAN CHAMPIONSHIPS 2018: 10-8-2018:

1.	Pascal M.-Lagarde (FRA)	(13.32)	13.17
2.	Sergey Shubenkov (ANA)	(13.24)	13.17
3.	Orlando Ortega (ESP)	(13.21)	13.34
4.	Damian Czykier (POL)	(13.45)	13.38
5.	Gregor Traber (GER)	(13.26)	13.46
6.	Andrew Pozzi (GBR)	(13.28)	13.48
7.	Aurel Manga (FRA)	(13.45)	13.51
8.	Balázs Baji (HUN)	(13.41)	13.55

9.	Garfield Darien (FRA)		13.46
10.	Lorenzo Perini (ITA)		13.50
11.	Hassane Fofana (ITA)	(13.50)	13.52
12.	Jason Joseph (SUI)		13.53
13.	David King (GBR)		13.55
14.	Konstadínos Douvalídis (GRE)		13.56
15.	Milan Trajkovic (CYP)		13.57
16.	Erik Balnuweit (GER)	(13.55)	13.59
17.	Elmo Lakka (FIN)		13.60
18.	Paolo Dal Molin (ITA)	(13.40)	13.61
19.	Artur Noga (POL)		13.66
20.	Vitali Parakhonka (BLR)		13.69
21.	Koen Smet (NED)	(13.61)	13.71
22.	Vladimir Vukicevic (NOR)	(13.67)	13.71
23.	Michael Obasuyi (BEL)		13.78
	Alexander John (GER)	(13.69)	dsq

25.	Artem Shamatryn (UKR)		14.02

WORLD RANKING 2018:

1.	Sergey Shubenkov (ANA)	12.92(Sze)
2.	Orlando Ortega (ESP)	13.08(Bir)
3.	Ronald Levy (JAM)	13.12(CON)
4.	Grant Holloway (USA)	13.15(Kno)
5.	Omar McLeod (JAM)	13.16(Sha)
6.	Pascal Martinot-Lagarde (FRA)	13.17(ECh)
7.	Hansle Parchment (JAM)	13.21(Mon)
8.	Gabriel Constantino (BRA)	13.23(Mnt)
	Devon Allen (USA)	13.23(Par)
10.	Gregor Traber (GER)	13.26(ECh)
11.	Daniel Roberts (USA)	13.27(Kno)
	Balázs Baji (HUN)	13.27(Sze)
	Freddie Crittenden (USA)	13.27(Bir)
14.	Andrew Pozzi (GBR)	13.28(ECh)
15.	Ruebin Walters (TTO)	13.31(Gai)
	Aurel Manga (FRA)	13.31(Par)
	Antonio Alkana (RSA)	13.31(Par)
18.	Jarret Eaton (USA)	13.33(Par)
19.	Johnathan Cabral (CAN)	13.34(Bel)
	Xie Wenjun (CHN)	13.34(Jak)
21.	Ryan Fontenot (USA)	13.35(Mtv)
22.	Milan Trajkovic (CYP)	13.36(GC)
	Ahmad Khader Almuwallad (KSA)	13.36(Pra)
	Taio Kanai (JPN)	13.36
25.	Aries Merritt (USA)	13.37(Sze)
	Aleec Harris (USA)	13.37(Bel)
	Damian Czykier (POL)	13.37
28.	Nicholas Hough (AUS)	13.38(GC)
	Ludovic Payen (FRA)	13.38
	Shane Brathwaite (BAR)	13.38
31.	Jason Joseph (SUI)	13.39
	Kuei-Ru Chen (TPE)	13.39(Jak)
33.	David Kendziera (USA)	13.40
	Vitali Parokhonka (BLR)	13.40
	Paolo Dal Molin (ITA)	13.40(ECh)
36.	Konstantinos Douvalidis (GRE)	13.41
37.	Damion Thomas (JAM)	13.44(NCA)
	Eduardo Santos (BRA)	13.44
	Yidiel Contreras (ESP)	13.44(Mad)
	Alexander John (GER)	13.44
41.	Shunya Takayama (JPN)	13.45
	Garfield Darien (FRA)	13.45

WORLD INDOOR CHAMPIONSHIPS: 4-3-2018:

1.	Andrew Pozzi (GBR)	(7.46)	7.46
2.	Jarret Eaton (USA)	(7.56)	7.47
3.	Aurel Manga (FRA)	(7.55)	7.54
4.	Aries Merritt (USA)	(7.60)	7.56
5.	Pascal Martinot-Lagarde (FRA)	(7.52)	7.68
6.	Gabriel Constantino (BRA)	(7.61)	7.71
7.	Roger Iribarne (CUB)	(7.58)	7.77
	Milan Trajkovic (CYP)	(7.51)	dsq

9.	Ronald Levy (JAM)		7.62
10.	Balázs Baji (HUN)		7.64
11.	Petr Svoboda (CZE)		7.64
12.	Ahmed Kh. A. Al-Molad (KSA)	(7.63)	7.66
13.	Yidiel Contreras (ESP)	(7.68)	7.68
14.	Konstadínos Douvalídis (GRE)	(7.66)	7.68
15.	Abdulaziz Al Mandeel (KUW)		7.69
16.	Koen Smet (NED)	(7.69)	7.69
17.	Erik Balnuweit (GER)	(7.67)	7.70
18.	David King (GBR)	(7.69)	7.70
19.	Johnathan Cabral (CAN)	(7.70)	7.71
20.	Xie Wenjun (CHN)	(7.71)	7.76
21.	Damian Czykier (POL)	(7.75)	7.78
22.	Nicholas Hough (AUS)	(7.76)	7.79
23.	Eddie Lovett (ISV)	(7.78)	7.90
24.	Vitali Parokhonka (BLR)	(7.71)	8.00

25.	Hassane Fofana (ITA)	7.81
26.	Vladimir Vukicevic (NOR)	7.81
27.	Paolo Dal Molin (ITA)	7.81
28.	Mikel Thomas (TTO)	7.84
29.	Ben Reynolds (IRL)	7.89
30.	Jason Joseph (SUI)	7.89

WORLD INDOOR RANKING 2018:

1.	Grant Holloway (USA)	7.42
2.	Jarret Eaton (USA)	7.43
3.	Omar McLeod (JAM)	7.46
	Aries Merritt (USA)	7.46
	Andrew Pozzi (GBR)	7.46
6.	Devon Allen (USA)	7.49
	Ronald Levy (JAM)	7.49
8.	Petr Svoboda (CZE)	7.51
	Milan Trajkovic (CYP)	7.51
10.	Pascal Martinot-Lagarde (FRA)	7.52
11.	Aurel Manga (FRA)	7.53
12.	Ahmad Khader AlMuwallad (KSA)	7.57
	Brendan Ames (USA)	7.57
14.	Roger Iribarne (CUB)	7.58
15.	Gabriel Constantino (BRA)	7.60
	Aleec Harris (USA)	7.60
	Erik Balnuweit (GER)	7.60
	Balázs Baji (HUN)	7.60
	Antoine Lloyd (USA)	7.60
20.	Ruebin Walters (TTO)	7.61
21.	Johnatan Cabral (CAN)	7.62
22.	Simon Krauss (FRA)	7.63
	David King (GBR)	7.63
	Ashlyn Davis (USA)	7.63

Commonwealth Games, Gold Coast, 10-4-2018:
1. Ronald Levy (JAM)   (13.35)   13.19
2. Hansle Parchment (JAM)   (13.30)   13.22
3. Nicholas Hough (AUS)   13.38
4. Milan Trajkovic (CYP)   (13.36)   13.42
5. Antonio Alkana (RSA)   (13.32)   13.49
6. Shane Brathwaite (BAR)   13.53
   Andrew Pozzi (GBR)   (13.29)   13.53

Shanghai, 12-5-2018:
1. Omar McLeod (JAM)   13.16
2. Orlando Ortega (ESP)   13.17
3. Sergey Shubenkov (ANA)   13.27
4. Ronald Levy (JAM)   13.33
5. Hansle Parchment (JAM)   13.48
6. Aries Merritt (USA)   13.65
7. Garfield Darien (FRA)   13.74

Knoxville, 13-5-2018:
1. Grant Holloway (USA)   13.15
2. Daniel Roberts (USA)   13.27
3. Damion Thomas (JAM)   13.64

Eugene, 26-5-2018: + 3 m/s:
1. Omar McLeod (JAM)   13.01
2. Sergey Shubenkov (ANA)   13.08
3. Devon Allen (USA)   13.13
4. Orlando Ortega (ESP)   13.17
5. Ronald Levy (JAM)   13.26
6. Aries Merritt (USA)   13.27
7. Andrew Pozzi (GBR)   13.51
8. Aleec Harris (USA)   13.52

Hengelo, 3-6-2018:
1. Sergey Shubenkov (ANA)   13.23
2. Orlando Ortega (ESP)   13.38
3. Pascal Martinot-Lagarde (FRA)   13.42
4. Gregor Traber (GER)   13.50
5. Balazs Baji (HUN)   13.54
6. Milan Trajkovic (CYP)   13.58

Eugene, NCAA, 9-6-2018:
1. Grant Holloway (USA)   (13.42+) 13.42
2. David Kendziera (USA)   (13.43)   13.43
3. Damion Thomas (JAM)   (13.44)   13.45
4. Trey Cunningham (USA)   13.64
5. Antoine Lloyd (USA)   (13.61)   13.94

Montreuil, 19-6-2018:
1. Sergey Shubenkov (RUS)   12.99
2. Gabriel Constantino (BRA)   13.23
3. Pascal Martinot-Lagarde (FRA)   13.28

US CHAMPIONSHIPS, Des Moines, 24-6-2018:
1. Devon Allen   (13.38)   13.46
2. Grant Holloway   (13.34)   13.46
3. Jarret Eaton   13.51
4. Aries Merritt   (13.43)   13.52
5. Trey Cunningham   (13.62)   13.71
6. Antoine Lloyd   (13.46)   13.72
7. Aleec Harris   (13.49)   13.76
8. David Kendziera   (13.53)   dnf
----
9. Ryan Fontenot   13.55

JAM CHAMPIONSHIPS, Kingston, 24-6-2018:
1. Ronald Levy   13.16
2. Hansle Parchment   13.40
3. Andrew Riley   13.53

Paris, 30-6-2018:
1. Ronald Levy (JAM)   (13.25)   13.18
2. Hansle Parchment (JAM)   (13.26)   13.22
3. Devon Allen (USA)   (13.34)   13.23
4. Antonio Alkana (RSA)   (13.31)   13.32
5. Jarret Eaton (USA)   (13.33)   13.40
6. Orlando Ortega (ESP)   (13.19)   13.44
7. Aurel Manga (FRA)   (13.31)   13.48
   Sergey Shubenkov (ANA)   (13.05)   dsq
----
9. Aleec Harris (USA)   13.42
10. Pascal Martinot-Lagarde (FRA)   13.42
11. Aries Merritt (USA)   13.51
12. Xie Wenjun (CHN)   13.53
13. Milan Trajkovic (CYP)   13.56

Szekesfehervar, 2-7-2018:
1. Sergey Shubenkov (ANA)   12.92
2. Balazs Baji (HUN)   13.27
3. Devon Allen (USA)   13.36
4. Aries Merritt (USA)   13.37
5. Aleec Harris (USA)   13.43
6. Omar McLeod (JAM)   13.45
7. Andrew Riley (JAM)   13.66

Lausanne, 5-7-2018:
1. Sergey Shubenkov (ANA)   12.95
2. Devon Allen (USA)   13.29
3. Pascal Martinot-Lagarde (FRA)   13.30
4. Balazs Baji (HUN)   13.36
5. Omar McLeod (JAM)   13.41
6. Aries Merritt (USA)   13.44

Luzern, 9-7-2018:
1. Balazs Baji (HUN)   13.33
2. Devon Allen (JAM)   13.35
3. Gregor Traber (ITA)   13.35
4. Milan Trajkovic (CYP)   13.37

London, World Cup, 15-7-2018:
1. Pascal Martinot-Lagarde (FRA)   13.22
2. Ronald Levy (JAM)   13.30
3. Devon Allen (JAM)   13.36
4. Antonio Alkana (RSA)   13.38

Monaco, 20-7-2018:
1. Sergey Shubenkov (ANA)   13.07
2. Orlando Ortega (ESP)   13.18
3. Pascal Martinot-Lagarde (FRA)   13.20
4. Hansle Parchment (JAM)   13.21
5. Devon Allen (USA)   13.38
6. Balazs Baji (HUN)   13.38
7. Aries Merritt (USA)   13.49

London, 22-7-2018:
1. Ronald Levy (JAM)   13.13
2. Devon Allen (USA)   13.30
3. Freddie Crittenden (USA)   13.33
4. Andrew Pozzi (GBR)   13.36
5. Antonio Alkana (RSA)   13.40
6. Shane Brathwaite (BAR)   13.41
7. Balazs Baji (HUN)   13.42
8. Aries Merritt (USA)   13.44

Birmingham, 18-8-2018:
1. Orlando Ortega (ESP)   13.08
2. Ronald Levy (JAM)   13.22
3. Pascal Martinot-Lagarde (FRA)   13.27
4. Freddie Crittenden (USA)   13.27
5. Andrew Pozzi (GBR)   13.35
6. Gabriel Constantino (BRA)   13.41
7. Johnathan Cabral (CAN)   13.46

Brussels, 31-8-2018:
1. Sergey Shubenkov (ANA)   12.97
2. Orlando Ortega (ESP)   13.10
3. Hansle Parchment (JAM)   13.35
4. Pascal Martinot-Lagarde (FRA)   13.36
5. Freddie Crittenden (USA)   13.39
6. Devon Allen (USA)   13.41
7. Ronald Levy (JAM)   13.47
8. Balazs Baji (HUN)   13.63

Berlin, 2-9-2018:
1. Orlando Ortega (ESP)   13.15
2. Freddie Crittenden (USA)   13.31
3. Pascal Martinot-Lagarde (FRA)   13.38
4. Ronald Levy (JAM)   13.47
5. Gregor Traber (GER)   13.52
6. Shane Brathwaite (BAR)   13.63
7. Balazs Baji (HUN)   13.67

Zagreb, 4-9-2018:
1. Orlando Ortega (ESP)   13.39
2. Devon Allen (USA)   13.50
3. Freddie Crittenden (USA)   13.52

CONTINENTAL CUP, Ostrava, 9-9-2018:
1. Sergey Shubenkov (EUR)   13.03
2. Ronald Levy (AME)   13.12
3. Pascal Martinot-Lagarde (EUR)   13.31
4. Antonio Alkana (AFR)   13.36
5. Devon Allen (AME)   13.57

OVERVIEW WORLDWIDE OUTDOOR CHAMPIONSHIP FINALISTS OF PAST 6 YEARS

	Wch 17	OG 16	Wch 15	Wch 13
Omar McLeod (JAM)	13.04 (1)	13.05 (1)	13.18 (6)	
Sergey Shubenkov (RUS)	13.14 (2)		12.98 (1)	13.24 (3)
Balázs Baji (HUN)	13.28 (3)			
Garfield Darien (FRA)	13.30 (4)		13.34 (8)	
Aries Merritt (USA)	13.31 (5)		13.04 (3)	13.31 (6)
Shane Brathwaite (BAR)	13.32 (6)			
Orlando Ortega (ESP)	13.37 (7)	13.17 (2)		
Hansle Parchment (JAM)	13.37 (8)		13.03 (2)	
Dimitri Bascou (FRA)		13.24 (3)	13.17 (5)	
Pascal Martinot-Lagarde (FRA)		13.29 (4)	13.17 (4)	
Devon Allen (USA)		13.31 (5)		
Johnathan Cabral (CAN)		13.40 (6)		
Milan Trajkovic (CYP)		13.41 (7)		
Ronnie Ash (USA)		dsq (8)		
David Oliver (USA)			13.33 (7)	13.00 (1)
Ryan Wilson (USA)				13.13 (2)
Jason Richardson (USA)				13.27 (4)
William Sharman (GBR)				13.30 (5)
Thomas Martinot-Lagarde (FRA)				13.42 (7)
Andrew Riley (JAM)				13.51 (8)

OVERVIEW WORLD INDOOR CHAMPIONSHIP FINALISTS OF 5 PAST YEARS

	Wch 18	Wch 16	Wch 14
Andrew Pozzi (GBR)	7.46 (1)		7.53 (4)
Jarret Eaton (USA)	7.47 (2)	7.50 (4)	
Aurel Manga (FRA)	7.54 (3)		
Aries Merritt (USA)	7.56 (4)		
Pascal Martinot-Lagarde (FRA)	7.68 (5)	7.46 (2)	7.46 (2)
Gabriel Constantino (BRA)	7.71 (6)		
Roger Iribarne (CUB)	7.77 (7)		
Milan Trajkovic (CYP)	dsq (8)		
Omar McLeod (JAM)		7.41 (1)	
Dimitri Bascou (FRA)		7.48 (3)	
Spencer Adams (USA)		7.64 (5)	
Balázs Baji (HUN)		7.65 (6)	
Eddie Lovett (ISV)		7.75 (7)	
Shane Brathwaite (BAR)		7.88 (8)	
Omo Osaghae (USA)			7.45 (1)
Garfield Darien (FRA)			7.47 (3)
Gregor Traber (GER)			7.56 (5)
Erik Balnuweit (GER)			7.56 (6)
William Sharman (GBR)			7.60 (7)
Andrew Riley (JAM)			dns (8)

OVERVIEW TOP 10 WORLD OUTDOOR RANKINGS OF PAST 5 YEARS

	2018	2017	2016	2015	2014
Sergey Shubenkov (RUS)	12.92 (1)	13.01 (2)		12.98 (3)	13.13 (5)
Orlando Ortega (ESP)	13.08 (2)	13.15 (9)	13.04 (3)	12.94 (1)	13.01 (4)
Ronald Levy (JAM)	13.12 (3)	13.05 (3)			
Grant Holloway (USA)	13.15 (4)				
Omar McLeod (JAM)	13.16 (5)	12.90 (1)	12.98 (1)	12.97 (2)	
Pascal Martinot-Lagarde (FRA)	13.17 (6)		13.12 (6)	13.06 (7)	12.95 (2)
Hansle Parchment (JAM)	13.21 (7)		13.10 (5)	13.03 (5)	12.94 (1)
Gabriel Constantino (BRA)	13.23 (8)				
Devon Allen (USA)	13.23 (8)	13.10 (6)	13.03 (2)		13.16 (7)
Gregor Traber (GER)	13.26 (10)				
Garfield Darien (FRA)		13.09 (4)			
Aries Merritt (USA)		13.09 (4)		13.04 (6)	
Antonio Alkana (RSA)		13.11 (7)			
Andrew Pozzi (GBR)		13.14 (8)	13.19 (9)		
Balázs Baji (HUN)		13.15 (9)			
David Oliver (USA)			13.09 (4)	12.98 (3)	
Dimitri Bascou (FRA)			13.12 (6)		
Ronnie Ash (USA)			13.18 (8)	13.13 (10)	12.99 (3)
Deuce Carter (JAM)			13.20 (10)		
Aleec Harris (USA)				13.11 (8)	13.14 (6)
Jason Richardson (USA)				13.12 (9)	
William Sharman (GBR)					13.16 (7)
Ryan Wilson (USA)					13.18 (9)
Yordan O'Farrill (CUB)					13.19 (10)
Andrew Riley (JAM)					13.19 (10)

OVERVIEW TOP 10 WORLD INDOOR RANKINGS OF PAST 5 YEARS

	2018	2017	2016	2015	2014
Grant Holloway (USA)	7.42 (1)				
Jarret Eaton (USA)	7.43 (2)		7.50 (5)		7.54 (8)
Andrew Pozzi (GBR)	7.46 (3)	7.43 (1)			7.53 (6)
Omar McLeod (JAM)	7.46 (3)	7.46 (2)	7.41 (1)	7.45 (1)	
Aries Merritt (USA)	7.46 (3)	7.51 (4)		7.52 (8)	
Devon Allen (USA)	7.49 (6)		7.56 (9)		
Ronald Levy (JAM)	7.49 (6)				
Petr Svoboda (CZE)	7.51 (8)	7.53 (7)			
Milan Trajkovic (CYP)	7.51 (8)				
Pascal Martinot-Lagarde (FRA)	7.52 (10)	7.51 (4)	7.46 (3)	7.49 (4)	7.45 (1)
Orlando Ortega (ESP)/(CUB)		7.48 (3)	7.49 (4)	7.45 (1)	
Dimitri Bascou (FRA)		7.51 (4)	7.41 (1)	7.46 (3)	
Garfield Darien (FRA)		7.53 (7)			7.47 (4)
Aurel Manga (FRA)		7.53 (7)			
Balázs Baji (HUN)		7.53 (7)	7.55 (8)		
Ashton Eaton (USA)			7.53 (6)	7.51 (6)	
Myles Hunter (USA)			7.53 (6)		
Jeff Porter (USA)			7.57 (10)		7.46 (3)
Aleec Harris (USA)				7.50 (5)	
Jason Richardson (USA)				7.51 (6)	
Wilhem Belocian (FRA)				7.52 (8)	
Dayron Robles (CUB)				7.53 (10)	7.51 (5)
Omo Osaghae (USA)					7.45 (1)
William Sharman (GBR)					7.53 (6)
Erik Balnuweit (GER)					7.54 (8)
Sergey Shubenkov (RUS)					7.55 (10)

WORLD RANKING ALL TIME:

1.	Aries Merritt (USA)	12.80 (2012)
2.	Dayron Robles (CUB)	12.87 (2008)
3.	Liu Xiang (CHN)	12.88 (2006)
4.	David Oliver (USA)	12.89 (2010)
5.	Dominique Arnold (USA)	12.90 (2006)
	Omar McLeod (JAM)	12.90 (2017)
7.	Colin Jackson (GBR)	12.91 (1993)
8.	Roger Kingdom (USA)	12.92 (1989)
	Allen Johnson (USA)	12.92 (1996)
	Sergey Shubenkov (ANA)	12.92 (2018)
11.	Renaldo Nehemiah (USA)	12.93 (1981)
12.	Jack Pierce (USA)	12.94 (1996)
	Hansle Parchment (JAM)	12.94 (2014)
	Orlando Ortega (CUB)	12.94 (2015)
15.	Terrence Trammell (USA)	12.95 (2007)
	Pascal Martinot-Lagarde (FRA)	12.95 (2014)
17.	Ladji Doucouré (FRA)	12.97 (2005)
18.	Mark Crear (USA)	12.98 (1999)
	Jason Richardson (USA)	12.98 (2012)
20.	Ronnie Ash (USA)	12.99 (2014)
21.	Anthony Jarrett (GBR)	13.00 (1993)
	Anier Garcia (CUB)	13.00 (2000)
23.	Larry Wade (USA)	13.01 (1999)
24.	Ryan Wilson (USA)	13.02 (2007)
	David Payne (USA)	13.02 (2007)
26.	Greg Foster (USA)	13.03 (1981)
	Reggie Torian (USA)	13.03 (1998)
	Devon Allen (USA)	13.03 (2016)
29.	Anthony Dees (USA)	13.05 (1991)
	Florian Schwarthoff (GER)	13.05 (1995)
	Ronald Levy (JAM)	13.05 (2017)
32.	Mark McKoy (CAN)	13.08 (1993)
	Stanislavs Olijars (LAT)	13.08 (2003)
	Jeff Porter (USA)	13.08 (2012)
35.	Antwon Hicks (USA)	13.09 (2008)
	Garfield Darien (FRA)	13.09 (2017)
37.	Falk Balzer (GER)	13.10 (1998)
38.	Aleec Harris (USA)	13.11 (2015)
	Antonio Alkana (RSA)	13.11 (2017)
40.	Duane Ross (USA)	13.12 (1999)
	Anwar Moore (USA)	13.12 (2007)
	Dimitri Bascou (FRA)	13.12 (2016)
43.	Igor Kovac (SVK)	13.13 (1997)
	Dexter Faulk (USA)	13.13 (2009)

WORLD RANKING ALL TIME INDOOR (60m):

1.	Colin Jackson (GBR)	7.30 (1994)
2.	Dayron Robles (CUB)	7.33 (2008)
3.	Greg Foster (USA)	7.36 (1987)
	Allen Johnson (USA)	7.36 (2004)
	Terrence Trammell (USA)	7.36 (2010)
6.	Roger Kingdom (USA)	7.37 (1989)
	Anier Garcia (CUB)	7.37 (2000)
	Anthony Dees (USA)	7.37 (2000)
	David Oliver (USA)	7.37 (2011)
10.	Mark Crear (USA)	7.38 (1998)
	Reggie Torian (USA)	7.38 (1999)
12.	Yoel Hernández (CUB)	7.40 (2000)
	Dexter Faulk (USA)	7.40 (2012)
14.	Mark McKoy (CAN)	7.41 (1993)
	Courtney Hawkins (USA)	7.41 (1995)
	Falk Balzer (GER)	7.41 (1999)
	Liu Xiang (CHN)	7.41 (2012)
	Dimitri Bascou (FRA)	7.41 (2016)
	Omar McLeod (JAM)	7.41 (2016)
20.	Igor Kazanov (URS)	7.42 (1989)
	Anthony Jarrett (GBR)	7.42 (1995)
	Ladji Doucouré (FRA)	7.42 (2005)
	Grant Holloway (USA)	7.42 (2018)
24.	Duane Ross (USA)	7.43 (1998)
	Aries Merritt (USA)	7.43 (2012)
	Andrew Pozzi (GBR)	7.43 (2017)
	Jarret Eaton (USA)	7.43 (2018)
28.	Elmar Lichtenegger (AUT)	7.44 (2002)
	Larry Wade (USA)	7.44 (2003)
	Yevgeniy Borisov (RUS)	7.44 (2008)
	Petr Svoboda (CZE)	7.44 (2010)
32.	Pascal Martinot-Lagarde (FRA)	7.45 (2014)
	Omoghan Osaghae (USA)	7.45 (2014)
	Orlando Ortega (CUB)	7.45 (2015)
35.	Yevgeniy Pechonkin (RUS)	7.46 (2002)
	Kevin Craddock (USA)	7.46 (2012)
	Jeff Porter (USA)	7.46 (2012)
38.	Ron Bramlett (USA)	7.47 (2007)
	Garfield Darien (FRA)	7.47 (2014)
40.	Thomas Munkelt (GER)	7.48 (1983)
	Maurice Wignall (JAM)	7.48 (2004)
	Joel Brown (USA)	7.48 (2009)

400 m Hurdles Men

EUROPEAN CHAMPIONSHIPS 2018: 9-8-2018:

1.	Karsten Warholm (NOR)	(48.67)	47.64
2.	Yasmani Copello (TUR)	(48.88)	47.81
3.	Thomas Barr (IRL)	(49.10)	48.31
4.	Ludvy Vaillant (FRA)	(48.88)	48.42
5.	Patryk Dobek (POL)	(48.75)	48.59
6.	Rasmus Mägi (EST)	(48.80)	48.75
7.	Sergio Fernández (ESP)	(49.19)	48.98
8.	Timofey Chalyy (ANA)	(48.89)	49.41

9.	Luka Campbell (GER)		49.20
10.	Tibor Koroknai (HUN)		49.24
11.	Victor Coroller (FRA)		49.34
12.	Lorenzo Vergani (ITA)		49.41
13.	Muhammad Kounta (FRA)		49.58
14.	Maté Koroknai (HUN)		49.77
15.	Jack Green (GBR)		49.84
16.	José Bencosme (ITA)		49.86
17.	Denys Nechyporenko (UKR)	(50.26)	50.27
18.	Martin Kucera (SVK)		50.30
19.	Michal Broz (CZE)		50.31
20.	Maksims Sincukovs (LAT)		50.33
21.	Jaak-Heinrich Jagor (EST)		50.41
22.	Alain-Hervé Mfomkpa (SUI)	(50.34)	50.71
23.	Emir Bekric (SRB)	(50.46)	50.96
	Aleksandr Skorobogatko (ANA)	(50.74)	dnf

25.	Dany Brand (SUI)		50.82
	Dai Greene (GBR)		dns

WORLD RANKING 2018:

1.	Abderrahman Samba (QAT)	46.98(Par)
2.	Rai Benjamin (USA)	47.02(NCA)
3.	Kyron McMaster (IVB)	47.54(Par)
4.	Karsten Warholm (NOR)	47.64(ECh)
5.	Yasmani Copello (TUR)	47.81(ECh)
6.	Kenneth Selmon (USA)	48.12(NCA)
7.	Andre Clarke (JAM)	48.29(Mtv)
8.	TJ Holmes (USA)	48.30(Par)
9.	Thomas Barr (IRL)	48.31(ECh)
10.	David Kendziera (USA)	48.42(NCA)
	Ludvy Vaillant (FRA)	48.42(ECh)
12.	Annsert Whyte (JAM)	48.46(CON)
13.	Patryk Dobek (POL)	48.59(ECh)
14.	Rasmus Mägi (EST)	48.60
15.	Khalifah Rosser (USA)	48.65(USC)
16.	Takatoshi Abe (JPN)	48.68
17.	Marcio Teles (BRA)	48.70
18.	Juander Santos (DOM)	48.77
19.	Kemar Mowatt (JAM)	48.83(NCA)
	Kerron Clement (USA)	48.83(Par)
21.	Nicholas Bett (KEN)	48.88(Pre)
22.	Timofey Chalyy (ANA)	48.89(ECh)
23.	Sharun Ayyasamy (IND)	48.96(Jak)
24.	Jeffery Gibson (BAH)	48.98(Heu)
	Sergio Fernández (ESP)	48.98(ECh)
26.	Mario Lambrughi (ITA)	48.99
27.	Quincy Downing (USA)	49.00(Hue)
28.	Abdelmalik Lahoulou (ALG)	49.01
29.	Byron Robinson (USA)	49.04(USC)
	Shawn Rowe (JAM)	49.04(JAC)
31.	Bershawn Jackson (USA)	49.08(Do)
32.	Leandro Zamora (CUB)	49.10
	Taylor McLaughlin (USA)	49.10(USC)
34.	Ziad Aziz (TUN)	49.13
35.	Jaheel Hyde (JAM)	49.14(GC)
	Luke Campbell (GER)	49.14(LCF)
37.	Lindsay Hanekom (RSA)	49.17(Pre)
38.	Jack Green (GBR)	49.18(GC)
	Artur Langowski Terezan (BRA)	49.18
40.	Le Roux Hamman (RSA)	49.22(Pre)
41.	Michael Stigler (USA)	49.24(USC)
	Tibor Koroknai (HUN)	49.24(ECh)
43.	Aron Koech (KEN)	49.28(GC)
	Guillermo Ruggeri (ARG)	49.28

Commonwealth Games, Gold Coast, 12-4-2018:
1. Kyron McMaster (IVB)   (48.78)   48.25
2. Jeffery Gibson (BAH)   49.10
3. Jaheel Hyde (JAM)   (49.14)   49.16
4. Jack Green (GBR)   (49.24)   49.18

    Andre Clarke (JAM)   49.10
    Nicholas Bett (KEN)   49.24
    Aron Koech (KEN)   49.28

Doha, 4-5-2018:
1. Abderrahman Samba (QAT)   47.57
2. Bershawn Jackson (USA)   49.08
3. Kyron McMaster (IVB)   49.46

Rome, 31-5-2018:
1. Abderrahman Samba (QAT)   47.48
2. Karsten Warholm (NOR)   47.82
3. Yasmani Copello (TUR)   48.63
4. TJ Holmes (USA)   49.00
5. Rasmus Mägi (EST)   49.19
6. Kerron Clement (USA)   49.48

Oslo, 7-6-2018:
1. Abderrahman Samba (QAT)   47.60
2. Karsten Warholm (NOR)   48.22
3. Yasmani Copello (TUR)   48.54
4. TJ Holmes (USA)   48.64
5. Kerron Clement (USA)   49.30
6. Rasmus Mägi (EST)   49.35
7. Mamadou Kasse Hann (FRA)   49.50
8. Thomas Barr (IRL)   49.53

Eugene, NCAA, 8-6-2018:
1. Rai Benjamin (USA)   47.02
2. Kenneth Selmon (USA)   48.12
3. David Kendziera (USA)   48.42
4. Kemar Mowatt (JAM)   48.83
5. Taylor McLaughlin (USA)   49.59

Stockholm, 10-6-2018:
1. Abderrahman Samba (QAT)   47.41
2. Karsten Warholm (NOR)   47.81
3. Yasmani Copello (TUR)   48.91
4. Mamadou Kasse Hann (FRA)   49.58

US CHAMPIONSHIPS, Des Moines, 23-6-2018:
1. Kenneth Selmon   48.21
2. TJ Holmes   48.51
3. Khallifah Rosser   48.65
4. Bershawn Jackson   49.14
5. David Kendziera   (49.15)   49.22
6. CJ Allen   49.58
7. Byron Robinson   (49.04)   49.79
8. Taylor McLaughlin   (49.10)   dns

    Quincy Downing   49.41

JAM CHAMPIONSHIPS, Kingston, 22-6-2018:
1. Annsert Whyte   48.80
2. Shawn Rowe   49.04
3. Kemar Mowatt   (48.96)   49.16
7. Andre Clarke   (48.46)   49.88

Paris, 30-6-2018:
1. Abderrahman Samba (QAT)   46.98
2. Kyron McMaster (IVB)   47.54
3. Karsten Warholm (NOR)   48.06
4. TJ Holmes (USA)   48.30
5. Kerron Clement (USA)   48.83
6. Bershawn Jackson (USA)   49.16

Lausanne, 5-7-2018:
1. Abderrahim Samba (QAT)   47.42
2. Karsten Warholm (NOR)   47.94
3. Yasmani Copello (TUR)   48.85
4. TJ Holmes (USA)   48.94
5. Rasmus Mägi (EST)   49.04
6. Bershawn Jackson (USA)   49.31
7. Jack Green (GBR)   49.52

London, 21-7-2018:
1. Karsten Warholm (NOR)   47.65
2. Yasmani Copello (TUR)   48.44
3. Thomas Barr (IRL)   48.99
4. David Kendziera (USA)   49.02
5. Rasmus Mägi (EST)   49.11
6. Kerron Clement (USA)   49.43
7. TJ Holmes (USA)   49.66

NACAC, Toronto, 12-8-2018:

1.	Kyron McMaster (IVB)	48.18
2.	Annsert Whyte (JAM)	48.91
3.	Khallifah Rosser (USA)	49.13
4.	Shawn Rowe (JAM)	49.40
5.	TJ Holmes (USA)	49.79

Zürich, 30-8-2018:

1.	Kyron McMaster (IVB)	48.08
2.	Karsten Warholm (NOR)	48.10
3.	Yasmani Copello (TUR)	48.73
4.	Rasmus Mägi (EST)	49.28

CONTINENTAL CUP, Ostrava, 8-9-2018:

1.	Abderrahman Samba (ASI)	47.37
2.	Annsert Whyte (AME)	48.46
3.	Karsten Warholm (EUR)	48.56
4.	Yasmani Copello (EUR)	48.65
5.	Abdelmalik Lahoulou (AFR)	49.12
6.	Takatoshi Abe (ASI)	49.80

OVERVIEW WORLDWIDE OUTDOOR CHAMPIONSHIP FINALISTS OF PAST 6 YEARS

	Wch 17	OG 16	Wch 15	Wch 13
Karsten Warholm (NOR)	48.35 (1)			
Yasmani Copello (TUR)	48.49 (2)	47.92 (3)	48.96 (6)	
Kerron Clement (USA)	48.52 (3)		48.18 (4)	49.08 (8)
Kemar Mowatt (JAM)	48.99 (4)			
TJ Holmes (USA)	49.00 (5)			
Juander Santos (DOM)	49.04 (6)			
Abderrahaman Samba (QAT)	49.74 (7)			
Kariem Hussein (SUI)	50.07 (8)			
Kerron Clement (USA)		47.73 (1)		
Boniface Mucheru Tumuti (KEN)		47.78 (2)	48.33 (5)	
Thomas Barr (IRL)		47.97 (4)		
Annsert Whyte (JAM)		48.07 (5)		
Rasmus Mägi (EST)		48.40 (6)		
Haron Koech (KEN)		49.09 (7)		
Javier Culson (PUR)		dsq (8)		48.38 (6)
Nicholas Bett (KEN)			47.79 (1)	
Denis Kudryavtsev (RUS)			48.05 (2)	
Jeffery Gibson (BAH)			48.17 (3)	
Patryk Dobek (POL)			49.14 (7)	
Michael Tinsley (USA)			50.02 (8)	47.70 (2)
Jehue Gordon (TRI)				47.69 (1)
Emir Bekric (SRB)				48.05 (3)
Omar Cisneros (CUB)				48.12 (4)
Felix Sanchez (DOM)				48.22 (5)
Mamadou Kasse Hann (SEN)				48.68 (7)

OVERVIEW TOP 10 WORLD OUTDOOR RANKINGS OF PAST 5 YEARS

	2018	2017	2016	2015	2014
Abderrahaman Samba (QAT)	46.98 (1)	48.31 (8)			
Rai Benjamin (ANT/USA)	47.02 (2)	48.33 (9)			
Kyron McMaster (IVB)	47.54 (3)	47.80 (1)			
Karsten Warholm (NOR)	47.64 (4)	48.22 (5)	48.49 (10)		
Yasmani Copello (TUR)	47.81 (5)	48.24 (6)	47.92 (3)		
Kenneth Selmon (USA)	48.12 (6)				
Andre Clarke (JAM)	48.29 (7)				
TJ Holmes (USA)	48.30 (8)				
Thomas Barr (IRL)	48.31 (9)		47.97 (4)		
David Kendziera (USA)	48.42 (10)				
Ludvy Vaillant (FRA)	48.42 (10)				
Kerron Clement (USA)		48.02 (2)	47.73 (1)	48.18 (6)	
Quincy Downing (USA)		48.13 (3)			
Eric Futch (USA)		48.18 (4)			
Michael Stigler (USA)		48.26 (7)		48.44 (10)	
Mamadou Kasse Hann (FRA)		48.40 (10)			
Boniface Mucheru Tumuti (KEN)			47.78 (2)	48.29 (7)	
Nicholas Kiplagat Bett (KEN)			48.01 (5)	47.79 (1)	
Annsert Whyte (JAM)			48.07 (6)		48.58 (7)
Johnny Dutch (USA)			48.10 (7)	48.13 (4)	
Rasmus Mägi (EST)			48.40 (8)		48.54 (6)
Javier Culson (PUR)			48.46 (9)		48.03 (1)
Haron Koech (KEN)			48.49 (10)		
Denis Kudryavtsev (RUS)				48.05 (2)	
Bershawn Jackson (USA)				48.09 (3)	
Jeffery Gibson (BAH)				48.17 (5)	
Michael Tinsley (USA)				48.34 (8)	48.25 (2)
Patryk Dobek (POL)				48.40 (9)	
Cornel Fredericks (RSA)					48.25 (2)
Kariem Hussein (SUI)					48.47 (4)
Roxroy Cato (JAM)					48.48 (5)
Andrés Silva (URU)					48.65 (8)
Ashton Eaton (USA)					48.69 (9)
Timofey Chalyy (RUS)					48.69 (9)

WORLD RANKING ALL TIME:

1.	Kevin Young (USA)	46.78 (1992)
2.	Abderrahman Samba (QAT)	46.98 (2018)
3.	Edwin Moses (USA)	47.02 (1983)
	Rai Benjamin (USA)	47.02 (2018)
5.	Bryan Bronson (USA)	47.03 (1998)
6.	Samuel Matete (ZAM)	47.10 (1991)
7.	André Phillips (USA)	47.19 (1988)
8.	Amadou Dia Ba (SEN)	47.23 (1988)
9.	Kerron Clement (USA)	47.24 (2005)
10.	Félix Sánchez (DOM)	47.25 (2003)
	Angelo Taylor (USA)	47.25 (2008)
12.	Bershawn Jackson (USA)	47.30 (2005)
13.	Stéphane Diagana (FRA)	47.37 (1995)
14.	Danny Harris (USA)	47.38 (1991)
15.	James Carter (USA)	47.43 (2005)
16.	Harald Schmid (FRG)	47.48 (1982)
17.	Hadi Soua'an Al Somaily (KSA)	47.53 (2000)
18.	Derrick Adkins (USA)	47.54 (1995)
	Fabrizio Mori (ITA)	47.54 (2001)
	Kyron McMaster (IVB)	47.54 (2018)
21.	Wintrop Graham (JAM)	47.60 (1993)
22.	Johnny Dutch (USA)	47.63 (2010)
23.	Karsten Warholm (NOR)	47.64 (2018)
24.	LJ van Zyl (RSA)	47.66 (2011)
25.	Bennie Brazell (USA)	47.67 (2005)
26.	Jehue Gordon (TTO)	47.69 (2013)
27.	Michael Tinsley (USA)	47.70 (2013)
28.	Javier Culson (PUR)	47.72 (2010)
29.	David Patrick (USA)	47.75 (1988)
30.	Boniface Mucheru (KEN)	47.78 (2016)
31.	Nicholas Bett (KEN)	47.79 (2015)
32.	Llewellyn Herbert (RSA)	47.81 (2000)
	Yasmani Copello (TUR)	47.81 (2018)
34.	John Akii-Bua (UGA)	47.82 (1972)
	Kriss Akabusi (GBR)	47.82 (1992)
	Periklis Iakovakis (GRE)	47.82 (2006)
37.	Bayano Kamani (PAN)	47.84 (2005)
	David Greene (GBR)	47.84 (2012)
39.	Dai Tamesue (JPN)	47.89 (2001)
40.	Calvin Davis (USA)	47.91 (1996)
41.	Aleksandr Vasilyev (URS)	47.92 (1985)
42.	Kenji Narisako (JPN)	47.93 (2006)
	Jeshua Anderson (USA)	47.93 (2011)
	Omar Cisneros (CUB)	47.93 (2013)
45.	Eric Thomas (USA)	47.94 (2000)

3000 m Steeple-chase Men

EUROPEAN CHAMPIONSHIPS 2018: 9-8-2018:

1. Mahiedine Mekhissi (FRA) (8.28.61) 8.31.66
2. Fernando Carro (ESP)   (8.29.63) 8.34.16
3. Yohanes Chiappinelli (ITA)(8.28.41) 8.35.81
4. Yoann Kowal (FRA)   (8.28.75) 8.36.77
5. Zak Seddon (GBR)   (8.30.00) 8.37.28
6. Daniel Arce (ESP)   (8.29.25) 8.38.12
7. Krystian Zalewski (POL)   (8.29.11) 8.38.59
8. Topi Raitanen (FIN)   (8.28.48) 8.40.11
9. Kaur Kivistik (EST)   (8.28.84) 8.40.32
10. Djilali Bedrani (FRA)   (8.29.75) 8.41.83
11. Tom Erling Karboe (NOR)   (8.29.90) 8.42.91
12. Napoleon Solomon (SWE)   (8.29.10) 8.43.66
13. Ahmed Abdelwahed (ITA)   (8.28.80) 8.44.77
14. Sebastián Martos (ESP)   (8.29.67) 8.46.76
15. Ole Hesselbjerg (DEN)   (8.30.44) 8.48.48

----

16. Jamaine Coleman (GBR)   8.33.78
17. Martin Grau (GER)   8.33.81
18. Mitko Tsenov (BUL)   8.36.39
19. Justinas Berzanskis (LTU)   8.36.88
20. Ieuan Thomas (GBR)   8.40.87
    Tarik Langat Akdag (TUR)   dnf

WORLD RANKING 2018:

1. Soufiane El Bakkali (MAR)   7.58.15(Mon)
2. Evan Jager (USA)   8.01.02(Mon)
3. Benjamin Kigen (KEN)   8.06.19(Rab)
4. Chala Beyo (ETH)   8.07.27(Rab)
5. Conseslus Kipruto (KEN)   8.08.40(Rom)
6. Abraham Kibiwot (KEN)   8.10.62(GC)
7. Hillary Bor (USA)   8.12.20(Rab)
8. Amos Kirui (KEN)   8.12.24(GC)
9. Matthew Hughes (CAN)   8.12.33(GC)
10. Nicholas Kiptanui Bett (KEN)   8.13.18
11. Ibrahim Ezzaydouny (MAR)   8.14.62(Rab)
12. Lawrence Kemboi Kipsang (KEN)   8.15.07(Do)
13. Emmanuel Kiprono (KEN)   8.16.24(Do)
14. Mahiedine Mekhissi (FRA)   8.16.97(Rom)
    Leonard Kipkemoi Bett (KEN)   8.16.97(Bir)
16. Barnabas Kipyego (KEN)   8.17.08(Nan)
17. Albert Chemutai (UGA)   8.17.17(Rom)
18. Tesfaye Deriba (ETH)   8.17.51(Do)
19. Kennedy Njiru (KEN)   8.18.04(Mon)
20. Jairus Kipchoge Birech (KEN)   8.18.76(Eug)
21. Fernando Carro (ESP)   8.19.30(Rab)
22. Hicham Sigueni (MAR)   8.19.51(Nan)
    Justus Lagat (KEN)   8.19.51(Nan)
24. Yemane Haileselassie (ERI)   8.19.61(Hue)
25. Mohamed Tindouft (MAR)   8.20.30(Rom)
26. Djilali Bedrani (FRA)   8.20.55(Nan)
27. Abdelkarim Ben Zahra (MAR)   8.21.08(Hue)
28. Hailemariyam Amare (ETH)   8.21.21(Do)
29. Tafese Soboka (ETH)   8.21.34
30. John Koech (KEN)   8.22.00(Rom)
31. Maksim Yakushev (RUS)   8.22.40

Commonwealth Games, Gold Coast, 13-4-2018:

1.	Conseslus Kipruto (KEN)	8.10.08
2.	Abraham Kibiwott (KEN)	8.10.62
3.	Amos Kirui (KEN)	8.12.24
4.	Matthew Hughes (CAN)	8.12.33
5.	Albert Chemutai (UGA)	8.19.89

Doha, 4-5-2018:

1.	Chala Beyo (ETH)	8.13.71
2.	Lawrence Kemboi Kipsang (KEN)	8.15.07
3.	Emmanuel Kiprono (KEN)	8.16.24
4.	Barnabas Kipyego (KEN)	8.17.30
5.	Tesfaye Deriba (ETH)	8.17.51
6.	Albert Chemutai (UGA)	8.18.80
7.	Hailemariyam Amare (ETH)	8.21.21
8.	Tolosa Nurgi (ETH)	8.24.11
9.	Mohamed Tindouft (MAR)	8.24.80
10.	Justus Lagat (KEN)	8.26.17
11.	Clement Kimutai Kemboi (KEN)	8.31.02

Eugene, 26-5-2018:

1.	Benjamin Kigen (KEN)	8.09.07
2.	Conseslus Kipruto (KEN)	8.11.71
3.	Evan Jager (USA)	8.11.71
4.	Amos Kirui (KEN)	8.15.23
5.	Nicholas Kiptanui Bett (KEN)	8.15.52
6.	Jairus Kipchoge Birech (KEN)	8.18.76
7.	Hillary Bor (USA)	8.21.51
8.	Paul Kipsiele Koech (KEN)	8.23.22

Rome, 31-5-2018:

1.	Conseslus Kipruto (KEN)	8.08.40
2.	Benjamin Kigen (KEN)	8.10.01
3.	Chala Beyo (ETH)	8.11.22
4.	Amos Kirui (KEN)	8.16.44
5.	Mahiedine Mekhissi (FRA)	8.16.97
6.	Albert Chemutai (UGA)	8.17.17
7.	Mohamed Tindouft (MAR)	8.20.30
8.	John Kibet Koech (KEN)	8.22.00
9.	Yemane Haileselassie (ERI)	8.22.15
10.	Justus Lagat (KEN)	8.23.23

Dessau, 8-6-2018:

1.	Nicholas Kiptanui Bett (KEN)	8.13.18
2.	Chala Beyo (ETH)	8.17.45
3.	Tolosa Nurgi (ETH)	8.24.91
4.	Ibrahim Ezzaydouny (MAR)	8.25.98

KEN Trials, Nairobi, 22-6-2018:

1.	Conseslus Kipruto	8.08.40
2.	Amos Kirui	8.18.37
3.	Kennedy Njiru	8.18.48
4.	Benjamin Kigen	8.22.64
5.	Emmanuel Kiprono Bett	8.25.10
6.	Ezekiel Kemboi	8.34.90
7.	Abraham Kibiwott	8.36.26
8.	Festu Kiprono	8.36.59

Nancy, 27-6-2018:

1.	Barnabas Kipyego (KEN)	8.17.08
2.	Mahiedine Mekhissi (FRA)	8.17.86
3.	Hicham Sigueni (MAR)	8.19.51
4.	Justus Lagat (KEN)	8.19.51
5.	Djilali Bedrani (FRA)	8.20.55
6.	Tafese Soboka (ETH)	8.22.68
7.	Lawrence Kemboi Kipsang (KEN)	8.22.73

Szekesfehervar, 2-7-2018:

1.	Benjamin Kigen (KEN)	8.10.48
2.	Nicholas Kiptanui Bett (KEN)	8.18.56
3.	Barnabas Kipyego (KEN)	8.21.11
4.	Amos Kirui (KEN)	8.24.52
5.	Jairus Kipchoge Birech (KEN)	8.26.74

Rabat, 13-7-2018:

1.	Benjamin Kigen (KEN)	8.06.19
2.	Chala Beyo (ETH)	8.07.27
3.	Soufiane El Bakkali (MAR)	8.09.58
4.	Hillary Bor (USA)	8.12.20
5.	Matthew Hughes (CAN)	8.13.13
6.	Abraham Kibiwott (KEN)	8.14.35
7.	Ibrahim Ezzaydouny (MAR)	8.14.62
8.	Nicholas Kiptanui Bett (KEN)	8.17.83
9.	Fernando Carro (ESP)	8.19.30
10.	Amos Kirui (KEN)	8.20.00
11.	Mohamed Tindouft (MAR)	8.21.13
12.	Conseslus Kipruto (KEN)	8.27.36

Monaco, 20-7-2018:
1.	Soufiane El Bakkali (MAR)	7.58.15
2.	Evan Jager (USA)	8.01.02
3.	Conseslus Kipruto (KEN)	8.09.78
4.	Benjamin Kigen (KEN)	8.09.98
5.	Hillary Bor (USA)	8.14.21
6.	Abraham Kibiwott (KEN)	8.17.40
7.	Kennedy Njiru (KEN)	8.18.04
8.	Ibrahim Ezzaydouny (MAR)	8.20.22
9.	Getnet Wale (ETH)	8.22.68
10.	Abdelkarim Ben Zahra (MAR)	8.23.41
11.	Matthew Hughes (CAN)	8.24.85

AFR CHAMPIONSHIPS, Assaba, 3-8-2018:
1.	Conseslus Kipruto (KEN)	8.26.38
2.	Soufiane El Bakkali (MAR)	8.28.01
3.	Getnet Wale Bayabl (ETH)	8.30.87
4.	Amos Kirui (KEN)	8.33.83
5.	Hailemariyam Amare Tegegn (ETH)	8.38.46
6.	Gigisa Tolosa Nugi (ETH)	8.42.14

Birmingham, 18-8-2018:
1.	Conseslus Kipruto (KEN)	8.14.33
2.	Chala Beyo (ETH)	8.14.61
3.	Nicholas Kiptanui Bett (KEN)	8.16.44
4.	Leonard Kipkemoi Bett (KEN)	8.16.97
5.	Benjamin Kigen (KEN)	8.17.43
6.	Abraham Kibiwott (KEN)	8.22.81
7.	Matthew Hughes (CAN)	8.23.67

Zürich, 30-8-2018:
1.	Conseslus Kipruto (KEN)	8.10.15
2.	Soufiane El Bakkali (MAR)	8.10.19
3.	Evan Jager (USA)	8.13.22
4.	Chala Beyo (ETH)	8.15.85
5.	Nicholas Kiptanui Bett (KEN)	8.19.74
6.	Abraham Kibiwott (KEN)	8.23.60

CONTINENTAL CUP, Ostrava, 8-9-2018:
1.	Conseslus Kipruto (AFR)	8.22.55
2.	Matthew Hughes (AME)	8.29.70
3.	Yohanes Chiappinelli (EUR)	8.32.89
4.	Fernando Carro (EUR)	8.33.76

OVERVIEW WORLDWIDE OUTDOOR CHAMPIONSHIP FINALISTS OF PAST 6 YEARS

	Wch 17	OG 16	Wch 15	Wch 13
Conseslus Kipruto (KEN)	8.14.12 (1)	8.03.28 (1)	8.12.38 (2)	8.06.37 (2)
Soufiane Elbakkali (MAR)	8.14.49 (2)	8.14.35 (4)		
Evan Jager (USA)	8.15.53 (3)	8.04.28 (2)	8.15.47 (6)	8.08.67 (5)
Mahiedine Mekhissi (FRA)	8.15.80 (4)	8.11.52 (3)		8.07.86 (3)
Stanley Kipkoech Kebenei (USA)	8.21.09 (5)			
Matthew Hughes (CAN)	8.21.84 (6)	8.36.83 (10)	8.18.63 (8)	8.11.64 (6)
Tesfaye Deriba (ETH)	8.22.12 (7)			
Tafese Seboka (ETH)	8.23.02 (8)			
Getnet Wale (ETH)	8.25.28 (9)			
Albert Chemutai (UGA)	8.25.94 (10)			
Ezekiel Kemboi (KEN)	8.29.38 (11)	dsq	8.11.28 (1)	8.06.01 (1)
Jairus Kipchoge Birech (KEN)	8.32.90 (12)		8.12.62 (4)	
Yoann Kowal (FRA)	8.34.53 (13)	8.16.75 (5)		8.17.41 (8)
Jacob Araptany (UGA)	8.49.18 (14)	dnf		8.25.86 (12)
Bilal Tabti (ALG)	dsq (15)		8.29.04 (13)	
Brimin Kiprop Kipruto (KEN)		8.18.79 (6)	8.12.54 (3)	
Hillary Bor (USA)		8.22.74 (7)		
Donald Cabral (USA)		8.25.81 (8)	8.24.94 (10)	
Altobeli da Silva (BRA)		8.26.30 (9)		
Yemane Haileselassie (ERI)		8.40.68 (10)		
Hamid Ezzine (MAR)		dnf	8.25.72 (11)	8.19.53 (9)
Amor Ben Yahia (TUN)		dsq		
Daniel Huling (USA)			8.14.39 (5)	
Brahim Taleb (MAR)			8.17.73 (7)	
Krystian Zalewski (POL)			8.21.22 (9)	
Hailemariyam Amare (ETH)			8.26.19 (12)	
Hicham Bouchicha (ALG)			8.33.79 (14)	
Tolosa Nurgi (ETH)			8.44.91 (15)	
Paul Kipsiele Koech (KEN)				8.08.62 (4)
Abel Kiprop Mutai (KEN)				8.17.04 (7)
Ion Luchianov (MDA)				8.19.99 (10)
Ángel Mullera (ESP)				8.20.93 (11)
Alex Genest (CAN)				8.27.01 (13)
Benjamin Kiplagat (UGA)				8.31.09 (14)
Nourredine Smaïl (FRA)				dnf (15)

OVERVIEW TOP 10 WORLD OUTDOOR RANKINGS OF PAST 5 YEARS

	2018	**2017**	**2016**	**2015**	**2014**
Soufiane Elbakkali (MAR)	7.58.15 (1)	8.04.83 (3)			
Evan Jager (USA)	8.01.02 (2)	8.01.29 (1)	8.04.01 (3)	8.00.45 (2)	8.04.71 (5)
Benjamin Kigen (KEN)	8.06.19 (3)	8.11.38 (9)			
Chala Beyo (ETH)	8.07.27 (4)				
Conseslus Kipruto (KEN)	8.08.40 (5)	8.04.63 (2)	8.00.12 (1)	8.05.20 (4)	8.09.81 (8)
Abraham Kibiwott (KEN)	8.10.62 (6)	8.10.62 (7)	8.09.25 (7)		
Hillary Bor (USA)	8.12.20 (7)	8.11.82 (10)			
Amos Kirui (KEN)	8.12.24 (8)	8.08.37 (6)			
Matthew Hughes (CAN)	8.12.33 (9)				
Nicholas Kiptanui Bett (KEN)	8.13.18 (10)		8.10.07 (9)		
Jairus Kipchoge Birech (KEN)		8.07.68 (4)	8.03.90 (2)	7.58.83 (1)	7.58.41 (1)
Stanley Kipkoech Kebenei (USA)		8.08.30 (5)			
Yemane Haileselassie (ERI)		8.11.22 (8)			
Mahiedine Mekhissi (FRA)			8.08.15 (4)		8.03.23 (2)
Paul Kipsiele Koech (KEN)			8.08.32 (5)	8.10.24 (6)	8.05.47 (6)
Barnabas Kipyego (KEN)			8.09.13 (6)		
John Kibet Koech (KEN)			8.09.62 (8)		
Clement Kimutai Kemboi (KEN)			8.10.65 (10)	8.12.68 (8)	
Ezekiel Kemboi (KEN)				8.01.71 (3)	8.04.12 (3)
Brimin Kiprop Kipruto (KEN)				8.10.09 (5)	8.04.64 (4)
Jonathan Muia Ndiku (KEN)				8.11.64 (7)	8.10.44 (9)
Hillary Kipsang Yego (KEN)				8.13.10 (9)	8.09.07 (7)
Donald Cabral (USA)				8.13.37 (10)	
Gilbert Kiplangat Kirui (KEN)					8.11.86 (10)

WORLD RANKING ALL TIME:

1.	Saif Saaeed Shaheen (QAT)	7.53.63 (2004)
2.	Brimin Kiprop Kipruto (KEN)	7.53.64 (2011)
3.	Paul Kipsiele Koech (KEN)	7.54.31 (2012)
4.	Brahim Boulami (MAR)	7.55.28 (2001)
5.	Bernard Barmasai (KEN)	7.55.72 (1997)
6.	Ezekiel Kemboi (KEN)	7.55.76 (2011)
7.	Moses Kiptanui (KEN)	7.56.16 (1997)
8.	Richard Kipkemboi Mateelong (KEN)	7.56.81 (2012)
9.	Reuben Kosgei (KEN)	7.57.29 (2001)
10.	Soufiane El Bakkali (MAR)	7.58.15 (2018)
11.	Jairus Kipchoge Birech (KEN)	7.58.41 (2014)
12.	Wilson Boit Kipketer (KEN)	7.59.08 (1997)
13.	Mahiedine Mekhissi Benabbad (FRA)	8.00.09 (2013)
14.	Conseslus Kipruto (KEN)	8.00.12 (2016)
15.	Evan Jager (USA)	8.00.45 (2015)
16.	Bouabdellah Tahri (FRA)	8.01.18 (2009)
17.	Abel Kiprop Mutai (KEN)	8.01.67 (2012)
18.	Kipkurui Misoi (KEN)	8.01.69 (2001)
19.	Patrick Sang (KEN)	8.03.41 (1997)
20.	Ali Ezzine (MAR)	8.03.57 (2000)
	Hillary Kipsang Yego (KEN)	8.03.57 (2013)
22.	Raymond Kipkorir Yator (KEN)	8.03.74 (2000)
23.	Benjamin Kiplagat (UGA)	8.03.81 (2010)
24.	John Kosgei (KEN)	8.03.89 (1997)
25.	Simon Vroemen (NED)	8.04.95 (2005)
26.	Eliud Barngetuny (KEN)	8.05.01 (1995)
27.	Peter Koech (KEN)	8.05.35 (1989)
28.	Philip Barkutwo (KEN)	8.05.37 (1992)
29.	Henry Rono (KEN)	8.05.4 (1978)
30.	Christopher Cherono Koskei (KEN)	8.05.43 (1999)
31.	Julius Kariuki (KEN)	8.05.51 (1988)
32.	Wesley Kiprotich (KEN)	8.05.68 (2004)
33.	Mustafa Mohamed (SWE)	8.05.75 (2007)
34.	Bernard Nganga (KEN)	8.05.88 (2011)
35.	Joseph Keter (KEN)	8.05.99 (1996)
36.	Tareq Mubarak Taher (BRN)	8.06.13 (2009)
37.	Roba Gari (ETH)	8.06.16 (2012)
38.	Benjamin Kigen (KEN)	8.06.19 (2018)
39.	Gideon Chirchir (KEN)	8.06.77 (1995)
40.	Christopher Kosgei (KEN)	8.06.86 (1995)
41.	Richard Kosgei (KEN)	8.06.88 (1995)
42.	Gilbert Kirui (KEN)	8.06.96 (2013)
43.	Brahim Taleb (MAR)	8.07.02 (2007)
44.	Paul Malakwen Kosgei (KEN)	8.07.13 (1999)
45.	Musa Amer Obaid (QAT)	8.07.18 (2004)

High Jump Men

EUROPEAN CHAMPIONSHIPS 2018: 11-8-2018:

1.	Mateusz Przybylko (GER)		2.35
2.	Maksim Nedasekau (BLR)		2.33
3.	Ilya Ivanyuk (ANA)		2.31
4.	Gianmarco Tamberi (ITA)		2.28
5.	Alperen Acet (TUR)	(2.25)	2.24
	Andrii Protsenko (UKR)	(2.25)	2.24
7.	Sylwester Bednarek (POL)	(2.25)	2.24
8.	Douwe Amels (NED)	(2.21)	2.19
	Eike Onnen (GER)	(2.25)	2.19
10.	Konstadínos Baniótis (GRE)	(2.21)	2.19
	Loïc Gasch (SUI)	(2.21)	2.19
	Dmytro Demyanyuk (UKR)	(2.25)	NM

13.	Marco Fassinotti (ITA)	2.21
	Viktor Lonskyy (UKR)	2.21
15.	Allan Smith (GBR)	2.21
16.	Chris Baker (GBR)	2.21
	Maciej Grynienko (POL)	2.21
	Dmitriy Kroytor (ISR)	2.21
	Tobias Potye (GER)	2.21

WORLD RANKING 2018:

1.	Mutaz Essa Barshim (QAT)	2.40(Do)
	Damil Lysenko (ANA)	2.40(Mon)
3.	Dzmitry Nabokau (BLR)	2.36
	Brandon Starc (AUS)	2.36(Ebe)
5.	Bryan McBride (USA)	2.35(CV)
	Mateusz Przybylko (GER)	2.35(ECh)
7.	Ivan Ukhov (RUS)	2.34
8.	Majd Eddin Ghazal (SYR)	2.33(Do)
	Fabian Delryd (SWE)	2.33
	Maksim Nedasekau (BLR)	2.33
	Gianmarco Tamberi (ITA)	2.33(Ebe)
12.	Michael Mason (CAN)	2.32
	Yu Wang (CHN)	2.32(Eug)
	Ricky Robertson (USA)	2.32(CV)
	Donald Thomas (BAH)	2.32(Sze)
	Naoto Tobe (JPN)	2.32
17.	Jeron Robinson (USA)	2.31
	Konstantinos Baniótis (GRE)	2.31
	Ilya Ivanyuk (ANA)	2.31(ECh)
	Andriy Protsenko (UKR)	2.31
21.	Jamal Wilson (BAH)	2.30(GC)
	Django Lovett (CAN)	2.30(GC)
	Alperen Acet (TUR)	2.30
	Mathew Sawe (KEN)	2.30

WORLD INDOOR CHAMPIONSHIPS: 1-3-2018:

1.	Danil Lysenko (ANA)	2.36
2.	Mutaz Essa Barshim (QAT)	2.33
3.	Mateusz Przybylko (GER)	2.29
4.	Erik Kynard (USA)	2.29
5.	Sylwester Bednarek (POL)	2.25
6.	Maksim Nedasekau (BLR)	2.20
	Donald Thomas (BAH)	2.20
	Yu Wang (CHN)	2.20
9.	Robert Grabarz (GBR)	2.20
	Tihomir Ivanov (BUL)	2.20
	Jamal Wilson (BAH)	2.20

WORLD INDOOR RANKING 2018:

1.	Mutaz Essa Barshim (QAT)	2.38
2.	Danil Lysenko (ANA)	2.37
3.	Ivan Ukhov (RUS)	2.35
4.	Trey Culver (USA)	2.33
	Sylwester Bednarek (POL)	2.33
	Vernon Turner (USA)	2.33
7.	Dzmitry Nabokau (BLR)	2.32
8.	Erik Kynard (USA)	2.31
	Yu Wang (CHN)	2.31
	Donald Thomas (BAH)	2.31
	Jamal Wilson (BAH)	2.31
	Ilya Ivanyuk (ANA)	2.31
	Maksim Nedasekau (BLR)	2.31
14.	Robbie Grabarz (GBR)	2.30
	Jeron Robinson (USA)	2.30
	Matus Bubeník (SVK)	2.30
	Mateusz Przybylko (GER)	2.30

OVERVIEW WORLDWIDE OUTDOOR CHAMPIONSHIP FINALISTS OF PAST 6 YEARS

	Wch 17	OG 16	Wch 15	Wch 13
Mutaz Essa Barshim (QAT)	2.35 (1)	2.36 (2)	2.33 (4)	2.38 (2)
Danil Lysenko (RUS)	2.32 (2)			
Majd Eddin Ghazal (SYR)	2.29 (3)	2.29 (7)		
Edgar Rivera (MEX)	2.29 (4)			
Mateusz Przybylko (GER)	2.29 (5)			
Robert Grabarz (GBR)	2.25 (6)	2.33 (4)		2.29 (8)
Ilya Ivanyuk (RUS)	2.25 (6)			
Bryan McBride (USA)	2.25 (8)			
Bohdan Bondarenko (UKR)	2.25 (9)	2.33 (3)	2.33 (2)	2.41 (1)
Eike Onnen (GER)	2.20 (10)		2.25 (12)	
Tihomir Ivanov (BUL)	NM	2.29 (10)		
Wang Yu (CHN)	dns			
Derek Drouin (CAN)		2.38 (1)	2.34 (1)	2.38 (3)
Andriy Protsenko (UKR)		2.33 (4)		
Erik Kynard (USA)		2.33 (6)	2.25 (8)	2.32 (5)
Kyriakos Ioannou (CYP)		2.29 (7)		
Donald Thomas (BAH)		2.29 (7)	2.29 (6)	2.32 (6)
Trevor Barry (BAH)		2.25 (11)	2.25 (10)	
Dimitrios Chondrokoukis (CYP)		2.25 (12)	2.25 (11)	
Luis Joel Castro (PUR)		2.25 (13)		
Jaroslav Baba (CZE)		2.20 (14)	2.29 (7)	
Brandon Starc (AUS)		2.20 (15)	2.25 (12)	
Zhang Guowei (CHN)			2.33 (2)	2.29 (9)
Daniil Tsyplakov (RUS)			2.29 (5)	
Gianmarco Tamberi (ITA)			2.25 (8)	
Konstádinos Baniótis (GRE)			2.20 (14)	2.25 (10)
Ivan Ukhov (RUS)				2.35 (4)
Aleksandr Shustov (RUS)				2.32 (7)
Kabele Kogosiemand (BOT)				2.25 (10)
Ryan Ingraham (BAH)				2.25 (10)

OVERVIEW WORLDWIDE INDOOR CHAMPIONSHIP FINALISTS OF PAST 5 YEARS

	Wch 18	Wch 16	Wch 14
Danil Lysenko (ANA)	2.37 (1)		
Mutaz Essa Barshim (QAT)	2.33 (2)	2.29 (4)	2.38 (1)
Mateusz Przybylko (GER)	2.29 (3)		
Erik Kynard (USA)	2.29 (4)	2.33 (3)	2.34 (4)
Sylwester Bednarek (POL)	2.25 (5)		
Maksim Nedasekau (BLR)	2.20 (6)		
Donald Thomas (BAH)	2.20 (6)	2.25 (10)	
Yu Wang (CHN)	2.20 (6)		
Robbie Grabarz (GBR)	2.20 (9)	2.33 (2)	
Tihomir Ivanov (BUL)	2.20 (9)		
Jamal Wilson (BAH)	2.20 (9)	2.20 (11)	
Gianmarco Tamberi (ITA)		2.36 (1)	
Konstadínos Baniótis (GRE)		2.29 (5)	
Zhang Guowei (CHN)		2.29 (6)	2.29 (7)
Andriy Protsenko (UKR)		2.29 (7)	2.36 (3)
Chris Baker (GBR)		2.29 (8)	
Marco Fassinotti (ITA)		2.25 (9)	2.29 (6)
Ricky Robertson (USA)		2.20 (12)	
Ivan Ukhov (RUS)			2.38 (2)
Daniil Tsyplakov (RUS)			2.32 (5)
Michael Mason (CAN)			2.25 (8)

OVERVIEW TOP 10 WORLD OUTDOOR RANKINGS OF PAST 5 YEARS

	2018	2017	2016	2015	2014
Mutaz Essa Barshim (QAT)	2.40 (1)	2.40 (1)	2.40 (1)	2.41 (1)	2.43 (1)
Danil Lysenko (RUS)	2.40 (1)	2.38 (2)			
Dzmitry Nabokau (BLR)	2.36 (3)				
Brandon Starc (AUS)	2.36 (3)				
Bryan McBride (USA)	2.35 (5)				
Mateusz Przybylko (GER)	2.35 (5)	2.35 (3)			
Ivan Ukhov (RUS)	2.34 (7)	2.32 (5)			2.41 (3)
Majd Eddin Ghazal (SYR)	2.33 (8)	2.32 (5)	2.36 (6)		
Fabian Delryd (SWE)	2.33 (8)				
Maksim Nedasekau (BLR)	2.33 (8)	2.33 (4)			
Gianmarco Tamberi (ITA)	2.33 (8)		2.39 (2)	2.37 (3)	
Sylwester Bednarek (POL)		2.32 (5)			
Bohdan Bondarenko (UKR)		2.32 (5)	2.37 (4)	2.37 (3)	2.42 (2)
Robert Grabarz (GBR)		2.31 (9)	2.33 (8)		
Zhang Guowei (CHN)		2.31 (9)	2.33 (8)	2.38 (2)	2.34 (8)
Eure Yánez (VEN)		2.31 (9)			
Tihomir Ivanov (BUL)		2.31 (9)			
Derek Drouin (CAN)			2.38 (3)	2.37 (3)	2.40 (4)
Donald Thomas (BAH)			2.37 (5)	2.34 (7)	
Erik Kynard (USA)			2.35 (7)	2.37 (3)	2.37 (6)
Wang Yu (CHN)			2.33 (8)		
Andriy Protsenko (UKR)			2.33 (8)		2.40 (4)
JaCorian Duffield (USA)				2.34 (7)	
Marco Fassinotti (ITA)				2.33 (9)	
Daniil Tsyplakov (RUS)				2.33 (9)	2.33 (10)
Michael Mason (CAN)				2.33 (9)	
Dusty Jonas (USA)					2.35 (7)
Mickael Hanany (FRA)					2.34 (8)

OVERVIEW TOP 10 WORLD INDOOR RANKINGS OF PAST 5 YEARS

	2018	**2017**	**2016**	**2015**	**2014**
Mutaz Essa Barshim (QAT)	2.38 (1)		2.36 (2)	2.41 (1)	2.38 (3)
Danil Lysenko (ANA)	2.37 (2)				
Ivan Ukhov (RUS)	2.35 (3)			2.31 (7)	2.42 (1)
Trey Culver (USA)	2.33 (4)				
Sylwester Bednarek (POL)	2.33 (4)	2.33 (1)			
Vernon Turner (USA)	2.33 (4)				
Dzmitry Nabokau (BLR)	2.32 (7)				
Erik Kynard (USA)	2.31 (8)	2.31 (4)	2.33 (5)	2.34 (2)	2.34 (5)
Yu Wang (CHN)	2.31 (8)				
Donald Thomas (BAH)	2.31 (8)	2.31 (4)	2.33 (5)	2.31 (7)	2.33 (8)
Jamal Wilson (BAH)	2.31 (8)		2.31 (10)		
Ilya Ivanyuk (ANA)	2.31 (8)				
Maksim Nedasekau (BLR)	2.31 (8)				
Derek Drouin (CAN)		2.33 (1)			
Pavel Seliverstau (BLR)		2.32 (3)			
Edgar Rivera (MEX)		2.30 (6)			
JaCorian Duffield (USA)		2.30 (6)			
Robert Grabarz (GBR)		2.30 (6)	2.33 (5)		
Mateusz Przybylko (GER)		2.28 (9)			
Lukas Beer (SVK)		2.28 (9)			
Tihomir Ivanov (BUL)		2.28 (9)			
Sun Zhao (CHN)		2.28 (9)			
Silvano Chesani (ITA)		2.28 (9)		2.31 (7)	
Matus Bubenik (SVK)		2.28 (9)		2.31 (7)	
Gianmarco Tamberi (ITA)			2.38 (1)		
Chris Baker (GBR)			2.36 (2)		
Marco Fassinotti (ITA)			2.35 (4)	2.34 (2)	2.34 (5)
Konstadínos Baniótis (GRE)			2.33 (5)		
Kyriakos Ioannou (CYP)			2.32 (9)		
Eike Onnen (GER)			2.31 (10)		
Andriy Protsenko (UKR)				2.33 (4)	2.36 (4)
Dimitrios Chondrokoukis (CYP)				2.32 (5)	
Zhang Guowei (CHN)				2.32 (5)	2.33 (8)
Aleksey Dmitrik (RUS)				2.31 (7)	2.40 (2)
Dmitriy Semenov (RUS)				2.31 (7)	
Daniil Tsyplakov (RUS)				2.31 (7)	2.34 (5)
Jesse Williams (USA)				2.31 (7)	
Michael Mason (CAN)				2.31 (7)	
Ricky Robertson (USA)				2.31 (7)	
Adónios Mástoras (GRE)				2.31 (7)	
Lev Missirov (RUS)					2.33 (8)

WORLD RANKING ALL TIME:

1.	Javier Sotomayor (CUB)	2.45 (1993)
2.	Mutaz Essa Barshim (QAT)	2.43 (2014)
3.	Patrik Sjöberg (SWE)	2.42 (1987)
	Bohdan Bondarenko (UKR)	2.42 (2014)
5.	Igor Paklin (URS)	2.41 (1985)
	Ivan Ukhov (RUS)	2.41 (2014)
7.	Rudolf Povarnitsyn (URS)	2.40 (1985)
	Sorin Matei (ROM)	2.40 (1990)
	Charles Austin (USA)	2.40 (1991)
	Vyacheslav Voronin (RUS)	2.40 (2000)
	Derek Drouin (CAN)	2.40 (2014)
	Andriy Protsenko (UKR)	2.40 (2014)
	Danil Lysenko (ANA)	2.40 (2018)
14.	Zhou Jianhua (CHN)	2.39 (1984)
	Hollis Conway (USA)	2.39 (1989)
	Gianmarco Tamberi (ITA)	2.39 (2016)
17.	Gennadiy Avdeyenko (URS)	2.38 (1987)
	Sergey Malchenko (URS)	2.38 (1988)
	Dragutin Topic (SRB)	2.38 (1993)
	Troy Kemp (BAH)	2.38 (1995)
	Artur Partyka (POL)	2.38 (1996)
	Jacques Freitag (RSA)	2.38 (2005)
	Andriy Sokolovskiy (UKR)	2.38 (2005)
	Andrey Silnov (RUS)	2.38 (2008)
	Zhang Guowei (CHN)	2.38 (2015)
26.	Valeriy Sereda (URS)	2.37 (1984)
	Carlo Thraenhardt (FRG)	2.37 (1984)
	Tom McCants (USA)	2.37 (1988)
	Jerome Carter (USA)	2.37 (1988)
	Sergiy Dymchenko (URS)	2.37 (1990)
	Steve Smith (GBR)	2.37 (1992)
	Stefan Holm (SWE)	2.37 (2008)
	Jesse Williams (USA)	2.37 (2011)
	Robbie Grabarz (GBR)	2.37 (2012)
	Erik Kynard (USA)	2.37 (2013)
	Donald Thomas (BAH)	2.37 (2016)

37 – 62, a.o.:

	Gerd Wessig (GDR)	2.36 (1980)
	Sergey Zasimovich (URS)	2.36 (1984)
	Dietmar Mögenburg (FRG)	2.36 (1984)
	Eddy Annys (BEL)	2.36 (1985)
	Dalton Grant (GBR)	2.36 (1991)
	Steinar Hoen (NOR)	2.36 (1997)
	Sergey Klyugin (RUS)	2.36 (1998)
	Konstantin Matusevich (ISR)	2.36 (2000)

WORLD RANKING ALL TIME INDOOR:

1.	Javier Sotomayor (CUB)	2.43 (1989)
2.	Carlo Thraenhardt (FRG)	2.42 (1988)
	Ivan Ukhov (RUS)	2.42 (2014)
4.	Patrik Sjöberg (SWE)	2.41 (1987)
	Mutaz Essa Barshim(QAT)	2.41 (2015)
6.	Hollis Conway (USA)	2.40 (1991)
	Stefan Holm (SWE)	2.40 (2005)
	Aleksey Dmitrik (RUS)	2.40 (2014)
9.	Dietmar Mögenburg (FRG)	2.39 (1985)
	Ralf Sonn (GER)	2.39 (1991)
11.	Igor Paklin (URS)	2.38 (1987)
	Gennadiy Avdeyenko (URS)	2.38 (1987)
	Steve Smith (GBR)	2.38 (1994)
	Wolf-Hendrik Beyer (GER)	2.38 (1994)
	Sorin Matei (ROM)	2.38 (1995)
	Matt Hemingway (USA)	2.38 (2000)
	Yaroslav Rybakov (RUS)	2.38 (2005)
	Linus Thörnblad (SWE)	2.38 (2007)
	Gianmarco Tamberi (ITA)	2.38 (2016)
20.	Artur Partyka (POL)	2.37 (1991)
	Dalton Grant (GBR)	2.37 (1994)
	Charles Austin (USA)	2.37 (1996)
	Vyacheslav Voronin (RUS)	2.37 (2000)
	Jaroslav Bába (CZE)	2.37 (2005)
	Andrey Silnov (RUS)	2.37 (2008)
	Danil Lysenko (ANA)	2.37 (2018)
27.	Jim Howard (USA)	2.36 (1986)
	Ján Zvara (TCH)	2.36 (1987)
	Sergey Malchenko (URS)	2.36 (1988)
	Gerd Nagel (FRG)	2.36 (1989)
	Steinar Hoen (NOR)	2.36 (1994)
	Troy Kemp (BAH)	2.36 (1994)
	Andriy Sokolovskiy (UKR)	2.36 (2006)
	Andrey Tereshin (RUS)	2.36 (2006)
	Jesse Williams (USA)	2.36 (2009)
	Andriy Protsenko (UKR)	2.36 (2014)
	Chris Baker (GBR)	2.36 (2016)

38 - 49:

	Volodymyr Yaschenko (URS)	2.35 (1978)
	Aleksandr Kotovich (URS)	2.35 (1985)
	Clarence Saunders (BER)	2.35 (1989)
	Brent Harken (USA)	2.35 (1991)
	Jean-Charles Gicquel (FRA)	2.35 (1994)
	Lambros Papakostas (GRE)	2.35 (1995)
	Dragutin Topic (SRB)	2.35 (1996)
	et al.	

Pole Vault Men

EUROPEAN CHAMPIONSHIPS 2018: 12-8-2018:		
1.	Armand Duplantis (SWE)	6.05
2.	Timur Morgunov (ANA)	6.00
3.	Renaud Lavillenie (FRA)	5.95
4.	Piotr Lisek (POL)	5.90
5.	Pawel Wojciechowski (POL)	5.80
6.	Konstadínos Filippídis (GRE)	5.75
	Sondre Guttormsen (NOR)	5.75
8.	Axel Chapelle (FRA)	5.65
9.	Arnaud Art (BEL)	5.65
10.	Adam Hague (GBR)	5.65
11.	Claudio Michel Stecchi (ITA)(5.51)	5.50
12.	Alioune Sene (FRA) (5.51)	5.30

13.	Tommi Holttinen (FIN)	5.51
	Torben Laidig (GER)	5.51
15.	Bo Kanda Lita Baehre (GER)	5.51
	Vladyslav Malykin (UKR)	5.51
25.	Jan Kudlicka (CZE)	5.36
	Robert Sobera (POL)	5.36
	Raphael Holzdeppe (GER)	NM
	Ilya Mudrov (ANA)	NM

WORLD RANKING 2018:		
1.	Armand Duplantis (SWE)	6.05(ECh)
2.	Timur Morgunov (ANA)	6.00(ECh)
3.	Sam Kendricks (USA)	5.96(Par)
4.	Renaud Lavillenie (FRA)	5.95(Aus)
5.	Piotr Lisek (POL)	5.94
6.	Shawnacy Barber (CAN)	5.92(Aus)
7.	Christopher Nilsen (USA)	5.86
8.	Pawel Wojciechowski (POL)	5.84(Lau)
9.	Raphael Holzdeppe (GER)	5.81
10.	Kurtis Marschall (AUS)	5.80(Per)
	Devin King (USA)	5.80(Aus)
12.	Cole Walsh (USA)	5.75(USC)
	Konstantinos Filippidis (GRE)	5.75(ECh)
	Sondre Guttormsen (NOR)	5.75(ECh)
15.	Stanley Joseph (FRA)	5.72(Par)
	Andrew Irwin (USA)	5.72
	Arnaud Art (BEL)	5.72
18.	Matt Ludwig (USA)	5.71
	Xue Changrui (CHN)	5.71(Sha)
	Ivan Horvat (CRO)	5.71(Zag)
21.	Scott Houston (USA)	5.70(USC)
	Axel Chapelle (FRA)	5.70
	Nate Richartz (USA)	5.70(CG)
	Alioun Sene (FRA)	5.70
	Rutger Koppelaar (NED)	5.70
	Melker Svärd Jacobsson (SWE)	5.70
	Seito Yamamoto (JPN)	5.70
	Thiago Braz (BRA)	5.70
	Georgiy Gorokhov (ANA)	5.70
	Huang Bokai (CHN)	5.70

WORLD INDOOR CHAMPIONSHIPS: 4-3-2018:

1. Renaud Lavillenie (FRA) — 5.90
2. Sam Kendricks (USA) — 5.85
3. Piotr Lisek (POL) — 5.85
4. Kurtis Marschall (AUS) — 5.80
5. Raphael Holzdeppe (GER) — 5.80
   Emmanouil Karalís (GRE) — 5.80
7. Armand Duplantis (SWE) — 5.70
   Konstadínos Filippídis (GRE) — 5.70
9. Melker Svärd Jacobsson (SWE) — 5.70
10. Axel Chapelle (FRA) — 5.60
11. Xue Changrui (CHN) — 5.60
12. Thiago Braz (BRA) — 5.60
13. Scott Houston (USA) — 5.60
    Pawel Wojciechowski (POL) — 5.60
15. Shawnacy Barber (CAN) — 5.45

WORLD INDOOR RANKING 2018:

1. Renaud Lavillenie (FRA) — 5.93
   Sam Kendricks (USA) — 5.93
3. Piotr Lisek (POL) — 5.91
   Timur Morgunov (ANA) — 5.91
5. Thiago Braz (BRA) — 5.90
6. Raphael Holzdeppe (GER) — 5.88
   Pawel Wojciechowski (POL) — 5.88
   Axel Chapelle (FRA) — 5.88
   Armand Duplantis (SWE) — 5.88
   Kévin Ménaldo (FRA) — 5.88
11. Shawnacy Barber (CAN) — 5.86
    Kurtis Marschall (AUS) — 5.86
13. Konstantinos Filippidis (GRE) — 5.85
14. Scott Houston (USA) — 5.83
15. Dmitriy Zhelyabin (RUS) — 5.80
    Christopher Nilsen (USA) — 5.80
    Emmanouil Karalís (GRE) — 5.80
18. Melker Svärd Jacobsson (SWE) — 5.78
    Mike Arnold (USA) — 5.78
20. Xue Changrui (CHN) — 5.75
21. Valentin Lavillenie (FRA) — 5.72
22. Menno Vloon (NED) — 5.70
    Hussein Assem Al Hizam (KSA) — 5.70

OVERVIEW WORLDWIDE OUTDOOR CHAMPIONSHIP FINALISTS OF PAST 6 YEARS

	Wch 17	OG 16	Wch 15	Wch 13
Sam Kendricks (USA)	5.95 (1)	5.85 (3)	5.65 (9)	
Piotr Lisek (POL)	5.89 (2)	5.75 (4)	5.80 (3)	
Renaud Lavillenie (FRA)	5.89 (3)	5.98 (2)	5.80 (3)	5.89 (2)
Xue Changrui (CHN)	5.82 (4)	5.65 (6)		5.50 (12)
Pawel Wojchiechowski (POL)	5.75 (5)		5.80 (3)	
Axel Chapelle (FRA)	5.65 (6)			
Kurtis Marschall (AUS)	5.65 (7)			
Shawnacy Barber (CAN)	5.65 (8)	5.50 (10)	5.90 (1)	
Armand Dupantis (SWE)	5.50 (9)			
Arnaud Art (BEL)	NM			
Raphael Holzdeppe (GER)	NM		5.90 (2)	5.89 (1)
Yao Jie (CHN)	NM			
Thiago Braz Da Silva (BRA)		6.03 (1)		
Jan Kudlicka (CZE)		5.75 (4)	5.50 (13)	5.75 (7)
Michal Balner (CZE)		5.50 (7)	5.65 (7)	
Konstadinos Filippidis (GRE)		5.50 (7)		5.65 (10)
Daichi Sawano (JPN)		5.50 (7)		
German Chiaraviglio (ARG)		5.50 (11)	5.65 (9)	
Pauls Pujats (LAT)		NM		
Kévin Ménaldo (FRA)			5.80 (6)	
Tobias Scherbarth (GER)			5.65 (7)	
Augusto de Oliveira (BRA)			5.65 (9)	5.65 (11)
Ivan Horvat (CRO)			5.65 (9)	
Robert Renner (SLO)			5.50 (13)	
Robert Sobera (POL)			5.50 (15)	
Ivan Gertlein (RUS)			NM	
Björn Otto (GER)				5.82 (3)
Brad Walker (USA)				5.82 (4)
Malte Mohr (GER)				5.82 (5)
Seito Yamamoto (JPN)				5.75 (6)
Sergey Kucheryanu (RUS)				5.65 (8)
Alhaji Jeng (SWE)				5.65 (9)
Valentin Lavillenie (FRA)				NM

OVERVIEW WORLDWIDE INDOOR CHAMPIONSHIP FINALISTS OF PAST 5 YEARS

	Wch18	Wch 16	Wch 14
Renaud Lavillenie (FRA)	5.90 (1)	6.02 (1)	
Sam Kendricks (USA)	5.85 (2)	5.80 (2)	
Piotr Lisek (POL)	5.85 (3)	5.75 (3)	
Kurtis Marschall (AUS)	5.80 (4)		
Raphael Holzdeppe (GER)	5.80 (5)		
Emmanouíl Karalís (GRE)	5.80 (5)		
Armand Duplantis (SWE)	5.70 (7)		
Konstadínos Filippidis (GRE)	5.70 (7)	5.65 (7)	5.80 (1)
Melker Svärd Jacobsson (SWE)	5.70 (9)		
Axel Chapelle (FRA)	5.60 (10)		
Xue Changrui (CHN)	5.60 (11)		5.75 (5)
Thiago Braz Da Silva (BRA)	5.60 (12)	5.55 (12)	5.75 (4)
Scott Houston (USA)	5.60 (13)		
Pawel Wojchiechowski (POL)	5.60 (13)		5.40 (12)
Shawnacy Barber (CAN)	5.45 (15)	5.75 (4)	
Jan Kudlicka (CZE)		5.75 (4)	5.80 (3)
Robert Sobera (POL)		5.65 (6)	5.65 (6)
Mike Arnold (USA)		5.65 (8)	
Michal Balner (CZE)		5.55 (9)	
Carlo Paech (GER)		5.55 (10)	
Seito Yamamoto (JPN)		5.55 (10)	
Jérôme Clavier (FRA)		5.55 (12)	5.55 (10)
Augusto de Oliveira (BRA)		5.40 (14)	5.65 (7)
Malte Mohr (GER)			5.80 (2)
Luke Cutts (GBR)			5.65 (8)
Yang Yancheng (CHN)			5.55 (9)
Kévin Ménaldo (FRA)			5.55 (11)

OVERVIEW TOP 10 WORLD OUTDOOR RANKINGS OF PAST 5 YEARS

	2018	2017	2016	2015	2014
Armand Duplantis (SWE)	6.05 (1)	5.90 (4)			
Timur Morgunov (ANA)	6.00 (2)	5.80 (9)			
Sam Kendricks (USA)	5.96 (3)	6.00 (1)	5.92 (3)	5.82 (7)	5.75 (7)
Renaud Lavillenie (FRA)	5.95 (4)	5.91 (3)	5.98 (2)	6.05 (1)	5.93 (1)
Piotr Lisek (POL)	5.94 (5)	5.89 (5)	5.75 (8)	5.82 (7)	5.82 (3)
Shawnacy Barber (CAN)	5.92 (6)		5.91 (4)	5.93 (3)	
Christopher Nilsen (USA)	5.86 (7)				
Pawel Wojchiechowski (POL)	5.84 (8)	5.93 (2)		5.84 (6)	5.80 (4)
Raphael Holzdeppe (GER)	5.81 (9)	5.80 (9)		5.94 (2)	
Kurtis Marschall (AUS)	5.80 (10)				
Devin King (USA)	5.80 (10)				
Menno Vloon (NED)		5.85 (6)			
Kévin Ménaldo (FRA)		5.83 (7)	5.80 (6)	5.81 (10)	
Xue Changrui (CHN)		5.82 (8)	5.75 (8)		5.80 (4)
Michal Balner (CZE)		5.80 (9)		5.82 (7)	5.75 (7)
Thiago Braz Da Silva (BRA)			6.03 (1)	5.92 (4)	5.73 (9)
Jan Kudlicka (CZE)			5.83 (5)		
Florian Gaul (GER)			5.77 (7)		
Tobias Scherbarth (GER)			5.75 (8)		5.73 (9)
Stanley Joseph (FRA)			5.75 (8)		
Daichi Sawano (JPN)			5.75 (8)		
Konstadinos Filippidis (GRE)				5.91 (5)	
Augusto de Oliveira (BRA)				5.81 (10)	
Mark Hollis (USA)					5.83 (2)
Robert Sobera (POL)					5.80 (4)

OVERVIEW TOP 10 WORLD INDOOR RANKINGS OF PAST 5 YEARS

	2018	2017	2016	2015	2014
Renaud Lavillenie (FRA)	5.93 (1)		6.03 (1)	6.04 (1)	6.16 (1)
Sam Kendricks (USA)	5.93 (1)	5.85 (3)	5.90 (4)	5.86 (4)	
Piotr Lisek (POL)	5.91 (3)	6.00 (1)	5.77 (9)	5.90 (3)	5.77 (6)
Timur Morgunov (RUS)	5.91 (3)				
Thiago Braz Da Silva (BRA)	5.90 (5)	5.86 (2)	5.93 (3)		5.76 (7)
Raphael Holzdeppe (GER)	5.88 (6)	5.80 (8)	5.84 (5)		
Pawel Wojchiechowski (POL)	5.88 (6)	5.85 (3)	5.84 (5)		5.76 (7)
Axel Chapelle (FRA)	5.88 (6)	5.80 (8)			
Armand Duplantis (SWE)	5.88 (6)	5.82 (7)			
Kévin Ménaldo (FRA)	5.88 (6)		5.77 (9)		
Konstadínos Filíppídis (GRE)		5.85 (3)	5.84 (5)		5.80 (4)
Shawnacy Barber (CAN)		5.83 (6)	6.00 (2)	5.91 (2)	
Jan Kudlicka (CZE)		5.80 (8)	5.77 (9)		5.80 (4)
Xue Changrui (CHN)			5.81 (8)		5.76 (7)
Seito Yamamoto (JPN)			5.77 (9)		
Carlo Paech (GER)			5.77 (9)		
Jérôme Clavier (FRA)			5.77 (9)		5.76 (7)
Robert Sobera (POL)			5.77 (9)	5.81 (6)	
Mike Arnold (USA)			5.77 (9)		
Aleksandr Gripich (RUS)				5.85 (5)	
Valentin Lavillenie (FRA)				5.80 (7)	
Jacob Blankenship (USA)				5.80 (7)	
Andrew Irwin (USA)				5.80 (7)	
Ilya Mudrov (RUS)				5.78 (10)	
Malte Mohr (GER)					5.90 (2)
Luke Cutts (GBR)					5.83 (3)

WORLD RANKING ALL TIME:

1.	Sergey Bubka (UKR)	6.14 (1994)
2.	Maxim Tarasov (RUS)	6.05 (1999)
	Dmitri Markov (AUS)	6.05 (2001)
	Renaud Lavillenie (FRA)	6.05 (2015)
	Armand Duplantis (SWE)	6.05 (2018)
6.	Brad Walker (USA)	6.04 (2008)
7.	Okkert Brits (RSA)	6.03 (1995)
	Jeff Hartwig (USA)	6.03 (2000)
	Thiago Braz (BRA)	6.03 (2016)
10.	Igor Trandenkov (RUS)	6.01 (1996)
	Timothy Mack (USA)	6.01 (2004)
	Yevgeniy Lukyanenko (RUS)	6.01 (2008)
	Björn Otto (GER)	6.01 (2012)
14.	Rodion Gataulin (URS)	6.00 (1989)
	Tim Lobinger (GER)	6.00 (1997)
	Toby Stevenson (USA)	6.00 (2004)
	Paul Burgess (AUS)	6.00 (2005)
	Steven Hooker (AUS)	6.00 (2008)
	Sam Kendricks (USA)	6.00 (2017)
	Timur Morgunov (ANA)	6.00 (2018)
21.	Lawrence Johnson (USA)	5.98 (1996)
	Jean Galfione (FRA)	5.98 (1999)
23.	Scott Huffman (USA)	5.97 (1994)
24.	Joe Dial (USA)	5.96 (1987)
25.	Andrej Tiwontschik (GER)	5.95 (1996)
	Michael Stolle (GER)	5.95 (2000)
	Romain Mesnil (FRA)	5.95 (2003)
28.	Raphael Holzdeppe (GER)	5.94 (2015)
	Piotr Lisek (POL)	5.94 (2018)
30.	Daniel Ecker (GER)	5.93 (1998)
	Aleksandr Averbukh (ISR)	5.93 (2003)
	Shawn Barber (CAN)	5.93 (2015)
	Pawel Wojciechowski (POL)	5.93 (2017)
34.	István Bagyula (HUN)	5.92 (1991)
	Igor Potapovich (KAZ)	5.92 (1992)
	Dean Starkey (USA)	5.92 (1994)
37.	Thierry Vigneron (FRA)	5.91 (1984)
	Riaan Botha (RSA)	5.91 (1997)
	Malte Mohr (GER)	5.91 (2012)
	Konstantinos Filippidis (GRE)	5.91 (2015)
41 – 52:		
	Pierre Quinon (FRA)	5.90 (1985)
	Miroslaw Chmara (POL)	5.90 (1988)
	Denis Petushinskiy (RUS)	5.90 (1993)
	Grigoriy Yegorov (KAZ)	5.90 (1993)
	et al.	

WORLD RANKING ALL TIME INDOOR:

1.	Renaud Lavillenie (FRA)	6.16 (2014)
2.	Sergey Bubka (UKR)	6.15 (1993)
3.	Steven Hooker (AUS)	6.06 (2009)
4.	Rodion Gataulin (URS)	6.02 (1989)
	Jeff Hartwig (USA)	6.02 (2002)
6.	Maxim Tarasov (RUS)	6.00 (1999)
	Jean Galfione (FRA)	6.00 (1999)
	Daniel Ecker (GER)	6.00 (2001)
	Shawnacy Barber (CAN)	6.00 (2016)
	Piotr Lisek (POL)	6.00 (2017)
11.	Lawrence Johnson (USA)	5.96 (2001)
12.	Tim Lobinger (GER)	5.95 (2000)
13.	Philippe Collet (FRA)	5.94 (1990)
14.	Billy Olson (USA)	5.93 (1986)
	Tye Harvey (USA)	5.93 (2001)
	Thiago Braz (BRA)	5.93 (2016)
	Sam Kendricks (USA)	5.93 (2018)
18.	Igor Potapovich (KAZ)	5.92 (1998)
	Björn Otto (GER)	5.92 (2012)
20.	Joe Dial (USA)	5.91 (1986)
	Viktor Ryzhenkov (URS)	5.91 (1991)
	Brian McGinty (USA)	5.91 (2007)
	Timur Morgunov (ANA)	5.91 (2018)
24.	Ferenc Salbert (FRA)	5.90 (1987)
	Grigoriy Yegorov (URS)	5.90 (1990)
	Igor Trandenkov (RUS)	5.90 (1993)
	Pyotr Bochkaryov (RUS)	5.90 (1994)
	Okkert Brits (RSA)	5.90 (1997)
	Michael Stolle (GER)	5.90 (2000)
	Igor Pavlov (RUS)	5.90 (2005)
	Yevgeniy Lukyanenko (RUS)	5.90 (2008)
	Dmitriy Starodubtsev (RUS)	5.90 (2011)
	Malte Mohr (GER)	5.90 (2014)
34.	Maksym Mazuryk (UKR)	5.88 (2011)
	Raphael Holzdeppe (GER)	5.88 (2018)
	Pawel Wojciechowski (POL)	5.88 (2018)
	Axel Chapelle (FRA)	5.88 (2018)
	Armand Duplantis (SWE)	5.88 (2018)
	Kévin Ménaldo (FRA)	5.88 (2018)
40.	Earl Bell (USA)	5.86 (1987)
	Aleksandr Averbukh (ISR)	5.86 (2001)
	Romain Mesnil (FRA)	5.86 (2001)
	Brad Walker (USA)	5.86 (2012)
	Kurtis Marschall (AUS)	5.86 (2018)

Long Jump Men

EUROPEAN CHAMPIONSHIPS 2018: 8-8-2018:

1.	Miltiádis Tentóglou (GRE)		8.25
2.	Fabian Heinle (GER)		8.13
3.	Serhii Nykyforov (UKR)		8.13
4.	Thobias Nilsson Montler (SWE)		8.10
5.	Tomasz Jaszczuk (POL)		8.08
6.	Dan Bramble (GBR)		7.90
7.	Michel Tornéus (SWE)	(7.91)	7.86
8.	Guillaume Victorin (FRA)		7.84
9.	Kafétien Gomis (FRA)		7.84
10.	Izmir Smajlaj (ALB)		7.83
11.	Kevin Ojiaku (ITA)	(7.90)	7.78
12.	Radek Juska (CZE)	(7.87)	7.73

13.	Vladyslav Mazur (UKR)	7.70
14.	Strahinja Jovancevic (SRB)	7.69
15.	Feron Sayers (GBR)	7.68
16.	Kristian Pulli (FIN)	7.68

WORLD RANKING 2018:

1.	Juan Miguel Echevarría (CUB)	8.68(BL)
2.	Luvo Manyonga (RSA)	8.58(Rom)
3.	Wang Jianan (CHN)	8.47
4.	Jeff Henderson (USA)	8.44
5.	Shi Yuhao (CHN)	8.43(Sha)
6.	Ruswahl Samaai (RSA)	8.42(Lon)
7.	Aleksandr Menkov (RUS)	8.41(Zhu)
8.	Zarck Visser (RSA)	8.40(BL)
9.	Zach Bazile (USA)	8.37(NCA)
10.	Henry Frayne (AUS)	8.34(GC)
11.	Zhang Yaoguang (CHN)	8.29
	Marquis Dendy (USA)	8.29(NAC)
13.	Jarvis Gotch (USA)	8.27(Tor)
	Radek Juska (CZE)	8.27
15.	Emiliano Lasa (URU)	8.26
16.	Miltiádis Tentóglou (GRE)	8.25
	Jarrion Lawson (USA)	8.25
18.	Tajay Gayle (JAM)	8.24(NAC)
19.	Andwuelle Wright (TTO)	8.23
	Serhiy Nykyforov (UKR)	8.23
21.	Stephan Hartmann (GER)	8.20
	Julian Howard (GER)	8.20
	Sreedhankar (IND)	8.20
24.	Huang Changzhou (CHN)	8.19
	Alexsandro do Nascimento (BRA)	8.19
26.	Terell McClain (USA)	8.18
	Corey Crawford (USA)	8.18
28.	Grant Holloway (USA)	8.17
29.	Dan Bramble (GBR)	8.15
30.	Jared Kerr (CAN)	8.14
	Janako Prasad (SRI)	8.14
32.	Kafétien Gomis (FRA)	8.13
	Ramone Bailey (JAM)	8.13(WC)
	Fabian Heinle (GER)	8.13(ECh)
35.	Cheswill Johnson (RSA)	8.12
	Paulo dos Santos (BRA)	8.12
	Maikel Vidal (CUB)	8.12
	Damarcus Simpson (USA)	8.12
39.	Fabian Edoki (NGR)	8.10
	Tomasz Jaszczuk (POL)	8.10
	Thobias Nilsson Montler (SWE)	8.10(ECh)
42.	Jie Lei (CHN)	8.09
	Yuki Hashioka (JPN)	8.09
	Sapwaturrahman Sapwaturahman (INA)	8.09

WORLD INDOOR CHAMPIONSHIPS: 2-3-2018:

1.	Juan Miguel Echevarría (CUB)	8.46
2.	Luvo Manyonga (RSA)	8.44
3.	Marquis Dendy (USA)	8.42
4.	Jarrion Lawson (USA)	8.14
5.	Shi Yuhao (CHN)	8.12
6.	Ruswahl Samaai (RSA)	8.05
7.	Radek Juska (CZE)	7.99
8.	Eusebio Cáceres (ESP)	7.91
9.	Miltiadis Tentoglou (GRE)	7.82
10.	Huang Changzhou (CHN)	7.75
11.	Tyrone Smith (BER)	7.75
12.	Emiliano Lasa (URU)	7.72
13.	Maykel Massó (CUB)	7.71
14.	Godfrey Khotso Mokoena (RSA)	7.53
15.	Damar Forbes (JAM)	7.21

WORLD INDOOR RANKING 2018:

1.	Juan Miguel Echevarría (CUB)	8.46
2.	Luvo Manyonga (RSA)	8.44
3.	Marquis Dendy (USA)	8.42
4.	Jarrion Lawson (USA)	8.38
5.	Aleksandr Menkov (ANA)	8.23
6.	William Williams (USA)	8.19
7.	Michael Hartfield (USA)	8.18
8.	Shi Yuhao (CHN)	8.16
9.	Jarvis Gotch (USA)	8.14
10.	Zach Bazile (USA)	8.13
	Grant Holloway (USA)	8.13
12.	Paulo dos Santos (BRA)	8.12
	Charles Brown (USA)	8.12
14.	Cristian Staicu (ROM)	8.09
15.	Damar Forbes (JAM)	8.07
16.	Ruswahl Samaai (RSA)	8.05
17.	Corion Knight (USA)	8.02
	Artyom Primak (RUS)	8.02
19.	Max Hess (GER)	8.00

OVERVIEW WORLDWIDE OUTDOOR CHAMPIONSHIP FINALISTS OF PAST 6 YEARS

	Wch 17	OG 16	Wch 15	Wch 13
Luvo Manyonga (RSA)	8.48 (1)	8.37 (2)		
Jarrion Lawson (USA)	8.44 (2)	8.25 (4)		
Ruswahl Samaai (RSA)	8.32 (3)	7.97 (9)		
Aleksandr Menkov (RUS)	8.27 (4)		8.02 (6)	8.56 (1)
Maykel Massó (CUB)	8.26 (5)			
Shi Yuhao (CHN)	8.23 (6)			
Wang Jianan (CHN)	8.23 (7)	8.17 (5)	8.18 (3)	
Michel Tornéus (SWE)	8.18 (8)			
Emiliano Lasa (URU)	8.11 (9)	8.10 (6)		
Radek Juska (CZE)	8.02 (10)		7.57 (11)	
Fabrice Lapierre (AUS)	7.93 (11)	7.87 (10)	8.24 (2)	
Damar Forbes (JAM)	7.91 (12)	7.82 (12)		8.02 (8)
Jeff Henderson (USA)		8.38 (1)	7.95 (9)	
Greg Rutherford (GBR)		8.29 (3)	8.41 (1)	
Henry Frayne (AUS)		8.06 (7)		
Kafétien Gomis (FRA)		8.05 (8)	8.02 (7)	
Huang Changzhou (CHN)		7.86 (11)		
Gao Xinglong (CHN)			8.14 (4)	
Li Jinzhe (CHN)			8.10 (5)	7.86 (12)
Sergey Polyanskiy (RUS)			7.97 (8)	
Tyrone Smith (BER)			7.79 (10)	
Mike Hartfield (USA)			NM (12)	
Ignisious Gaisah (NED)				8.29 (2)
Luis Rivera (MEX)				8.27 (3)
Eusebio Cáceres (ESP)				8.26 (4)
Mauro Vinicius da Silva (BRA)				8.24 (5)
Christian Reif (GER)				8.22 (6)
Godfrey Khotso Mokoena (RSA)				8.10 (7)
Sebastian Bayer (GER)				7.98 (9)
Loúis Tsátoumas (GRE)				7.98 (10)
Dwight Phillips (USA)				7.88 (11)

OVERVIEW WORLDWIDE INDOOR CHAMPIONSHIP FINALISTS OF PAST 5 YEARS

	Wch18	Wch 16	Wch 14
Juan Miguel Echevarría (CUB)	8.46 (1)		
Luvo Manyonga (RSA)	8.44 (2)		
Marquis Dendy (USA)	8.42 (3)	8.26 (1)	
Jarrion Lawson (USA)	8.14 (4)		
Shi Yuhao (CHN)	8.12 (5)		
Rushwal Samaai (RSA)	8.05 (6)	8.18 (5)	
Radek Juska (CZE)	7.99 (7)	7.88 (10)	
Eusebio Cáceres (ESP)	7.91 (8)		
Miltiadis Tentoglou (GRE)	7.82 (9)		
Huang Changzhou (CHN)	7.75 (10)	8.21 (3)	
Fabrice Lapierre (AUS)		8.25 (2)	
Jeff Henderson (USA)		8.19 (4)	
Daniel Bramble (GBR)		8.14 (6)	
Emiliano Lasa (URU)		7.94 (7)	
Wang Jianan (CHN)		7.93 (8)	
Kafétien Gomis (FRA)		7.88 (9)	
Mauro Vinicius Da Silva (BRA)			8.28 (1)
Li Jinzhe (CHN)			8.23 (2)
Michel Tornéus (SWE)			8.21 (3)
Loúis Tsátoumas (GRE)			8.13 (4)
Aleksandr Menkov (RUS)			8.08 (5)
Adrian Strzalkowski (POL)			7.96 (6)
Luis Rivera (MEX)			7.93 (7)
Christian Reif (GER)			7.75 (8)

OVERVIEW TOP 10 WORLD OUTDOOR RANKINGS OF PAST 5 YEARS

	2018	2017	2016	2015	2014
Juan Miguel Echevarría (CUB)	8.68 (1)				
Luvo Manyonga (RSA)	8.58 (2)	8.65 (1)	8.48 (2)		
Wang Jianan (CHN)	8.47 (3)				
Jeff Henderson (USA)	8.44 (4)		8.38 (6)	8.52 (1)	8.43 (4)
Shi Yuhao (CHN)	8.43 (5)	8.31 (7)			
Ruswahl Samaai (RSA)	8.42 (6)	8.49 (2)	8.38 (6)	8.38 (5)	
Aleksandr Menkov (RUS)	8.41 (7)	8.32 (6)		8.27 (9)	
Zarck Visser (RSA)	8.40 (8)			8.41 (2)	8.31 (7)
Zach Bazile (USA)	8.37 (9)				
Henry Frayne (AUS)	8.34 (10)				
Jarrion Lawson (USA)		8.44 (3)	8.58 (1)	8.34 (6)	
Tyrone Smith (BER)		8.34 (4)			
Maykel Massó (CUB)		8.33 (5)			
Eusebio Cáceres (ESP)		8.31 (7)			
Radek Juska (CZE)		8.31 (7)			
Michel Tornéus (SWE)		8.30 (10)	8.44 (4)		
Miltiádis Tentóglou (GRE)		8.30 (10)			
Marquise Goodwin (USA)			8.45 (3)		
Marquis Dendy (USA)			8.42 (5)	8.39 (4)	
Mike Hartfield (USA)			8.34 (8)	8.27 (9)	
Fabrice Lapierre (AUS)			8.31 (9)	8.29 (7)	
Greg Rutherford (GBR)			8.31 (9)	8.41 (2)	8.51 (1)
Markus Rehm (GER)				8.29 (7)	8.24 (9)
Christian Reif (GER)					8.49 (2)
Li Jinzhe (CHN)					8.47 (3)
Tyron Stewart (USA)					8.39 (5)
Salim Sdiri (FRA)					8.35 (6)
Loúis Tsátoumas (GRE)					8.25 (8)
Luis Rivera (MEX)					8.24 (9)

OVERVIEW TOP 10 WORLD INDOOR RANKINGS OF PAST 5 YEARS

	2018	2017	2016	2015	2014
Juan Miguel Echevarría (CUB)	8.46 (1)				
Luvo Manyonga (RSA)	8.44 (2)				
Marquis Dendy (USA)	8.42 (3)		8.41 (1)	8.28 (2)	
Jarrion Lawson (USA)	8.38 (4)		8.17 (10)	8.27 (3)	8.39 (1)
Aleksandr Menkov (RUS)	8.23 (5)				8.30 (2)
William Williams (USA)	8.19 (6)				
Michael Hartfield (USA)	8.18 (7)				
Shi Yuhao (CHN)	8.16 (8)				
Jarvis Gotch (USA)	8.14 (9)			8.12 (8)	
Zach Bazile (USA)	8.13 (10)				
Serhiy Nykyforov (UKR)		8.18 (1)			
Julian Harvey (USA)		8.17 (2)			
Zhang Yaoguang (CHN)		8.16 (3)			
Huang Changzhou (CHN)		8.13 (4)	8.21 (6)	8.14 (7)	
Jean-Pierre Bertrand (FRA)		8.08 (5)			
Izmir Smajlaj (ALB)		8.08 (5)			
Michel Tornéus (SWE)		8.08 (5)		8.30 (1)	8.21 (8)
Lamont Marcell Jacobs (ITA)		8.07 (8)			
Grant Holloway (USA)		8.05 (9)			
Godfrey Khotso Mokoena (RSA)		8.05 (9)			
Filippo Randazzo (ITA)		8.05 (9)			
Greg Rutherford (GBR)			8.26 (2)	8.17 (5)	
Bachana Khorava (GEO)			8.25 (3)		
Fabrice Lapierre (AUS)			8.25 (3)		
Kafétien Gomis (FRA)			8.23 (5)	8.18 (4)	
Jeff Henderson (USA)			8.19 (7)		
Wang Jianan (CHN)			8.18 (8)		
Ruswahl Samaai (RSA)			8.18 (8)		
Jonathan Addison (USA)			8.17 (10)		
Eusebio Cáceres (ESP)				8.16 (6)	
Gao Xinglong (CHN)				8.12 (8)	
Li Jinzhe (CHN)				8.10 (10)	8.23 (4)
Radek Juska (CZE)				8.10 (10)	
Mauro Vinicius Da Silva (BRA)					8.28 (3)
Loúis Tsátoumas (GRE)					8.23 (4)
Tyron Stewart (USA)					8.22 (6)
Corey Crawford (USA)					8.22 (6)
Ngonidzashe Makusha (ZIM)					8.18 (9)
Adrian Strzalkowski (POL)					8.18 (9)

WORLD RANKING ALL TIME OUTDOOR:

1.	Mike Powell (USA)	8.95 (1991)
2.	Bob Beamon (USA)	8.90 (1968)
3.	Carl Lewis (USA)	8.87 (1991)
4.	Robert Emmiyan (URS)	8.86 (1987)
5.	Larry Myricks (USA)	8.74 (1988)
	Erick Walder (USA)	8.74 (1994)
	Dwight Phillips (USA)	8.74 (2009)
8.	Irving Saladino (PAN)	8.73 (2008)
9.	Iván Pedroso (CUB)	8.71 (1995)
10.	Juan Miguel Echevarría (CUB)	8.68 (2018)
11.	Louis Tsatoumas (GRE)	8.66 (2007)
12.	Luvo Manyonga (RSA)	8.65 (2017)
13.	Kareem Streete-Thompson (USA)	8.63 (1994)
14.	James Beckford (JAM)	8.62 (1997)
15.	Jarrion Lawson (USA)	8.58 (2016)
16.	Yago Lamela (ESP)	8.56 (1999)
	Aleksandr Menkov (RUS)	8.56 (2013)
18.	Lutz Dombrowski (GDR)	8.54 (1980)
	Michell Watt (AUS)	8.54 (2011)
20.	Jaime Jefferson (CUB)	8.53 (1990)
21.	Savanté Stringfellow (USA)	8.52 (2002)
	Jeff Henderson (USA)	8.52 (2015)
23.	Roland McGhee (USA)	8.51 (1995)
	Greg Rutherford (GBR)	8.51 (2014)
25.	Llewellyn Starks (USA)	8.50 (1991)
	Godfrey Khotso Mokoena (RSA)	8.50 (2009)
27.	Melvin Lister (USA)	8.49 (2000)
	Jai Taurima (AUS)	8.49 (2000)
	Sebastian Bayer (GER)	8.49 (2009)
	Christian Reif (GER)	8.49 (2014)
	Rushwahl Samaai (RSA)	8.49 (2017)
32.	Joe Greene (USA)	8.48 (1995)
	Moh. Salman Al Khuwalidi (KSA)	8.48 (2006)
34.	Kevin Dilworth (USA)	8.47 (1996)
	John Moffitt (USA)	8.47 (2004)
	Andrew Howe (ITA)	8.47 (2007)
	Li Jinzhe (CHN)	8.47 (2014)
	Wang Jianan (CHN)	8.47 (2018)
39.	Leonid Voloshin (URS)	8.46 (1988)
	Mike Conley (USA)	8.46 (1996)
	Cheikh Tidiane Toure (SEN)	8.46 (1997)
	Miguel Pate (USA)	8.46 (2003)
	Ibrahim Camejo (CUB)	8.46 (2008)
	Luis Alberto Rivera (MEX)	8.46 (2013)
45.	Nenad Stekic (YUG)	8.45 (1975)
	et al.	

WORLD RANKING ALL TIME INDOOR:

1.	Carl Lewis (USA)	8.79 (1984)
2.	Sebastian Bayer (GER)	8.71 (2009)
3.	Iván Pedroso (CUB)	8.62 (1999)
4.	Miguel Pate (USA)	8.59 (2002)
5.	Yago Lamela (ESP)	8.56 (1999)
6.	Robert Emmiyan (URS)	8.49 (1987)
7.	Juan Miguel Echevarría (CUB)	8.46 (2018)
8.	Larry Myricks (USA)	8.44 (1984)
	Mike Powell (USA)	8.44 (1993)
	Luvo Manyonga (RSA)	8.44 (2018)
11.	Stanislav Tarasenko (RUS)	8.43 (1994)
	Erick Walder (USA)	8.43 (1994)
13.	Irving Saladino (PAN)	8.42 (2008)
	Marquis Dendy (USA)	8.42 (2018)
15.	Kirill Sosunov (RUS)	8.41 (1997)
	Joe Greene (USA)	8.41 (1997)
	Savanté Stringfellow (USA)	8.41 (2004)
18.	James Beckford (JAM)	8.40 (1996)
19.	Jarrion Lawson (USA)	8.39 (2014)
20.	Vitaliy Shkurlatov (RUS)	8.38 (2000)
21.	Joan Lino Martínez (ESP)	8.37 (2005)
22.	Ignisious Gaisah (GHA)	8.36 (2006)
23.	Llewellyn Starks (USA)	8.34 (1992)
24.	Reggie Kelly (USA)	8.33 (1983)
	Roman Shchurenko (UKR)	8.33 (2002)
26.	Vladimir Ochkan (URS)	8.32 (1988)
27.	Mike Conley (USA)	8.31 (1986)
	Aleksandr Menkov (RUS)	8.31 (2013)
29.	Bob Beamon (USA)	8.30 (1968)
	Ivailo Mladenov (BUL)	8.30 (1994)
	Bogdan Tarus (ROM)	8.30 (2000)
	Andrew Howe (ITA)	8.30 (2007)
	Michel Tornéus (SWE)	8.30 (2015)
34.	Dwight Phillips (USA)	8.29 (2003)
35.	Roland McGhee (USA)	8.28 (1995)
	Gregor Cankar (SLO)	8.28 (1999)
	Brian Johnson (USA)	8.28 (2003)
	Mauro Vinicius Da Silva (BRA)	8.28 (2012)
39.	Yuriy Naumkin (RUS)	8.27 (1995)
	Petar Dachev (BUL)	8.27 (2002)
	John Moffitt (USA)	8.27 (2004)
	Salim Sdiri (FRA)	8.27 (2006)
	Su Xiongfeng (CHN)	8.27 (2010)
44.	Charlton Ehizuelen (NGR)	8.26 (1975)
	Giovanni Evangelisti (ITA)	8.26 (1987)
	Greg Rutherford (GBR)	8.26 (2016)

Triple Jump Men

EUROPEAN CHAMPIONSHIPS 2018: 12-8-2018:

1.	Nelson Évora (POR)		17.10
2.	Alexis Copello (AZE)		16.93
3.	Dimitrios Tsiámis (GRE)		16.78
4.	Nazim Babayev (AZE)		16.76
5.	Pablo Torrijos (ESP)	(16.79)	16.74
6.	Nathan Douglas (GBR)		16.71
7.	Jean-Marc Pontvianne (FRA)	(16.77)	16.61
8.	Tomas Veszelka (SVK)		16.48
9.	Simo Lipsanen (FIN)	(16.51)	16.46
10.	Marcos Ruiz (ESP)	(16.59)	16.44
11.	Harold Correia (FRA)	(16.43)	16.33
12.	Can Özüpek (TUR)	(16.66)	15.88

13.	Simone Forte (ITA)	16.35
14.	Levon Aghasyan (ARM)	16.34
15.	Max Hess (GER)	16.32
16.	Aleksey Fyodorov (ANA)	16.29
17.	Elvijs Misans (LAT)	16.26
18.	Necati Er (TUR)	16.26
19.	Kevin Luron (FRA)	16.25
20.	Fabrizio Donato (ITA)	16.15
21.	Marian Oprea (ROM)	15.93
	Karol Hoffmann (POL)	NM

WORLD RANKING 2018:

1.	Pedro Pablo Pichardo (POR)	17.95(Do)
2.	Christian Taylor (USA)	17.81(Do)
3.	Almir dos Santos (BRA)	17.53(BM)
4.	Will Claye (USA)	17.44(Eug)
5.	Jordan Díaz (CUB)	17.41
6.	Omar Craddock (USA)	17.40(CV)
	Chris Benard (USA)	17.40(CV)
8.	Donald Scott (USA)	17.37(USC)
9.	Cristian Nápoles (CUB)	17.34
10.	Lázaro Martínez (CUB)	17.28
11.	Alexis Copello (AZE)	17.24(Eug)
12.	Dong Bin (CHN)	17.22(Eug)
13.	Chris Carter (USA)	17.18
14.	Keandre Bates (USA)	17.16(USC)
15.	Aleksandr Yurchenko (RUS)	17.15(Zhu)
16.	Zhu Yaming (CHN)	17.11
17.	Nelson Évora (POR)	17.10(ECh)
18.	Arpinder Singh (IND)	17.09
19.	Harold Correa (FRA)	17.05
20.	Henry Rosique (CUB)	17.02
	Hugues Fabrice Zango (BDI)	17.02(CON)

WORLD INDOOR CHAMPIONSHIPS: 3-3-2018:

1. Will Claye (USA)   17.43
2. Almir dos Santos (BRA)   17.41
3. Nelson Évora (POR)   17.40
4. Alexis Copello (AZE)   17.17
5. Chris Carter (USA)   17.15
6. Hugues Fabrice Zango (BDI)   17.11
7. Zhu Yaming (CHN)   16.87
8. Dong Bin (CHN)   16.84
9. Cristian Nápoles (CUB)   16.70
10. Elvijs Misans (LAT)   16.55
11. Max Hess (GER)   16.47
12. Momchil Karailiev (BUL)   16.14
13. Clive Pullen (JAM)   16.13
14. Fabrizio Donato (ITA)   15.96
15. Andy Díaz (CUB)   15.37

WORLD INDOOR RANKING 2018:

1. Will Claye (USA)   17.43
2. Almir dos Santos (BRA)   17.41
3. Nelson Ëvora (POR)   17.40
4. Hugues Fabrice Zango (BDI)   17.23
5. Chris Carter (USA)   17.20
6. Pedro Pablo Pichardo (POR)   17.19
7. Omar Craddock (USA)   17.18
8. Alexis Copello (AZE)   17.17
9. Aleksandr Yurchenko (RUS)   17.12
10. Donald Scott (USA)   17.06
11. Cristian Nápoles (CUB)   17.02

OVERVIEW WORLDWIDE OUTDOOR CHAMPIONSHIP FINALISTS OF PAST 6 YEARS

	Wch 17	OG 16	Wch 15	Wch 13
Christian Taylor (USA)	17.68 (1)	17.86 (1)	18.21 (1)	17.20 (4)
Will Claye (USA)	17.63 (2)	17.76 (2)		17.52 (3)
Nelson Évora (POR)	17.19 (3)	17.03 (6)	17.52 (3)	
Cristian Nápoles (CUB)	17.16 (4)			
Alexis Copello (AZE)	17.16 (5)			
Chris Benard (USA)	17.16 (6)			
Andy Diaz (CUB)	17.13 (7)			
Jean-Marc Pontvianne (FRA)	16.79 (8)			
Wu Ruiting (CHN)	16.66 (9)			
Pablo Torrijos (ESP)	16.60 (10)			
Yordanys Duranona (DMA)	16.42 (11)			
Lázaro Martinez (CUB)	16.25 (12)	16.68 (8)		
Dong Bin (CHN)		17.58 (3)		16.73 (9)
Cao Shuo (CHN)		17.13 (4)		
John Murillo (COL)		17.09 (5)		
Troy Doris (GUY)		16.90 (7)		
Alberto Alvarez (MEX)		16.56 (9)		
Benjamin Compaoré (FRA)		16.54 (10)	16.63 (12)	
Xu Xiaolong (CHN)		16.41 (11)		
Karol Hoffmann (POL)		16.31 (12)		
Pedro Pablo Pichardo (CUB)			17.73 (2)	17.68 (2)
Omar Craddock (USA)			17.37 (4)	
Lyukman Adams (RUS)			17.28 (5)	
Marian Oprea (ROM)			17.06 (6)	16.82 (6)
Dmitriy Sorokin (RUS)			16.99 (7)	
Tosin Oke (NGR)			16.81 (8)	
Godfrey Khotso Mokoena (RSA)			16.81 (9)	
Leevan Sands (BAH)			16.68 (10)	
Jonathan Drack (MRI)			16.64 (11)	
Teddy Tamgho (FRA)				18.04 (1)
Aleksey Fedorov (RUS)				16.90 (5)
Gaëtan Saku Bafuanga Baya (FRA)				16.79 (7)
Fabrizio Schembri (ITA)				16.74 (8)
Dimitrios Tsiámis (GRE)				16.66 (10)
Samyr Laine (HAI)				16.09 (11)
Yoann Rapinier (FRA)				15.17 (12)

OVERVIEW WORLDWIDE INDOOR CHAMPIONSHIP FINALISTS OF PAST 5 YEARS

	Wch 18	Wch 16	Wch 14
Will Claye (USA)	17.43 (1)		
Almir dos Santos (BRA)	17.41 (2)		
Nelson Évora (POR)	17.40 (3)	16.89 (4)	
Alexis Copello (AZE)	17.17 (4)		
Chris Carter (USA)	17.15 (5)		16.74 (6)
Hugues Fabrize Zango (BDI)	17.11 (6)		
Zhu Yaming (CHN)	16.87 (7)		
Dong Bin (CHN)	16.84 (8)	17.33 (1)	
Cristian Nápoles (CUB)	16.70 (9)		
Elvijs Misans (LAT)	16.55 (10)		
Max Hess (GER)		17.14 (2)	
Benjamin Compaoré (FRA)		17.09 (3)	
Omar Craddock (USA)		16.87 (5)	
Tosin Oke (NGR)		16.73 (6)	
Pablo Torrijos (ESP)		16.67 (7)	
Nazim Babayev (AZE)		16.43 (8)	
Harold Correa (FRA)		16.30 (9)	
Marian Oprea (ROM)		16.27 (10)	17.21 (4)
Lyukman Adams (RUS)			17.37 (1)
Ernesto Revé (CUB)			17.33 (2)
Pedro Pablo Pichardo (CUB)			17.24 (3)
Karol Hoffmann (POL)			16.89 (5)
Cao Shuo (CHN)			16.55 (7)
Viktor Kuznetsov (UKR)			16.51 (8)

OVERVIEW TOP 10 WORLD OUTDOOR RANKINGS OF PAST 5 YEARS

	2018	2017	2016	2015	2014
Pedro Pablo Pichardo (POR/CUB)	17.95 (1)	17.60 (3)		18.08 (2)	17.76 (1)
Christian Taylor (USA)	17.81 (2)	18.11 (1)	17.86 (1)	18.21 (1)	17.51 (4)
Almir dos Santos (BRA)	17.53 (3)				
Will Claye (USA)	17.44 (4)	17.91 (2)	17.76 (2)	17.48 (6)	17.75 (2)
Jordan Díaz (CUB)	17.41 (5)	17.30 (7)			
Omar Craddock (USA)	17.40 (6)		17.16 (9)	17.53 (3)	
Chris Benard (USA)	17.40 (6)	17.48 (4)	17.21 (5)		
Donald Scott (USA)	17.37 (8)	17.25 (10)			
Crístian Nápoles (CUB)	17.34 (9)	17.27 (8)			
Lázaro Martinez (CUB)	17.28 (10)				17.24 (10)
Andy Diaz (CUB)		17.40 (5)			
Fabrizio Donato (ITA)		17.32 (6)			
Dong Bin (CHN)		17.27 (8)	17.58 (3)		
Renjith Maheswary (IND)			17.30 (4)		
Max Hess (GER)			17.20 (6)		
Troy Doris (GUY)			17.18 (7)		
Chris Carter (USA)			17.18 (7)		
Karol Hoffmann (POL)			17.16 (9)		
Nelson Évora (POR)				17.52 (4)	
Marquis Dendy (USA)				17.50 (5)	
Aleksey Fedorov (RUS)				17.42 (7)	
Lyukman Adams (RUS)				17.34 (8)	17.29 (8)
Dmitriy Sorokin (RUS)				17.29 (9)	
Teddy Tamgho (FRA)				17.24 (10)	
Ernesto Revé (CUB)					17.58 (3)
Benjamin Compaoré (FRA)					17.48 (5)
Godfrey Khotso Mokoena (RSA)					17.35 (6)
Cao Shuo (CHN)					17.30 (7)
Samyr Laine (HAI)					17.27 (9)

OVERVIEW TOP 10 WORLD INDOOR RANKINGS OF PAST 5 YEARS

	2018	2017	2016	2015	2014
Will Claye (USA)	17.43 (1)			16.93 (7)	17.04 (6)
Almir dos Santos (BRA)	17.41 (2)				
Nelson Évora (POR)	17.40 (3)	17.20 (3)		17.21 (2)	
Hugues Fabrice Zango (BDI)	17.23 (4)				
Chris Carter (USA)	17.20 (5)	17.10 (8)	17.06 (4)		17.15 (5)
Pedro Pablo Pichardo (CUB)	17.19 (6)				17.32 (3)
Omar Craddock (USA)	17.18 (7)		16.96 (8)		
Alexis Copello (AZE)/(CUB)	17.17 (8)	17.10 (8)	16.99 (6)	17.07 (3)	
Aleksandr Yurchenko (RUS)	17.12 (9)				
Donald Scott (USA)	17.06 (10)				
Max Hess (GER)		17.52 (1)	17.14 (2)		
Melvin Raffin (FRA)		17.20 (2)			
Clive Pullen (JAM)		17.19 (4)			
Jean-Marc Pontvianne (FRA)		17.13 (5)			
Fabrizio Donato (ITA)		17.13 (5)			
Dong Bin (CHN)		17.12 (7)	17.41 (1)		
Elvijs Misans (LAT)		17.02 (10)			
Benjamin Compaoré (FRA)			17.09 (3)		
Eric Sloan (USA)			17.03 (5)		
Teddy Tamgho (FRA)			16.98 (7)		
Chris Benard (USA)			16.93 (9)		16.99 (7)
Harold Corréa (FRA)			16.91 (10)		
Marquis Dendy (USA)				17.37 (1)	
Pablo Torrijos (ESP)				17.04 (4)	
Roman Valiyev (KAZ)				17.00 (5)	
Dmitriy Sorokin (RUS)				16.94 (6)	
Aleksey Fedorov (RUS)				16.91 (8)	
Marian Oprea (ROM)				16.91 (8)	17.30 (4)
Dmitriy Chizhikov (RUS)				16.89 (10)	
Lyukman Adams (RUS)					17.37 (1)
Ernesto Revé (CUB)					17.33 (2)
Karol Hoffmann (POL)					16.89 (8)
Julian Reid (GBR)					16.87 (9)
Troy Doris (USA)					16.84 (10)

WORLD RANKING ALL TIME OUTDOOR:

1.	Jonathan Edwards (GBR)	18.29 (1995)
2.	Christian Taylor (USA)	18.21 (2015)
3.	Kenny Harrison (USA)	18.09 (1996)
4.	Pedro Pablo Pichardo (CUB)	18.08 (2015)
5.	Teddy Tamgho (FRA)	18.04 (2013)
6.	Willie Banks (USA)	17.97 (1985)
7.	Khristo Markov (BUL)	17.92 (1987)
	James Beckford (JAM)	17.92 (1995)
9.	Will Claye (USA)	17.91 (2017)
10.	Volodimir Inozemtsev (URS)	17.90 (1990)
	Jadel Gregório (BRA)	17.90 (2007)
12.	João Carlos de Oliveira (BRA)	17.89 (1975)
13.	Mike Conley (USA)	17.87 (1987)
14.	Charles Simpkins (USA)	17.86 (1985)
15.	Yoelbi Quesada (CUB)	17.85 (1997)
16.	Marian Oprea (ROM)	17.81 (2005)
	Phillips Idowu (GBR)	17.81 (2010)
18.	Christian Olsson (SWE)	17.79 (2004)
19.	Nikolay Musiyenko (URS)	17.78 (1986)
	Melvin Lister (USA)	17.78 (2004)
21.	Aleksandr Kovalenko (URS)	17.77 (1987)
22.	Oleg Protsenko (URS)	17.75 (1990)
	Leonid Voloshin (URS)	17.75 (1991)
24.	Nelson Évora (POR)	17.74 (2007)
25.	Seref Osmanoglu (UKR)	17.72 (2011)
26.	Walter Davis (USA)	17.71 (2006)
27.	Aliecer Urrutia (CUB)	17.70 (1996)
28.	Igor Lapshin (URS)	17.69 (1988)
29.	Danil Burkenya (RUS)	17.68 (2004)
	Alexis Copello (CUB)	17.68 (2011)
31.	Ralf Jaros (GER)	17.66 (1991)
32.	Aleksandr Yakovlev (URS)	17.65 (1987)
	Denis Kapustin (RUS)	17.65 (1998)
	Yoandri Betanzos (CUB)	17.65 (2009)
35.	Nathan Douglas (GBR)	17.64 (2005)
36.	Kenta Bell (USA)	17.63 (2002)
37.	Brian Wellman (BER)	17.62 (1995)
	David Girat (CUB)	17.62 (2009)
39.	Vladimir Plekhanov (URS)	17.60 (1985)
	Fabrizio Donato (ITA)	17.60 (2000)
41.	Vasily Sokov (RUS)	17.59 (1993)
	Charles Friedek (GER)	17.59 (1997)
	Leevan Sands (BAH)	17.59 (2008)
	Li Yanxi (CHN)	17.59 (2009)
45.	Oleg Sakirkin (URS) et al.	17.58 (1989)

WORLD RANKING ALL TIME INDOOR:

1.	Teddy Tamgho (FRA)	17.92 (2011)
2.	Aliecer Urrutia (CUB)	17.83 (1997)
	Christian Olsson (SWE)	17.83 (2004)
4.	Leonid Voloshin (RUS)	17.77 (1994)
5.	Mike Conley (USA)	17.76 (1987)
6.	Phillips Idowu (GBR)	17.75 (2008)
7.	Marian Oprea (ROM)	17.74 (2006)
8.	Walter Davis (USA)	17.73 (2006)
	Fabrizio Donato (ITA)	17.73 (2011)
10.	Brian Wellman (BER)	17.72 (1995)
11.	Will Claye (USA)	17.70 (2012)
	Daniele Greco (ITA)	17.70 (2013)
13.	Yoandri Betanzos (CUB)	17.69 (2010)
14.	Oleg Protsenko (URS)	17.67 (1987)
15.	Jonathan Edwards (GBR)	17.64 (1998)
16.	Christian Taylor (USA)	17.63 (2012)
17.	Yoelbi Quesada (CUB)	17.62 (1995)
	Yoel García (CUB)	17.62 (1997)
19.	Pierre Camara (FRA)	17.59 (1993)
20.	Jadel Gregório (BRA)	17.56 (2006)
21.	Maris Bruziks (URS)	17.54 (1986)
22.	Volodimir Inozemtsev (URS)	17.53 (1991)
23.	Max Hess (GER)	17.52 (2017)
24.	Charles Simpkins (USA)	17.50 (1986)
25.	Denis Kapustin (RUS)	17.47 (1994)
	Nathan Douglas (GBR)	17.47 (2007)
	David Girat (CUB)	17.47 (2008)
28.	Kenny Harrison (USA)	17.46 (1990)
29.	Khristo Markov (BUL)	17.45 (1988)
	Tim Rusan (USA)	17.45 (2003)
31.	Willie Banks (USA)	17.41 (1982)
	Jorge Reyna (CUB)	17.41 (1989)
	Danil Burkenya (RUS)	17.41 (2004)
	Dong Bin (CHN)	17.41 (2016)
	Almir dos Santos (BRA)	17.41 (2018)
36.	Nelson Évora (POR)	17.40 (2018)
37.	Nikolay Musiyenko (URS)	17.39 (1987)
38.	Vasif Asadov (URS)	17.37 (1988)
	Vasiliy Sokov (RUS)	17.37 (1994)
	Lyukman Adams (RUS)	17.37 (2014)
	Marquis Dendy (USA)	17.37 (2015)
42.	Oleg Sakirkin (URS)	17.36 (1990)
43.	Vladimir Chemikov (URS)	17.35 (1987)
	Igor Lapshin (URS)	17.35 (1990)
45.	Grigoriy Yemets (URS) et al.	17.33 (1984)

Javelin Throw Men

EUROPEAN CHAMPIONSHIPS 2018: 9-8-2018:

1.	Thomas Röhler (GER)	(85.47)	89.47
2.	Andreas Hofmann (GER)	(82.36)	87.60
3.	Magnus Kirt (EST)	(83.15)	85.96
4.	Marcin Krukowski (POL)	(84.35)	84.55
5.	Johannes Vetter (GER)	(87.39)	83.27
6.	Antti Ruuskanen (FIN)	(79.93)	81.70
7.	Andrian Mardare (MDA)	(80.46)	81.54
8.	Jakub Vadlejch (CZE)	(80.28)	80.64
9.	Cyprian Mrzygłód (POL)	(83.85)	80.20
10.	Edis Matusevicius (LTU)	(81.08)	77.64
11.	Rolands Strobinders (LAT)	(81.93)	76.59
12.	Petr Frydrych (CZE)	(79.74)	72.79

13.	Gatis Cakss (LAT)	78.13
14.	Patriks Gailums (LAT)	78.10
15.	Tanel Laanmäe (EST)	77.21
16.	Oliver Helander (FIN)	76.64

WORLD RANKING 2018:

1.	Johannes Vetter (GER)	92.70
2.	Andreas Hofmann (GER)	92.06
3.	Thomas Röhler (GER)	91.78(Do)
4.	Magnus Kirt (EST)	89.75(Rab)
5.	Jakub Vadlejch (CZE)	89.02(Pra)
6.	Neeraj Chopra (IND)	88.06(Jak)
7.	Oliver Helander (FIN)	88.02
8.	Julian Weber (GER)	86.63(Bir)
9.	Alexandru Novac (ROM)	86.37
10.	Paraskevas Batzavalis (GRE)	85.46
11.	Dmitriy Tarabin (RUS)	85.38(Zhu)
12.	Marcin Krukowski (POL)	85.32(Zü)
13.	Bernhard Seifert (GER)	85.17
14.	Keshorn Walcott (TTO)	84.96
15.	Rolands Strobinders (LAT)	84.80
	Chao-Tsun Cheng (TPE)	84.60
17.	Andrian Mardare (MDA)	84.43(Pra)
18.	Gatis Cakss (LAT)	83.89
19.	Petr Frydrych (CZE)	83.85
	Cyprian Mrzygłód (POL)	83.85(ECh)
21.	Ahmed Bader Magour (QAT)	83.71(Do)
22.	Hamish Peacock (AUS)	83.63
23.	Anderson Peters (GRN)	82.82(NCA)
24.	Edis Matusevicius (LTU)	82.67
25.	Tero Pitkämäki (FIN)	82.64
26.	Antti Ruuskanen (FIN)	82.59
27.	Ma Qun (CHN)	82.46
28.	Tanel Laanmäe (EST)	82.36
29.	Vitezslav Veselý (CZE)	82.30
30.	Shivpal Singh (IND)	82.28
31.	Liu Qizhen (CHN)	82.22
32.	Pavel Milaleshka (BLR)	82.05

OVERVIEW WORLDWIDE OUTDOOR CHAMPIONSHIP FINALISTS OF PAST 6 YEARS

	Wch 17	OG 16	Wch 15	Wch 13
Johannes Vetter (GER)	89.89 (1)	85.32 (4)	83.79 (7)	
Jakub Vadlejch (CZE)	89.73 (2)	82.42 (8)		
Petr Frydrych (CZE)	88.32 (3)	79.12 (12)		
Thomas Röhler (GER)	88.26 (4)	90.30 (1)	87.41 (4)	
Tero Pitkämäki (FIN)	86.94 (5)		87.64 (3)	87.07 (2)
Ioánnis Kiriazis (GRE)	84.52 (6)			
Keshorn Walcott (TTO)	84.48 (7)	85.38 (3)		
Andreas Hofmann (GER)	83.98 (8)		86.01 (6)	
Marcin Krukowski (POL)	82.01 (9)			
Ahmed Bader Magour (QAT)	81.77 (10)			
Magnus Kirt (EST)	80.48 (11)			
Davinder Singh (IND)	80.02 (12)			
Julius Yego (KEN)	76.29 (13)	88.24 (2)	92.72 (1)	85.40 (4)
Dmytro Kosynskyy (UKR)		83.95 (5)		
Antti Ruuskanen (FIN)		83.05 (6)	87.12 (5)	81.44 (6)
Vitezslav Vesely (CZE)		82.51 (7)	83.13 (8)	87.17 (1)
Julian Weber (GER)		81.36 (9)		
Braian Toledo (ARG)		79.81 (10)	80.27 (10)	
Ryohei Arai (JPN)		79.47 (11)	83.07 (9)	
Ihab Abdelrahman El Sayed (EGY)			88.99 (2)	80.94 (8)
Kim Amb (SWE)			78.51 (11)	78.91 (11)
Risto Mätas (EST)			76.79 (12)	80.03 (9)
Dmitri Tarabin (RUS)				86.23 (3)
Roman Avramenko (UKR)				82.05 (5)
Andreas Thorkildsen (NOR)				81.06 (7)
Stuart Farquhar (NZL)				79.24 (10)
Ivan Zaytsev (UZB)				78.33 (12)

OVERVIEW TOP 10 WORLD OUTDOOR RANKINGS OF PAST 5 YEARS

	2018	2017	2016	2015	2014
Johannes Vetter (GER)	92.70 (1)	94.44 (1)	89.57 (2)		
Andreas Hofmann (GER)	92.06 (2)	91.07 (4)			86.13 (9)
Thomas Röhler (GER)	91.78 (3)	93.90 (2)	91.28 (1)	89.27 (3)	87.63 (4)
Magnus Kirt (EST)	89.75 (4)			86.65 (9)	
Jakub Vadlejch (CZE)	89.02 (5)	89.73 (5)	88.02 (7)	86.21 (10)	
Neeraj Chopra (IND)	88.06 (6)				
Oliver Helander (FIN)	88.02 (7)				
Julian Weber (GER)	86.63 (8)		88.29 (4)		
Alexandru Novac (ROM)	86.37 (9)				
Paraskevas Batzavalis (GRE)	85.46 (10)				
Chao-Tsun Cheng (TPE)		91.36 (3)			
Petr Frydrych (CZE)		88.32 (6)			
Tero Pitkämäki (FIN)		88.27 (7)		89.09 (4)	86.63 (7)
Marcin Krukowski (POL)		88.09 (8)			
Ioánnis Kiriazís (GRE)		88.01 (9)	87.14 (9)		
Julius Yego (KEN)		87.97 (10)	88.23 (5)	92.72 (1)	
Keshorn Walcott (TTO)			88.68 (3)	90.16 (2)	
Antti Ruuskanen (FIN)			88.23 (6)	88.98 (6)	88.01 (3)
Ihab Abdelrahman El Sayed (EGY)			87.37 (8)	88.99 (5)	89.21 (1)
Zigismunds Sirmais (LAT)			86.66 (10)		86.61 (8)
Vitezslav Veselý (CZE)				88.18 (7)	87.38 (5)
Ari Mannio (FIN)				86.82 (8)	
Zhao Qinggang (CHN)					89.15 (2)
Ryohei Arai (JPN)					86.83 (6)
Dmitri Tarabin (RUS)					85.92 (10)

WORLD RANKING ALL TIME:

1.	Jan Zelezný (CZE)	98.48 (1996)
2.	Johannes Vetter (GER)	94.44 (2017)
3.	Thomas Röhler (GER)	93.90 (2017)
4.	Aki Parviainen (FIN)	93.09 (1999)
5.	Julius Yego (KEN)	92.72 (2015)
6.	Sergey Makarov (RUS)	92.61 (2002)
7.	Raymond Hecht (GER)	92.60 (1995)
8.	Andreas Hofmann (GER)	92.06 (2018)
9.	Konstantinos Gatsioudis (GRE)	91.69 (2000)
10.	Andreas Thorkildsen (NOR)	91.59 (2006)
11.	Tero Pitkämäki (FIN)	91.53 (2005)
12.	Steve Backley (GBR)	91.46 (1992)
13.	Chao-Tsun Cheng (TPE)	91.36 (2017)
14.	Breaux Greer (USA)	91.29 (2007)
15.	Kimmo Kinnunen (FIN)	90.82 (1991)
16.	Vadims Vasilevskis (LAT)	90.73 (2007)
17.	Seppo Räty (FIN)	90.60 (1992)
18.	Boris Henry (GER)	90.44 (1997)
19.	Keshorn Walcott (TTO)	90.16 (2015)
20.	Magnus Kirt (EST)	89.75 (2018)
21.	Jakub Vadlejch (CZE)	89.73 (2017)
22.	Ihab Abdelrahman (EGY)	89.21 (2014)
23.	Tom Petranoff (RSA)	89.16 (1991)
24.	Zhao Qinggang (CHN)	89.15 (2014)
25.	Patrik Bodén (SWE)	89.10 (1990)
26.	Jarrod Bannister (AUS)	89.02 (2008)
27.	Antti Ruuskanen (FIN)	88.98 (2015)
28.	Aleksandr Ivanov (RUS)	88.90 (2003)
29.	Dmitriy Tarabin (RUS)	88.84 (2013)
30.	Marius Corbett (RSA)	88.75 (1998)
31.	Peter Blank (GER)	88.70 (2001)
32.	Matthias de Zordo (GER)	88.36 (2011)
33.	Vitezslav Veselý (CZE)	88.34 (2012)
34.	Petr Frydrych (CZE)	88.32 (2017)
35.	Julian Weber (GER)	88.29 (2016)
36.	Matti Närhi (FIN)	88.24 (1997)
37.	Juha Laukkanen (FIN)	88.22 (1992)
38.	Gavin Lovegrove (NZL)	88.20 (1996)
39.	Marcin Krukowski (POL)	88.09 (2017)
40.	Neeraj Chopra (IND)	88.06 (2018)
41.	Oliver Helander (FIN)	88.02 (2018)
42.	Ioannis Kyriazis (GRE)	88.01 (2017)
43.	Vladimir Ovchinnikov (RUS)	88.00 (1995)
44.	Andrus Värnik (EST)	87.83 (2003)
45.	Harri Hakkarainen (FIN)	87.82 (1995)

Discus Throw Men

EUROPEAN CHAMPIONSHIPS 2018: 8-8-2018:

1. Andrius Gudzius (LTU) (64.30) 68.46
2. Daniel Stahl (SWE) (67.07) 68.23
3. Lukas Weisshaidinger (AUT) (62.26) 65.14
4. Simon Pettersson (SWE) (64.82) 64.55
5. Gerd Kanter (EST) (64.18) 64.34
6. Robert Harting (GER) (63.29) 64.33
7. Alin Firfirica (ROM) (64.79) 63.73
8. Apostolos Parellis (CYP) (62.32) 63.62
9. Viktor Butenko (ANA) (62.63) 62.24
10. Lolassonn Djouhan (FRA) (62.54) 61.89
11. Ola Stunes Isene (NOR) (62.19) 59.56
12. Mykyta Nesterenko (UKR) (63.34) 57.66

----

13. Martin Kupper (EST) 62.13
14. Robert Urbanek (POL) 62.00
15. Róbert Szikszai (HUN) 61.82
16. Gudni Valur Gudnason (ISL) 61.36
17. Axel Härstedt (SWE) 61.19
18. Hannes Kirchler (ITA) 60.42
19. Daniel Jasinski (GER) 60.10
20. Zoltán Kovágó (HUN) 59.29
21. Giovanni Faloci (ITA) 59.27
22. Erik Cadée (NED) 57.97
23. Nazzareno Di Marco (ITA) 57.49
24. Lois Maikel Martinez (ESP) 54.56
    Christoph Harting (GER) NM
    Piotr Malachowski (POL) NM

WORLD RANKING 2018:

1. Daniel Stahl (SWE) 69.72
2. Fedrick Dacres (JAM) 69.67(Sto)
3. Andrius Gudzius (LTU) 69.59(Sto)
4. Lukas Weisshaidinger (AUT) 68.98
5. Ehsan Hadadi (IRI) 68.85(CV)
6. Reggie Jagers (USA) 68.61(USC)
7. Traves Smikle (JAM) 67.72
8. Christoph Harting (GER) 67.59
9. Mason Finley (USA) 67.06(USC)
10. Martin Wierig (GER) 66.98
11. Daniel Jasinski (GER) 66.59
12. Philip Milanov (BEL) 66.51(Sto)
    Lois Maikel Martínez (ESP) 66.51
14. Sam Mattis (USA) 66.32
15. Mauricio Ortega (COL) 66.30
16. Alin Firfirica (ROM) 66.22
17. Andrew Evans (USA) 66.04
18. David Wrobel (GER) 65.98
19. Simon Pettersson (SWE) 65.84
20. Piotr Malachowski (POL) 65.78
21. Zoltán Kövagó (HUN) 65.66
22. Gudni Valur Gudnason (ISL) 65.53
23. Jason Harrell (USA) 65.48(CV)
24. Chad Wright (JAM) 65.47
25. Rodney Brown (USA) 65.33
26. Jorge Fernández (CUB) 65.27
27. Victor Hogan (RSA) 65.20
28. Robert Urbanek (POL) 65.15
29. Robert Harting (GER) 65.13
30. Aleksey Khudyakov (RUS) 64.73
31. Matthew Denny (AUS) 64.67(GC)
32. Gerd Kanter (EST) 64.46
33. Róbert Szikszai (HUN) 64.37
34. Giovanni Faloci (ITA) 64.19
35. Lolassonn Djouhan (FRA) 64.05

OVERVIEW WORLDWIDE OUTDOOR CHAMPIONSHIP FINALISTS OF PAST 6 YEARS

	Wch 17	OG 16	Wch 15	Wch 13
Andrius Gudzius (LTU)	69.21 (1)	60.66 (12)		
Daniel Stahl (SWE)	69.19 (2)		64.73 (5)	
Mason Finley (USA)	68.03 (3)	62.05 (11)		
Fedrick Dacres (JAM)	65.83 (4)		64.22 (7)	
Piotr Malachowski (POL)	65.24 (5)	67.55 (2)	67.40 (1)	68.36 (2)
Robert Harting (GER)	65.10 (6)			69.11 (1)
Robert Urbanek (POL)	64.15 (7)		65.18 (3)	64.32 (6)
Traves Smikle (JAM)	64.04 (8)			
Lukas Weisshaidinger (AUT)	63.76 (9)	64.95 (6)		
Apostolos Parellis (CYP)	63.17 (10)	63.72 (8)	64.55 (6)	
Simon Pettersson (SWE)	60.39 (11)			
Gerd Kanter (EST)	60.00 (12)	65.10 (5)	64.82 (4)	65.19 (3)
Christoph Harting (GER)		68.37 (1)	63.94 (8)	
Daniel Jasinski (GER)		67.05 (3)		
Martin Kupper (EST)		66.58 (4)		
Zoltan Kövagó (HUN)		64.50 (7)		
Philip Milanov (BEL)		62.22 (9)	66.90 (2)	
Axel Härstedt (SWE)		62.12 (10)		
Vikas Gowda (IND)			62.24 (9)	64.03 (7)
Benn Harradine (AUS)			62.05 (10)	
Mauricio Ortega (COL)			62.01 (11)	
Julian Wruck (AUS)			60.01 (12)	62.40 (11)
Martin Wierig (GER)				65.02 (4)
Victor Hogan (RSA)				64.35 (5)
Victor Butenko (RUS)				63.38 (8)
Jennifer Frank Casañas (ESP)				62.89 (9)
Jorge Fernández (CUB)				62.88 (10)
Mario Pestano (ESP)				61.88 (12)

OVERVIEW TOP 10 WORLD OUTDOOR RANKINGS OF PAST 5 YEARS

	2018	2017	2016	2015	2014
Daniel Stahl (SWE)	69.72 (1)	71.29 (1)	68.72 (1)		66.89 (4)
Fedrick Dacres (JAM)	69.67 (2)	68.88 (3)	68.02 (5)	66.40 (10)	66.75 (5)
Andrius Gudzius (LTU)	69.59 (3)	69.21 (2)			66.11 (10)
Lukas Weisshaidinger (AUT)	68.98 (4)	66.52 (10)		67.24 (5)	
Ehsan Hadadi (IRI)	68.85 (5)				
Reggie Jagers (USA)	68.61 (6)				
Travis Smikle (JAM)	67.72 (7)				
Christoph Harting (GER)	67.59 (8)		68.37 (2)	67.93 (3)	
Mason Finley (USA)	67.06 (9)	68.03 (4)			
Martin Wierig (GER)	66.98 (10)		67.60 (7)		66.59 (6)
Piotr Malachowski (POL)		67.68 (5)	68.15 (3)	68.29 (1)	69.28 (1)
Philip Milanov (BEL)		67.05 (6)	67.26 (9)	66.90 (7)	
Robert Urbanek (POL)		66.73 (7)			
Lois Maikel Martínez (ESP)/(CUB)		66.67 (8)			
Andrew Evans (USA)		66.61 (9)			66.37 (8)
Robert Harting (GER)			68.04 (4)		68.47 (2)
Victor Hogan (RSA)			67.62 (6)		
Sam Mattis (USA)			67.45 (8)		
Daniel Jasinski (GER)			67.16 (10)		
Jason Morgan (JAM)				68.19 (2)	
Zoltan Kövágó (HUN)				67.39 (4)	
Gerhard Mayer (AUT)				67.20 (6)	
Ben Harradine (AUS)				66.75 (8)	
Martin Kupper (EST)				66.67 (9)	
Martin Maric (CRO)					67.92 (3)
Jorge Fernández (CUB)					66.50 (7)
Gerd Kanter (EST)					66.28 (9)

WORLD RANKING ALL TIME:

1.	Jürgen Schult (GDR)	74.08 (1986)
2.	Virgilijus Alekna (LTU)	73.88 (2000)
3.	Gerd Kanter (EST)	73.38 (2006)
4.	Yuriy Dumchev (URS)	71.86 (1983)
5.	Piotr Malachowski (POL)	71.84 (2013)
6.	Róbert Fazekas (HUN)	71.70 (2002)
7.	Lars Riedel (GER)	71.50 (1997)
8.	Daniel Stahl (SWE)	71.29 (2017)
9.	John Powell (USA)	71.26 (1984)
	Rickard Bruch (SWE)	71.26 (1984)
	Imrich Bugár (TCH)	71.26 (1985)
12.	Art Burns (USA)	71.18 (1983)
13.	Wolfgang Schmidt (GDR)	71.16 (1978)
14.	Anthony Washington (USA)	71.14 (1996)
15.	Luis Delis (CUB)	71.06 (1983)
16.	Mac Wilkins (USA)	70.98 (1980)
17.	Aleksander Tammert (EST)	70.82 (2006)
18.	Robert Harting (GER)	70.66 (2012)
19.	Dmitriy Shevchenko (RUS)	70.54 (2002)
20.	Jay Silvester (USA)	70.38 (1971)
21.	Frantz Kruger (RSA)	70.32 (2002)
22.	Romas Ubartas (URS)	70.06 (1988)
23.	Juan Martinez (CUB)	70.00 (1983)
24.	Zoltán Kövagó (HUN)	69.95 (2006)
25.	John Godina (USA)	69.91 (1998)
26.	Jason Young (USA)	69.90 (2010)
27.	Gejza Valent (TCH)	69.70 (1984)
28.	Fedrick Dacres (JAM)	69.67 (2018)
29.	Knut Hjeltnes (NOR)	69.62 (1985)
	Timo Tompuri (FIN)	69.62 (2001)
31.	Andrius Gudzius (LTU)	69.59 (2018)
32.	Mario Pestano (ESP)	69.50 (2008)
33.	Al Oerter (USA)	69.46 (1980)
34.	Georgiy Kolnootchenko (URS)	69.44 (1982)
35.	Art Swarts (USA)	69.40 (1979)
36.	Mike Buncic (USA)	69.36 (1991)
37.	Ehsan Hadadi (IRI)	69.32 (2008)
38.	Vladimir Dubrovshchik (BLR)	69.28 (2000)
39.	Ken Stadel (USA)	69.26 (1979)
40.	Lukas Weisshaidinger (AUT)	68.98 (2018)
41.	Adam Setliff (USA)	68.94 (2001)
42.	Ian Waltz (USA)	68.91 (2006)
43.	Jean-Claude Retel (FRA)	68.90 (2002)
44.	Volodimir Zinchenko (URS)	68.88 (1988)
45.	Jarred Rome (USA)	68.76 (2011)

Hammer Throw Men

EUROPEAN CHAMPIONSHIPS 2018: 7-8-2018:

1. Wojciech Nowicki (POL) (76.03) 80.12
2. Pawel Fajdek (POL) (77.86) 78.69
3. Bence Halasz (HUN) (76.81) 77.36
4. Pavel Bareisha (BLR) (76.47) 77.02
5. Eivind Henriksen (NOR) (75.14) 76.86
6. Ivan Tikhon (BLR) (74.67) 75.79
7. Hlib Piskunov (UKR) (74.18) 74.62
8. Serghei Marghiev (MDA) (75.10) 74.47
9. Mihail Anastasákis (GRE) (75.61) 73.33
10. Nick Miller (GBR) (73.79) 73.16
11. Marcel Lomnický (SVK) (75.08) 72.74
12. Denis Lukyanov (ANA) (73.19) 71.71

----

13. Marco Linghua (ITA) 73.07
14. Aleksy Sokirskiy (ANA) 72.97
15. Javier Cienfuegos (ESP) 72.76
16. Quentin Bigot (FRA) 72.73
17. Esref Apak (TUR) 72.70
18. Hleb Dudarau (BLR) 72.19
19. Özkan Baltaci (TUR) 71.55
20. Henri Liipola (FIN) 71.34
21. Simone Falloni (ITA) 71.03
22. Denzel Comenentia (NED) 70.70
23. Volodymyr Myslyvchuk (UKR) 70.59
24. Chris Bennett (GBR) 70.57
25. Serhiy Reheda (UKR) 70.39
26. Bence Pásztor (HUN) 69.66
27. Anders Eriksson (SWE) 69.19
28. David Söderberg (FIN) 69.18
29. Nejc Plesko (SLO) 68.29
30. Pedro Martín (ESP) 67.56

WORLD RANKING 2018:

1. Wojciech Nowicki (POL) 81.85(Sze
2. Pawel Fajdek (POL) 81.14(Sze
3. Nick Miller (GBR) 80.26(GC
4. Bence Halász (HUN) 79.57
5. Esref Apak (TUR) 78.59
6. Dilshod Nazarov (TJK) 78.18
7. Siarhei Kalamoyets (BLR) 78.13
8. Hleb Dudarau (BLE) 78.04
9. Mostafa Elgamel (EGY) 77.71
10. Pavel Bareisha (BLR) 77.37
11. Ashraf Amgad El Seify (QAT) 77.04
12. Denis Lukyanov (RUS) 77.02
13. Marcel Lomnický (SVK) 77.00

OVERVIEW WORLDWIDE OUTDOOR CHAMPIONSHIP FINALISTS OF PAST 6 YEARS

	Wch 17	OG 16	Wch 15	Wch 13
Pawel Fajdek (POL)	79.81 (1)		80.88 (1)	81.97 (1)
Valeriy Pronkin (RUS)	78.16 (2)			
Wojciech Nowicki (POL)	78.03 (3)	77.73 (3)	78.55 (3)	
Quentin Bigot (FRA)	77.67 (4)			
Aleksei Sokyrskii (RUS)	77.50 (5)			
Nick Miller (GBR)	77.31 (6)		72.94 (11)	
Dilshod Nazarov (TJK)	77.22 (7)	78.68 (1)	78.55 (2)	78.31 (5)
Serghei Marghiev (MDA)	75.87 (8)	74.14 (10)		
Pavel Bareisha (BLR)	75.86 (9)			
Martco Linghua (ITA)	75.13 (10)			
Bence Halász (HUN)	74.45 (11)			
Özkan Baltaci (TUR)	74.39 (12)			
Ivan Tsikhan (BLR)		77.79 (2)		
Diego del Real (MEX)		76.05 (4)		
Marcel Lomnicky (SVK)		75.97 (5)	75.79 (8)	77.57 (8)
Ashraf Amgad Elseify (QAT)		75.46 (6)	74.09 (9)	
Krisztian Pars (HUN)		75.28 (7)	77.32 (4)	80.30 (2)
David Soderberg (FIN)		74.61 (8)	76.92 (6)	
Siarhei Kalamoyets (BLR)		74.22 (9)		
Yevhen Vynohradov (UKR)		74.11 (11)		
Wagner Domingos (BRA)		72.28 (12)		
Sergej Litvinov (RUS)			77.24 (5)	75.90 (11)
Mostafa El Gamel (EGY)			76.81 (7)	
Tuomas Seppänen (FIN)			73.18 (10)	
Roberto Janet (CUB)			72.50 (12)	
Lukás Melich (CZE)				79.36 (3)
Primoz Kozmus (SLO)				79.22 (4)
Koji Murofushi (JPN)				78.03 (6)
Nicola Vizzoni (ITA)				77.61 (7)
Szymon Ziólkowski (POL)				76.84 (9)
Markus Esser (GER)				76.25 (10)
Yury Shayunou (BLR)				73.68 (12)

OVERVIEW TOP 10 WORLD OUTDOOR RANKINGS OF PAST 5 YEARS

	2018	2017	2016	2015	2014
Wojciech Nowicki (POL)	81.85 (1)	80.47 (2)	78.36 (8)	78.71 (7)	
Pawel Fajdek (POL)	81.14 (2)	83.44 (1)	82.47 (1)	83.93 (1)	83.48 (1)
Nick Miller (GBR)	80.26 (3)				
Bence Halász (HUN)	79.57 (4)	78.85 (4)			
Esref Apak (TUR)	78.59 (5)	78.00 (6)			
Dilshod Nazarov (TJK)	78.18 (6)	77.81 (9)	78.87 (3)	79.36 (4)	80.62 (4)
Siarhei Kalamoyets (BLR)	78.13 (7)				
Hleb Dudarau (BLR)	78.04 (8)				
Mostafa El Gamel (EGY)	77.71 (9)			79.90 (3)	81.27 (3)
Pavel Bareisha (BLR)	77.37 (10)	78.04 (5)	78.60 (5)		
Valeriy Pronkin (RUS)		79.32 (3)			
Marcel Lomnický (SVK)		77.92 (7)			79.16 (7)
Quentin Bigot (FRA)		77.87 (8)			
Mihail Anastasákis (GRE)		77.72 (10)			
Ivan Tsikhan (BLR)			80.04 (2)		
Wagner Domingos (BRA)			78.63 (4)		
Serghei Marghiev (MDA)			78.48 (6)	78.72 (6)	78.27 (9)
Hassan Mohamed Mahmoud (EGY)			78.39 (7)		
Ashraf Amgad Elseify (QAT)			78.19 (9)		
Oleksandr Drygol (ISR)			77.70 (10)		
Krisztián Pars (HUN)				79.91 (2)	82.69 (2)
Yevhen Vynohradov (UKR)				79.25 (5)	
Dzmitry Marshin (AZE)				78.52 (8)	
Marco Linghua (ITA)				78.29 (9)	
Suhrob Khodjaev (UZB)				78.22 (10)	
Sergej Litvinov (RUS)					79.35 (5)
Pavel Kryvitski (BLR)					79.21 (6)
Szymon Ziólkowski (POL)					78.41 (8)
Olexiy Sokyrskiyy (UKR)					77.86 (10)

WORLD RANKING ALL TIME:

1.	Yuriy Sedykh (URS)	86.74 (1986)
2.	Sergey Litvinov (URS)	86.04 (1986)
3.	Vadim Devyatovskiy (BLR)	84.90 (2005)
4.	Koji Murofushi (JPN)	84.86 (2003)
5.	Igor Astapkovich (BLR)	84.62 (1992)
6.	Ivan Tikhon (BLR)	84.51 (2008)
7.	Igor Nikulin (URS)	84.48 (1990)
8.	Juri Tamm (URS)	84.40 (1984)
9.	Adrián Annus (HUN)	84.19 (2003)
10.	Pawel Fajdek (POL)	83.93 (2015)
11.	Tibor Gécsek (HUN)	83.68 (1998)
12.	Andrey Abduvaliyev (URS)	83.46 (1990)
13.	Aleksey Zagorniy (RUS)	83.43 (2002)
14.	Ralf Haber (GDR)	83.40 (1988)
15.	Szymon Ziólkowski (POL)	83.38 (2001)
16.	Olli-Pekka Karjalainen (FIN)	83.30 (2004)
17.	Heinz Weis (GER)	83.04 (1997)
18.	Balázs Kiss (HUN)	83.00 (1998)
19.	Karsten Kobs (GER)	82.78 (1999)
20.	Krisztián Pars (HUN)	82.69 (2014)
21.	Günther Rodehau (GDR)	82.64 (1985)
22.	Sergey Kirmasov (RUS)	82.62 (1998)
	Andriy Skvaruk (UKR)	82.62 (2002)
24.	Primoz Kozmus (SLO)	82.58 (2009)
25.	Vasiliy Sidorenko (RUS)	82.54 (1992)
26.	Lance Deal (USA)	82.52 (1996)
27.	Plamen Minev (BUL)	82.40 (1991)
28.	Gilles Dupray (FRA)	82.38 (2000)
29.	Ilya Konovalov (RUS)	82.28 (2003)
30.	Benjaminas Viluckis (URS)	82.24 (1986)
	Vyacheslav Korovin (URS)	82.24 (1987)
32.	Vladislav Piskunov (UKR)	82.23 (2002)
33.	Holger Klose (GER)	82.22 (1998)
34.	Vitaliy Alisevich (URS)	82.16 (1988)
35.	Ivan Tanev (BUL)	82.08 (1988)
36.	Sergey Alay (BLR)	82.00 (1992)
37.	Jud Logan (USA)	81.88 (1988)
38.	Wojciech Nowicki (POL)	81.85 (2018)
39.	Libor Charfreitag (SVK)	81.81 (2003)
40.	Christophe Epalle (FRA)	81.79 (2000)
41.	Christopher Sahner (FRG)	81.78 (1988)
42.	Aleksandr Seleznyov (RUS)	81.70 (1993)
43.	Oleksandr Krikun (UKR)	81.66 (2004)
44.	Enrico Sgrulletti (ITA)	81.64 (1997)
45.	Sergey Gavrilov (RUS)	81.56 (1996)
	Zsolt Németh (HUN)	81.56 (1999)

Shot Put Men

EUROPEAN CHAMPIONSHIPS 2018: 7-8-2018:

1.	Michal Haratyk (POL)	(20.59)	21.72
2.	Konrad Bukowiecki (POL)		21.66
3.	David Storl (GER)	(20.63)	21.41
4.	Tomás Stanek (CZE)		21.16
5.	Aleksandr Lesnoy (ANA)	(20.47)	21.04
6.	Bob Bertemes (LUX)		21.00
7.	Stipe Zunic (CRO)	(20.61)	20.73
8.	Maksim Afonin (ANA)	(20.33)	20.68
9.	Tsanko Arnaudov (POR)		20.33
10.	Aliaksei Nichypar (BLR)		20.27
11.	Nikólaos Skarvélis (GRE)	(20.24)	20.11
12.	Mesud Pezer (BIH)	(20.16)	19.91

13.	Jakub Szyszkowski (POL)	19.67
14.	Francisco Belo (POR)	19.66
15.	Ihor Musiyenko (UKR)	19.61
16.	Marcus Thomsen (NOR)	19.59
17.	Frederic Dagee (FRA)	19.56
18.	Carlos Tobalina (ESP)	19.41
19.	Georgi Ivanov (BUL)	19.40
20.	Hamza Alic (BIH)	19.34
21.	Tomas Djurovic (MNT)	19.33
22.	Filip Mihaljevic (CRO)	19.32
23.	Andrei Gag (ROM)	19.26
24.	Giorgi Mujaridze (GEO)	19.18
25.	Blaz Zupancic (SLO)	18.83
26.	Osman Özdeveci (TUR)	18.77
27.	Kemal Mesic (BIH)	18.70
28.	Arttu Kangas (FIN)	18.17
29.	Leonardo Fabbri (ITA)	18.04
	Asmir Kolasinac (SRB)	NM

WORLD RANKING 2018:

1.	Tomas Walsh (NZL)	22.67
2.	Ryan Crouser (USA)	22.53(Eug)
3.	Darrell Hill (USA)	22.40(Zü)
4.	Michal Haratyk (POL)	22.08(Ost)
5.	Darlan Romani (BRA)	22.00
6.	Tomás Stanek (CZE)	21.87(Zü)
7.	Konrad Bukowiecki (POL)	21.66(ECh)
8.	Curtis Jensen (USA)	21.63
9.	David Storl (GER)	21.62
10.	Aleksandr Lesnoy (ANA)	21.58
11.	Stipe Zunic (CRO)	21.36
12.	Filip Mihaljevic (CRO)	21.33
13.	Chukwuebuka Enekwechi (NGR)	21.22
14.	Joe Kovacs (USA)	21.02(Ost)
	O'Dayne Richards (JAM)	21.02
	Tim Nedow (CAN)	21.02(NAC)
17.	Bob Bertemes (LUX)	21.00(ECh)
18.	Ryan Whiting (USA)	20.99
19.	Payton Otterdahl (USA)	20.96
20.	Ashinia Miller (JAM)	20.93
21.	Denzel Comenentia (NED)	20.88(Kno)
22.	Francisco Belo (POR)	20.86
23.	Franck Elemba (COD)	20.81
24.	Maksim Afonin (ANA)	20.80
25.	Mesud Pezer (BIH)	20.79
26.	Damien Birkinhead (AUS)	20.77(GC)
	Josh Olayinka Awotunde (NGR)	20.77(Kno)
28.	Tejinderpal Singh Toor (IND)	20.75(Jak)
29.	Orazio Cremona (RSA)	20.71(Pre)
30.	Jakub Szyszkowski (POL)	20.68(Pra)
31.	Jonathan Jones (USA)	20.65
	Tsanko Arnaudov (POR)	20.65
33.	Andrzej Gudro (POL)	20.63
	Eldred Henry (IVB)	20.63(NAC)
35.	Asmir Kolasinac (SRB)	20.48
36.	Hamza Alic (BIH)	20.45
37.	Mostafa Amr Hassan (EGY)	20.44(NCA)
38.	Aliaksei Nichypar (BLR)	20.43
39.	Joshua Freeman (USA)	20.42(USC)
40.	Jordan Geist (USA)	20.41
	Garrett Appier (USA)	20.41
	Adrian Piperi (USA)	20.41
43.	Jared Kern (USA)	20.39
44.	David Pless (USA)	20.37

WORLD INDOOR CHAMPIONSHIPS: 3-3-2018:

1. Tomas Walsh (NZL) — 22.31
2. David Storl (GER) — 21.44
3. Tomás Stanek (CZE) — 21.44
4. Darlan Romani (BRA) — 21.37
5. Mesud Pezer (BIH) — 21.15
6. Darrell Hill (USA) — 21.06
7. Ryan Whiting (USA) — 21.03
8. Konrad Bukowiecki (POL) — 20.99
9. Tim Nedow (CAN) — 20.82
10. Michal Haratyk (POL) — 20.69
11. O'Dayne Richards (JAM) — 19.93
12. Tsanko Arnaudov (POR) — 19.93
13. Maksim Afonin (ANA) — 19.84
14. Chukwuebuka Enekwechi (NGR) — 19.78
15. Asmir Kolasinac (SRB) — 19.34
16. Damien Birkinhead (AUS) — 19.11

WORLD INDOOR RANKING 2018:

1. Tomas Walsh (NZL) — 22.31
2. Tomas Stanek (CZE) — 22.17
3. Konrad Bukowiecki (POL) — 22.00
4. Michal Haratyk (POL) — 21.47
5. Jordan Geist (USA) — 21.45
6. David Storl (GER) — 21.44
7. Maksim Afonin (RUS) — 21.39
8. Darlan Romani (BRA) — 21.37
9. Josh Olayinka Awotunde (NGR) — 21.33
10. Tsanko Arnaudov (POR) — 21.27
11. Mesud Pezer (BIH) — 21.15
12. Stipe Zunic (CRO) — 21.13
13. Tyson Jones (USA) — 21.09
14. Darrell Hill (USA) — 21.06
15. Aleksandr Lesnoy (ANA) — 21.05
16. Ryan Whiting (USA) — 21.03
17. Chukwuebuka Enekwechi (NGR) — 20.89
18. Mostafa Amr Hassan (EGY) — 20.86
19. Tim Nedow (CAN) — 20.82
20. Nicholas Vena (USA) — 20.68
21. Andrei Marius Gag (ROM) — 20.60
22. Ashinia Miller (JAM) — 20.49
23. Denzel Comenentia (NED) — 20.44
24. Aliaksei Nichypar (BLR) — 20.40
25. Frederic Dagee (FRA) — 20.36
26. Borja Vivas (ESP) — 20.27
27. Curtis Jensen (USA) — 20.19
28. Hamza Alic (BIH) — 20.18
29. Nicholas Scarvelis (GRE) — 20.15
30. Patrick Müller (GER) — 20.14
31. Carlos Tobalina (ESP) — 20.12
32. Asmir Kolasinac (SRB) — 20.11
33. Austin Droogsma (USA) — 20.10

OVERVIEW WORLDWIDE OUTDOOR CHAMPIONSHIP FINALISTS OF PAST 6 YEARS

	Wch 17	OG 16	Wch 15	Wch 13
Tomas Walsh (NZL)	22.03 (1)	21.36 (3)	21.58 (4)	
Joe Kovacs (USA)	21.66 (2)	21.78 (2)	21.93 (1)	
Stipe Zunic (CRO)	21.46 (3)	20.04 (11)		
Tomás Stanek (CZE)	21.41 (4)			
Michal Haratyk (POL)	21.41 (5)			
Ryan Crouser (USA)	21.20 (6)	22.52 (1)		
Ryan Whiting (USA)	21.09 (7)			21.57 (2)
Konrad Bukowiecki (POL)	20.89 (8)	NM (12)		
Jacko Gill (NZL)	20.82 (9)	20.50 (9)	20.11 (8)	
David Storl (GER)	20.80 (10)	20.64 (7)	21.74 (2)	21.73 (1)
Darrell Hill (USA)	20.79 (11)			
Andrei Gag (ROM)	19.96 (12)			
Franck Elemba (CGO)		21.20 (4)		
Darlan Romani (BRA)		21.02 (5)		
Tomasz Majewski (POL)		20.72 (6)	20.82 (6)	20.98 (6)
O'Dayne Richards (JAM)		20.64 (8)	21.69 (3)	
Damien Birkinhead (AUS)		20.45 (10)		
Reese Hoffa (USA)			21.00 (5)	21.12 (4)
Asmir Kolasinac (SRB)			20.71 (7)	19.96 (10)
Germán Lauro (ARG)			19.70 (9)	20.40 (7)
Jan Marcell (CZE)			19.69 (10)	
Inderjeet Singh (IND)			19.52 (11)	
Christian Cantwell (USA)			dns (12)	
Dylan Armstrong (CAN)				21.34 (3)
Ladislav Prásil (CZE)				20.98 (5)
Georgi Ivanov (BUL)				20.39 (8)
Cory Martin (USA)				20.09 (9)
Antonin Zalský (CZE)				19.54 (11)
Martin Stasek (CZE)				19.10 (12)

OVERVIEW WORLDWIDE INDOOR CHAMPIONSHIP FINALISTS OF PAST 5 YEARS

	Wch 18	Wch 16	Wch 14
Tomas Walsh (NZL)	22.31 (1)	21.78 (1)	21.26 (3)
David Storl (GER)	21.44 (2)		21.79 (2)
Tomas Stanek (CZE)	21.44 (3)		
Darlan Romani (BRA)	21.37 (4)		
Mesud Pezer (BIH)	21.15 (5)		
Darrell Hill (USA)	21.06 (6)		
Ryan Whiting (USA)	21.03 (7)		22.05 (1)
Konrad Bukowiecki (POL)	20.99 (8)	20.53 (4)	
Tim Nedow (CAN)	20.82 (9)	20.23 (7)	
Michal Haratyk (POL)	20.69 (10)		
O'Dayne Richards (JAM)	19.93 (11)		
Tsanko Arnaudov (POR)	19.03 (12)		
Andrei Gag (ROM)		20.89 (2)	
Filip Mihaljevic (CRO)		20.87 (3)	
Jonathan Jones (USA)		20.31 (5)	
Germán Lauro (ARG)		20.24 (6)	20.50 (6)
Tobias Dahm (GER)		20.22 (8)	
Jacko Gill (NZL)		19.93 (9)	
Carlos Tobalina (ESP)		19.86 (10)	
Borja Vivas (ESP)		19.85 (11)	
Stephen Mozia (NGR)		19.84 (12)	
Tomasz Majewski (POL)			21.04 (4)
Georgi Ivanov (BUL)			21.02 (5)
Orazio Cremona (RSA)			20.49 (7)
Aleksandr Lesnoi (RUS)			20.16 (8)

OVERVIEW TOP 10 WORLD OUTDOOR RANKINGS OF PAST 5 YEARS

	2018	2017	2016	2015	2014
Tomas Walsh (NZL)	22.67 (1)	22.14 (4)	22.21 (2)	21.62 (5)	
Ryan Crouser (USA)	22.53 (2)	22.65 (1)	22.52 (1)		21.27 (10
Darrell Hill (USA)	22.40 (3)	22.44 (3)	21.63 (5)		
Michal Haratyk (POL)	22.08 (4)	21.88 (7)	21.23 (9)		
Darlan Romani (BRA)	22.00 (5)	21.82 (9)			
Tomás Stanek (CZE)	21.87 (6)	22.01 (5)	21.26 (8)		
Konrad Bukowiecki (POL)	21.66 (7)				
Curtis Jensen (USA)	21.63 (8)				
David Storl (GER)	21.62 (9)	21.87 (8)	21.39 (7)	22.20 (2)	21.97 (2)
Alexandr Lesnoi (RUS)	21.58 (10)				21.40 (7)
Joe Kovacs (USA)		22.57 (2)	22.13 (3)	22.56 (1)	22.03 (1)
O'Dayne Richards (JAM)		21.96 (6)		21.69 (3)	21.61 (5)
Ryan Whiting (USA)		21.65 (10)		21.37 (8)	21.31 (9)
Stephen Mozia (NGR)			21.76 (4)		
Kurt Roberts (USA)			21.40 (6)		21.47 (6)
Damien Birkinhead (AUS)			21.21 (10)		
Christian Cantwell (USA)				21.64 (4)	21.85 (4)
Asmir Kolasinac (SRB)				21.58 (6)	
Jordan Clarke (USA)				21.49 (7)	21.37 (8)
Thomas Schmitt (GER)				21.35 (9)	
Reese Hoffa (USA)				21.30 (10)	21.88 (3)

OVERVIEW TOP 10 WORLD INDOOR RANKINGS OF PAST 5 YEARS

	2018	2017	2016	2015	2014
Tomas Walsh (NZL)	22.31 (1)		21.78 (1)		21.26 (5)
Tomás Stanek (CZE)	22.17 (2)	21.43 (2)	21.30 (6)	20.94 (5)	
Konrad Bukowiecki (POL)	22.00 (3)	21.97 (1)			
Michal Haratyk (POL)	21.47 (4)		21.35 (4)		
Jordan Geist (USA)	21.45 (5)	20.82 (10)			
David Storl (GER)	21.44 (6)	21.37 (3)		21.26 (2)	21.79 (2)
Maksim Afonin (RUS)	21.39 (7)				
Darlan Romani (BRA)	21.37 (8)				
Josh Olayinka Awotunde (NGR)	21.33 (9)				
Tsanko Arnaudov (POR)	21.27 (10)	21.08 (5)			
Mostafa Amr Hassan (EGY)		21.30 (4)			
Stipe Zunic (CRO)		21.04 (6)		21.11 (4)	
Asmir Kolasinac (SRB)		20.87 (7)		20.91 (6)	
Franck Elemba (COD)		20.86 (8)			
Ladislav Prasil (CZE)		20.84 (9)		20.66 (10)	20.82 (10)
Ryan Crouser (USA)			21.73 (2)	21.14 (3)	21.23 (6)
Kurt Roberts (USA)			21.57 (3)		21.50 (3)
Tim Nedow (CAN)			21.33 (5)		
Stephen Mozia (NGR)			21.11 (7)		
Reese Hoffa (USA)			21.02 (8)		
Andrei Gag (ROM)			20.89 (9)		
Filip Mihaljevic (CRO)			20.87 (10)		
Ryan Whiting (USA)				21.80 (1)	22.23 (1)
Christian Cantwell (USA)				20.83 (7)	
Jan Marcell (CZE)				20.71 (8)	
Alexandr Lesnoi (RUS)				20.70 (9)	
Borja Vivas (ESP)				20.66 (10)	
Joe Kovacs (USA)					21.46 (4)
Germán Lauro (ARG)					21.04 (7)
Tomasz Majewski (POL)					21.04 (7)
Georgi Ivanov (BUL)					21.02 (9)

WORLD RANKING ALL TIME OUTDOOR:

1.	Randy Barnes (USA)	23.12 (1990)
2.	Ulf Timmermann (GDR)	23.06 (1988)
3.	Alessandro Andrei (ITA)	22.91 (1987)
4.	Brian Oldfield (USA)	22.86 (1975)
5.	Werner Günthör (SUI)	22.75 (1988)
6.	Kevin Toth (USA)	22.67 (2003)
	Tomas Walsh (NZL)	22.67 (2018)
8.	Ryan Crouser (USA)	22.65 (2017)
9.	Udo Beyer (GDR)	22.64 (1986)
10.	Joe Kovacs (USA)	22.57 (2017)
11.	Christian Cantwell (USA)	22.54 (2004)
12.	John Brenner (USA)	22.52 (1987)
13.	Adam Nelson (USA)	22.51 (2002)
14.	Darrell Hill (USA)	22.44 (2017)
15.	Reese Hoffa (USA)	22.43 (2007)
16.	Ryan Whiting (USA)	22.28 (2013)
17.	Sergey Smirnov (URS)	22.24 (1986)
18.	Dylan Armstrong (CAN)	22.21 (2011)
19.	John Godina (USA)	22.20 (2005)
	David Storl (GER)	22.20 (2015)
21.	Sergey Gavryushin (URS)	22.10 (1986)
	Cory Martin (USA)	22.10 (2010)
23.	Sergey Kasnauskas (URS)	22.09 (1984)
24.	Michal Haratyk (POL)	22.08 (2018)
25.	Dave Laut (USA)	22.02 (1982)
26.	Tomás Stanek (CZE)	22.01 (2017)
27.	Aleksandr Baryshnikov (URS)	22.00 (1976)
	Darlan Romani (BRA)	22.00 (2018)
29.	Gregg Tafralis (USA)	21.98 (1992)
30.	Janus Robberts (RSA)	21.97 (2001)
31.	Mikhail Kostin (URS)	21.96 (1986)
	O'Dayne Richards (JAM)	21.96 (2017)
33.	Tomasz Majewski (POL)	21.95 (2009)
34.	Remigius Machura (TCH)	21.93 (1987)
35.	Carl Myerscough (GBR)	21.92 (2003)
36.	C.J. Hunter (USA)	21.86 (2000)
37.	Terry Albritton (USA)	21.85 (1976)
38.	Al Feuerbach (USA)	21.82 (1973)
	Andy Bloom (USA)	21.82 (2000)
40.	Yuriy Bilonoh (UKR)	21.81 (2000)
41.	Randy Matson (USA)	21.78 (1967)
	Daniel Taylor (USA)	21.78 (2009)
43.	Dragan Peric (SRB)	21.77 (1998)
44.	Michael Carter (USA)	21.76 (1984)
	Stephen Mozia (NGR)	21.76 (1984)

WORLD RANKING ALL TIME INDOOR:

1.	Randy Barnes (USA)	22.66 (1989)
2.	Ulf Timmermann (GDR)	22.55 (1989)
3.	Adam Nelson (USA)	22.40 (2008)
4.	Tomas Walsh (NZL)	22.31 (2018)
5.	Werner Günthör (SUI)	22.26 (1987)
6.	Ryan Whiting (USA)	22.23 (2014)
7.	Christian Cantwell (USA)	22.18 (2008)
8.	Tomás Stanek (CZE)	22.17 (2018)
9.	Reese Hoffa (USA)	22.11 (2006)
10.	Mika Halvari (FIN)	22.09 (2000)
11.	George Woods (USA)	22.02 (1974)
12.	Konrad Bukowiecki (POL)	22.00 (2018)
13.	David Storl (GER)	21.88 (2012)
14.	Oleksandr Bagach (UKR)	21.83 (1999)
	John Godina (USA)	21.83 (2005)
16.	Remigius Machura (TCH)	21.79 (1985)
17.	Mike Stulce (USA)	21.77 (1993)
18.	Ryan Crouser (USA)	21.73 (2016)
19.	Tomasz Majewski (POL)	21.72 (2012)
20.	Kevin Toth (USA)	21.70 (2003)
21.	Brian Oldfield (USA)	21.64 (1981)
22.	Joachim Olsen (DEN)	21.63 (2004)
	Dylan Armstrong (CAN)	21.63 (2011)
24.	Andy Bloom (USA)	21.60 (2000)
25.	Daniel Taylor (USA)	21.57 (2007)
	Mikulas Konopka (SVK)	21.57 (2007)
	Kurt Roberts (USA)	21.57 (2016)
28.	Jim Doehring (USA)	21.56 (1993)
29.	Alessandro Andrei (ITA)	21.54 (1987)
30.	Terry Albritton (USA)	21.50 (1977)
31.	Carl Myerscough (GBR)	21.49 (2003)
32.	Oliver-Sven Buder (GER)	21.47 (1998)
	Janus Robberts (RSA)	21.47 (2001)
	Michal Haratyk (POL)	21.47 (2018)
35.	Kevin Akins (USA)	21.46 (1983)
	Sergey Kasnauskas (URS)	21.46 (1984)
	Yuriy Bilonoh (UKR)	21.46 (2003)
	Joe Kovacs (USA)	21.46 (2014)
39.	Jordan Geist (USA)	21.45 (2018)
40.	Al Feuerbach (USA)	21.44 (1974)
	C.J. Hunter (USA)	21.44 (1999)
	Ralf Bartels (GER)	21.44 (2010)
43.	Sergey Smirnov (URS)	21.40 (1987)
44.	Udo Beyer (GDR)	21.39 (1985)
	Mikhail Kostin (URS)	21.39 (1988)

4 x 100 m Men

EUROPEAN CHAMPIONSHIPS 2018: 12-8-2018:

1.	GBR	(37.84)	37.80

Ujah/Hughes/Gemili/Aikines-Aryeetey

2.	TUR	(38.30)	37.98

Barnes/Harvey/Hekimoglu/Guliyev

3.	NED	(38.30)	38.03

Garia/Martina/Paulina/Burnet

4.	FRA	(38.62)	38.51

Zeze/Rene/Dutamby/Fall

5.	UKR	(38.86)	38.71

Sokolov/Ibrahimov/Suprun/Smelyk

6.	FIN	(39.11)	38.92

Rantala/Ahlfors/Lehtonen/Purola

7.	POR	(39.09)	39.07

Lopes/Antunes/Curvelo/Nascimento

	CZE	(38.94)	dns

Stromsik/Veleba/Jirka/Maslák

9.	ESP	39.12

Ike/Retamal/D. Rodriguez/A. Rodriguez

10.	SUI	39.13

Somasundaram/Eicki/Clivaz/Wilson

11.	GRE	39.49

Steryioulis/Nifadopoulos/Trivizas/Tsakonas

12.	ROM	39.63

Homiuc/Terpezan/Neagoe/Rezmives

	SWE	dnf

Leal/Tarnhuvud/Svensson/Darkwah

	GER	dnf

Kranz/Domogala/Reus/Jakubczyk

	ITA	dsq

Cattaneo/Desalu/Manenti/Tortu

	POL	dsq

Hampel/Olszewski/Kopec/Slowikowski

WORLD RANKING 2018:

1.	GBR	37.61(Lon)
2.	JPN	37.85(Osa)
3.	TUR	37.98(ECh)
4.	NED	38.03(ECh)
5.	USA	38.08(Kno)
6.	RSA	38.24(GC)
7.	JAM	38.35(GC)
8.	BAR	38.41
9.	CAN	38.42
10.	ITA	38.49
11.	FRA	38.51(ECh)
12.	NGR	38.52(GC)
13.	GER	38.56(WC)
14.	AUS	38.58(GC)
15.	DOM	38.71
	UKR	38.71(ECh)
17.	CHN	38.72(Osa)
18.	POL	38.77
	INA	38.77(Jak)
20.	BRA	38.78
21.	TTO	38.89
22.	FIN	38.92(ECh)
23.	CZE	38.94(ECh)
24.	COL	38.97
25.	TPE	38.98(Jak)
26.	VEN	39.03
	CUB	39.03
28.	POR	39.07(ECh)
29.	SRI	39.08(GC)
30.	KOR	39.10
31.	ESP	39.12(ECh)
32.	SUI	39.13(ECh)

OVERVIEW WORLDWIDE OUTDOOR CHAMPIONSHIP FINALISTS OF PAST 6 YEARS

	Wch 17	OG 16	Wch 15	Wch 13
GBR	37.47 (1)	37.98 (5)		dsq
USA	37.52 (2)	dsq	37.38 (1)	37.66 (2)
JPN	38.04 (3)	37.60 (2)	38.20 (3)	38.39 (6)
CHN	38.34 (4)	37.90 (4)		
FRA	38.48 (5)		38.81 (5)	
CAN	38.59 (6)	37.64 (3)		37.92 (3)
TUR	38.73 (7)			
JAM	dnf (8)	37.27 (1)	37.68 (2)	37.36 (1)
BRA		38.41 (6)	38.63 (4)	
TTO		dsq	38.92 (7)	38.57 (7)
SKN			38.85 (6)	
GER			39.40 (8)	38.04 (4)
NED				38.37 (5)

OVERVIEW TOP 10 WORLD OUTDOOR RANKINGS OF PAST 5 YEARS

	2018	2017	2016	2015	2014
GBR	37.61 (1)	37.47 (1)	37.78 (5)	38.20 (8)	37.93 (2)
JPN	37.85 (2)	38.04 (5)	37.60 (2)	38.20 (8)	38.34 (8)
TUR	37.98 (3)	38.44 (9)	38.30 (10)		
NED	38.03 (4)				
USA	38.08 (5)	37.52 (2)	37.65 (4)	37.38 (2)	
RSA	38.24 (6)	38.47 (10)			38.35 (9)
JAM	38.35 (7)	37.95 (3)	37.27 (1)	37.36 (1)	37.58 (1)
BAR	38.41 (8)				
CAN	38.42 (9)	38.15 (6)	37.64 (3)	38.03 (6)	38.41 (10)
ITA	38.49 (10)				
FRA		38.03 (4)		37.88 (3)	38.33 (7)
CHN		38.16 (7)	37.82 (6)	37.92 (4)	37.99 (3)
GER		38.30 (8)	38.22 (9)	38.15 (7)	38.09 (5)
TTO			37.96 (7)	38.32 (10)	38.04 (4)
BRA			38.19 (8)		38.10 (6)
ANT				38.01 (5)	

WORLD RANKING ALL TIME:

1.	JAM	36.84 (2012)
2.	USA	37.38 (2015)
3.	GBR	37.47 (2017)
4.	JPN	37.60 (2016)
5.	TTO	37.62 (2009)
6.	CAN	37.64 (2016)
7.	FRA	37.79 (1990)
8.	CHN	37.82 (2016)
9.	BRA	37.90 (2000)
10.	NGR	37.94 (1997)
11.	TUR	37.98 (2018)
12.	CUB	38.00 (1992)
13.	ANT	38.01 (2015)
14.	URS	38.02 (1987)
	GER	38.02 (2012)
16.	NED	38.03 (2018)
17.	GHA	38.12 (1997)
18.	AUS	38.17 (1995)
	ITA	38.17 (2010)
20.	RSA	38.24 (2018)
21.	GDR	38.29 (1982)
22.	POL	38.31 (2012)
23.	SKN	38.41 (2012)
	BAR	38.41 (2018)
25.	AHO	38.45 (2005)
26.	ESP	38.46 (2013)
27.	HKG	38.47 (2012)

4 x 400 m Men

EUROPEAN CHAMPIONSHIPS 2018: 11-8-2018:

1.	BEL	(3.02.55)	2.59.47

D. Borlée/J. Borlée/Sacoor/K. Borlée

2.	GBR	(3.01.62)	3.00.36

Yousif/Cowan/Hudson-Smith/Rooney

3.	ESP	(3.04.62)	3.00.78

Husillos/Bua/Garcia/Hortelano

4.	FRA	(3.01.67)	3.02.08

Vaillant/Hanne/Atine/Jordier
(Anne/Hanne/Atine/Jordier)

5.	POL	(3.02.75)	3.02.27

Zalewski/Omelko/Krawczuk/Duszynski

6.	ITA	(3.04.08)	3.02.34

Scotti/Tricca/Re/Galvan

7.	CZE	(3.02.52)	3.03.00

Tesar/Maslák/Sorm/Snejdr
(Sorm/Desensky/Müller/Maslák)

8.	GER	(3.03.37)	3.04.69

Schneider/Junker/Dammermann/Trefz

9.	NED	3.04.93

Van Diepen/Bonevacia/Angela/Smidt

10.	UKR	3.05.95

Pozdnyakov/Danylenko/Senyk/Butrym

11.	IRL	3.06.55

O'Donnell/Arrey/Reid/Barr

12.	CRO	3.07.80

Ruzic/Cukman/Cepus/Kovacic

13.	TUR	3.07.83

Tütünci/Can/Ozyürek/Altintas

14.	ROM	3.10.08

Radu/Trofin/Nastase/Parge

	SWE	dsq

Bengtström/Martinsson/Forsman/Groth

	SUI	dsq

Gehrig/Petrucciani/Burgunder/Devantay

WORLD RANKING 2018:

1.	BEL	2.59.47(ECh)
2.	USA	2.59.78(WC)
3.	GBR	3.00.36(ECh)
4.	QAT	3.00.56(Jak)
5.	ESP	3.00.78(ECh)
6.	FRA	3.01.67(ECh)
7.	BOT	3.01.78(GC)
8.	IND	3.01.85(Jak)
9.	BAH	3.01.92(GC)
10.	JPN	3.01.94(Jak)
11.	JAM	3.01.97(GC)
12.	ITA	3.02.11
13.	POL	3.02.27(ECh)
14.	CZE	3.02.52(ECh)
15.	SRI	3.02.74(Jak)
16.	TTO	3.02.85(GC)
17.	GER	3.03.16(WC)
18.	NED	3.03.51
19.	CUB	3.03.87
20.	DOM	3.03.92
21.	BRN	3.03.97(Jak)

WORLD INDOOR CHAMPIONSHIPS: 4-3-2018:

1. POL   3.01.77
Zalewski/Omelko/Krawczuk/Krzewina
2. USA   3.01.97
F. Kerley/Cherry/Bailey/Norwood
3. BEL   3.02.51
D. Borlée/J. Borlée/Sacoor/K. Borlée
4. TTO   3.02.52
Lendore/Richards/Guevara/Gordon
5. CZE   3.04.87
Desenský/Sorm/Snejdr/Maslák
6. GBR   3.05.08
Smith/Plenderleith/Rhoden-Stevens/Thompson

----

7. ESP   3.07.52
8. DOM   3.10.45
    JAM   dns
    UKR   dns

WORLD INDOOR RANKING 2018:

1. POL   3.01.77
2. USA   3.01.97
3. BEL   3.02.51
4. TTO   3.02.52
5. CZE   3.04.87
6. GBR   3.05.08
7. ESP   3.07.52

OVERVIEW WORLDWIDE OUTDOOR CHAMPIONSHIP FINALISTS OF PAST 6 YEARS

	Wch 17	OG 16	Wch 15	Wch 13
TTO	2.58.12 (1)		2.58.20 (2)	3.01.74 (6)
USA	2.58.61 (2)	2.57.30 (1)	2.57.82 (1)	2.58.71 (1)
GBR	2.59.00 (3)		2.58.51 (3)	3.00.88 (4)
BEL	3.00.04 (4)	2.58.52 (4)	3.00.24 (5)	3.01.02 (5)
ESP	3.00.65 (5)			
CUB	3.01.10 (6)	2.59.53 (6)	3.03.05 (7)	
POL	3.01.59 (7)	3.00.50 (7)		
FRA	3.01.79 (8)		3.00.65 (6)	
JAM		2.58.16 (2)	2.58.51 (4)	2.59.88 (2)
BAH		2.58.49 (3)		
BOT		2.59.06 (5)		
BRA		3.03.28 (8)		3.02.19 (7)
RUS			3.03.05 (8)	2.59.90 (3)
AUS				3.02.26 (8)

OVERVIEW TOP 10 WORLD OUTDOOR RANKINGS OF PAST 5 YEARS

	2018	2017	2016	2015	2014
BEL	2.59.47 (1)	2.59.47 (4)	2.58.52 (4)	2.59.28 (6)	
USA	2.59.78 (2)	2.58.61 (2)	2.57.30 (1)	2.57.82 (1)	2.57.25 (1)
GBR	3.00.36 (3)	2.59.00 (3)		2.58.51 (3)	2.58.79 (4)
QAT	3.00.56 (4)				
ESP	3.00.78 (5)	3.00.65 (5)			
FRA	3.01.67 (6)	3.00.93 (6)	3.00.82 (9)	2.59.42 (7)	2.59.89 (7)
BOT	3.01.78 (7)	3.02.28 (10)	2.59.06 (5)	2.59.95 (10)	
IND	3.01.85 (8)				
BAH	3.01.92 (9)		2.58.49 (3)	2.58.91 (5)	2.57.59 (2)
JPN	3.01.94 (10)				
TTO		2.58.12 (1)		2.58.20 (2)	2.58.34 (3)
CUB		3.01.10 (7)	2.59.53 (6)	2.59.80 (9)	3.00.61 (8)
POL		3.01.59 (8)	2.59.58 (7)		2.59.85 (6)
JAM		3.01.98 (9)	2.58.16 (2)	2.58.51 (3)	3.01.17 (9)
BRA			3.00.43 (8)		
IND			3.00.91 (10)		
RUS				2.59.45 (8)	2.59.38 (5)
VEN					3.01.44 (10)

OVERVIEW WORLDWIDE INDOOR CHAMPIONSHIP FINALISTS OF PAST 5 YEARS

	Wch 18	Wch 16	Wch 14
POL	3.01.77 (1)		3.04.39 (4)
USA	3.01.97 (2)	3.02.45 (1)	3.02.13 (1)
BEL	3.02.51 (3)	3.09.71 (6)	
TTO	3.02.52 (4)	3.05.51 (3)	
CZE	3.04.87 (5)		
GBR	3.05.08 (6)		3.03.49 (2)
BAH		3.04.75 (2)	
JAM		3.06.02 (4)	3.03.69 (3)
NGR		3.08.55 (5)	
RUS			3.07.12 (5)
UKR			3.08.79 (6)

OVERVIEW TOP 10 WORLD INDOOR RANKINGS OF PAST 5 YEARS

	2018	2017	2016	2015	2014
POL	3.01.77 (1)	3.06.99 (2)		3.02.97 (3)	3.04.39 (4)
USA	3.01.97 (2)	3.02.52 (1)	3.02.45 (1)	3.02.86 (1)	3.02.13 (1)
BEL	3.02.51 (3)	3.07.80 (3)	3.07.39 (5)	3.02.87 (2)	
TTO	3.02.52 (4)		3.05.51 (3)	3.04.09 (4)	
CZE	3.04.87 (5)	3.08.60 (4)			
GBR	3.05.08 (6)			3.08.56 (6)	3.03.49 (2)
ESP	3.07.52 (7)				
FRA		3.08.99 (5)			
BAH			3.04.75 (2)		3.09.79 (8)
JAM			3.06.02 (4)		3.03.69 (3)
NGR			3.07.98 (6)		3.07.95 (7)
QAT			3.08.20 (7)		
RSA			3.08.45 (8)		
RUS				3.08.00 (5)	3.06.63 (5)
UKR					3.07.54 (6)

WORLD RANKING ALL TIME OUTDOOR:

1.	USA	2.54.29 (1993)
2.	GBR	2.56.60 (1996)
3.	BAH	2.56.72 (2012)
4.	JAM	2.56.75 (1997)
5.	POL	2.58.00 (1998)
6.	TTO	2.58.12 (2017)
7.	BEL	2.58.52 (2016)
8.	BRA	2.58.56 (1999)
9.	NGR	2.58.68 (2000)
10.	FRA	2.58.96 (2003)
11.	BOT	2.59.06 (2016)
12.	CUB	2.59.13 (1992)
13.	RSA	2.59.21 (2011)
14.	RUS	2.59.38 (2014)
15.	KEN	2.59.63 (1992)
16.	AUS	2.59.70 (1984)
17.	GDR	2.59.86 (1985)
18.	YUG	2.59.95 (1991)
19.	FRG	2.59.96 (1987)
20.	GER	2.59.99 (1993)
21.	DOM	3.00.15 (2015)
22.	URS	3.00.16 (1984)
23.	QAT	3.00.56 (2018)
24.	SEN	3.00.64 (1996)
25.	ESP	3.00.65 (2017)
26.	JPN	3.00.76 (1996)
27.	ZIM	3.00.79 (1997)
28.	VEN	3.00.82 (2011)
29.	IND	3.00.91 (2016)
30.	FIN	3.01.12 (1972)
31.	COL	3.01.16 (2016)
32.	ITA	3.01.37 (1986)
33.	BAR	3.01.60 (1984)
34.	BUL	3.01.61 (1993)

WORLD RANKING ALL TIME INDOOR:

1.	POL	3.01.77 (2018)
2.	USA	3.01.96 (2006)
3.	BEL	3.02.51 (2018)
4.	TTO	3.02.52 (2018)
5.	GER	3.03.05 (1991)
6.	GBR	3.03.20 (1999)
7.	JAM	3.03.69 (2014)
8.	CZE	3.04.09 (2015)
9.	BAH	3.04.75 (2016)
10.	RUS	3.04.82 (2001)
11.	ITA	3.05.51 (1991)
12.	JPN	3.05.90 (1999)

Decathlon Outdoor / Heptathlon Indoor

EUROPEAN CHAMPIONSHIPS 2018: 8-8-2018:

1. Arthur Abele (GER)   8431
10.86-7.42-15.64-1.93-48.01
13.94-45.42-4.60-68.10-4.30.84
2. Ilya Shkurenkov (ANA)   8321
11.12-7.55-13.43-2.02-48.95
14.44-45.53-5.30-59.13-4.31.38
3. Vitali Zhuk (BLR)   8290
11.12-7.05-15.65-1.99-48.41
14.66-45.46-4.90-66.19-4.30.81
4. Niklas Kaul (GER)   8220
11.36-7.20-13.85-2.08-49.28
14.78-46.30-4.70-67.72-4.23.67
5. Tim Duckworth (GBR)   8160
10.65-7.57-13.61-2.17-49.87
14.55-41.94-5.10-54.78-4.58.28
6. Martin Roe (NOR)   8131
7. Pieter Braun (NED)   8105
8. Jan Dolezal (CZE)   8067
9. Fredrik Samuelsson (SWE)   8005
10. Simone Cairoli (ITA)   7949
11. Yury Yaremich (BLR)   7875
12. Marcus Nilsson (SWE)   7819
13. Pawel Wiesiolek (POL)   7696
14. Marek Lukas (CZE)   7683
15. Elmo Savola (FIN)   7655
    Dominik Distelberger (AUT)   dnf
    Maicel Uibo (EST)   dnf
    Mathias Brugger (GER)   dnf
    Eelco Sintnicolaas (NED)   dnf
    Thomas van der Plaetsen (BEL)   dnf
    Kevin Mayer (FRA)   dnf

WORLD RANKING 2018:

1. Kevin Mayer (FRA)   **WR**   9126(Tal)
10.55-7.80-16.00-2.05-48.42
13.75-50.54-5.45-71.90-4.36.11
2. Damian Warner (CAN)   8795(Gtz)
10.31-7.81-14.83-2.03-47.72
13.56-47.32-4.80-61.94-4.26.59
3. Marcel Uibo (EST)   8514(Gtz)
11.04-7.57-14.78-2.12-50.32
14.66-46.58-5.30-61.75-4.27.54
4. Arthur Abele (GER)   8481(Rat)
10.85-7.28-15.93-1.89-48.40
14.01-44.77-4.90-67.61-4.22.22
5. Pieter Braun (NED)   8342(Gtz)
11.12-7.62-15.28-2.00-49.25
14.40-45.52-4.90-58.77-4.24.29
6. Timothy Duckworth (GBR)   8336(NCA)
10.57-8.01-13.15-2.13-48.78
14.37-42.76-5.11-57.27-5.01.27
7. Kai Kazmirek (GER)   8329(Gtz)
10.99-7.56-14.03-2.06-47.27
14.42-43.76-4.70-61.53-4.30.75
8. Ilya Shkurenyov (ANA)   8321(ECh)
9. Mathias Brugger (GER)   8304(Gtz)
10.98-7.32-15.11-2.00-48.02
14.24-46.04-5.00-51.72-4.23.93
10. Lindon Victor (GRN)   8303(GC)
10.70-7.24-15.79-2.01-49.48
14.87-52.32-4.60-71.10-5.04.75
11. Zachery Ziemek (USA)   8294(USC)
10.65-7.23-13.92-2.02-49.99
14.63-50.90-5.35-56.54-4.47.38
12. Vitaliy Zhuk (BLR)   8290(ECh)
13. Cedric Dubler (AUS)   8229(GC)
10.63-7.58-13.01-2.10-49.01
14.21-41.03-5.20-56.37-4.50.53
    Tim Nowak (GER)   8229(Tal)
11.19-7.56-14.50-1.96-49.29
14.72-45.31-4.85-64.00-4.26.80
15. Martin Roe (NOR)   8228
10.82-7.53-15.46-1.92-49.78
15.15-48.26-4.75-66.64-4.40.97
16. Niklas Kaul (GER)   8220(ECh)
17. Pierce Lepage (CAN)   8171(GC)
18. Fredrik Samuelsson (SWE)   8165(Gtz)

WORLD INDOOR CHAMPIONSHIPS: 3-3-2018:

1. Kevin Mayer (FRA)		6348
6.85-7.55-15.67-2.02-7.83-5.00-2.39.64		
2. Damian Warner (CAN)		6343
6.74-7.39-14.90-2.02-7.67-4.90-2.37.12		
3. Maicel Uibo (EST)		6265
7.20-7.41-14.30-2.17-8.19-5.30-2.38.51		
4. Kai Kazmirek (GER)		6238
7.15-7.68-14.55-2.05-7.95-5.20-2.42.15		
5. Eelco Sintnicolaas (NED)		5997
6.96-7.15-14.09-1.90-7.97-5.30-2.45.93		
6. Zachery Ziemek (USA)		5941
6.89-7.21-13.48-2.02-8.14-5.10-2.51.73		
7. Ruben Gado (FRA)		5927
6.99-7.26-13.61-1.96-8.47-5.10-2.38.86		
8. Dominik Distelberger (AUT)		5908
6.93-7.35-13.04-1.93-7.98-4.80-2.41.49		
9. Jan Dolezal (CZE)		5775
7.04-7.04-14.82-1.96-8.20-4.70-2.47.99		
Oleksiy Kasyanov (UKR)		dnf
6.95-7.43-14.16-2.02-dsq -dns		
Lindon Victor (GRN)		dnf
6.98-5.55-15.54- NM-dns		

WORLD INDOOR RANKING 2018:

1. Kevin Mayer (FRA)		6348
2. Damian Warner (CAN)		6343
3. Maicel Uibo (EST)		6265
4. Kai Kazmirek (GER)		6238
5. Timothy Duckworth (GBR)		6188
6.84-7.74-13.59-2.17-8.23-5.16-2.56.23		
6. Hunter Veith (USA)		6090
6.90-7.54-13.39-2.08-7.99-4.76-2.43.33		
7. Tyler Adams (USA)		6081
6.99-7.38-12.12-2.20-7.97-4.56-2.36.14		
8. Zachery Ziemek (USA)		6043
6.89-7.10-14.02-2.03-8.08-5.27-2.49.95		
9. Jan Dolezal (CZE)		6021
7.01-7.59-14.31-1.99-7.96-4.90-2.49.42		
10. Oleksiy Kasyanov (UKR)		6016
6.92-7.45-13.78-2.02-7.80-4.66-2.46.22		
11. Ruben Gado (FRA)		6014
6.99-7.33-12.91-2.00-8.32-5.30-2.40.96		
12. Eelco Sintnicolaas (NED)		5997
13. Johannes Erm (EST)		5988
7.11-7.64-13.77-1.99-8.38-4.96-2.39.45		
14. Samuel Remedios (POR)		5980
6.92-7.52-13.70-2.03-7.98-5.00-2.57.33		
15. Dominik Distelberger (AUT)		5973
6.93-7.40-12.84-1.95-7.96-4.90-2.40.42		
16. Adam Sebastian Helcelet (CZE)		5951
7.05-7.41-14.65-2.05-7.97-4.60-2.48.98		
Martin Roe (NOR)		5951
6.92-7.81-15.71- ? -8.43-4.80-2.51.03		
18. Jeremy Taiwo (USA)		5935
7.15-7.10-12.75-2.10-8.19-5.05-2.41.36		
19. TJ Lawson (USA)		5934
7.09-7.40-14.46-2.02-8.36-4.76-2.40.89		
20. Wolf Mahler (USA)		5923
6.99-7.24-13.07-1.92-8.18-5.15-2.40.43		
21. Fredrik Samuelsson (SWE)		5908
7.09-7.28-13.43-2.08-8.14-4.85-2.47.44		
22. Tim Nowak (GER)		5906
7.23-6.96-14.30-2.02-8.21-5.06-2.40.12		
23. Artyom Makarenko (RUS)		5904
6.91-7.05-13.85-2.02-7.81-4.60-2.46.53		

OVERVIEW WORLDWIDE OUTDOOR CHAMPIONSHIP FINALISTS OF PAST 6 YEARS

	Wch 17	OG 16	Wch 15	Wch 13
Kevin Mayer (FRA)	8768 (1)	8834 (2)		8446 (4)
Rico Freimuth (GER)	8564 (2)		8561 (3)	8382 (7)
Kai Kazmirek (GER)	8488 (3)	8580 (4)	8448 (6)	
Janek Oiglane (EST)	8371 (4)			
Damian Warner (CAN)	8309 (5)	8666 (3)	8695 (2)	8512 (3)
Oleksiy Kasyanov (UKR)	8234 (6)		8262 (9)	
Kurt Felix (GRN)	8227 (7)	8323 (9)	8302 (8)	
Adam Sebastian Helcelet (CZE)	8222 (8)			
Jorge Urena (ESP)	8125 (9)			
Devon Williams (USA)	8088 (10)			
Ashton Eaton (USA)		8893 (1)	9045 (1)	8809 (1)
Larbi Bourrada (ALG)		8521 (5)	8461 (5)	
Leonel Suarez (CUB)		8460 (6)		8317 (10)
Zach Ziemek (USA)		8392 (7)		
Thomas van der Plaetsen (BEL)		8332 (8)		
Luiz Alberto de Araujo (BRA)		8315 (10)		
Ilya Shkurenev (RUS)			8538 (4)	8370 (8)
Michael Schrader (GER)			8418 (7)	8670 (2)
Marcel Uibo (EST)			8245 (10)	
Eelco Sintnicolaas (NED)				8391 (5)
Carlos Chinin (BRA)				8388 (6)
Willem Coertzen (RSA)				8343 (9)

OVERVIEW WORLDWIDE INDOOR CHAMPIONSHIP FINALISTS OF PAST 5 YEARS

	Wch 18	Wch 16	Wch 14
Kevin Mayer (FRA)	6348 (1)		
Damian Warner (CAN)	6343 (2)		6129 (7)
Marcel Uibo (EST)	6265 (3)		
Kai Kazmirek (GER)	6238 (4)		6173 (6)
Eelco Sintnicolaas (NED)	5997 (5)		6198 (4)
Zachery Ziemek (USA)	5941 (6)		
Ashton Eaton (USA)		6470 (1)	6632 (1)
Oleksiy Kasyanov (UKR)		6182 (2)	6176 (5)
Mathias Brugger (GER)		6126 (3)	
Curtis Beach (USA)		6118 (4)	
Adam Sebastian Helcelet (CZE)		6003 (5)	
Kurt Felix (GRN)		5986 (6)	
Andrei Krauchanka (BLR)			6303 (2)
Thomas van der Plaetsen (BEL)			6259 (3)

OVERVIEW TOP 10 WORLD OUTDOOR RANKINGS OF PAST 5 YEARS

	2018	2017	2016	2015	2014
Kevin Mayer (FRA)	9126 (1)	8768 (1)	8834 (2)	8469 (6)	8521 (2)
Damian Warner (CAN)	8795 (2)	8591 (4)	8666 (3)	8695 (3)	
Maicel Uibo (EST)	8514 (3)				
Arthur Abele (GER)	8481 (4)		8605 (4)		8477 (6)
Pieter Braun (NED)	8342 (5)				
Timothy Duckworth (GBR)	8336 (6)				
Kai Kazmirek (GER)	8329 (7)	8478 (8)	8580 (5)	8462 (7)	8471 (7)
Ilya Shkurenyov (RUS)	8321 (8)	8601 (3)		8538 (5)	8498 (4)
Matthias Brugger (GER)	8304 (9)				
Lindon Victor (GRN)	8303 (10)	8539 (5)	8446 (8)		
Rico Freimuth (GER)		8663 (2)		8561 (4)	8356 (8)
Eelco Sintnicolaas (NED)		8539 (5)			8478 (5)
Kurt Felix (GRN)		8509 (7)			
Janek Oiglane (EST)		8371 (9)			
Devon Williams (USA)		8345 (10)			
Ashton Eaton (USA)			8893 (1)	9045 (1)	
Larbi Bourada (ALG)			8521 (6)	8461 (8)	8311 (10)
Leonel Suarez (CUB)			8460 (7)		
Jeremy Taiwo (USA)			8425 (9)		
Zach Ziemek (USA)			8413 (10)		
Trey Hardee (USA)				8725 (2)	8518 (3)
Michael Schrader (GER)				8419 (9)	
Willem Coertzen (RSA)				8398 (10)	
Andrei Krauchanka (BLR)					8616 (1)
Yordani Garcia (CUB)					8337 (9)

OVERVIEW TOP 10 WORLD INDOOR RANKINGS OF PAST 5 YEARS

	2018	2017	2016	2015	2014
Kevin Mayer (FRA)	6348 (1)	6479 (1)			
Damian Warner (CAN)	6343 (2)				6129 (8)
Maicel Uibo (EST)	6265 (3)				6044 (10)
Kai Kazmirek (GER)	6238 (4)		6111 (6)	6049 (10)	6173 (7)
Timothy Duckworth (GBR)	6188 (5)	6165 (5)			
Hunter Veith (USA)	6090 (6)				
Tyler Adams (USA)	6081 (7)				
Zachery Ziemek (USA)	6043 (8)		6173 (3)		
Jan Dolezal (CZE)	6021 (9)				
Oleksiy Kasyanov (UKR)	6016 (10)		6182 (2)		6176 (6)
Jorge Ureña (ESP)		6249 (2)	6076 (7)	6051 (9)	
Adam Sebastian Helcelet (CZE)		6188 (3)		6164 (5)	
Devon Williams (USA)		6177 (4)			
Dominik Distelberger (AUT)		6063 (6)			
Karl Robert Saluri (EST)		6051 (7)			
Fredrik Samuelsson (SWE)		6015 (8)			
Hunter Price (USA)		5996 (7)			
Kristjan Rosenberg (EST)		5986 (8)			
Ashton Eaton (USA)			6470 (1)		6632 (1)
Mathias Brugger (GER)			6126 (4)		
Curtis Beach (USA)			6118 (5)		
Pau Tonnesen (ESP)			6027 (8)		
Garrett Scantling (USA)			6020 (9)	6068 (8)	
Mihail Dudas (SRB)			6015 (10)		
Ilya Shkurenev (RUS)				6353 (1)	
Arthur Abele (GER)				6279 (2)	
Jeremy Taiwo (USA)				6273 (3)	
Eelco Sintnicolaas (NED)				6185 (4)	6242 (4)
Gaël Quérin (FRA)				6115 (6)	
Luca Wieland (GER)				6070 (7)	
Andrei Krauchanka (BLR)					6303 (2)
Thomas van der Plaetsen (BEL)					6259 (3)
Curtis Beach (USA)					6190 (5)
Gray Horn (USA)					6071 (9)

WORLD RANKING ALL TIME OUTDOOR:

1.	Kevin Mayer (FRA)	9126 (2018)
2.	Ashton Eaton (USA)	9045 (2015)
3.	Roman Sebrle (CZE)	9026 (2001)
4.	Tomás Dvorák (CZE)	8994 (1999)
5.	Dan O'Brien (USA)	8891 (1992)
6.	Daley Thompson (GBR)	8847 (1984)
7.	Bryan Clay (USA)	8832 (2008)
8.	Erki Nool (EST)	8815 (2001)
9.	Damian Warner (CAN)	8795 (2018)
10.	Trey Hardee (USA)	8790 (2009)
11.	Tom Pappas (USA)	8784 (2003)
12.	Siegfried Wentz (FRG)	8762 (1983)
13.	Eduard Hämäläinen (BLR)	8735 (1994)
14.	Jürgen Hingsen (FRG)	8730 (1986)
15.	Dmitriy Karpov (KAZ)	8725 (2004)
16.	Frank Busemann (GER)	8706 (1996)
17.	Dave Johnson (USA)	8705 (1992)
18.	Chris Huffins (USA)	8694 (1998)
19.	Torsten Voss (GER)	8680 (1987)
20.	Michael Schrader (GER)	8670 (2013)
21.	Guido Kratschmer (FRG)	8667 (1980)
22.	Rico Freimuth (GER)	8663 (2017)
23.	Leonle Suárez (CUB)	8654 (2009)
24.	Steve Fritz (USA)	8644 (1996)
	Maurice Smith (JAM)	8644 (2007)
26.	Bruce Jenner (USA)	8634 (1976)
27.	Robert Zmelik (TCH)	8627 (1992)
28.	Michael Smith (CAN)	8626 (1996)
29.	Andrey Krauchanka (BLR)	8617 (2007)
30.	Arthur Abele (GER)	8605 (2016)
31.	Dean Macey (GBR)	8603 (2001)
32.	Ilya Shkurenyov (RUS)	8601 (2017)
33.	Kai Kazmirek (GER)	8580 (2016)
34.	Christian Plaziat (FRA)	8574 (1990)
	Oleksandr Yurkov (UKR)	8574 (2000)
36.	Jon Arnar Magnússon (ISL)	8573 (1998)
37.	Lev Lobodin (RUS)	8571 (1998)
38.	Sebastian Chmara (POL)	8566 (1998)
39.	Pascal Behrenbruch (GER)	8558 (2012)
40.	Attila Zsivocky-Pandel (HUN)	8554 (2000)
41.	Paul Meier (GER)	8548 (1993)
42.	Lindon Victor (GRN)	8539 (2017)
	Eelco Sintnicolaas (NED)	8539 (2017)
44.	Aleksandr Pogorelov (RUS)	8528 (2009)

WORLD RANKING ALL TIME INDOOR:

1.	Ashton Eaton (USA)	6645 (2012)
2.	Kevin Mayer (FRA)	6479 (2017)
3.	Dan O'Brien (USA)	6476 (1993)
4.	Roman Sebrle (CZE)	6438 (2004)
5.	Tomás Dvorak (CZE)	6424 (2000)
6.	Christian Plaziat (FRA)	6418 (1992)
7.	Sebastian Chmara (POL)	6415 (1998)
8.	Lev Lobodin (RUS)	6412 (2003)
9.	Erki Nool (EST)	6374 (1999)
10.	Eelco Sintnicolaas (NED)	6372 (2013)
11.	Bryan Clay (USA)	6371 (2008)
12.	Mikk Pahapill (EST)	6362 (2009)
13.	Tom Pappas (USA)	6361 (2003)
14.	Ilya Shkurenyov (RUS)	6353 (2015)
15.	Damian Warner (CAN)	6343 (2018)
16.	Andrey Krauchanka (BLR)	6303 (2014)
17.	Aleksey Drozdov (RUS)	6300 (2010)
18.	Jón Arnar Magnússon (ISL)	6293 (1999)
19.	Frank Busemann (GER)	6291 (2002)
20.	Michael Smith (CAN)	6279 (1993)
	Arthur Abele (GER)	6279 (2015)
22.	Jeremy Taiwo (USA)	6273 (2015)
23.	Maicel Uibo (EST)	6265 (2018)
24.	Thomas van der Plaetsen (BEL)	6259 (2014)
25.	Oleksiy Kasyanov (UKR)	6254 (2010)
26.	Dezsö Szabó (HUN)	6249 (1998)
	Jorge Ureña (ESP)	6249 (2017)
28.	Kai Kazmirek (GER)	6238 (2018)
29.	Nadir El Fassi (FRA)	6237 (2011)
30.	Gunnar Nixon (USA)	6232 (2013)
31.	Aleksandr Pogorelov (RUS)	6229 (2006)
	Dmitriy Karpov (KAZ)	6229 (2008)
33.	Robert Zmelík (CZE)	6228 (1997)
34.	Steve Fritz (USA)	6213 (1996)
35.	Trey Hardee (USA)	6208 (2006)
36.	André Niklaus (GER)	6192 (2006)
37.	Curtis Beach (USA)	6190 (2014)
38.	Adam Helcelet (CZE)	6188 (2017)
	Timothy Duckworth (GBR)	6188 (2018)
40.	Kamil Damasek (CZE)	6182 (1997)
41.	Devon Williams (USA)	6177 (2017)
42.	Kevin Lazas (USA)	6175 (2013)
43.	Zachery Ziemek (USA)	6173 (2016)
44.	Japheth Cato (USA)	6165 (2013)
45.	Siegfried Wentz (FRG)	6163 (1986)

Marathon Men

EUROPEAN CHAMPIONSHIPS 2018: 12-8-2018:

1.	Koen Naert (BEL)	2.09.51
2.	Tadesse Abraham (SUI)	2.11.24
3.	Yassine Rachik (ITA)	2.12.09
4.	Javier Guerra (ESP)	2.12.22
5.	Eyob Ghebrehiwet Faniel (ITA)	2.12.43
6.	Jesús España (ESP)	2.12.58
7.	Maru Teferi (ISR)	2.13.00
8.	Lemawork Ketema (AUT)	2.13.22
9.	Tiidrek Nurme (EST)	2.15.16
10.	Peter Herzog (AUT)	2.15.29
11.	Tom Gröschel (GER)	2.15.48
12.	Stefano La Rosa (ITA)	2.15.57
13.	Mariusz Gizynski (POL)	2.16.02
14.	Ihor Olefirenko (UKR)	2.16.35
15.	Kevin Seaward (IRL)	2.16.58
16.	Camilo Santiago (ESP)	2.17.24
17.	Roman Fosti (EST)	2.17.57
18.	Mick Clohisey (IRL)	2.18.00
19.	Henryk Szost (POL)	2.18.09
20.	Valdas Dopolskas (LTU)	2.18.12
30.	Abdellatif Meftah (FRA)	2.19.23
	Sondre Moen (NOR)	dnf

WORLD RANKING 2018:

1.	Eliud Kipchoge (KEN)	2.01.39(Ber)
2.	Mosinet Geremew (ETH)	2.04.00(Dub)
3.	Leule Gebrselassie (ETH)	2.04.02(Dub)
4.	Tamirat Tola (ETH)	2.04.06(Dub)
	Asefa Mengstu (ETH)	2.04.06(Dub)
	Lawrence Cherono (KEN)	2.04.06(Ams)
7.	Sisay Lemma (ETH)	2.04.08(Dub)
8.	Birhanu Legese (ETH)	2.04.15(Dub)
9.	Mule Wasihun (ETH)	2.04.37(Ams)
10.	Soloman Deksisa (ETH)	2.04.40(Ams)
11.	El Hassan El Abbassi (BRN)	2.04.43(Val)
12.	Seifu Tura (ETH)	2.04.44(Dub)
13.	Tola Shura Kitata (ETH)	2.04.49(Lon)
14.	Matthew Kipkoech Kisorio (KEN)	2.04.53(Val)
15.	Mo Farah (GBR)	2.05.11(Chi)
16.	Emmanuel Saina (KEN)	2.05.21(BA)
	Tsegaye Kebede (ETH)	2.05.21(Val)
18.	Nobert Kigen (KEN)	2.05.22(Val)
19.	Al Mahjoub Dazza (MAR)	2.05.26(Val)
20.	Dickson Chumba (KEN)	2.05.30(Tok)
21.	Kenneth Kiprop Kipkemoi (KEN)	2.05.44(Rot)
22.	Abera Kuma (ETH)	2.05.50(Rot)
	Suguru Osako (JPN)	2.05.50(Chi)
24.	Kelkile Gezahegn (ETH)	2.05.56(Rot)
25.	Laban Korir (KEN)	2.05.58(Rot)
26.	Lelisa Desisa (ETH)	2.05.59(NY)
27.	Galen Rupp (USA)	2.06.07(Pra)
28.	Yuta Shitara (JPN)	2.06.11(Tok)
29.	Gideon Kipkemoi Kipketer (KEN)	2.06.15(Ams)
30.	Sammy Kitwara (KEN)	2.06.21(Val)
31.	Amos Kipruto (KEN)	2.06.23(Ber)
32.	Kaan Kigen Özbilen (TUR)	2.06.24(Ams)
	Solomon Kirwa Yego (KEN)	2.06.24(Val)
34.	Paul Lonyangata (KEN)	2.06.25(Par)
35.	Geoffrey Kamworor (KEN)	2.06.26(NY)
36.	Abraham Kiptum (KEN)	2.06.29(Dae)
37.	Evans Korir (KEN)	2.06.35(Dae)
38.	Ernest Ngeno (KEN)	2.06.41(Par)
	Martin Kiprugut Kosgey (KEN)	2.06.41(Fra)
40.	Geoffrey Kirui (KEN)	2.06.45(Chi)
41.	Deme Tadu Abate (ETH)	2.06.47(Ams)
42.	Wilson Kipsang Kiprotich (KEN)	2.06.48(Ber)
43.	Peter Kimeli Some (KEN)	2.06.49(Dae)
44.	Jonathan Korir (KEN)	2.06.51(Ams)

Houston, 14-1-2018:

1.	Bazu Worku Hayla (ETH)	2.08.30
2.	Yitayal Atnafu Zerihun (ETH)	2.09.07
3.	Elisha Kiprop Barno (KEN)	2.09.32

Dubai, 26-1-2018:

1.	Mosinet Geremew Bayih (ETH)	2.04.00
2.	Leule Gebrselassie Aleme (ETH)	2.04.02
3.	Tamirat Tola Adere (ETH)	2.04.06
4.	Asefa Mengstu Negewo (ETH)	2.04.06
5.	Sisay Lemma Kasaye (ETH)	2.04.08
6.	Birhanu Legese Gurmesa (ETH)	2.04.15
7.	Seyefu Tura Abdiwak (ETH)	2.04.44
8.	Yenew Alamirew Getahun (ETH)	2.08.56
9.	Mekuant Ayenew Gebre (ETH)	2.09.20
10.	Birhanu Teshome Demisie (ETH)	2.10.27

Mumbai, 21-1-2018:

1.	Solomon Deksisa (ETH)	2.09.34
2.	Shumet Mengistu (ETH)	2.10.00
3.	Joshua Kipkorir (KEN)	2.10.30
4.	Shumi Dechasa (BRN)	2.12.24

Oita, 4-2-2018:

1.	Desmond Mokgobu (RSA)	2.09.31
2.	Hayato Sonoda (JPN)	2.09.34
3.	Shotei Otsuka (JPN)	2.10.12
4.	Josphat Leting (KEN)	2.10.54
5.	Tsukasa Komaya (JPN)	2.11.20
6.	Takuya Fujikawa (JPN)	2.11.59
7.	Ryu Takaku (JPN)	2.12.12
8.	Abraham Kiplimo (UGA)	2.12.18
9.	Ezekiel Kimalel Cheboitibin (KEN)	2.12.32
10.	Ayumi Sato (JPN)	2.12.37

Sevilla, 25-2-2018:

1.	Dickson Tuwei (KEN)	2.08.22
2.	Laban Mutai (KEN)	2.08.23
3.	Andrew Kimutai (KEN)	2.08.32
4.	Javier Guerra (ESP)	2.08.36
5.	Douglas Chebii (KEN)	2.08.43
6.	Kipkemoi Kipsang (KEN)	2.09.59
7.	Stefano La Rosa (ITA)	2.11.08
8.	Jesús Espana (ESP)	2.13.24
9.	Gezaw Bekele Megerssa (ETH)	2.14.17
10.	Tujuba Beyu Megersa (ETH)	2.14.37

Tokyo, 25-2-2018:

1.	Dickson Chumba (KEN)	2.05.30
2.	Yuta Shitara (JPN)	2.06.11
3.	Amos Kipruto (KEN)	2.06.33
4.	Gideon Kipkemoi Kipketer (KEN)	2.06.47
5.	Hiroto Inoue (JPN)	2.06.54
6.	Feyisa Lelisa (ETH)	2.07.30
7.	Ryo Kiname (JPN)	2.08.08
8.	Chihiro Miyawaki (JPN)	2.08.45
9.	Kenji Yamamoto (JPN)	2.08.48
10.	Yuki Sato (JPN)	2.08.58
11.	Mohamed Reda El Aaraby (MAR)	2.09.18
12.	Kohei Ogino (JPN)	2.09.36
13.	Tadashi Isshiki (JPN)	2.09.43
14.	Akinobu Murasawa (JPN)	2.09.47
15.	Simon Kariuki (KEN)	2.10.00
16.	Asuka Tanaka (JPN)	2.10.13
17.	Hiroko Yamagishi (JPN)	2.10.14
18.	Daichi Kamno (JPN)	2.10.18
19.	Kengo Suzuki (JPN)	2.10.21
20.	Tsegaye Mekonnen (ETH)	2.10.26
21.	Juan Luis Barrios (MEX)	2.10.55

Otsu, 4-3-2018:

1.	Joseph Mana Ndirangu (KEN)	2.07.53
2.	Albert Korir (KEN)	2.08.17
3.	Jake Robertson (NZL)	2.08.26
4.	Michel Githae (KEN)	2.09.21
5.	Abera Kuma (ETH)	2.09.31
6.	Daniele Meucci (ITA)	2.10.45
7.	Shogo Nakamura (JPN)	2.10.51
8.	Ezekiel Chebii (KEN)	2.11.00
9.	Masato Imai (JPN)	2.11.38
10.	Takuya Noguchi (JPN)	2.11.48

Barcelona, 11-3-2018:

1.	Anthony Maritim (KEN)	2.08.08
2.	Silas Too (KEN)	2.08.26
3.	Hillary Kipsambu (KEN)	2.08.53
4.	Tariku Kinfu (ETH)	2.09.25
5.	Tsegaye Kebede (ETH)	2.09.25
6.	Tsedat Abege Ayana (ETH)	2.09.26
7.	Benson Seurei (KEN)	2.11.27
8.	Tsegay Hiluf (ETH)	2.12.30
9.	Reuben Limaa (KEN)	2.13.02
10.	Alemu Gemechu (ETH)	2.14.32

Seoul, 18-3-2018:
1. Wilson Loyanae Erupe (KEN) — 2.06.57
2. Mark Korir (KEN) — 2.07.03
3. Benson Kipruto (KEN) — 2.07.11
4. Marius Kimutai (KEN) — 2.07.45
5. Felix Kiprotich (KEN) — 2.07.57
6. Saïd Aït Addi (MAR) — 2.08.43
7. Deriba Robi (ETH) — 2.08.51
8. Paul Kipkorir Kipkemboi (KEN) — 2.08.53
9. Oleksandr Sitkovskiy (UKR) — 2.10.12
10. Bernard Kiprop Kipyego (KEN) — 2.10.16

Daegu, 1-4-2018:
1. Abraham Kiptum (KEN) — 2.06.29
2. Evans Korir (KEN) — 2.06.35
3. Peter Kimeli Some (KEN) — 2.06.49
4. Elisha Kipchirchir Rotich (KEN) — 2.07.50
5. Al Mahjoub Dazza (MAR) — 2.08.33
6. Jacob Kibet (KEN) — 2.10.08
7. Weldu Negash Gebretsadik (ETH) — 2.10.39
8. Reuben Kiprop (KEN) — 2.11.02
9. Mike Kiptum (KEN) — 2.11.25
10. Julius Tuwei (KEN) — 2.14.20

Paris, 8-4-2018:
1. Paul Lonyangata (KEN) — 2.06.25
2. Matthew Kipkoech Kisorio (KEN) — 2.06.36
3. Ernest Ngeno (KEN) — 2.06.41
4. Yitayal Atnafu Zerihun (ETH) — 2.07.00
5. Eliud Kiptanui (KEN) — 2.08.20
6. Martin Kiprugut Kosgei (KEN) — 2.08.31
7. Kiprotich Kirui (KEN) — 2.08.48
8. Thomas Kiplagat (KEN) — 2.08.55
9. Asbel Kipsang (KEN) — 2.09.06
10. Birhanu Teshome (ETH) — 2.09.59
11. Shumet Mengistu (ETH) — 2.10.15
12. Abraham Niyonkuru (BDI) — 2.11.19
13. Mark Kosgei Kiptoo (KEN) — 2.11.55

Rotterdam, 8-4-2018:
1. Kenneth Kiprop Kipkemoi (KEN) — 2.05.44
2. Abera Kuma (ETH) — 2.05.50
3. Kelkile Gezahegn (ETH) — 2.05.56
4. Laban Korir (KEN) — 2.05.58
5. Marius Kipserem (KEN) — 2.07.22
6. Mule Wasihun (ETH) — 2.08.13
7. Samuel Kalalei (KEN) — 2.10.44
8. Bashir Abdi (BEL) — 2.10.46
9. Daniel Kibet (KEN) — 2.11.13
10. Joash Mutai (KEN) — 2.12.58

Roma, 8-4-2018:
1. Jairus Kipchoge Birech (KEN) — 2.08.03
2. Abdi Ibrahim Abdo (BRN) — 2.08.32
3. Paul Kios Kangogo (KEN) — 2.09.20
4. Motlokoa Mkhabutlane (LES) — 2.10.32
5. Birhanu Tefera Girma (ETH) — 2.10.57
6. Mathew Kipsaat (KEN) — 2.11.35
7. Dejene Debela Gonfa (ETH) — 2.12.01

Milano, 8-4-2018:
1. Seyefu Tura (ETH) — 2.09.04
2. Justus Kimutai Kipkosgei (KEN) — 2.10.00
3. Barnabas Kiptum (KEN) — 2.10.17

Hannover, 8-4-2018:
1. Seboka Nigusse (ETH) — 2.09.44
2. Michael Kunyuga Njenga (KEN) — 2.10.16
3. Duncan Cheruiyot Koech (KEN) — 2.10.19
4. Justus Kiprotich (KEN) — 2.11.11

Boston, 18-4-2018:
1. Yuki Kawauchi (JPN) — 2.15.58
2. Geoffrey Kirui (KEN) — 2.18.23
3. Shadrack Kiptoo Biwott (USA) — 2.18.35
4. Tyler Pennel (USA) — 2.18.57
5. Andrew Bumbalough (USA) — 2.19.52
6. Scott Smith (USA) — 2.21.47
7. Abdi Nageeye (NED) — 2.23.16
8. Elkanah Kibet (USA) — 2.23.37
9. Reid Coolsaet (CAN) — 2.25.02
10. Daniel Vassallo (USA) — 2.27.50
11. Daniel Daly (USA) — 2.27.54
12. Matthew Herzig (USA) — 2.28.03
13. Benjamin Zywicki (USA) — 2.28.06
14. Stephen Sambu (KEN) — 2.28.07
15. Abdi Abdirahman (USA) — 2.28.18

London, 22-4-2018:

1.	Eliud Kipchoge (KEN)	2.04.17
2.	Tola Shura Kitata (ETH)	2.04.49
3.	Mo Farah (GBR)	2.06.21
4.	Abel Kirui (KEN)	2.07.07
5.	Bedan Karoki (KEN)	2.08.34
6.	Kenenisa Bekele (ETH)	2.08.53
7.	Lawrence Cherono (KEN)	2.09.25
8.	Daniel Wanjiru Kinyua (KEN)	2.10.35
9.	Amanuel Mesel (ERI)	2.11.52
10.	Yohanes Gebregergish (ERI)	2.12.09

Wien, 22-4-2018:

1.	Salaheddine Bounaser (MAR)	2.09.29
2.	Ishimael Bushendich (KEN)	2.10.03
3.	Samwel Maswai (KEN)	2.11.08
4.	Nicholas Rotich (KEN)	2.12.00
5.	Noah Kigen (KEN)	2.12.03

Madrid, 22-4-2018:

1.	Eliud Barngetuny (KEN)	2.10.15
2.	Kenneth Kiplagat (KEN)	2.10.24
3.	Alfonce Kibiwott (KEN)	2.10.32
4.	Julius Tuwei (KEN)	2.11.10
5.	Ezekiel Kimeli (KEN)	2.11.16
6.	Alemu Bekele (BRN)	2.11.20

Hamburg, 29-4-2018:

1.	Solomon Deksisa (ETH)	2.06.34
2.	Deme Tadu Abate (ETH)	2.06.54
3.	Ayele Abshero (ETH)	2.07.19
4.	Yego Solomon Kirwa (KEN)	2.07.37
5.	Stephen Kiprotich (UGA)	2.07.57
6.	Vincent Kipruto (KEN)	2.10.31
7.	Stephen Chebogut (KEN)	2.10.33
8.	Aychew Bantie (ETH)	2.11.16
9.	Emmanuel Mutai (KEN)	2.11.57
10.	Ezekiel Chepkorom (UGA)	2.13.12

Praha, 6-5-2018:

1.	Galen Rupp (USA)	2.06.07
2.	Sisay Lemma (ETH)	2.07.03
3.	Stephen Chemlany (KEN)	2.09.42
4.	Barselius Kipyego (KEN)	2.10.18
5.	Yuma Hattori (JPN)	2.10.26
6.	Mekuant Ayenew Gebre (ETH)	2.10.43

Dalian, 13-5-2018:

1.	Edwin Koech (KEN)	2.09.44
2.	Willy Ngelel (KEN)	2.10.31
3.	Habtamu Arega (ETH)	2.12.17

Ottawa, 27-5-2018:

1.	Yemane Adhane Tsegay (ETH)	2.08.52
2.	Ishimael Bushendich (KEN)	2.10.03
3.	Samwel Maswai (KEN)	2.11.08
4.	Nicholas Rotich (KEN)	2.12.00
5.	Noah Kigen (KEN)	2.12.03

Gold Coast, 1-7-2018:

1.	Kenneth Mburu Mungara (KEN)	2.09.49
2.	Kenta Murayama (JPN)	2.09.50
3.	Jo Fukuda (JPN)	2.09.52

Berlin, 16-9-2018:

1.	Eliud Kipchoge (KEN)	2.01.39**WR**
2.	Amos Kipruto (KEN)	2.06.23
3.	Wilson Kipsang Kiprotich (KEN)	2.06.48
4.	Shogo Nakamura (JPN)	2.08.16
5.	Zersenay Tadese (ERI)	2.08.46
6.	Yuki Sato (JPN)	2.09.18
7.	Okubay Tsegay Gebretnsae (ERI)	2.09.56
8.	Daisuke Uekado (JPN)	2.11.07
9.	Wily Canchanya (PER)	2.12.57
10.	Bart van Nunen (NED)	2.13.09

Buenos Aires, 23-9-2018:

1.	Emmanuel Saina (KEN)	2.05.21
2.	Barnabas Kiptum (KEN)	2.09.19
3.	Christian Pacheco (PER)	2.11.19

Cape Town, 23-9-2018:

1.	Stephen Mokoka (RSA)	2.08.31
2.	Albert Korir (KEN)	2.09.02
3.	Philemon Kacheran (KEN)	2.09.13
4.	Kipkemoi Kipsang (KEN)	2.09.21
5.	Nicholas Rotich (KEN)	2.12.39

Hengshui, 29-9-2018:

1.	Hayle Lemi (ETH)	2.08.51
2.	Herpasa Negasa (ETH)	2.09.14
3.	Dominic Ruto (KEN)	2.09.49
4.	Mathew Kipsaat (KEN)	2.11.31
5.	Benson Seurei (KEN)	2.12.50

Kosice, 7-10-2018:
1. Raymond Kipchumba Choge (KEN) — 2.08.11
2. Aychew Bantie Dessie (ETH) — 2.08.15
3. Shumet Mengistu Akahew (ETH) — 2.08.50

Chicago, 7-10-2018:
1. Mo Farah (GBR) — 2.05.11**ER**
2. Mosinet Geremew Bayih (ETH) — 2.05.24
3. Suguru Osako (JPN) — 2.05.50
4. Kenneth Kiprop Kipkemoi (KEN) — 2.05.57
5. Galen Rupp (USA) — 2.06.21
6. Geoffrey Kirui (KEN) — 2.06.45
7. Abel Kirui (KEN) — 2.07.52
8. Taku Fujimoto (JPN) — 2.07.57
9. Bedan Karoki (KEN) — 2.07.59
10. Birhanu Legese (ETH) — 2.08.41
11. Mohamed Reda El Aaraby (MAR) — 2.09.16
12. Yohei Suzuki (JPN) — 2.12.18

Eindhoven, 14-10-2018:
1. Elisha Kipchirchir Rotich (KEN) — 2.07.32
2. Laban Mutai (KEN) — 2.07.38
3. Vincent Rono (KEN) — 2.07.50
4. Silas Too (KEN) — 2.08.34

Amsterdam, 21-10-2018:
1. Lawrence Cherono (KEN) — 2.04.06
2. Mule Wasihun (ETH) — 2.04.37
3. Solomon Deksisa (ETH) — 2.04.40
4. Gideon Kipkemoi Kipketer (KEN) — 2.06.15
5. Kaan Kigen Özbilen (TUR) — 2.06.24
6. Laban Korir (KEN) — 2.06.33
7. Demu Tadu Abate (ETH) — 2.06.47
8. Jonathan Korir (KEN) — 2.06.51
9. Hillary Kipsambu (KEN) — 2.07.20
10. Yenew Alamirew (ETH) — 2.10.35

Toronto, 21-10-2018:
1. Benson Kipruto (KEN) — 2.07.24
2. Augustino Paulo Sulle (TAN) — 2.07.46
3. Felix Kipchirchir Kandie (KEN) — 2.08.30
4. Cameron Levins (CAN) — 2.09.25
5. Jake Robertson (NZL) — 2.09.52
6. Daniel Teklebrhan Mesfun (ERI) — 2.10.06
7. Stephen Kiprotich (UGA) — 2.11.06
8. Anthony Maritim (KEN) — 2.13.07
9. Philemon Rono (KEN) — 2.13.37
10. Reid Coolsaet (CAN) — 2.17.37

Gyeongju, 21-10-2018:
1. Kennedy Cheboror (KEN) — 2.08.26
2. Samuel Kiplimo Kosgei (KEN) — 2.09.07
3. Robert Kiplimo Kipkemboi (KEN) — 2.09.24
4. Mike Kiptum (KEN) — 2.09.34
5. Richard Kiprop (KEN) — 2.10.24
6. Mark Korir (KEN) — 2.11.00
7. Meshak Koech (KEN) — 2.11.39
8. Lani Rutto (KEN) — 2.12.16
9. Pius Karanja (KEN) — 2.12.53
10. Philip Sanga Kimutai (KEN) — 2.14.03

Frankfurt, 28-10-2018:
1. Kelkile Gezahegn Woldaregay (ETH) — 2.06.37
2. Martin Kiprugut Kosgei (KEN) — 2.06.41
3. Alex Kibet (KEN) — 2.07.09
4. Amos Kiplimo Mitei (KEN) — 2.07.28
5. Kenneth Keter (KEN) — 2.07.34
6. Mark Kosgei Kiptoo (KEN) — 2.07.50
7. Asefa Tefera Mengisa (ETH) — 2.08.34
8. Tsedat Abeye Ayana (ETH) — 2.09.39
9. Arne Gabius (GER) — 2.11.45
10. Vincent Kipsegechi Yator (KEN) — 2.12.03

Ljubljana, 28-10-2018:
1. Sisay Lemma Kasaye (ETH) — 2.04.58
2. Gebretsadik Abraha Adihana (ETH) — 2.08.36
3. Hiskel Tewelde (ERI) — 2.08.49
4. Ayele Abshero (ETH) — 2.09.12
5. Geoffrey Kusuro (UGA) — 2.10.53
6. Peter Kimeli Some (KEN) — 2.12.57
7. Douglas Kipsanai Chebii (KEN) — 2.13.10
8. Stephen kibiwott Chebogut (KEN) — 2.13.56
9. Roman Romanenko (UKR) — 2.15.38
10. Alfers Lagat (KEN) — 2.18.08

Chuncheon, 28-10-2018:
1. Gudeta Tamrat Shifera (ETH) — 2.08.50
2. Adugna Tekele Bikila (ETH) — 2.11.27
3. William Yegon (KEN) — 2.14.38

Hangzhou, 4-11-2018:
1. Michael Njenga Kunyuga (KEN) — 2.10.37
2. Douglas Kimeli (KEN) — 2.11.06
3. Mike Kiprotich Mutai (KEN) — 2.11.12

New York, 4-11-2018:

1.	Lelisa Desisa (ETH)	2.05.59
2.	Tola Shura Kitata (ETH)	2.06.01
3.	Geoffrey Kamworor (KEN)	2.06.26
4.	Tamirat Tola (ETH)	2.08.30
5.	Daniel Wanjiru Kinyua (KEN)	2.10.21
6.	Jared Ward (USA)	2.12.24
7.	Scott Fauble (USA)	2.12.28
8.	Festus Talam (KEN)	2.12.40
9.	Shadrack Kiptoo Biwott (KEN)	2.12.52
10.	Chris Derrick (USA)	2.13.08
11.	Juan Luis Barrios (MEX)	2.13.55
12.	Tadesse Yae Dabi (ETH)	2.13.57
13.	Tim Ritchie (USA)	2.15.22
14.	Ryan Vail (USA)	2.15.31
15.	Jonny Mellor (GBR)	2.16.09
16.	Harbert Okuti (UGA)	2.16.51
17.	Scott Smith (USA)	2.17.12
18.	Bernard Lagat (USA)	2.17.20
19.	Girma Bekele Gebre (ETH)	2.18.18
20.	Birhanu Dare Kemal (ETH)	2.18.20

Cannes, 4-11-2018:

1.	Abrha Milaw Asefa (ETH)	2.07.25
2.	Nixson Kurgat (KEN)	2.10.41
3.	Bernard Too (KEN)	2.11.55

Porto, 4-11-2018:

1.	Robert Chemonges (UGA)	2.09.05
2.	Olivier Irabaruta (BDI)	2.09.48
3.	Fikadu Kebede (ETH)	2.10.41

Seoul, 4-11-2018:

1.	Asefa Mengstu Negewo (ETH)	2.08.11
2.	Tariku Kinfu (ETH)	2.08.19
3.	Abdela Godana (ETH)	2.08.32
4.	Barselius Kipyego (KEN)	2.08.42
5.	Fred Musobo (UGA)	2.09.04
6.	Zelalem Bacha Regasa (BRN)	2.09.16
7.	Tariku Bekele (ETH)	2.09.30
8.	Stephano Gwandu Huche (TAN)	2.12.24
9.	Bernard Kitur (KEN)	2.12.44
10.	Evans Korir (KEN)	2.13.45

Beirut, 11-11-2018:

1.	Mohamed Reda El Aaraby (MAR)	2.10.41
2.	Felix Chemonges (UGA)	2.11.57
3.	Deresa Geleta (ETH)	2.12.33

Hefei, 11-11-2018:

1.	Leonard Langat (KEN)	2.10.49
2.	Hillary Kipkoech Bett (KEN)	2.11.41
3.	Tesfaye Lencho Anbesa (ETH)	2.11.46

Athens, 11-11-2018:

1.	Brimin Kipkorir Misoi (KEN)	2.10.56
2.	Tiruneh Workneh Tesfa (ETH)	2.12.52
3.	Azmeraw Mengistu Gereme (ETH)	2.13.20

Shanghai, 18-11-2018:

1.	Seifu Tura Abdiwak (ETH)	2.09.18
2.	Tsegaye Mekonnen (ETH)	2.09.18
3.	Dickson Tuwei (KEN)	2.09.21
4.	Tsegaye Getachew (ETH)	2.09.24
5.	Abdi Fufa (ETH)	2.09.24
6.	Solomon Mutai (UGA)	2.09.27
7.	Asbel Kipsang (KEN)	2.09.28
8.	Berga Birhanu Bekele (ETH)	2.11.46
9.	Jackson Kiprop (KEN)	2.13.31
10.	Dennis Kimetto (KEN)	2.14.54

Valencia, 2-12-2018:

1.	Leul Gebrselassie Aleme (ETH)	2.04.31
2.	El Hassan El Abbassi (BRN)	2.04.43
3.	Matthew Kipkoech Kisorio (KEN)	2.04.53
4.	Tsegaye Kebede Wordofa (ETH)	2.05.21
5.	Norbert Kipkoech Kigen (KEN)	2.05.22
6.	Al Mahjoub Dazza (MAR)	2.05.26
7.	Sammy Kirop Kitwara (KEN)	2.06.21
8.	Solomon Kirwa Yego (KEN)	2.06.24
9.	Deriba Robi Melka (ETH)	2.07.33
10.	Benson Kiplagat Seurei (KEN)	2.07.37
11.	Tesfamriam Samuel Tsegay (ERI)	2.08.20
12.	Hamid Ben Daoud (MAR)	2.10.21
13.	Julius Kipkorir Tuwei (KEN)	2.10.22
14.	Yohanes Ghebregergis (ERI)	2.11.27
15.	Girmaw Amare (ETH)	2.12.37

Istanbul, 11-11-2018:
1. Felix Kimutai (KEN)   2.09.57
2. Abdi Ibrahim Abdo (BRN)   2.10.37
3. Abraham Kiprotich (FRA)   2.10.55

Fukuoka, 2-12-2018:
1. Yuma Hattori (JPN)   2.07.27
2. Yemane Tsegay (ETH)   2.08.54
3. Amanuel Mesel (ERI)   2.09.45
4. Yuta Shitara (JPN)   2.10.25
5. Hayato Sonoda (JPN)   2.10.31
6. Hiroki Yamagishi (JPN)   2.10.42
7. Jo Fukuda (JPN)   2.10.54
8. Satoru Sasaki (JPN)   2.11.40
9. Ryo Hashimoto (JPN)   2.11.40
10. Yuki Kawauchi (JPN)   2.12.03

Abu Dhabi, 7-12-2018: (course too short?)
1. Marius Kipserem (KEN)   2.04.04
2. Abraham Kiptum (KEN)   2.04.16
3. Dejena Debela Gonfa (ETH)   2.07.06
4. Thomas Kiplagat Rono (KEN)   2.07.12
5. Stanley Kipleting Biwott (KEN)   2.09.18
6. Beshah Yersiie Eskezia (ETH)   2.10.01
7. Anouar El Ghouz (MAR)   2.10.19
8. Emmanuel Kipchirchir Mutai (KEN) 2.12.38
9. Ghebrezgiabhier Weldemicael Kibrom (ERI) 2.17.15
10. Wendwesen Tilahun Damte (ETH)   2.18.31

Guangzhou. 9-12-2018:
1. Mohammed Ziani (MAR)   2.10.44
2. Shumie Gadisa (ETH)   2.10.44
3. Balew Yihunle Derseh (ETH)   2.10.53
4. Tsegay Tuemay (ERI)   2.10.55

OVERVIEW WORLD OUTDOOR CHAMPIONSHIP FINALISTS OF PAST 6 YEARS

	Wch 17	OG 16	Wch 15	Wch 13
Geoffrey Kipkorir Kirui (KEN)	2.08.27 (1)			
Tamirat Tola (ETH)	2.09.49 (2)			
Alphonce Felix Simbu (TAN)	2.09.51 (3)	2.11.15 (5)		
Callum Hawkins (GBR)	2.10.17 (4)	2.11.52 (9)		
Gideon Kipkemoi Kipketer (KEN)	2.10.56 (5)			
Daniele Meucci (ITA)	2.10.56 (6)		2.14.54 (8)	
Yohanes Ghebregergis (ERI)	2.12.07 (7)			
Daniel Kinyua Wanjiru (KEN)	2.12.16 (8)			
Yuki Kawauchi (JPN)	2.12.19 (9)			
Kentaro Nakamoto (JPN)	2.12.41 (10)			2.10.50 (5)
Eliud Kipchoge (KEN)		2.08.44 (1)		
Feyisa Lilesa (ETH)		2.09.54 (2)		
Galen Rupp (USA)		2.10.05 (3)		
Ghirmay Ghebreslassie (ERI)		2.11.04 (4)	2.12.28 (1)	
Jared Ward (USA)		2.11.30 (6)		
Tadesse Abraham (SUI)		2.11.42 (7)		
Munyo Solomon Mutai (UGA)		2.11.49 (8)	2.13.30 (3)	
Eric Gillis (CAN)		2.12.29 (10)		
Yemane Tsegay (ETH)			2.13.08 (2)	2.11.43 (8)
Ruggero Pertile (ITA)			2.14.23 (4)	
Shumi Dechasa (BRN)			2.14.36 (5)	
Stephen Kiprotich (UGA)			2.14.43 (6)	
Lelisa Desisa (ETH)			2.14.54 (7)	2.10.12 (2)
Amanuel Mesel (ERI)			2.15.07 (9)	
Jackson Kiprop (UGA)			2.15.16 (10)	2.12.12 (10)
Stephen Kiprotich (UGA)				2.09.51 (1)
Tadese Tola (ETH)				2.10.23 (3)
Tsegay Kebede (ETH)				2.10.47 (4)
Solonei da Silva (BRA)				2.11.40 (6)
Paulo Roberto Paula (BRA)				2.11.40 (7)
Peter Kimeli Some (KEN)				2.11.47 (9)

OVERVIEW TOP 10 WORLD OUTDOOR RANKINGS OF PAST 5 YEARS

	2018	2017	2016	2015	2014
Eliud Kipchoge (KEN)	2.01.39 (1)	2.03.32 (1)	2.03.05 (2)	2.04.00 (1)	2.04.11 (3)
Mosinet Geremew (ETH)	2.04.00 (2)				
Leule Gebrselassie (ETH)	2.04.02 (3)				
Tamirat Tola (ETH)	2.04.06 (4)	2.04.11 (4)			
Asefa Mengistu (ETH)	2.04.06 (4)				
Lawrence Cherono (KEN)	2.04.06 (4)	2.05.09 (5)			
Sisay Lemma (ETH)	2.04.08 (7)		2.05.16 (9)		
Birhanu Legese (ETH)	2.04.15 (8)				
Mule Wasihun (ETH)	2.04.37 (9)	2.05.39 (10)			
Soloman Deksisa (ETH)	2.04.40 (10)				
Guye Adola (ETH)		2.03.46 (2)			
Wilson Kipsang Kiprotich (KEN)		2.03.58 (3)	2.03.13 (3)	2.04.47 (2)	2.04.29 (5)
Norbert Kipkoech Kigen (KEN)		2.05.13 (6)			
Sammy Kirop Kitwara (KEN)		2.05.15 (7)			2.04.28 (4)
Abraham Kiptum (KEN)		2.05.26 (8)			
Evans Kiplagat Chebet (KEN)		2.05.30 (9)			
Kenenisa Bekele (ETH)			2.03.03 (1)		2.05.04 (9)
Stanley Kiplliting Biwott (KEN)			2.03.51 (4)		2.04.55 (8)
Tesfaye Abera (ETH)			2.04.24 (5)		
Lemi Berhanu (ETH)			2.04.33 (6)		
Tsegaye Mekonnen (ETH)			2.04.46 (7)		
Wilson Loyanae Erupe (KEN)			2.05.13 (8)		
Daniel Kinyua Wanjiru (KEN)			2.05.21 (10)		
Eliud Kiptanui (KEN)				2.05.21 (3)	
Berhanu Lemi (ETH)				2.05.28 (4)	
Mark Korir (KEN)				2.05.49 (5)	
Dennis Kipruto Kimetto (KEN)				2.05.50 (6)	2.02.57 (1)
Lelisa Desisa (ETH)				2.05.52 (7)	
Stephen Kibiwott Chebogut (KEN)				2.05.52 (7)	
Deribe Robi (ETH)				2.05.58 (9)	
Endeshaw Negesse (ETH)				2.06.00 (10)	
Mark Kosgei Kiptoo (KEN)				2.06.00 (10)	
Emmanuel Kipchirchir Mutai (KEN)					2.03.13 (2)
Tsegaye Mekonnen (ETH)					2.04.32 (6)
Dickson Kiptolo Chumba (KEN)					2.04.32 (6)
Markos Geneti (ETH)					2.05.12 (10)

WORLD RANKING ALL TIME:

1.	Eliud Kipchoge (KEN)	2.01.39 (2018)
2.	Dennis Kimetto (KEN)	2.02.57 (2014)
3.	Kenenisa Bekele (ETH)	2.03.03 (2016)
4.	Emmanuel Mutai (KEN)	2.03.13 (2014)
	Wilson Kipsang Kiprotich (KEN)	2.03.13 (2016)
6.	Patrick Makau Musyoki (KEN)	2.03.38 (2011)
7.	Guye Idemo Adola (ETH)	2.03.46 (2017)
8.	Stanley Kipleting Biwott (KEN)	2.03.51 (2016)
9.	Haile Gebrselassie (ETH)	2.03.59 (2008)
10.	Mosinet Geremew (ETH)	2.04.00 (2018)
11.	Leule Gebrselassie (ETH)	2.04.02 (2018)
12.	Tamirat Tola (ETH)	2.04.06 (2018)
	Asefa Mengstu (ETH)	2.04.06 (2018)
	Lawrence Cherono (KEN)	2.04.06 (2018)
15.	Sisay Lemma (ETH)	2.04.08 (2018)
16.	Geoffrey Mutai (KEN)	2.04.15 (2012)
	Birhanu Legese (ETH)	2.04.15 (2018)
18.	Ayele Abshero (ETH)	2.04.23 (2012)
19.	Tesfaye Abera (ETH)	2.04.24 (2016)
20.	Duncan Kibet (KEN)	2.04.27 (2009)
	James Kipsang Kwambai (KEN)	2.04.27 (2009)
22.	Sammy Kitwara (KEN)	2.04.28 (2014)
23.	Tsegaye Mekonnen (ETH)	2.04.32 (2014)
	Dickson Chumba (KEN)	2.04.32 (2014)
25.	Hayle Lemi (ETH)	2.04.33 (2016)
26.	Mule Wasihun (ETH)	2.04.37 (2018)
27.	Tsegaye Kebede (ETH)	2.04.38 (2012)
28.	Soloman Deksisa (ETH)	2.04.40 (2018)
29.	El Hassan El Abbassi (BRN)	2.04.43 (2018)
30.	Seifu Tura (ETH)	2.04.44 (2018)
31.	Lelisa Desisa (ETH)	2.04.45 (2013)
32.	Yemane Adhane Tsegay (ETH)	2.04.48 (2012)
	Berhanu Shiferaw (ETH)	2.04.48 (2013)
34.	Tadesse Tola (ETH)	2.04.49 (2013)
	Tola Shura Kitata (ETH)	2.04.49 (2018)
36.	Dino Sefir (ETH)	2.04.50 (2012)
	Getu Feleke (ETH)	2.04.50 (2012)
38.	Feyisa Lilesa (ETH)	2.04.52 (2012)
	Endeshaw Negesse (ETH)	2.04.52 (2013)
40.	Bernard Kiprop Koech (KEN)	2.04.53 (2013)
	Matthew Kipkoech Kisorio (KEN)	2.04.53 (2018)
42.	Markos Geneti (ETH)	2.04.54 (2012)
43.	Paul Tergat (KEN)	2.04.55 (2003)
44.	Sammy Kipchoge Korir (KEN)	2.04.56 (2003)
	Jonathan Maiyo (KEN)	2.04.56 (2012)

100 m Women Outdoor / 60 m Women Indoor

EUROPEAN CHAMPIONSHIPS 2018: 7-8-2018:

1.	Dina Asher-Smith (GBR)	(10.93)	10.85
2.	Gina Lückenkemper (GER)	(10.98)	10.98
3.	Dafne Schippers (NED)	(11.05)	10.99
4.	Mujinga Kambundji (SUI)	(11.14)	11.05
5.	Jamile Samuel (NED)	(11.10)	11.14
6.	Imani Lansiquot (GBR)	(11.14)	11.14
7.	Carolle Zahi (FRA)	(11.18)	11.20
8.	Orlann Ombissa-Dzangue(FRA)	(11.20)	11.29

9.	Tatjana Pinto (GER)		11.26
10.	Daryll Neita (GBR)		11.27
11.	Ewa Swoboda (POL)		11.30
12.	Orphee Neola (FRA)		11.33
13.	Krystsina Tsimanouskaya (BLR)		11.34
14.	Lisa Marie Kwayie (GER)	(11.30)	11.36
15.	Salomé Kora (SUI)		11.36
16.	Ezinne Okparaebo (NOR)		11.37
17.	Ajla del Ponte (SUI)		11.38
18.	Naomi Sedney (NED)		11.42
19.	Lorène Bazolo (POR)		11.46
20.	Phil Healy (IRL)	(11.44)	11.46
21.	Marije van Hunenstijn (NED)	(11.48)	11.49
22.	Inna Eftimova (BUL)	(11.45)	11.52
23.	Irene Siragusa (ITA)		11.60
24.	Anna Bongiorni (ITA)	(11.53)	11.62

25.	Klára Seidlová (CZE)	11.63
26.	Rafailia Spanoudáki-Hatziríga (GRE)	11.63
27.	Gina Akpe-Moses (IRL)	11.63
28.	Cristina Lara (ESP)	11.65

WORLD RANKING 2018:

1.	Marie-Josée Ta Lou (CIV)	10.85(Do)
	Dina Asher-Smith (GBR)	10.85(ECh)
3.	Blessing Okagbare (NGR)	10.90(Do)
	Aleia Hobbs (USA)	10.90(Tam)
	Murielle Ahouré (CIV)	10.90(Eug)
6.	Elaine Thompson (JAM)	10.93(Do)
7.	Mujinga Kambundji (SUI)	10.95
8.	Ashley Henderson (USA)	10.96(USC)
	Jenna Prandini (USA)	10.96(NAC)
10.	Carina Horn (RSA)	10.98(Do)
	Shania Collins (USA)	10.98(NCA)
	Shelly-Ann Fraser-Pryce (JAM)	10.98(Lon)
	Gina Lückenkemper (GER)	10.98(ECh)
14.	Twanisha Terry (USA)	10.99(Tor)
	Dezerea Bryant (USA)	10.99(USC)
	Wei Yongli (CHN)	10.99(LCF)
	Dafne Schippers (NED)	10.99(ECh)
18.	Ángela Tenorio (ECU)	11.01
	Carolle Zahi (FRA)	11.01
20.	Tamara Clark (USA)	11.02(Kno)
	English Gardner (USA)	11.02(Rov)
22.	Tori Bowie (USA)	11.03(Eug)
	Vitoria Rosa (BRA)	11.03
24.	Natalliah Whyte (JAM)	11.04(Kno)
	Jada Baylark (USA)	11.04
26.	Mikiah Brisco (USA)	11.05(Tam)
27.	Michelle-Lee Ahye (TTO)	11.06(Osl)
	Orlann Ombissa-Dzangue (FRA)	11.06
29.	Semoy Hackett (TTO)	11.07(Mtv)
	Jonielle Smith (JAM)	11.07(Lon)
31.	Arianna Washington (USA)	11.08(USC)
32.	Krystsina Tsimanouskaya (BLR)	11.09
33.	Kortnei Johnson (USA)	11.10(Tam)
	Javianne Oliver (USA)	11.10
	Jamile Samuel (NED)	11.10(ECh)
36.	Teahna Daniels (USA)	11.11(Wac)
	Tatjana Pinto (GER)	11.11
	Imani Lansiquot (GBR)	11.11(Lon)
	Crystal Emmanuel (CAN)	11.11(NAC)
40.	Marisol Landázuri (ECU)	11.12
41.	Briana Williams (JAM); Kiara Parker (USA); Taylor Bennett (USA); Ka'Tia Seymour (USA); Tamari Davis (USA); Aaliyah Brown (USA); Shericka Jackson (JAM)	11.13

WORLD INDOOR CHAMPIONSHIPS: 2-3-2018:

1. Murielle Ahouré (CIV)   (7.01)   6.97
2. Marie-Josée Ta Lou (CIV)   (7.08)   7.05
3. Mujinga Kambundji (SUI)   (7.10)   7.05
4. Elaine Thompson (JAM)   (7.07)   7.08
5. Dafne Schippers (NED)   (7.09)   7.10
6. Michelle-Lee Ahye (TTO)   (7.15)   7.13
7. Carolle Zahi (FRA)   (7.11)   7.19
8. Remona Burchell (JAM)   (7.15)   7.50

----

9. Javianne Oliver (USA)   7.10
10. Asha Philip (GBR)   7.13
11. Carina Horn (RSA)   7.18
12. Tatjana Pinto (GER)   7.18
13. Ezinne Okparaebo (NOR)   7.19
14. Kelly-Ann Baptiste (TTO)   7.21
15. Anna Kielbasinska (POL)   7.23
16. Ewa Swoboda (POL)   (7.24)   7.25
17. Bianca Williams (GBR)   7.26
18. Crystal Emmanuel (CAN)   (7.26)   7.27
19. Destiny Carter (USA)   (7.24)   7.28
20. Anna Bongiorni (ITA)   (7.24)   7.30
21. Liang Xiaojing (CHN)   (7.24)   7.30
22. Klára Seidlová (CZE)   (7.30)   7.35
23. Ajla del Ponte (SUI)   (7.31)   7.40
24. Gayon Evans (JAM)   (7.33)   dns

----

25. Rosângela Santos (BRA)   7.32
26. Jamile Samuel (NED)   7.34
27. Hrystyna Stuy (UKR)   7.34
28. Wei Yongli (CHN)   7.35
29. Andrea Purica (VEN)   7.36
30. Krystsina Tsimanouskaya (BLR)   7.37
31. Isidora Jiménez (CHI)   7.38
32. Vitoria Rosa (BRA)   7.39
33. Lorène Bazolo (POR)   7.39
34. Rafailia Spanoudáki-Hatziríga (GRE) 7.40
35. Mathilde Kramer (DEN)   7.43
36. Ciara Neville (IRL)   7.47
37. Tahesia Harrigan-Scott (IVB)   7.50

WORLD INDOOR RANKING 2018:

1. Murielle Ahouré (CIV)   6.97
2. Javianne Oliver (USA)   7.02
3. Mujinga Kambundji (SUI)   7.03
4. Marie-Josée Ta Lou (CIV)   7.05
5. Tatjana Pinto (GER)   7.06
6. Elaine Thompson (JAM)   7.07
    Aleia Hobbs (USA)   7.07
8. Mikiah Brisco (USA)   7.08
    Dina Asher-Smith (GBR)   7.08
10. Carina Horn (RSA)   7.09
    Dafne Schippers (NED)   7.09
12. Gina Lückenkemper (GER)   7.11
    Carolle Zahi (FRA)   7.11
14. Lisa Mayer (GER)   7.12
    Asha Philip (GBR)   7.12
    Nataliah Whyte (JAM)   7.12
17. Remona Burchell (JAM)   7.13
    Michelle-Lee Ahye (TTO)   7.13
19. Tori Bowie (USA)   7.14
    Christania Williams (JAM)   7.14
21. Jonielle Smith (JAM)   7.15
22. Ezinne Okparaebo (NOR)   7.17
    Jamile Samuel (NED)   7.17
    Kate Hall (USA)   7.17
25. Kortnei Johnson (USA)   7.18
    Morolake Akinosun (USA)   7.18
    Ewa Swoboda (POL)   7.18
    Makenzie Dunmore (USA)   7.18
29. Ashley Henderson (USA)   7.19
    Destiny Carter (USA)   7.19
31. Liang Xiaojing (CHN)   7.20
    Rosângela Santos (BRA)   7.20
    Quanesha Burks (USA)   7.20

Torrance, 21-4-2018:

1.	Twanisha Terry (USA)	10.99
2.	Ashley Henderson (USA)	11.06
3.	Jenna Prandini (USA)	11.09
4.	Aaliyah Brown (USA)	11.15
5.	Ariana Washington (USA)	11.17

Doha, 4-5-2018:

1.	Marie-Josée Ta Lou (CIV)	10.85
2.	Blessing Okagbare (NGR)	10.90
3.	Elaine Thompson (JAM)	10.93
4.	Murielle Ahouré (CIV)	10.96
5.	Carina Horn (RSA)	10.98
6.	Dafne Schippers (NED)	11.03

Knoxville, 12-5-2018:

1.	Aleia Hobbs (USA)	(10.93)	10.92
2.	Shania Collins (USA)	(11.06)	10.99
3.	Tamara Clark (USA)		11.03
4.	Natalliah Whyte (JAM)		11.04
5.	Mikiah Brisco (USA)	(11.09)	11.07
6.	Kortnei Johnson (USA)		11.12
7.	Kiara Parker (USA)		11.13
8.	Cassondra Hall (USA)		11.29

Eugene, 26-5-2018:

1.	Marie-Josée Ta Lou (CIV)	10.88
2.	Murielle Ahouré (CIV)	10.90
3.	Elaine Thompson (JAM)	10.98
4.	Dafne Schippers (NED)	11.01
5.	Torie Bowie (USA)	11.03
6.	Dina Asher-Smith (GBR)	11.06
7.	Blessing Okagbare (NGR)	11.07
8.	Javianne Oliver (USA)	11.10

Oslo, 7-6-2018:

1.	Murielle Ahouré (CIV)	10.91
2.	Dina Asher-Smith (GBR)	10.92
3.	Michelle-Lee Ahye (TTO)	11.06
4.	Blessing Okagbare (NGR)	11.12
5.	Gina Lückenkemper (GER)	11.12
6.	Carina Horn (RSA)	11.22

Eugene, NCAA, 9-6-2018:

1.	Aleia Hobbs (USA)	(10.91)	11.01
2.	Natallia Whyte (JAM)	(11.11)	11.24
3.	Twanisha Terry (USA)	(11.08)	11.39
4.	Jonielle Smith (JAM)	(11.11)	11.40
5.	Shania Collins (USA)	(10.98)	11.41
6.	Mikiah Brisco (USA)	(11.18)	11.44
7.	Deanna Hill (USA)	(11.17)	11.45
8.	Ariana Washington (USA)	(11.08)	11.50

Kingston, 9-6-2018:

1.	Shelly-Ann Fraser-Pryce (JAM)	11.10
2.	Jenna Prandini (USA)	11.14
3.	Briana Williams (JAM)	11.26

Stockholm, 10-6-2018:

1.	Dina Asher-Smith (GBR)	10.93
2.	Murielle Ahouré (CIV)	11.03
3.	Michelle-Lee Ahye (TTO)	11.11
4.	Gina Lückenkemper (GER)	11.23
5.	Blessing Okagbare (NGR)	11.29
6.	Carina Horn (RSA)	11.29

US CHAMPIONSHIPS, Des Moines, 22-6-2018:

1.	Aleia Hobbs	(10.97)	10.91
2.	Ashley Henderson	(11.03)	10.96
3.	Jenna Prandini	(11.00)	10.98
4.	Mikiah Brisco		11.10
5.	Aaliyah Brown		11.13
6.	Dezerea Bryant	(10.99)	11.17
7.	Shania Collins	(11.10)	11.21
8.	Kiara Parker		11.22
---	---	---	---
9.	Tawanna Meadows	(11.27)	11.19+
10.	Ariana Washington		11.20
11.	Lekeisha Lawson	(11.19)	11.21+
12.	Barbara Pierre		11.23
13.	Deajah Stevens	(11.18)	11.26+
14.	Destinee Brown	(11.33)	11.36
15.	Gabrielle Cunningham	(11.21)	11.40
16.	Candyce McGrone		11.52+
---	---	---	---
17.	Jada Baylark		11.34
18.	Kimberlyn Duncan		11.34+
19.	Kaylin Whitney		11.37
20.	Jeneba Tarmoh		11.40
21.	Felicia Brown		11.53

JAM CHAMPIONSHIPS, Kingston, 22-6-2018:

1.	Elaine Thompson		11.01
2.	Shelly-Ann Fraser		11.09
3.	Shericka Jackson		11.13
4.	Jonielle Smith		11.15
5.	Briana Williams		11.21
6.	Jura Levy	(11.22)	11.33
7.	Natasha Morrison		11.34
8.	Jodean Williams	(11.32)	11.36

Lausanne, 5-7-2018:

1.	Marie-Josée Ta Lou (CIV)	10.90
2.	Elaine Thompson (JAM)	10.99
3.	Jenna Prandini (USA)	11.00
4.	Dafne Schippers (NED)	11.02
5.	Mujinga Kambundji (SUI)	11.03
6.	Murielle Ahouré (CIV)	11.03

Monaco, 20-7-2018:

1.	Marie-Josée Ta Lou (CIV)	10.89
2.	Murielle Ahouré (CIV)	11.01
3.	Elaine Thompson (JAM)	11.02
4.	Jenna Prandini (USA)	11.09
5.	Dafne Schippers (NED)	11.12
6.	Mujinga Kambundji (SUI)	11.15
7.	Carina Horn (RSA)	11.21
8.	Blessing Okagbare (NGR)	11.32

London, 21-7-2018:

1.	Shelly-Ann Fraser-Pryce (JAM)	10.98
2.	Dezerea Bryant (USA)	11.04
3.	Jonielle Smith (JAM)	11.07
4.	Wei Yongli (CHN)	11.10
5.	Imani-Lara Lansiquot (GBR)	11.11
6.	Jamile Samuel (NED)	11.14

NACAC, Toronto, 11-8-2018:

1.	Jenna Prandini (USA)	(11.01)	10.96
2.	Jonielle Smith (JAM)		11.07
3.	Crystal Emmanuel (CAN)		11.11
4.	Dezerea Bryant (USA)		11.17
5.	Shelly-Ann Fraser-Pryce (JAM)		11.18

Zürich, 30-8-2018:

1.	Murielle Ahouré (CIV)	11.01
2.	Dina Asher-Smith (GBR)	11.08
3.	Marie-Josée Ta Lou (CIV)	11.10
4.	Mujinga Kambundji (SUI)	11.14
5.	Dafne Schippers (NED)	11.15
6.	Michelle-Lee Ahye (TTO)	11.27

Berlin, 2-9-2018:

1.	Marie-Josée Ta Lou (CIV)	11.08
2.	Michelle-Lee Ahye (TTO)	11.13
3.	Gina Lückenkemper (GER)	11.18
4.	Daryll Neita (GBR)	11.24
5.	Dezerea Bryant (USA)	11.29

CONTINENTAL CUP, Ostrava, 8-9-2018:

1.	Marie-Josée Ta Lou (AFR)	11.14
2.	Dina Asher-Smith (EUR)	11.16
3.	Jenna Prandini (AME)	11.21
4.	Dafne Schippers (EUR)	11.23

OVERVIEW WORLD OUTDOOR CHAMPIONSHIP FINALISTS OF PAST 6 YEARS

	Wch 17	OG 16	Wch 15	Wch 13
Tori Bowie (USA)	10.85 (1)	10.83 (2)	10.86 (3)	
Marie-Josée Ta Lou (CIV)	10.86 (2)	10.86 (4)		
Dafne Schippers (NED)	10.96 (3)	10.90 (5)	10.81 (2)	
Murielle Ahouré (CIV)	10.98 (4)			10.93 (2)
Elaine Thompson (JAM)	10.98 (5)	10.71 (1)		
Michelle-Lee Ahye (TTO)	11.01 (6)	10.92 (6)	10.98 (5)	
Rosangela Santos (BRA)	11.06 (7)			
Kelly-Ann Baptiste (TTO)	11.09 (8)		11.01 (6)	
Shelly-Ann Fraser-Pryce (JAM)		10.86 (3)	10.76 (1)	10.71 (1)
English Gardner (USA)		10.94 (7)		10.97 (4)
Christania Williams (JAM)		11.80 (8)		
Veronica Campbell-Brown (JAM)			10.91 (4)	
Natasha Morrison (JAM)			11.02 (7)	
Blessing Okagbare (NGR)			11.02 (8)	11.04 (6)
Carmelita Jeter (USA)				10.94 (4)
Kerron Stewart (JAM)				10.97 (5)
Alexandria Anderson (USA)				11.10 (7)
Octavious Freeman (USA)				11.16 (8)

OVERVIEW WORLD INDOOR CHAMPIONSHIP FINALISTS OF PAST 5 YEARS

	Wch 18	Wch 16	Wch 14
Murielle Ahouré (CIV)	6.97 (1)		7.01 (2)
Marie-Josée Ta Lou (CIV)	7.05 (2)	7.29 (7)	
Mujinga Kambundji (SUI)	7.05 (3)		
Elaine Thompson (JAM)	7.08 (4)	7.06 (3)	
Dafne Schippers (NED)	7.10 (5)	7.04 (2)	
Michelle-Lee Ahye (TTO)	7.13 (6)	7.11 (4)	7.16 (6)
Carolle Zahi (FRA)	7.19 (7)		
Remona Burchell (JAM)	7.50 (8)		
Barbara Pierre (USA)		7.02 (1)	
Asha Philip (GBR)		7.14 (5)	7.11 (4)
Tori Bowie (USA)		7.14 (5)	
Dina Asher-Smith (GBR)		dns (8)	
Shelly-Ann Fraser-Pryce (JAM)			6.98 (1)
Tianna Bartoletta (USA)			7.06 (3)
Veronica Campbell-Brown (JAM)			7.13 (5)
Gloria Asumnu (NGR)			7.18 (7)
Verena Sailer (GER)			7.18 (8)

OVERVIEW TOP 10 WORLD OUTDOOR RANKINGS OF PAST 5 YEARS

	2018	2017	2016	2015	2014
Marie-Josée Ta Lou (CIV)	10.85 (1)	10.86 (7)	10.86 (8)		
Dina Asher-Smith (GBR)	10.85 (1)				
Blessing Okagbare (NGR)	10.90 (3)			10.80 (3)	10.85 (2)
Aleia Hobbs (USA)	10.90 (3)	10.85 (5)			
Murielle Ahouré (CIV)	10.90 (3)	10.83 (3)	10.78 (3)	10.81 (4)	10.97 (6)
Elaine Thompson (JAM)	10.93 (6)	10.71 (1)	10.70 (1)	10.84 (7)	
Mujinga Kambundji (SUI)	10.95 (7)				
Ashley Henderson (USA)	10.96 (8)				
Jenna Prandini (USA)	10.96 (8)			10.92 (10)	
Carina Horn (RSA)	10.98 (10)				
Shania Collins (USA)	10.98 (10)				
Shelly-Ann Fraser-Pryce (JAM)	10.98 (10)		10.86 (8)	10.74 (1)	11.01 (8)
Gina Lückenkemper (GER)	10.98 (10)				
Michelle-Lee Ahye (TTO)		10.82 (2)	10.90 (10)		10.85 (2)
Veronica Campbell-Brown (JAM)		10.84 (4)	10.83 (6)	10.89 (9)	10.86 (4)
Tori Bowie (USA)		10.85 (5)	10.78 (3)	10.81 (4)	10.80 (1)
Kelly-Ann Baptiste (TTO)		10.88 (8)		10.84 (7)	
Rosangela Santos (BRA)		10.91 (9)			
Schillonie Schalvert (JAM)		10.94 (10)			
English Gardner (USA)			10.74 (2)	10.79 (2)	11.01 (8)
Tianna Bartoletta (USA)			10.78 (3)		10.92 (5)
Dafne Schippers (NED)			10.83 (6)	10.81 (4)	
Jasmine Todd (USA)				10.92 (10)	
Barbara Pierre (USA)				10.92 (10)	
Samantha Henry-Robinson (JAM)					11.00 (7)
Allyson Felix (USA)					11.01 (8)

OVERVIEW TOP 10 WORLD INDOOR RANKINGS OF PAST 5 YEARS

	2018	**2017**	**2016**	**2015**	**2014**
Murielle Ahouré (CIV)	6.97 (1)			7.05 (1)	7.01 (2)
Javianne Oliver (USA)	7.02 (2)				
Mujinga Kambundji (SUI)	7.03 (3)			7.11 (8)	
Marie-Josée Ta Lou (CIV)	7.05 (4)		7.06 (4)		
Tatjana Pinto (GER)	7.06 (5)		7.07 (5)		
Elaine Thompson (JAM)	7.07 (6)	6.98 (1)	7.04 (3)		
Aleia Hobbs (USA)	7.07 (6)				
Mikiah Brisco (USA)	7.08 (8)				
Dina Asher-Smith (GBR)	7.08 (8)	7.13 (9)	7.11 (9)	7.08 (3)	
Carina Horn (RSA)	7.09 (10)				
Dafne Schippers (NED)	7.09 (10)		7.00 (1)	7.05 (1)	
Asha Philip (GBR)		7.06 (2)	7.10 (8)		7.09 (4)
Hannah Cunliffe (USA)		7.07 (3)			
Morolake Akinosun (USA)		7.08 (4)			
Olesya Povh (UKR)		7.10 (5)		7.11 (8)	
Ewa Swoboda (POL)		7.10 (5)	7.07 (5)		
Barbara Pierre (USA)		7.11 (7)	7.00 (1)		7.10 (6)
Dezerea Bryant (USA)		7.11 (7)			
Ezinne Okparaebo (NOR)		7.13 (9)		7.10 (7)	
Michelle-Lee Ahye (TTO)			7.09 (7)	7.11 (8)	7.10 (6)
Teahna Daniels (USA)			7.11 (9)		
Tori Bowie (USA)			7.11 (9)		
Remona Burchell (JAM)				7.08 (3)	7.11 (8)
Tianna Bartoletta (USA)				7.08 (3)	7.06 (3)
Verena Sailer (GER)				7.08 (3)	
Shelly-Ann Fraser-Pryce (JAM)					6.98 (1)
LaKeisha Lawson (USA)					7.09 (4)
LaKya Brookins (USA)					7.11 (8)
Gloria Asumnu (NGR)					7.11 (8)

WORLD RANKING ALL TIME OUTDOOR:

1.	Florence Griffith-Joyner (USA)	10.49 (1988)
2.	Carmelita Jeter (USA)	10.64 (2009)
3.	Marion Jones (USA)	10.65 (1998)
4.	Shelly-Ann Fraser-Pryce (JAM)	10.70 (2012)
	Elaine Thompson (JAM)	10.70 (2016)
6.	Christine Arron (FRA)	10.73 (1998)
7.	Merlene Ottey (JAM)	10.74 (1996)
	English Gardner (USA)	10.74 (2016)
9.	Kerron Stewart (JAM)	10.75 (2009)
10.	Evelyn Ashford (USA)	10.76 (1984)
	Veronica Campbell-Brown (JAM)	10.76 (2011)
12.	Irina Privalova (RUS)	10.77 (2014)
	Ivet Lalova-Collio (BUL)	10.77 (2004)
14.	Dawn Sowell (USA)	10.78 (1989)
	Torri Edwards (USA)	10.78 (2008)
	Murielle Ahouré (CIV)	10.78 (2016)
	Tianna Bartoletta (USA)	10.78 (2016)
	Tori Bowie (USA)	10.78 (2016)
19.	Li Xuemei (CHN)	10.79 (1997)
	Inger Miller (USA)	10.79 (1999)
	Blessing Okagbare (NGR)	10.79 (2013)
22.	Marlies Göhr (GDR)	10.81 (1983)
	Dafne Schippers (NED)	10.81 (2015)
24.	Gail Devers (USA)	10.82 (1992)
	Gwen Torrence (USA)	10.82 (1994)
	Zhanna Block (UKR)	10.82 (2001)
	Sherone Simpson (JAM)	10.82 (2006)
	Michelle-Lee Ahye (TTO)	10.82 (2017)
29.	Marita Koch (GDR)	10.83 (1983)
	Sheila Echols (USA)	10.83 (1988)
	Juliet Cuthbert (JAM)	10.83 (1992)
	Katerina Thanou (GRE)	10.83 (1999)
33.	Chandra Sturrup (BAH)	10.84 (2005)
	Kelly-Ann Baptiste (TTO)	10.84 (2010)
35.	Anelia Nuneva (BUL)	10.85 (1988)
	Muna Lee (USA)	10.85 (2008)
	Barbara Pierre (USA)	10.85 (2013)
	Aleia Hobbs (USA)	10.85 (2017)
	Marie-Josée Ta Lou (CIV)	10.85 (2018)
	Dina Asher-Smith (GBR)	10.85 (2018)
41.	Silke Möller (GDR)	10.86 (1987)
	Diane Williams (USA)	10.86 (1988)
	Chryste Gaines (USA)	10.86 (2003)
	Marshevet Hooker (USA)	10.86 (2011)
45.	Octavious Freeman (USA)	10.87 (2013)

WORLD RANKING ALL TIME INDOOR:

1.	Irina Privalova (RUS)	6.92 (1993)
2.	Gail Devers (USA)	6.95 (1993)
	Marion Jones (USA)	6.95 (1998)
4.	Merlene Ottey (JAM)	6.96 (1992)
	Katerina Thanou (GRE)	6.96 (1999)
6.	LaVerne Jones-Ferrette (ISV)	6.97 (2010)
	Murielle Ahouré (CIV)	6.97 (2018)
8.	Shelly-Ann Fraser-Pryce (JAM)	6.98 (2014)
	Elaine Thompson (JAM)	6.98 (2017)
10.	Nelli Cooman (NED)	7.00 (1986)
	Veronica Campbell-Brown (JAM)	7.00 (2010)
	Dafne Schippers (NED)	7.00 (2016)
	Barbara Pierre (USA)	7.00 (2016)
14.	Savatheda Fynes (BAH)	7.01 (1999)
	Me'Lisa Barber (USA)	7.01 (2006)
	Lauryn Williams (USA)	7.01 (2006)
17.	Gwen Torrence (USA)	7.02 (1996)
	Christy Opara-Thompson (NGR)	7.02 (1997)
	Chioma Ajunwa (NGR)	7.02 (1998)
	Philomena Mensah (CAN)	7.02 (1999)
	Carmelita Jeter (USA)	7.02 (2010)
	Tianna Bartoletta (USA)	7.02 (2012)
	Javianne Oliver (USA)	7.02 (2018)
24.	Anelia Nuneva (BUL)	7.03 (1987)
	Mujinga Kambundji (SUI)	7.03 (2018)
26.	Marita Koch (GDR)	7.04 (1985)
	Silke Möller (GDR)	7.04 (1988)
	Carlette Guidry (USA)	7.04 (1995)
	Natalya Safronnikova (BLR)	7.04 (2001)
	Petya Pendareva (BUL)	7.04 (2001)
	Mariya Bolikova (RUS)	7.04 (2006)
32.	Chandra Sturrup (BAH)	7.05 (2001)
	Marie-Josée Ta Lou (CIV)	7.05 (2018)
34.	Katrin Krabbe (GER)	7.06 (1991)
	Natalya Voronova (RUS)	7.06 (1993)
	Olga Bogoslovskaya (RUS)	7.06 (1994)
	Yuliya Tabakova (RUS)	7.06 (2004)
	Christine Arron (FRA)	7.06 (2006)
	Angela Williams (USA)	7.06 (2008)
	Asha Philip (GBR)	7.06 (2017)
	Tatjana Pinto (GER)	7.06 (2018)
42 – 51.:		
	Marlies Göhr (GDR)	7.07 (1986)
	Michelle Burrell-Finn (USA)	7.07 (1992)
	Zhanna Block (UKR)	7.07 (1993)
	et al.	

200 m Women

EUROPEAN CHAMPIONSHIPS 2018: 11-8-2018:

1.	Dina Asher-Smith (GBR)	(22.33)	21.89
2.	Dafne Schippers (NED)	(22.69)	22.14
3.	Jamile Samuel (NED)	(22.58)	22.37
4.	Mujinga Kambundji (SUI)	(22.84)	22.45
5.	Ivet Lalova-Collio (BUL)	(22.65)	22.82
6.	Bianca Williams (GBR)	(22.83)	22.88
7.	Beth Dobbin (GBR)	(22.84)	22.93
8.	Laura Müller (GER)	(22.87)	23.08

9.	Sarah Atcho (SUI)		22.88
10.	Krystsina Tsimanouskaya (BLR)		23.03
11.	Phil Healy (IRL)		23.23
12.	Jessica-Bianca Wessolly (GER)		23.26
13.	Jodie Williams (GBR)		23.28
14.	Anna Kielbasinska (POL)	(23.20)	23.29
15.	Irene Siragusa (ITA)		23.30
16.	Martyna Kotwila (POL)		23.41
17.	Rebekka Haase (GER)		23.42
18.	Gloria Hooper (ITA)	(23.28)	23.43
19.	Estela Garcia (ESP)		23.46
20.	Manon Depuydt (BEL)	(23.59)	23.60
21.	Inna Eftimova (BUL)	(23.56)	23.62
22.	Lorène Bazolo (POR)	(23.60)	23.80
23.	Cornelia Halbheer (SUI)	(23.63)	23.98
	Sindija Buksa (LAT)	(23.36)	dns

25.	Marcela Pirková (CZE)	23.72
26.	Alina Kalistratova (UKR)	23.79
27.	Ezinne Okparaebo (NOR)	23.84
28.	Paula Sevilla (ESP)	23.91

WORLD RANKING 2018:

1.	Dina Asher-Smith (GBR)	21.89(ECh)
2.	Blessing Okagbare (NGR)	22.04
3.	Shericka Jackson (JAM)	22.05(Par)
4.	Shaunae Miller-Uibo (BAH)	22.06(Sha)
5.	Dafne Schippers (NED)	22.14(ECh)
6.	Jenna Prandini (USA)	22.16(Lon)
7.	Gabrielle Thomas (USA)	22.19(Lon)
8.	Lynna Irby (USA)	22.25(Kno)
9.	Elaine Thompson (JAM)	22.30(GC)
10.	Shakima Wimbley (USA)	22.34(Cle)
	Marie-Josée Ta Lou (CIV)	22.34(Lon)
12.	Jamile Samuel (NED)	22.37(Lon)
13.	Sydney McLaughlin (USA)	22.39(Gai)
14.	Brittany Brown (USA)	22.42(USC)
	Phyllis Francis (USA)	22.42(USC)
16.	Mujinga Kambundji (SUI)	22.45(ECh)
17.	Jeneba Tarmoh (USA)	22.46(USC)
18.	Shania Collins (USA)	22.47(Kno)
19.	Tamari Davis (USA)	22.48
	Kyra Jefferson (USA)	22.48(USC)
21.	Ashley Henderson (USA)	22.49(NCA)
22.	Briana Williams (JAM)	22.50
23.	Lauren Rain Williams (USA)	22.51(Tuc)
24.	Makenzie Dunmore (USA)	22.53(PA)
	Tamara Clark (USA)	22.53
26.	Arianna Washington (USA)	22.54(USC)
27.	Natalliah Whyte (JAM)	22.55(Aub)
28.	Kortnei Johnson (USA)	22.56
29.	Mikiah Brisco (USA)	22.59
	Beth Dobbin (GBR)	22.59
31.	Murielle Ahouré (CIV)	22.60(Ost)
	Bianca Williams (GBR)	22.60
33.	Joanna Atkins (USA)	22.62(Cle)
	Edidiong Ofinome Odiong (BRN)	22.62(CON)
35.	Ivet Lalova-Collio (BUL)	22.63(Sto)
	Kimberlyn Duncan (USA)	22.63(USC)
37.	Anglerne Annelus (USA)	22.64(PA)
	Semoy Hackett (TTO)	22.64
39.	Janet Amponsah (GHA)	22.67(Aub)
	Deanna Hill (USA)	22.67
	Crystal Emmanuel (CAN)	22.67(NAC)
42.	Jasmine Camacho-Quinn (PUR)	22.69

WORLD INDOOR RANKING 2018:

1.	Gabrielle Thomas (USA)	22.38
2.	Ashley Henderson (USA)	22.41
3.	Lynna Irby (USA)	22.55
4.	Sydney McLaughlin (USA)	22.68
5.	Mikiah Brisco (USA)	22.81
6.	Deanna Hill (USA)	22.82
7.	Kayelle Clarke (TTO)	22.83
8.	Ka'Tia Seymour (USA)	22.85
9.	Léa Sprunger (SUI)	22.88
	Kortnei Johnson (USA)	22.88
11.	Payton Stumbaugh Chadwick (USA)	22.99
	Kendall Ellis (USA)	22.99
13.	Jasmine Camacho-Quinn (PUR)	23.00
14.	Quanera Hayes (USA)	23.02
	Maria Belimpasaki (GRE)	23.02
	Shauna Helps (JAM)	23.02
17.	Daija Lampkin (USA)	23.03
18.	Danyel White (USA)	23.07
19.	Tamara Clark (USA)	23.10
20.	Anna Kielbasinska (POL)	23.12
21.	Shania Collins (USA)	23.14
	Felicia Brown (USA)	23.14
	Hannah Jackson (USA)	23.14
24.	Brenessa Thompson (GUY)	23.15
25.	Anna Cockrell (USA)	23.16
	Lauren Rain Williams (USA)	23.16
	Diamond Spaulding (USA)	23.16
	Brittany Brown (USA)	23.16
29.	LaTessa Johnson (USA)	23.17
30.	Twanisha Terry (USA)	23.19
	Tatjana Pinto (GER)	23.19
32.	Khianna Gray (USA)	23.20

Commonwealth Games, Gold Coast, 12-4-2018:
1.	Shaunae Miller-Uibo (BAH)	22.09
2.	Shericka Jackson (JAM)	22.18
3.	Dina Asher-Smith (GBR)	22.29
4.	Elaine Thompson (JAM)	22.30
5.	Crystal Emmanuel (CAN)	22.70

Shanghai, 12-5-2018:
1.	Shaunae Miller-Uibo (BAH)	22.06
2.	Dafne Schippers (NED)	22.34
3.	Shericka Jackson (JAM)	22.36
4.	Marie-Josée Ta Lou (CIV)	22.58
5.	Mujinga Kambundji (SUI)	22.72

Knoxville, 13-5-2018:
1.	Lynna Irby (USA)	22.25
2.	Shania Collins (USA)	22.47
3.	Tamara Clark (USA)	22.64
4.	Mikiah Brisco (USA)	22.88
5.	Kortnei Johnson (USA)	22.95

NCAA, Eugene, 9-6-2018:
1.	Anglerne Annelus (USA)	(22.52+)	22.76
2.	Gabrielle Thomas (USA)	(22.36+)	22.86
3.	Lynna Irby (USA)	(22.37)	22.92
4.	Ka'Tia Seymour (USA)	(22.74)	23.10
5.	Kortnei Johnson (USA)	(22.71)	23.20
6.	Ashley Henderson (USA)	(22.49)	23.34
7.	Deanna Hill (USA)	(22.78)	23.53
8.	Shania Collins (USA)	(22.67)	24.01

Kingston, 9-6-2018:
1.	Shaunae Miller-Uibo (BAH)	22.11
2.	Shericka Jackson (JAM)	22.62
3.	Shashalee Forbes (JAM)	22.86

JAM CHAMPIONSHIPS, 24-6-2018:
1.	Shericka Jackson	22.28
2.	Shashalee Forbes	22.95
3.	Jodean Williams	23.23

US CHAMPIONSHIPS, Des Moines, 24-6-2018:
1.	Jenna Prandini	(22.22)	22.62
2.	Phyllis Francis	(22.42)	22.83
3.	Kyra Jefferson	(22.48)	22.89
4.	Shania Collins	(22.54)	23.08
5.	Brittany Brown	(22.42)	23.08
6.	Kimberlyn Duncan	(22.63)	23.13
7.	Ariana Washington	(22.54)	23.22
8.	Jeneba Tarmoh	(22.46)	23.33
---	---	---	---
9.	Kortnei Johnson		22.58
10.	Joanna Atkins		22.70
11.	Jaide Stepter		22.87
12.	Kaylin Whitney		23.05
13.	Ashton Purvis		23.39
14.	Gabrielle Cunningham		23.45
	Mikiah Brisco		dns
	Deajah Stevens		dns

Paris, 30-6-2018:
1.	Shericka Jackson (JAM)	22.05
2.	Jenna Prandini (USA)	22.30
3.	Marie Josée Ta Lou (CIV)	22.50
4.	Jamile Samuel (NED)	22.63
5.	Kyra Jefferson (USA)	22.69
6.	Kimberlyn Duncan (USA)	22.95

Rabat, 13-7-2018:
1.	Shaunae Miller-Uibo (BAH)	22.29
2.	Dina Asher-Smith (GBR)	22.40
3.	Jenna Prandini (USA)	22.60
4.	Gabrielle Thomas (USA)	22.70
5.	Murielle Ahouré (CIV)	22.70

London, 22-7-2018:
1.	Jenna Prandini (USA)	22.16
2.	Gabrielle Thomas (USA)	22.19
3.	Shericka Jackson (JAM)	22.22
4.	Dina Asher-Smith (GBR)	22.25
5.	Marie-Josée Ta Lou (CIV)	22.34
6.	Jamile Samuel (NED)	22.37
7.	Dafne Schippers (NED)	22.42

Birmingham, 18-8-2018:
1. Shaunae Miller-Uibo (BAH)   22.15
2. Dina Asher-Smith (GBR)   22.31
3. Dafne Schippers (NED)   22.41
4. Shericka Jackson (JAM)   22.55
5. Jenna Prandini (USA)   22.58
6. Gabrielle Thomas (USA)   22.85
7. Marie-José Ta Lou (CIV)   22.88

Brussels, 31-8-2018:
1. Shaunae Miller-Uibo (BAH)   22.12
2. Dafne Schippers (NED)   22.53
3. Jamile Samuel (NED)   22.64
4. Shericka Jackson (JAM)   22.72
5. Jenna Prandini (USA)   22.96
6. Gabrielle Thomas (USA)   23.18

CONTINENTAL CUP, Ostrava, 9-9-2018:
1. Shaunae Miller-Uibo (AME)   22.16
2. Dafne Schippers (EUR)   22.28
3. Marie-Josée Ta Lou (AFR)   22.61
4. Shericka Jackson (AME)   22.62
5. Edidiong Odiong (ASI)   22.62

OVERVIEW WORLD OUTDOOR CHAMPIONSHIP FINALISTS OF PAST 6 YEARS

	Wch 17	OG 16	Wch 15	Wch 13
Dafne Schippers (NED)	22.05 (1)	21.88 (2)	21.63 (1)	
Marie-Josée Ta Lou (CIV)	22.08 (2)	22.21 (4)		
Shaunae Miller-Uibo (BAH)	22.15 (3)			22.74 (4)
Dina Asher-Smith (GBR)	22.22 (4)	22.31 (5)	22.07 (5)	
Deajah Stevens (USA)	22.44 (5)	22.65 (7)		
Kimberlyn Duncan (USA)	22.59 (6)			
Crystal Emmanuel (CAN)	22.60 (7)			
Tynia Gaither (BAH)	23.07 (8)			
Elaine Thompson (JAM)		21.78 (1)	21.66 (2)	
Tori Bowie (USA)		22.15 (3)		
Michelle-Lee Ahye (TTO)		22.34 (6)		
Ivet Lalova-Collio (BUL)		22.69 (8)	22.41 (7)	
Veronica Campbell-Brown (JAM)			21.97 (3)	
Candyce McGrone (USA)			22.01 (4)	
Jeneba Tarmoh (USA)			22.31 (6)	22.78 (5)
Sherone Simpson (JAM)			22.50 (8)	
Shelly-Ann Fraser-Pryce (JAM)				22.17 (1)
Murielle Ahouré (CIV)				22.32 (2)
Blessing Okagbare (NGR)				22.32 (3)
ChaRonda Williams (USA)				22.81 (6)
Mariya Ryemyen (UKR)				22.84 (7)
Allyson Felix (USA)				dnf (8)

OVERVIEW TOP 10 WORLD OUTDOOR RANKINGS OF PAST 5 YEARS

	2018	**2017**	**2016**	**2015**	**2014**
Dina Asher-Smith (GBR)	21.89 (1)	22.22 (8)		22.07 (6)	
Blessing Okagbare (NGR)	22.04 (2)				22.23 (5)
Shericka Jackson (JAM)	22.05 (3)				
Shaunae Miller-Uibo (BAH)	22.06 (4)	21.88 (2)	22.05 (5)	22.14 (7)	
Dafne Schippers (NED)	22.14 (5)	22.05 (5)	21.86 (2)	21.63 (1)	22.03 (2)
Jenna Prandini (USA)	22.16 (6)			22.20 (9)	
Gabrielle Thomas (USA)	22.19 (7)				
Lynna Irby (USA)	22.25 (8)				
Elaine Thompson (JAM)	22.30 (9)	21.98 (3)	21.78 (1)	21.66 (2)	
Shakima Wimbley (USA)	22.34 (10)				
Marie-Josée Ta Lou (CIV)	22.34 (10)	22.08 (6)	22.21 (6)		
Tori Bowie (USA)		21.77 (1)	21.99 (3)	22.23 (10)	22.18 (4)
Kyra Jefferson (USA)		22.02 (4)			
Deajah Stevens (USA)		22.09 (7)	22.25 (8)		
Allyson Felix (USA)		22.33 (9)	22.02 (4)	21.98 (4)	22.02 (1)
Ariana Washington (USA)		22.39 (10)	22.21 (6)		
Michelle-Lee Ahye (TTO)			22.25 (8)		
Felecia Brown (USA)			22.26 (10)		
Veronica Campbell-Brown (JAM)				21.97 (3)	
Candyce McGrone (USA)				22.01 (5)	
Dezerea Bryant (USA)				22.18 (8)	
Jeneba Tarmoh (USA)				22.23 (10)	22.41 (9)
Myriam Soumaré (FRA)					22.11 (3)
Olivia Ekpone (USA)					22.23 (5)
Joanna Atkins (USA)					22.27 (7)
Murielle Ahouré (CIV)					22.36 (8)
Jodie Williams (GBR)					22.46 (10)

OVERVIEW TOP 10 WORLD INDOOR RANKINGS OF PAST 5 YEARS

	2018	2017	2016	2015	2014
Gabrielle Thomas (USA)	22.38 (1)	22.88 (9)			
Ashley Henderson (USA)	22.41 (2)	22.81 (6)			
Lynna Irby (USA)	22.55 (3)				
Sydney McLaughlin (USA)	22.68 (4)				
Mikiah Brisco (USA)	22.81 (5)				
Deanna Hill (USA)	22.82 (6)	22.54 (3)	23.03 (6)		
Kayelle Clarke (TTO)	22.83 (7)				
Ka'Tia Seymour (USA)	22.85 (8)				
Léa Sprunger (SUI)	22.88 (9)				
Kortnei Johnson (USA)	22.88 (9)				
Ariana Washington (USA)		22.42 (1)		23.07 (7)	
Hannah Cunliffe (USA)		22.53 (2)	22.85 (3)		
Deajah Stevens (USA)		22.65 (4)	22.98 (5)		
Rebekka Haase (GER)		22.77 (5)	23.10 (10)	23.12 (10)	
Jada Martin (USA)		22.85 (7)	22.92 (4)		
Brittany Brown (USA)		22.86 (8)			
Ashley Spencer (USA)		22.94 (10)			
Diamond Spaulding (USA)		22.94 (10)			
Felecia Brown (USA)			22.45 (1)		
Kyra Jefferson (USA)			22.72 (2)	22.63 (2)	22.79 (3)
Taylor Ellis-Watson (USA)			23.03 (6)	23.08 (8)	
DayeShon Robertson (USA)			23.05 (8)		
Kali Davis-White (USA)			23.08 (9)		
Robin Reynolds (USA)			23.10 (10)		
Jenna Prandini (USA)				22.52 (1)	
Dezerea Bryant (USA)				22.74 (3)	22.69 (2)
Cierra White (USA)				22.90 (4)	
Akeyla Mitchell (USA)				22.96 (5)	
Kamaria Brown (USA)				22.97 (6)	22.50 (1)
Shakima Wimbley (USA)				23.08 (8)	
Phyllis Francis (USA)					22.92 (4)
Mahagony Jones (USA)					22.93 (5)
Regine Williams (USA)					23.06 (6)
Olivia Ekpone (USA)					23.10 (7)
Patricia Hall (JAM)					23.11 (8)
Ashton Purvis (USA)					23.11 (8)
Dina Asher-Smith (GBR)					23.15 (10)

WORLD RANKING ALL TIME OUTDOOR:

1.	Florence Griffith-Joyner (USA)	21.34 (1988)
2.	Marion Jones (USA)	21.62 (1998)
3.	Dafne Schippers (NED)	21.63 (2015)
4.	Merlene Ottey (JAM)	21.64 (1991)
5.	Elaine Thompson (JAM)	21.66 (2015)
6.	Allyson Felix (USA)	21.69 (2012)
7.	Marita Koch (GDR)	21.71 (1979)
	Heike Drechsler (GDR)	21.71 (1986)
9.	Grace Jackson-Small (JAM)	21.72 (1988)
	Gwen Torrence (USA)	21.72 (1992)
11.	Marlies Göhr (GDR)	21.74 (1984)
	Silke Möller (GDR)	21.74 (1987)
	Veronica Campbell-Brown (JAM)	21.74 (2008)
14.	Juliet Cuthbert (JAM)	21.75 (1992)
15.	Inger Miller (USA)	21.77 (1999)
	Tori Bowie (USA)	21.77 (2017)
17.	Valerie Brisco-Hooks (USA)	21.81 (1984)
18.	Evelyn Ashford (USA)	21.83 (1979)
19.	Bärbel Wöckel (GDR)	21.85 (1984)
20.	Irina Privalova (RUS)	21.87 (1995)
21.	Shaunae Miller-Uibo (BAH)	21.88 (2017)
22.	Dina Asher-Smith (GBR)	21.89 (2018)
23.	Pam Marshall (USA)	21.93 (1988)
24.	Katrin Krabbe (GDR)	21.95 (1990)
25.	Jarmila Kratochvilova (TCH)	21.97 (1981)
26.	Chandra Cheeseborough (USA)	21.99 (1983)
	Marie-Josée Perec (FRA)	21.99 (1993)
	Kerron Stewart (JAM)	21.99 (2008)
29.	Sherone Simpson (JAM)	22.00 (2006)
30.	Anelia Nuneva (BUL)	22.01 (1987)
	Li Xuemei (CHN)	22.01 (1997)
	Muna Lee (USA)	22.01 (2008)
	Candyce McGrone (USA)	22.01 (2015)
34.	Kyra Jefferson (USA)	22.02 (2017)
35.	Dawn Sowell (USA)	22.04 (1989)
	Blessing Okagbare (NGR)	22.04 (2018)
37.	Shericka Jackson (JAM)	22.05 (2018)
38.	Evette De Klerk (RSA)	22.06 (1989)
39.	Mary Onyali (NGR)	22.07 (1996)
40.	Marie-Josée Ta Lou (CIV)	22.08 (2017)
41.	Sanya Richards-Ross (USA)	22.09 (2012)
	Shelly-Ann Fraser-Pryce (JAM)	22.09 (2012)
	Deajah Stevens (USA)	22.09 (2017)
44.	Kathy Cook (GBR)	22.10 (1984)
45.	Carmelita Jeter (USA)	22.11 (2012)
	Myriam Soumaré (FRA)	22.11 (2014)

WORLD RANKING ALL TIME INDOOR:

1.	Merlene Ottey (JAM)	21.87 (1993)
2.	Irina Privalova (RUS)	22.10 (1995)
3.	Heike Drechsler (GDR)	22.27 (1987)
4.	Gwen Torrence (USA)	22.33 (1996)
5.	Veronica Campbell-Brown (JAM)	22.38 (2005)
	Gabrielle Thomas (USA)	22.38 (2018)
7.	Marita Koch (GER)	22.39 (1983)
	Ionela Tirlea (ROM)	22.39 (1999)
9.	Bianca Knight (USA)	22.40 (2008)
10.	Galina Malchugina (RUS)	22.41 (1994)
	Ashley Henderson (USA)	22.41 (2018)
12.	Arianna Washington (USA)	22.42 (2017)
13.	Svetlana Goncharenko (RUS)	22.43 (1998)
14.	Felicia Brown (USA)	22.45 (2016)
15.	Muriel Hurtis (FRA)	22.49 (2003)
	Muna Lee (USA)	22.49 (2003)
	Sanya Richards-Ross (USA)	22.49 (2004)
18.	Melanie Paschke (GER)	22.50 (1998)
	Kamaria Brown (USA)	22.50 (2014)
20.	Nanceen Perry (USA)	22.52 (2000)
	Jenna Prandini (USA)	22.52 (2015)
22.	Hannah Cunliffe (USA)	22.53 (2017)
23.	Kimberlyn Duncan (USA)	22.54 (2013)
	Deanna Hill (USA)	22.54 (2017)
25.	Lynna Irby (USA)	22.55 (2018)
26.	Shalonda Solomon (USA)	22.57 (2006)
27.	Grit Breuer (GER)	22.58 (1991)
	Kerron Stewart (JAM)	22.58 (2007)
29.	Anastasiya Kapachinskaya (RUS)	22.59 (2003)
30.	Juliet Cuthbert (JAM)	22.60 (1995)
	Consuella Moore (USA)	22.60 (2004)
32.	Nickeisha Anderson (JAM)	22.62 (2008)
33.	Kyra Jefferson (USA)	22.63 (2015)
34.	Gesine Walther (GDR)	22.64 (1982)
	Melinda Gainsford-Taylor (AUS)	22.64 (1995)
	Juliet Campbell (JAM)	22.64 (2001)
	Michelle Collins (USA)	22.64 (2003)
38.	Deajah Stevens (USA)	22.65 (2017)
39.	Pauline Davis-Thompson (BAH)	22.68 (1995)
	Aurieyall Scott (USA)	22.68 (2013)
	Sydney McLaughlin (USA)	22.68 (2018)
42.	Ewa Kasprzyk (POL)	22.69 (1988)
	Christine Arron (FRA)	22.69 (2005)
	Dezerea Bryant (USA)	22.69 (2014)
45.	Karin Mayr-Krifka (AUT)	22.70 (2002)
	Ashton Purvis (USA)	22.70 (2013)

400 m Women

EUROPEAN CHAMPIONSHIPS 2018: 11-8-2018:

1. Justyna Swiety-Ersetic (POL)(51.23) 50.41
2. Maria Belibasáki (GRE) (51.23) 50.45
3. Lisanne de Witte (NED) (51.24) 50.77
4. Laviai Nielsen (GBR) (51.21) 51.21
5. Inga Baumgart-Witan (POL)(51.35) 51.24
6. Agne Serksniene (LTU) (51.41) 51.42
7. Floria Guei (FRA) (51.50) 51.57
8. Madiea Ghafoor (NED) (51.29) 51.57

----

9. Libania Grenot (ITA) 51.54
10. Gunta Latiseva-Cudare (LAT) 51.60
11. Polina Miller (ANA) 51.65
12. Malgorzata Holub-Kowalik (POL) 51.74
13. Anyika Onuora (GBR) 51.77
14. Anita Horvat (SLO) 51.89
15. Amy Allcock (GBR) 51.91
16. Cynthia Bolingo Mbongo (BEL)(51.69)51.92
17. Tetyana Melnyk (UKR) 52.20
18. Cátia Azevedo (POR) (51.84) 52.23
19. Maria Chigbolu (ITA) (51.76) 52.26
20. Bianca Razor (ROM) (52.19) 52.27
21. Camille Laus (BEL) (52.40) 52.40
22. Laura Bueno (ESP) (52.14) 52.46
23. Andrea Miklos (ROM) (52.40) 52.49
24. Tamara Salaski (SRB) (52.39) 53.20

----

25. Nadine Gonska (GER) 52.54
26. Laura de Witte (NED) 52.57
27. Matilda Hellqvist (SWE) 52.68
28. Modesta Morauskaite (LTU) 52.68
29. Alena Mamina (ANA) 52.72
30. Alexandra Bezeková (SVK) 52.88

WORLD RANKING 2018:

1. Shaunae Miller-Uibo (BAH) 48.97(Mon)
2. Salwa Eid Naser (BRN) 49.08(Mon)
3. Shakima Wimbley (USA) 49.52(USC)
4. Caster Semenya (RSA) 49.62(CON)
5. Lynna Irby (USA) 49.80(NCA)
6. Kendall Ellis (USA) 49.99(PA)
7. Sydney McLaughlin (USA) 50.07(Gai)
   Phyllis Francis (USA) 50.07(Sto)
9. Jessica Beard (USA) 50.08(USC)
10. Amantle Montsho (BOT) 50.15(GC)
11. Stephenie Ann McPherson (JAM) 50.31(Lon)
12. Justyna Swiety-Ersetic (POL) 50.41(ECh)
13. Maria Belimpasaki (GRE) 50.45(ECh)
14. Léa Sprunger (SUI) 50.52(LCF)
15. Anastasia Le-Roy (JAM) 50.57(GC)
16. Makenzie Dunmore (USA) 50.63(PA)
    Jaide Stepter (USA) 50.63(Lau)
18. Courtney Okolo (USA) 50.65(USC)
19. Sharrika Barnett (USA) 50.69(Kno)
    Aminatou Seyni (NGR) 50.69(Rov)
21. Lisanne de Witte (NED) 50.77(ECh)
22. Brionna Thomas (USA) 50.78(NCA)
23. Hima Das (IND) 50.79(Jak)
24. Shamier Little (USA) 50.82(Sto)
25. Christine Botlogetswe (BOT) 50.89
26. Agne Serksniene (LTU) 50.99(LCF)
27. Madiea Ghafoor (NED) 51.12(Bel)
28. Anyika Onuora (GBR) 51.13(Lon)
29. Eleni Artymata (CYP) 51.14(Bel)
30. Malgorzata Holub-Kowalik (POL) 51.18

WORLD INDOOR CHAMPIONSHIPS: 3-3-2018:

1. Courtney Okolo (USA)   (51.54)   50.55
2. Shakima Wimbley (USA)   (51.34)   51.47
3. Eilidh Doyle (GBR)   (52.15)   51.60
4. Justyna Swiety-Ersetic (POL)   51.85
5. Tovea Jenkins (JAM)   52.12
6. Zoey Clark (GBR)   52.16

----

7. Agne Serksniene (LTU)   52.62
8. Anna Yaroshchuk-Ryzhykova (UKR)   52.74
9. Alexandra Bezeková (SVK)   (52.78)   53.05
10. Madiea Ghafoor (NED)   (52.54)   53.14
11. Raphaela Boaheng Lukudo (ITA)(52.98)53.18
12. Phil Healy (IRL)   (52.75)   53.26
13. Lala Vondrová (CZE)   (53.05)   53.32
14. Nadine Gonska (GER)   (52.77)   53.45
15. Iveta Putalová (SVK)   53.46
16. Stephenie Ann McPherson (JAM)(52.18)dsq
    Léa Sprunger (SUI)   (52.46)   dsq
    Maria Belimpasaki (GRE)   (52.27)   dsq

----

19. Patrycja Wyciskiewicz (POL)   53.22
20. Ayomide Folorunso (ITA)   53.24
21. Kelsey Balkwill (CAN)   53.29
22. Travia Jones (CAN)   53.31
23. Svetlana Golendova (KAZ)   53.44
24. Anita Horvat (SLO)   53.52

WORLD INDOOR RANKING 2018:

1. Kendall Ellis (USA)   50.34
2. Sydney McLaughlin (USA)   50.36
3. Courtney Okolo (USA)   50.55
4. Lynna Irby (USA)   50.62
5. Sharrika Barnett (USA)   51.07
6. Shakima Wimbley (USA)   51.17
7. Phyllis Francis (USA)   51.19
8. Léa Sprunger (SUI)   51.28
9. Georganne Moline (USA)   51.39
10. Quanera Hayes (USA)   51.46
11. Brionna Thomas (USA)   51.56
12. Eilidh Doyle (GBR)   51.60
13. Briana Guillory (USA)   51.68
14. Justyna Swiety-Ersetic (POL)   51.78
15. Joanna Atkins (USA)   51.87
16. Ama Pipi (GBR)   52.07
17. Phil Healy (IRL)   52.08
18. Natasha Hastings (USA)   52.11
19. Zoey Clark (GBR)   52.12
    Tovea Jenkins (USA)   52.12
21. Stephenie Ann McPherson (JAM)   52.18
22. Morgan Burks-Magee (USA)   52.20

Commonwealth Games, Gold Coast, 11-4-2018:
1. Amantle Montsho (BOT)   50.15
2. Anastasia Le-Roy (JAM)   50.57
3. Stephenie Ann McPherson (JAM)(50.80) 50.93

Kingston, 19-5-2018:
1. Jessica Beard (USA)   50.52
2. Jaide Stepter (USA)   50.72
3. Stephenie Ann McPherson (JAM)   50.82
4. Chrisann Gordon (JAM)   51.23

Eugene, 26-5-2018:
1. Shaunae Miller-Uibo (BAH)   49.52
2. Phyllis Francis (USA)   50.81
3. Shakima Wimbley (USA)   50.84
4. Jessica Beard (USA)   50.89
5. Stephenie Ann McPherson (JAM)   51.01
6. Jaide Stepter (USA)   51.17

Oslo, 7-6-2018:
1. Salwa Eid Naser (BRN)   49.98
2. Phyllis Francis (USA)   50.47
3. Shakima Wimbley (USA)   50.53
4. Jessica Beard (USA)   50.57
5. Jaide Stepter (USA)   50.78
6. Courtney Okolo (USA)   51.22

NCAA, Eugene, 9-6-2018:
1. Lynna Irby (USA)   (50.11)   49.80
2. Kendall Ellis (USA)   50.19
3. Brionna Thomas (USA)   50.78
4. Sharrika Barnett (USA)   51.16

Stockholm, 10-6-2018:
1. Salwa Eid Naser (BRN)   49.84
2. Phyllis Francis (USA)   50.07
3. Jessica Beard (USA)   50.55
4. Shamier Little (USA)   50.82
5. Jaide Stepter (USA)   50.99
6. Courtney Okolo (USA)   51.28

US CHAMPIONSHIPS, Des Moines, 23-6-2018:
1. Shakima Wimbley   49.52
2. Jessica Beard   50.08
3. Kendall Ellis   50.37
4. Courtney Okolo   50.65
5. Brionna Thomas   51.16

JAM CHAMPIONSHIPS, Kingston, 24-6-2018:
1. Stephenie Ann McPherson   50.74
2. Christine Day   51.41
3. Anastasia Le-Roy   52.00

Paris, 30-6-2018:
1. Salwa Eid Naser (BRN)   49.55
2. Jessica Beard (USA)   50.39
3. Phyllis Francis (USA)   50.50
4. Shakima Wimbley (USA)   50.81
5. Stephenie Ann McPherson (JAM)   50.85
6. Anastasia Le-Roy (JAM)   51.12

Szekesfehervar, 2-7-2018:
1. Shaunae Miller-Uibo (BAH)   49.53
2. Phyllis Francis (USA)   50.95
   Shakima Wimbley (USA)   50.95
4. Courtney Okolo (USA)   51.58

Lausanne, 5-7-2018:
1. Salwa Eid Naser (BRN)   49.78
2. Jessica Beard (USA)   50.40
3. Shakima Wimbley (USA)   50.58
4. Jaide Stepter (USA)   50.63
5. Stephenie Ann McPherson (JAM)   50.84
6. Anastasia Le-Roy (JAM)   51.12

Monaco, 20-7-2018:
1. Shaunae Miller-Uibo (BAH)   48.97
2. Salwa Eid Naser (BRN)   49.08
3. Shakima Wimbley (USA)   50.85
4. Phyllis Francis (USA)   51.05
5. Anita Horvat (SLO)   51.22
6. Libania Grenot (ITA)   51.56
7. Jessica Beard (USA)   51.58
8. Floria Guei (FRA)   51.66

London, 22-7-2018:
1. Stephenie Ann McPherson (JAM)   50.31
2. Anastasia Le-Roy (JAM)   50.85
3. Courtney Okolo (USA)   50.93
4. Lisanne de Witte (NED)   51.08
5. Anyika Onuora (GBR)   51.13

Brussels, 31-8-2018:

1. Salwa Eid Naser (BRN)   49.33
2. Phyllis Francis (USA)   50.55
3. Shakima Wimbley (USA)   50.77
4. Jaide Stepter (USA)   51.17

CONTINENTAL CUP, Ostrava, 8-9-2018:

1. Salwa Eid Naser (ASI)   49.32
2. Caster Semenya (AFR)   49.62
3. Stephenie Ann McPherson (AME) 50.82

OVERVIEW WORLD OUTDOOR CHAMPIONSHIP FINALISTS OF PAST 6 YEARS

	Wch 17	OG 16	Wch 15	Wch 13
Phyllis Francis (USA)	49.92 (1)	50.41 (5)	50.51 (7)	
Salwa Eid Naser (BRN)	50.06 (2)			
Allyson Felix (USA)	50.08 (3)	49.51 (2)	49.26 (1)	
Shaunae Miller-Uibo (BAH)	50.49 (4)	49.44 (1)	49.67 (2)	
Shericka Jackson (JAM)	50.76 (5)	49.85 (3)	49.99 (3)	
Stephenie Ann McPherson (JAM)	50.86 (6)	50.97 (6)	50.42 (5)	49.99 (4)
Kabange Mupopo (ZAM)	51.15 (7)			
Novlene Williams-Mills (JAM)	51.48 (8)		50.47 (6)	51.49 (8)
Natasha Hastings (USA)		50.34 (4)		50.30 (5)
Olha Zemlyak (UKR)		51.24 (7)		
Libania Grenot (ITA)		51.25 (8)		
Christine Day (JAM)			50.14 (4)	
Christine Ohuruogu (GBR)			50.63 (8)	49.41 (1)
Amantle Montsho (BOT)				49.41 (1)
Antonina Krivoshapka (RUS)				49.78 (3)
Francena McCorory (USA)				50.68 (6)
Kseniya Ryzhova (RUS)				50.98 (7)

OVERVIEW WORLD INDOOR CHAMPIONSHIP FINALISTS OF PAST 5 YEARS

	Wch 18	Wch 16	Wch 14
Courtney Okolo (USA)	50.55 (1)		
Shakima Wimbley (USA)	51.47 (2)		
Eilidh Doyle (GBR)	51.60 (3)		
Justyna Swiety (POL)	51.85 (4)	52.46 (5)	52.20 (4)
Tovea Jenkins (JAM)	52.12 (5)		
Zoey Clark (GBR)	52.16 (6)		
Oluwakemi Adekoya (BRN)		51.45 (1)	
Ashley Spencer (USA)		51.72 (2)	
Quanera Hayes (USA)		51.76 (3)	
Stephenie Ann McPherson (JAM)		52.20 (4)	
Iveta Putalová (SVK)		54.39 (6)	
Francena McCorory (USA)			51.12 (1)
Kaliese Spencer (JAM)			51.54 (2)
Shaunae Miller (BAH)			52.06 (3)
Patricia Hall (JAM)			52.51 (5)
Joanna Atkins (USA)			52.55 (6)

OVERVIEW TOP 10 WORLD OUTDOOR RANKINGS OF PAST 5 YEARS

	2018	2017	2016	2015	2014
Shaunae Miller-Uibo (BAH)	48.97 (1)	49.46 (1)	49.44 (1)	49.67 (2)	
Salwa Eid Naser (BRN)	49.08 (2)	49.88 (4)			
Shakima Wimbley (USA)	49.52 (3)				
Caster Semenya (RSA)	49.62 (4)				
Lynna Irby (USA)	49.80 (5)				
Kendall Ellis (USA)	49.99 (6)	50.00 (6)			
Sydney McLaughlin (USA)	50.07 (7)				
Phyllis Francis (USA)	50.07 (7)	49.92 (5)	49.94 (7)		
Jessica Beard (USA)	50.08 (9)				
Amantle Montsho (BOT)	50.15 (10)				50.37 (7)
Allyson Felix (USA)		49.65 (2)	49.51 (2)	49.26 (1)	
Quanera Hayes (USA)		49.72 (3)	49.91 (6)		
Shericka Jackson-Johnson (JAM)		50.05 (7)	49.83 (4)	49.99 (5)	
Chrisann Gordon (JAM)		50.13 (8)			
Natasha Hastings (USA)		50.14 (9)	49.90 (5)	50.24 (9)	50.53 (9)
Novlene Williams-Mills (JAM)		50.14 (9)			50.05 (4)
Courtney Okolo (USA)			49.71 (3)		50.03 (3)
Stephenie Ann McPherson (JAM)			50.04 (8)	50.32 (10)	50.12 (5)
Francena McCorory (USA)			50.23 (9)	49.83 (3)	49.48 (1)
Taylor Ellis-Watson (USA)			50.25 (10)		
Sanya Richards-Ross (USA)				49.95 (4)	49.66 (2)
Christine Day (JAM)				50.14 (6)	50.16 (6)
Christine Ohuruogu (GBR)				50.16 (7)	
Kabange Mupopo (ZAM)				50.22 (8)	
Kendall Baisden (USA)					50.46 (8)
Libania Grenot (ITA)					50.55 (10)

OVERVIEW TOP 10 WORLD INDOOR RANKINGS OF PAST 5 YEARS

	2018	2017	2016	2015	2014
Kendall Ellis (USA)	50.34 (1)	51.07 (1)			
Sydney McLaughlin (USA)	50.36 (2)	51.61 (4)	51.84 (10)		
Courtney Okolo (USA)	50.55 (3)		50.69 (1)	51.12 (1)	
Lynna Irby (USA)	50.62 (4)				
Sharrika Barnett (USA)	51.07 (5)				
Shakima Wimbley (USA)	51.17 (6)	51.07 (1)			
Phyllis Francis (USA)	51.19 (7)				50.46 (1)
Léa Sprunger (SUI)	51.28 (8)	51.46 (3)			
Georganne Moline (USA)	51.39 (9)				
Quanera Hayes (USA)	51.46 (10)		51.09 (2)		
Chrisann Gordon (JAM)		51.71 (5)	51.69 (8)		
Zuzana Hejnova (CZE)		51.77 (6)			
Carly Muscaro (USA)		51.78 (7)			
Sage Watson (CAN)		51.84 (8)			
Eilidh Doyle-Child (GBR)		51.86 (9)			
Laviai Nielsen (GBR)		51.90 (10)			
Floria Guei (FRA)		51.90 (10)			
Ashley Spencer (USA)			51.29 (3)	51.85 (5)	51.71 (10)
Natasha Hastings (USA)			51.34 (4)		51.34 (6)
Oluwakemi Adekoya (BRN)			51.45 (5)		
Taylor Ellis-Watson (USA)			51.51 (6)	51.52 (2)	
Seren Bundy-Davies (GBR)			51.60 (7)	51.72 (4)	
Shamier Little (USA)			51.74 (9)	51.92 (6)	
Francena McCorory (USA)				51.70 (3)	50.85 (2)
Nataliia Pyhyda (UKR)				51.96 (7)	
Shapri Romero (USA)				52.06 (8)	
Ekaterina Renzhina (RUS)				52.08 (9)	
Margaret Bamgbose (USA)				52.10 (10)	
Kamaria Brown (USA)					50.94 (3)
Kseniya Ryzhova (RUS)					51.03 (4)
Joanna Atkins (USA)					51.13 (5)
Kaliese Spencer (JAM)					51.54 (7)
Regina George (NGR)					51.60 (8)
Shaunae Miller (BAH)					51.63 (9)

WORLD RANKING ALL TIME OUTDOOR:

1.	Marita Koch (GDR)	47.60 (1985)
2.	Jarmila Kratochvílová (TCH)	47.99 (1983)
3.	Marie-Josée Perec (FRA)	48.25 (1996)
4.	Olga Bryzgina (URS)	48.27 (1985)
5.	Tatiana Kocembová (TCH)	48.59 (1983)
6.	Cathy Freeman (AUS)	48.63 (1996)
7.	Sanya Richards-Ross (JAM)	48.70 (2006)
8.	Valerie Brisco-Hooks (USA)	48.83 (1984)
9.	Ana Guevara (MEX)	48.89 (2003)
10.	Shaunae Miller-Uibo (BAH)	48.97 (2018)
11.	Chandra Cheeseborough (USA)	49.05 (1984)
12.	Tonique Williams-Darling (BAH)	49.07 (2004)
13.	Salwa Eid Naser (BRN)	49.08 (2018)
14.	Falilat Ogunkoya (NGR)	49.10 (1996)
15.	Olga Nazarova (URS)	49.11 (1988)
16..	Antonina Krivoshapka (RUS)	49.16 (2012)
17.	Mariya Pinigina (URS)	49.19 (1983)
18.	Sabine Busch (GDR)	49.24 (1984)
19.	Allyson Felix (USA)	49.26 (2015)
20.	Pauline Davis-Thompson (BAH)	49.28 (1996)
	Yuliya Gushchina (RUS)	49.28 (2012)
22.	Irena Szewinska (POL)	49.29 (1976)
	Charity Opara (NGR)	49.29 (1998)
24.	Petra Schersing (GDR)	49.30 (1988)
	Lorraine Fenton (JAM)	49.30 (2002)
26.	Shericka Williams (JAM)	49.32 (2009)
27.	Amantle Montsho (BOT)	49.33 (2013)
28.	Jearl Miles-Clark (USA)	49.40 (1997)
29.	Christine Ohuruogu (GBR)	49.41 (2013)
30.	Grit Breuer (GER)	49.42 (1991)
31.	Kathy Cook (GBR)	49.43 (1984)
	Fatima Yusuf (NGR)	49.43 (1995)
33.	Aelita Yurchenko (URS)	49.47 (1988)
34.	Francena McCorory (USA)	49.48 (2014)
35.	Olga Zaytseva (RUS)	49.49 (2006)
36.	Shakima Wimbley (USA)	49.52 (2018)
37.	Vanya Stambolova (BUL)	49.53 (2006)
38.	Bärbel Wöckel (GDR)	49.56 (1982)
	Monique Hennagan (USA)	49.56 (2004)
40.	Grace Jackson-Small (JAM)	49.57 (1988)
41.	Dagmar Neubauer (GDR)	49.58 (1984)
42.	Marion Jones (USA)	49.59 (2000)
	Katharine Merry (GBR)	49.59 (2001)
44	Ana Quirot (CUB)	49.61 (1991)
45.	Caster Semenya (RSA)	49.62 (2018)

WORLD RANKING ALL TIME INDOOR:

1.	Jarmila Kratochvílová (TCH)	49.59 (1982)
2.	Natalya Nazarova (RUS)	49.68 (2004)
3.	Tatiana Kocembová (TCH)	49.76 (1984)
4.	Sabine Busch (GDR)	50.01 (1984)
5.	Nicola Sanders (GBR)	50.02 (2007)
6.	Olesya Krasnomovets (RUS)	50.04 (2006)
7.	Olga Zaytseva (RUS)	50.15 (2006)
8.	Vanya Stambolova (BUL)	50.21 (2006)
9.	Irina Privalova (RUS)	50.23 (1995)
10.	Petra Schersing (GDR)	50.28 (1988)
11.	Christine Amertil (BAH)	50.34 (2006)
	Kendall Ellis (USA)	50.34 (2018)
13.	Sydney McLaughlin (USA)	50.36 (2018)
14.	Natalya Antyukh (RUS)	50.37 (2006)
15.	Dagmar Neubauer (GDR)	50.40 (1984)
16.	Svetlana Pospelova (RUS)	50.41 (2005)
17.	Olga Kotlyarova (RUS)	50.42 (2001)
18.	Grit Breuer (GER)	50.45 (1998)
19.	Phyllis Francis (USA)	50.46 (2014)
20.	Katharine Merry (GBR)	50.53 (2001)
21.	Francena McCorory (USA)	50.54 (2010)
22.	Svetlana Usovich (BLR)	50.55 (2005)
	Antonina Krivoshapka (RUS)	50.55 (2009)
	Courtney Okolo (USA)	50.55 (2018)
25.	Ionela Tirlea (ROM)	50.56 (1998)
26.	Lynna Irby (USA)	50.62 (2018)
27.	Diane Dixon (USA)	50.64 (1991)
28.	Sanya Richards-Ross (USA)	50.71 (2012)
29.	Charity Opara (NGR)	50.73 (1998)
30.	Jessica Beard (USA)	50.79 (2011)
31.	Natasha Hastings (USA)	50.80 (2007)
32.	Olga Bryzgina (URS)	50.81 (1987)
33.	Jearl Miles-Clark (USA)	50.83 (1999)
34.	Helga Arendt (FRG)	50.84 (1988)
35.	Perri Shakes-Drayton (GBR)	50.85 (2013)
36.	Debbie Dunn (USA)	50.86 (2010)
37.	Tonique Williams-Darling (BAH)	50.87 (2004)
38.	Shaunae Miller-Uibo (BAH)	50.88 (2013)
39.	Tiandra Ponteen (SKN)	50.91 (2005)
40.	Hazel-Ann Regis (GRN)	50.92 (2005)
41.	Sandie Richards (USA)	50.93 (1993)
	Ana Guevara (MEX)	50.93 (1999)
43.	Kamaria Brown (USA)	50.94 (2014)
44.	Sandra Myers (ESP)	50.99 (1991)
	Helena Fuchsová (CZE)	50.99 (1998)

800 m Women

EUROPEAN CHAMPIONSHIPS 2018: 10-8-2018:

1. Nataliya Pryshchepa (UKR)   2.00.38
2. Renelle Lamote (FRA)   (1.59.44)   2.00.62
3. Olha Lyakhova (UKR)   (2.00.26)   2.00.79
4. Adelle Tracey (GBR)   (1.59.86)   2.00.86
5. Anna Sabat (POL)   (2.00.32)   2.01.26
6. Lynsey Sharp (GBR)   (2.00.32)   2.01.83
7. Selina Büchel (SUI)   (2.00.42)   2.02.05
8. Shelayna Oskan-Clarke (GBR)(2.00.39)2.02.26
9. Lovisa Lindh (SWE)   2.02.36
----
10. Hanna Hermansson (SWE)   2.00.52
11. Lore Hoffmann (SUI)   2.01.67
12. Charline Mathias (LUX)   2.02.01
13. Angelika Cichocka (POL)   (2.01.01)   2.03.14
14. Christina Hering (GER)   (2.01.57)   2.04.04
15. Egle Balciunaité (LTU)   (2.02.18)   2.04.60
    Anita Hinriksdóttir (ISL)   (2.02.15)   dsq
----
17. Cynthia Anais (FRA)   2.02.27
18. Yusneysi Santiusti (ITA)   2.02.46
19. Gabriela Gajanová (SVK)   2.02.57
20. Sara Kuivisto (FIN)   2.02.62
21. Sanne Wolters-Verstegen (NED)   2.02.72
22. Elena Bellò (ITA)   2.02.77
23. Siofra Cléirigh Büttner (IRL)   2.02.80
24. Natalia Evangelidou (CYP)   2.03.38
25. Bianka Kéri (HUN)   2.03.44
26. Claire Mooney (IRL)   2.04.26

WORLD RANKING 2018:

1. Caster Semenya (RSA)   1.54.25(Par)
2. Francine Niyonsaba (BDI)   1.55.86(Par)
3. Natoya Goule (JAM)   1.56.15(Mon)
4. Ajee Wilson (USA)   1.56.45(Mon)
5. Habitam Alemu (ETH)   1.56.71(Mon)
6. Rababe Arafi (MAR)   1.57.47(Mon)
7. Raevyn Rogers (USA)   1.57.69(Mon)
8. Ce'Aira Brown (USA)   1.58.01
9. Emily Cherotich Tuei (KEN)   1.58.04(Nan)
10. Charlene Lipsey (USA)   1.58.05(Par)
11. Margaret Nyairera Wambui (KEN)   1.58.07(GC)
12. Halimah Nakaayi (UGA)   1.58.39(Nan)
13. Renelle Lamote (FRA)   1.58.83(Mon)
14. Nelly Jepkosgei (KEN)   1.58.96(Osl)
15. Laura Muir (GBR)   1.59.09(Osl)
16. Eunice Jepkoech Sum (KEN)   1.59.25(Par)
17. Malika Akkaoui (MAR)   1.59.27(Rab)
18. Lynsey Sharp (GBR)   1.59.34(Lon)
19. Sifan Hassan (NED)   1.59.35(Par)
20. Nataliya Pryshchepa (UKR)   1.59.58(Ost)
21. Kaela Edwards (USA)   1.59.68(SC)
22. Diribe Welteji (ETH)   1.59.74
23. Mahelet Mulugeta (ETH)   1.59.84(Nan)
24. Sanne Verstegen (NED)   1.59.85(Bru))
25. Adelle Tracey (GBR)   1.59.86(ECh)
26. Aleksandra Gulyayeva (RUS)   1.59.87(Zhu)
27. Alexandra Bell (GBR)   1.59.93

WORLD INDOOR CHAMPIONSHIPS: 4-3-2018:

1. Francine Niyonsaba (BDI)   1.58.31
2. Ajee Wilson (USA)   1.58.99
3. Shelayna Oskan-Clarke (GBR)   1.59.81
4. Habitam Alemu (ETH)   2.01.10
5. Raevyn Rogers (USA)   2.01.44
6. Selina Büchel (SUI)   (2.01.84)   2.03.01
----
7. Angelika Cichocka (POL)   2.02.25
8. Natoya Goule (JAM)   2.02.49
9. Mhairi Hendry (GBR)   2.02.65
10. Liga Velvere (LAT)   2.02.98
11. Olha Lyakhova (UKR)   2.03.81
12. Jenna Westaway (CAN)   2.03.91
13. Esther Guerrero Puigdevall (ESP)   2.04.06
14. Winny Chebet (KEN)   2.18.31
     Margaret Nyairera Wambui (KEN)   dsq

WORLD INDOOR RANKING 2018:

1. Francine Niyonsaba (BDI)   1.58.31
2. Ajee Wilson (USA)   1.58.99
3. Laura Muir (GBR)   1.59.69
     Habitam Alemu (ETH)   1.59.69
5. Shelayna Oskan-Clarke (GBR)   1.59.81
6. Natoya Goule (JAM)   1.59.86
7. Raevyn Rogers (USA)   1.59.99
8. Margaret Nyairera Wambui (KEN)   2.00.48
9. Angelika Cichocka (POL)   2.00.70
10. Ce'Aira Brown (USA)   2.00.86
11. Olha Lyakhova (UKR)   2.01.08
12. Jenna Westaway (CAN)   2.01.22
13. Mhairi Hendry (GBR)   2.01.30
14. Kaela Edwards (USA)   2.01.49
15. Sabrina Southerland (USA)   2.01.55
16. Cecilia Barowski (USA)   2.01.61
17. Nelly Jepkosgei (KEN)   2.01.68
18. Selina Büchel (SUI)   2.01.80
19. Charlene Lipsey (USA)   2.01.89

Commonwealth Games, Gold Coast, 13-4-2018:
1. Caster Semenya (RSA)   1.56.68
2. Margaret Nyairera Wambui (KEN)   1.58.07
3. Natoya Goule (JAM)   1.58.82

Eugene, 26-5-2018:
1. Caster Semenya (RSA)   1.55.92
2. Ajee Wilson (USA)   1.56.86
3. Francine Niyonsaba (BDI)   1.56.88
4. Habitam Alemu (ETH)   1.57.78
5. Charlene Lipsey (USA)   1.58.35
6. Margaret Nyairera Wambui (KEN)   1.58.67
7. Raevyn Rogers (USA)   1.59.36
8. Eunice Jepkoech Sum (KEN)   2.00.41

Oslo, 7-6-2018:
1. Caster Semenya (RSA)   1.57.25
2. Francine Niyonsaba (BDI)   1.58.57
3. Habitam Alemu (ETH)   1.58.58
4. Nelly Jepkosgei (KEN)   1.58.96
5. Laura Muir (GBR)   1.59.09
6. Brenda Martinez (USA)   2.00.74
7. Selina Büchel (SUI)   2.00.78

KEN TRIALS, Nairobi, 23-6-2018:
1. Emily Cherotich Tuei   1.59.52
2. Eunice Jepkoech Sum   2.00.76
3. Margaret Nyairera Wambui   2.00.86

US CHAMPIONSHIPS, Des Moines, 24-6-2018:
1. Ajee Wilson   1.58.18
2. Raevyn Rogers   1.58.57
3. Ce'Aira Brown   1.58.65
4. Kaela Edwards   1.59.68
5. Charlene Lipsey   1.59.95
6. Olivia Baker   2.00.08
7. Hanna Green   2.00.09
8. Sabrina Southerland   2.01.62

Nancy, 27-6-2018:
1. Emily Cherotich Tuei (KEN)   1.58.04
2. Halimah Nakaayi (UGA)   1.58.39
3. Mahelet Mulugeta (ETH)   1.59.84

Paris, 30-6-2018:
1. Caster Semenya (RSA)   1.54.25
2. Francine Niyonsaba (BDI)   1.55.86
3. Ajee Wilson (USA)   1.57.11
4. Habitam Alemu (ETH)   1.57.17
5. Natoya Goule (JAM)   1.57.69
6. Charlene Lipsey (USA)   1.58.05
7. Emily Cherotich Tuei (KEN)   1.58.99
8. Renelle Lamote (FRA)   1.59.25
9. Eunice Jepkoech Sum (KEN)   1.59.25
10. Sifan Hassan (NED)   1.59.35

Lausanne, 5-7-2018:
1. Francine Niyonsaba (BDI)   1.57.80
2. Ajee Wilson (USA)   1.58.20
3. Habitam Alemu (ETH)   1.58.38
4. Margaret Nyairera Wambui (KEN)   1.59.03
5. Raevyn Rogers (USA)   2.00.12
6. Nelly Jepkosgei (KEN)   2.00.26
7. Eunice Jepkoech Sum (KEN)   2.00.33
8. Lynsey Sharp (GBR)   2.01.02

Rabat, 13-7-2018:
1. Francine Niyonsaba (BDI)   1.57.90
2. Natoya Goule (JAM)   1.58.33
3. Rababe Arafi (MAR)   1.58.84
4. Margaret Nyairera Wambui (KEN)   1.59.09
5. Emily Cherotich Tuei (KEN)   1.59.19
6. Malika Akkaoui (MAR)   1.59.27
7. Lynsey Sharp (GBR)   1.59.86
8. Laura Roesler (USA)   2.00.56

Monaco, 20-7-2018:
1. Caster Semenya (RSA)   1.54.60
2. Francine Niyonsaba (BDI)   1.55.96
3. Natoya Goule (JAM)   1.56.15
4. Ajee Wilson (USA)   1.56.45
5. Habitam Alemu (ETH)   1.56.71
6. Rababe Arafi (MAR)   1.57.47
7. Raevyn Rogers (USA)   1.57.69
8. Charlene Lipsey (USA)   1.58.42
9. Renelle Lamote (FRA)   1.58.83
10. Emily Cherotich Tuei (KEN)   1.59.45
11. Margaret Nyairera Wambui (KEN)   1.59.70
12. Selina Büchel (SUI)   2.00.75

London, 22-7-2018:
1. Ce'Aira Brown (USA)   1.58.57
2. Natoya Goule (JAM)   1.58.67
3. Lynsey Sharp (GBR)   1.59.34
4. Laura Roesler (USA)   2.00.45

NACAC, Toronto, 11-8-2018:
1. Ajee Wilson (USA)   1.57.52
2. Natoya Goule (JAM)   1.57.95
3. Rose Mary Almanza (CUB)   2.00.15
4. Raevyn Rogers (USA)   2.00.75

Zürich, 30-8-2018:
1. Caster Semenya (RSA)   1.55.27
2. Ajee Wilson (USA)   1.57.86
3. Natoya Goule (JAM)   1.58.49
4. Habitam Alemu (ETH)   1.58.63
5. Raevyn Rogers (USA)   1.59.05
6. Francine Niyonsaba (BDI)   1.59.11
7. Selina Büchel (SUI)   2.00.64

CONTINENTAL CUP, Ostrava, 9-9-2018:
1. Caster Semenya (AFR)   1.54.77
2. Ajee Wilson (AME)   1.57.16
3. Natoya Goule (AME)   1.57.36
4. Nataliya Prishchepa (EUR)   1.59.58

OVERVIEW WORLD OUTDOOR CHAMPIONSHIP FINALISTS OF PAST 6 YEARS

	Wch 17	OG 16	Wch 15	Wch 13
Caster Semenya (RSA)	1.55.16 (1)	1.55.28 (1)		
Francine Niyonsaba (BDI)	1.55.92 (2)	1.56.49 (2)		
Ajee Wilson (USA)	1.56.65 (3)			1.58.21 (6)
Margaret Wambui (KEN)	1.57.54 (4)	1.56.89 (3)		
Melissa Bishop (CAN)	1.57.68 (5)	1.57.02 (4)	1.58.12 (2)	
Angelika Cichocka (POL)	1.58.41 (6)			
Charlene Lipsey (USA)	1.58.73 (7)			
Lynsey Sharp (GBR)	1.58.98 (8)	1.57.69 (6)		
Joanna Jozwik (POL)		1.57.37 (5)	1.59.09 (7)	
Maryna Arzamasova (BLR)		1.59.10 (7)	1.58.03 (1)	
Kate Grace (USA)		1.59.57 (8)		
Eunice Jepkoech Sum (KEN)			1.58.18 (3)	1.57.38 (1)
Rababe Arafi (MAR)			1.58.90 (4)	
Shelayna Osman-Clarke (GBR)			1.58.99 (5)	
Nataliia Lupu (UKR)			1.58.99 (5)	1.59.79 (7)
Renelle Lamote (FRA)			1.59.70 (8)	
Mariya Savinova (RUS)				1.57.80 (2)
Brenda Martinez (USA)				1.57.91 (3)
Alysia Johnson Montano (USA)				1.57.95 (4)
Ekaterina Poistogova (RUS)				1.58.05 (5)
Lenka Masná (CZE)				2.00.59 (8)

OVERVIEW WORLD INDOOR CHAMPIONSHIP FINALISTS OF PAST 5 YEARS

	Wch 18	Wch 16	Wch 14
Francine Niyonsaba (BDI)	1.58.31 (1)	2.00.01 (1)	
Ajee Wilson (USA)	1.58.99 (2)	2.00.27 (2)	
Shelayna Oskan-Clarke (GBR)	1.59.81 (3)		
Habitam Alemu (ETH)	2.01.10 (4)	2.04.61 (6)	
Raevyn Rogers (USA)	2.01.44 (5)		
Selina Büchel (SUI)	2.03.01 (6)		2.01.06 (4)
Margaret Wambui (KEN)		2.00.44 (3)	
Laura Roesler (USA)		2.00.80 (4)	
Anita Hinriksdóttir (ISL)		2.02.58 (5)	
Chanelle Price (USA)			2.00.09 (1)
Angelika Cichocka (POL)			2.00.45 (2)
Maryna Arzamasova (BLR)			2.00.79 (3)
Nataliia Lupu (UKR)			2.01.17 (5)
Lenka Masná (CZE)			2.02.46 (6)

OVERVIEW TOP 10 WORLD OUTDOOR RANKINGS OF PAST 5 YEARS

	2018	2017	2016	2015	2014
Caster Semenya (RSA)	1.54.25 (1)	1.55.16 (1)	1.55.28 (1)		
Francine Niyonsaba (BDI)	1.55.86 (2)	1.55.47 (2)	1.56.24 (2)	1.57.62 (4)	
Natoya Goule (JAM)	1.56.15 (3)				
Ajee Wilson (USA)	1.56.45 (4)	1.55.61 (3)		1.57.87 (7)	1.57.67 (1)
Habitam Alemu (ETH)	1.56.71 (5)		1.57.05 (7)		
Rababe Arafi (MAR)	1.57.47 (6)				
Raevyn Rogers (USA)	1.57.69 (7)				
Ce'Aira Brown (USA)	1.58.01 (8)				
Emily Cherotich Tuei (KEN)	1.58.04 (9)				
Charlene Lipsey (USA)	1.58.05 (10)	1.57.38 (8)			
Sifan Hassan (NED)		1.56.81 (4)			
Margaret Wambui (KEN)		1.56.87 (5)	1.56.89 (3)		
Melissa Bishop (CAN)		1.57.01 (6)	1.57.02 (4)	1.57.52 (2)	
Eunice Jepkoech Sum (KEN)		1.57.78 (9)	1.57.47 (6)	1.56.99 (1)	1.57.92 (3)
Lynsey Sharp (GBR)		1.58.01 (10)	1.57.69 (8)	1.57.71 (6)	1.58.80 (9)
Joanna Józwik (POL)			1.57.37 (5)		
Molly Beckwith-Ludlow (USA)			1.57.68 (7)		
Renelle Lamote (FRA)			1.58.01 (9)		
Kate Grace (USA)			1.58.28 (10)		
Maryna Arzamasova (BLR)				1.57.54 (3)	1.58.15 (4)
Rose Mary Almanza (CUB)				1.57.70 (5)	
Selina Büchel (SUI)				1.57.95 (8)	
Faith Chepngetich Kipyegon (KEN)				1.58.02 (9)	
Fabienne Kohlmann (GER)				1.58.34 (10)	
Sahily Diago (CUB)					1.57.74 (2)
Ekaterina Poistogova (RUS)					1.58.55 (5)
Winnie Nanyondo (UGA)					1.58.63 (6)
Svetlana Karamasheva (RUS)					1.58.70 (7)
Janeth Jepkosgei Busienei (KEN)					1.58.70 (7)
Brenda Martinez (USA)					1.58.84 (10)

OVERVIEW TOP 10 WORLD INDOOR RANKINGS OF PAST 5 YEARS

	2018	2017	2016	2015	2014
Francine Niyonsaba (BDI)	1.58.31 (1)		2.00.01 (1)		
Ajee Wilson (USA)	1.58.99 (2)		2.00.09 (2)	2.01.57 (5)	2.00.43 (3)
Laura Muir (GBR)	1.59.69 (3)		2.00.70 (10)		2.00.94 (7)
Habitam Alemu (ETH)	1.59.69 (4)				
Shelayna Oskan-Clarke (GBR)	1.59.81 (5)	2.00.39 (4)			
Natoya Goule (JAM)	1.59.86 (6)			2.01.64 (6)	
Raevyn Rogers (USA)	1.59.99 (7)	2.01.09 (9)			
Margaret Wambui (KEN)	2.00.48 (8)		2.00.44 (8)		
Angelika Cichocka (POL)	2.00.70 (9)				2.00.37 (2)
Ce'Aira Brown (USA)	2.00.86 (10)				
Charlene Lipsey (USA)		1.58.64 (1)			
Joanna Józwik (POL)		1.59.29 (2)	2.00.12 (3)	2.00.01 (2)	
Selina Büchel (SUI)		2.00.38 (3)		2.01.87 (9)	2.00.93 (6)
Genzebe Dibaba (ETH)		2.00.62 (5)			
Jazmine Fray (USA)		2.00.69 (6)			
Malika Akkaoui (MAR)		2.00.91 (7)			
Olha Lyakhova (UKR)		2.00.92 (8)			
Lynsey Sharp (GBR)		2.01.14 (10)	2.00.30 (6)		
Brenda Martinez (USA)			2.00.14 (4)		
Melissa Bishop (CAN)			2.00.19 (5)		
Nataliia Lupu (UKR)			2.00.36 (7)		2.00.65 (4)
Laura Roesler (USA)			2.00.49 (9)		
Jennifer Meadows (GBR)				1.59.21 (1)	
Ekaterina Poistogova (RUS)				2.01.44 (3)	
Anita Hinriksdóttir (ISL)				2.01.56 (4)	
Ayvika Malanova (RUS)				2.01.71 (7)	
Treniere Moser (USA)				2.01.79 (8)	
Renelle Lamote (FRA)				2.01.97 (10)	
Chanelle Price (USA)					2.00.09 (1)
Maryna Arzamasova (BLR)					2.00.79 (5)
Lenka Masná (CZE)					2.01.25 (8)
Anna Shchagina (RUS)					2.01.29 (9)
Yekaterina Kupina (RUS)					2.01.46(10)

WORLD RANKING ALL TIME OUTDOOR:

1.	Jarmila Kratochvilova (TCH)	1.53.28 (1983)
2.	Nadezhda Olizarenko (URS)	1.53.43 (1980)
3.	Pamela Jelimo (KEN)	1.54.01 (2008)
4.	Caster Semenya (RSA)	1.54.25 (2018)
5.	Ana Fidelia Quirot (CUB)	1.54.81 (1980)
6.	Olga Mineyeva (URS)	1.54.81 (1980)
7.	Tatyana Kazankina (URS)	1.54.94 (1976)
8.	Doina Melinte (ROM)	1.55.05 (1982)
9.	Maria Mutola (MOZ)	1.55.19 (1994)
	Jolanda Ceplak (SLO)	1.55.19 (2002)
11.	Sigrun Wodars-Grau (GDR)	1.55.26 (1987)
12.	Christine Wachtel (GDR)	1.55.32 (1987)
13.	Nikolina Shtereva (BUL)	1.55.42 (1976)
14.	Tatyana Providokhina (URS)	1.55.46 (1980)
15.	Francine Niyonsaba (BDI)	1.55.47 (2017)
16.	Ellen van Langen (NED)	1.55.54 (1992)
	Liu Dong (CHN)	1.55.54 (1993)
18.	Lyubov Gurina (URS)	1.55.56 (1987)
19.	Elfi Zinn (GDR)	1.55.60 (1976)
20.	Ajee Wilson (USA)	1.55.61 (2017)
21.	Ella Kovács (ROM)	1.55.68 (1985)
22.	Irina Podyalovskaya (URS)	1.55.69 (1984)
23.	Anita Weiss (GDR)	1.55.74 (1976)
24.	Svetlana Masterkova (RUS)	1.55.87 (1999)
25.	Lyudmila Veselkova (URS)	1.55.96 (1982)
	Yekaterina Podkopaeva (URS)	1.55.96 (1983)
27.	Liliya Nurutdinova (RUS)	1.55.99 (1992)
28.	Tatyana Andrianova (RUS)	1.56.00 (2008)
29.	Janeth Jepkosgei (KEN)	1.56.04 (2007)
30.	Zulia Calatayud (CUB)	1.56.09 (2002)
31.	Natoya Goule (JAM)	1.56.15 (2018)
32.	Martina Kämpfert-Steuk (GDR)	1.56.21 (1980)
	Zamira Zaytseva (URS)	1.56.21 (1983)
	Kelly Holmes (GBR)	1.56.21 (1995)
35.	Ravilya Agletdinova (URS)	1.56.24 (1985)
	Qu Yunxia (CHN)	1.56.24 (1993)
37.	Jearl Miles-Clark (USA)	1.56.40 (1999)
38.	Paula Ivan (ROM)	1.56.42 (1988)
39.	Hasna Benhassi (MAR)	1.56.43 (2004)
40.	Svetlana Styrkina (URS)	1.56.44 (1976)
41.	Slobodanka Colovic (YUG)	1.56.51 (1987)
42.	Patricia Djate-Taillard (FRA)	1.56.53 (1995)
43.	Ludmila Formanová (CZE)	1.56.56 (1999)
44.	Zoya Rigel (URS)	1.56.57 (1978)
45.	Totka Petrova (BUL)	1.56.59 (1978)
	Natalya Khrushchelyova (RUS)	1.56.59 (2004)

WORLD RANKING ALL TIME INDOOR:

1.	Jolanda Ceplak (SLO)	1.55.82 (2002)
2.	Stephanie Graf (AUT)	1.55.85 (2002)
3.	Christine Wachtel (GDR)	1.56.40 (1988)
4.	Ludmila Formanová (CZE)	1.56.90 (1999)
5.	Maria Mutola (MOZ)	1.57.06 (1999)
6.	Inna Yevseyeva (UKR)	1.57.23 (1992)
7.	Natalya Tsyganova (RUS)	1.57.47 (1999)
8.	Olga Kotlyarova (RUS)	1.57.51 (2006)
9.	Larisa Chzhao (RUS)	1.57.53 (2005)
10.	Sigrun Wodars-Grau (GDR)	1.57.67 (1988)
11.	Mariya Savinova (RUS)	1.58.10 (2009)
12.	Yuliya Stepanova (RUS)	1.58.14 (2011)
13.	Francine Niyonsabo (BDI)	1.58.31 (2018)
14.	Svetlana Cherkasova (RUS)	1.58.34 (2006)
15.	Helena Fuchsová (CZE)	1.58.37 (2001)
16.	Jennifer Meadows (GBR)	1.58.43 (2010)
17.	Irina Vashentseva (RUS)	1.58.48 (2005)
18.	Yelena Soboleva (RUS)	1.58.53 (2006)
19.	Charlene Lipsey (USA)	1.58.64 (2017)
20.	Yevgeniya Zinurova (RUS)	1.58.65 (2010)
21.	Tetyana Petlyuk (UKR)	1.58.67 (2007)
22.	Nicole Teter (USA)	1.58.71 (2002)
23.	Yelena Afanasyeva (RUS)	1.58.73 (2001)
24.	Pamela Jelimo (KEN)	1.58.83 (2012)
25.	Natalya Ignatova (RUS)	1.58.84 (2008)
26.	Suzy Favor Hamilton (USA)	1.58.92 (1999)
27.	Olga Kuznetsova (RUS)	1.58.94 (2001)
28.	Ajee Wilson (USA)	1.58.99 (2018)
29.	Doina Melinte (ROM)	1.59.00 (1987)
30.	Malika Akkaoui (MAR)	1.59.01 (2012)
31.	Jearl Miles-Clark (USA)	1.59.09 (2002)
32.	Meredith Rainey-Valmon (USA)	1.59.11 (1999)
	Oksana Zbrozhek (RUS)	1.59.11 (2007)
34.	Natalya Gorelova (RUS)	1.59.15 (2001)
35.	Kutre Dulecha (ETH)	1.59.17 (1999)
36.	Milena Strnadová (TCH)	1.59.18 (1986)
	Svetlana Masterkova (RUS)	1.59.18 (1993)
38.	Lyubov Gurina (URS)	1.59.21 (1990)
	Letitia Vriesde (SUR)	1.59.21 (1997)
	Kelly Holmes (GBR)	1.59.21 (2003)
41.	Martina Kämpfert-Steuk (GDR)	1.59.24 (1982)
42.	Elisa Cusma (ITA)	1.59.25 (2009)
43.	Marilyn Okoro (GBR)	1.59.27 (2009)
44.	Joanna Józwik (POL)	1.59.29 (2017)
45.	Violeta Beclea-Szekely (ROM)	1.59.30 (1994)

1500 m Women

EUROPEAN CHAMPIONSHIPS 2018: 12-8-2018:

1.	Laura Muir (GBR)	4.02.32
2.	Sofia Ennaoui (POL)	4.03.08
3.	Laura Weightman (GBR)	4.03.75
4.	Ciara Mageean (IRL)	4.04.63
5.	Simona Vrzalová (CZE)	4.06.47
6.	Marta Pen (POR)	4.06.54
7.	Hanna Hermansson (SWE)	4.07.16
8.	Daryla Barysevich (BLR)	4.07.52
9.	Marta Pérez (ESP)	4.07.65
10.	Diana Mezuliáníková (CZE)	4.07.82
11.	Esther Guerrero (ESP)	4.09.88
12.	Angelika Cichocka (POL) (4.10.04)	4.10.93

13.	Elise Vanderelst (BEL)	4.10.30
14.	Kristiina Mäki (CZE)	4.10.35
15.	Jemma Reekie (GBR)	4.10.35
16.	Solange Pereira (ESP)	4.10.63
17.	Sara Kuivisto (FIN)	4.11.39
18.	Caterina Granz (GER)	4.11.46
19.	Diana Sujew (GER)	4.12.08
20.	Anna Silvander (SWE)	4.12.61
21.	Delia Sclabas (SUI)	4.13.47
22.	Claudia Bobocea (ROM)	4.16.20
23.	Amela Terzic (SRB)	4.17.22

WORLD RANKING 2018:

1.	Genzebe Dibaba (ETH)	3.56.68(Cho)
2.	Shelby Houlihan (USA)	3.57.34(Lau)
3.	Sifan Hassan (NED)	3.57.41(Lon)
4.	Gudaf Tsegay (ETH)	3.57.64(Sto)
5.	Laura Muir (GBR)	3.58.18(Lau)
6.	Hellen Obiri (KEN)	3.58.88(Lon)
7.	Rababe Arafi (MAR)	3.59.15(Lau)
8.	Jenny Simpson (USA)	3.59.37(Eug)
9.	Caster Semenya (RSA)	3.59.92(Do)
10.	Winny Chebet (KEN)	4.00.60(Eug)
11.	Linden Hall (USA)	4.00.86(Eug)
12.	Nelly Jepkosgei (KEN)	4.00.99(Do)
13.	Habitam Alemu (ETH)	4.01.41(Do)
14.	Besu Sado (ETH)	4.01.75(Do)
15.	Laura Weightman (GBR)	4.01.76(Lau)
16.	Alemaz Samuel (ETH)	4.01.78(Do)
17.	Eilish McColgan (GBR)	4.01.98(Lau)
18.	Sofia Ennaoui (POL)	4.02.06(Bir)
19.	Meraf Bahta (SWE)	4.02.31(Sto)
20.	Axumawit Embaye (ETH)	4.02.44(Bir)
21.	Brenda Martinez (USA)	4.02.65(Eug)
22.	Dawit Seyaum (ETH)	4.02.81(Eug)
23.	Colleen Quigley (USA)	4.03.02(Cho)
24.	Beatrice Chepkoech (KEN)	4.03.09(GC)
25.	Sarah McDonald (GBR)	4.03.17(Bir)
26.	Melissa Courtney (GBR)	4.03.44(GC)
27.	Judith Kiyeng (KEN)	4.03.87(Do)
28.	Marta Pen (POR)	4.03.99(Bir)
29.	Kate Grace (USA)	4.04.05(Lon)
30.	Ciara Mageean (IRL)	4.04.13
31.	Georgie Griffith (AUS)	4.04.17(GC)
32.	Aleksandra Gulyayeva (RUS)	4.04.76(Zhu)
33.	Simonna Vrzalová (CZE)	4.04.80(Ost)
34.	Marta Pérez (ESP)	4.04.88(Mad)
35.	Charlene Lipsey (USA)	4.04.98
36.	Maureen Koster (NED)	4.05.12(Mad)
37.	Ajee Wilson (USA)	4.05.18
38.	Eunice Jepkoech Sum (KEN)	4.05.38(Do)

WORLD INDOOR CHAMPIONSHIPS: 3-3-2018:

1. Genzebe Dibaba (ETH)   (4.06.25)   4.05.27
2. Laura Muir (GBR)   (4.06.54)   4.06.23
3. Sifan Hassan (NED)   (4.05.46)   4.07.26
4. Shelby Houlihan (USA)   (4.06.21)   4.11.93
5. Winny Chebet (KEN)   (4.05.81)   4.12.08
6. Aisha Praught (JAM)   (4.07.51)   4.12.86
7. Beatrice Chepkoech (KEN) (4.09.12)   4.13.59
8. Rababe Arafi (MAR)   (4.06.12)   4.14.94
9. Colleen Quigley (USA)   (4.09.31)   4.15.97
10. Meraf Bahta (SWE)   (4.22.40)   4.23.05
----
11. Kate van Buskirk (CAN)   4.09.42
12. Dominique Scott (RSA)   4.09.80
13. Marta Pérez (ESP)   4.09.90
14. Gabriela Stafford (CAN)   4.09.94
15. Dawit Seyaum (ETH)   4.10.20
16. Linn Nilsson (SWE)   4.10.36
17. Diana Sujew (GER)   4.10.64
18. Luiza Gega (ALB)   4.10.65
19. Ciara Mageean (IRL)   4.11.81
20. Hanna Klein (GER)   4.12.11
21. Eilish McColgan (GBR)   4.13.32
22. Simona Vrzalová (CZE)   4.14.11
23. Malika Akkaoui (MAR)   4.15.09
24. Anita Hinríksdottir (ISL)   4.15.73
25. Claudia Bobocea (ROM)   4.24.60

WORLD INDOOR RANKING 2018:

1. Genzebe Dibaba (ETH)   3.57.45
2. Beatrice Chepkoech (KEN)   4.02.21
3. Konstanze Klosterhalfen (GER)   4.04.00
4. Dawit Seyaum (ETH)   4.04.38
5. Rababe Arafi (MAR)   4.04.76
6. Meraf Bahta (SWE)   4.04.89
7. Aisha Praught (JAM)   4.04.95
8. Hellen Obiri (KEN)   4.05.04
9. Alemaz Samuel (ETH)   4.05.36
10. Laura Muir (GBR)   4.05.37
11. Sifan Hassan (NED)   4.05.46
12. Habitam Alemu (ETH)   4.05.51
13. Axumawit Embaye (ETH)   4.05.64
14. Winny Chebet (KEN)   4.05.81
15. Gudaf Tsegay (ETH)   4.05.91
16. Shelby Houlihan (USA)   4.06.21
17. Angelika Cichocka (POL)   4.06.35
18. Dominique Scott (RSA)   4.07.25
19. Sarah McDonald (GBR)   4.07.62
20. Linn Nilsson (SWE)   4.07.71
21. Eilish McColgan (GBR)   4.08.07
22. Diana Sujew (GER)   4.08.33
23. Sofia Ennaoui (POL)   4.08.70
24. Cory Ann McGee (USA)   4.08.84
25. Marta Pérez (ESP)   4.09.24
26. Yelena Korobkina (RUS)   4.09.25
27. Malika Akkaoui (MAR)   4.09.31
    Collen Quigley (USA)   4.09.31
29. Kate van Buskirk (CAN)   4.09.42
30. Ciara Mageean (IRL)   4.09.47
31. Aleksandra Gulyayeva (RUS)   4.09.48
32. Aníta Hinríksdottír (ISL)   4.09.54
33. Gabriela Stafford (CAN)   4.09.94
34. Nelly Jepkosgei (KEN)   4.09.99
35. Stacey Smith (GBR)   4.10.05
36. Katie Snowden (GBR)   4.10.09
37. Hanna Klein (GER)   4.10.12
38. Josephine Chelangat Kiplangat (KEN) 4.10.14
39. Simona Vrzalová (CZE)   4.10.36
    Luiza Gega (ALB)   4.10.36
41. Claudia Bobocea (ROM)   4.10.37
42. Zoe Buckman (AUS)   4.10.52
    Gesa Felicitas Krause (GER)   4.10.85
44. Hannah England (GBR)   4.11.25
45. Adanech Anbesa (ETH)   4.11.57

Commonwealth Games, Gold Coast, 10-4-2018:

1.	Caster Semenya (RSA)	4.00.71
2.	Beatrice Chepkoech (KEN)	4.03.09
3.	Melissa Courtney (GBR)	4.03.44
4.	Linden Hall (AUS)	4.03.67
5.	Georgia Griffith (AUS)	4.04.17
6.	Eilish McColgan (GBR)	4.04.30
7.	Stephanie Twell (GBR)	4.05.56
8.	Sarah McDonald (GBR)	4.05.77
9.	Mary Kuria (KEN)	4.05.88
10.	Winnie Nanyondo (UGA)	4.06.05
11.	Katie Snowden (GBR)	4.06.55
12.	Zoe Buckman (AUS)	4.06.76
13.	Ciara Mageean (IRL)	4.07.41

Doha, 4-5-2018:

1.	Caster Semenya (RSA)	3.59.92
2.	Nelly Jepkosgei (KEN)	4.00.99
3.	Habitam Alemu (ETH)	4.01.41
4.	Besu Sado (ETH)	4.01.75
5.	Alemaz Samuel (ETH)	4.01.78
6.	Gudaf Tsegay (ETH)	4.01.81
7.	Rababe Arafi (MAR)	4.03.69
8.	Judith Kimutai Kiyeng (KEN)	4.03.87
9.	Eunice Jepkoech Sum (KEN)	4.05.38
10.	Winny Chebet (KEN)	4.05.76
11.	Linden Hall (AUS)	4.07.07
12.	Zoe Buckman (AUS)	4.07.25

Eunice, 26-5-2018:

1.	Shelby Houlihan (USA)	3.59.06
2.	Laura Muir (GBR)	3.59.30
3.	Jennifer Simpson (USA)	3.59.37
4.	Rababe Arafi (MAR)	3.59.51
5.	Winny Chebet (KEN)	4.00.60
6.	Linden Hall (AUS)	4.00.86
7.	Brenda Martinez (USA)	4.02.65
8.	Dawit Seyaum (ETH)	4.02.81
9.	Beatrice Chepkoech (KEN)	4.05.36
10.	Mary Wangari Kuria (KEN)	4.06.07
11.	Kate Grace (USA)	4.07.10
12.	Laura Weightman (GBR)	4.07.48
13.	Zoe Buckman (AUS)	4.08.75
14.	Angelika Cichocka (POL)	4.11.50

Chorzow, 8-6-2018:

1.	Genzebe Dibaba (ETH)	3.56.68
2.	Axumawit Embaye (ETH)	4.04.90
3.	Diana Sujew (GER)	4.05.95
4.	Sofia Ennaoui (POL)	4.07.04
5.	Simona Vrzalová (CZE)	4.07.32

Stockholm, 10-6-2018:

1.	Gudaf Tsegay (ETH)	3.57.64
2.	Laura Muir (GBR)	3.58.53
3.	Rababe Arafi (MAR)	4.00.28
4.	Jennifer Simpson (USA)	4.00.34
5.	Nelly Jepkosgei (KEN)	4.01.95
6.	Meraf Bahta (SWE)	4.02.31
7.	Besu Sado (ETH)	4.02.81
8.	Linden Hall (AUS)	4.02.89
9.	Laura Weightman (GBR)	4.02.90
10.	Karoline Grövdal (NOR)	4.05.57
11.	Brenda Martinez (USA)	4.06.54
12.	Habitam Alemu (ETH)	4.08.19

Ostrava, 13-6-2018:

1.	Gudaf Tsegay (ETH)	4.02.45
2.	Sarah McDonald (GBR)	4.04.41
3.	Simona Vrzalová (CZE)	4.04.80
4.	Sofia Ennaoui (POL)	4.05.06
5.	Nelly Jepkosgei (KEN)	4.05.17
6.	Fantu Worku (ETH)	4.06.01
7.	Diana Mezulianikova (CZE)	4.06.12

Madrid, 22-6-2018:

1.	Gudaf Tsegay (ETH)	3.59.60
2.	Sofia Ennaoui (POL)	4.02.93
3.	Meraf Bahta (SWE)	4.03.36
4.	Linden Hall (AUS)	4.04.48
5.	Marta Pérez (ESP)	4.04.88
6.	Maureen Koster (NED)	4.05.12
7.	Simona Vrzalová (CZE)	4.06.03

KEN Trials, Nairobi, 23-6-2018:

1.	Winny Chebet	4.09.69
2.	Mary Kuria	4.10.81
3.	Judith Kimutai Kiyeng	4.10.83
4.	Nelly Jepkosgei	4.11.76
5.	Winfredah Mbithe	4.14.28

Lausanne, 5-7-2018:

1.	Shelby Houlihan (USA)	3.57.34
2.	Laura Muir (GBR)	3.58.18
3.	Sifan Hassan (NED)	3.58.39
4.	Gudaf Tsegay (ETH)	3.59.07
5.	Rababe Arafi (MAR)	3.59.15
6.	Caster Semenya (RSA)	4.00.44
7.	Laura Weightman (GBR)	4.01.76
8.	Eilish McColgan (GBR)	4.01.98
9.	Winny Chebet (KEN)	4.06.10
10.	Melissa Courtney (GBR)	4.06.27
11.	Meraf Bahta (SWE)	4.06.96
12.	Malika Akkaoui (MAR)	4.07.08
13.	Linden Hall (AUS)	4.07.26

Barcelona, 11-7-2018:

1.	Ciara Mageean (IRL)	4.04.13
2.	Marta Pen (POR)	4.04.53
3.	Linden Hall (AUS)	4.04.88
4.	Sara Vaughn (USA)	4.05.88

AFR CHAMPIONSHIPS, Assaba, 3-8-2018:

1.	Winny Chebet (KEN)	4.14.02
2.	Rababe Arafi (MAR)	4.14.12
3.	Malika Akkaoui (MAR)	4.14.17
4.	Besu Sado Deko (ETH)	4.15.74
5.	Winnie Nanyondo (UGA)	4.16.55
6.	Judith Kimutai Kiyeng (KEN)	4.17.26
7.	Mary Kuria (KEN)	4.17.70

Birmingham, 18-8-2018:

1.	Sifan Hassan (NED)	4.00.60
2.	Gudaf Tsegay (ETH)	4.01.03
3.	Sofia Ennaoui (POL)	4.02.06
4.	Axumawit Embaye (ETH)	4.02.44
5.	Sarah McDonald (GBR)	4.03.17
6.	Winny Chebet (KEN)	4.03.64
7.	Marta Pen (POR)	4.03.99
8.	Kate Grace (USA)	4.04.64

Chorzow, 22-8-2018:

1.	Colleen Quigley (USA)	4.03.02
2.	Sofia Ennaoui (POL)	4.03.28
3.	Sarah McDonald (GBR)	4.03.36
4.	Simona Vrzalová (CZE)	4.05.05
5.	Kristina Mäki (EST)	4.06.71

Brussels, 31-8-2018:

1.	Laura Muir (GBR)	3.58.49
2.	Shelby Houlihan (USA)	3.58.94
3.	Sifan Hassan (NED)	3.59.41
4.	Gudaf Tsegay (ETH)	3.59.68
5.	Axumawit Embaye (ETH)	4.02.75
6.	Winny Chebet (KEN)	4.03.37
7.	Sofia Ennaoui (POL)	4.03.49
8.	Rababe Arafi (MAR)	4.03.82
9.	Laura Weightman (GBR)	4.04.36
10.	Jennifer Simpson (USA)	4.04.57
11.	Elise Vanderelst (BEL)	4.05.75

CONTINENTAL CUP, Ostrava, 8-9-2018:

1.	Winny Chebet (AFR)	4.16.01
2.	Shelby Houlihan (AME)	4.16.36
3.	Rababe Arafi (AFR)	4.17.19
4.	Unnikrishnan Chitra (ASI)	4.18.45
5.	Linden Hall (ASI)	4.18.82
6.	Simona Vrzalová (EUR)	4.19.46
7.	Sofia Ennaoui (EUR)	4.22.56

OVERVIEW WORLD OUTDOOR CHAMPIONSHIP FINALISTS OF PAST 6 YEARS

	Wch 17	OG 16	Wch 15	Wch 13
Faith Kipyegon (KEN)	4.02.59 (1)	4.08.92 (1)	4.08.96 (2)	4.05.08 (5)
Jennifer Simpson (USA)	4.02.76 (2)	4.10.53 (3)	4.16.28 (11)	4.02.99 (2)
Caster Semenya (RSA)	4.02.90 (3)			
Laura Muir (GBR)	4.02.97 (4)	4.12.88 (7)	4.11.48 (5)	
Sifan Hassan (NED)	4.03.34 (5)	4.11.23 (5)	4.09.34 (3)	
Laura Weightman (GBR)	4.04.11 (6)	4.14.95 (11)		
Angelika Cichocka (POL)	4.04.16 (7)		4.13.22 (8)	
Rababe Arafi (MAR)	4.04.35 (8)	4.15.16 (12)	4.13.66 (9)	
Meraf Bahta (SWE)	4.04.76 (9)	4.12.59 (6)		
Malika Akkaoui (MAR)	4.05.87 (10)		4.16.98 (12)	
Hanna Klein (GER)	4.06.22 (11)			
Genzebe Dibaba (ETH)	4.06.72 (12)	4.10.27 (2)	4.08.09 (1)	4.05.99 (8)
Shannon Rowbury (USA)		4.11.05 (4)	4.12.39 (7)	
Dawit Seyaum (ETH)		4.13.14 (8)	4.10.26 (4)	
Besu Sado (ETH)		4.13.58 (9)		
Sofia Ennaoui (POL)		4.14.72 (10)		
Abeba Aregawi (SWE)			4.12.16 (6)	4.02.67 (1)
Tatyana Tomashova (RUS)			4.14.18 (10)	
Hellen Onsando Obiri (KEN)				4.03.86 (3)
Hannah England (GBR)				4.04.98 (4)
Ekaterina Sharmina (RUS)				4.05.49 (6)
Zoe Buckman (AUS)				4.05.77 (7)
Nancy Jebet Langat (KEN)				4.06.01 (9)
Mary Cain (USA)				4.07.19 (10)
Siham Hilali (MAR)				4.09.16 (11)
Elena Korobkina (RUS)				4.10.18 (12)

OVERVIEW WORLD INDOOR CHAMPIONSHIP FINALISTS OF 5 PAST YEARS

	Wch 18	Wch 16	Wch 14
Genzebe Dibaba (ETH)	4.05.27 (1)		
Laura Muir (GBR)	4.06.23 (2)		
Sifan Hassan (NED)	4.07.26 (3)	4.04.96 (1)	
Shelby Houlihan (USA)	4.11.93 (4)		
Winny Chebet (KEN)	4.12.08 (5)		
Aisha Praught (JAM)	4.12.86 (6)		
Beatrice Chepkoech (KEN)	4.13.59 (7)		
Rababe Arafi (MAR)	4.14.94 (8)		dsq
Colleen Quigley (USA)	4.15.97 (9)		
Meraf Bahta (SWE)	4.23.05 (10)		
Dawit Seyaum (ETH)		4.05.30 (2)	
Gudaf Tsegay (ETH)		4.05.71 (3)	
Axumawit Embaye (ETH)		4.09.37 (4)	4.07.12 (2)
Brenda Martinez (USA)		4.09.57 (5)	
Melissa Duncan (AUS)		4.09.69 (6)	
Renata Plis (POL)		4.10.14 (7)	
Viola Cheptoo Lagat (KEN)		4.10.45 (7)	
Danuta Urbanik (POL)		4.12.59 (8)	
Abeba Aregawi (SWE)			4.00.61 (1)
Nicole Sifuentes (CAN)			4.07.61 (3)
Siham Hilali (MAR)			4.07.62 (4)
Treniere Moser (USA)			4.07.84 (5)
Luiza Gega (ALB)			4.08.24 (6)
Svetlana Karamasheva (RUS)			4.13.89 (7)
Heather Kampf (USA)			dsq

OVERVIEW TOP 10 WORLD OUTDOOR RANKINGS OF PAST 5 YEARS

	2018	2017	2016	2015	2014
Genzebe Dibaba (ETH)	3.56.68 (1)	3.57.82 (3)	3.57.31 (4)	3.50.07 (1)	
Shelby Houlihan (USA)	3.57.34 (2)				
Sifan Hassan (NED)	3.57.41 (3)	3.56.14 (1)	3.57.13 (3)	3.56.05 (2)	3.57.00 (1)
Gudaf Tsegay (ETH)	3.57.64 (4)	3.59.55 (6)	4.00.18 (10)		
Laura Muir (GBR)	3.58.18 (5)	4.00.35 (7)	3.55.22 (1)	3.58.66 (5)	4.00.07 (8)
Hellen Onsando Obiri (KEN)	3.58.88 (6)	4.00.44 (8)	3.59.34 (8)		3.57.05 (2)
Rababe Arafi (MAR)	3.59.15 (7)				
Jennifer Simpson (USA)	3.59.37 (8)		3.58.19 (7)	3.57.30 (4)	3.57.22 (3)
Caster Semenya (RSA)	3.59.92 (9)				
Winny Chebet (KEN)	4.00.60 (10)	3.59.16 (5)			
Faith Kipyegon (KEN)		3.57.04 (2)	3.56.41 (2)	3.59.32 (6)	3.58.01 (5)
Konstanze Klosterhalfen (GER)		3.58.92 (4)			
Meraf Bahta (SWE)		4.00.49 (9)			
Dawit Seyaum (ETH)		4.00.52 (10)	3.58.09 (6)	3.59.76 (7)	3.59.53 (7)
Shannon Rowbury (USA)			3.57.78 (5)	3.56.29 (3)	3.59.49 (6)
Besu Sado (ETH)			3.59.47 (9)	4.00.65 (9)	
Maureen Koster (NED)				3.59.79 (8)	
Mercy Cherono (KEN)				4.01.26 (10)	
Abeba Aregawi (SWE)					3.57.57 (4)
Mimi Belete (BRN)					4.00.08 (9)
Laura Weightman (GBR)					4.00.17 (10)

OVERVIEW TOP 10 WORLD INDOOR RANKINGS OF PAST 5 YEARS

	2018	2017	2016	2015	2014
Genzebe Dibaba (ETH)	3.57.45 (1)	3.58.80 (1)	3.56.46 (1)		3.55.17 (1)
Beatrice Chepkoech (KEN)	4.02.21 (2)				
Konstanze Klosterhalfen (GER)	4.04.00 (3)	4.04.45 (4)			
Dawit Seyaum (ETH)	4.04.38 (4)		4.00.28 (2)		
Rababe Arafi (MAR)	4.04.76 (5)			4.07.91 (8)	4.07.53 (10)
Meraf Bahta (SWE)	4.04.89 (6)	4.06.40 (8)		4.06.42 (5)	
Aisha Praught (JAM)	4.04.95 (7)				
Hellen Onsando Obiri (KEN)	4.05.04 (8)				4.05.82 (7)
Alemaz Samuel (ETH)	4.05.36 (9)				
Laura Muir (GBR)	4.05.37 (10)	4.02.39 (2)			4.05.32 (3)
Sifan Hassan (NED)		4.03.05 (3)	4.01.40 (3)	4.00.46 (1)	4.05.34 (4)
Shannon Rowbury (USA)		4.04.56 (5)	4.07.30 (10)	4.05.08 (3)	
Kate Grace (USA)		4.04.86 (6)	4.06.75 (7)		
Axumawit Embaye (ETH)		4.04.95 (7)	4.06.11 (6)	4.02.92 (2)	4.07.12 (9)
Sofia Ennaoui (POL)		4.06.59 (9)			
Luiza Gega (ALB)		4.06.66 (10)	4.06.89 (8)		
Gudaf Tsegay (ETH)			4.01.81 (4)	4.07.69 (7)	
Brenda Martinez (USA)			4.04.58 (5)		
Melissa Duncan (AUS)			4.06.93 (9)		
Betlhem Desalegn (UAE)				4.05.61 (4)	
Angelika Cichocka (POL)				4.06.44 (6)	
Jordan Hasay (USA)				4.07.93 (9)	
Federica Del Buono (ITA)				4.08.87 (10)	
Abeba Aregawi (SWE)					3.57.91 (2)
Kim Conley (USA)					4.05.70 (5)
Elena Korobkina (RUS)					4.05.78 (6)
Mary Cain (USA)					4.06.63 (8)

WORLD RANKING ALL TIME OUTDOOR:

1.	Genzebe Dibaba (ETH)	3.50.07 (2015)
2.	Qu Yunxia (CHN)	3.50.46 (1993)
3.	Bo Jiang (CHN)	3.50.98 (1997)
4.	Lang Yinglai (CHN)	3.51.34 (1997)
5.	Wang Junxia (CHN)	3.51.92 (1993)
6.	Tatyana Kazankina (URS)	3.52.47 (1980)
7.	Yin Lili (CHN)	3.53.91 (1997)
8.	Paula Ivan (ROM)	3.53.96 (1988)
9.	Lan Lixin (CHN)	3.53.97 (1997)
10.	Olga Dvirna (URS)	3.54.23 (1982)
11.	Zhang Ling (CHN)	3.54.52 (1997)
12.	Dong Yanmei (CHN)	3.55.07 (1997)
13.	Laura Muir (GBR)	3.55.22 (2016)
14.	Hassiba Boulmerka (ALG)	3.55.30 (1992)
15.	Süreyya Ayhan (TUR)	3.55.33 (2003)
16.	Yuliya Chizhenko (RUS)	3.55.68 (2006)
17.	Sifan Hassan (NED)	3.56.05 (2015)
18.	Zamira Zaytseva (URS)	3.56.14 (1982)
19.	Maryam Yusuf Jamal (BRN)	3.56.18 (2006)
20.	Shannon Rowbury (USA)	3.56.29 (2015)
21.	Liu Dong (CHN)	3.56.31 (1997)
22.	Faith Kipyegon (KEN)	3.56.41 (2016)
23.	Yelena Soboleva (RUS)	3.56.43 (2006)
24.	Tetyana Pozdnyakova (URS)	3.56.50 (1982)
25.	Abeba Aregawi (ETH)	3.56.54 (2012)
26.	Nadezhda Ralldugina (URS)	3.56.63 (1984)
27.	Yekaterina Podkopaeva (URS)	3.56.65 (1984)
28.	Doina Melinte (ROM)	3.56.7 (1986)
29.	Lyudmila Rogachova (RUS)	3.56.91 (1992)
	Tatyana Tomashova (RUS)	3.56.91 (2006)
31.	Gabriela Szabo (ROM)	3.56.97 (1998)
32.	Jing Liu (CHN)	3.57.03 (1997)
33.	Svetlana Guskova (URS)	3.57.05 (1982)
	Hellen Obiri (KEN)	3.57.05 (2014)
35.	Svetlana Masterkova (RUS)	3.57.11 (1998)
36.	Mary Slaney-Decker (USA)	3.57.12 (1983)
37.	Maricica Puica (ROM)	3.57.22 (1984)
	Jenny Simpson (USA)	3.57.22 (2014)
39.	Shelby Houlihan (USA)	3.57.34 (2018)
40.	Suzy Favor Hamilton (USA)	3.57.40 (2000)
41.	Jackline Maranga (KEN)	3.57.41 (1998)
42.	Zhang Linli (CHN)	3.57.46 (1993)
43.	Gudaf Tsegay (ETH)	3.57.64 (2018)
44.	Christine Wardenberg (GDR)	3.57.71 (1980)
	Carla Sacramento (POR)	3.57.71 (1998)

WORLD RANKING ALL TIME INDOOR:

1.	Genzebe Dibaba (ETH)	3.55.17 (2014)
2.	Abeba Aregawi (SWE)	3.57.91 (2014)
3.	Yelena Soboleva (RUS)	3.58.28 (2006)
4.	Gelete Burka (ETH)	3.59.75 (2008)
5.	Maryam Yusuf Jamal (BRN)	3.59.79 (2008)
6.	Regina Jacobs (USA)	3.59.98 (2003)
7.	Doina Mehlinte (ROM)	4.00.27 (1990)
8.	Dawit Seyaum (ETH)	4.00.28 (2016)
9.	Sifan Hassan (NED)	4.00.46 (2015)
10.	Natalya Gorelova (RUS)	4.00.72 (2003)
11.	Mary Decker (USA)	4.00.8 (1980)
12.	Yuliya Chizenko (RUS)	4.01.26 (2006)
13.	Nuria Fernández (ESP)	4.01.77 (2009)
14.	Gudaf Tsegay (ETH)	4.01.81 (2016)
15.	Kutre Dulecha (ETH)	4.01.90 (2004)
16.	Beatrice Chepkoech (KEN)	4.02.21 (2018)
17.	Lyudmila Rogachova (RUS)	4.02.3 (1990)
18.	Laura Muir (GBR)	4.02.39 (2017)
19.	Yekaterina Rozenberg (RUS)	4.02.58 (2003)
20.	Kelly Holmes (GBR)	4.02.66 (2003)
21.	Axumawit Embaye (ETH)	4.02.92 (2015)
22.	Natalia Marasescu (ROM)	4.03.0 (1979)
23.	Elena Buhaianu-Antoci (ROM)	4.03.09 (2005)
24.	Gabriela Szabo (ROM)	4.03.23 (1999)
25.	Kalkidan Gezahegne (ETH)	4.03.28 (2010)
26.	Fita Lovin (ROM)	4.03.46 (1985)
27.	Yelena Kanales (RUS)	4.03.53 (2006)
	Liliana Barbulescu-Popescu (ROM)	4.03.53 (2008)
29.	Lidia Chojecka (POL)	4.03.58 (2003)
30.	Violeta Beclea-Szekely (ROM)	4.03.61 (2001)
31.	Brigitte Kraus (GER)	4.03.64 (1985)
32.	Mariem Alaoui Selsouli (MAR)	4.03.67 (2012)
33.	Yekaterina Sharmina (RUS)	4.03.68 (2008)
34.	Oksana Zbrozhek (RUS)	4.03.86 (2009)
35.	Zamira Zaytseva (URS)	4.03.9 (1979)
36.	Konstanze Klosterhalfen (GER)	4.04.00 (2018)
37.	Gabriella Dorio (ITA)	4.04.01 (1982)
38.	Carla Sacramento (POR)	4.04.11 (2001)
39.	Daniela Yordanova (BUL)	4.04.19 (2008)
40.	Olga Kuznetsova (RUS)	4.04.26 (2001)
41.	Olga Komyagina (RUS)	4.04.33 (2006)
42.	Olesya Chumakova (RUS)	4.04.39 (2006)
43.	Alesya Turava (BLR)	4.04.42 (2004)
44.	Hasna Benhassi (MAR)	4.04.48 (2001)
45.	Siham Hilali (MAR)	4.04.53 (2012)

Mile Women

WORLD RANKING OUTDOOR 2018:

1.	Sifan Hassan (NED)	4.14.71(Lon)
2.	Gudaf Tsegay (ETH)	4.16.14(Lon)
3.	Hellen Obiri (KEN)	4.16.15(Lon)
4.	Jennifer Simpson (USA)	4.17.30(Lon)
5.	Laura Muir (GBR)	4.19.28(Lon)
6.	Laura Weightman (GBR)	4.20.49(Lon)
7.	Winny Chebet (KEN)	4.20.51(Lon)
	Genzebe Dibaba (ETH)	4.20.51(Pad)
9.	Kate Grace (USA)	4.20.70(Lon)
10.	Sarah McDonald (GBR)	4.20.85(Lon)
11.	Linden Hall (AUS)	4.21.40(Lon)
12.	Simona Vrzalová (CZE)	4.21.54(Lon)
13.	Marta Pen (POR)	4.22.45(Ber)
14.	Sofia Ennaoui (POL)	4.23.34(Lon)
15.	Konstanze Klosterhalfen (GER)	4.24.27(Ber)
16.	Alexa Efraimson (USA)	4.24.82(Ber)
17.	Eilish McColgan (GBR)	4.25.07(Ber)
18.	Shannon Osika (USA)	4.25.47
19.	Besu Sado (ETH)	4.25.99(Hen)
20.	Stephanie Twell (GBR)	4.26.05(Ber)
21.	Dominique Scott (RSA)	4.26.63
22.	Ciara Mageean (IRL)	4.26.75(Ber)
23.	Meraf Bahta (SWE)	4.27.03(Hen)
24.	Helen Schlachtenhaufen (USA)	4.27.09
25.	Jemma Reekie (GBR)	4.27.16(Lon)
26.	Rachel Schneider (USA)	4.27.23
27.	Charlene Lipsey (USA)	4.27.28(Ral)
28.	Melissa Courtney (GBR)	4.27.29(Hen)
29.	Sara Vaughn (USA)	4.27.31(Ral)
30.	Judith Kiyeng (KEN)	4.27.32(Hen)
31.	Cory Ann McGee (USA)	4.27.78(Ral)
32.	Nicole Sifuentes (CAN)	4.27.81(Ral)
33.	Winnie Nanyondo (UGA)	4.28.16(Hen)
	Lauren Johnson (USA)	4.28.16
35.	Marta Pérez (ESP)	4.28.25(Hen)
36.	Renata Plis (POL)	4.28.36(Ber)
37.	Diana Sujew (GER)	4.28.38(Hen)
38.	Kate van Buskirk (CAN)	4.28.67
39.	Sanne Verstegen-Wolters (NED)	4.29.11(Hen)
40.	Aníta Hinríksdóttír (ISL)	4.29.20(Hen)
41.	Katie Snowden (GBR)	4.29.56(Hen)
42.	Birri Abera (ETH)	4.29.74(Hen)
43.	Katie Mackey (USA)	4.29.81(Ber)
44.	Mary Kuria (KEN)	4.29.82(Sze)

WORLD RANKING INDOOR 2018:

1.	Elinor Purrier (USA)	4.26.55
2.	Kate van Buskirk (CAN)	4.26.92
3.	Rachel Schneider (USA)	4.27.30
4.	Gabriela Stafford (CAN)	4.27.44
5.	Karissa Schweizer (USA)	4.27.54
6.	Shannon Osika (USA)	4.27.55
7.	Nicole Sifuentes (CAN)	4.27.69
8.	Marta Pen (POR)	4.29.65
9.	Colleen Quigley (USA)	4.30.05
10.	Kate Grace (USA)	4.30.08
11.	Nicole Tully (USA)	4.30.98
12.	Ciara Mageean (IRL)	4.30.99
13.	Rebecca Addison (USA)	4.31.09
14.	Lauren Johnson (USA)	4.31.63
15.	Lucia Stafford (CAN)	4.31.66
16.	Danielle Jones (USA)	4.31.82
17.	Sara Vaughn (USA)	4.31.98
	Millie Paladino (USA)	4.31.98
19.	Helen Schlachtenhaufen (USA)	4.32.17
20.	Nikki Hiltz (USA)	4.32.59
21.	Natalija Piliusina (LTU)	4.32.67
22.	Alexa Efraimson (USA)	4.32.73
23.	Rhianwedd Price-Weimer (GBR)	4.33.00
24.	Kellyn Johnson (USA)	4.33.40
25.	Kaela Edwards (USA)	4.33.98

Hengelo, 3-6-2018:

1.	Jennifer Simpson (USA)	4.25.71
2.	Besu Sado (ETH)	4.25.99
3.	Meraf Bahta (SWE)	4.27.03
4.	Sarah McDonald (GBR)	4.27.12
5.	Melissa Courtney (GBR)	4.27.29
6.	Judith Jemutai Kiyeng (CHN)	4.27.32
7.	Winnie Nanyondo (UGA)	4.28.16
8.	Marta Pérez (ESP)	4.28.25
9.	Diana Sujew (GER)	4.28.38
10.	Sanne Verstegen (NED)	4.29.11
11.	Aníta Hinríksdóttír (ISL)	4.29.20
12.	Katie Snowden (GBR)	4.29.56
13.	Birri Abera (ETH)	4.29.74

London, 22-7-2018:

1.	Sifan Hassan (NED)	4.14.71
2.	Gudaf Tsegay (ETH)	4.16.14
3.	Hellen Obiri (KEN)	4.16.15
4.	Jennifer Simpson (USA)	4.17.30
5.	Laura Muir (GBR)	4.19.28
6.	Laura Weightman (GBR)	4.20.49
7.	Winny Chebet (KEN)	4.20.51
8.	Kate Grace (USA)	4.20.70
9.	Sarah McDonald (GBR)	4.20.85
10.	Linden Hall (AUS)	4.21.40
11.	Simona Vrzalová (CZE)	4.21.54
12.	Sofia Ennaoui (POL)	4.23.34
13.	Jemma Reekie (GBR)	4.27.16

Berlin, 2-9-2018:

1.	Marta Pen (POR)	4.22.45
2.	Kate Grace (USA)	4.23.23
3.	Konstanze Klosterhalfen (GER)	4.24.27
4.	Alexa Efraimson (USA)	4.24.82
5.	Eilish McColgan (GBR)	4.25.07
6.	Stephanie Twell (GBR)	4.26.05
7.	Ciara Mageean (IRL)	4.26.75
8.	Renata Plis (POL)	4.28.36
9.	Katie Mackey (USA)	4.29.81

WORLD RANKING OUTDOOR ALL TIME:

1.	Svetlana Masterkova (RUS)	4.12.56 (1996)
2.	Genzebe Dibaba (ETH)	4.14.30 (2016)
3.	Sifan Hassan (NED)	4.14.71 (2018)
4.	Paula Ivan (ROM)	4.15.61 (1989)
5.	Natalya Artyomova (URS)	4.15.8 (1984)
6.	Gudaf Tsegay (ETH)	4.16.14 (2018)
7.	Hellen Obiri (KEN)	4.16.56 (2017)
8.	Mary Slaney-Decker (USA)	4.16.71 (1985)
	Faith Kipyegon (KEN)	4.16.71 (2015)
10.	Sonia O'Sullivan (IRL)	4.17.25 (1994)
11.	Jennifer Simpson (USA)	4.17.30 (2018)
12.	Maricica Puica (ROM)	4.17.33 (1985)
13.	Zola Budd (GBR)	4.17.57 (1985)
14.	Maryam Yusuf-Jamal (BRN)	4.17.75 (2007)
15.	Laura Muir (GBR)	4.18.03 (2017)
16.	Doina Melinte (ROM)	4.18.13 (1990)
17.	Gelete Burka (ETH)	4.18.23 (2008)
18.	Gabriela Szabo (ROM)	4.19.30 (1998)
19.	Kirsty Wade (GBR)	4.19.41 (1985)
20.	Winny Chebet (KEN)	4.19.55 (2017)
21.	Angelika Cichocka (POL)	4.19.58 (2017)
22.	Gulnara Galkina (RUS)	4.20.23 (2007)
23.	Shannon Rowbury (USA)	4.20.34 (2008)
24.	Lisa Dobriskey (GBR)	4.20.35 (2008)
25.	Laura Weightman (GBR)	4.20.49 (2018)
26.	Kate Grace (USA)	4.20.70 (2018)
27.	Hassiba Boulmerka (ALG)	4.20.79 (1991)
28.	Sarah McDonald (GBR)	4.20.85 (2018)
29.	Anna Alminova (RUS)	4.20.86 (2007)
30.	Lyudmila Veselkova (URS)	4.20.89 (1981)
31.	Regina Jacobs (USA)	4.20.93 (1998)
32.	Nuria Fernández (ESP)	4.21.13 (2008)
33.	Olesya Chumakova (RUS)	4.21.29 (2007)
34.	Lyudmila Rogachova (RUS)	4.21.30 (1992)
35.	Fita Lovin (ROM)	4.21.40 (1981)
	Linden Hall (AUS)	4.21.40 (2018)
37.	Vesela Yatsinska (BUL)	4.21.52 (1982)
38.	Simona Vrzalová (CZE)	4.21.54 (2018)
39.	Yelena Zadorozhnaya (RUS)	4.21.57 (2004)
40.	Ulrike Bruns (GDR)	4.21.59 (1985)
41.	Violeta Beclea-Szekely (ROM)	4.21.69 (1993)
42.	Vanya Gospodinova (BUL)	4.21.78 (1982)
	Ruth Wysocki (USA)	4.21.78 (1984)
44.	Tamara Sorokina (URS)	4.21.89 (1982)
45.	Natalía Rodríguez (ESP)	4.21.92 (2008)

WORLD RANKING INDOOR ALL TIME:

1.	Genzebe Dibaba (ETH)	4.13.31 (2016)
2.	Doina Melinte (ROM)	4.17.14 (1990)
3.	Paula Ivan (ROM)	4.18.99 (1989)
4.	Sifan Hassan (NED)	4.19.89 (2017)
5.	Mary Tabb (Decker) (USA)	4.20.5 (1982)
6.	Regina Jacobs (USA)	4.21.79 (2000)
7.	Shannon Rowbury (USA)	4.22.66 (2015)
8.	Kate Grace (USA)	4.22.93 (2017)
9.	Carla Sacramento (POR)	4.23.00 (2002)
10.	Gabriela Szabo (ROM)	4.23.19 (2001)
11.	Kutre Dulecha (ETH)	4.23.33 (2001)
12.	Olga Komyagina (RUS)	4.23.49 (2008)
13.	Axumawit Embaye (ETH)	4.23.50 (2015)
14.	Gelete Burka (ETH)	4.23.53 (2010)
15.	Kirsty Wade (GBR)	4.23.86 (1988)
16.	Kalkidan Gezahegne (ETH)	4.24.10 (2010)
17.	Yelena Zadorozhnaya (RUS)	4.24.11 (2001)
	Mary Cain (USA)	4.24.11 (2014)
19.	Kimberley Smith (NZL)	4.24.14 (2008)
20.	Shelby Houlihan (USA)	4.24.16 (2017)
21.	Lidia Chojecka (POL)	4.24.44 (2000)
22.	Yelena Orlova (RUS)	4.24.53 (2008)
23.	Kim Conley (USA)	4.24.54 (2014)
24.	Maryam Yusuf Jamal (BRN)	4.24.71 (2010)
25.	Colleen Quigley (USA)	4.24.88 (2017)
26.	Natalya Artyomova (RUS)	4.24.98 (1992)
	Gudaf Tsegay (ETH)	4.24.98 (2016)
28.	Olga Yegorova (RUS)	4.25.54 (2000)
29.	Rachel Schneider (USA)	4.25.62 (2017)
30.	Jennifer Simpson (USA)	4.25.91 (2009)
31.	Kerri Gallagher (USA)	4.26.18 (2016)
32.	Amanda Rego (USA)	4.26.28 (2014)
33.	Hayley Parry-Tullett (GBR)	4.26.50 (2000)
34.	Elinor Purrier (USA)	4.26.55 (2018)
35.	Amanda Eccleston (USA)	4.26.63 (2016)
36.	Kate van Buskirk (CAN)	4.26.92 (2018)
37.	Sheila Reid (CAN)	4.27.02 (2013)
38.	Viorica Ghican (ROM)	4.27.10 (1990)
39.	Christin Wurth-Thomas (USA)	4.27.18 (2008)
	Leah O'Connor (USA)	4.27.18 (2015)
41.	Sally Kipyego (KEN)	4.27.19 (2009)
42.	Heather Kampf (USA)	4.27.26 (2016)
43.	Olesya Chumakova (RUS)	4.27.36 (2008)
44.	Lyudmila Vasilyeva (RUS)	4.27.39 (2002)
45.	Gabriela Stafford (CAN)	4.27.44 (2018)

3000 m Women

WORLD RANKING 2018:

1.	Sifan Hassan (NED)	8.27.50(CON)
2.	Caroline Chepkoech Kipkirui (KEN)	8.29.05(Do)
3.	Agnes Jebet Tirop (KEN)	8.29.09(Do)
4.	Hyvin Kiyeng (KEN)	8.30.51(Do)
5.	Jennifer Simpson (USA)	8.30.83(Do)
6.	Letesenbet Gidey (ETH)	8.30.96(Do)
7.	Senbere Teferi (ETH)	8.32.49(CON)
8.	Lilian Kasait Rengeruk (KEN)	8.33.13(Do)
9.	Norah Jeruto (KEN)	8.33.61(Zag)
10.	Meskerem Mamo (ETH)	8.33.63(Do)
11.	Gudaf Tsegay (ETH)	8.33.78(Zag)
12.	Kalkidan Gezahegne (BRN)	8.34.65(Zag)
13.	Beyenu Degefa (ETH)	8.35.76(Do)
14.	Hellen Obiri (KEN)	8.36.20(CON)
15.	Yasemin Can (TUR)	8.36.24(Do)
16.	Susan Krumins (NED)	8.37.21(Zag)
17.	Alemaz Samuel (ETH)	8.37.68(Zag)
18.	Konstanze Klosterhalfen (GER)	8.38.04(CON)
19.	Eilish McColgan (GBR)	8.38.49(Bir)
20.	Gloriah Kite (KEN)	8.39.07(Tur)
21.	Melissa Courtney (GBR)	8.39.20(Bir)
22.	Eva Cherono (KEN)	8.41.69(Tur)
23.	Lonah Chemtai Salpeter (ISR)	8.42.88(Bir)
24.	Loice Chemnung (KEN)	8.43.00(Rov)
25.	Axumawit Embaye (ETH)	8.43.83(Zag)
26.	Ejgayehu Taye (ETH)	8.44.13(Bir)
27.	Rosemary Monica Wanjiru (KEN)	8.44.24
28.	Katie Mackey (USA)	8.44.47(Lon)
29.	Genzebe Dibaba (ETH)	8.45.33(Eug)
30.	Elena Burkard (GER)	8.45.43(Bir)
31.	Gabriela Stafford (CAN)	8.45.67(Lon)
32.	Camille Buscomb (NZL)	8.45.97
33.	Ellinor Purrier (USA)	8.46.43
34.	Stephanie Twell (GBR)	8.46.79(Bir)
35.	Jessica O'Connell (CAN)	8.46.86
36.	Shuru Bulo (ETH)	8.47.24
37.	Fotyen Tesfay (ETH)	8.47.73(Do)
38.	Rina Nabeshima (JPN)	8.48.21(Lon)
39.	Lauren Paquette (USA)	8.48.65(Lon)
40.	Hellen Ekarare Lobun (KEN)	8.48.69
41.	Genevieve Gregson-Lacaze (AUS)	8.49.38(Zag)
42.	Emily Sisson (USA)	8.49.61
43.	Ann Karindi Mwangi (KEN)	8.50.58
44.	Martha Mokaya (KEN)	8.51.11

WORLD INDOOR CHAMPIONSHIPS: 1-3-2018:

1. Genzebe Dibaba (ETH)   8.45.05
2. Sifan Hassan (NED)   8.45.68
3. Laura Muir (GBR)   8.45.78
4. Hellen Obiri (KEN)   8.49.66
5. Shelby Houlihan (USA)   8.50.38
6. Fantu Worku (ETH)   8.50.54
7. Konstanze Klosterhalfen (GER) 8.51.79
8. Katie Mackey (USA)   8.56.62
9. Dominique Scott (RSA)   8.59.93
10. Eilish McColgan (GBR)   9.01.32
11. Geneviève Lalonde (CAN)   9.03.91
12. Meraf Bahta (SWE)   9.05.94
13. Claudia Bobocea (ROM)   9.23.70
14. Tamara Armoush (JOR)   9.45.68

WORLD RANKING INDOOR 2018:

1. Genzebe Dibaba (ETH)   8.31.23
2. Shelby Houlihan (USA)   8.36.01
   Konstanze Klosterhalfen (GER) 8.36.01
4. Hellen Obiri (KEN)   8.38.81
5. Beatrice Chepkoech (KEN)   8.39.15
6. Fantu Worku (ETH)   8.39.55
7. Marielle Hall (USA)   8.40.20
8. Jenny Simpson (USA)   8.40.31
9. Fotyen Tesfay (ETH)   8.41.08
10. Aisha Praught (JAM)   8.41.10
11. Emma Coburn (USA)   8.41.16
12. Dominique Scott (RSA)   8.41.18
13. Karissa Schweizer (USA)   8.41.60
14. Stephanie Twell (GBR)   8.41.94
15. Meraf Bahta (SWE)   8.42.46
16. Katie Mackey (USA)   8.43.15
17. Meskerem Mamo (ETH)   8.43.56
18. Sifan Hassan (NED)   8.45.68
19. Laura Muir (GBR)   8.45.78
20. Rosie Clarke (GBR)   8.47.30
21. Lauren Paquette (USA)   8.47.81
22. Ruth Jebet (BRN)   8.48.99
23. Kate van Buskirk (CAN)   8.49.02
24. Geneviève Lalonde (CAN)   8.49.78
25. Norah Jeruto (KEN)   8.49.89
26. Hawi Feysa (ETH)   8.50.80
27. Eilish McColgan (GBR)   8.50.87
28. Mel Lawrence (USA)   8.50.96
29. Emily Lipari (USA)   8.51.07
30. Yelena Korobkina (RUS)   8.51.90
31. Sofia Ennaoui (MAR)   8.53.63
32. Claudia Bobocea (ROM)   8.53.97
33. Gesa Felicitas Krause (GER) 8.54.08
34. Allie Ostrander (USA)   8.54.35
35. Margherita Magnani (ITA)   8.54.56
36. Melissa Courtney (GBR)   8.55.10
37. Elinor Purrier (USA)   8.55.68
38. Caterina Granz (GER)   8.56.29
39. Yekaterina Ivonina (RUS)   8.56.34
40. Simona Vrzalová (CZE)   8.57.07
41. Yelena Sedova (RUS)   8.57.15
42. Linn Nilsson (SWE)   8.58.31
43. Sarah Pagano (USA)   8.58.42
44. Erin Finn (USA)   8.58.69

Doha, 4-5-2018:

1.	Caroline Chepkoech Kipkirui (KEN)	8.29.05
2.	Agnes Jebet Tirop (KEN)	8.29.09
3.	Hyvin Kiyeng (KEN)	8.30.51
4.	Jennifer Simpson (USA)	8.30.83
5.	Letesenbet Gidey (ETH)	8.30.96
6.	Lilian Kasait Rengeruk (KEN)	8.33.13
7.	Meskerem Mamo (ETH)	8.33.63
8.	Beyenu Degefa (ETH)	8.35.76
9.	Yasemin Can (TUR)	8.36.24
10.	Norah Jeruto (KEN)	8.37.09
11.	Fotyen Tesfay (ETH)	8.47.73
12.	Eilish McColgan (GBR)	8.48.03
13.	Abersh Minsewo (ETH)	8.51.93
14.	Hellen Obiri (KEN)	8.53.65
15.	Sandrafelis Chebet Tuei (KEN)	8.58.04

Turku, 5-6-2018:

1.	Meskerem Mamo (ETH)	8.38.65
2.	Norah Jeruto (KEN)	8.39.03
3.	Gloria Chebiwatt Kite (KEN)	8.39.07
4.	Beyenu Degefa (ETH)	8.39.46
5.	Eva Cherono (KEN)	8.41.69
6.	Sandra Eriksson (FIN)	8.57.11

London, 21-7-2018:

1.	Lilian Kasait Rengeruk (KEN)	8.41.51
2.	Susan Krumins (NED)	8.41.83
3.	Katie Mackey (USA)	8.44.47
4.	Gabriela Stafford (CAN)	8.45.67
5.	Melissa Courtney (GBR)	8.46.33
6.	Stephanie Twell (GBR)	8.47.93
7.	Eva Cherono (KEN)	8.48.14
8.	Rina Nabeshima (JPN)	8.48.21
9.	Lauren Paquette (USA)	8.48.65
10.	Genevieve Lacaze (AUS)	8.50.09
11.	Jessica Judd (GBR)	8.53.29
12.	Dana Giordano (USA)	8.55.14
13.	Sheila Chalangat (KEN)	8.55.19

Birmingham, 18-8-2018:

1.	Agnes Jebet Tirop (KEN)	8.32.21
2.	Lilian Kasait Rengeruk (KEN)	8.33.43
3.	Hellen Obiri (KEN)	8.36.26
4.	Eilish McColgan (GBR)	8.38.49
5.	Melissa Courtney (GBR)	8.39.20
6.	Konstanze Klosterhalfen (GER)	8.41.37
7.	Lonah Chemtai Salpeter (ISR)	8.42.88
8.	Ejgayehu Taye (ETH)	8.44.13
9.	Elena Burkard (GER)	8.45.43
10.	Eva Cherono (KEN)	8.45.65
11.	Stephanie Twell (GBR)	8.46.79
12.	Susan Krumins (NED)	8.49.60
13.	Genevieve Lacaze (AUS)	8.50.19
14.	Katie Mackey (USA)	8.53.18
15.	Beatrice Chebet (KEN)	8.59.72

Zagreb, 4-9-2018:

1.	Lilian Kasait Rengeruk (KEN)	8.33.37
2.	Norah Jeruto (KEN)	8.33.61
3.	Gudaf Tsegay (ETH)	8.33.78
4.	Kalkidan Gezahegne (BRN)	8.34.65
5.	Susan Krumins (NED)	8.37.21
6.	Alemaz Samuel (ETH)	8.37.68
7.	Axumawit Embaye (ETH)	8.43.83
8.	Loice Chemnung (KEN)	8.45.28
9.	Gloria Chebiwatt Kite (KEN)	8.46.52
10.	Eilish McColgan (GBR)	8.47.36
11.	Genevieve Lacaze (AUS)	8.49.38

CONTINENTAL CUP, Ostrava, 8-9-2018:

1.	Sifan Hassan (EUR)	8.27.50
2.	Senbere Teferi (AFR)	8.32.49
3.	Hellen Obiri (AFR)	8.36.20
4.	Konstanze Klosterhalfen (EUR)	8.38.04

OVERVIEW WORLD INDOOR CHAMPIONSHIP FINALISTS OF PAST 5 YEARS

	Wch 18	Wch 16	Wch 14
Genzebe Dibaba (ETH)	8.45.05 (1)	8.47.43 (1)	8.55.04 (1)
Sifan Hassan (NED)	8.45.68 (2)		9.03.22 (5)
Laura Muir (GBR)	8.45.78 (3)		
Hellen Onsando Obiri (KEN)	8.49.66 (4)		8.57.72 (2)
Shelby Houlihan (USA)	8.50.38 (5)		
Fantu Worku (ETH)	8.50.54 (6)		
Konstanze Klosterhalfen (GER)	8.51.79 (7)		
Katie Mackey (USA)	8.56.62 (8)		
Dominique Scott (RSA)	8.59.93 (9)		
Eilish McColgan (GBR)	9.01.32 (10)		
Geneviève Lalonde (CAN)	9.03.91 (11)		
Meraf Bahta (SWE)	9.05.94 (12)		
Claudia Bobocea (ROM)	9.23.70 (13)		
Meseret Defar (ETH)		8.54.26 (2)	
Shannon Rowbury (USA)		8.55.55 (3)	9.07.82 (8)
Maureen Koster (NED)		8.56.44 (4)	
Abbey d'Agostino (USA)		8.58.40 (5)	
Stephanie Twell (GBR)		9.00.38 (6)	
Betsy Saina (KEN)		9.01.86 (7)	
Betlhem Desalegn (UAE)		9.03.30 (8)	9.04.06 (6)
Jessica O'Connell (CAN)		9.05.71 (9)	
Nancy Chepkwemoi (KEN)		9.07.63 (10)	
Sviatlana Kudzelich (BLR)		9.17.45 (11)	
Sheila Reid (CAN)		9.19.67 (12)	
Josephine Moultrie (GBR)		9.29.10 (13)	
Maryam Yusuf Jamal (BRN)			8.59.16 (3)
Irene Jelagat (KEN)			9.02.67 (4)
Renata Plis (POL)			9.07.05 (7)
Margherita Magnani (ITA)			9.10.13 (9)
Gabrielle Grunewald (USA)			9.11.76 (10)
Hiwot Ayalew (ETH)			9.12.51 (11)
Alia Saeed Mohammed (UAE)			9.21.23 (12)

OVERVIEW TOP 10 WORLD OUTDOOR RANKINGS OF PAST 5 YEARS

	2018	2017	2016	2015	2014
Sifan Hassan (NED)	8.27.50 (1)	8.28.90 (3)			8.29.38 (8)
Caroline Chepkoech Kipkirui (KEN)	8.29.05 (2)				
Agnes Jebet Tirop (KEN)	8.29.09 (3)				
Hyvin Kiyeng (KEN)	8.30.51 (4)				
Jennifer Simpson (USA)	8.30.83 (5)			8.34.43 (4)	8.29.58 (9)
Letesenbet Gidey (ETH)	8.30.96 (6)				
Senbere Teferi (ETH)	8.32.49 (7)			8.34.32 (3)	
Lilian Kasait Rengeruk (KEN)	8.33.13 (8)	8.32.73 (8)			
Norah Jeruto (KEN)	8.33.61 (9)				
Meskerem Mamo (ETH)	8.33.62 (10)				
Hellen Onsando Obiri (KEN)		8.23.14 (1)	8.24.27 (2)		8.20.68 (1)
Beatrice Chepkoech (KEN)		8.28.66 (2)			
Konstanze Klosterhalfen (GER)		8.29.89 (4)			
Margaret Chelimo Kipkemboi (KEN)		8.30.11 (5)	8.37.54 (9)		
Laura Muir (GBR)		8.30.64 (6)		8.38.47 (7)	
Eilish McColgan (GBR)		8.31.00 (7)			
Shannon Rowbury (USA)		8.33.38 (9)			8.29.93 (10)
Susan Krumins (NED)		8.34.41 (10)			
Almaz Ayana (ETH)			8.23.11 (1)	8.22.22 (1)	8.24.58 (5)
Mercy Cherono (KEN)			8.26.36 (3)	8.35.48 (5)	8.21.14 (2)
Janet Kisa (ETH)			8.28.33 (4)		
Gelete Burka (ETH)			8.28.49 (5)		
Genzebe Dibaba (ETH)			8.31.84 (6)	8.26.54 (2)	8.26.21 (6)
Vivian Jepkemoi Cheruiyot (KEN)			8.31.86 (7)	8.38.91 (8)	
Viola Jelagat Kibiwot (KEN)			8.34.50 (8)		8.24.41 (4)
Etenesh Diro (ETH)			8.38.32 (10)		
Irene Jelagat (KEN)				8.36.90 (6)	8.28.51 (7)
Faith Chepngetich Kipyegon (KEN)				8.38.91 (8)	8.23.55 (3)
Alamitu Heroye (ETH)				8.39.85 (10)	

OVERVIEW TOP 10 WORLD INDOOR RANKINGS OF PAST 5 YEARS

	2018	2017	2016	2015	2014
Genzebe Dibaba (ETH)	8.31.23 (1)		8.22.50 (1)		8.16.60 (1)
Shelby Houlihan (USA)	8.36.01 (2)				
Konstanze Klosterhalfen (GER)	8.36.01 (2)				
Hellen Onsando Obiri (KEN)	8.38.81 (4)	8.29.41 (2)			8.29.99 (2)
Beatrice Chepkoech (KEN)	8.39.15 (5)				
Fantu Worku (ETH)	8.39.55 (6)				
Marielle Hall (USA)	8.40.20 (7)				
Jennifer Simpson (USA)	8.40.31 (8)				8.44.28 (8)
Fotyen Tesfay (ETH)	8.41.08 (9)				
Aisha Praught (JAM)	8.41.10 (10)				
Laura Muir (GBR)		8.26.41 (1)		8.49.73 (8)	
Sifan Hassan (NED)		8.30.76 (3)			8.45.32 (10)
Dawit Seyaum (ETH)		8.37.65 (4)			
Shannon Rowbury (USA)		8.41.94 (5)			
Meraf Bahta (SWE)		8.43.00 (6)			
Eilish McColgan (GBR)		8.43.02 (7)			
Yasemin Can (TUR)		8.43.46 (8)			
Maureen Koster (NED)		8.44.63 (9)	8.49.18 (9)	8.51.10 (10)	
Sofia Ennaoui (POL)		8.45.29 (10)	8.49.07 (8)		
Meseret Defar (ETH)			8.30.83 (2)		
Gelete Burka (ETH)			8.33.76 (3)		
Betlhem Desalegn (UAE)			8.44.59 (4)		
Ruth Jebet (BRN)			8.47.24 (5)		
Alia Saeed Mohammed (UAE)			8.48.62 (6)		
Nancy Chepkwemoi (KEN)			8.49.06 (7)		
Gesa Felicitas Krause (GER)			8.49.43 (10)		
Sally Jepkosgei Kipyego (KEN)				8.41.72 (1)	8.44.69 (9)
Betsy Saina (KEN)				8.43.19 (2)	
Gotytom Gebreslase (ETH)				8.45.05 (3)	
Habiba Ghribi (TUN)				8.46.61 (4)	
Senbere Teferi (ETH)				8.46.84 (5)	
Elena Korobkina (RUS)				8.47.61 (6)	
Sviatlana Kudzelich (BLR)				8.48.02 (7)	
Jordan Hasay (USA)				8.50.21 (9)	
Irene Jelagat (KEN)					8.40.75 (3)
Maryam Yusuf Jamal (BRN)					8.43.16 (4)
Hiwot Ayalew (ETH)					8.43.29 (5)
Viola Jelagat Kibiwot (KEN)					8.43.42 (6)
Almaz Ayana (ETH)					8.43.47 (7)

WORLD RANKING OUTDOOR ALL TIME:

1.	Wang Junxia (CHN)	8.06.11 (1993)
2.	Qu Yunxia (CHN)	8.12.18 (1993)
3.	Zhang Linli (CHN)	8.16.50 (1993)
4.	Ma Liyan (CHN)	8.19.78 (1993)
5.	Hellen Obiri (KEN)	8.20.68 (2014)
6.	Mercy Cherono (KEN)	8.21.14 (2014)
7.	Gabriela Szabo (ROM)	8.21.42 (2002)
8.	Sonia O'Sullivan (IRL)	8.21.64 (1994)
9.	Zhou Yihong (CHN)	8.21.84 (1993)
10.	Paula Radcliffe (GBR)	8.22.20 (2002)
11.	Almaz Ayana (ETH)	8.22.22 (2015)
12.	Tatyana Kazankina (URS)	8.22.62 (1984)
13.	Edith Masai (KEN)	8.23.23 (2002)
14.	Olga Yegorova (RUS)	8.23.26 (2001)
15.	Faith Kipyegon (KEN)	8.23.55 (2014)
16.	Viola Jelagat Kibiwot (KEN)	8.24.41 (2014)
17.	Meseret Defar (ETH)	8.24.51 (2007)
18.	Yelena Zadorozhnaya (RUS)	8.25.40 (2001)
19.	Tatyana Tomashova (RUS)	8.25.56 (2001)
20.	Berhane Adere (ETH)	8.25.62 (2001)
21.	Mary Slaney-Decker (USA)	8.25.83 (1985)
22.	Gelete Burka (ETH)	8.25.92 (2006)
23.	Genzebe Dibaba (ETH)	8.26.21 (2014)
24.	Zahra Ouaziz (MAR)	8.26.48 (1999)
25.	Tatyana Dorovskikh (URS)	8.26.53 (1988)
26.	Svetlana Ulmasova (URS)	8.26.78 (1982)
27.	Lyudmila Bragina (URS)	8.27.12 (1976)
28.	Paula Ivan (ROM)	8.27.15 (1988)
29.	Sifan Hassan (NED)	8.27.50 (2018)
30.	Gete Wami (ETH)	8.27.62 (2001)
31.	Maricica Puica (ROM)	8.27.83 (1985)
32.	Janet Kisa (KEN)	8.28.33 (2016)
33.	Sentayehu Ejigu (ETH)	8.28.41 (2010)
34.	Irene Jelagat (KEN)	8.28.51 (2014)
35.	Vivian Jepkemoi Cheruiyot (KEN)	8.28.66 (2007)
	Beatrice Chepkoech (KEN)	8.28.66 (2017)
37.	Marta Domínguez (ESP)	8.28.80 (2000)
38.	Zola Budd (GBR)	8.28.83 (1985)
39.	Maryam Yusuf Jamal (BRN)	8.28.87 (2005)
40.	Yvonne Murray (GBR)	8.29.02 (1988)
41.	Caroline Chepkoech Kipkirui (KEN)	8.29.05 (1018)
42.	Priscah Jepleting Cherono (KEN)	8.29.06 (2007)
43.	Agnes Jebet Tirop (KEN)	8.29.09 (2018)
44.	Lydia Cheromei (KEN)	8.29.14 (2000)
45.	Svetlana Guskova (URS)	8.29.36 (1982)

WORLD RANKING INDOOR ALL TIME:

1.	Genzebe Dibaba (ETH)	8.16.60 (2014)
2.	Meseret Defar (ETH)	8.23.72 (2007)
3.	Meselech Melkamu (ETH)	8.23.74 (2007)
4.	Sentayehu Ejigu (ETH)	8.25.27 (2010)
5.	Laura Muir (GBR)	8.26.41 (2017)
6.	Liliya Shobukhova (RUS)	8.27.86 (2006)
7.	Anna Alminova (RUS)	8.28.49 (2009)
8.	Olesya Syreva (RUS)	8.29.00 (2006)
9.	Berhane Adere (ETH)	8.29.15 (2002)
10.	Hellen Obiri (KEN)	8.29.41 (2017)
11.	Vivian Jepkemoi Cheruiyot (KEN)	8.30.53 (2009)
12.	Sifan Hassan (NED)	8.30.76 (2017)
13.	Joanne Pavey (GBR)	8.31.50 (2007)
14.	Gelete Burka (ETH)	8.31.94 (2008)
15.	Gabriela Szabo (ROM)	8.32.88 (2001)
16.	Shalane Flanagan (USA)	8.33.25 (2007)
17.	Tirunesh Dibaba (ETH)	8.33.37 (2008)
18.	Elly van Hulst (NED)	8.33.82 (1989)
19.	Liz McColgan (GBR)	8.34.80 (1989)
20.	Olga Komyagina (RUS)	8.35.68 (2006)
21.	Mariem Alaoui Selsouli (MAR)	8.35.86 (2008)
22.	Shelby Houlihan (USA)	8.36.01 (2018)
	Konstanze Klosterhafen (GER)	8.36.01 (2018)
24.	Ejegayehu Dibaba (ETH)	8.36.59 (2008)
25.	Carla Sacramento (POR)	8.36.79 (2002)
26.	Kalkidan Gezahegne (ETH)	8.37.47 (2011)
27.	Olga Yegorova (RUS)	8.37.48 (2001)
28.	Dawit Seyaum (ETH)	8.37.65 (2017)
29.	Kimberley Smith (NZL)	8.38.14 (2007)
30.	Lidia Chojecka (POL)	8.38.21 (2007)
31.	Zahria Ouaziz (MAR)	8.38.43 (1999)
32.	Regina Jacobs (USA)	8.39.14 (1999)
33.	Beatrice Chepkoech (KEN)	8.39.15 (2018)
34.	Zhor El Kamch (MAR)	8.39.27 (2003)
35.	Kim McGreevy (USA)	8.39.40 (1997)
36.	Fernanda Ribeiro (POR)	8.39.49 (1996)
37.	Fantu Worku (ETH)	8.39.55 (2018)
38.	Mercy Wanjiku Njoroge (KEN)	8.39.70 (2011)
39.	Zola Budd (GBR)	8.39.79 (1986)
40.	Helen Clitheroe (GBR)	8.39.81 (2011)
41.	Yelena Zadorozhnaya (RUS)	8.40.15 (2001)
42.	Marielle Hall (USA)	8.40.20 (2018)
43.	Jennifer Simpson (USA)	8.40.31 (2018)
44.	Lynn Jennings (USA)	8.40.45 (1990)
45.	Sylvia Jebiwot Kibet (KEN)	8.40.50 (2012)

5000 m Women

EUROPEAN CHAMPIONSHIPS 2018: 12-8-2018:

1. Sifan Hassan (NED) — 14.46.12
2. Eilish McColgan (GBR) — 14.53.05
3. Yasemin Can (TUR) — 14.57.63
4. Konstanze Klosterhalfen (GER) — 15.03.73
5. Melissa Courtney (GBR) — 15.04.75
6. Susan Krumins (NED) — 15.09.65
7. Ancuta Bobocel (ROM) — 15.16.13
8. Maureen Koster (NED) — 15.21.64
9. Charlotta Fougberg (SWE) — 15.24.36
10. Stephanie Twell (GBR) — 15.41.10
11. Katarzyna Rutkowska (POL) — 15.41.52
12. Paulina Kaczynska (POL) — 15.49.21
13. Louise Carton (BEL) — 15.53.27
14. Denise Krebs (GER) — 16.07.98
15. Yuliya Shmatenko (UKR) — 16.41.37
Linn Nilsson (SWE) — dnf
Hanna Klein (GER) — dnf
Lonah Salpeter (ISR) — dsq

WORLD RANKING 2018:

1. Hellen Obiri (KEN) — 14.21.75(Rab)
2. Sifan Hassan (NED) — 14.22.34(Rab)
3. Letesenbet Gidey (ETH) — 14.23.14(Rab)
4. Senbere Teferi (ETH) — 14.23.33(Rab)
5. Agnes Jebet Tirop (KEN) — 14.24.24(Rab)
6. Genzebe Dibaba (ETH) — 14.26.89(Eug)
7. Shelby Houlihan (USA) — 14.34.45(Heu)
8. Caroline Chepkoech Kipkirui (KEN) — 14.43.96(Zü)
9. Gudaf Tsegay (ETH) — 14.51.30(Eug)
10. Eilish McColgan (GBR) — 14.52.83(Rab)
11. Loice Chemnung (KEN) — 14.53.14(Bel)
12. Yasemin Can (TUR) — 14.57.63(ECh)
13. Lilian Kasait Rengeruk (KEN) — 15.01.15(Eug)
14. Molly Huddle (USA) — 15.01.44(Heu)
15. Margaret Chelimo Kipkemboi (KEN) — 15.01.98(Eug)
16. Karissa Schweizer (USA) — 15.02.44(Heu)
17. Konstanze Klosterhalfen (GER) — 15.03.73(ECh)
18. Dominique Scott (RSA) — 15.04.14(Heu)
19. Melissa Courtney (GBR) — 15.04.75(ECh)
20. Meskerem Mamo (ETH) — 15.05.21(Tub)
21. Madeline Hills (AUS) — 15.06.19(Heu)
22. Gloria Kite (KEN) — 15.06.84(Tub)
23. Abersh Minsewo (ETH) — 15.07.90(Tub)
24. Kalkidan Gezahegne (BRN) — 15.08.08(Jak)
25. Meraf Bahta (SWE) — 15.08.17(Zü)
26. Marielle Hall (USA) — 15.08.20(Heu)
27. Rosemary Monica Wanjiru (KEN) — 15.08.61

Eugene, 26-5-2018:
1. Genzebe Dibaba (ETH)   14.26.89
2. Letesenbet Gidey (ETH)   14.30.29
3. Hellen Obiri (KEN)   14.35.03
4. Gudaf Tsegay (ETH)   14.51.30
5. Lilian Kasait Rengeruk (KEN)   15.01.15
6. Margaret Chelimo Kipkemboi (KEN) 15.01.98
7. Meraf Bahta (SWE)   15.10.20
8. Dominique Scott (RSA)   15.10.23
9. Rina Nabeshima (JPN)   15.10.91
10. Alice Aprot Nawowuna (KEN)   15.11.00
11. Lauren Paquette (USA)   15.15.23

US CHAMPIONSHIPS, Des Moines, 24-6-2018:
1. Shelby Houlihan   15.31.03
2. Rachel Schneider   15.32.71
3. Karissa Schweizer   15.34.31
4. Lauren Paquette   15.36.83
5. Vanessa Fraser   15.36.89
6. Katie Mackey   15.39.25

KEN Trials, Nairobi, 23-6-2018:
1. Hellen Obiri   15.09.82
2. Lilian Kasait Rengeruk   15.14.52
3. Beatrice Chepkoech   15.15.34
4. Loise Chemnung   15.16.99
5. Pascalia Chepkorir   15.32.26
6. Margaret Wangari Muriuki   15.37.20

Rabat, 13-7-2018:
1. Hellen Obiri (KEN)   14.21.75
2. Sifan Hassan (NED)   14.22.34
3. Letesenbet Gidey (ETH)   14.23.14
4. Senbere Teferi (ETH)   14.23.33
5. Agnes Jebet Tirop (KEN)   14.24.24
6. Genzebe Dibaba (ETH)   14.42.98
7. Eilish McColgan (GBR)   14.52.83
8. Caroline Ch. Chepkirui (KEN) 14.55.63

Heusden, 21-7-2018:
1. Shelby Houlihan (USA)   14.34.45
2. Molly Huddle (USA)   15.01.44
3. Karissa Schweizer (USA)   15.02.44
4. Dominique Scott (RSA)   15.04.14
5. Madeline Hills (AUS)   15.06.19
6. Marielle Hall (USA)   15.08.20
7. Vanessa Fraser (USA)   15.09.62
8. Sarah Pagano (USA)   15.11.27
9. Emily Sisson (USA)   15.13.66
10. Jip Vastenburg (NED)   15.15.77

AFR CHAMPIONSHIPS, Assaba, 2-8-2018:
1. Hellen Obiri (KEN)   15.47.18
2. Senbere Teferi Sora (ETH)   15.54.48
3. Meskerem Mamo Hayile (ETH)   15.57.38
4. Hawi Feysa Gejia (ETH)   15.59.23
5. Lilian Kasait Rengeruk (KEN) 16.04.51
6. Loice Chemnung (KEN)   16.25.78

Zürich, 30-8-2018:
1. Hellen Obiri (KEN)   14.38.39
2. Sifan Hassan (NED)   14.38.77
3. Senbere Teferi (ETH)   14.40.97
4. Caroline Ch. Chepkirui (KEN) 14.43.96
5. Agnes Jebet Tirop (KEN)   14.44.24
6. Genzebe Dibaba (ETH)   14.50.24
7. Letesenbet Gidey (ETH)   14.57.52
8. Lilian Kasait Rengeruk (KEN) 15.03.11
9. Konstanze Klosterhalfen (GER) 15.04.16
10. Meraf Bahta (SWE)   15.08.17
11. Eilish McColgan (GBR)   15.09.00

OVERVIEW WORLD OUTDOOR CHAMPIONSHIP FINALISTS OF PAST 6 YEARS

	Wch 17	OG 16	Wch 15	Wch 13
Hellen Onsando Obiri (KEN)	14.34.86 (1)	14.29.77 (2)		
Almaz Ayana (ETH)	14.40.35 (2)	14.33.59 (3)	14.26.83 (1)	14.51.33 (3)
Sifan Hassan (NED)	14.42.73 (3)			
Senbere Teferi (ETH)	14.47.45 (4)	14.43.75 (5)	14.44.07 (2)	
Margaret Kipkemboi (KEN)	14.48.74 (5)			
Laura Muir (GBR)	14.52.07 (6)			
Sheila Chepkirui Kiprotich (KEN)	14.54.05 (7)			
Susan Krumins-Kuijken (NED)	14.58.33 (8)	15.00.69 (8)	15.08.00 (8)	15.14.70 (8)
Shannon Rowbury (USA)	14.59.92 (9)			15.06.10 (7)
Eilish McColgan (GBR)	15.00.43 (10)	15.12.09 (13)		
Letesenbet Gidey (ETH)	15.04.99 (11)			
Molly Huddle (USA)	15.05.28 (12)			15.05.73 (6)
Shelby Houlihan (USA)	15.06.40 (13)	15.08.89 (11)		
Kalkidan Gezahegne (BRN)	15.28.21 (14)			
Karoline Bjerkeli Grövdal (NOR)	dnf (15)	14.57.53 (7)		15.48.87 (13)
Vivian Jepkemoi Cheruiyot (KEN)		14.26.17 (1)		
Mercy Cherono (KEN)		14.42.89 (4)	15.01.36 (5)	14.51.22 (2)
Yasemin Can (TUR)		14.56.96 (6)		
Eloise Wellings (AUS)		15.01.59 (9)	15.09.62 (10)	
Madeline Heiner Hills (AUS)		15.04.05 (10)		
Genevieve Lacaze (AUS)		15.10.35 (12)		
Ababel Yeshaneh (ETH)		15.18.26 (14)		
Miyuki Uehara (JPN)		15.34.97 (15)		
Jennifer Wenth (AUT)		15.56.11 (16)	15.35.46 (15)	
Genzebe Dibaba (ETH)			14.44.14 (3)	
Viola Jelagat Kibiwot (KEN)			14.46.16 (4)	15.01.67 (4)
Janet Kisa (KEN)			15.02.68 (6)	
Irene Chepet Cheptai (KEN)			15.03.41 (7)	
Ayuko Suzuki (JPN)			15.08.29 (9)	
Mimi Belete (BRN)			15.17.01 (11)	
Stephanie Twell (GBR)			15.26.24 (12)	
Nicole Tully (USA)			15.27.42 (13)	
Misaki Onishi (JPN)			15.29.63 (14)	
Meseret Defar (ETH)				14.50.19 (1)
Buze Diriba (ETH)				15.05.38 (5)
Elena Nagovitsyna (RUS)				15.24.83 (9)
Dolores Checa (ESP)				15.30.42 (10)
Tejitu Daba (BRN)				15.33.89 (11)
Kim Conley (USA)				15.36.58 (12)
Dominika Nowakowska (POL)				15.58.26 (14)
Jackie Areson (AUS)				16.08.32 (15)

OVERVIEW TOP 10 WORLD OUTDOOR RANKINGS OF PAST 5 YEARS

	2018	**2017**	**2016**	**2015**	**2014**
Hellen Onsando Obiri (KEN)	14.21.75 (1)	14.18.37 (1)	14.25.78 (2)		
Sifan Hassan (NED)	14.22.34 (2)				
Letesenbet Gidey (ETH)	14.23.14 (3)	14.33.32 (7)			
Senbere Teferi (ETH)	14.23.33 (4)	14.31.76 (4)	14.29.82 (5)	14.36.44 (6)	
Agnes Jebet Tirop (KEN)	14.24.24 (5)	14.33.09 (6)			
Genzebe Dibaba (ETH)	14.26.89 (6)	14.25.22 (2)		14.15.41 (2)	14.28.88 (1)
Shelby Houlihan (USA)	14.34.45 (7)				
Caroline Kipkirui (KEN)	14.43.96 (8)	14.27.55 (3)			
Gudaf Tsegay (ETH)	14.51.30 (9)				
Eilish McColgan (GBR)	14.52.83 (10)				
Margaret Kipkemboi (KEN)		14.32.82 (5)			
Lilian Kasait Rengeruk (KEN)		14.36.80 (8)			
Yasemin Can (TUR)		14.36.82 (9)	14.37.61 (8)		
Beatrice Chepkoech (KEN)		14.39.33 (10)			
Almaz Ayana (ETH)			14.12.59 (1)	14.14.32 (1)	14.29.19 (2)
Vivian Jepkemoi Cheruiyot (KEN)			14.26.17 (3)	14.46.69 (9)	
Viola Jelagat Kibiwot (KEN)			14.29.50 (4)	14.34.22 (5)	14.33.73 (3)
Etenesh Diro (ETH)			14.33.30 (6)		
Mercy Cherono (KEN)			14.33.95 (7)	14.34.10 (4)	14.43.11 (7)
Janet Kisa (KEN)			14.38.70 (9)		14.52.59 (9)
Shannon Rowbury (USA)			14.38.92 (10)		14.48.68 (8)
Faith Chepngetich Kipyegon (KEN)				14.31.95 (3)	
Gelete Burka (ETH)				14.40.50 (7)	
Alemitu Heroye (ETH)				14.43.28 (8)	14.52.67 (10)
Sally Jepkosgei Kipyego (KEN)				14.47.75 (10)	14.37.18 (4)
Betsy Saina (KEN)					14.39.49 (5)
Molly Huddle (USA)					14.42.64 (6)

WORLD RANKING ALL TIME:

1.	Tirunesh Dibaba (ETH)	14.11.15 (2008)
2.	Almaz Ayana (ETH)	14.12.59 (2016)
3.	Meseret Defar (ETH)	14.12.88 (2008)
4.	Genzebe Dibaba (ETH)	14.15.41 (2015)
5.	Hellen Onsando Obiri (KEN)	14.18.37 (2017)
6.	Vivian Jepkemoi Cheruiyot (KEN)	14.20.87 (2011)
7.	Sifan Hassan (NED)	14.22.34 (2018)
8.	Letesenbet Gidey (ETH)	14.23.14 (2018)
9.	Senbere Teferi (ETH)	14.23.33 (2018)
10.	Liliya Shobukhova (RUS)	14.23.75 (2008)
11.	Agnes Jebet Tirop (KEN)	14.24.24 (2018)
12.	Elvan Abeylegesse (TUR)	14.24.68 (2004)
13.	Caroline Chepkoech Kipkirui (KEN)	14.27.55 (2017)
14.	Bo Jiang (CHN)	14.28.09 (1997)
15.	Sentayehu Ejigu (ETH)	14.28.39 (2010)
16.	Paula Radcliffe (GBR)	14.29.11 (2004)
17.	Olga Yegorova (RUS)	14.29.32 (2001)
	Berhane Adere (ETH)	14.29.32 (2003)
19.	Viola Jelagat Kibiwot (KEN)	14.29.50 (2016)
20.	Dong Yanmei (CHN)	14.29.82 (1997)
21.	Sally Kipyego (KEN)	14.30.42 (2011)
22.	Gete Wami (ETH)	14.30.88 (2000)
23.	Linet Chepkwemoi Masai (KEN)	14.31.14 (2010)
24.	Gelete Burka (ETH)	14.31.20 (2007)
25.	Gabriela Szabo (ROM)	14.31.48 (1998)
26.	Meselech Melkamu (ETH)	14.31.91 (2010)
	Sylvia Jebiwot Kibet (KEN)	14.31.91 (2010)
28.	Faith Kipyegon (KEN)	14.31.95 (2015)
29.	Zahra Ouaziz (MAR)	14.32.08 (1998)
30.	Liu Shixiang (CHN)	14.32.33 (1997)
31.	Ejegayehu Dibaba (ETH)	14.32.74 (2004)
32.	Margaret Chelimo Kipkemboi (KEN)	14.32.82 (2017)
33.	Werknesh Kidane (ETH)	14.33.04 (2003)
34.	Gulnara Galkina (RUS)	14.33.13 (2008)
35.	Etenesh Diro (ETH)	14.33.30 (2016)
36.	Lucy Kabuu Wangui (KEN)	14.33.49 (2008)
37.	Edith Masai (KEN)	14.33.84 (2006)
38.	Mercy Cherono (KEN)	14.33.95 (2016)
39.	Shelby Houlihan (USA)	14.34.45 (2018)
40.	Priscah Jepleting Cherono (KEN)	14.35.30 (2006)
41.	Fernanda Ribeiro (POR)	14.36.45 (1995)
42.	Mariem Alaoui Selsouli (MAR)	14.36.52 (2007)
43.	Lilian Kasait Rengeruk (KEN)	14.36.80 (2017)
44.	Yasemin Can (TUR)	14.36.82 (2017)
45.	Jessica Augusto (POR)	14.37.07 (2010)

10.000 m Women

EUROPEAN CHAMPIONSHIPS 2018: 8-8-2018:

1. Lonah Salpeter (ISR) — 31.43.29
2. Susan Krumins (NED) — 31.52.55
3. Meraf Bahta (SWE) — 32.19.34
4. Alina Reh (GER) — 32.28.48
5. Yasemin Can (TUR) — 32.34.34
6. Alice Wright (GBR) — 32.36.45
7. Charlotta Fougberg (SWE) — 32.43.04
8. Sviatlana Kudzelich (BLR) — 32.46.34
9. Maitane Melero (ESP) — 32.52.59
10. Sara Ribeiro (POR) — 32.53.71
11. Nuria Lugueros (ESP) — 32.55.30
12. Roxana Barca (ROM) — 33.17.61
13. Krisztina Papp (HUN) — 33.20.27
14. Natalie Tanner (GER) — 33.22.21
15. Jip Vastenburg (NED) — 33.41.79
16. Sophie Duarte (FRA) — 33.56.57
17. Emma Mitchell (IRL) — 34.08.61
18. Yevheniya Prokofyeva (UKR) — 34.15.81
    Ancuta Bobocel (ROM) — dnf
    Sara Moreira (POR) — dnf
    Ines Monteiro (POR) — dnf

WORLD RANKING 2018:

1. Pauline Kamulu (KEN) — 30.41.85(Fka)
2. Minami Yamanouchi (JPN) — 31.16.48(Yam)
3. Grace Mbuthye Kimanzi (KEN) — 31.17.28(Yam)
4. Harumi Okamoto (JPN) — 31.18.20(Yam)
5. Rina Nabeshima (JPN) — 31.28.81(Yam)
6. Stacey Chepkemboi Ndiwa (KEN) — 31.31.17(Ass)
7. Hiromi Niiya (JPN) — 31.32.50(Mel)
8. Lona Chemtai Salpeter (ISR) — 31.33.03
9. Alice Aprot Nawowuna (KEN) — 31.36.12(Ass)
10. Mercyline Chelangat (UGA) — 31.38.4
11. Stella Chesang (UGA) — 31.39.0
12. Gloria Kite (KEN) — 31.41.47
13. Ancuta Bobocel (ROM) — 31.43.12
14. Shiori Yano (JPN) — 31.44.13(Yam)
15. Gete Alemayehu (ETH) — 31.45.32
16. Yuka Hori (JPN) — 31.48.93(Yam)
17. Beatrice Mutai (KEN) — 31.49.81(GC)
18. Natsuki Sekiya (JPN) — 31.50.17(Yam)
19. Natasha Wodak (CAN) — 31.50.189GC)
20. Celia Sullohern (AUS) — 31.50.75(GC)
21. Sinead Diver (AUS) — 31.50.98(Mel)
22. Pauline Ch. Korikwiang (KEN) — 31.51.1
23. Molly Huddle (USA) — 31.51.32(USC)
24. Mizuki Matsuda (JPN) — 31.52.42(Yam)
25. Susan Krumins (NED) — 31.52.55(ECh)
26. Jessica Tonn (USA) — 31.54.83(PA)
27. Gwen Jorgensen (USA) — 31.55.68(PA)
28. Sarah Pagano (USA) — 31.56.43(PA)
29. Marielle Hall (USA) — 31.56.68(USC)
30. Rachel Cliff (CAN) — 31.56.86(PA)
31. Chelsea Blaase (USA) — 31.57.56(PA)
32. Rosemary Monica Wanjiru (KEN) — 31.57.66
33. Ayako Suzuki (JPN) — 31.57.82(Yam)
34. Carrie Dimoff (USA) — 31.57.85(PA)
35. Mao Ichiyama (JPN) — 31.57.91(PA)
36. Kaori Morita (JPN) — 31.57.95(Yam)
37. Juliet Chekwel (UGA) — 31.57.97(GC)

Commonwealth Games, Gold Coast, 9-4-2018:
1. Stella Chesang (UGA)   31.45.30
2. Stacey Chepkemboi Ndiwa (KEN)   31.46.36
3. Mercyline Chelangat (UGA)   31.48.41
4. Beatrice Mutai (KEN)   31.49.81
5. Natasha Wodak (CAN)   31.50.18
6. Celia Sullohern (AUS)   31.50.75

US CHAMPIONSHIPS, Des Moines, 21-6-2018:
1. Molly Huddle   31.52.32
2. Marielle Hall   31.56.68
3. Stephanie Bruce   32.05.05
4. Emily Sisson   23.06.31

KEN Trials, Nairobi, 21-6-2018:
1. Pauline Chemning Korikwiang   31.51.1
2. Alice Aprot Nawowuna   31.59.1
3. Sandrafelis Chebet Tuei   32.16.5
4. Perine Nengampi   32.43.3
5. Rosemary Monica Wanjiru   32.59.3

AFR CHAMPIONSHIPS, Assaba, 4-8-2018:
1. Stacey Chepkemboi Ndiwa (KEN)   31.31.17
2. Alice Aprot Nawowuna (KEN)   31.36.12
3. Gete Alemayehu Teknemichael (ETH) 32.10.68
4. Stella Chesang (UGA)   32.29.54
5. Mercyline Chelangat (UGA)   32.36.39

Yamaguchi, 8-12-2018:
1. Minami Yamanouchi (JPN)   31.16.48
2. Grace Mbutthye Kimanzi (KEN)   31.17.28
3. Harumi Okamoto (JPN)   31.28.20
4. Rina Nabeshima (JPN)   31.28.81
5. Shiori Yano (JPN)   31.44.13
6. Yuka Hori (JPN)   31.48.93
7. Natsuki Sekiya (JPN)   31.50.17

OVERVIEW WORLD OUTDOOR CHAMPIONSHIP FINALISTS OF PAST 6 YEARS

	Wch 17	OG 16	Wch 15	Wch 13
Almaz Ayana (ETH)	30.16.32 (1)	29.17.45 (1)		
Tirunesh Dibaba (ETH)	31.02.69 (2)	29.42.56 (3)		30.43.35 (1)
Agnes Jebet Tirop (KEN)	31.03.50 (3)			
Alice Aprot Nawowuna (KEN)	31.11.86 (4)	29.53.51 (4)		
Susan Krumins-Kuijken (NED)	31.20.24 (5)	31.32.43 (14)	31.54.32 (10)	
Emily Infeld (USA)	31.20.45 (6)	31.26.94 (11)	31.43.49 (3)	
Irene Chepet Cheptai (KEN)	31.21.11 (7)			
Molly Huddle (USA)	31.24.78 (8)	30.13.17 (6)	31.43.58 (4)	
Emily Sisson (USA)	31.26.36 (9)			
Ayuko Suzuki (JPN)	31.27.30 (10)			
Yasemin Can (TUR)	31.35.48 (11)	30.26.41 (7)		
Shitaye Eshete (BRN)	31.38.66 (12)			31.13.79 (6)
Mercyline Chelangat (UGA)	31.40.48 (13)			
Dera Dida (ETH)	31.51.75 (14)			
Desi Mokonin (BRN)	31.55.34 (15)			
Vivian Jepkemoi Cheruiyot (KEN)		29.32.53 (2)	31.41.31 (1)	
Betsy Saina (KEN)		30.07.78 (5)	31.51.35 (8)	
Gelete Burka (ETH)		30.26.66 (8)	31.41.77 (2)	
Karoline Bjerkeli Grövdal (NOR)		31.14.07 (9)		
Eloise Wellings (AUS)		31.14.94 (10)		
Sarah Lahti (SWE)		31.28.43 (12)		
Diane Nukuri (BDI)		31.28.69 (13)		
Joanne Pavey (GBR)		31.33.44 (15)		
Sally Jepkosgei Kipyego (KEN)			31.44.42 (5)	
Shalane Flanagan (USA)			31.46.23 (6)	31.34.83 (8)
Alemitu Heroye (ETH)			31.49.73 (7)	
Belaynesh Oljira (ETH)			31.53.01 (9)	30.46.98 (3)
Jip Vastenburg (NED)			32.03.03 (11)	
Sara Moreira (POR)			32.06.14 (12)	
Kasumi Nishihara (JPN)			32.12.95 (13)	
Brenda Flores (MEX)			32.15.26 (14)	
Kate Avery (GBR)			32.16.19 (15)	
Gladys Cherono (KEN)				30.45.17 (2)
Emily Chebet (KEN)				30.47.02 (4)
Hitomi Niiya (JPN)				30.56.70 (5)
Sally Kaptich Chepyego (KEN)				31.22.11 (7)
Ababel Yeshaneh (ETH)				32.02.09 (9)
Christelle Daunay (FRA)				32.04.44 (10)
Marisol Romero (MEX)				32.16.36 (11)
Jordan Hasay (USA)				32.17.93 (12)
Ana Dulce Félix (POR)				32.36.73 (13)
Amy Hastings (USA)				32.51.19 (14)
Karolina Jarzynska (POL)				32.54.15 (15)

OVERVIEW TOP 10 WORLD OUTDOOR RANKINGS OF PAST 5 YEARS

	2018	2017	2016	2015	2014
Pauline Kamulu (KEN)	30.41.85 (1)				
Minami Yamanouchi (JPN)	31.16.48 (2)				
Grace Mbuthye Kimanzi (KEN)	31.17.28 (3)				
Harumi Okamoto (JPN)	31.28.20 (4)				
Rina Nabeshima (JPN)	31.28.81 (5)				
Stacey Chepkemboi Ndiwa (KEN)	31.31.17 (6)				
Hitomi Niiya (JPN)	31.32.50 (7)				
Lonah Chemtai Salpeter (ISR)	31.33.03 (8)				
Alice Aprot Nawowuna (KEN)	31.36.12 (9)	31.11.86 (10)	29.53.51 (4)		
Mercyline Chelangat (UGA)	31.38.4 (10)				
Almaz Ayana (ETH)		30.16.32 (1)	29.17.45 (1)		
Gelete Burka (ETH)		30.40.87 (2)	30.26.66 (8)	30.49.68 (1)	
Senbere Teferi (ETH)		30.41.68 (3)			
Belaynesh Oljira (ETH)		30.44.57 (4)		30.53.69 (3)	
Dera Dida (ETH)		30.56.48 (5)			
Tirunesh Dibaba (ETH)		31.02.69 (6)	29.42.56 (3)		
Agnes Jebet Tirop (KEN)		31.03.50 (7)			
Rahma Tusa (ETH)		31.05.14 (8)			
Veronica Nyaruai Wanjiru (KEN)		31.07.56 (9)			
Vivian Jepkemoi Cheruiyot (KEN)			29.32.53 (2)	31.13.29 (10)	
Betsy Saina (KEN)			30.07.78 (5)		30.57.30 (3)
Molly Huddle (USA)			30.13.17 (6)		30.47.59 (2)
Yasemin Can (TUR)			30.26.41 (7)		
Netsanet Gudeta (ETH)			30.36.75 (9)		
Genet Yalew (ETH)			30.37.38 (10)	31.08.82 (7)	
Alemitu Heroye (ETH)				30.50.83 (2)	
Mamitu Daska (ETH)				30.55.56 (4)	
Wude Ayalew (ETH)				30.58.03 (5)	
Netsanet Gudeta (ETH)				31.06.53 (6)	
Shalane Flanagan (USA)				31.09.02 (8)	
Sara Moreira (POR)				31.12.93 (9)	
Sally Jepkosgei Kipyego (KEN)					30.42.26 (1)
Selly Chepyego Kaptich (KEN)					31.28.07 (4)
Jordan Hasay (USA)					31.39.67 (5)
Ayumi Hagiwara (JPN)					31.41.80 (7)
Julia Bleasdale (GBR)					31.42.02 (7)
Almensh Belete (BEL)					31.43.05 (8)
Doricah Obare Kerubo (KEN)					31.45.24 (9)
Kim Conley (USA)					31.48.71 (10)

WORLD RANKING ALL TIME:

1.	Almaz Ayana (ETH)	29.17.45 (2016)
2.	Wang Junxia (CHN)	29.31.78 (1993)
3.	Vivian Jepkemoi Cheruiyot (KEN)	29.32.53 (2016)
4.	Tirunesh Dibaba (ETH)	29.42.56 (2016)
5.	Alice Aprot Nawowuna (KEN)	29.53.51 (2016)
6.	Meselech Melkamu (ETH)	29.53.80 (2009)
7.	Meseret Defar (ETH)	29.59.20 (2009)
8.	Paula Radcliffe (GBR)	30.01.09 (2002)
9.	Berhane Adere (ETH)	30.04.18 (2003)
10.	Werknesh Kidane (ETH)	30.07.15 (2003)
11.	Sun Yingjie (CHN)	30.07.20 (2003)
12.	Betsy Saina (KEN)	30.07.78 (2016)
13.	Florence Kiplagat (KEN)	30.11.53 (2009)
14.	Wude Ayalew (ETH)	30.11.87 (2009)
15.	Lornah Kiplagat (NED)	30.12.53 (2003)
16.	Molly Huddle (USA)	30.13.17 (2016)
17.	Zhong Huandi (CHN)	30.13.37 (1993)
18.	Ingrid Kristiansen (NOR)	30.13.74 (1986)
19.	Derartu Tulu (ETH)	30.17.49 (2000)
20.	Ejegayehu Dibaba (ETH)	30.18.39 (2005)
21.	Elvan Abeylegesse (TUR)	30.21.67 (2006)
22.	Shalane Flanagan (USA)	30.22.22 (2008)
23.	Gete Wami (ETH)	30.22.48 (2000)
24.	Fernanda Ribeiro (POR)	30.22.88 (2000)
25.	Alla Zhilyayeva (RUS)	30.23.07 (2003)
26.	Xing Huina (CHN)	30.24.36 (2004)
27.	Galina Bogomolova (RUS)	30.26.20 (2003)
28.	Sally Kipyego (KEN)	30.26.37 (2012)
29.	Yasemin Can (TUR)	30.26.41 (2016)
30.	Linet Chepkwemoi Masai (KEN)	30.26.50 (2008)
31.	Gelete Burka (ETH)	30.26.66 (2016)
32.	Belaynesh Oljira (ETH)	30.26.70 (2012)
33.	Chiemi Takahashi (JPN)	30.27.62 (1999)
34.	Gladys Cherono (KEN)	30.29.23 (2013)
35.	Liliya Shobukhova (RUS)	30.29.36 (2009)
36.	Edith Masai (KEN)	30.30.26 (2005)
37.	Mariya Konovalova (RUS)	30.31.03 (2009)
38.	Inga Abitova (RUS)	30.31.42 (2006)
39.	Tegla Loroupe (KEN)	30.32.03 (1999)
40.	Susanne Wigene (NOR)	30.32.36 (2006)
41.	Lidiya Grigoryeva (RUS)	30.32.72 (2006)
42.	Kimberley Smith (NZL)	30.35.54 (2008)
43.	Ababel Yeshaneh (ETH)	30.35.91 (2013)
44.	Netsanet Gudeta (ETH)	30.36.75 (2016)
45.	Genet Yalew (ETH)	30.37.38 (2016)

100 m Hurdles Women outdoor / 60 m Hurdles Women indoor

EUROPEAN CHAMPIONSHIPS 2018: 9-8-2018:

1.	Elvira Herman (BLR)	(12.76)	12.67
2.	Pamela Dutkiewicz (GER)	(12.71)	12.72
3.	Cindy Roleder (GER)	(12.83)	12.77
4.	Nadine Visser (NED)	(12.84)	12.88
5.	Ricarda Lobe (GER)	(12.90)	13.00
6.	Karolina Koleczek (POL)	(12.94)	13.11
	Solène Ndama (FRA)	(12.77)	dsq
	Alina Talay (BLR)	(12.96)	dsq

9.	Nooralotta Neziri (FIN)	12.94
10.	Eline Berings (BEL)	12.94
11.	Eefje Boons (NED)	12.94
12.	Luca Kozák (HUN)	12.96
13.	Elisávet Pesirídou (GRE)	13.00
14.	Isabelle Pedersen (NOR)	13.04
15.	Luminosa Bogliolo (ITA)	13.09
16.	Klaudia Siciarz (POL)	13.12
17.	Andrea Ivancevic (CRO)	13.13
18.	Reetta Hurske (FIN)	13.20
19.	Laura Valette (FRA)	(13.16) 13.22
20.	Gréta Kerekes (HUN)	13.23
21.	Beate Schrott (AUT)	(13.06) 13.23
22.	Anamaria Nesteriuc (ROM)	(13.16) 13.26
23.	Stephanie Bendrat (AUT)	13.43
24.	Caridad Jerez (ESP)	(13.19) 15.34

25.	Franziska Hofmann (GER)	13.23
26.	Ivana Loncarek (CRO)	13.23
27.	Hanna Plotitsyna (UKR)	13.23
28.	Annimari Korte (FIN)	13.31
29.	Elisa Di Lazzaro (ITA)	13.42
30.	Elin Westerlund (SWE)	13.42

WORLD RANKING 2017:

1.	Kendra Harrison (USA)	12.36(Lon)
2.	Brianna McNeal (USA)	12.38(Sto)
3.	Jasmine Camacho-Quinn (PUR)	12.40(Kno)
4.	Alina Talay (BLR)	12.41
5.	Danielle Williams (JAM)	12.48(Sto)
6.	Sharika Nelvis (USA)	12.51(Lon)
7.	Christina Manning (USA)	12.56(Lon)
8.	Queen Harrison (USA)	12.63(Lon)
9.	Elvira Herman (BLR)	12.64
10.	Rushelle Burton (JAM)	12.65(Wac)
11.	Pamela Dutkiewicz (GER)	12.67(Luz)
12.	Sally Pearson (AUS)	12.68
	Tobi Amusan (NGR)	12.68(GC)
14.	Devynne Charlton (BAH)	12.70(BR)
	Alaysha Johnson (USA)	12.70(NCA)
16.	Jasmin Stowers (USA)	12.71(Sha)
	Nadine Visser (NED)	12.71(Sto)
18.	Pedrya Seymour (BAH)	12.72(Wac)
	Eline Berings (BEL)	12.72
	Isabelle Pedersen (NOR)	12.72(Lon)
21.	Yanique Thompson (JAM)	12.74(JAC)
22.	Chanel Brissett (USA)	12.75(PA)
	Dawn Harper-Nelson (USA)	12.75(Sze)
24.	Cindy Roleder (GER)	12.77(ECh)
	Solène Ndama (FRA)	12.77(ECh)
26.	Kori Carter (USA)	12.78(USC)
27.	Bridgette Owens (USA)	12.79(Tor)
	Alexis Duncan (USA)	12.79(Kno)
	Jeanine Williams (JAM)	12.79(JAC)
30.	Erica Bougard (USA)	12.80(Gtz)
	Janeek Brown (JAM)	12.80(NCA)
32.	Rikenette Steenkamp (RSA)	12.81(LCF)
33.	Dior Hall (USA)	12.83(PA)
34.	Evonne Britton (USA)	12.84(Bel)
35.	Andrea Ivancevic (CRO)	12.85(Zag)
36.	Ebony Morrison (USA)	12.86(CG)
	Cortney Jones (USA)	12.86(NCA)
	Luca Kozák (HUN)	12.86
	Nooralotta Neziri (FIN)	12.86
	Eefje Boons (NED)	12.86
41.	Anna Cockrell (USA)	12.88(PA)
	Tonea Marshall (USA)	12.88(NCA)
43.	Tia Jones (USA)	12.89

WORLD INDOOR CHAMPIONSHIPS: 3-3-2018:

1.	Kendra Harrison (USA)	(7.77)	7.70
2.	Christina Manning (USA)	(7.83)	7.79
3.	Nadine Visser (NED)	(7.83)	7.84
4.	Sharika Nelvis (USA)	(7.86)	7.86
5.	Cindy Roleder (GER)	(7.86)	7.87
6.	Isabelle Pedersen (NOR)	(7.86)	7.94
7.	Oluwatobiloba Amusan (NGR)	(7.91)	8.05
8.	Devynne Charlton (BAH)	(7.89)	8.18

9.	Sally Pearson (AUS)		7.92
10.	Elvira Herman (BLR)		8.06
11.	Andrea Ivancevic (CRO)		8.07
12.	Alina Talay (BLR)		8.07
13.	Lindsay Lindley (NGR)		8.08
14.	Hanna Plotitsyna (UKR)		8.09
15.	Stephanie Bendrat (AUT)	(8.06)	8.10
16.	Eline Berings (BEL)		8.14
17.	Gréta Kerekes (HUN)		8.17
18.	Reetta Hurske (FIN)		8.20
19.	Nooralotta Neziri (FIN)	(8.13)	8.20
20.	Ivana Loncarek (CRO)	(8.16)	8.21
21.	Karolina Koleczek (POL)	(8.16)	8.21
22.	Michelle Jenneke (AUS)	(8.20)	8.22
23.	Luca Kozák (HUN)	(8.16)	8.24
24.	Eefje Boons (NED)	(8.16)	8.24

25.	Angela Whyte (CAN)	8.21
26.	Marilyn Nwawulor (GBR)	8.22
27.	Beate Schrott (AUT)	8.27
28.	Veronica Borsi (ITA)	8.27
29.	Megan Marrs (GBR)	8.28
30.	Anamaria Nesteriuc (ROM)	8.32
31.	Ricarda Lobe (GER)	8.33
32.	Andrea Vargas (CRC)	8.34
33.	Elisa di Lazzaro (ITA)	8.35
34.	Elin Westerlund (SWE)	8.36

WORLD INDOOR RANKING 2018:

1.	Kendra Harrison (USA)	7.70
	Sharika Nelvis (USA)	7.70
3.	Christina Manning (USA)	7.73
4.	Pamela Dutkiewicz (GER)	7.83
	Nadine Visser (NED)	7.83
6.	Cindy Roleder (GER)	7.84
7.	Isabelle Pedersen (NOR)	7.86
8.	Alina Talay (BLR)	7.88
	Jasmin Stowers (USA)	7.88
10.	Tobi Amusan (NGR)	7.89
	Deveynne Charlton (BAH)	7.89
12.	Queen Harrison (USA)	7.91
13.	Sally Pearson (AUS)	7.92
14.	Payton Stumbaugh Chadwick (USA)	7.93
	Anna Cockrell (USA)	7.93
16.	Dior Hall (USA)	7.94
	Kristi Castlin (USA)	7.94
	Bridgette Owens (USA)	7.94
19.	Jasmine Camacho-Quinn (PUR)	7.95
20.	Erica Bougard (USA)	7.98
	Tara Davis (USA)	7.98
22.	Nadine Hildebrand (GER)	7.99
23.	Kori Carter (USA)	8.00
	Tiffani McReynolds (USA)	8.00

Commonwealth Games, Gold Coast, 13-4-2018:
1.	Tobi Amusan (NGR)	(12.73)	12.68
2.	Danielle Williams (JAM)	(12.69)	12.78
3.	Yanique Thompson (JAM)		12.97

Doha, 4-5-2018:
1.	Kendra Harrison (USA)	12.53
2.	Brianna McNeal (USA)	12.58
3.	Sharika Nelvis (USA)	12.75
4.	Jasmin Stowers (USA)	12.77
5.	Danielle Williams (JAM)	12.82
	Isabelle Pedersen (NOR)	12.82
7.	Nadine Visser (NED)	12.94
8.	Dawn Harper-Nelson (USA)	13.21

Shanghai, 12-5-2018:
1.	Brianna McNeal (USA)	12.50
2.	Sharika Nelvis (USA)	12.52
3.	Kendra Harrison (USA)	12.56
4.	Jasmin Stowers (USA)	12.71
5.	Isabelle Pedersen (NOR)	12.76
6.	Nadine Visser (NED)	12.81
7.	Cindy Roleder (GER)	12.81
8.	Dawn Harper-Nelson (USA)	12.94

Oslo, 7-6-2018:
1.	Danielle Williams (JAM)	12.60
2.	Alina Talay (BLR)	12.63
3.	Queen Harrison (USA)	12.71
4.	Isabelle Pedersen (NOR)	12.78
5.	Cindy Roleder (GER)	12.81
6.	Eline Berings (BEL)	12.89
7.	Bridgette Owens-Mitchell (USA)	12.98
8.	Jasmin Stowers (USA)	12.99

NCAA, Eugene, 8-6-2018:
1.	Jasmine Camacho-Quinn (PUR)	(12.54)	12.70
2.	Devynne Charlton (BAH)	(12.86)	12.77
3.	Cortney Jones (USA)	(12.86)	13.04
4.	Pedrya Seymour (BAH)	(12.81)	13.04
5.	Janeek Brown (JAM)	(12.80)	13.05
6.	Tonea Marshall (USA)	(12.88)	13.09
7.	Alaysha Johnson (USA)	(12.70)	13.22
8.	Rushelle Burton (JAM)	(12.77)	13.51
-----	-----------------------	-------	-----
9.	Anna Cockrell (USA)		12.88
10.	Alexis Duncan (USA)		12.93
11.	Macca McGlaston (USA)		12.98

Stockholm, 10-6-2018:
1.	Brianna McNeal (USA)	12.38
2.	Danielle Williams (JAM)	12.48
3.	Alina Talay (BLR)	12.55
4.	Nadine Visser (NED)	12.71
5.	Christina Manning (USA)	12.75
6.	Dawn Harper-Nelson (USA)	12.80
7.	Isabelle Pedersen (NOR)	12.82

US CHAMPIONSHIPS, Des Moines, 23-6-2018:
1.	Kendra Harrison	(12.46)	12.46
2.	Christina Manning	(12.68)	12.65
3.	Sharika Nelvis		12.68
4.	Queen Harrison	(12.66)	12.76
5.	Dawn Harper-Nelson	(12.81)	12.93
6.	Kori Carter	(12.78)	13.11
7.	Alaysha Johnson		13.23
	Jasmin Stowers	(12.89)	dns

JAM CHAMPIONSHIPS, Kingston, 24-6-2018:
1.	Danielle Williams		12.63
2.	Yanique Thompson	(12.74)	12.78
3.	Jeanine Williams	(12.79)	12.94
4.	Nickiesha Wilson	(12.93)	12.95

Szekesfehervar, 2-7-2018:
1.	Sharika Nelvis (USA)	12.55
2.	Kendra Harrison (USA)	12.58
3.	Christina Manning (USA)	12.65
4.	Dawn Harper-Nelson (USA)	12.75
5.	Kristi Castlin (USA)	13.03
6.	Cindy Roleder (GER)	13.05

B-race:
1.	Elvira Herman (BLR)	12.90

Luzern, 9-7-2018:
1.	Brianna McNeal (USA)	12.44
2.	Pamela Dutkiewicz (GER)	12.67
3.	Christina Manning (USA)	12.71
4.	Queen Harrison (USA)	12.75
5.	Tobi Amusan (NGR)	12.80
6.	Cindy Roleder (GER)	12.81
7.	Yanique Thompson (JAM)	13.00

B-race:
1.	Nooralotta Neziri (FIN)	12.89

Rabat, 13-7-2018:
1.	Brianna McNeal (USA)	12.51
2.	Sharika Nelvis (USA)	12.58
3.	Christina Manning (USA)	12.72
4.	Dawn Harper-Nelson (USA)	12.86
5.	Tobi Amusan (NGR)	12.87
6.	Cindy Roleder (GER)	12.87
7.	Pamela Dutkiewicz (GER)	12.89
8.	Yanique Thompson (JAM)	12.93

Monaco, 20-7-2018:
1.	Queen Harrison (USA)	12.64
2.	Dawn Harper-Nelson (USA)	12.90
3.	Yanique Thompson (JAM)	12.92
4.	Eline Berings (BEL)	12.94

London, 22-7-2018:
1.	Kendra Harrison (USA)	(12.50)	12.36
2.	Brianna McNeal (USA)	(12.41)	12.47
3.	Sharika Nelvis (USA)	(12.61)	12.51
4.	Danielle Williams (JAM)	(12.67)	12.55
5.	Christina Manning (USA)	(12.56)	12.57
6.	Queen Harrison (USA)	(12.85)	12.63
7.	Tobi Amusan (NGR)	(12.69)	12.68
8.	Isabelle Pedersen (NOR)	(12.72)	12.73
9.	Elvira Herman (BLR)	(12.87)	12.78

NACAC, Toronto, 11-8-2018:
1.	Kendra Harrison (USA)	12.55
2.	Danielle Williams (JAM)	12.67
3.	Andrea Vargas (CRC)	12.91
4.	Queen Harrison (USA)	12.93

Brussels, 31-8-2018:
1.	Brianna McNeal (USA)	12.61
2.	Kendra Harrison (USA)	12.63
3.	Danielle Williams (JAM)	12.64
4.	Tobi Amusan (NGR)	12.69
5.	Sharika Nelvis (USA)	12.80
6.	Nadine Visser (NED)	12.81
7.	Eline Berings (BEL)	12.94

Berlin, 2-9-2018:
1.	Christina Manning (USA)	12.72
2.	Pamela Dutkiewicz (GER)	12.73
3.	Cindy Roleder (GER)	12.73
4.	Elvira Herman (BLR)	12.90
5.	Dawn Harper-Nelson (USA)	12.94
6.	Nadine Hildebrand (GER)	12.97

Zagreb, 4-9-2018:
1.	Sharika Nelvis (USA)	12.65
2.	Brianna McNeal (USA)	12.66
3.	Christina Manning (USA)	12.79
4.	Andrea Ivancevic (CRO)	12.85
5.	Cindy Roleder (GER)	12.99
6.	Elvira Herman (BLR)	13.10

CONTINENTAL CUP, Ostrava, 8-9-2018:

1. Danielle Williams (AME)   12.49
2. Kendra Harrison (AME)   12.52
3. Pamela Dutkiewicz (EUR)   12.82
4. Elvira Herman (EUR)   12.91
5. Tobi Amusan (AFR)   12.96

OVERVIEW WORLD OUTDOOR CHAMPIONSHIP FINALISTS OF PAST 6 YEARS

	Wch 17	OG 16	Wch 15	Wch 13
Sally Pearson (AUS)	12.59 (1)			12.50 (2)
Dawn Harper Nelson (USA)	12.63 (2)			12.59 (4)
Pamela Dutkiewicz (GER)	12.72 (3)			
Kendra Harrison (USA)	12.74 (4)			
Christina Manning (USA)	12.74 (5)			
Alina Talay (BLR)	12.81 (6)		12.66 (3)	
Nadine Visser (NED)	12.83 (7)			
Nia Ali (USA)	13.04 (8)	12.59 (2)		
Brianna McNeal-Rollins (USA)		12.48 (1)	12.67 (4)	12.44 (1)
Kristi Castlin (USA)		12.61 (3)		
Cindy Ofili (GBR)		12.63 (4)		
Cindy Roleder (GER)		12.74 (5)	12.59 (2)	
Pedrya Seymour (BAH)		12.76 (6)		
Tiffany Porter (GBR)		12.76 (7)	12.68 (5)	12.55 (3)
Phylicia George (CAN)		12.89 (8)		
Danielle Williams (JAM)			12.57 (1)	
Noemi Zbären (SUI)			12.95 (6)	
Shermaine Williams (JAM)			12.95 (7)	
Sharika Nelvis (USA)			13.06 (8)	
Queen Harrison (USA)				12.73 (5)
Angela Whyte (CAN)				12.78 (6)
Cindy Billaud (FRA)				12.84 (7)
Yuliya Kondakova (RUS)				12.86 (8)

OVERVIEW WORLD INDOOR CHAMPIONSHIP FINALISTS OF PAST 5 YEARS

	Wch 18	Wch 16	Wch 14
Kendra Harrison (USA)	7.70 (1)	8.87 (8)	
Christina Manning (USA)	7.79 (2)		
Nadine Visser (NED)	7.84 (3)		
Sharika Nelvis (USA)	7.86 (4)		
Cindy Roleder (GER)	7.87 (5)		8.01 (6)
Isabelle Pedersen (NOR)	7.94 (6)		
Oluwatobiloba Amusan (NGR)	8.05 (7)		
Devynne Charlton (BAH)	8.18 (8)		
Nia Ali (USA)		7.81 (1)	7.80 (1)
Brianna McNeal-Rollins (USA)		7.82 (2)	
Tiffany Porter (GBR)		7.90 (3)	7.86 (3)
Andrea Ivancevic (CRO)		7.95 (4)	
Angela Whyte (CAN)		7.99 (5)	
Alina Talay (BLR)		8.00 (6)	
Serita Solomon (GBR)		8.29 (7)	
Sally Pearson (AUS)			7.85 (2)
Cindy Billaud (FRA)			7.89 (4)
Janay Deloach Soukup (USA)			7.90 (5)
Nadine Hildebrand (GER)			8.02 (7)
Yuliya Kondakova (RUS)			8.08 (8)

OVERVIEW TOP 10 WORLD OUTDOOR RANKINGS OF PAST 5 YEARS

	2018	2017	2016	2015	2014
Kendra Harrison (USA)	12.36 (1)	12.28 (1)	12.20 (1)	12.50 (4)	12.71 (10)
Brianna McNeal-Rollins (USA)	12.38 (2)		12.34 (2)	12.56 (6)	12.53 (4)
Jasmine Camacho-Quinn (PUR)	12.40 (3)	12.58 (9)			
Alina Talay (BLR)	12.41 (4)		12.63 (9)		
Danielle Williams (JAM)	12.48 (5)	12.56 (7)		12.57 (8)	
Sharika Nelvis (USA)	12.51 (6)	12.52 (4)	12.60 (7)	12.34 (1)	12.71 (10)
Christina Manning (USA)	12.56 (7)	12.54 (6)			
Queen Harrison (USA)	12.63 (8)		12.57 (6)	12.52 (5)	12.46 (2)
Elvira Herman (BLR)	12.64 (9)				
Rushelle Burton (JAM)	12.65 (10)				
Jasmin Stowers (USA)		12.47 (2)	12.55 (4)	12.35 (2)	12.71 (10)
Sally Pearson (AUS)		12.48 (3)		12.59 (9)	12.59 (8)
Nia Ali (USA)		12.52 (4)	12.55 (4)		
Oluwatobiloba Amusan (NGR)		12.57 (8)			
Pamela Dutkiewicz (GER)		12.61 (10)			
Kristi Castlin (USA)		12.61 (10)	12.50 (3)		12.58 (7)
Cindy Roleder (GER)			12.62 (8)	12.59 (9)	
Cindy Ofili (GBR)			12.63 (9)		
Dawn Harper Nelson (USA)				12.48 (3)	12.44 (1)
Tiffany Porter (GBR)				12.56 (6)	12.51 (3)
LoLo Jones (USA)					12.55 (5)
Cindy Billaud (FRA)					12.56 (6)
Kellie Wells (USA)					12.68 (9)
Nadine Hildebrand (GER)					12.71 (10)

OVERVIEW TOP 10 WORLD INDOOR RANKINGS OF PAST 5 YEARS

	2018	2017	2016	2015	2014
Kendra Harrison (USA)	7.70 (1)	7.74 (1)	7.77 (2)	7.87 (4)	
Sharika Nelvis (USA)	7.70 (1)	7.87 (7)	7.90 (9)	7.83 (1)	7.93 (9)
Christina Manning (USA)	7.73 (3)	7.82 (3)	7.90 (9)		
Pamela Dutkiewicz (GER)	7.83 (4)	7.79 (2)			
Nadine Visser (NED)	7.83 (4)	7.92 (10)			
Cindy Roleder (GER)	7.84 (6)	7.84 (5)	7.88 (6)	7.93 (7)	
Isabelle Pedersen (NOR)	7.86 (7)			7.95 (9)	
Alina Talay (BLR)	7.88 (8)	7.86 (6)		7.85 (3)	
Jasmin Stowers (USA)	7.88 (8)	7.82 (3)		7.84 (2)	
Tobi Amusan (NGR)	7.89 (10)				
Deveynne Charlton (BAH)	7.89 (10)				
Sasha Wallace (USA)		7.87 (7)			
Sally Pearson (AUS)		7.91 (9)			7.79 (1)
Hanna Plotitsyna (UKR)		7.92 (10)			
Brianna McNeal-Rollins (USA)			7.76 (1)		
Nia Ali (USA)			7.81 (3)		7.80 (2)
Queen Harrison (USA)			7.83 (4)		
Janay Deloach (USA)			7.85 (5)		7.82 (3)
Tiffany Porter (GBR)			7.89 (7)		7.86 (4)
Cindy Ofili (GBR)			7.89 (7)		
Bridgette Owens-Mitchell (USA)				7.88 (5)	
Lucy Hatton (GBR)				7.90 (6)	
Serita Solomon (GBR)				7.93 (7)	
Eline Berings (BEL)				7.95 (9)	
Cindy Billaud (FRA)					7.87 (5)
Kristi Castlin (USA)					7.88 (6)
Nadine Hildebrand (GER)					7.91 (7)
Yvette Lewis (PAN)/(USA)					7.91 (7)
Ekaterina Galitskaia (RUS)					7.93 (9)
Tiffany McReynolds (USA)					7.93 (9)

WORLD RANKING OUTDOOR ALL TIME:

1.	Kendra Harrison (USA)	12.20 (2016)
2.	Yordanka Donkova (BUL)	12.21 (1988)
3.	Ginka Zagorcheva (BUL)	12.25 (1987)
4.	Ludmila Narozhilenko (RUS)	12.26 (1992)
	Brianna Rollins (USA)	12.26 (2013)
6.	Sally Pearson (AUS)	12.28 (2011)
7.	Gail Devers (USA)	12.33 (2000)
8.	Sharika Nelvis (USA)	12.34 (2015)
9.	Jasmin Stowers (USA)	12.35 (2015)
10.	Grazyna Rabsztyn (POL)	12.36 (1980)
11.	Joanna Hayes (USA)	12.37 (2004)
	Dawn Harper-Nelson (USA)	12.37 (2012)
13.	Vera Komisova (URS)	12.39 (1980)
	Natalya Grigoryeva (URS)	12.39 (1991)
15.	Jasmine Camacho-Quinn (PUR)	12.40 (2018)
16.	Alina Talay (BLR)	12.41 (2018)
17.	Bettine Jahn (GDR)	12.42 (1983)
	Anjanette Kirkland (USA)	12.42 (2001)
19.	Lucyna Langer (POL)	12.43 (1984)
	Michelle Perry (USA)	12.43 (2005)
	Lolo Jones (USA)	12.43 (2008)
	Queen Harrison (USA)	12.43 (2013)
23.	Gloria Siebert (GDR)	12.44 (1987)
	Olga Shishigina (KAZ)	12.44 (1995)
	Glory Alozie (NGR)	12.44 (1998)
	Damu Cherry (USA)	12.44 (2006)
27.	Cornelia Oschkenat (GDR)	12.45 (1987)
	Brigitte Foster (JAM)	12.45 (2003)
	Olena Krasovska (UKR)	12.45 (2004)
	Virginia Crawford (USA)	12.45 (2007)
31.	Perdita Felicien (CAN)	12.46 (2004)
32.	Marina Azyabina (RUS)	12.47 (1993)
	Danielle Carruthers (USA)	12.47 (2011)
34.	Kellie Wells (USA)	12.48 (2012)
	Nia Ali (USA)	12.48 (2013)
	Danielle Williams (JAM)	12.48 (2018)
37.	Susanna Kallur (SWE)	12.49 (2007)
	Priscilla Schliep (CAN)	12.49 (2009)
39.	Vera Akimova (URS)	12.50 (1984)
	Delloreen Ennis (JAM)	12.50 (2007)
	Josephine Onyia (ESP)	12.50 (2008)
	Kristi Castlin (USA)	12.50 (2016)
43.	Miesha McKelvy-Jones (USA)	12.51 (2003)
	Tiffany Porter (GBR)	12.51 (2014)
45.	Michelle Freeman (JAM)	12.52 (1997)

WORLD RANKING INDOOR ALL TIME:

1.	Susanna Kallur (SWE)	7.68 (2008)
2.	Ludmila Narozhilenko (URS)	7.69 (1990)
3.	Sharika Nelvis (USA)	7.70 (2018)
	Kendra Harrison (USA)	7.70 (2018)
5.	Lolo Jones (USA)	7.72 (2010)
6.	Cornelia Oschkenat (GDR)	7.73 (1989)
	Sally Pearson (AUS)	7.73 (2012)
	Christina Manning (USA)	7.73 (2018)
9.	Yordanka Donkova (BUL)	7.74 (1987)
	Michelle Freeman (JAM)	7.74 (1998)
	Gail Devers (USA)	7.74 (2003)
12.	Bettina Jahn (GDR)	7.75 (1983)
	Perdita Felicien (CAN)	7.75 (2004)
14.	Gloria Siebert (GDR)	7.76 (1988)
	Brianna McNeal-Rollins (USA)	7.76 (2016)
16.	Zofia Bielczyk (POL)	7.77 (1980)
17.	Brigita Bukovec (SLO)	7.78 (1999)
18.	Kellie Wells (USA)	7.79 (2011)
	Pamela Dutkiewicz (GER)	7.79 (2017)
20.	Carolin Dietrich (GER)	7.80 (2011)
	Tiffany Porter (GBR)	7.80 (2011)
	Nia Ali (USA)	7.80 (2014)
23.	Jackie Joyner-Kersee (USA)	7.81 (1989)
24.	Yelizaveta Chernyshova (URS)	7.82 (1989)
	Monique Éwanje-Épée (FRA)	7.82 (1991)
	Glory Alozie (NGR)	7.82 (1999)
	Olga Shishigina (KAZ)	7.82 (1999)
	Kimberly Carson (USA)	7.82 (2000)
	Linda Ferga (FRA)	7.82 (2004)
	Priscilla Schliep (CAN)	7.82 (2010)
	Janay Deloach (USA)	7.82 (2014)
	Jasmin Stowers (USA)	7.82 (2017)
33.	Melissa Morrison (USA)	7.83 (1998)
	Joanna Hayes (USA)	7.83 (2004)
	Lacena Golding-Clarke (JAM)	7.83 (2006)
	Christina Vukicevic (NOR)	7.83 (2011)
	Queen Harrison (USA)	7.83 (2016)
	Nadine Visser (NED)	7.83 (2018)
39. :		
	Grazyna Rabsztyn (POL)	7.84 (198)
	Patricia Girard (FRA)	7.84 (1995)
	Patricia Russell (JAM)	7.84 (1997)
	Cheryl Dickey (USA)	7.84 (1997)
	Virginia Crawford (USA)	7.84 (2006)
	Derval O'Rourke (IRL)	7.84 (2006)
	et al.	

400 m Hurdles Women

EUROPEAN CHAMPIONSHIPS 2018: 10-8-2018:

1. Léa Sprunger (SUI)   (55.04)   54.33
2. Anna Ryzhykova (UKR)   (54.82)   54.51
3. Meghan Beesley (GBR)   (55.21)   55.31
4. Hanne Claes (BEL)   (55.75)   55.75
5. Yadisleidis Pedroso (ITA)   (55.13)   55.80
6. Vera Rudakova (ANA)   (55.24)   55.89
7. Viktoriya Tkachuk (UKR)   (55.37)   56.15
8. Eilidh Doyle (GBR)   (55.16)   56.23
----
9. Ayomide Folorunso (ITA)   55.69
10. Line Kloster (NOR)   55.78
11. Amalie Hammild Iuel (NOR)   55.81
12. Robine Schürmann (SUI)   55.89
13. Zuzana Hejnová (CZE)   56.03
14. Joanna Linkiewicz (POL)   56.06
15. Aurelie Chaboudez (FRA)   56.19
16. Mariya Mykolenko (UKR)   56.35
17. Yasmin Giger (SUI)   56.81
18. Sara Slott Petersen (DEN)   56.91
19. Sara Gallego (ESP)   (57.18)   57.25
20. Kirsten Mcaslan (GBR)   (56.78)   57.33
21. Justien Grillet (BEL)   (56.94)   57.40
22. Sanda Belgyan (ROM)   (56.68)57.51
23. Justyna Saganiak (POL)   (57.24)   57.71
   Margo van Puyvelde (BEL)(56.70)   dns
----
25. Elif Gören (TUR)   57.53
26. Johanna Holmén (SWE)   57.55
27. Anna Runia (NED)   57.76
28. Daniela Ledecká (SVK)   57.81

WORLD RANKING 2018:

1. Sydney McLaughlin (USA)   52.75(Kno)
2. Shamier Little (USA)   53.32(NAC)
3. Janieve Russell (JAM)   53.46(Lau)
4. Dalilah Muhammad (USA)   53.65(Osl)
5. Georganne Moline (USA)   53.90(Lau)
6. Léa Sprunger (SUI)   54.33(ECh)
7. Anna Yaroshchuk-Ryzhykova (UKR) 54.47(CON)
8. Kemi Adekoya (BRN)   54.48(Jak)
9. Sage Watson (CAN)   54.55(Osl)
10. Wenda Nel (RSA)   54.61(GC)
11. Ashley Spencer (USA)   54.66(Luz)
12. Leah Nugent (JAM)   54.67(Kin)
13. Eilidh Doyle (IRL)   54.80(GC)
14. Rhonda Whyte (JAM)   54.90(JAC)
15. Cassandra Tate (USA)   54.94(Pra)
16. Yadisleidis Pedroso (ITA)   54.98
17. Glory Onome Nathaniel (NGR)   55.01(GC)
18. Zenéy van der Walt (RSA)   55.05(Pre)
19. Rushell Clayton (JAM)   55.08(JAC)
20. Zundike Rodriguez (MEX)   55.11
21. Zurian Hechavarría (CUB)   55.13
22. Sparkle McKnight (TTO)   55.15(GC)
23. Ayomide Folorunso (ITA)   55.16(Rom)
   Zuzana Hejnová (CZE)   55.16(Osl)
25. Hanne Claes (BEL)   55.20
26. Meghan Beesley (GBR)   55.21(ECh)
27. Irina Davydova (RUS)   55.23(Zhu)
28. Vera Rudakova (ANA)   55.24(ECh)
29. Amalie Iuel (NOR)   55.26(Osl)
30. Viktoriya Tkachuk (UKR)   55.28
31. Thi Lan Quach (VIE)   55.30(Jak)
32. Ristananna Tracey (JAM)   55.38
33. Nikita Tracey (JAM)   55.41(JAC)
34. Sara Slott Petersen (DEN)   55.48
35. Line Kloster (NOR)   55.49(LCF)
36. Robine Schürmann (SUI)   55.53
37. Aminat Jamal (BRN)   55.54
   Kymber Payne (USA)   55.54(USC)
39. Gianna Woodruff (PAN)   55.60
40. Katrina Seymour (BAH)   55.69(GC)
41. Anna Cockrell (USA)   55.71(NCA)
42. Lauren Wells (AUS)   55.73(GC)
43. Yanique Haye-Smith (JAM)   55.74
44. Shiann Salmon (JAM)   55.78

Commonwealth Games, Gold Coast, 12-4-2018:
1. Janieve Russell (JAM)   54.33
2. Eilidh Doyle (GBR)   54.80
3. Wenda Nel (RSA)   54.96
4. Rhonda Whyte (JAM)   55.02
5. Sage Watson (CAN)   55.55
6. Glory Onome Nathaniel (NGR)   56.39
7. Sparkle McKnight (TTO)   57.45
8. Ristananna Tracey (JAM)   57.50

Shanghai, 12-5-2018:
1. Dalilah Muhammad (USA)   53.77
2. Janieve Russell (JAM)   53.78
3. Sage Watson (CAN)   55.23
4. Wenda Nel (RSA)   55.63
5. Joanna Linkiewicz (POL)   55.84
6. Leah Nugent (JAM)   56.54

Kingston, 19-5-2018:
1. Janieve Russell (JAM)   54.26
2. Ashley Spencer (USA)   55.23
3. Leah Nugent (JAM)   55.37
4. Rushell Clayton (JAM)   55.50
5. Sparkle McKnight (TTO)   55.60
6. Ristananna Tracey (JAM)   56.38

Eugene, 26-5-2018:
1. Janieve Russell (JAM)   54.06
2. Dalilah Muhammad (USA)   54.09
3. Georganne Moline (USA)   54.33
4. Sage Watson (CAN)   54.81
5. Shamier Little (USA)   55.23
6. Zuzana Hejnová (CZE)   55.36
7. Ashley Spencer (USA)   55.58
8. Cassandra Tate (USA)   55.97

Rome, 31-5-2018:
1. Georganne Moline (USA)   53.97
2. Janieve Russell (JAM)   54.08
3. Dalilah Muhammad (USA)   54.65
4. Ayomide Folorunso (ITA)   55.16
5. Yadisleidis Pedroso (ITA)   55.43
6. Viktoriya Tkachuk (UKR)   55.69

Oslo, 7-6-2018:
1. Dalilah Muhammad (USA)   53.65
2. Shamier Little (USA)   53.94
3. Sage Watson (CAN)   54.55
4. Léa Sprunger (SUI)   55.07
5. Zuzana Hejnová (CZE)   55.16
6. Amalie Iuel (NOR)   55.26
7. Yadisleidis Pedroso (ITA)   55.47

JAM CHAMPIONSHIPS, Kingston, 22-6-2018:
1. Janieve Russell   54.18
2. Leah Nugent   54.70
3. Rhonda Whyte   54.90
4. Rushell Clayton   55.08
5. Ristananna Tracey   (55.55) 55.65
6. Nikita Tracey   (55.41) 55.84

US CHAMPIONSHIPS, Des Moines, 24-6-2018:
1. Shamier Little   53.61
2. Georganne Moline   54.12
3. Cassandra Tate   55.00
4. Kymber Payne   55.54
5. Anna Cockrell   56.14
6. Kiah Seymour   57.70
7. Deonca Bookman   58.02
   Ashley Spencer   dnf

Szekesfehervar, 2-7-2018:
1. Janieve Russell (JAM)   54.16
2. Dalilah Muhammad (USA)   54.46
3. Ashley Spencer (USA)   55.29
4. Georganne Moline (USA)   55.37
5. Kemi Adekoya (BRN)   56.34
6. Leah Nugent (JAM)   56.49
7. Cassandra Tate (USA)   56.52

Lausanne, 5-7-2018:
1. Shamier Little (USA)   53.41
2. Janieve Russell (JAM)   53.46
3. Georganne Moline (USA)   53.90
4. Dalilah Muhammad (USA)   54.61
5. Ashley Spencer (USA)   54.74
6. Léa Sprunger (SUI)   54.79
7. Cassandra Tate (USA)   55.45

Luzern, 9-7-2018:

1.	Janieve Russell (JAM)	53.63
2.	Dalilah Muhammad (USA)	53.79
3.	Ashley Spencer (USA)	54.66
4.	Léa Sprunger (SUI)	54.92
5.	Leah Nugent (JAM)	54.94
6.	Cassandra Tate (USA)	55.45
7.	Line Kloster (NOR)	55.61
8.	Rhonda Whyte (JAM)	56.57

London, 21-7-2018:

1.	Shamier Little (USA)	53.95
2.	Janieve Russell (JAM)	53.96
3.	Dalilah Muhammad (USA)	54.86
4.	Georganne Moline (USA)	55.47
5.	Wenda Nel (RSA)	55.67
6.	Ristananna Tracey (JAM)	56.07
7.	Eilidh Doyle (GBR)	56.18
8.	Sage Watson (CAN)	56.21

NACAC, Toronto, 12-8-2018:

1.	Shamier Little (USA)	53.32
2.	Janieve Russell (JAM)	53.81
3.	Georganne Moline (USA)	54.26
4.	Zurian Hechevarría (CUB)	55.71
5.	Lean Nugent (JAM)	55.74

Zürich, 30-8-2018:

1.	Dalilah Muhammad (USA)	53.88
2.	Shamier Little (USA)	54.21
3.	Janieve Russell (JAM)	54.38
4.	Georganne Moline (USA)	55.00
5.	Eilidh Doyle (GBR)	55.05
6.	Léa Sprunger (SUI)	55.36
7.	Sage Watson (CAN)	55.57
8.	Wenda Nel (RSA)	57.23

CONTINENTAL CUP, Ostrava, 9-9-2018:

1.	Janieve Russell (AME)	53.61
2.	Shamier Little (AME)	53.86
3.	Anna Yaroshchuk (EUR)	54.47
4.	Meghan Beesley (EUR)	55.58
5.	Aminat Yusuf Jamal (ASI)	55.65
6.	Wenda Nel (AFR)	56.54

OVERVIEW WORLD OUTDOOR CHAMPIONSHIP FINALISTS OF PAST 6 YEARS

	Wch 17	OG 16	Wch 15	Wch 13
Kori Carter (USA)	53.07 (1)			
Dalilah Muhammad (USA)	53.50 (2)	53.13 (1)		54.09 (2)
Ristananna Tracey (JAM)	53.74 (3)	54.15 (5)		
Zuzana Hejnova (CZE)	54.20 (4)	53.92 (4)	53.50 (1)	52.83 (1)
Léa Sprunger (SUI)	54.59 (5)			
Sage Watson (CAN)	54.92 (6)			
Cassandra Tate (USA)	55.43 (7)		54.02 (3)	
Eilidh Doyle-Child (GBR)	55.71 (8)	54.61 (8)	54.78 (6)	54.86 (5)
Sara Slott Petersen (DEN)		53.55 (2)	54.20 (4)	
Ashley Spencer (USA)		53.72 (3)		
Leah Nugent (JAM)		54.45 (6)		
Janieve Russell (JAM)		54.56 (7)	54.64 (5)	
Shamier Little (USA)			53.94 (2)	
Wenda Nel (RSA)			54.94 (7)	
Kaliese Spencer (JAM)			55.47 (8)	
Lashinda Demus (USA)				54.27 (3)
Anna Titimets (UKR)				54.72 (4)
Anna Yaroshchuk (UKR)				55.01 (6)
Perri Shakes-Drayton (GBR)				56.25 (7)
Nickiesha Wilson (JAM)				57.34 (8)

OVERVIEW TOP 10 WORLD OUTDOOR RANKINGS OF PAST 5 YEARS

	2018	**2017**	**2016**	**2015**	**2014**
Sydney McLaughlin (USA)	52.75 (1)	53.82 (7)	54.15 (9)		
Shamier Little (USA)	53.32 (2)	52.75 (2)	53.51 (2)	53.74 (2)	
Janieve Russell (JAM)	53.46 (3)	54.02 (9)	53.96 (6)		
Dalilah Muhammad (USA)	53.65 (4)	52.64 (1)	52.88 (1)		
Georganne Moline (USA)	53.90 (5)	53.14 (5)	53.97 (7)	54.24 (8)	54.00 (3)
Léa Sprunger (SUI)	54.33 (6)	54.29 (10)			
Anna Yaroshchuk (UKR)	54.47 (7)				
Oluwakemi Adekoya (BRN)	54.48 (8)			54.12 (6)	54.59 (7)
Sage Watson (CAN)	54.55 (9)				
Wenda Nel (RSA)	54.61 (10)			54.37 (10)	
Kori Carter (USA)		52.95 (3)			53.84 (2)
Ashley Spencer (USA)		53.11 (4)	53.72 (4)		
Ristananna Tracey (JAM)		53.74 (6)	54.15 (9)		
Zuzana Hejnová (CZE)		53.93 (8)	53.92 (5)	53.50 (1)	
Rhonda Whyte (JAM)		54.29 (10)			
Sara Slott Petersen (DEN)			53.55 (3)	53.99 (3)	
Eilidh Doyle-Child (GBR)			54.09 (8)		54.39 (4)
Cassandra Tate (USA)				54.01 (4)	54.70 (9)
Kendra Harrison (USA)				54.09 (5)	
Kaliese Spencer (JAM)				54.15 (7)	53.41 (1)
Tiffany Williams (USA)				54.27 (9)	54.74 (10)
Denisa Rosolová (CZE)					54.54 (5)
Anna Titimets (UKR)					54.56 (6)
Irina Davydova (RUS)					54.60 (8)

WORLD RANKING ALL TIME:

1.	Yuliya Nosova-Pechonkina (RUS)	52.34 (2003)
2.	Melaine Walker (JAM)	52.42 (2009)
3.	Lashinda Demus (USA)	52.47 (2011)
4.	Kim Batten (USA)	52.61 (1995)
5.	Tonja Buford-Bailey (USA)	52.62 (1995)
6.	Dalilah Muhammad (USA)	52.64 (2017)
7.	Natalya Antyukh (RUS)	52.70 (2012)
8.	Sally Gunnell (GBR)	52.74 (1993)
9.	Shamier Little (USA)	52.75 (2017)
	Sydney McLaughlin (USA)	52.75 (2018)
11.	Fani Chalkia (GRE)	52.77 (2004)
12.	Sandra Farmer-Patrick (USA)	52.79 (1993)
	Kaliese Spencer (JAM)	52.79 (2011)
14.	Deon Hemmings (JAM)	52.82 (1996)
15.	Zuzana Hejnová (CZE)	52.83 (2013)
16.	Daimí Pernía (CUB)	52.89 (1999)
	Nezha Bidouane (MAR)	52.90 (1999)
18.	Marina Stepanova (URS)	52.94 (1986)
19.	Sheena Johnson (USA)	52.95 (2004)
	Kori Carter (USA)	52.95 (2017)
21.	Irina Privalova (RUS)	53.02 (2000)
22.	Tatyana Ledovskaya (URS)	53.11 (1991)
	Ashley Spencer (USA)	53.11 (2017)
24.	Georganne Moline (USA)	53.14 (2017)
25.	Debbie Flintoff (AUS)	53.17 (1988)
26.	Josanne Lucas (TTO)	53.20 (2009)
27.	Marie-Josée Perec (FRA)	53.21 (1995)
28.	Jana Pittman (AUS)	53.22 (2003)
29.	Sabine Busch (GDR)	53.24 (1987)
30.	Ionela Tirlea (ROM)	53.25 (1999)
31.	Tiffany Williams (USA)	53.28 (2007)
32.	Sandra Glover (USA)	53.32 (2005)
33.	Andrea Blackett (BAR)	53.36 (1999)
	Brenda Taylor (USA)	53.36 (2004)
35.	Tetyana Tereshchuk-Antipova (UKR)	53.37 (2004)
36.	Janieve Russell (JAM)	53.46 (2018)
37.	Janeene Vickers (USA)	53.47 (1991)
38.	Margarita Ponomariova (RUS)	53.48 (1993)
39.	Sara Slott Petersen (DEN)	53.55 (2016)
40.	Cornelia Feuerbach (GDR)	53.58 (1987)
41.	Ellen Fiedler (GDR)	53.63 (1988)
42.	Perri Shakes-Drayton (GBR)	53.67 (2013)
43.	Vanya Stambolova (BUL)	53.68 (2011)
44.	Yekaterina Bikert (RUS)	53.72 (2004)
45.	Myrtle Bothma (RSA)	53.74 (1986)
	Ristananna Tracey (JAM)	53.74 (2017)

3000 m Steeple-chase Women

EUROPEAN CHAMPIONSHIPS 2018: 12-8-2018:

1. Gesa-Felicitas Krause (GER)(9.33.51) 9.19.80
2. Fabienne Schlumpf (SUI)   (9.32.32) 9.22.29
3. Karoline Grövdal (NOR)   (9.34.23) 9.24.46
4. Luiza Gega (ALB)   (9.33.11) 9.24.78
5. Adva Cohen (ISR)   (9.36.13) 9.29.74
6. Elena Burkard (GER)   (9.34.63) 9.29.76
7. Anna Emilie Möller (DEN)(9.34.46) 9.31.66
8. Irene Sanchez (ESP)   (9.34.69) 9.31.84
9. Ophélie Cl.-Boxberger (FRA)(9.34.50) 9.31.84
10. Rosic Clarke (GBR)   (9.33.78) 9.32.15
11. Marusa Mismas (SLO)   (9.34.28) 9.34.50
12. Nataliya Strebkova (UKR)   (9.37.28) 9.40.03
13. Viktória Gyürkés (HUN)   (9.38.56) 9.40.41
14. Emma Oudiou (FRA)   (9.36.15) 9.43.26
15. Isabel Mattuzzi (ITA)   (9.34.02) 9.43.90
----
16. Martina Merlo (ITA)   9.41.05
17. Alicja Konieczek (POL)   9.41.16
18. Jana Sussmann (GER)   9.41.18
19. Janica Rauma (FIN)   9.41.70
20. Maria José Pérez (ESP)   9.44.72
21. Chiara Scherrer (SUI)   9.47.46
22. Francesca Bertoni (ITA)   9.47.75
23. Sviatlana Kudzelich (BLR)   9.47.89
24. Matylda Kowal (POL)   9.49.27
25. Lucie Sekanová (CZE)   9.50.38
26. Özlem Kaya (TUR)   9.50.80
27. Antje Möldner-Schmidt (GER)   9.52.79
28. Zita Kácser (HUN)   9.53.36
29. Katarzyna Kowalska (POL)   9.54.83
30. Caroline Högardh (SWE)   9.55.61
31. Irene van der Reijken (NED)   9.57.10

WORLD RANKING 2018:

1. Beatrice Chepkoech (KEN)   8.44.32(Mon)
2. Norah Jeruto (KEN)   8.59.62(Bru)
3. Courtney Frerichs (USA)   9.00.85(Mon)
4. Hyvin Kiyeng (KEN)   9.01.60(Bru)
5. Celliphine Chepteek Chespol (KEN) 9.01.82(Par)
6. Emma Coburn (USA)   9.05.06(Mon)
7. Peruth Chemutai (UGA)   9.07.94(Mon)
8. Roseline Chepngetich (KEN)   9.08.23(Mon)
9. Colleen Quigley (USA)   9.10.27(Ber)
10. Daisy Jepkemei (KEN)   9.10.71(Mon)
11. Winfred Mutile Yavi (BRN)   9.10.74(Mon)
12. Aisha Praught (JAM)   9.14.09(Bru)
13. Yekaterina Ivonina (RUS)   9.16.68
14. Karoline Bjerkeli Grövdal (NOR)   9.18.36(Mon)
15. Gesa Felicitas Krause (GER)   9.19.80(ECh)
16. Purity Kirui (KEN)   9.21.34(Sha)
17. Luiza Gega (ALB)   9.22.00(Rom)
18. Fabienne Schlumpf (SUI)   9.22.29(ECh)
19. Joan Chepkemoi (KEN)   9.22.85(Sha)
20. Mary Wanjiru (KEN)   9.23.4
21. Genevieve Gregson-Lacaze (AUS)   9.23.69(Ber)
22. Marusa Mismas (SLO)   9.28.61(Ber)
23. Mercy Chepkurui (KEN)   9.29.42
24. Adva Cohen (ISR)   9.29.74(ECh)
25. Elena Burkard (GER)   9.29.76(ECh)
26. Caroline Tuigong (KEN)   9.30.62(Ost)
27. Habiba Ghribi (TUN)   9.31.36(Rom)
28. Anna Emilie Möller (DEN)   9.31.66(ECh)
29. Irene Sánchez (ESP)   9.31.84(ECh)
     Ophélie Claude-Boxberger (FRA)   9.31.84(ECh)
31. Rosie Clarke (GBR)   9.32.08(Rom)
32. Naomi Chepkemoi (KEN)   9.32.3
33. Mel Lawrence (USA)   9.32.68
34. Fancy Cherono (KEN)   9.32.85(Ber)
35. Isabel Mattuzzi (ITA)   9.34.02(ECh)
36. Geneviève Lalonde (CAN)   9.35.19
37. Viktória Gyürkés (HUN)   9.35.42(Ber)
38. Özlem Kaya (TUR)   9.35.47(Ber)
39. Weynshet Ansa (ETH)   9.35.59(Ost)

Commonwealth Games, Gold Coast, 11-4-2018:

1.	Aisha Praught (JAM)	9.21.00
2.	Celliphine Chepteek Chespol (KEN)	9.22.61
3.	Purity Kirui (KEN)	9.25.74
4.	Rosie Clarke (GBR)	9.36.29
5.	Genevieve Lacaze (CAN)	9.42.69
6.	Fancy Cherono (KEN)	9.46.27
7.	Geneviève Lalonde (CAN)	9.46.68

Shanghai, 12-5-2018:

1.	Beatrice Chepkoech (KEN)	9.07.27
2.	Norah Jeruto (KEN)	9.09.30
3.	Daisy Jepkemei (KEN)	9.15.56
4.	Roseline Chepngetich (KEN)	9.21.05
5.	Purity Kirui (KEN)	9.21.34
6.	Joan Chepkemoi (KEN)	9.22.85
7.	Peruth Chemutai (UGA)	9.22.94
8.	Winfred Mutile Yavi (BRN)	9.44.02
9.	Caren Chebet (KEN)	9.46.58
10.	Fancy Cherono (KEN)	9.47.48
11.	Ann Gathoni (KEN)	9.47.71
12.	Birtukan Adamu (ETH)	9.48.38

Rome, 31-5-2018:

1.	Hyvin Kiyeng (KEN)	9.04.96
2.	Celliphine Chepteek Chespol (KEN)	9.05.14
3.	Norah Jeruto (KEN)	9.07.17
4.	Emma Coburn (USA)	9.08.13
5.	Beatrice Chepkoech (KEN)	9.15.85
6.	Winfred Mutile Yavi (BRN)	9.16.38
7.	Daisy Jepkemei (KEN)	9.18.44
8.	Aisha Praught (JAM)	9.19.33
9.	Luiza Gega (ALB)	9.22.00
10.	Habiba Ghribi (TUN)	9.31.36
11.	Purity Kirui (KEN)	9.31.96
12.	Rosie Clarke (GBR)	9.32.08
13.	Ophélie Claude-Boxberger (FRA)	9.34.43
14.	Gesa Felicitas Krause (GER)	9.39.52
15.	Tugba Güvenc (TUR)	9.39.68

Oslo, 7-6-2018:

1.	Hyvin Kiyeng (KEN)	9.09.63
2.	Emma Coburn (USA)	9.09.70
3.	Daisy Jepkemei (KEN)	9.16.87
4.	Courtney Frerichs (USA)	9.20.84
5.	Aisha Praught (JAM)	9.23.33
6.	Winfred Mutile Yavi (BRN)	9.27.76
7.	Karoline Bjerkeli Grövdal (NOR)	9.29.94
8.	Purity Kirui (KEN)	9.39.23
9.	Rosie Clarke (GBR)	9.42.80
10.	Birtukan Adamu (ETH)	9.58.48

Ostrava, 13-6-2018:

1.	Norah Jeruto (KEN)	9.11.33
2.	Peruth Chemutai (UGA)	9.16.89
3.	Daisy Jepkemei (KEN)	9.23.70
4.	Caroline Tuigong (KEN)	9.30.62
5.	Joan Chepkemoi (KEN)	9.30.70
6.	Marusa Mismas (SLO)	9.35.49
7.	Purity Kirui (KEN)	9.35.51
8.	Weynshet Ansa (ETH)	9.35.59
9.	Ophélie Claude-Boxberger (FRA)	9.35.94
10.	Viktória Gyürkes (HUN)	9.38.23
11.	Katarzyna Kowalska (POL)	9.43.38
12.	Antje Möldner-Schmidt (GER)	9.43.38
13.	Maya Rehberg (GER)	9.44.82
14.	Anna Emilie Möller (DEN)	9.45.32
15.	Matylda Kowal (POL)	9.47.65
16.	Birtukan Adamu (ETH)	9.48.68

KEN Trials, Nairobi, 22-6-2018:

1.	Beatrice Chepkoech	9.23.73
2.	Celliphine Chepteek Chespol	9.28.36
3.	Nancy Cherono	9.37.62
4.	Joan Chepkemboi	9.42.99
5.	Mercy Wanjiru	9.45.62
6.	Caroline Tuigong	9.55.61
7.	Naomi Chepkemoi	9.58.40
8.	Elizabeth Mueni	10.07.61

US CHAMPIONSHIPS, Des Moines, 23-6-2018:

1. Emma Coburn   9.17.70
2. Courtney Frerichs   9.18.69
3. Mel Lawrence   9.33.30
4. Shalaya Kipp   9.41.24

Paris, 30-6-2018:

1. Beatrice Chepkoech (KEN)   8.59.36
2. Celliphine Chepteek Chespol (KEN) 9.01.82
3. Hyvin Kiyeng (KEN)   9.03.86
4. Norah Jeruto (KEN)   9.04.17
5. Winfred Mutile Yavi (BRN)   9.12.74
6. Roseline Chepngetich (KEN)   9.17.08
7. Daisy Jepkemei (KEN)   9.17.35
8. Aisha Praught (JAM)   9.20.89
9. Karoline Bjerkeli Grövdal (NOR)   9.28.50
10. Fabienne Schlumpf (SUI)   9.39.89
11. Elena Burkard (GER)   9.40.18
12. Geneviève Lalonde (CAN)   9.40.34

Tampere, 13-7-2018:

1. Celliphine Chepteek Chespol (KEN) 9.12.78
2. Peruth Chemutai (UGA)   9.18.87
3. Winfred Mutile Yavi (BRN)   9.23.47
4. Mercy Chepkurui (KEN)   9.43.65
5. Agrie Belachew (ETH)   9.44.79
6. Ethlemahu Sintayehu (ETH)   9.50.96

Monaco, 20-7-2018:

1. Beatrice Chepkoech (KEN)   8.44.32**WR**
2. Courtney Frerichs (USA)   9.00.85
3. Hyvin Kiyeng (CHN)   9.04.41
4. Emma Coburn (USA)   9.05.06
5. Noah Jeruto (KEN)   9.07.20
6. Peruth Chemutai (UGA)   9.07.94
7. Roseline Chepngetich (KEN)   9.08.23
8. Daisy Jepkemei (KEN)   9.10.71
9. Winfred Mutile Yavi (BRN)   9.10.74
10. Celliphine Chepteek Chespol (KEN) 9.12.05
11. Karoline Bjerkeli Grövdal (NOR)   9.18.36
12. Colleen Quigley (USA)   9.20.99
13. Aisha Praught (JAM)   9.25.48
14. Rosie Clarke (GBR)   9.38.71

Brussels, 31-8-2018:

1. Beatrice Chepkoech (KEN)   8.55.10
2. Noah Jeruto (KEN)   8.59.62
3. Hyvin Kiyeng (KEN)   9.01.60
4. Emma Coburn (USA)   9.06.51
5. Celliphine Chepteek Chespol (KEN) 9.06.75
6. Courtney Frerichs (USA)   9.07.07
7. Peruth Chemutai (UGA)   9.13.58
8. Aisha Praught (JAM)   9.14.09
9. Winfred Mutile Yavi (BRN)   9.14.52
10. Daisy Jepkemei (KEN)   9.17.08
11. Roseline Chepngetich (KEN)   9.28.94
12. Karoline Bjerkeli Grövdal (NOR)   9.38.34

Berlin, 2-9-2018:

1. Colleen Quigley (USA)   9.10.27
2. Daisy Jepkemei (KEN)   9.14.66
3. Genevieve Lacaze (AUS)   9.23.69
4. Marusa Mismas (SLO)   9.28.61
5. Fancy Cherono (KEN)   9.32.85
6. Ophélie Claude-Boxberger (FRA)   9.33.47
7. Viktoria Gyürkes (HUN)   9.35.42
8. Özlem Kaya (TUR)   9.35.47
9. Jana Sussmann (GER)   9.36.26
10. Rosie Clarke (GBR)   9.40.00
11. Lucie Sekanova (CZE)   9.47.14

CONTINENTAL CUP, Ostrava, 9-9-2018:

1. Beatrice Chepkoech (AFR)   9.07.92
2. Courtney Frerichs (AME)   9.15.22
3. Winfred Mutile Yavi (ASI)   9.17.86
4. Anna Emilie Möller (EUR)   9.42.57

OVERVIEW WORLD OUTDOOR CHAMPIONSHIP FINALISTS OF PAST 6 YEARS

	Wch 17	OG 16	Wch 15	Wch 13
Emma Coburn (USA)	9.02.58 (1)	9.07.63 (3)	9.21.78 (5)	
Courtney Frerichs (USA)	9.03.77 (2)	9.22.87 (11)		
Hyvin Kiyeng Jepkemoi (KEN)	9.04.03 (3)	9.07.12 (2)	9.19.11 (1)	9.22.05 (6)
Beatrice Chepkoech (KEN)	9.10.45 (4)	9.16.05 (4)		
Ruth Jebet (BRN)	9.13.96 (5)	8.59.75 (1)	9.33.41 (11)	
Celliphine Chespol (KEN)	9.15.04 (6)			
Etenesh Diro (ETH)	9.22.46 (7)	9.38.77 (15)		9.16.97 (5)
Winfred Mutile Yavi (BRN)	9.22.67 (8)			
Gesa Felicitas Krause (GER)	9.23.87 (9)	9.18.41 (6)	9.19.25 (3)	9.37.11 (9)
Purity Cherotich Kirui (KEN)	9.25.62 (10)			
Belén Casetta (ARG)	9.25.99 (11)			
Genevieve Lacaze (AUS)	9.26.25 (12)	9.21.21 (9)		
Genevieve Lalonde (CAN)	9.29.99 (13)	9.41.88 (16)		
Aisha Praught (JAM)	dsq (14)	9.34.20 (14)		
Birtukan Fente (ETH)	dns (15)			
Sofia Assefa (ETH)		9.17.15 (5)	9.20.01 (4)	9.12.84 (3)
Madeline Heiner Hills (AUS)		9.20.38 (7)		
Colleen Quigley (USA)		9.21.10 (8)	9.34.29 (12)	
Lalita Shivaji Babar (IND)		9.22.74 (10)	9.29.64 (8)	
Habiba Ghribi (TUN)		9.28.75 (12)	9.19.24 (2)	
Lydia Chebet Rotich (KEN)		9.29.90 (13)		
Sara Louise Treacy (IRL)		9.52.70 (17)		
Fabienne Schlumpf (SUI)		9.59.30 (18)		
Hiwot Ayalew (ETH)			9.24.27 (6)	9.15.25 (4)
Virginia Nganga (KEN)			9.26.21 (7)	
Stephanie Garcia (USA)			9.31.06 (9)	
Salima Elouali Alami (MAR)			9.32.15 (10)	10.08.36 (15)
Özlem Kaya (TUR)			9.34.66 (13)	
Fadwa Sidi Madane (MAR)			9.41.45 (14)	
Roseline Chepngetich (KEN)			9.46.08 (15)	
Milcah Chemos Cheywa (KEN)				9.11.65 (1)
Lydia Chepkurui (KEN)				9.12.55 (2)
Valentyna Zhudina (UKR)				9.33.73 (7)
Antje Möldner-Schmidt (GER)				9.34.06 (8)
Eilish McColgan (GBR)				9.37.33 (10)
Diana Martin (ESP)				9.38.30 (11)
Natalya Gorchakova (RUS)				9.38.57 (12)
Ancuta Bobocel (ROM)				9.53.35 (13)
Silvia Danekova (BUL)				9.58.57 (14)

OVERVIEW TOP 10 WORLD OUTDOOR RANKINGS OF PAST 5 YEARS

	2018	2017	2016	2015	2014
Beatrice Chepkoech (KEN)	8.44.32 (1)	8.59.84 (3)	9.10.86 (4)		
Norah Jeruto Tanui (KEN)	8.59.62 (2)	9.03.70 (6)			
Courtney Frerichs (USA)	9.00.85 (3)	9.03.77 (7)			
Hyvin Kiyeng Jepkemoi (KEN)	9.01.60 (4)	9.00.12 (4)	9.00.01 (2)	9.10.15 (2)	9.22.58 (9)
Celliphine Chespol (KEN)	9.01.82 (5)	8.58.78 (2)			
Emma Coburn (USA)	9.05.06 (6)	9.02.58 (5)	9.07.63 (3)	9.15.59 (6)	9.11.42 (3)
Peruth Chemutai (UGA)	9.07.94 (7)				
Roseline Chepngetich (KEN)	9.08.23 (8)				
Colleen Quigley (USA)	9.10.27 (9)				
Daisy Jepkemei (KEN)	9.10.71 (10)				
Ruth Jebet (BRN)		8.55.29 (1)	8.52.78 (1)		9.20.55 (6)
Sofia Assefa (ETH)		9.07.06 (8)	9.13.09 (5)	9.12.63 (3)	9.11.39 (2)
Gesa Felicitas Krause (GER)		9.11.85 (9)	9.18.41 (8)	9.19.25 (8)	
Etenesh Diro (ETH)		9.13.25 (10)	9.16.87 (7)		9.19.71 (5)
Genevieve Lacaze (AUS)			9.14.28 (6)		
Habiba Ghribi (TUN)			9.18.71 (9)	9.05.36 (1)	9.15.23 (4)
Leah O'Connor (USA)			9.18.85 (10)		
Virginia Nganga (KEN)				9.13.85 (4)	
Hiwot Ayalew (ETH)				9.14.73 (5)	9.10.64 (1)
Purity Kirui (KEN)				9.17.74 (7)	9.23.43 (10)
Lydia Chepkurui (KEN)				9.20.44 (9)	
Salima Elouali Alami (MAR)				9.20.64 (10)	9.21.24 (7)
Milcah Cheywa (KEN)					9.21.91 (8)

WORLD RANKING ALL TIME:

1.	Beatrice Chepkoech (KEN)	8.44.32 (2018)
2.	Ruth Jebet (BRN)	8.52.78 (2016)
3.	Celliphine Chepteek Chespol (KEN)	8.58.78 (2017)
4.	Gulnara Galkina (RUS)	8.58.81 (2008)
5.	Norah Jeruto Tanui (KEN)	8.59.62 (2018)
6.	Hyvin Kiyeng Jepkemoi (KEN)	9.00.01 (2016)
7.	Courtney Frerichs (USA)	9.00.85 (2018)
8.	Emma Coburn (USA)	9.02.58 (2017)
9.	Habiba Ghribi (TUN)	9.05.36 (2015)
10.	Yekaterina Volkova (RUS)	9.06.57 (2007)
11.	Sofia Assefa (ETH)	9.07.06 (2017)
12.	Milcah Cheywa Chemos (KEN)	9.07.14 (2012)
13.	Eunice Jepkorir (KEN)	9.07.41 (2008)
14.	Peruth Chemutai (UGA)	9.07.94 (2018)
15.	Roseline Chepngetich (KEN)	9.08.23 (2018)
16.	Yuliya Zaripova (RUS)	9.08.39 (2009)
17.	Tatyana Petrova (RUS)	9.09.19 (2007)
18.	Marta Domínguez (ESP)	9.09.39 (2009)
19.	Hiwot Ayalew (ETH)	9.09.61 (2012)
20.	Colleen Quigley (USA)	9.10.27 (2018)
21.	Daisy Jepkemei (KEN)	9.10.71 (2018)
22.	Winfred Mutile Yavi (BRN)	9.10.74 (2018)
23.	Gesa Felicitas Krause (GER)	9.11.85 (2017)
24.	Jennifer Simpson (USA)	9.12.50 (2009)
25.	Lydia Chepkurui (KEN)	9.12.55 (2013)
26.	Ruth Bosibori Nyangau (KEN)	9.13.16 (2009)
27.	Gladys Jerotich Kipkemoi (KEN)	9.13.22 (2010)
28.	Etenesh Diro (ETH)	9.13.25 (2017)
29.	Karoline Bjerkeli Grövdal (NOR)	9.13.35 (2017)
30.	Gülcan Mingir (TUR)	9.13.53 (2012)
31.	Virginia Nyambura Nganga (KEN)	9.13.85 (2015)
32.	Aisha Praught (JAM)	9.14.09 (2018)
33.	Genevieve Gregson-Lacaze (AUS)	9.14.28 (2016)
34.	Dorcus Inzikuru (UGA)	9.15.04 (2005)
35.	Alesya Turava (BLR)	9.16.51 (2002)
36.	Yekaterina Ivonina (RUS)	9.16.68 (2018)
37.	Cristina Casandra (ROM)	9.16.85 (2008)
38.	Mercy Wanjiku Njoroge (KEN)	9.16.94 (2011)
39.	Wioletta Frankiewicz (POL)	9.17.15 (2006)
40.	Purity Kirui (KEN)	9.17.74 (2015)
41.	Zemzem Ahmed (ETH)	9.17.85 (2008)
42.	Lydia Chebet Rotich (KEN)	9.18.03 (2010)
43.	Donna MacFarlane (AUS)	9.18.35 (2008)
44.	Antje Möldner-Schmidt (GER)	9.18.54 (2009)
	Jessica Augusto (POR)	9.18.54 (2010)

High Jump Women

EUROPEAN CHAMPIONSHIPS 2018: 10-8-2018:

1.	Maria Lasitskene (ANA)		2.00
2.	Mirela Demireva (BUL)		2.00
3.	Marie-Laurence Jungfleisch (GER)		1.96
4.	Airine Palsyte (LTU)		1.96
5.	Kateryna Tabashnyk (UKR)		1.94
6.	Michaela Hruba (CZE)		1.91
7.	Morgan Lake (GBR)		1.91
8.	Alessia Trost (ITA)		1.91
9.	Yuliya Levchenko (UKR)		1.91
10.	Oksana Okuneva (UKR)		1.87
	Ana Simic (CRO)	(1.90)	1.87
12.	Karina Taranda (BLR)		1.87
13.	Erika Kinsey (SWE)	(1.90)	1.87
14.	Imke Onnen (GER)	(1.90)	1.82

15.	Elena Vallortigara (ITA)	1.86
16.	Sofie Skoog (SWE)	1.86
17.	Ella Junnila (FIN)	1.86
18.	Nikki Manson (GBR)	1.81
	Lada Pejchalová (CZE)	1.81
	Desirée Rossit (ITA)	1.81
	Daniela Stanciu (ROM)	1.81
	Marija Vukovic (MNT)	1.81
23.	Claire Orcel (BEL)	1.81
24.	Tonje Angelsen (NOR)	1.81
25.	Eierlin Haas (EST)	1.76

WORLD RANKING 2018:

1.	Maria Lasitskene (ANA)	2.04(Par)
2.	Elena Vallortigara (ITA)	2.02(Lon)
3.	Nafissatou Thiam (BEL)	2.01(Gtz)
4.	Mirela Demireva (BUL)	2.00(Sto)
5.	Anna Chicherova (RUS)	1.98
6.	Yuliya Levchenko (UKR)	1.97(Par)
	Morgan Lake (GBR)	1.97(Bir)
8.	Levern Spencer (LCA)	1.96
	Marie-Laurence Jungfleisch (GER)	1.96
	Kateryna Tabashnyk (UKR)	1.96
	Vashti Cunningham (USA)	1.96(Lon)
	Ariné Palsyté (LTU)	1.96(ECh)
	Svetlana Radzivil (UZB)	1.96
14.	Yaroslava Mahuchikh (UKR)	1.95
15.	Yuliya Chumachenko (UKR)	1.94
	Erika Kinsey (USA)	1.94
	Oksana Okuneva (UKR)	1.94
	Nadezhda Dusanova (UZB)	1.94(Jak)

WORLD INDOOR CHAMPIONSHIPS: 1-3-2018:

1.	Mariya Lasitskene (ANA)	2.01
2.	Vashti Cunningham (USA)	1.93
3.	Alessia Trost (ITA)	1.93
4.	Morgan Lake (GBR)	1.93
5.	Yuliya Levchenko (UKR)	1.89
6.	Mirela Demireva (BUL)	1.89
7.	Iryna Gerashchenko (UKR)	1.84
	Erika Kinsey (SWE)	1.84
	Inika McPherson (USA)	1.84
10.	Michaela Hrubá (CZE)	1.84
	Sofie Skoog (SWE)	1.84
	Levern Spencer (LCA)	1.84
13.	Yorgelis Rodríguez (CUB)	1.84

WORLD INDOOR RANKING 2018:

1.	Mariya Lasitskene (ANA)	2.04
2.	Yuliya Levchenko (UKR)	1.97
	Vashti Cunningham (USA)	1.97
4.	Levern Spencer (LCA)	1.95
	Mirela Demireva (BUL)	1.95
6.	Iryna Gerashchenko (UKR)	1.93
	Michaela Hrubá (CZE)	1.93
	Katarina Johnson-Thompson (GBR)	1.93
	Yuliya Chumachenko (UKR)	1.93
	Alessia Trost (ITA)	1.93
	Morgan Lake (GBR)	1.93

OVERVIEW WORLD OUTDOOR CHAMPIONSHIP FINALISTS OF PAST 6 YEARS

	Wch 17	OG 16	Wch 15	Wch 13
Maria Lasitskene-Kuchina (RUS)	2.03 (1)		2.01 (1)	
Yuliia Levchenko (UKR)	2.01 (2)			
Kamila Licwinko (POL)	1.99 (3)	1.93 (9)	1.99 (4)	
Marie-Laurence Jungfleisch (GER)	1.95 (4)	1.93 (7)	1.99 (6)	NM (13)
Katarina Johnson-Thompson (GBR)	1.95 (5)			
Morgan Lake (GBR)	1.95 (6)	1.93 (10)		
Mirela Demireva (BUL)	1.92 (7)	1.97 (2)	1.88 (9)	
Airiné Palsyté (LTU)	1.92 (7)	1.88 (13)		1.89 (11)
Inika McPherson (USA)	1.92 (9)	1.93 (10)		
Vashti Cunningham (USA)	1.92 (10)	1.88 (13)		
Michaela Hrubá (CZE)	1.92 (11)			
Ruth Beitia (ESP)	1.88 (12)	1.97 (1)	1.99 (5)	1.97 (3)
Blanka Vlasic (CRO)		1.97 (3)	2.01 (2)	
Chaunté Lowe (USA)		1.97 (4)		
Alessia Trost (ITA)		1.93 (5)		1.93 (7)
Levern Spencer (LCA)		1.93 (6)	1.88 (12)	1.89 (11)
Sofie Skoog (SWE)		1.93 (7)		
Iryna Gerashchenko (UKR)		1.93 (10)		
Svetlana Radzivil (UZB)		1.88 (13)	1.88 (9)	
Desiree Rossit (ITA)		1.88 (16)		
Ayxandria Treasure (CAN)		1.88 (17)		
Anna Chicherova (RUS)			2.01 (3)	1.97 (3)
Jeanelle Scheper (LCA)			1.92 (7)	
Eleanor Patterson (AUS)			1.92 (8)	
Ana Simic (CRO)			1.88 (9)	
Doreen Amata (NGR)			1.88 (12)	
Svetlana Shkolina (RUS)				2.03 (1)
Brigetta Barrett (USA)				2.00 (2)
Emma Green Tregaro (SWE)				1.97 (5)
Justyna Kasprzycka (POL)				1.97 (6)
Kamila Stepaniuk (POL)				1.93 (7)
Irina Gordeeva (RUS)				1.93 (9)
Zheng Xingjuan (CHN)				1.93 (9)

OVERVIEW WORLD INDOOR CHAMPIONSHIP FINALISTS OF PAST 5 YEARS

	Wch 18	Wch 16	Wch 14
Marira Lasitskene-Kuchina (RUS)	2.01 (1)		2.00 (1)
Vashti Cunningham (USA)	1.93 (2)	1.96 (1)	
Alessia Trost (ITA)	1.93 (3)	1.93 (7)	
Morgan Lake (GBR)	1.93 (4)		
Yuliya Levchenko (UKR)	1.89 (5)		
Mirela Demireva (BUL)	1.89 (6)		
Iryna Gerashchenko (UKR)	1.84 (7)		
Erika Kinsey (SWE)	1.84 (7)	1.93 (8)	
Inika McPherson (USA)	1.84 (7)		
Michaela Hrubá (CZE)	1.84 (10)		
Sofie Skoog (SWE)	1.84 (10)	1.93 (5)	
Levern Spencer (LCA)	1.84 (10)		
Ruth Beitia (ESP)		1.96 (2)	2.00 (3)
Kamila Licwinko (POL)		1.96 (3)	2.00 (1)
Airiné Palsyté (LTU)		1.96 (4)	
Levern Spencer (LCA)		1.93 (5)	1.94 (7)
Doreen Amata (NGR)		1.89 (9)	
Lissa Labiche (SEY)		1.89 (10)	
Isobel Pooley (GBR)		1.89 (10)	
Justyna Kasprzycka (POL)			1.97 (4)
Emma Green Tregaro (SWE)			1.94 (5)
Blanka Vlasic (CRO)			1.94 (6)
Marie-Laurence Jungfleisch (GER)			1.90 (8)
Nafissatou Thiam (BEL)			1.90 (8)

OVERVIEW TOP 10 WORLD OUTDOOR RANKINGS OF PAST 5 YEARS

	2018	2017	2016	2015	2014
Maria Lasitskene-Kuchina (RUS)	2.04 (1)	2.06 (1)		2.01 (2)	2.00 (3)
Elena Vallortigara (ITA)	2.02 (2)				
Nafissatou Thiam (BEL)	2.01 (3)	1.98 (6)	1.98 (4)		1.97 (10)
Mirela Demireva (BUL)	2.00 (4)		1.97 (7)		
Anna Chicherova (RUS)	1.98 (5)			2.03 (1)	2.01 (1)
Yuliia Levchenko (UKR)	1.97 (6)	2.01 (2)			
Morgan Lake (GBR)	1.97 (6)	1.96 (8)			
Levern Spencer (LCA)	1.96 (8)				
Marie-Laurence Jungfleisch (GER)	1.96 (8)	2.00 (3)	2.00 (2)	1.99 (5)	1.97 (10)
Kateryna Tabashnyk (UKR)	1.96 (8)	1.95 (10)			
Vashti Cunningham (USA)	1.96 (8)	1.99 (4)	1.97 (7)	1.96 (9)	
Airiné Palsyté (LTU)	1.96 (8)				1.98 (8)
Svetlana Radzivil (UZB)	1.96 (8)				
Kamila Licwinko (POL)		1.99 (4)	1.99 (3)	1.99 (5)	1.97 (10)
Oksana Okuneva (UKR)		1.97 (7)	1.97 (7)		1.98 (8)
Inika McPherson (USA)		1.96 (8)			2.00 (3)
Katarina Johnson-Thompson (GBR)		1.95 (10)	1.98 (4)		
Iryna Gerashchenko (UKR)		1.95 (10)			
Yorgelis Rodríguez (CUB)		1.95 (10)			
Chaunté Lowe (USA)			2.01 (1)		1.97 (10)
Ruth Beitia (ESP)			1.98 (4)	2.00 (4)	2.01 (1)
Desiree Rossit (ITA)			1.97 (7)		
Blanka Vlasic (CRO)			1.97 (7)	2.01 (2)	2.00 (3)
Erika Kinsey (SWE)				1.97 (7)	
Isobel Pooley (GBR)				1.97 (7)	
Eleanor Patterson (AUS)				1.96 (9)	
Jeanelle Scheper (LCA)				1.96 (9)	
Justyna Kasprzycka (POL)					1.99 (6)
Ana Simic (CRO)					1.99 (6)

OVERVIEW TOP 10 WORLD INDOOR RANKINGS OF PAST 5 YEARS

	2018	2017	2016	2015	2014
Mariya Lasitskene (RUS)	2.04 (1)	2.03 (1)		1.99 (2)	2.01 (1)
Yuliia Levchenko (UKR)	1.97 (2)	1.94 (7)			
Vashti Cunningham (USA)	1.97 (2)	1.96 (5)	1.99 (1)		
Levern Spencer (LCA)	1.95 (4)		1.95 (6)		
Mirela Demireva (BUL)	1.95 (4)				
Iryna Gerashchenko (UKR)	1.93 (6)	1.93 (9)			
Michaela Hrubá (CZE)	1.93 (6)		1.95 (6)		
Katarina Johnson-Thompson (GBR)	1.93 (6)			1.97 (4)	1.96 (9)
Yuliya Chumachenko (UKR)	1.93 (6)				
Alessia Trost (ITA)	1.93 (6)		1.95 (6)	1.97 (4)	1.96 (9)
Morgan Lake (GBR)	1.93 (6)				
Airiné Palsyté (LTU)		2.01 (2)	1.97 (4)	1.98 (3)	1.97 (5)
Ruth Beitia (ESP)		1.98 (3)	1.98 (2)	1.96 (6)	2.00 (2)
Kamila Licwinko (POL)		1.97 (4)	1.97 (4)	2.02 (1)	2.00 (2)
Nafissatou Thiam (BEL)		1.96 (5)			
Oksana Okuneva (UKR)		1.94 (7)			
Madeline Fagan (USA)		1.93 (9)			
Akela Jones (BAR)			1.98 (2)		
Blanka Vlasic (CRO)			1.95 (6)		2.00 (2)
Chaunté Lowe (USA)			1.95 (6)		
Marie-Laurence Jungfleisch (GER)			1.95 (6)		1.97 (5)
Irina Gordeeva (RUS)				1.96 (6)	
Svetlana Shkolina (RUS)				1.95 (8)	
Yana Maksimava (BLR)				1.95 (8)	
Ana Simic (CRO)				1.95 (8)	
Emma Green Tregaro (SWE)					1.97 (5)
Justyna Kasprzycka (POL)					1.97 (5)
Svetlana Radzivil (UZB)					1.96 (9)

WORLD RANKING OUTDOOR ALL TIME:

1.	Stefka Kostadinova (BUL)	2.09 (1987)
2.	Blanka Vlasic (CRO)	2.08 (2009)
3.	Lyudmila Andonova (BUL)	2.07 (1984)
	Anna Chicherova (RUS)	2.07 (2011)
5.	Kajsa Bergqvist (SWE)	2.06 (2003)
	Hestrie Cloete (RSA)	2.06 (2003)
	Yelena Slesarenko (RUS)	2.06 (2004)
	Ariane Friedrich (GER)	2.06 (2009)
	Mariya Lasitskene (RUS)	2.06 (2017)
10.	Tamara Bykova (URS)	2.05 (1984)
	Heike Henkel (GER)	2.05 (1991)
	Inga Babakova (UKR)	2.05 (1995)
	Tia Hellebaut (BEL)	2.05 (2008)
	Chaunte Lowe (USA)	2.05 (2010)
15.	Silvia Costa (CUB)	2.04 (1989)
	Venelina Veneva (BUL)	2.04 (2001)
	Irina Gordeyeva (RUS)	2.04 (2012)
	Brigetta Barrett (USA)	2.04 (2013)
19.	Ulrike Meyfarth (FRG)	2.03 (1983)
	Louise Ritter (USA)	2.03 (1988)
	Tatyana Babashkina (RUS)	2.03 (1995)
	Niki Bakogianni (RUS)	2.03 (1996)
	Antonietta Di Martino (ITA)	2.03 (2007)
	Svetlana Shkolina (RUS)	2.03 (2012)
25.	Yelena Yelesina (URS)	2.02 (1990)
	Monica Iagar (ROM)	2.02 (1998)
	Marina Kuptsova (RUS)	2.02 (2003)
	Vita Styopina (UKR)	2.02 (2004)
	Ruth Beitia (ESP)	2.02 (2007)
	Elena Vallortigara (ITA)	2.02 (2018)
31.	Sara Simeoni (ITA)	2.01 (1978)
	Olga Turchak (URS)	2.01 (1986)
	Desiré du Plessis (RSA)	2.01 (1986)
	Heike Balck (GER)	2.01 (1989)
	Alina Astafei (GER)	2.01 (1995)
	Hanne Haugland (NOR)	2.01 (1997)
	Yelena Gulyayeva (RUS)	2.01 (1998)
	Vita Palamar (UKR)	2.01 (2003)
	Amy Acuff (USA)	2.01 (2003)
	Irina Mikhalchenko (UKR)	2.01 (2004)
	Emma Green (SWE)	2.01 (2010)
	Yuliya Levchenko (UKR)	2.01 (2017)
	Nafissatou Thiam (BEL)	2.01 (2018)
44 – 63:		
	Rosemarie Ackermann (GDR) et al.	2.00 (1977)

WORLD RANKING INDOOR ALL TIME:

1.	Kajsa Bergqvist (SWE)	2.08 (2006)
2.	Heike Henkel (GER)	2.07 (1992)
3.	Stefka Kostadinova (BUL)	2.06 (1988)
	Blanka Vlasic (CRO)	2.06 (2010)
	Anna Chicherova (RUS)	2.06 (2012)
6.	Tia Hellebaut (BEL)	2.05 (2007)
	Ariane Friedrich (GER)	2.05 (2009)
8.	Alina Astafei (GER)	2.04 (1995)
	Yelena Slesarenko (RUS)	2.04 (2004)
	Antonietta Di Martino (ITA)	2.04 (2011)
	Mariya Lasitskene (RUS)	2.04 (2018)
12.	Tamara Bykova (URS)	2.03 (1983)
	Monica Iagar (ROM)	2.03 (1999)
	Marina Kuptsova (RUS)	2.03 (2002)
15.	Susanne Beyer (GDR)	2.02 (1987)
	Venelina Veneva (BUL)	2.02 (2002)
	Yelena Yelesina (RUS)	2.02 (2003)
	Chaunte Lowe (USA)	2.02 (2012)
	Kamila Licwinko (POL)	2.02 (2015)
20.	Gabriele Günz (GDR)	2.01 (1988)
	Ioamnet Quintero (CUB)	2.01 (1993)
	Tisha Waller (USA)	2.01 (1998)
	Ruth Beitia (ESP)	2.01 (2007)
	Vita Palamar (UKR)	2.01 (2008)
	Irina Gordeyeva (RUS)	2.01 (2009)
	Airiné Palsyté (LTU)	2.01 (2017)
27.	Coleen Sommer (USA)	2.00 (1982)
	Emilia Dragieva (BUL)	2.00 (1987)
	Lyudmila Avdeyenko (URS)	2.00 (1988)
	Larisa Kositsyna (URS)	2.00 (1988)
	Inga Babakova (UKR)	2.00 (1993)
	Yelena Gulyayeva (RUS)	2.00 (1994)
	Britta Bilac (SLO)	2.00 (1994)
	Tatyana Babashkina (RUS)	2.00 (1995)
	Hanne Haugland (NOR)	2.00 (1995)
	Yuliya Lyakhova (RUS)	2.00 (1999)
	Viktoriya Seryogina (RUS)	2.00 (2003)
	Svetlana Lapina (RUS)	2.00 (2003)
	Daniela Rath (GER)	2.00 (2004)
	Yekaterina Savchenko (RUS)	2.00 (2008)
	Viktoriya Klyugina (RUS)	2.00 (2009)
	Svetlana Shkolina (RUS)	2.00 (2010)
	Meike Kröger (GER)	2.00 (2010)
	Alessia Trost (ITA)	2.00 (2013)

Pole Vault Women

EUROPEAN CHAMPIONSHIPS 2018: 9-8-2018:

1. Ekateríni Stefanídi (GRE) — 4.85
2. Nikoléta Kiriakopoúlou (GRE) — 4.80
3. Holly Bradshaw (GBR) — 4.75
4. Anzhelika Sidorova (ANA) — 4.70
5. Ninon Guillon-Romarin (FRA) — 4.65
6. Angelica Bengtsson (SWE) — 4.65
7. Iryna Zhuk (BLR) — 4.55
8. Maryna Kylypko (UKR) — 4.45
9. Carolin Hingst (GER) (4.35) 4.30
   Amálie Svábíková (CZE) (4.45) 4.30
11. Olga Mullina (ANA) (4.45) 4.30
    Eléni-Klaoúdia Pólak (GRE) (4.45) NM

----

13. Lisa Gunnarsson (SWE) — 4.35
    Minna Nikkanen (FIN) — 4.35
15. Lucy Bryan (GBR) — 4.35
    Marion Lotout (FRA) — 4.35
17. Wilma Murto (FIN) — 4.35
    Jacqueline Otchere (GER) — 4.35
19. Maialen Axpe (ESP) — 4.35
20. Angelica Moser (SUI) — 4.20
    Justyna Smietanka (POL) — 4.20
22. Monica Clemente (ESP) — 4.20
    Lene Retzius (NOR) — 4.20
24. Molly Caudery (GBR) — 4.20
25. Femke Pluim (NED) — 4.20
    Tina Sutej (SLO) — 4.20
27. Stefanie Dauber (GER) — 4.00

WORLD RANKING 2018:

1. Sandi Morris (USA) — 4.95
2. Eliza McCartney (NZL) — 4.94
3. Jennifer Suhr (USA) — 4.93(Aus)
4. Katerina Stefanidi (GRE) — 4.87(Zü)
5. Anzhelika Sidorova (ANA) — 4.85(Mon)
6. Holly Bradshaw (GBR) — 4.80
   Yarisley Silva (CUB) — 4.80(Mon)
   Nikoleta Kiriakopoulou (GRE) — 4.80(ECh)
   Katie Nageotte (USA) — 4.80
10. Alysha Newman (CAN) — 4.75(GC)
    Ninon Guillon-Romarin (FRA) — 4.75(Mon)
12. Angelica Bengtsson (SWE) — 4.73
13. Nina Kennedy (AUS) — 4.71
14. Robeilys Peinado (VEN) — 4.70
15. Iryna Zhuk (BLR) — 4.67(Sze)
16. Lexi Jacobus (USA) — 4.65(Kno)
    Olga Mullina (ANA) — 4.65
18. Emily Grove (USA) — 4.61(CV)
    Kristen Hixson (USA) — 4.61(Osa)
    Megan Clark (USA) — 4.61(CV)
21. Lisa Gunnarsson (SWE) — 4.60(Aus)
    Morgann Leleux Romero (USA) — 4.60
    Jacqueline Otchere (GER) — 4.60
    Li Ling (CHN) — 4.60
    Wilma Murto (FIN) — 4.60
26. Juliana de Menis (BRA) — 4.56
27. Olivia Gruver (USA) — 4.55(NCA)
    Annie Rhodes-Johnigan (USA) — 4.55(USC)
    Aksana Gataullina (ANA) — 4.55
30. Molly Caudery (GBR) — 4.53
31. Tori Hoggard (USA) — 4.51
    Anicka Newell (CAN) — 4.51(Osa)
    Amálie Svábíková (CZE) — 4.51(Tmp)
34. Kortney Ross (USA) — 4.50
    Angelina Krasnova (RUS) — 4.50
    Lene Onsrud Retzius (NOR) — 4.50(Osl)
    Marion Lotout (FRA) — 4.50
    Tina Sutej (SLO) — 4.50
    Maryna Kylypko (UKR) — 4.50
    Justyna Smietanka (POL) — 4.50

WORLD INDOOR CHAMPIONSHIPS: 3-3-2018:

1.	Sandi Morris (USA)	4.95
2.	Anzhelika Sidorova (ANA)	4.90
3.	Katerina Stefanidi (GRE)	4.80
4.	Eliza McCartney (NZL)	4.75
5.	Katie Nageotte (USA)	4.70
6.	Alysha Newman (CAN)	4.70
7.	Yarisley Silva (CUB)	4.60
8.	Nina Kennedy (AUS)	4.60
9.	Olga Mullina (ANA)	4.60
10.	Ninon Guillon-Romarin (FRA)	4.50
11.	Angelica Bengtsson (SWE)	4.50
	Lisa Ryzih (GER)	NM

WORLD INDOOR RANKING 2018:

1.	Sandi Morris (USA)	4.95
2.	Katie Nageotte (USA)	4.91
3.	Anzhelika Sidorova (ANA)	4.90
4.	Katerina Stefanidi (GRE)	4.83
5.	Jennifer Suhr (USA)	4.81
6.	Eliza McCartney (NZL)	4.75
7.	Ninon Guillon-Romarin (FRA)	4.72
8.	Alysha Newman (CAN)	4.70
9.	Olivia Gruver (USA)	4.67
10.	Lexi Jacobus (USA)	4.66
11.	Nikoleta Kiriakopoulou (GRE)	4.65
12.	Kristen Hixson (USA)	4.62
	Maryna Kylypko (UKR)	4.62
	Lisa Ryzih (GER)	4.62
	Iryna Zhuk (BLR)	4.62
	Nina Kennedy (AUS)	4.62
17.	Angelina Krasnova (RUS)	4.61
	Morgann Leleux Romero (USA)	4.61
	Tori Hoggard (USA)	4.61
20.	Holly Bradshaw (GBR)	4.60
	Anicka Newell (CAN)	4.60
	Yarisley Silva (CUB)	4.60
	Olga Mullina (ANA)	4.60
24.	Annie Rhodes-Johnigan (USA)	4.57
25.	Jirina Ptácniková (CZE)	4.55
	Aksana Gataullina (ANA)	4.55
27.	Katharina Bauer (GER)	4.52
28.	Friedelinde Petershofen (GER)	4.51
	Kristen Brown (USA)	4.51
30.	Anjuli Knäsche (GER)	4.50
	Polina Knoroz (RUS)	4.50
	Angelica Bengtsson (SWE)	4.50

OVERVIEW WORLD OUTDOOR CHAMPIONSHIP FINALISTS OF PAST 6 YEARS

	Wch 17	OG 16	Wch 15	Wch 13
Ekateríni Stefanídi (GRE)	4.91 (1)	4.85 (1)		
Sandi Morris (USA)	4.75 (2)	4.85 (2)	4.70 (4)	
Robeilys Peinado (VEN)	4.65 (3)			
Yarisley Silva (CUB)	4.65 (3)	4.60 (7)	4.90 (1)	4.82 (3)
Lisa Ryzih (GER)	4.65 (5)	4.50 (10)	4.60 (12)	4.55 (8)
Holly Bradshaw-Bleasdale (GBR)	4.65 (6)	4.70 (5)	4.70 (7)	
Alysha Newman (CAN)	4.65 (7)			
Olga Mullina (RUS)	4.55 (8)			
Eliza McCartney (NZL)	4.55 (9)	4.80 (3)		
Angelica Bengtsson (SWE)	4.55 (10)		4.70 (4)	
Nicole Büchler (SUI)	4.45 (11)	4.70 (6)		
Anicka Newell (CAN)	4.45 (12)			
Alana Boyd (AUS)		4.80 (4)	4.60 (11)	
Jennifer Suhr (USA)		4.60 (7)	4.70 (4)	4.82 (2)
Martina Strutz (GER)		4.60 (9)	4.60 (8)	
Tina Sutej (SLO)		4.50 (11)		
Kelsie Ahbe (CAN)		4.50 (12)		
Fabiana Murer (BRA)			4.85 (2)	4.65 (5)
Nikoléta Kyriakopoúlou (GRE)			4.80 (3)	
Li Ling (CHN)			4.60 (9)	4.45 (11)
Minna Nikkanen (FIN)			4.60 (10)	
Anzhelika Sidorova (RUS)			NM (13)	
Michaela Meijer (SWE)			NM (13)	
Elena Isinbaeva (RUS)				4.89 (1)
Silke Spiegelburg (GER)				4.75 (4)
Anastasia Savchenko (RUS)				4.65 (5)
Angelina Zhuk-Krasnova (RUS)				4.65 (7)
Jirina Ptácniková-Svobodová (CZE)				4.55 (8)
Kristina Gadschiew (GER)				4.45 (10)
Marion Lotout (FRA)				4.45 (12)

OVERVIEW WORLD INDOOR CHAMPIONSHIP FINALISTS OF PAST 5 YEARS

	Wch 18	Wch 16	Wch 14
Sandi Morris (USA)	4.95 (1)	4.85 (2)	
Anzhelika Sidorova (RUS)	4.90 (2)		4.70 (2)
Ekateríni Stefanídi (GRE)	4.80 (3)	4.80 (3)	
Eliza McCartney (NZL)	4.75 (4)	4.70 (5)	
Katie Nageotte (USA)	4.70 (5)		
Alysha Newman (CAN)	4.70 (6)		
Yarisley Silva (CUB)	4.60 (7)		4.70 (1)
Nina Kennedy (AUS)	4.60 (8)		
Olga Mullina (ANA)	4.60 (9)		
Ninon Guillon-Romarin (FRA)	4.50 (10)		
Angelica Bengtsson (SWE)	4.50 (11)		
Jennifer Suhr (USA)		4.90 (1)	4.65 (5)
Nicole Büchler (SUI)		4.80 (4)	
Nikoléta Kyriakopoúlou (GRE)		4.60 (6)	4.30 (12)
Fabiana Murer (BRA)		4.60 (6)	4.70 (4)
Romana Malácová (CZE)		4.50 (8)	
Marta Onofre (POR)		NM (9)	
Alana Boyd (AUS)		dns (10)	
Jirina Svobodová (CZE)			4.70 (3)
Anna Rogowska (POL)			4.65 (5)
Silke Spiegelburg (GER)			4.65 (7)
Mary Saxer (USA)			4.55 (8)
Holly Bradshaw-Bleasdale (GBR)			4.55 (9)
Tina Sutej (SLO)			4.55 (10)
Anastasia Savchenko (RUS)			4.45 (11)

OVERVIEW TOP 10 WORLD OUTDOOR RANKINGS OF PAST 5 YEARS

	2018	2017	2016	2015	2014
Sandi Morris (USA)	4.95 (1)	4.84 (2)	5.00 (1)	4.76 (6)	
Eliza McCartney (NZL)	4.94 (2)	4.82 (4)	4.80 (9)		
Jennifer Suhr (USA)	4.93 (3)	4.83 (3)	4.82 (7)	4.82 (4)	4.71 (2)
Ekateríni Stefanídi (GRE)	4.87 (4)	4.91 (1)	4.86 (4)	4.71 (9)	4.71 (2)
Anzhelika Sidorova (RUS)	4.85 (5)	4.75 (7)	4.85 (5)	4.79 (5)	4.70 (5)
Yarisley Silva (CUB)	4.80 (6)	4.81 (5)	4.84 (6)	4.91 (1)	4.70 (5)
Holly Bradshaw-Bleasdale (GBR)	4.80 (6)	4.81 (5)			
Nikoléta Kyriakopoúlou (GRE)	4.80 (6)			4.83 (3)	4.67 (7)
Katie Nageotte (USA)	4.80 (6)	4.73 (9)			
Alysha Newman (CAN)	4.75 (10)	4.75 (7)			
Ninon Guillon-Romarin (FRA)	4.75 (10)				
Nicole Büchler (SUI)		4.73 (9)	4.78 (10)	4.71 (9)	4.67 (7)
Lisa Ryzih (GER)		4.73 (9)			4.71 (2)
Elena Isinbaeva (RUS)			4.90 (2)		
Fabiana Murer (BRA)			4.87 (3)	4.85 (2)	4.80 (1)
Alana Boyd (AUS)			4.81 (8)		4.65 (9)
Silke Spiegelburg (GER)				4.75 (7)	
Jirina Ptácniková-Svobodova (CZE)				4.72 (8)	
Demi Payne (USA)				4.71 (9)	
Angelina Zhuk-Krasnova (RUS)					4.65 (9)

OVERVIEW TOP 10 WORLD INDOOR RANKINGS OF PAST 5 YEARS

	2018	2017	2016	2015	2014
Sandi Morris (USA)	4.95 (1)	4.72 (4)	4.95 (2)	4.66 (10)	
Katie Nageotte (USA)	4.91 (2)	4.65 (7)			
Anzhelika Sidorova (RUS)	4.90 (3)			4.80 (2)	4.72 (4)
Ekateríni Stefanídi (GRE)	4.83 (4)	4.85 (1)	4.90 (3)	4.77 (4)	
Jennifer Suhr (USA)	4.81 (5)	4.81 (2)	5.03 (1)		4.73 (2)
Eliza McCartney (NZL)	4.75 (6)	4.70 (5)	4.70 (10)		
Ninon Guillon-Romarin (FRA)	4.72 (7)				
Alysha Newman (CAN)	4.70 (8)	4.65 (7)			
Olivia Gruver (USA)	4.67 (9)				
Lexi Jacobus (USA)	4.66 (10)				
Lisa Ryzih (GER)		4.75 (3)		4.72 (6)	
Wilma Murto (FIN)		4.66 (6)	4.71 (7)		
Mary Saxer (USA)		4.65 (7)	4.71 (7)		4.71 (7)
Nicole Büchler (SUI)		4.61 (10)	4.80 (6)		
Demi Payne (USA)			4.90 (3)	4.75 (5)	
Nikoléta Kyriakopoúlou (GRE)			4.81 (5)	4.80 (2)	4.72 (4)
Fabiana Murer (BRA)			4.71 (7)	4.83 (1)	4.70 (10)
Li Ling (CHN)			4.70 (10)		
Marion Fiack (FRA)				4.71 (7)	
Angelica Bengtsson (SWE)				4.70 (8)	
Angelina Zhuk-Krasnova (RUS)				4.67 (9)	
Anna Rogowska (POL)					4.76 (1)
Holly Bradshaw-Bleasdale (GBR)					4.73 (2)
Silke Spiegelburg (GER)					4.72 (4)
Jirina Ptacnikova-Svobodová (CZE)					4.71 (7)
Tina Sutej (SLO)					4.71 (7)
Yarisley Silva (CUB)					4.70 (10)

WORLD RANKING OUTDOOR ALL TIME:

1.	Yelena Isinbayeva (RUS)	5.06 (2009)
2.	Sandi Morris (USA)	5.00 (2016)
3.	Eliza McCartney (NZL)	4.94 (2018)
4.	Jennifer Suhr (USA)	4.93 (2018)
5.	Yarisley Silva (CUB)	4.91 (2015)
	Katerina Stefanidi (GRE)	4.91 (2017)
7.	Svetlana Feofanova (RUS)	4.88 (2004)
8.	Fabiana Murer (BRA)	4.87 (2016)
9.	Anzhelika Sidorova (RUS)	4.85 (2016)
10.	Stacy Dragila (USA)	4.83 (2004)
	Anna Rogowska (POL)	4.83 (2005)
	Nikoleta Kiriakopoulou (GRE)	4.83 (2015)
13.	Monika Pyrek (POL)	4.82 (2007)
	Silke Spiegelburg (GER)	4.82 (2012)
15.	Alana Boyd (AUS)	4.81 (2016)
	Holly Bradshaw (GBR)	4.81 (2017)
17.	Martina Strutz (GER)	4.80 (2011)
	Katie Nageotte (USA)	4.80 (2018)
19.	Tatyana Polnova (RUS)	4.78 (2004)
	Nicole Büchler (SUI)	4.78 (2016)
21.	Annika Becker (GER)	4.77 (2002)
22.	Jirina Ptácniková (CZE)	4.76 (2013)
23.	Katerina Badurová (CZE)	4.75 (2007)
	Yuliya Golubchikova (RUS)	4.75 (2008)
	Alysha Newman (CAN)	4.75 (2017)
	Ninon Guillon-Romarin (FRA)	4.75 (2018)
27.	Chelsea Johnson (USA)	4.73 (2008)
	Anastasiya Savchenko (RUS)	4.73 (2013)
	Lisa Ryzih (GER)	4.73 (2016)
	Angelica Bengtsson (SWE)	4.73 (2018)
31.	Jillian Schwartz (USA)	4.72 (2008)
	Carolin Hingst (GER)	4.72 (2010)
33.	Demi Payne (USA)	4.71 (2015)
	Michaela Meijer (SWE)	4.71 (2017)
	Nina Kennedy (AUS)	4.71 (2018)
36.	Yvonne Buschbaum (GER)	4.70 (2003)
	Vanessa Boslak (FRA)	4.70 (2006)
	Mary Saxer (USA)	4.70 (2013)
	Kylie Hutson (USA)	4.70 (2013)
	Angelina Krasnova (RUS)	4.70 (2013)
	Kristen Brown (USA)	4.70 (2016)
	Lexi Weeks (USA)	4.70 (2016)
	Robeilys Peinado (VEN)	4.70 (2018)
44.	Anna Battke (GER)	4.68 (2009)

WORLD RANKING INDOOR ALL TIME:

1.	Jennifer Suhr (USA)	5.03 (2016)
2.	Yelena Isinbayeva (RUS)	5.01 (2012)
3.	Sandi Morris (USA)	4.95 (2016)
4.	Katie Nageotte (USA)	4.91 (2018)
5.	Katerina Stefanidi (GRE)	4.90 (2016)
	Demi Payne (USA)	4.90 (2016)
	Anzhelika Sidorova (ANA)	4.90 (2018)
8.	Holly Bradshaw (GBR)	4.87 (2012)
9.	Svetlana Feofanova (RUS)	4.85 (2004)
	Anna Rogowska (POL)	4.85 (2011)
11.	Fabiana Murer (BRA)	4.83 (2015)
12.	Yarisley Silva (CUB)	4.82 (2013)
13.	Stacy Dragila (USA)	4.81 (2004)
	Nikoleta Kiriakopoulou (GRE)	4.81 (2016)
15.	Nicole Büchler (SUI)	4.80 (2016)
16.	Silke Spiegelburg (GER)	4.77 (2012)
17.	Monika Pyrek (POL)	4.76 (2006)
18.	Yuliya Golubchikova (RUS)	4.75 (2008)
	Kylie Hutson (USA)	4.75 (2013)
	Lisa Ryzih (GER)	4.75 (2017)
	Eliza McCartney (NZL)	4.75 (2018)
22.	Kym Howe (AUS)	4.72 (2007)
	Ninon Guillon-Romarin (FRA)	4.72 (2018)
24.	Tatyana Polnova (RUS)	4.71 (2004)
	Anastasiya Savchenko (RUS)	4.71 (2013)
	Jirina Ptácníková (CZE)	4.71 (2014)
	Tina Sutej (SLO)	4.71 (2014)
	Mary Saxer (USA)	4.71 (2014)
	Marion Fiack (FRA)	4.71 (2015)
	Wilma Murto (FIN)	4.71 (2016)
31.	Carolin Hingst (GER)	4.70 (2007)
	Vanessa Boslak (FRA)	4.70 (2012)
	Angelica Bengtsson (SWE)	4.70 (2015)
	Li Ling (CHN)	4.70 (2016)
	Alysha Newman (CAN)	4.70 (2018)
36.	Annika Becker (GER)	4.68 (2004)
37.	Angelina Krasnova (RUS)	4.67 (2015)
	Olivia Gruver (USA)	4.67 (2018)
39.	Christine Adams (GER)	4.66 (2002)
	Lacy Janson (USA)	4.66 (2010)
	Kristina Gadschiew (GER)	4.66 (2011)
	Lexi Weeks (USA)	4.66 (2018)
43. :		
	Yvonne Buschbaum (GER) et al.	4.65 (2002)

Long Jump Women

WORLD CHAMPIONSHIPS 2018: 11-8-2018:

1.	Malaika Mihambo (GER)	(6.71)	6.75
2.	Maryna Bekh (UKR)	(6.64)	6.73
3.	Shara Proctor (GBR)	(6.75)	6.70
4.	Jazmin Sawyers (GBR)	(6.64)	6.67
5.	Nastassia Mironchyk (BLR)	(6.68)	6.58
6.	Ksenija Balta (EST)	(6.63)	6.49
7.	Khaddi Sagnia (SWE)	(6.69)	6.47
8.	Evelise Veiga (POR)	(6.61)	6.47
9.	Lorraine Ugen (GBR)	(6.70)	6.45
10.	Juliet Itoya (ESP)	(6.65)	6.38
11.	Nektaria Panagi (CYP)	(6.62)	6.29
	Ivana Spanovic (SRB)	(6.84)	dns

13.	Laura Strati (ITA)	6.60
14.	Angela Morosanu (ROM)	6.55
15.	Alina Rotaru (ROM)	6.55
	Alexandra Wester (GER)	6.55
17.	Sosthene Moguenara (GER)	6.54
18.	Lauma Griva (LAT)	6.47
19.	Krystyna Hryshutyna (UKR)	6.31
20.	Milena Mitkova (BUL)	6.29
21.	Milica Gardasevic (SRB)	6.26
22.	Fatima Diame (ESP)	6.24
23.	Háido Alexoúli (GRE)	6.21
24.	Karin Melis Mey (TUR)	6.18
25.	Fiorentina Iusco (ROM)	6.17
	Neja Filipic (SLO)	NM
	Éloyse Lesueur-Aymonin (FRA)	NM

WORLD RANKING 2018:

1.	Lorraine Ugen (GBR)	7.05(Bir)
2.	Malaika Mihambo (GER)	6.99
	Ivana Spanovic (SRB)	6.99
4.	Caterine Ibargüen (COL)	6.93(CON)
5.	Christabel Nettey (CAN)	6.92(Bri)
6.	Shara Proctor (GBR)	6.91(Lon)
7.	Brooke Stratton (AUS)	6.88(Bri)
8.	Brittney Reese (USA)	6.87(Cho)
9.	Jazmin Sawyers (GBR)	6.86(Bir)
10.	Sosthene Moguenara-Taroum (GER)	6.84
11.	Ese Brume (NGR)	6.82
12.	Keturah Orji (USA)	6.81(Kno)
	Krystyna Hryshutyna (UKR)	6.81
14.	Éloyse Lesueur (FRA)	6.80
	Juliet Itoya (ESP)	6.80
16.	Taliyah Brooks (USA)	6.78
17.	Kylie Price (USA)	6.77(CV)
	Sha'Keela Saunders (USA)	6.77(Sze)
	Nastassia Mironchyk-Ivanova (BLR)	6.77
20.	Chanice Porter (JAM)	6.75
21.	Bianca Stuart (BAH)	6.74
	Tianna Bartoletta (USA)	6.74
23.	Maryna Bekh (UKR)	6.73(ECh)
24.	Nektaria Panagi (CYP)	6.72
	Alina Rotaru (ROM)	6.72
26.	Tara Davis (USA)	6.71
	Khaddi Sagnia (SWE)	6.71
28.	Nadja Käther (GER)	6.70
	Yelena Sokolova (RUS)	6.70
	Katarina Johnson-Thompson (GBR)	6.70(Lon)

WORLD INDOOR CHAMPIONSHIPS: 4-3-2018:

1. Ivana Spanovic (SRB)   6.96
2. Brittney Reese (USA)   6.89
3. Sosthene Moguenara-Taroum (GER)   6.85
4. Quanesha Burks (USA)   6.81
5. Malaika Mihambo (GER)   6.64
6. Khaddi Sagnia (SWE)   6.64
7. Christabel Nettey (CAN)   6.63
8. Ksenija Balta (EST)   6.57
9. Alina Rotariu (ROM)   6.41
10. Maryna Bekh (UKR)   6.37
11. Lauma Griva (LAT)   6.34
12. Éloyse Lesueur (FRA)   6.34
13. Jessamyn Sauceda (MEX)   5.99

WORLD INDOOR RANKING 2018:

1. Ivana Spanovic (SRB)   6.96
2. Khaddi Sagnia (SWE)   6.92
3. Brittney Reese (USA)   6.89
4. Sosthene Moguenara-Taroum (GER)   6.85
5. Quanesha Burks (USA)   6.81
6. Kate Hall (USA)   6.73
7. Malaika Mihambo (GER)   6.72
8. Katarina Johnson-Thompson (GBR)   6.71
9. Éloyse Lesueur (FRA)   6.69
10. Maryna Bekh (UKR)   6.67

OVERVIEW WORLD OUTDOOR CHAMPIONSHIP FINALISTS OF PAST 6 YEARS

	Wch 17	OG 16	Wch 15	Wch 13
Brittney Reese (USA)	7.02 (1)	7.15 (2)		7.01 (1)
Darya Klishina (RUS)	7.00 (2)	6.63 (9)	6.65 (10)	6.76 (7)
Tianna Bartoletta (USA)	6.97 (3)	7.17 (1)	7.14 (1)	
Ivana Spanovic (SRB)	6.96 (4)	7.08 (3)	7.01 (3)	6.82 (3)
Lorraine Ugen (GBR)	6.72 (5)	6.58 (11)	6.85 (5)	
Brooke Stratton (AUS)	6.67 (6)	6.74 (7)		
Chantel Malone (IVB)	6.57 (7)			
Blessing Okagbare (NGR)	6.55 (8)			6.99 (2)
Lauma Griva (LAT)	6.54 (9)			
Claudia Salman-Rath (GER)	6.54 (10)			
Eliane Martins (BRA)	6.52 (11)			
Alina Rotaru (ROM)	6.46 (12)			
Malaika Mihambo (GER)		6.95 (4)	6.79 (6)	
Ese Brume (NGR)		6.81 (5)		
Ksenija Balta (EST)		6.79 (6)		
Jazmin Sawyers (GBR)		6.69 (8)		
Sosthene Moguenara (GER)		6.61 (10)		6.42 (12)
Maryna Bekh (UKR)		NM (12)		
Shara Proctor (GBR)			7.07 (2)	6.79 (6)
Christabel Nettey (CAN)			6.95 (4)	
Khaddi Sagnia (SWE)			6.78 (7)	
Janay Deloach Soukup (USA)			6.67 (8)	6.44 (11)
Nastassia Mironchyk-Ivanova (BLR)			6.66 (9)	
Katarina Johnson-Thompson (GBR)			6.63 (11)	
Erica Jarder (SWE)			6.48 (12)	6.47 (10)
Volha Sudarava (BLR)				6.82 (4)
Olga Kucherenko (RUS)				6.81 (5)
Tori Polk (USA)				6.73 (8)
Elena Sokolova (RUS)				6.65 (9)

OVERVIEW WORLD INDOOR CHAMPIONSHIP FINALISTS OF 5 PAST YEARS

	Wch 18	Wch 16	Wch 14
Ivana Spanovic (SRB)	6.96 (1)	7.07 (2)	6.77 (3)
Brittney Reese (USA)	6.89 (2)	7.22 (1)	
Sosthene Moguenara-Taroum(GER)	6.85 (3)		
Quanesha Burks (USA)	6.81 (4)		
Malaika Mihambo (GER)	6.64 (5)		
Khaddi Sagnia (SWE)	6.64 (6)		
Christabel Nettey (CAN)	6.63 (7)		
Ksenija Balta (EST)	6.57 (8)	6.60 (7)	
Alina Rotaru (ROM)	6.41 (9)	6.45 (10)	
Maryna Bekh (UKR)	6.37 (10)		
Lorraine Ugen (GBR)		6.93 (3)	
Janay Deloach (USA)		6.89 (4)	
Brooke Stratton (AUS)		6.75 (5)	
Alexandra Wester (GER)		6.67 (6)	
Shara Proctor (GBR)		6.57 (8)	6.68 (4)
Nastassia Mironchyk-Ivanov (BLR)		6.56 (9)	
Éloyse Lesueur (FRA)			6.85 (1)
Katarina Johnson-Thompson (GBR)			6.81 (2)
Tori Polk (USA)			6.61 (5)
Teresa Dobija (POL)			6.52 (6)
Darya Klishina (RUS)			6.51 (7)
Erica Jarder (SWE)			6.36 (8)

OVERVIEW TOP 10 WORLD OUTDOOR RANKINGS OF PAST 5 YEARS

	2018	2017	2016	2015	2014
Lorraine Ugen (GBR)	7.05 (1)				
Malaika Mihambo (GER)	6.99 (2)		6.95 (6)		6.90 (6)
Ivana Spanovic (SRB)	6.99 (2)	6.96 (4)	7.10 (4)	7.02 (3)	6.88 (8)
Caterine Ibargüen (COL)	6.93 (4)				
Christabel Nettey (CAN)	6.92 (5)	6.92 (5)		6.99 (4)	
Shara Proctor (GBR)	6.91 (6)			7.07 (2)	
Brooke Stratton (AUS)	6.88 (7)	6.79 (10)	7.05 (5)		
Brittney Reese (USA)	6.87 (8)	7.13 (1)	7.31 (1)	6.97 (5)	6.92 (3)
Jazmin Sawyers (GBR)	6.86 (9)				
Sosthene Moguenara (GER)	6.84 (10)		7.16 (3)	6.94 (8)	
Tianna Bartoletta (USA)		7.01 (2)	7.17 (2)	7.14 (1)	7.02 (1)
Darya Klishina (RUS)		7.00 (3)		6.95 (6)	6.90 (6)
Claudia Salman-Rath (GER)		6.86 (6)			
Elena Sokolova (RUS)		6.85 (7)			
Jasmine Todd (USA)		6.83 (8)			
Quanesha Burks (USA)		6.83 (8)		6.93 (10)	
Shakeela Saunders (USA)		6.79 (10)	6.89 (9)		
Alexandra Wester (GER)		6.79 (10)			
Maryna Bekh (UKR)			6.93 (7)		
Janay Deloach Soukup (USA)			6.93 (7)	6.95 (6)	
Concepcíon Montaner (ESP)			6.88 (10)		
Lena Malkus (GER)				6.94 (8)	6.88 (8)
Anna Nazarova-Klyashtornaya (RUS)				6.93 (2)	
Éloyse Lesueur (FRA)				6.92 (3)	
Katarina Johnson-Thompson (GBR)				6.92 (3)	
Blessing Okagbare (NGR)				6.86 (10)	

OVERVIEW TOP 10 WORLD INDOOR RANKINGS OF PAST 5 YEARS

	2018	2017	2016	2015	2014
Ivana Spanovic (SRB)	6.96 (1)	7.24 (1)	7.07 (2)	6.98 (2)	6.92 (3)
Khaddi Sagnia (SWE)	6.92 (2)				
Brittney Reese (USA)	6.89 (3)		7.22 (1)		
Sosthene Moguenara-Taroum (GER)	6.85 (4)				6.86 (4)
Quanesha Burks (USA)	6.81 (5)	6.76 (7)	6.80 (8)		
Kate Hall (USA)	6.73 (6)				
Malaika Mihambo (GER)	6.72 (7)				
Katarina Johnson-Thompson (GBR)	6.71 (8)			6.93 (3)	6.81 (5)
Éloyse Lesueur (FRA)	6.69 (9)			6.74 (8)	6.86 (4)
Maryna Bekh (UKR)	6.67 (10)	6.71 (9)			
Lorraine Ugen (GBR)		6.97 (2)	6.93 (4)		6.73 (8)
Claudia Salman (GER)		6.94 (3)			
Shakeela Saunders (USA)		6.90 (4)			
Darya Klishina (RUS)		6.84 (5)			6.76 (6)
Ksenija Balta (EST)		6.79 (6)	6.76 (10)		
Keturah Orji (USA)		6.72 (8)			
Alexandra Wester (GER)		6.71 (9)	6.95 (3)		
Jazmin Sawyers (GBR)		6.71 (9)			
Shara Proctor (GBR)			6.91 (5)		6.69 (10)
Janay Deloach Soukup (USA)			6.89 (6)		
Nastassia Mironchyk-Ivanova (BLR)			6.84 (7)		
Akela Jones (BAR)			6.80 (8)		
Christabel Nettey (CAN)				6.99 (1)	
Ekaterina Koneva (RUS)				6.82 (5)	
Aiga Grabuste (LAT)				6.82 (5)	
Florentina Marincu (ROM)				6.79 (7)	
Funmi Jimoh (USA)				6.74 (8)	
Alina Rotaru (ROM)				6.74 (8)	
Svetlana Biryukova (RUS)					6.98 (1)
Tori Bowie (USA)					6.95 (2)
Yulia Pidluzhnaya (RUS)					6.75 (7)
Tori Polk (USA)					6.70 (9)
Olga Kucherenko (RUS)					6.69 (10)

WORLD RANKING OUTDOOR ALL TIME:

1.	Galina Chistyakova (URS)	7.52 (1988)
2.	Jackie Joyner-Kersee (USA)	7.49 (1994)
3.	Heike Drechsler (GDR)	7.48 (1988)
4.	Anisoara Cusmir-Stanciu (ROM)	7.43 (1983)
5.	Tatyana Kotova (RUS)	7.42 (2002)
6.	Yelena Belevskaya (URS)	7.39 (1987)
7.	Inessa Kravets (UKR)	7.37 (1992)
8.	Tatyana Lebedeva (RUS)	7.33 (2004)
9.	Olena Khlopotnova (URS)	7.31 (1985)
	Marion Jones (USA)	7.31 (1998)
	Brittney Reese (USA)	7.31 (2016)
12.	Irína Meleshina (RUS)	7.27 (2004)
13.	Maurren Higa Maggi (BRA)	7.26 (1999)
14.	Larisa Berezhnaya (URS)	7.24 (1991)
15.	Helga Radtke (GDR)	7.21 (1984)
	Lyudmila Kolchanova (RUS)	7.21 (2007)
17.	Valy Ionescu (ROM)	7.20 (1982)
	Irena Ozhenko (URS)	7.20 (1986)
	Yelena Sinchukova (URS)	7.20 (1991)
	Irina Mushayilova (RUS)	7.20 (1994)
21.	Irina Valyukevich (URS)	7.17 (1987)
	Tianna Bartoletta (USA)	7.17 (2016)
23.	Yolanda Chen (URS)	7.16 (1988)
	Elva Goulbourne (JAM)	7.16 (2004)
	Sosthene Moguenara-Taroum (GER)	7.16 (2016)
26.	Nijolé Medvedeva (URS)	7.14 (1988)
	Mirela Dulgheru (ROM)	7.14 (1992)
28.	Olga Kucherenko (RUS)	7.13 (2010)
29.	Sabine John (GDR)	7.12 (1984)
	Chioma Ajunwa (NGR)	7.12 (1996)
	Naide Gomes (POR)	7.12 (2008)
32.	Fiona May (ITA)	7.11 (1998)
	Anna Klyashtornaya (RUS)	7.11 (2012)
34.	Chelsea Hayes (USA)	7.10 (2012)
	Ivana Spanovic (SRB)	7.10 (2016)
36.	Vilma Bardauskiené (URS)	7.09 (1978)
	Ludmila Ninova (BUL)	7.09 (1994)
38.	Marieta Ilcu (ROM)	7.08 (1989)
	Nastassia Mironchyk-Ivanova (BLR)	7.08 (2012)
40.	Svetlana Zorina (URS)	7.07 (1987)
	Yelena Sokolova (RUS)	7.07 (2012)
	Shara Proctor (GBR)	7.07 (2015)
43.	Tatyana Kolpakova (URS)	7.06 (1980)
	Niurka Montalvo (ESP)	7.06 (1999)
	Tatyana Ter-Mesrobyan (RUS)	7.06 (2002)

WORLD RANKING INDOOR ALL TIME:

1.	Heike Drechsler (GDR)	7.37 (1988)
2.	Galina Chistyakova (URS)	7.30 (1989)
3.	Ivana Spanovic (SRB)	7.24 (2017)
4.	Brittney Reese (USA)	7.23 (2012)
5.	Larisa Berezhnaya (URS)	7.20 (1989)
6.	Olena Khlopotnova (URS)	7.17 (1985)
7.	Jackie Joyner-Kersee (USA)	7.13 (1994)
8.	Helga Radtke (GDR)	7.09 (1985)
	Inessa Kravets (UKR)	7.09 (1992)
10.	Yolanda Chen (URS)	7.05 (1989)
11.	Dawn Burrell (USA)	7.03 (2001)
12.	Nijolé Medvedeva (URS)	7.01 (1987)
	Yelena Belevskaya (URS)	7.01 (1987)
	Tatyana Kotova (RUS)	7.01 (2002)
	Darya Klishina (RUS)	7.01 (2013)
16.	Lyudmila Galkina (RUS)	7.00 (2001)
	Naide Gomes (POR)	7.00 (2008)
18.	Eva Murková (TCH)	6.99 (1985)
	Mirela Dulgheru (ROM)	6.99 (1993)
	Janay Deloach (USA)	6.99 (2011)
	Christabel Nettey (CAN)	6.99 (2015)
22.	Tatyana Lebedeva (RUS)	6.98 (2004)
	Svetlana Biryukova (RUS)	6.98 (2014)
24.	Chioma Ajunwa (NGR)	6.97 (1997)
	Lorraine Ugen (GBR)	6.97 (2017)
26.	Valy Ionescu (ROM)	6.96 (1988)
	Irina Meleshina (RUS)	6.96 (2008)
28.	Marieta Ilcu (ROM)	6.95 (1989)
	Tori Bowie (USA)	6.95 (2014)
	Alexandra Wester (GER)	6.95 (2016)
31.	Anisoara Cusmir-Stanciu (ROM)	6.94 (1983)
	Irina Mushayilova (RUS)	6.94 (1993)
	Claudia Salman-Rath (GER)	6.94 (2017)
34.	Katarina Johnson-Thompson (GBR)	6.93 (2015)
35.	Carolina Klüft (SWE)	6.92 (2004)
	Khaddi Sagnia (SWE)	6.92 (2018)
37.	Irina Valyukevich (URS)	6.91 (1985)
	Niki Xanthou (GRE)	6.91 (1997)
	Magdalena Khristova (BUL)	6.91 (1998)
	Fiona May (ITA)	6.91 (1998)
	Elva Goulbourne (JAM)	6.91 (2002)
	Whitney Gipson (USA)	6.91 (2012)
	Shara Proctor (GBR)	6.91 (2016)
44.	Galina Baranovskaya (URS)	6.90 (1991)
	Susen Tiedtke (GER)	6.90 (1995)
	et al.	

Triple Jump Women

EUROPEAN CHAMPIONSHIPS 2018: 10-8-2018:

1. Paraskevi Papahristou (GRE) (14.49) 14.60
2. Kristin Gierisch (GER) (14.31) 14.45
3. Ana Peleteiro (ESP) (14.27) 14.44
4. Elena Panturoiu (ROM) (14.20) 14.38
5. Hanna Minenko (ISR) (14.41) 14.37
6. Gabriela Petrova (BUL) (14.05) 14.26
7. Jeanine Assani Issouf (FRA) (14.30) 14.12
8. Rouguy Diallo (FRA) (14.31) 14.08
9. Kristiina Mäkelä (FIN) (14.24) 14.01
10. Neele Eckhardt (GER) (14.33) 14.01
11. Susana Costa (POR) (14.17) 13.97
12. Naomi Ogbeta (GBR) (14.15) 13.94

----

13. Olha Saladukha (UKR) 14.04
14. Anna Jagaciak Michalska (POL) 14.01
15. Jessie Maduka (GER) 13.94
16. Patricia Mamona (POR) 13.92
17. Iryna Vaskouskaya (BLR) 13.90
18. Hanna Krasutska (UKR) 13.88
19. Lecabela Quaresma (POR) 13.87
20. Patricia Sarrapio (ESP) 13.87
21. Violetta Skvartsova (BLR) 13.82
22. Tähti Alver (EST) 13.76
23. Dovile Dzindzaletaite (LTU) 13.75
24. Merilyn Uudmäe (EST) 13.74
25. Maria Vicente (ESP) 13.50
26. Aleksandra Nacheva (BUL) 13.39
27. Anna Krylova (ANA) 13.05
    Ottavia Cestonaro (ITA) NM
    Dariya Derkach (ITA) NM

WORLD RANKING 2018:

1. Caterine Ibargüen (COL) 14.96(Rab)
2. Tori Franklin (USA) 14.84(BM)
3. Nubia Soares (BRA) 14.69
4. Yekaterina Koneva (RUS) 14.66
5. Kimberly Williams (JAM) 14.64(GC)
6. Keturah Orji (USA) 14.62(Kno)
7. Shanieka Ricketts (JAM) 14.61(WC)
8. Paraskevi Papachristou (GRE) 14.60
9. Ana Peleteiro (ESP) 14.55
10. Andreea Panturoiu (ROM) 14.47(Mnt)
    Yosiris Urrutia (COL) 14.47
12. Kristin Gierisch (GER) 14.45(ECh)
13. Jeanine Assani Issouf (FRA) 14.43
14. Hanna Knyazheva-Minenko (ISR) 14.41(ECh)
15. Gabriela Petrova (BUL) 14.40
16. Neele Eckhardt (GER) 14.33(ECh)
17. Kristiina Mäkelä (FIN) 14.31
    Rouguy Diallo (FRA) 14.31(ECh)
19. Liadagmis Povea (CUB) 14.30
20. Olga Rypakova (KAZ) 14.26(Jak)
21. Anna Jagaciak (POL) 14.24
22. Ama Lucia Jose Tima (DOM) 14.22
23. Olha Saladukha (UKR) 14.20
    Darya Nidbaykina (RUS) 14.20(Zhu)
25. Patricia Mamona (POR) 14.19
26. Aleksandra Nacheva (BUL) 14.18
27. Parinya Chuaimaroeng (THA) 14.17
    Susana Costa (POR) 14.17
29. Yanis David (FRA) 14.15
    Anna Krasutska (UKR) 14.15
    Naomi Ogbeta (GBR) 14.15
32. Valentina Kosolapova (RUS) 14.14
33. Patricia Sarrapio (ESP) 14.08
34. Irina Yektova (KAZ) 14.07
35. Ottavia Cestonaro (ITA) 14.05
    Dariya Derkach (ITA) 14.05
    Tähti Alver (EST) 14.05
38. Ivonne Rangel (MEX) 14.02
39. Thea Lafond (DOM) 14.01
40. Marie-Jose Ebwea Bile (FRA) 14.00

WORLD INDOOR CHAMPIONSHIPS: 3-3-2018:

1.	Yulimar Rojas (VEN)	14.63
2.	Kimberly Williams (JAM)	14.48
3.	Ana Peleteiro (ESP)	14.40
4.	Elena Andreea Panturoiu (ROM)	14.33
5.	Keturah Orji (USA)	14.31
6.	Paraskevi Papachristou (GRE)	14.05
7.	Viktoriya Prokopenko (ANA)	14.05
8.	Tori Franklin (USA)	14.03
9.	Nubia Soares (BRA)	14.00
10.	Shanieka Ricketts (JAM)	13.93
11.	Gabriela Petrova (BUL)	13.91
12.	Dovilé Dzindzaletaité (LTU)	13.90
13.	Neele Eckhardt (GER)	13.87
14.	Iryna Vaskouskaya (BLR)	13.81
15.	Anna Krylova (ANA)	13.75
16.	Kristiina Mäkelä (FIN)	13.73
17.	Thea Lafond (DMA)	13.68

WORLD INDOOR RANKING 2018:

1.	Yulimar Rojas (VEN)	14.63
2.	Keturah Orji (USA)	14.53
3.	Kimberly Williams (JAM)	14.48
4.	Viktoriya Prokopenko (ANA)	14.44
5.	Ana Peleteiro (ESP)	14.40
6.	Elena Panturoiu (ROM)	14.33
7.	Iryna Vaskouskaya (BLR)	14.30
8.	Paraskevi Papachristou (GRE)	14.25
9.	Rouguy Diallo (FRA)	14.22
10.	Tori Franklin (USA)	14.15
11.	Dovilé Dzindzaletaité (LTU)	14.13
	Neele Eckhardt (GER)	14.13
13.	Yekaterina Koneva (RUS)	14.11
	Yanis Esmeralda David (FRA)	14.11
15.	Thea Lafond (DMA)	14.08
16.	Patricia Sarrapio (ESP)	14.07
	Ilionis Guillaume (FRA)	14.07
18.	Jeanine Assani Issouf (FRA)	14.06
19.	Anna Krylova (RUS)	14.02
	Natalya Yevdokimova (RUS)	14.02
21.	Nubia Soares (BRA)	14.00

OVERVIEW WORLD OUTDOOR CHAMPIONSHIP FINALISTS OF PAST 6 YEARS

	Wch 17	OG 16	Wch 15	Wch 13
Yulimar Rojas (VEN)	14.91 (1)	14.98 (2)		
Caterine Ibargüen (COL)	14.89 (2)	15.17 (1)	14.90 (1)	14.85 (1)
Olga Rypakova (KAZ)	14.77 (3)	14.74 (3)	14.77 (3)	
Hanna Knyazyeva-Minenko (ISR)	14.42 (4)	14.68 (5)	14.78 (2)	14.33 (6)
Kristin Gierisch (GER)	14.33 (5)	13.96 (11)	14.25 (8)	
Anna Jagaciak (POL)	14.25 (6)	14.07 (10)		13.95 (10)
Ana Peleteiro (ESP)	14.23 (7)			
Shanieka Ricketts-Thomas (JAM)	14.13 (8)		14.08 (11)	
Patricia Mamona (POR)	14.12 (9)	14.65 (6)		
Kimberly Williams (JAM)	14.01 (10)	14.53 (7)	14.45 (5)	14.62 (4)
Susana Costa (POR)	13.99 (11)	14.12 (9)		
Neele Eckhardt (GER)	13.97 (12)			
Keturah Orji (USA)		14.71 (4)		
Paraskevi Papahristou (GRE)		14.26 (8)		
Kristiina Mäkelä (FIN)		13.95 (12)		
Gabriela Petrova (BUL)			14.66 (4)	
Olha Saladukha (UKR)			14.41 (6)	14.65 (3)
Ekaterina Koneva (RUS)			14.37 (7)	14.81 (2)
Jeanine Assani Issouf (FRA)			14.12 (9)	
Yosiry Urrutia (COL)			14.09 (10)	
Keila Costa (BRA)			13.90 (12)	
Mabel Gay (CUB)				14.45 (5)
Anna Pyatykh (RUS)				14.29 (7)
Irina Gumenyuk (RUS)				14.15 (8)
Snezana Rodic (SLO)				14.13 (9)
Dana Veldáková (SVK)				13.84 (11)
Athanasia Pérra (GRE)				13.75 (12)

OVERVIEW WORLD INDOOR CHAMPIONSHIP FINALISTS OF PAST 5 YEARS

	Wch 18	Wch 16	Wch 14
Yulimar Rojas (VEN)	14.63 (1)	14.41 (1)	
Kimberly Williams (JAM)	14.48 (2)		14.39 (3)
Ana Peleteiro (ESP)	14.40 (3)	13.59 (11)	
Elena Panturoiu (ROM)	14.33 (4)	14.11 (5)	
Keturah Orji (USA)	14.31 (5)	14.14 (4)	
Paraskevi Papahristou (GRE)	14.05 (6)	14.15 (3)	
Viktoriya Prokopenko (ANA)	14.05 (7)		
Tori Franklin (USA)	14.03 (8)		
Nubia Soares (BRA)	14.00 (9)		
Shanieka Ricketts-Thomas (JAM)	13.93 (10)	13.95 (8)	
Kristin Gierisch (GER)		14.30 (2)	
Kristiina Mäkelä (FIN)		14.07 (6)	
Jeanine Assani Issouf (FRA)		14.07 (7)	
Keila Costa (BRA)		13.94 (9)	
Christina Epps (USA)		13.68 (10)	
Ekaterina Koneva (RUS)			14.46 (1)
Olha Saladukha (UKR)			14.45 (2)
Patricia Mamona (POR)			14.26 (4)
Li Yanmei (CHN)			14.19 (5)
Kseniya Dziatsuk (BLR)			14.13 (6)
Yarianna Martínez (CUB)			13.99 (7)
Dana Veldákova (SVK)			13.75 (8)

OVERVIEW TOP 10 WORLD OUTDOOR RANKINGS OF PAST 5 YEARS

	2018	2017	2016	2015	2014
Caterine Ibargüen (COL)	14.96 (1)	14.89 (2)	15.17 (1)	14.90 (2)	15.31 (1)
Tori Franklin (USA)	14.84 (2)				
Nubia Soares (BRA)	14.69 (3)	14.56 (4)			
Yekaterina Koneva (RUS)	14.66 (4)			15.04 (1)	14.89 (2)
Kimberly Williams (JAM)	14.64 (5)	14.54 (5)	14.56 (9)	14.45 (7)	14.59 (4)
Keturah Orji (USA)	14.62 (6)		14.71 (5)		
Shanieka Ricketts-Thomas (JAM)	14.61 (7)	14.45 (6)	14.57 (8)		
Paraskevi Papahristou (GRE)	14.60 (8)		14.73 (4)		
Ana Peleteiro (ESP)	14.55 (9)				
Andreea Panturoiu (ROM)	14.47 (10)				
Yosiris Urrutia (COL)	14.47 (10)				14.58 (5)
Yulimar Rojas (VEN)		14.96 (1)	15.02 (2)		
Olga Rypakova (KAZ)		14.77 (3)	14.74 (3)	14.77 (4)	14.37 (10)
Liadagmis Povea (CUB)		14.45 (6)	14.56 (9)		
Patrícia Mamona (POR)		14.42 (8)	14.65 (7)		
Hanna Knyazyeva-Minenko (ISR)		14.42 (8)	14.68 (6)	14.78 (3)	
Kristin Gierisch (GER)		14.40 (10)		14.38 (8)	
Gabriela Petrova (BUL)				14.66 (5)	
Olha Saladukha (UKR)				14.62 (6)	14.73 (3)
Susana Costa (POR)				14.32 (9)	
Irina Litvinenko-Yektova (KAZ)				14.32 (9)	
Mabel Gay (CUB)					14.53 (6)
Alsu Murtazina (RUS)					14.50 (7)
Irina Gumenyuk (RUS)					14.46 (8)
Dailenys Alcantara (CUB)					14.45 (9)

OVERVIEW TOP 10 WORLD INDOOR RANKINGS OF PAST 5 YEARS

	2018	**2017**	**2016**	**2015**	**2014**
Yulimar Rojas (VEN)	14.63 (1)	14.79 (1)	14.69 (1)		
Keturah Orji (USA)	14.53 (2)	14.32 (4)			
Kimberly Williams (JAM)	14.48 (3)				14.39 (3)
Viktoriya Prokopenko (ANA)	14.44 (4)				
Ana Peleteiro (ESP)	14.40 (5)	14.20 (8)			
Elena Panturoiu (ROM)	14.33 (6)	14.33 (3)	14.15 (10)		
Iryna Vaskouskaya (BLR)	14.30 (7)		14.23 (5)		
Paraskeví Papahrístou (GRE)	14.25 (8)	14.24 (7)	14.21 (6)		
Rouguy Diallo (FRA)	14.22 (9)		14.16 (9)		
Tori Franklin (USA)	14.15 (10)				
Kristin Gierisch (GER)		14.37 (2)	14.30 (4)	14.46 (4)	14.24 (7)
Patrícia Mamona (POR)		14.32 (5)		14.32 (5)	14.36 (4)
Jenny Elbe (GER)		14.27 (6)	14.15 (10)		
Kristiina Mäkelä (FIN)		14.18 (9)	14.20 (7)	14.20 (9)	
Anna Jagaciak (POL)		14.15 (10)			
Olga Rypakova (KAZ)			14.32 (2)		
Gabriela Petrova (BUL)			14.32 (2)	14.55 (2)	
Jeanine Assani Issouf (FRA)			14.17 (8)		
Ekaterina Koneva (RUS)				14.69 (1)	14.65 (1)
Hanna Knyazyeva-Minenko (ISR)				14.49 (3)	
Cristina Bujin (ROM)				14.28 (6)	
Natallia Viatkina (BLR)				14.21 (7)	
Li Yanmei (CHN)				14.21 (7)	14.19 (8)
Katja Demut (GER)				14.16 (10)	
Olha Saladukha (UKR)					14.65 (1)
Kseniya Dziatsuk (BLR)					14.34 (5)
Irina Gumenyuk (RUS)					14.25 (6)
Dana Veldáková (SVK)					14.10 (9)
Irina Kosko (RUS)					14.09 (10)
Veronika Mosina (RUS)					14.09 (10)

WORLD RANKING OUTDOOR ALL TIME:

1. Inessa Kravets (UKR) — 15.50 (1995)
2. Francoise Mbango Etone (CMR) — 15.39 (2008)
3. Tatyana Lebedeva (RUS) — 15.34 (2004)
4. Chrysopigi Devetzi (GRE) — 15.32 (2004)
5. Caterine Ibargüen (COL) — 15.31 (2014)
6. Yamilé Aldama (CUB) — 15.29 (2003)
7. Yargelis Savigne (CUB) — 15.28 (2007)
8. Olga Rypakova (KAZ) — 15.25 (2010)
9. Sárka Kaspárková (CZE) — 15.20 (1997)
    Tereza Marinova (BUL) — 15.20 (2000)
11. Iva Prandzheva (BUL) — 15.18 (1995)
12. Rodica Petrescu (ROM) — 15.16 (1997)
    Trecia Kaye Smith (JAM) — 15.16 (2004)
14. Ashia Hansen (GBR) — 15.15 (1997)
15. Nadezhda Alyokhina (RUS) — 15.14 (2009)
16. Anna Biryukova (RUS) — 15.09 (1993)
    Inna Lasovskaya (RUS) — 15.09 (1997)
18. Paraskevi Tsiamita (GRE) — 15.07 (1999)
19. Yekaterina Koneva (RUS) — 15.04 (2015)
20. Magdelín Martínez (ITA) — 15.03 (2004)
    Marija Sestak (SLO) — 15.03 (2008)
22. Anna Pyatykh (RUS) — 15.02 (2006)
    Yulimar Rojas (VEN) — 15.02 (2016)
24. Kéne Ndoye (SEN) — 15.00 (2004)
25. Olha Saladukha (UKR) — 14.99 (2012)
26. Sofiya Boshanova (BUL) — 14.98 (1994)
    Baya Rahouli (ALG) — 14.98 (2005)
28. Yolanda Chen (RUS) — 14.97 (1993)
29. Olena Govorova (UKR) — 14.96 (2000)
30. Xie Limei (CHN) — 14.90 (2007)
31. Viktoriya Gurova (RUS) — 14.85 (2008)
    Oksana Udmurtova (RUS) — 14.85 (2008)
33. Tori Franklin (USA) — 14.84 (2018)
34. Yelena Oleynikova (RUS) — 14.83 (2002)
35. Irina Mushayilova (RUS) — 14.79 (1993)
36. Hanna Knyazheva-Minenko (ISR) — 14.78 (2015)
37. Galina Chistyakova (RUS) — 14.76 (1995)
    Gundega Sproge (LAT) — 14.76 (1997)
    Kseniya Dziatsuk (BLR) — 14.76 (2012)
40. Adelina Gavrila (ROM) — 14.75 (2003)
41. Paraskevi Papachristou (GRE) — 14.73 (2016)
42. Huang Qiuyan (CHN) — 14.72 (2001)
43. Athanasia Perra (GRE) — 14.71 (2012)
    Keturah Orji (USA) — 14.71 (2016)
45. Cristina Nicolau (ROM) — 14.70 (1999)

WORLD RANKING INDOOR ALL TIME:

1. Tatyana Lebedeva (RUS) — 15.36 (2004)
2. Ashia Hansen (GBR) — 15.16 (1998)
3. Olga Rypakova (KAZ) — 15.14 (2010)
4. Marija Sestak (SLO) — 15.08 (2008)
5. Yargelis Savigne (CUB) — 15.05 (2008)
6. Yolanda Chen (RUS) — 15.03 (1995)
7. Inna Lasovskaya (RUS) — 15.01 (1997)
8. Iva Prandzheva (BUL) — 14.94 (1999)
    Cristina Nicolau (ROM) — 14.94 (2000)
    Oksana Udmurtova (RUS) — 14.94 (2008)
11. Anna Pyatykh (RUS) — 14.93 (2006)
12. Rodica Petrescu (ROM) — 14.91 (1997)
    Tereza Martinova (BUL) — 14.91 (2001)
14. Yamilé Aldama (SUD) — 14.90 (2004)
15. Francoise Mbango Etone (CMR) — 14.88 (2003)
    Olha Saladukha (UKR) — 14.88 (2013)
17. Sarka Kaspárková (CZE) — 14.87 (1999)
18. Chrysopiqi Devetzi (GRE) — 14.84 (2003)
    Trecia Kaye Smith (JAM) — 14.84 (2006)
20. Yelena Lebedyenko (RUS) — 14.83 (2001)
21. Magdelín Martínez (ITA) — 14.81 (2004)
22. Yulimar Rojas (VEN) — 14.79 (2017)
23. Adelina Gavrila (ROM) — 14.76 (2003)
24. Anna Biryukova (RUS) — 14.75 (1995)
25. Viktoriya Gurova (RUS) — 14.74 (2005)
26. Kéne Ndoye (SEN) — 14.72 (2003)
27. Oksana Rogova (RUS) — 14.70 (2002)
28. Yekaterina Koneva (RUS) — 14.69 (2015)
29. Anastasiya Potapova (RUS) — 14.68 (2009)
30. Inessa Kravets (UKR) — 14.67 (1995)
31. Nadezhda Alyokhina (RUS) — 14.65 (2002)
32. Carlota Castrejana (ESP) — 14.64 (2007)
33. Paraskevi Tsiamita (GRE) — 14.63 (1999)
34. Yelena Oleynikova (RUS) — 14.60 (2002)
    Simona La Mantia (ITA) — 14.60 (2011)
36. Olena Govorova (UKR) — 14.59 (2004)
37. Mabel Gay (CUB) — 14.57 (2004)
38. Fiona May (ITA) — 14.56 (1998)
39. Gabriela Petrova (BUL) — 14.55 (2015)
40. Mariya Sokova (RUS) — 14.54 (1995)
41. Teresa Nzola Meso Ba (FRA) — 14.53 (2008)
    Keturah Orji (USA) — 14.53 (2018)
43. Sofiya Boshanova (BUL) — 14.52 (1994)
44. Olga Vasdeki (GRE) — 14.51 (1999)

Javelin Throw Women

EUROPEAN CHAMPIONSHIPS 2018: 10-8-2018:

1.	Christin Hussong (GER)	(67.29)	67.90
2.	Nikola Ogrodníkova (CZE)	(61.27)	61.85
3.	Liveta Jasiunaite (LTU)	(61.61)	61.59
4.	Martina Ratej (SLO)	(61.69)	61.41
5.	Tatsiana Khaladovich (BLR)	(61.21)	60.92
6.	Alexie Alais (FRA)		60.01
7.	Irena Sedivá (CZE)		59.76
8.	Sigrid Borge (NOR)		59.60
9.	Madara Palameika (LAT)	(60.21)	57.98
10.	Sofi Flink (SWE)	(59.58)	56.91
11.	Marija Vucenovic (SRB)	(59.98)	55.23
12.	Jenni Kangas (FIN)	(59.96)	54.92

13.	Ásdis Hjálmsdóttir (ISL)	58.64
14.	Lidia Parada (ESP)	58.08
15.	Katharina Molitor (GER)	58.00
16.	Eda Tugsuz (TUR)	57.77
17.	Anete Kocina (LAT)	57.48
18.	Arantxa Moreno (ESP)	56.33
19.	Lina Muze (LAT)	53.95
20.	Dana Bergrath (GER)	53.61
21.	Hanna Hatsko-Fedusova (UKR)	53.08
22.	Sofia Ifantídou (GRE)	52.26
	Liina Laasma (EST)	NM

WORLD RANKING 2018:

1.	Kathryn Mitchell (AUS)	68.92(GC)
2.	Christin Hussong (GER)	67.90(ECh)
3.	Lyu Huihui (CHN)	67.69
4.	Tatsiana Khaladovich (BLR)	67.47(Osl)
5.	Liu Shiying (CHN)	67.12(Osa)
6.	Marcelina Witek (POL)	66.53
7.	Martina Ratej (SLO)	66.10
8.	Nikola Ogrodníková (CZE)	65.61
9.	Eda Tugsuz (TUR)	65.20
10.	Kara Winger (USA)	64.75(Zü)
11.	Kelsey-Lee Roberts (AUS)	64.57(Bri)
12.	Lina Muze (LAT)	63.18
13.	Madara Palameika (LAT)	62.98
14.	Anete Kocina (LAT)	62.58
15.	Sunette Viljoen (RSA)	62.46
16.	Sigrid Borge (NOR)	62.42
17.	Laila de Silva (BRA)	62.39
18.	Sinta Sprudzane (LAT)	62.21

OVERVIEW WORLD OUTDOOR CHAMPIONSHIP FINALISTS OF PAST 6 YEARS

	Wch 17	OG 16	Wch 15	Wch 13
Barbora Spotáková (CZE)	66.76 (1)	64.80 (3)	60.08 (9)	
Li Lingwei (CHN)	66.25 (2)		64.10 (5)	61.30 (8)
Lyu Huihui (CHN)	65.26 (3)	64.04 (7)	66.13 (2)	
Sara Kolak (CRO)	64.95 (4)	66.18 (1)		
Eda Tugsuz (TUR)	64.52 (5)			
Tatsiana Khaladovich (BLR)	64.05 (6)	64.60 (5)		
Katharina Molitor (GER)	63.75 (7)		67.69 (1)	
Liu Shiying (CHN)	62.84 (8)			
Martina Ratej (SLO)	61.05 (9)			
Kelsey-Lee Roberts (AUS)	60.76 (10)			
Ásdis Hjálmsdóttir (ISL)	60.16 (11)			
Elizabeth Gleadle (CAN)	60.12 (12)		59.82 (11)	
Sunette Viljoen (RSA)		64.92 (2)	65.79 (3)	63.58 (6)
Maria Andrejczyk (POL)		64.78 (4)		
Kathryn Mitchell (AUS)		64.36 (6)		63.77 (5)
Christina Obergföll (GER)		62.92 (8)	64.61 (4)	69.05 (1)
Flor Ruiz (COL)		61.54 (9)		
Madara Palameika (LAT)		60.14 (10)		
Linda Stahl (GER)		59.71 (11)	59.88 (10)	64.78 (4)
Christin Hussong (GER)		57.70 (12)	62.98 (6)	
Sinta Ozolina (LAT)			62.20 (7)	
Kara Winger (USA)			60.88 (8)	
Brittany Borman (USA)			58.26 (12)	
Kimberley Mickle (AUS)				66.60 (2)
Maria Abakumova (RUS)				65.09 (3)
Viktoriya Sudarushkina (RUS)				62.21 (7)
Tatjana Jelaca (SRB)				60.81 (9)
Sofi Flinck (SWE)				59.52 (10)
Vira Rebryk (UKR)				58.33 (11)
Nadeeka Babaranda (SRI)				58.16 (12)

OVERVIEW TOP 10 WORLD OUTDOOR RANKINGS OF PAST 5 YEARS

	2018	**2017**	**2016**	**2015**	**2014**
Kathryn Mitchell (AUS)	68.92 (1)	66.12 (8)			66.10 (7)
Christin Hussong (GER)	67.90 (2)		66.41 (4)	65.92 (6)	
Lyu Huihui (CHN)	67.69 (3)	67.59 (3)		66.13 (5)	
Tatsiana Khaladovich (BLR)	67.47 (4)	66.30 (6)	66.34 (5)		
Liu Shiying (CHN)	67.12 (5)	66.47 (5)	65.64 (8)		
Marcelina Witek (POL)	66.53 (6)				
Martina Ratej (SLO)	66.10 (7)	65.64 (9)		65.75 (7)	66.13 (6)
Nikola Ogrodníková (CZE)	65.61 (8)				
Eda Tugsuz (TUR)	65.20 (9)	67.21 (4)			
Kara Winger (USA)	64.75 (10)			66.47 (4)	
Sara Kolak (CRO)		68.43 (1)	66.18 (6)		
Barbora Spotáková (CZE)		68.26 (2)	66.87 (3)	65.66 (8)	67.99 (1)
Li Lingwei (CHN)		66.25 (7)		65.07 (9)	
Katharina Molitor (GER)		65.37 (10)		67.69 (1)	
Vera Rebryk (RUS)/(UKR)			67.30 (1)		
Maria Andrejczyk (POL)			67.11 (2)		
Madara Palameika (LAT)			66.18 (6)	65.01 (10)	66.15 (5)
Linda Stahl (GER)			65.25 (9)		67.32 (2)
Sunette Viljoen (RSA)			65.14 (10)	66.62 (2)	65.32 (9)
Kimberley Mickle (AUS)				66.57 (3)	66.83 (4)
Hanna Hatsko-Fedusova (UKR)					67.29 (3)
Zhang Li (CHN)					65.47 (8)
Elizabeth Gleadle (CAN)					64.50 (10)

WORLD RANKING ALL TIME:

1.	Barbora Spotáková (CZE)	72.28 (2008)
2.	Mariya Abakumova (RUS)	71.99 (2011)
3.	Olisdeilys Menéndez (CUB)	71.70 (2005)
4.	Christina Obergföll (GER)	70.20 (2007)
5.	Trine Solberg-Hattestad (NOR)	69.48 (2000)
6.	Kathryn Mitchell (AUS)	68.92 (2018)
7.	Sunette Viljoen (RSA)	69.35 (2012)
8.	Sara Kolak (CRO)	68.43 (2017)
9.	Steffi Nerius (GER)	68.34 (2008)
10.	Christin Hussong (GER)	67.90 (2018)
11.	Katharina Molitor (GER)	67.69 (2015)
	Lyu Huihui (CHN)	67.69 (2018)
13.	Sonia Bisset (CUB)	67.67 (2005)
14.	Mirela Manjani (GRE)	67.51 (2000)
15.	Tatsiana Khaladovich (BLR)	67.47 (2018)
16.	Linda Stahl (GER)	67.32 (2014)
17.	Vera Rebrik (RUS)	67.30 (2016)
18.	Hanna Hatsko-Fedusova (UKR)	67.29 (2014)
19.	Eda Tugsuz (TUR)	67.21 (2017)
20.	Tatyana Shikolenko (RUS)	67.20 (2000)
21.	Martina Ratej (SLO)	67.16 (2010)
22.	Liu Shiying (CHN)	67.12 (2018)
23.	Maria Andrejczyk (POL)	67.11 (2016)
24.	Tanja Damaske (GER)	66.91 (1999)
25.	Kimberley Mickle (AUS)	66.83 (2014)
26.	Louise McPaul-Currey (AUS)	66.80 (2000)
27.	Kara Winger (USA)	66.67 (2010)
28.	Marcelina Witek (POL)	66.53 (2018)
29.	Li Lingwei (CHN)	66.25 (2017)
30.	Madara Palameika (LAT)	66.18 (2016)
31.	Goldie Sayers (GBR)	66.17 (2012)
32.	Elena Révayová (TCH)	66.16 (1989)
33.	Nikola Tomecková-Brejchová (CZE)	65.91 (2004)
34.	Natalya Yermolovich (URS)	65.80 (1987)
35.	Nikola Ogrodníková (CZE)	65.61 (2018)
36.	Zhang Li (CHN)	65.47 (2014)
37.	Claudia Coslovich (ITA)	65.30 (2000)
38.	Xiomara Rivero (CUB)	65.29 (2001)
39.	Karen Forkel (GER)	65.17 (1999)
40.	Ana Mirela Termure (ROM)	65.08 (2001)
41.	Paula Huhtaniemi (FIN)	64.90 (2003)
42.	Yekaterina Krasnikova-Ivakina (RUS)	64.89 (2000)
43.	Kelly Morgan (GBR)	64.87 (2002)
44.	Christina Scherwin (DEN)	64.83 (2006)
	Elizabeth Gleadle (CAN)	64.83 (2015)

Discus Throw Women

EUROPEAN CHAMPIONSHIPS 2018: 11-8-2018:

1. Sandra Perkovic (CRO)   (64.54) 67.62
2. Nadine Müller (GER)   (60.64) 63.00
3. Shanice Craft (GER)   (61.13) 62.46
4. Claudine Vita (GER)   61.25
5. Daisy Osakue (ITA)   59.32
6. Dragana Tomasevic (SRB)   58.94
7. Liliana Cá (POR)   58.91
8. Alexandra Emilianov (MDA)   (58.83) 58.10
9. Irina Rodrigues (POR)   (59.22) 58.00
10. Hrisoúla Anagnostopoúlou (GRE)   57.34
11. Jade Lally (GBR)   (57.71) 57.33
12. Eliska Stankova (CZE)   (57.81) 57.04
----
13. Kristina Rakocevic (MNT)   55.90
14. Corinne Nugter (NED)   55.70
15. Sabina Asenjo (ESP)   55.57
16. Marija Tolj (CRO)   55.52
17. Valentine Aniballi (ITA)   55.06
18. Vanessa Kamga (SWE)   54.88
19. Sanna Kämäräinen (FIN)   54.76
20. Jorinde van Klinken (NED)   54.33
21. Salla Sipponen (FIN)   54.00
22. Daria Zabawska (POL)   53.94
23. Ieva Zarankaite (LTU)   53.91
24. Helena Leveelahti (FIN)   53.56
25. Yuliya Maltseva (ANA)   53.50
26. Kirsty Law (GBR)   52.37

WORLD RANKING 2018:

1. Sandra Perkovic (CRO)   71.38(Do)
2. Dani Stevens (AUS)   68.26(GC)
3. Yaimé Pérez (CUB)   67.82
4. Chen Yang (CHN)   67.03
5. Denia Caballero (CUB)   66.09
6. Claudine Vita (GER)   65.15
7. Andressa de Morais (BRA)   65.10
8. Fernanda Borges (BRA)   64.66
9. Feng Bin (CHN)   64.58
10. Yelena Panova (RUS)   63.92
11. Su Xinyue (CHN)   63.73
12. Valarie Allman (USA)   63.55(USC)
13. Nadine Müller (GER)   63.00(ECh)

OVERVIEW WORLD OUTDOOR CHAMPIONSHIP FINALISTS OF PAST 6 YEARS

	Wch 17	OG 16	Wch 15	Wch 13
Sandra Perkovic (CRO)	70.31 (1)	69.21 (1)	67.39 (2)	67.99 (1)
Dani Stevens-Samuels (AUS)	69.64 (2)	64.90 (4)	63.14 (6)	62.42 (10)
Mélina Robert-Michon (FRA)	66.21 (3)	66.73 (2)	60.92 (10)	66.28 (2)
Yaimé Pérez (CUB)	64.82 (4)	NM	65.46 (4)	62.39 (11)
Denia Caballero (CUB)	64.37 (5)	65.34 (3)	69.28 (1)	62.80 (8)
Nadine Müller (GER)	64.13 (6)	63.13 (6)	65.53 (3)	64.47 (4)
Su Xinyue (CHN)	63.37 (7)	64.37 (5)	62.90 (8)	
Feng Bin (CHN)	61.56 (8)	63.06 (8)		
Julia Harting-Fischer (GER)	61.34 (9)	62.67 (9)	63.88 (5)	
Chen Yang (CHN)	61.28 (10)	63.11 (7)		
Andressa de Morais (BRA)	60.00 (11)			
Zinaida Sendriuté (LTU)	NM	61.89 (10)		62.42 (9)
Shanice Craft (GER)		59.85 (11)	63.10 (7)	
Whitney Ashley (USA)			61.05 (9)	
Gia Lewis-Smallwood (USA)			60.55 (11)	64.23 (5)
Natalia Semenova (UKR)			59.54 (12)	
Yarelys Barrios (CUB)				64.96 (3)
Tan Jian (CHN)				63.34 (6)
Zaneta Glanc (POL)				62.90 (7)
Rocio Comba (ARG)				59.83 (12)

OVERVIEW TOP 10 WORLD OUTDOOR RANKINGS OF PAST 5 YEARS

	2018	2017	2016	2015	2014
Sandra Perkovic (CRO)	71.38 (1)	71.41 (1)	70.88 (1)	70.08 (2)	71.08 (1)
Dani Stevens-Samuels (AUS)	68.26 (2)	69.64 (2)	67.77 (4)	66.21 (4)	67.99 (3)
Yaimé Pérez (CUB)	67.82 (3)	69.19 (3)	68.86 (2)	67.13 (3)	66.03 (6)
Chen Yang (CHN)	67.03 (4)				
Denia Caballero (CUB)	66.09 (5)	67.04 (4)	67.62 (5)	70.65 (1)	
Claudine Vita (GER)	65.15 (6)				
Andressa de Morais (BRA)	65.10 (7)	64.68 (9)			
Fernanda Borges (BRA)	64.66 (8)				
Feng Bin (CHN)	64.58 (9)		65.14 (9)		
Yelena Panova (RUS)	63.92 (10)				
Mélina Robert-Michon (FRA)		66.21 (5)	66.73 (7)	65.04 (8)	65.51 (10)
Gia Lewis-Smallwood (USA)		65.81 (6)			69.17 (2)
Nadine Müller (GER)		65.76 (7)	66.84 (6)	65.72 (7)	67.30 (4)
Valarie Allman (USA)		64.69 (8)			
Su Xinyue (CHN)		64.56 (10)	65.59 (8)		
Julia Fischer (GER)			68.49 (3)	65.98 (6)	66.46 (5)
Jade Lally (GBR)			65.10 (10)		
Anna Rüh (GER)				66.14 (5)	
Whitney Ashley (USA)				64.80 (9)	
Shanice Craft (GER)				64.79 (10)	65.88 (7)
Zinaida Sendriuté (LTU)					65.83 (8)
Ekaterina Strokova (RUS)					65.78 (9)

WORLD RANKING ALL TIME:

1.	Gabriele Reinsch (GDR)	76.80 (1988)
2.	Zdenka Silhavá (TCH)	74.56 (1984)
	Ilke Wyludda (GDR)	74.56 (1989)
4.	Diana Gansky (GDR)	74.08 (1987)
5.	Daniela Costian (ROM)	73.84 (1988)
6.	Irina Meszynski (GDR)	73.36 (1984)
7.	Galina Savinkova (URS)	73.28 (1984)
8.	Tsvetanka Khristova (BUL)	73.22 (1987)
9.	Gisela Beyer (GDR)	73.10 (1984)
10.	Martina Hellmann (GER)	72.92 (1987)
11.	Galina Murashova (URS)	72.14 (1984)
12.	Mariya Vergova-Petkova (BUL)	71.80 (1980)
13.	Xiao Yanling (CHN)	71.68 (1992)
14.	Ellina Zvereva (URS)	71.58 (1988)
15.	Evelin Jahl (GDR)	71.50 (1980)
16.	Sandra Perkovic (CRO)	71.41 (2017)
17.	Larisa Korotkevich (RUS)	71.30 (1992)
18.	Ria Stalman (NED)	71.22 (1984)
19.	Hilda Ramos (CUB)	70.88 (1992)
20.	Larisa Mikhalchenko (URS)	70.80 (1988)
21.	Maritza Marten (CUB)	70.68 (1992)
22.	Denia Caballero (CUB)	70.65 (2015)
23.	Faina Melnik (URS)	70.50 (1976)
24.	Silvia Madetzky (GDR)	70.34 (1988)
25.	Natalya Sadova (RUS)	70.02 (1999)
26.	Valentina Kharchenko (URS)	69.86 (1981)
27.	Svetla Mitkova-Sinirtas (BUL)	69.72 (1987)
28.	Mette Bergmann (NOR)	69.68 (1995)
29.	Dani Stevens (AUS)	69.64 (2017)
30.	Franka Dietzsch (GER)	69.51 (1999)
31.	Florenta Craciunescu (ROM)	69.50 (1985)
32.	Yaimé Pérez (CUB)	69.19 (2017)
33.	Gia Lewis-Smallwood (USA)	69.17 (2014)
34.	Irina Yatchenko (BLR)	69.14 (2004)
35.	Carmen Romero (CUB)	69.08 (1976)
	Mariana Lengyel (ROM)	69.08 (1986)
37.	Sabine Engel (GDR)	68.92 (1977)
38.	Nadine Müller (GER)	68.89 (2012)
39.	Nicoleta Grasu (ROM)	68.80 (1999)
40.	Margitta Pufe (GDR)	68.64 (1979)
41.	Yu Hourun (CHN)	68.62 (1988)
	Hou Xuemei (CHN)	68.62 (1988)
43.	Nadezhda Kugayevskikh (URS)	68.60 (1983)
44.	Lyubov Zverkova (URS)	68.58 (1984)
45.	Beatrice Faumuina (NZL)	68.52 (1997)

Hammer Throw Women

EUROPEAN CHAMPIONSHIPS 2018: 12-8-2018:

1. Anita Wlodarczyk (POL) (75.10) 78.94
2. Alexandra Tavernier (FRA) (72.88) 74.78
3. Joanna Fiodorow (POL) (71.46) 74.00
4. Malwina Kopron (POL) (71.14) 72.20
5. Hanna Skydan (AZE) (74.02) 72.10
6. Zalina Petrivskaya (MDA) 71.80
7. Kathrin Klaas (GER) 71.50
8. Sophie Hitchon (GBR) 70.52
9. Réka Gyurátz (HUN) 70.48
10. Sofiya Palkina (ANA) (69.74) 68.64
11. Iryna Klymets (UKR) (69.44) 68.11
    Hanna Malyshik (BLR) (72.39) NM

----

13. Yelizaveta Tsareva (ANA) 68.35
14. Kivilcim Salman (TUR) 68.10
15. Stamatia Skarvélis (GRE) 67.97
16. Anna Maria Orel (EST) 67.22
17. Ida Storm (SWE) 66.66
18. Martina Hrasnová (SVK) 66.37
19. Bianca Ghelber (ROM) 66.17
20. Inga Linna (FIN) 65.46
21. Krista Tervo (FIN) 65.37
22. Katerina Safránková (CZE) 64.85
23. Iryna Novozhylova (UKR) 64.70
24. Marina Nikisenko (MDA) 64.37
25. Anamari Kozul (CRO) 62.55
26. Nicole Zihlmann (SUI) 61.67
27. Alyona Shamotina (UKR) 61.66
28. Éva Orbán (HUN) 59.16

WORLD RANKING 2018:

1. Anita Wlodarczyk (POL) 79.59
2. DeAnna Price (USA) 78.12(USC)
3. Gwen Berry (USA) 77.78(Cho)
4. Hanna Malyshik (BLR) 76.26
5. Joanna Fiodorow (POL) 75.63
6. Luo Na (CHN) 75.02
7. Alexandra Tavernier (FRA) 74.78(ECh)
8. Maggie Ewen (USA) 74.53(Tem)
9. Brooke Andersen (USA) 74.20(Tuc)
10. Hanna Skydan (AZE) 74.02(ECh)
11. Wang Zheng (CHN) 73.73(Ost)
12. Sophie Hitchon (GBR) 73.48(WC)
13. Martina Hrasnová (SVK) 73.25
14. Yelizaveta Tsareva (RUS) 73.22(Zhu)
15. Janeah Stewart (USA) 72.92(NCA)
16. Malwina Kopron (POL) 72.88(Ost)
17. Zalina Petrivskaya (MDA) 72.70
18. Iryna Klymets (UKR) 72.63
19. Réka Gyurátz (HUN) 72.52
20. Liu Tingting (CHN) 72.24
21. Jillian Weir (CAN) 71.96(NAC)
22. Kivilcim Salman (TUR) 71.66
23. Kathrin Klaas (GER) 71.50(ECh)
24. Jennifer Dahlgren (ARG) 70.98
25. Bianca Ghelber (ROM) 70.96
26. Rosa Rodríguez (VEN) 70.93
27. Barbara Spiler (SLO) 70.92
28. Ida Storm (SWE) 70.62
29. Jessica Ramsey (USA) 70.41(USC)
30. Jeneva Stevens (USA) 70.05

OVERVIEW WORLD OUTDOOR CHAMPIONSHIP FINALISTS OF PAST 6 YEARS

	Wch 17	OG 16	Wch 15	Wch 13
Anita Wlodarczyk (POL)	77.90 (1)	82.29 (1)	80.85 (1)	78.46 (2)
Wang Zheng (CHN)	75.98 (2)	NM (12)	73.83 (5)	74.90 (4)
Malwina Kopron (POL)	74.76 (3)			
Zhang Wenxiu (CHN)	74.53 (4)	76.75 (2)	76.33 (2)	75.58 (3)
Hanna Skydan (AZE)	73.38 (5)			
Joanna Fiodorow (POL)	73.04 (6)	69.87 (9)		
Sophie Hitchon (GBR)	72.32 (7)	74.54 (3)	73.86 (4)	
Katerina Safránková (CZE)	71.34 (8)			
DeAnna Price (USA)	70.04 (9)	70.95 (8)		
Hanna Malyshik (BLR)	69.43 (10)	71.90 (7)		
Kathrin Klaas (GER)	68.91 (11)		73.18 (6)	
Alexandra Tavernier (FRA)	66.21 (12)	65.18 (11)	74.02 (3)	
Betty Heidler (GER)		73.71 (4)	72.56 (7)	
Zalina Marghieva (MDA)		73.50 (5)	72.38 (8)	
Amber Campbell (USA)		72.74 (6)	NM (12)	
Rosa Rodriguez (VEN)		69.26 (10)	67.78 (11)	
Amanda Bingson (USA)			72.35 (9)	72.56 (10)
Alena Sobaleva (BLR)			70.09 (10)	
Tatyana Lysenko (RUS)				78.80 (1)
Anna Bulgakova (RUS)				74.62 (5)
Yipsi Moreno (CUB)				74.16 (6)
Oksana Kondrateva (RUS)				72.76 (7)
Éva Orbán (HUN)				72.70 (8)
Jeneva McCall (USA)				72.65 (9)
Bianca Perie (ROM)				71.25 (11)
Gulfiya Khanafeyeva (RUS)				71.07 (12)

OVERVIEW TOP 10 WORLD OUTDOOR RANKINGS OF PAST 5 YEARS

	2018	2017	2016	2015	2014
Anita Wlodarczyk (POL)	79.59 (1)	82.87 (1)	82.98 (1)	81.08 (1)	79.58 (1)
DeAnna Price (USA)	78.12 (2)	74.91 (9)	73.09 (9)		
Gwen Berry (USA)	77.78 (3)	76.77 (3)	73.09 (9)		
Hanna Malyshik (BLR)	76.26 (4)	74.94 (8)			
Joanna Fiodorow (POL)	75.63 (5)	75.09 (7)			74.39 (9)
Luo Na (CHN)	75.02 (6)				
Alexandra Tavernier (FRA)	74.78 (7)			74.39 (4)	
Magdalyn Ewen (USA)	74.53 (8)	74.56 (10)			
Brooke Andersen (USA)	74.20 (9)				
Hanna Skydan (AZE)	74.02 (10)	75.29 (6)	73.87 (8)		
Malwina Kopron (POL)		76.85 (2)			
Wang Zheng (CHN)		76.25 (4)	74.50 (5)	73.99 (6)	77.68 (3)
Zhang Wenxiu (CHN)		75.48 (5)	76.75 (2)	76.33 (2)	77.33 (4)
Betty Heidler (GER)			75.77 (3)	75.73 (3)	78.00 (2)
Sophie Hitchon (GBR)			74.54 (4)	73.86 (8)	
Zalina Petrivskaya-Marghieva (MDA)			74.21 (6)	73.97 (7)	
Amber Campbell (USA)			74.03 (7)		
Martina Hrasnová (SVK)				74.27 (5)	75.27 (6)
Mariya Bespalova (RUS)				73.74 (9)	
Sultana Frizell (CAN)				73.66 (10)	75.73 (5)
Amanda Bingson (USA)					75.12 (7)
Kathrin Klaas (GER)					74.62 (8)
Jessica Cosby-Toruga (USA)					74.20 (10)

WORLD RANKING ALL TIME:

1.	Anita Wlodarczyk (POL)	82.98 (2016)
2.	Betty Heidler (GER)	79.42 (2011)
3.	Tatyana Lysenko (RUS)	78.80 (2013)
4.	DeAnna Price (USA)	78.12 (2018)
5.	Gwen Berry (USA)	77.78 (2018)
6.	Wang Zheng (CHN)	77.68 (2014)
7.	Zhang Wenxiu (CHN)	77.33 (2014)
8.	Oksana Miankova (BLR)	77.32 (2008)
9.	Gulfiya Agafonova (RUS)	77.26 (2006)
10.	Oksana Kondratyeva (RUS)	77.13 (2013)
11.	Martina Hrasnová (SVK)	76.90 (2009)
12.	Malwina Kopron (POL)	76.85 (2017)
13.	Kamila Skolimowska (POL)	76.83 (2007)
14.	Mariya Bespalova (RUS)	76.72 (2012)
15.	Olga Tsander (BLR)	76.66 (2005)
16.	Yekaterina Khoroshikh (RUS)	76.63 (2006)
17.	Yipsi Moreno (CUB)	76.62 (2008)
18.	Yelena Matoshko (BLR)	76.56 (2012)
19.	Darya Pchelnik (BLR)	76.33 (2008)
20.	Hanna Malyshik (BLR)	76.26 (2018)
21.	Yelena Konyevtsova (RUS)	76.21 (2007)
22.	Anna Bulgakova (RUS)	76.17 (2013)
23.	Mihaela Melinte (ROM)	76.07 (1999)
24.	Kathrin Klaas (GER)	76.05 (2012)
25.	Amanda Bingson (USA)	75.73 (2013)
	Sultana Frizell (CAN)	75.73 (2014)
27.	Olga Kuzenkova (RUS)	75.68 (2000)
28.	Joanna Fiodorow (POL)	75.63 (2018)
29.	Hanna Skydan (AZE)	75.29 (2017)
30.	Yelena Rigert (RUS)	75.09 (2013)
31.	Ivana Brkljacic (CRO)	75.08 (2007)
32.	Luo Na (CHN)	75.02 (2018)
33.	Alexandra Tavernier (FRA)	74.78 (2018)
34.	Jeneva Stevens (USA)	74.77 (2013)
35.	Manuela Montebrun (FRA)	74.66 (2005)
36.	Marina Smolyachkova (BLR)	74.65 (2008)
37.	Maggie Ewen (USA)	74.56 (2017)
38.	Sophie Hitchon (GBR)	74.54 (2016)
39.	Iryna Sekachova (UKR)	74.52 (2008)
40.	Zalina Petrivskaya (MDA)	74.21 (2016)
41.	Jessica Cosby-Toruga (USA)	74.20 (2014)
	Brooke Andersen (USA)	74.20 (2018)
43.	Tugce Sahutoglu (TUR)	74.17 (2012)
44.	Iryna Novozhylova (UKR)	74.10 (2012)
45.	Amber Campbell (USA)	74.03 (2016)

Shot Put Women

EUROPEAN CHAMPIONSHIPS 2018: 8-8-2018:

1.	Paulina Guba (POL)	(18.66)	19.33
2.	Christina Schwanitz (GER)	(18.83)	19.19
3.	Aliona Dubitskaya (BLR)	(18.67)	18.81
4.	Klaudia Kardasz (POL)	(18.00)	18.48
5.	Sara Gambetta (GER)		18.13
6.	Radoslava Mavrodieva (BUL)		18.03
7.	Sophie McKinna (GBR)		17.69
8.	Viktoryia Kolb (BLR)		17.50
9.	Alina Kenzel (GER)	(17.46)	17.26
10.	Amelia Strickler (GBR)	(17.31)	17.15
11.	Fanny Roos (SWE)	(17.71)	17.09
12.	Alena Abramchuk (BLR)	(17.17)	16.90

13.	Úrsula Ruiz (ESP)	17.06
14.	Melissa Boekelman (NED)	16.90
15.	Dimitriana Surdu (MDA)	16.87
16.	Olha Golodna (UKR)	16.69
17.	Markéta Cervenková (CZE)	16.62
18.	Viktoriya Klochko (UKR)	16.27
19.	Frida Akerström (SWE)	16.20
20.	Senja Mäkitörmä (FIN)	16.04
21.	Divine Oladipo (GBR)	15.78
22.	Eliana Bandeira (POR)	15.18
23.	Ieva Zarankaite (LTU)	15.13

WORLD RANKING 2018:

1.	Gong Lijao (CHN)	20.38
2.	Christina Schwanitz (GER)	19.78
3.	Raven Saunders (USA)	19.74(CON)
4.	Maggie Ewen (USA)	19.46(Tuc)
5.	Paulina Guba (POL)	19.38
6.	Danniel Thomas-Dodd (JAM)	19.36(GC)
7.	Valerie Adams (NZL)	19.31(Mon)
8.	Jessica Ramsey (USA)	19.23(USC)
9.	Aliona Dubitskaya (BLR)	19.21(Rab)
10.	Anita Márton (HUN)	19.12
11.	Natalia Ducó (CHI)	18.97
12.	Radoslava Mavrodieva (BUL)	18.95
13.	Monique Riddick (USA)	18.70

WORLD INDOOR CHAMPIONSHIPS: 2-3-2018:

1.	Anita Márton (HUN)	19.62
2.	Danniel Thomas-Dodd (JAM)	19.22
3.	Gong Lijiao (CHN)	19.08
4.	Gao Yang (CHN)	18.77
5.	Paulina Guba (POL)	18.54
6.	Aliona Dubitskaya (BLR)	18.21
7.	Yaniuvis López (CUB)	18.19
8.	Jeneva Stevens (USA)	18.18
9.	Cleopatra Borel (TTO)	17.80
10.	Brittany Crew (CAN)	17.61
11.	Yuliya Leantsiuk (BLR)	17.44
12.	Daniella Hill (USA)	17.26
13.	Fanny Roos (SWE)	17.23
14.	Dimitriana Surdu (MDA)	17.22
15.	Radoslava Mavrodieva (BUL)	16.33

WORLD INDOOR RANKING 2018:

1.	Anita Márton (HUN)	19.62
2.	Danniel Thomas-Dodd (JAM)	19.22
3.	Maggie Ewen (USA)	19.20
4.	Gong Lijiao (CHN)	19.08
5.	Paulina Guba (POL)	18.77
	Gang Yao (CHN)	18.77
7.	Jeneva Stevens (USA)	18.55
8.	Irina Tarasova (RUS)	18.28
9.	Aliona Dubitskaya (BLR)	18.21
10.	Brittany Crew (CAN)	18.20

OVERVIEW WORLD OUTDOOR CHAMPIONSHIP FINALISTS OF PAST 6 YEARS

	Wch 17	OG 16	Wch 15	Wch 13
Gong Lijiao (CHN)	19.94 (1)	19.39 (4)	20.30 (2)	19.95 (3)
Anita Márton (HUN)	19.49 (2)	19.87 (3)	19.48 (4)	
Michelle Carter (USA)	19.14 (3)	20.63 (1)	19.76 (3)	19.94 (4)
Danniel Thomas-Dodd (JAM)	18.91 (4)			
Gao Yang (CHN)	18.25 (5)		19.04 (5)	
Brittany Crew (CAN)	18.21 (6)			
Yuliya Leantsiuk (BLR)	18.12 (7)		18.25 (7)	
Yaniuvis López (CUB)	18.03 (8)			
Geisa Arcanjo (BRA)	18.03 (9)	18.16 (9)		
Raven Saunders (USA)	17.86 (10)	19.35 (5)		
Melissa Boekelman (NED)	17.73 (11)			
Bian Ka (CHN)	17.60 (12)			
Valerie Adams (NZL)		20.42 (2)		20.88 (1)
Christina Schwanitz (GER)		19.03 (6)	20.37 (1)	20.41 (2)
Cleopatra Borel (TTO)		18.37 (7)	17.43 (12)	
Aliona Dubitskaya (BLR)		18.23 (8)	18.52 (6)	
Natalia Ducó (CHI)		18.07 (10)	17.98 (9)	18.02 (11)
Alena Abramchuk (BLR)		17.37 (11)		
Aurione Dongmo (CMR)		16.99 (12)		
Natallia Mikhnevich (BLR)			18.24 (8)	
Jeneva Stevens (USA)			17.84 (10)	
Paulina Guba (POL)			17.52 (11)	
Evgeniia Kolodko (RUS)				19.81 (5)
Li Ling (CHN)				18.39 (6)
Irina Tarasova (RUS)				18.37 (7)
Tia Brooks (USA)				18.09 (8)
Galyna Obleshchuk (UKR)				18.08 (9)
Liu Xiangrong (CHN)				18.04 (10)
Alena Kopets (BLR)				17.70 (12)

OVERVIEW WORLD INDOOR CHAMPIONSHIP FINALISTS OF PAST 5 YEARS

	Wch 18	Wch 16	Wch 14
Anita Márton (HUN)	19.62 (1)	19.33 (2)	18.17 (6)
Danniel Thomas-Dodd (JAM)	19.22 (2)		
Gong Lijiao (CHN)	19.08 (3)		19.24 (3)
Gao Yang (CHN)	18.77 (4)	17.67 (8)	
Paulina Guba (POL)	18.54 (5)		
Aliona Dubitskaya (BLR)	18.21 (6)	17.45 (9)	
Yaniuvis López (CUB)	18.19 (7)		
Jeneva Stevens-McCall (USA)	18.18 (8)		18.05 (8)
Cleopatra Borel (TTO)	17.80 (9)	18.38 (4)	
Brittany Crew (CAN)	17.61 (10)		
Yuliya Leantsiuk (BLR)	17.44 (11)		18.16 (7)
Michelle Carter (USA)		20.21 (1)	19.10 (5)
Valerie Adams (NZL)		19.25 (3)	20.67 (1)
Jillian Camarena-Williams (USA)		18.17 (5)	
Radoslava Mavrodieva (BUL)		18.00 (6)	
Lena Urbaniak (GER)		17.91 (7)	
Bian Ka (CHN)		17.34 (10)	
Chiara Rosa (ITA)		17.10 (11)	
Christina Schwanitz (GER)			19.94 (2)
Evgeniia Kolodko (RUS)			19.11 (4)

OVERVIEW TOP 10 WORLD OUTDOOR RANKINGS OF PAST 5 YEARS

	2018	2017	2016	2015	2014
Gong Lijiao (CHN)	20.38 (1)	20.11 (1)	20.43 (2)	20.34 (2)	19.65 (4)
Christina Schwanitz (GER)	19.78 (2)		20.17 (4)	20.77 (1)	20.22 (2)
Raven Saunders (USA)	19.74 (3)	19.76 (2)	19.35 (7)		
Maggie Ewen (USA)	19.46 (4)				
Paulina Guba (POL)	19.38 (5)				
Danniel Thomas-Dodd (JAM)	19.36 (6)	19.15 (6)			
Valerie Adams (NZL)	19.31 (7)		20.42 (3)		20.59 (1)
Jessica Ramsey (USA)	19.23 (8)				
Aliona Dubitskaya (BLR)	19.21 (9)	19.01 (7)		18.88 (10)	
Anita Márton (HUN)	19.12 (10)	19.63 (4)	19.87 (5)	19.48 (4)	19.04 (9)
Daniella Bunch (USA)		19.64 (3)		18.89 (9)	
Michelle Carter (USA)		19.34 (5)	20.63 (1)	20.02 (3)	19.84 (3)
Yaniuvis López (CUB)		18.92 (8)			
Monique Riddick (USA)		18.89 (9)			
Manpreet Kaur (IND)		18.86 (10)			
Tia Brooks (USA)			19.73 (6)	19.00 (7)	
Felisha Johnson (USA)			19.26 (8)		19.18 (7)
Gao Yang (CHN)			19.20 (9)	19.04 (6)	
Jeneva Stevens (USA)			19.11 (10)		
Cleopatra Borel (TTO)				19.26 (5)	19.13 (8)
Brittany Smith (USA)				18.96 (8)	
Evgeniia Kolodko (RUS)				19.52 (5)	
Galyna Obleshchuk (UKR)				19.22 (6)	
Yuliya Leantsiuk (BLR)					18.87 (10)

OVERVIEW TOP 10 WORLD INDOOR RANKINGS OF PAST 5 YEARS

	2018	2017	2016	2015	2014
Anita Márton (HUN)	19.62 (1)	19.28 (2)	19.33 (3)	19.23 (2)	18.63 (9)
Danniel Thomas-Dodd (JAM)	19.22 (2)	18.40 (9)			
Maggie Ewen (USA)	19.20 (3)				
Gong Lijiao (CHN)	19.08 (4)	18.95 (4)	19.37 (2)		19.24 (3)
Paulina Guba (POL)	18.77 (5)		18.63 (9)		
Gang Yao (CHN)	18.77 (5)				
Jeneva Stevens-McCall (USA)	18.55 (7)	18.54 (6)		18.83 (5)	
Irina Tarasova (RUS)	18.28 (8)				
Aliona Dubitskaya (BLR)	18.21 (9)				
Brittany Crew (CAN)	18.20 (10)				
Raven Saunders (USA)		19.56 (1)	19.23 (5)	18.62 (6)	
Michelle Carter (USA)		19.03 (3)	20.21 (1)	19.45 (1)	19.10 (5)
Felisha Johnson (USA)		18.72 (5)		18.32 (10)	
Christina Schwanitz (GER)		18.50 (7)			20.05 (2)
Daniella Bunch (USA)		18.45 (8)	18.87 (6)		
Yuliya Leantsiuk (BLR)		18.39 (10)	18.68 (7)	19.00 (4)	18.85 (7)
Valerie Adams (NZL)			19.25 (4)		20.67 (1)
Jillian Camarena-Williams (USA)			18.64 (8)		
Brittany Smith (USA)			18.57 (10)	19.01 (3)	
Tori Bliss (USA)				18.47 (7)	
Radoslava Mavrodieva (BUL)				18.34 (8)	
Rebecca O'Brien (USA)				18.34 (8)	
Evgeniia Kolodko (RUS)					19.11 (4)
Anca Heltne (ROM)					18.88 (6)
Alena Kopets (BLR)					18.74 (8)
Tia Brooks (USA)					18.51 (10)

WORLD RANKING OUTDOOR ALL TIME:

1.	Natalia Lisovskaya (URS)	22.63 (1987)
2.	Ilona Slupianek (GDR)	22.45 (1980)
3.	Helena Fibingerová (TCH)	22.32 (1977)
4.	Claudia Losch (FRG)	22.19 (1987)
5.	Ivanka Khristova (BUL)	21.89 (1976)
6.	Marianne Adam (GDR)	21.86 (1979)
7.	Li Meisu (CHN)	21.76 (1988)
8.	Natalya Akhrimenko (URS)	21.73 (1988)
9.	Vita Pavlysh (UKR)	21.69 (1998)
10.	Sui Xinmei (CHN)	21.66 (1990)
11.	Verzhiniya Veselinova (BUL)	21.61 (1982)
12.	Margitta Pufe (GDR)	21.58 (1978)
13.	Ines Müller (GDR)	21.57 (1988)
14.	Nunu Abashidze (URS)	21.53 (1984)
15.	Huang Zhihong (CHN)	21.52 (1990)
16.	Larisa Peleshenko (RUS)	21.46 (2000)
17.	Nadezhda Chizhova (URS)	21.45 (1973)
18.	Eva Wilms (FRG)	21.43 (1977)
19.	Svetlana Krachevskaya (URS)	21.42 (1980)
20.	Heike Hartwig (GDR)	21.31 (1988)
21.	Liane Schmuhl (GDR)	21.27 (1982)
22.	Valerie Adams (NZL)	21.24 (2011)
23.	Astrid Kumbernuss (GER)	21.22 (1995)
24.	Kathrin Neimke (GDR)	21.21 (1987)
25.	Helma Knorscheidt (GDR)	21.19 (1984)
26.	Heidi Krieger (GDR)	21.10 (1986)
27.	Nadezhda Ostapchuk (BLR)	21.09 (2005)
28.	Valentina Fedyushina (URS)	21.08 (1988)
29.	Svetlana Krivelyova (RUS)	21.06 (1992)
30.	Zdenka Silhavá (TCH)	21.05 (1983)
31.	Ivanka Petrova (BUL)	21.01 (1979)
32.	Mihaela Loghin (ROM)	21.00 (1984)
	Cordula Schulze (GDR)	21.00 (1984)
34.	Belsy Laza (CUB)	20.96 (1992)
35.	Elena Stoyanova (BUL)	20.95 (1980)
36.	Svetla Mitkova (BUL)	20.91 (1987)
37.	Irina Korzhanenko (RUS)	20.82 (1998)
38.	Sona Vasicková (TCH)	20.80 (1988)
39.	Christina Schwanitz (GER)	20.77 (2015)
40.	Grit Hammer (GDR)	20.72 (1987)
41.	Natalya Mikhnevich (BLR)	20.70 (2008)
42.	Michelle Carter (USA)	20.63 (2016)
43.	Maria Elena Sarría (CUB)	20.61 (1982)
	Yanina Korolchik (BLR)	20.61 (2001)
45.	Marina Antonyuk (URS)	20.60 (1986)

WORLD RANKING INDOOR ALL TIME:

1.	Helena Fibingerová (TCH)	22.50 (1977)
2.	Natalia Lisovskaya (URS)	22.14 (1987)
3.	Valentina Fedyushina (UKR)	21.60 (1991)
4.	Ilona Slupianek (GDR)	21.59 (1979)
5.	Claudia Losch (FRG)	21.46 (1986)
6.	Ines Müller (GDR)	21.26 (1985)
	Natalya Akhrimenko (URS)	21.26 (1987)
8.	Margitta Pufe (GDR)	21.23 (1978)
9.	Irina Korzhanenko (RUS)	21.15 (1999)
10.	Sui Xinmei (CHN)	21.10 (1990)
11.	Li Meisu (CHN)	21.08 (1988)
12.	Eva Wilms (FRG)	21.06 (1977)
	Nunu Abashidze (URS)	21.06 (1984)
14.	Helma Knorscheidt (FRG)	21.03 (1983)
15.	Valerie Adams (NZL)	20.98 (2013)
16.	Kathrin Neimke (GDR)	20.94 (1988)
17.	Heidi Krieger (GDR)	20.85 (1987)
18.	Ivanka Khristova (BUL)	20.78 (1976)
19.	Heike Hartwig (GDR)	20.75 (1987)
20.	Verzhiniya Veselinova (BUL)	20.74 (1982)
21.	Vita Pavlysh (UKR)	20.73 (2004)
22.	Larisa Peleshenko (URS)	20.71 (1988)
23.	Liane Schmuhl (GDR)	20.70 (1982)
24.	Svetlana Krivelyova (RUS)	20.69 (1999)
25.	Nadezhda Chizhova (URS)	20.62 (1974)
26.	Marianne Adam (GDR)	20.58 (1979)
27.	Mihaela Loghin (ROM)	20.57 (1987)
28.	Nadezhda Ostapchuk (BLR)	20.56 (2003)
29.	Christa Wiese (GDR)	20.50 (1989)
30.	Sona Vasickova (TCH)	20.37 (1989)
31.	Cordula Schulze (GDR)	20.35 (1982)
32.	Marina Antonyuk (URS)	20.34 (1987)
33.	Huang Zhihong (CHN)	20.33 (1991)
34.	Stephanie Storp (FRG)	20.30 (1989)
	Astrid Kumbernuss (GDR)	20.30 (1996)
36.	Michelle Carter (USA)	20.21 (2016)
37.	Danguolé Urbikiené (URS)	20.20 (1987)
38.	Iris Plotzitzka (FRG)	20.17 (1988)
39.	Svetla Mitkova (BUL)	20.13 (1992)
40.	Li Xiaoyun (CHN)	20.08 (1993)
41.	Svetlana Krachevskaya (URS)	20.06 (1976)
42.	Christina Schwanitz (GER)	20.05 (2014)
43.	Anna Romanova (RUS)	20.01 (1992)
44.	Simone Rüdrich (GDR)	19.96 (1983)
45.	Gong Lijiao (CHN)	19.93 (2011)

4 x 100 m Women

EUROPEAN CHAMPIONSHIPS 2018: 12-8-2018:

1. GBR   (42.19)   41.88
Philip/Lansiquot/B. Williams/Asher-Smith
2. NED   (42.62)   42.15
Schippers/Van Hunenstijn/Samuel/Sedney
3. GER   (42.34)   42.23
Kwakyie/Lückenkemper/Pinto/Haase
4. SUI   (42.62)   42.30
Del Ponte/Atcho/Kambundji/Kora
5. FRA   (43.06)   43.10
Ombissa-Dzangue/Akakpo/Galais/Zahi
6. POL   (43.20)   43.34
Ciba/Kielbasinska/Kotwila/Swoboda
7. ITA   (43.74)   43.42
Herrera/Hooper/Siragusa/Alloh
8. ESP   (43.38)   43.54
Pérez/Garcia/Sevilla/Lara

----

9. IRL   43.80
J. Healy/P. Healy/Neville/Akpe-Moses
10. UKR   43.90
Plotitsyna/Kalistratova/Kachur/Holeneva
11. DEN   44.09
Östergard/Karstoft/Graversgaard/Kramer
12. CZE   44.12
Domská/Plisková/Slaninová/Seidlová
13. HUN   44.15
Nguyen/Kaptur/Kerekes/Kozák
14. GRE   44.48
Keramida/Pesirídou/Spanoudáki/Politi
15. SWE   44.51
Payton/Adriansson/Ström/Östlund

WORLD RANKING 2018:

1.	GBR	41.88(ECh)
2.	NED	42.15(ECh)
3.	GER	42.23(ECh)
4.	SUI	42.29(Lau)
5.	USA	42.50(NAC)
6.	JAM	42.52(GC)
7.	CHN	42.59(Lon)
8.	BRN	42.73(Jak)
9.	NGR	42.75(GC)
10.	FRA	43.06(ECh)
11.	POL	43.20(ECh)
12.	ESP	43.31
13.	ITA	43.42(ECh)
14.	TTO	43.50(GC)
15.	GHA	43.64(GC)
16.	RSA	43.68(Lon)
	DOM	43.68
18.	AUS	43.76(Bri)
19.	IRL	43.80(ECh)
20.	KAZ	43.82(Jak)
21.	UKR	43.90(ECh)

OVERVIEW WORLD OUTDOOR CHAMPIONSHIP FINALISTS OF PAST 6 YEARS

	Wch 17	OG 16	Wch 15	Wch 13
USA	41.82 (1)	41.01 (1)	41.68 (2)	42.75 (2)
GBR	42.12 (2)	41.77 (3)	42.10 (4)	42.87 (3)
JAM	42.19 (3)	41.36 (2)	41.07 (1)	41.29 (1)
GER	42.36 (4)	42.10 (4)	42.64 (5)	42.90 (4)
SUI	42.51 (5)			
TTO	42.62 (6)	42.12 (5)	42.03 (3)	
BRA	42.63 (7)			dnf
NED	43.07 (8)		dsq	
UKR		42.36 (6)		
CAN		43.15 (7)	43.05 (6)	43.28 (6)
NGR		43.21 (8)		
RUS			dnf	42.93 (5)
FRA				dsq

OVERVIEW TOP 10 WORLD OUTDOOR RANKINGS OF PAST 5 YEARS

	2018	2017	2016	2015	2014
GBR	41.88 (1)	41.86 (3)	41.77 (4)	42.10 (4)	42.21 (3)
NED	42.15 (2)	42.64 (8)	42.04 (5)	42.32 (5)	42.40 (5)
GER	42.23 (3)	42.17 (4)	41.62 (3)	42.64 (8)	42.63 (7)
SUI	42.29 (4)	42.50 (5)			
USA	42.50 (5)	41.82 (1)	41.01 (1)	41.68 (2)	41.88 (2)
JAM	42.52 (6)	41.85 (2)	41.36 (2)	41.07 (1)	41.83 (1)
CHN	42.59 (7)		42.65 (10)		42.83 (9)
BRN	42.73 (8)				
NGR	42.75 (9)		42.55 (8)	42.99 (10)	42.67 (8)
FRA	43.06 (10)	42.92 (9)			42.29 (4)
TTO		42.62 (6)	42.12 (6)	42.03 (3)	42.59 (6)
BRA		42.63 (7)	42.59 (9)	42.92 (9)	42.92 (10)
KAZ		43.03 (10)			
UKR			42.36 (7)	42.50 (6)	
CAN				42.60 (7)	
RUS				42.99 (10)	

WORLD RANKING ALL TIME:

1.	USA	40.82 (2012)
2.	JAM	41.07 (2015)
3.	GDR	41.37 (1985)
4.	RUS	41.49 (1993)
5.	GER	41.62 (2016)
6.	GBR	41.77 (2016)
7.	FRA	41.78 (2003)
8.	BAH	41.92 (1999)
9.	URS	42.00 (1985)
10.	TTO	42.03 (2015)
11.	UKR	42.04 (2012)
	NED	42.04 (2016)
13.	BUL	42.29 (1988)
	BRA	42.29 (2013)
	SUI	42.29 (2018)
16.	NGR	42.39 (1992)
17.	BEL	42.54 (2008)
18.	BLR	42.56 (2005)
19.	FRG	42.59 (1976)
	CHN	42.59 (2018)
21.	CAN	42.60 (2015)
22.	GHA	42.67 (2016)
23.	POL	42.68 (2010)
24.	BRN	42.73 (2018)
25.	CUB	42.89 (1993)
26.	KAZ	42.92 (2016)
27.	UKR	42.97 (1986)
28.	TCH	42.98 (1982)
29.	AUS	42.99 (2000)

4 x 400 m Women

EUROPEAN CHAMPIONSHIPS 2018: 11-8-2018:

1. POL   (3.28.52)   3.26.59
Holub-Kowalik/Baumgart/Wyciskiewicz/Swiety-Ersetic
2. FRA   (3.28.61)   3.27.17
Diarra/Sananes/Raharolahy/Guei
3. GBR   3.27.40
Clark/Onuora/Allcock/Doyle
4. BEL   3.27.69
Bolingo Mbongo/Claes/Grillet/Laus
5. ITA   (3.27.63)   3.28.62
Chigbolu/Folorunso/Lukudo/Grenot
6. GER   3.30.33
Gonska/Müller/Pahlitzsch/Mergenthaler
7. ROM   (3.31.95)   3.32.15
Miklos/Balan/Belgyan/Razor
8. SVK   (3.32.11)   3.32.22
Zapetalová/Putalová/Ledecká/Bezeková
----
9. SWE   3.32.61
Hellqvist/Hjelmer/Magnusson/Duffy
10. SUI   3.32.86
Humair/Schürmann/Pellaud/Giger
11. ESP   3.33.18
Bueno/Parra/Sánchez/Bokesa
12. POR   3.33.35
Mentai/Monteiro/Azevedo/Évora
13. GRE   3.34.69
Vasilíou/Mourtá/Zigóri/Vasilíou
14. IRL   3.35.96
Denny/Becker/Patterson/Mooney
15. LTU   3.37.73
Misiunaite/Morauskaite/Galvydyte/Kruminaite
    UKR   dsq
Klymyuk/Mykolenko/Bryzhina/Melnyk

WORLD RANKING 2018:

1.	JAM	3.24.00(GC)
2.	USA	3.24.28(WC)
3.	NGR	3.25.29(GC)
4.	FRA	3.25.91(WC)
5.	POL	3.26.17(WC)
6.	GBR	3.26.48(WC)
7.	BOT	3.26.86(GC)
8.	AUS	3.27.43(GC)
9.	ITA	3.27.63(ECh)
10.	BEL	3.27.69(ECh)
11.	CAN	3.28.04(NAC)
12.	IND	3.28.72(Jak)
13.	SUI	3.29.46
14.	CUB	3.29.48

WORLD INDOOR CHAMPIONSHIPS: 4-3-2018:

  1. USA   3.23.85
Hayes/Moline/Wimbley/Okolo
  2. POL   3.26.09
Swiety-Ersetic/Wyciskiewicz/Gaworska/Holub-Kowalik
  3. GBR   3.29.38
Beesley/Williams/Allcock/Clark
  4. UKR   3.31.32
Melnyk/Klymiuk/Yaroshchuk-Ryzhykova/Bryzhina
  5. ITA   3.31.55
Lukudo/Folorunso/Bazzoni/Spacca
      JAM   (3.32.01)   dsq
Jenkins/Russell/Le-Roy/McPherson

----

  7. CZE   3.34.90
  8. POR   3.35.43
  9. KAZ   3.40.54
      NGR   dns

WORLD INDOOR RANKING 2018:

1.	USA	3.23.85
2.	POL	3.26.09
3.	GBR	3.29.38
4.	UKR	3.31.32
5.	ITA	3.31.55
6.	JAM	3.32.01

OVERVIEW WORLD OUTDOOR CHAMPIONSHIP FINALISTS OF PAST 6 YEARS

	Wch 17	OG 16	Wch 15	Wch 13
USA	3.19.02 (1)	3.19.06 (1)	3.19.39 (1)	3.20.41 (2)
GBR	3.25.00 (2)	3.25.88 (3)	3.26.38 (3)	3.22.61 (3)
POL	3.25.41 (3)	3.27.28 (7)	3.29.30 (5)	
FRA	3.26.56 (4)		3.26.68 (4)	3.24.21 (4)
NGR	3.26.72 (5)			3.27.57 (6)
GER	3.27.45 (6)			
BOT	3.28.00 (7)			
JAM	dnf	3.20.34 (2)	3.22.49 (2)	
CAN		3.26.43 (4)	3.29.65 (6)	
UKR		3.26.64 (5)		3.27.38 (5)
ITA		3.27.05 (6)		dsq
AUS		3.27.45 (8)	3.30.03 (7)	
BRA			3.31.30 (8)	
RUS				3.20.19 (1)
ROM				3.28.40 (7)

OVERVIEW WORLD INDOOR CHAMPIONSHIP FINALISTS OF PAST 5 YEARS

	Wch 18	Wch 16	Wch 14
USA	3.23.85 (1)	3.26.38 (1)	3.24.83 (1)
POL	3.26.09 (2)	3.31.15 (2)	3.29.89 (5)
GBR	3.29.38 (3)		3.27.90 (3)
UKR	3.31.32 (4)	3.40.42 (5)	
ITA	3.31.55 (5)		
JAM	dsq (6)	dnf (6)	3.26.54 (2)
ROM		3.31.51 (3)	
NGR		3.34.03 (4)	3.31.59 (6)
RUS			3.28.39 (4)

OVERVIEW TOP 10 WORLD OUTDOOR RANKINGS OF PAST 5 YEARS

	2018	2017	2016	2015	2014
JAM	3.24.00 (1)	3.23.64 (2)	3.20.34 (2)	3.19.13 (1)	3.23.26 (2)
USA	3.24.28 (2)	3.19.02 (1)	3.19.06 (1)	3.19.39 (2)	3.21.73 (1)
NGR	3.25.29 (3)	3.25.40 (4)		3.23.27 (3)	3.23.41 (3)
FRA	3.25.91 (4)	3.26.56 (7)	3.25.96 (9)	3.24.86 (6)	3.24.27 (4)
POL	3.26.17 (5)	3.25.41 (5)	3.25.34 (7)		3.25.73 (8)
GBR	3.26.48 (6)	3.24.74 (3)	3.24.81 (4)	3.23.62 (4)	3.24.34 (6)
BOT	3.26.86 (7)	3.26.90 (8)			
AUS	3.27.43 (8)	3.28.02 (10)	3.25.71 (8)		
ITA	3.27.63 (9)	3.27.81 (9)	3.25.16 (6)	3.27.07 (9)	3.27.44 (9)
BEL	3.27.69 (10)				
GER		3.26.24 (6)	3.26.02 (10)		3.27.69 (10)
UKR		3.28.02 (10)	3.24.54 (3)	3.25.94 (7)	3.24.32 (5)
CAN			3.24.94 (5)	3.26.14 (8)	
RUS				3.23.75 (5)	3.25.02 (7)
CUB				3.28.15 (10)	

OVERVIEW TOP 10 WORLD INDOOR RANKINGS OF PAST 5 YEARS

	2018	2017	2016	2015	2014
USA	3.23.85 (1)	3.27.07 (1)	3.26.38 (1)	3.28.48 (1)	3.24.83 (1)
POL	3.26.09 (2)	3.29.94 (2)	3.31.15 (2)	3.31.90 (4)	3.29.48 (5)
GBR	3.29.38 (3)	3.31.05 (3)		3.31.79 (3)	3.27.90 (3)
UKR	3.31.32 (4)			3.32.39 (6)	
ITA	3.31.55 (5)				
JAM	3.32.01 (6)				3.26.54 (2)
ROM			3.31.51 (3)		
FRA				3.31.61 (2)	
CZE				3.32.08 (5)	
RUS				3.32.53 (7)	3.28.39 (4)
NGR					3.29.67 (6)

WORLD RANKING OUTDOOR ALL TIME:

1.	URS	3.15.17 (1988)
2.	USA	3.15.51 (1988)
3.	GDR	3.15.92 (1984)
4.	RUS	3.18.38 (1993)
5.	JAM	3.18.71 (2011)
6.	GBR	3.20.04 (2007)
7.	TCH	3.20.32 (1983)
8.	GER	3.20.92 (1997)
9.	NGR	3.21.04 (1996)
10.	CAN	3.21.21 (1984)
11.	BLR	3.21.88 (2007)
12.	UKR	3.21.94 (1986)
13.	FRA	3.22.34 (1994)
14.	FRG	3.22.49 (1988)
15.	CUB	3.23.21 (2008)
16.	UKR	3.23.57 (2012)
17.	CZE	3.23.73 (1997)
18.	AUS	3.23.81 (2000)
19.	POL	3.24.49 (2005)
20.	ITA	3.25.16 (2016)
21.	ROM	3.25.68 (1999)
22.	BUL	3.25.81 (1983)
23.	FIN	3.25.87 (1976)
24.	GRE	3.26.33 (2004)
25.	BAH	3.26.36 (2016)
26.	BRA	3.26.82 (2005)
27.	BOT	3.26.86 (2018)
28.	IND	3.26.89 (2004)
29.	NED	3.26.98 (2016)

WORLD RANKING INDOOR ALL TIME:

1.	RUS	3.23.37 (2006)
2.	USA	3.23.85 (2018)
3.	POL	3.26.09 (2018)
4.	JAM	3.26.54 (2014)
5.	AUS	3.26.87 (1999)
6.	GER	3.27.22 (1991)
7.	GBR	3.27.56 (2013)
8.	BLR	3.27.83 (2007)
9.	URS	3.27.95 (1991)
10.	CZE	3.28.47 (1997)
11.	FRA	3.28.71 (2013)
12.	NGR	3.29.67 (2014)

Heptathlon Women Outdoor / Pentathlon Women Indoor

EUROPEAN CHAMPIONSHIPS 2018: 10-8-2018:
1. Nafissatou Thiam (BEL)　　6816
13.69-1.91-15.35-24.81-6.60-57.91-2.19.35
2. Katarina Johnson-Thompson (GBR)　6759
13.34-1.91-13.09-22.88-6.68-42.16-2.09.84
3. Carolin Schäfer (GER)　　6602
13.33-1.79-14.12-23.75-6.24-53.73-2.14.65
4. Ivona Dadic (AUT)　　6552
13.66-1.82-14.06-23.61-6.35-47.42-2.11.87
5. Anouk Vetter (NED)　　6414
13.55-1.76-14.79-23.97-6.30-51.25-2.22.84
6. Katerina Cachová (CZE)　　6400
13.29-1.85-12.71-24.25-6.36-44.64-2.14.91
7. Xénia Krizsán (HUN)　　6367
13.64-1.79-13.99-25.05-6.24-45.45-2.07.61
8. Verena Preiner (AUT)　　6337
13.58-1.73-13.76-24.12-6.09-48.79-2.11.29
9. Géraldine Rukcstuhl (SUI)　　6260
13.90-1.79-12.96-25.04-5.90-56.31-2.15.13
10. Hanne Maudens (BEL)　　6104
11. Esther Turpin (FRA)　　6093
12. Grit Sadeiko (EST)　　6060
13. Sarah Lagger (AUT)　　6058
14. Daryna Sloboda (UKR)　　5999
15. Alina Shukh (UKR)　　5985
16. Lecabela Quaresma (POR)　　5950
17. Rimma Hordiyenko (UKR)　　5894
18. Diane Marie-Hardy (FRA)　　5794
19. Maria Huntington (FIN)　　5731
20. Noor Vidts (BEL)　　5598
21. Annik Kälin (SUI)　　5572

WORLD RANKING 2018:
1. Nafissatou Thiam (BEL)　　6816(ECh)
2. Katarina Johnson-Thompson (GBR)　6759(ECh)
3. Yorgelis Rodríguez (CUB)　　6742(Gtz)
13.48-1.86-14.95-23.96-6.58-48.65-2.12.73
4. Erica Bougard (USA)　　6725(Gtz)
12.80-1.86-13.02-23.31-6.62-41.97-2.08.42
5. Carolin Schäfer (GER)　　6602(Gtz)
6. Ivona Dadic (AUT)　　6552(ECh)
7. Anouk Vetter (NED)　　6426(Gtz)
13.46-1.71-15.91-23.89-6.25-51.27-2.23.41
8. Katerina Cachová (CZE)　　6400(ECh)
9. Géraldine Ruckstuhl (SUI)　　6391(Tal)
13.85-1.83-13.82-24.96-5.96-55.11-2.13.98
10. Xénia Krizsan (HUN)　　6367(ECh)
11. Verena Preiner (AUT)　　6337(ECh)
12. Evelis Aguilar (COL)　　6285
13.92-1.77-13.64-23.95-6.47-43.01-2.16.18

WORLD INDOOR CHAMPIONSHIPS: 2-3-2018:

1. Katarina Johnson-Thompson (GBR)   4750
8.36-1.91-12.68-6.50-2.16.63

2. Ivona Dadic (AUT)   4700
8.32-1.82-14.27-6.40-2.17.82

3. Yorgelis Rodríguez (CUB)   4637
8.57-1.88-14.15-6.15-2.17.70

4. Eliska Klucinova (CZE)   4579
8.65-1.82-14.76-6.20-2.19.16

5. Erica Bougard (USA)   4571
8.07-1.85-12.31-6.18-2.19.51

6. Xénia Krizsán (HUN)   4559
8.38-1.82-13.88-6.09-2.18.12

7. Alina Shukh (UKR)   4466
8.85-1.82-14.08-6.09-2.18.36

8. Lecabela Quaresma (POR)   4424
8.51-1.76-14.12-6.01-2.19.85

9. Kendell Williams (USA)   4414
8.08-1.76-12.13-6.30-2.24.60

10. Caroline Agnou (SUI)   4397
8.56-1.73-14.92-5.96-2.21.08

11. Katerina Cachová (CZE)   4282
8.20-1.70-12.18-5.94-2.18.90

WORLD INDOOR RANKING 2018:

1. Erica Bougard (USA)   4760
7.98-1.89-12.76-6.20-2.13.77

2. Katarina Johnson-Thompson (GBR)   4750

3. Ivona Dadic (AUT)   4700

4. Eliska Klucinová (CZE)   4663
8.51-1.84-14.52-6.26-2.17.34

5. Yorgelís Rodríguez (CUB)   4637

6. Xénia Krizsán (HUN)   4583
8.39-1.79-14.21-6.14-2.16.28

7. Taliyah Brooks (USA)   4572
8.05-1.84-12.16-6.36-2.22.44

8. Kendell Williams (USA)   4508
8.11-1.74-12.55-6.38-2.19.22

9. Nina Schultz (CAN)   4502
8.28-1.82-11.61-6.39-2.19.79

10. Alina Shukh (UKR)   4472
8.88-1.85-13.48-6.05-2.16.47

OVERVIEW WORLD OUTDOOR CHAMPIONSHIP FINALISTS OF PAST 6 YEARS

	Wch 17	OG 16	Wch 15	Wch 13
Nafissatou Thiam (BEL)	6784 (1)	6810 (1)		
Carolin Schäfer (GER)	6696 (2)	6540 (5)		
Anouk Vetter (NED)	6636 (3)	6394 (10)		
Yorgelis Rodríguez (CUB)	6594 (4)	6481 (7)		
Katarina Johnson-Thompson (GBR)	6558 (5)	6523 (6)		6449 (5)
Ivona Dadic (AUT)	6417 (6)			
Nadine Visser (NED)	6370 (7)		6344 (8)	
Claudia Salman-Rath (GER)	6362 (8)		6441 (5)	6462 (4)
Xénia Krizsán (HUN)	6356 (9)		6322 (9)	
Eliska Klucinová (CZE)	6313 (10)			6332 (7)
Jessica Ennis-Hill (GBR)		6775 (2)	6669 (1)	
Brianne Theisen-Eaton (CAN)		6653 (3)	6554 (2)	6530 (2)
Laura Ikauniece-Admidina (LAT)		6617 (4)	6516 (3)	
Gyorgyi Zsivocky-Farkas (HUN)		6442 (8)	6389 (6)	
Jennifer Oeser (GER)		6401 (9)	6308 (10)	
Nadine Broersen (NED)			6491 (4)	6224 (10)
Anastasiya Mokhnyuk (UKR)			6359 (7)	
Ganna Melnichenko (UKR)				6586 (1)
Dafne Schippers (NED)				6477 (3)
Sharon Day (USA)				6407 (6)
Antoinette Nana Djimou Ida (FRA)				6326 (8)
Karolina Tyminska (POL)				6270 (9)

OVERVIEW WORLD INDOOR CHAMPIONSHIP FINALISTS OF PAST 5 YEARS

	Wch 18	Wch 16	Wch 14
Katarina Johnson-Thompson (GBR)	4750 (1)		
Ivona Dadic (AUT)	4700 (2)		
Yorgelis Rodríguez (CUB)	4637 (3)		
Eliska Klucinová (CZE)	4579 (4)		
Erica Bougard (USA)	4571 (5)		
Xénia Krizsán (HUN)	4559 (6)		
Alina Shukh (UKR)	4466 (7)		
Lecabela Quaresma (POR)	4424 (8)		
Kendell Williams (USA)	4414 (9)	4586 (6)	
Brianne Theisen Eaton (CAN)		4881 (1)	4768 (2)
Anastasiya Mokhnyuk (UKR)		4847 (2)	
Alina Fodorova (UKR)		4770 (3)	4724 (3)
Barbara Nwaba (USA)		4661 (4)	
Györgyi Zsivocky-Farkas (HUN)		4656 (5)	
Morgan Lake (GBR)		4499 (7)	
Katerina Cachová (CZE)		4403 (8)	
Nadine Broersen (NED)			4830 (1)
Sharon Day-Monroe (USA)			4718 (4)
Claudia Rath (GER)			4681 (5)
Yana Maksimava (BLR)			4651 (6)
Ganna Melnichenko (UKR)			4587 (7)
Karolina Tyminska (POL)			4557 (8)

OVERVIEW TOP 10 WORLD OUTDOOR RANKINGS OF PAST 5 YEARS

	2018	2017	2016	2015	2014
Nafissatou Thiam (BEL)	6816 (1)	7013 (1)	6810 (1)		6508 (6)
Katarina Johnson-Thompson (GBR)	6759 (2)	6691 (4)	6523 (7)		6682 (1)
Yorgelis Rodríguez (CUB)	6742 (3)	6594 (6)	6481 (9)		
Erica Bougard (USA)	6725 (4)	6557 (9)			
Carolin Schäfer (GER)	6602 (5)	6836 (2)	6557 (6)	6547 (3)	6395 (10)
Ivona Dadic (AUT)	6552 (6)				
Anouk Vetter (NED)	6426 (7)	6636 (5)	6626 (4)	6458 (8)	
Katerina Cachová (CZE)	6400 (8)				
Géraldine Ruckstuhl (SUI)	6391 (9)				
Xénia Krizsán (HUN)	6367 (10)				
Laura Ikauniece-Admidina (LAT)		6815 (3)	6622 (5)	6516 (5)	
Claudia Salman-Rath (GER)		6580 (7)		6458 (8)	
Kendell Williams (USA)		6564 (8)			
Sharon Day-Monroe (USA)		6421 (10)		6458 (8)	6470 (7)
Jessica Ennis-Hill (GBR)			6775 (2)	6669 (2)	
Brianne Theisen Eaton (CAN)			6765 (3)	6808 (1)	6641 (2)
Barbara Nwaba (USA)			6494 (8)	6500 (6)	
Antoinette Djimou Ida (FRA)			6458 (10)		6551 (3)
Nadine Broersen (NED)				6531 (4)	6539 (5)
Nadine Visser (NED)				6467 (7)	
Dafne Schippers (NED)					6545 (4)
Eliska Klucinová (CZE)					6460 (8)
Lilli Schwarzkopf (GER)					6426 (9)

OVERVIEW TOP 10 WORLD INDOOR RANKINGS OF PAST 5 YEARS

	2018	2017	2016	2015	2014
Erica Bougard (USA)	4760 (1)	4558 (8)			4586 (9)
Katharina Johnson-Thompson(GBR)	4750 (2)				5000 (1)
Ivona Dadic (AUT)	4700 (3)	4767 (2)			
Eliska Klucinova (CZE)	4663 (4)			4687 (6)	
Yorgelís Rodríguez (CUB)	4637 (5)				
Xénia Krizsán (HUN)	4583 (6)	4631 (5)			
Taliyah Brooks (USA)	4572 (7)	4580 (7)			
Kendell Williams (USA)	4508 (8)	4682 (4)	4703 (4)	4678 (7)	4635 (7)
Nina Schultz (CAN)	4502 (9)				
Alina Shukh (UKR)	4472 (10)	4550 (9)			
Nafissatou Thiam (BEL)		4870 (1)	4678 (6)	4696 (4)	
Györgyi Zsivocky-Farkas (HUN)		4723 (3)	4656 (8)	4691 (5)	
Nadine Broersen (NED)		4582 (6)			
Verena Preiner (AUT)		4486 (10)			
Brianne Theisen Eaton (CAN)			4881 (1)		4768 (3)
Anastasiya Mokhnyuk (UKR)			4847 (2)	4707 (3)	
Alina Fyodorova (UKR)			4770 (3)	4609 (9)	4724 (4)
Claudia Rath (GER)			4688 (5)		4681 (6)
Barbara Nwaba (USA)			4661 (7)		
Akela Jones (BAR)			4643 (9)		
Morgan Lake (GBR)			4519 (10)		
Yana Maksimava (BLR)				4742 (2)	4686 (5)
Sharon Day-Monroe (USA)				4654 (8)	4805 (2)
Antoinette Nana Djimou Ida (FRA)				4591 (10)	
Nadine Broersen (NED)					4830 (1)
Ganna Melnichenko (UKR)					4587 (8)
Karolina Tyminska (POL)					4557 (10)

WORLD RANKING OUTDOOR ALL TIME:

1.	Jackie Joyner-Kersee (USA)	7291 (1988)
2.	Carolina Klüft (SWE)	7032 (2007)
3.	Nafissatou Thiam (BEL)	7013 (2017)
4.	Larissa Nikitina (URS)	7007 (1989)
5.	Sabine Braun (GER)	6985 (1992)
6.	Jessica Ennis-Hill (GBR)	6955 (2012)
7.	Sabine John (GDR)	6946 (1984)
8.	Ghada Shouaa (SYR)	6942 (1996)
9.	Ramona Neubert (GDR)	6935 (1983)
10.	Eunice Barber (FRA)	6889 (2005)
11.	Natalya Shubenkova (URS)	6859 (1994)
12.	Anke Vater (GDR)	6858 (1988)
13.	Irina Belova (RUS)	6845 (1992)
14.	Carolin Schäfer (GER)	6836 (2017)
15.	Lyudmila Blonska (UKR)	6832 (2007)
16.	Denise Lewis (GBR)	6831 (2000)
17.	Laura Ikauniece-Admidina (LAT)	6815 (2017)
18.	Brianne Theisen-Eaton (CAN)	6808 (2015)
19.	Jane Frederick (USA)	6803 (1984)
20.	Nataliya Dobrynska (UKR)	6778 (2010)
21.	Yelena Prokhorova (RUS)	6765 (2000)
22.	Katarina Johnson-Thompson (GBR)	6759 (2018)
23.	Ma Miaolan (CHN)	6750 (1993)
24.	Yorgelis Rodríguez (CUB)	6742 (2018)
25.	Heike Drechsler (GER)	6741 (1994)
26.	Hyleas Fountain (USA)	6735 (2010)
27.	Erica Bougard (USA)	6725 (2018)
28.	Tatyana Blokhina (RUS)	6703 (1993)
29.	Chantal Beaugeant (FRA)	6702 (1988)
30.	Jane Flemming (AUS)	6695 (1990)
31.	Jennifer Oeser (GER)	6683 (2010)
32.	Kristina Savitskaya (RUS)	6681 (2012)
33.	Ines Schulz (GER)	6660 (1988)
34.	Svetla Dimitrova (BUL)	6658 (1992)
35.	Lilli Schwarzkopf (GER)	6649 (2012)
36.	Natalya Grachova (URS)	6646 (1982)
37.	Anouk Vetter (NED)	6636 (2017)
38.	Sibylle Thiele (GDR)	6635 (1986)
	Svetlana Buraga (BLR)	6635 (1993)
40.	Natalya Roshchupkina (RUS)	6633 (2000)
41.	Judy Simpson (GBR)	6623 (1986)
42.	Liliana Nastase (ROM)	6619 (1992)
43.	Tatyana Chernova (RUS)	6618 (2008)
44.	Malgorzata Nowak (POL)	6616 (1985)
45.	Remigija Nazarovienė (URS)	6604 (1989)

WORLD RANKING INDOOR ALL TIME:

1.	Nataliya Dobrynska (UKR)	5013 (2012)
2.	Katarina Johnson-Thompson (GBR)	5000 (2015)
3.	Irina Belova (RUS)	4991 (1992)
4.	Jessica Ennis-Hill (GBR)	4965 (2012)
5.	Carolina Klüft (SWE)	4948 (2005)
6.	Kelly Sotherton (GBR)	4927 (2007)
7.	Yekaterina Bolshova (RUS)	4896 (2012)
8.	Brianne Theisen (CAN)	4881 (2016)
9.	Tia Hellebaut (BEL)	4877 (2007)
10.	Nafissatou Thiam (BEL)	4870 (2017)
11.	Svetlana Moskalets (RUS)	4866 (1995)
12.	Yekaterina Lobakina (RUS)	4851 (2013)
13.	Natalya Sazanovich (BLR)	4850 (2001)
14.	Anastasia Mokhnyuk (UKR)	4847 (2016)
15.	Nadine Broersen (NED)	4830 (2014)
16.	Urszula Wlodarczyk (POL)	4808 (1998)
17.	Sharon Day-Monroe (USA)	4805 (2014)
18.	Austra Skujyte (LTU)	4802 (2012)
19.	Larisa Nikitina (RUS)	4801 (1994)
	Karin Rückstuhl (NED)	4801 (2007)
21.	Olga Kurban (RUS)	4792 (2012)
22.	Anna Bogdanova (RUS)	4784 (2009)
23.	Sabine Braun (GER)	4780 (1997)
24.	Rita Ináncsi (HUN)	4775 (1994)
25.	Lyudmila Blonska (UKR)	4771 (2008)
26.	Alina Fyodorova (UKR)	4770 (2016)
27.	Karolina Tyminska (POL)	4769 (2008)
28.	Sabine John (GDR)	4768 (1985)
29.	Ivona Dadic (AUT)	4767 (2017)
30.	Erica Bougard (USA)	4760 (2018)
31.	Naide Gomes (POR)	4759 (2004)
32.	Liliana Nastase (ROM)	4753 (1993)
	DeDee Nathan (USA)	4753 (1999)
	Hyleas Fountain (USA)	4753 (2010)
35.	Hanna Kasyanova (UKR)	4748 (2012)
36.	Yana Maksimava (BLR)	4742 (2015)
37.	Yelena Lebedyenko (RUS)	4735 (1996)
38.	Ida Antoinette Nana Djimou (FRA)	4723 (2011)
	Györgyi Zsivocky-Farkas (HUN)	4723 (2017)
40.	Tatyana Chernova (RUS)	4717 (2008)
41.	Lyubov Ratsu (URS)	4714 (1985)
42.	Olga Levenkova (RUS)	4713 (2006)
43.	Yelena Prokhorova (RUS)	4711 (2001)
44.	Kendell Williams (USA)	4703 (2016)
45.	Claudia Salman-Rath (GER)	4688 (2016)

Marathon Women

EUROPEAN CHAMPIONSHIPS 2018: 12-8-2018:

1.	Volha Mazuronak (BLR)	2.26.22
2.	Clémence Calvin (FRA)	2.26.28
3.	Eva Vrabcova-Nývltová (CZE)	2.26.31
4.	Maryna Damantsevich (BLR)	2.27.44
5.	Nastassia Ivanova (BLR)	2.27.49
6.	Sara Dossena (ITA)	2.27.53
7.	Martina Strähl (SUI)	2.28.07
8.	Catherine Bertone (ITA)	2.30.06
9.	Trihas Gebre (ESP)	2.32.13
10.	Izabela Trzaskalska (POL)	2.33.43
11.	Fabienne Amrhein (GER)	2.33.44
12.	Nina Savina (BLR)	2.33.50
13.	Maria Díaz (ESP)	2.34.00
14.	Fatna Maraoui (ITA)	2.34.48
15.	Tracy Barlow (GBR)	2.35.00
16.	Katharina Heinig (GER)	2.35.00
17.	Mikaela Larsson (SWE)	2.35.06
18.	Ruth van der Meijden (NED)	2.35.44
19.	Olha Kotovska (UKR)	2.35.56
20.	Bojana Bjeljac (CRO)	2.37.31
21.	Sonia Samuels (GBR)	2.37.36
22.	Hanna Lindholm (SWE)	2.37.44
23.	Elena Loyo (ESP)	2.37.54
24.	Marta Galimany (ESP)	2.38.25
25.	Darya Mykhaylova (UKR)	2.38.30
26.	Glória Privilétzio (GRE)	2.38.39
27.	Milda Eimonte (LTU)	2.38.58
28.	Laura Hrebec (SUI)	2.39.03
29.	Lizzie Lee (IRL)	2.40.12
30.	Caryl Jones (GBR)	2.40.41
	Lily Partridge (GBR)	dnf
	Charlotte Purdue (GBR)	dnf

WORLD RANKING 2018:

1.	Gladys Cherono Kiprono (KEN)	2.18.11(Ber)
2.	Vivian Jepkemoi Cheruiyot (KEN)	2.18.31(Lon)
3.	Ruti Aga (ETH)	2.18.34(Ber)
4.	Brigid Kosgei (KEN)	2.18.35(Chi)
	Ruth Chepngetich (KEN)	2.18.35(Ist)
6.	Tirunesh Dibaba (ETH)	2.18.55(Ber)
7.	Roza Dereje (ETH)	2.19.17(Dub)
8.	Boru Feyse Tadese (ETH)	2.19.30(Dub)
9.	Yebrgual Melese (ETH)	2.19.36(Dub)
10.	Birhane Dibaba (ETH)	2.19.51(Tok)
11.	Debele Degafa (ETH)	2.19.53(Dub)
12.	Haftamnesh Tesfaye (ETH)	2.20.13(Dub)
13.	Meskerem Assefa (ETH)	2.20.36(Fra)
14.	Gelete Burka (ETH)	2.20.45(Dub)
15.	Ashete Dido (ETH)	2.21.14(Val)
16.	Edna Neringwony Kiplagat (KEN)	2.21.18(Ber)
17.	Bedatu Hirpa (ETH)	2.21.32(Fra)
18.	Valary Jemeli (KEN)	2.21.38(Bei)
19.	Tadelech Bekele Alemu (ETH)	2.21.40(Lon)
20.	Amy Cragg (USA)	2.21.42(Tok)
21.	Dera Dida (ETH)	2.21.45(Dub)
22.	Azmera Abreha (ETH)	2.21.51(Sha)
23.	Belaynesh Oljira (ETH)	2.21.53(Fra)
24.	Shure Demise Ware (ETH)	2.22.07(Tok)
25.	Lydia Cheromei (KEN)	2.22.11(Val)
26.	Mizuki Matsuda (JPN)	2.22.23(Ber)
27.	Mimi Belete (BRN)	2.22.29(Tor)
28.	Marta Megra (ETH)	2.22.35(Tor)
29.	Sentayehu Lewetegn (ETH)	2.22.45(Fra)
30.	Nancy Jepkosgei Kiprop (KEN)	2.22.46(Fra)
31.	Helen Tola (ETH)	2.22.48(Ber)
	Mary Jepkosgei Keitany (KEN)	2.22.48(NY)
33.	Betsy Saina (KEN)	2.22.56(Par)
34.	Visiline Jepkesho (KEN)	2.22.58(Lju)
35.	Gulume Chala (ETH)	2.23.06(Par)
36.	Hanami Sekine (JPN)	2.23.07(Nag)
37.	Selly Chepyego Kaptich (KEN)	2.23.15(Lju)
38.	Shashi Insermu (ETH)	2.23.28(Ams)
39.	Ruth Chebitok (KEN)	2.23.29(Tor)
40.	Azmera Gebru (ETH)	2.23.31(Ams)
41.	Dibabe Kuma (ETH)	2.23.34(Lju)
42.	Tinbit Weldegebril (ETH)	2.23.37(Val)
43.	Desi Jisa Mokonin (BRN)	2.23.39(Ams)
44.	Betty Lembus (KEN)	2.23.40(Sha)

Xiamen, 7-1-2018:
1. Fatuma Sado (ETH)   2.26.41
2. Hirut Gebremichael Alemayehu (ETH) 2.30.09
3. Meseret Mengistu (ETH)   2.30.15

Houston, 14-1-2018:
1. Biruktayit Eshetu (ETH)   2.24.51
2. Belaynesh Oljira (ETH)   2.24.57
3. Tsegaye Meselech (ETH)   2.27.21
4. Gladys Kipsoi (KEN)   2.27.32
5. Yetsehay Desalegn (ETH)   2.32.00
6. Veronica Nyaruai (KEN)   2.32.06

Mumbai, 21-1-2018:
1. Amane Godena (ETH)   2.25.49
2. Bornes Chrpkirui (KEN)   2.28.48
3. Shuko Genemo (ETH)   2.29.41
4. Birke Debele (ETH)   2.29.45

Hongkong, 21-1-2018:
1. Gulume Chala (ETH)   2.29.37
2. Meskerem Assefa (ETH)   2.29.42
3. Fantu Jimma (ETH)   2.30.10
4. Betelhem Moges (ETH)   2.30.54
5. Meseret Legese (ETH)   2.31.00
6. Lucy Kabuu Wangui (KEN)   2.31.21

Dubai, 26-1-2018:
1. Roza Dereje Bekele (ETH)   2.19.17
2. Boru Feyse Tadese (ETH)   2.19.30
3. Yebrgual Melese (ETH)   2.19.36
4. Debele Degafa (ETH)   2.19.53
5. Haftamnesh Tesfaye (ETH)   2.20.13
6. Gelete Burka (ETH)   2.20.45
7. Dera Dida (ETH)   2.21.45
8. Desi Jisa Mokonin (BRN)   2.24.05
9. Senbere Teferi (ETH)   2.24.11
10. Muliye Dekebo (ETH)   2.26.52
11. Genet Yalew (ETH)   2.27.46
12. Azmera Abreha (ETH)   2.28.12
13. Anne-Marie Hyryläinen (FIN)   2.28.53

Osaka. 28-1-2018:
1. Mizuki Matsuda (JPN)   2.22.44
2. Honami Maeda (JPN)   2.23.48
3. Yuka Ando (JPN)   2.27.37
4. Anja Scherl (GER)   2.29.29
5. Kaori Yoshida (JPN)   2.29.53
6. Mari Ozaki (JPN)   2.30.03
7. Gladys Tejeda (PER)   2.30.44
8. Hitomi Mizuguchi (JPN)   2.33.10
9. Asami Furuse (JPN)   2.33.58
10. Ayano Ikemitsu (JPN)   2.36.18

Marrakesh, 28-1-2018:
1. Tinbit Weldegebril (ETH)   2.26.48
2. Truphena Chepchirchir (KEN)   2.28.11
3. Ruth Wanjiru (KEN)   2.28.27
4. Nurit Ymam Shimels (ETH)   2.28.41
5. Mulunesh Zewdu (ETH)   2.32.14
6. Ruth Matebo (KEN)   2.32.15

Sevilla, 25-2-2018:
1. Kawtar Boulaid (MAR)   2.25.35
2. Haimanot Alemayehu (ETH)   2.25.51
3. Bedatu Hirpa (ETH)   2.25.54
4. Zinash Debebe Getachew (ETH)   2.27.47
5. Sechale Dalasa Adugna (ETH)   2.29.21
6. Giovanna Epis (ITA)   2.29.41
7. Marta Esteban (ESP)   2.31.24

Tokyo, 25-2-2018:
1. Birhane Dibaba (ETH)   2.19.51
2. Ruti Aga (ETH)   2.21.19
3. Amy Cragg (USA)   2.21.42
4. Shure Demise Ware (ETH)   2.22.07
5. Helah Jelagat Kiprop (KEN)   2.28.58
6. Hiroko Yoshitomi (JPN)   2.30.16
7. Madoka Nakano (JPN)   2.31.41
8. Mao Uesugi (JPN)   2.31.49
9. Marie Imada (JPN)   2.32.00
10. Zhang Meixia (CHN)   2.33.02

Barcelona, 11-3-2018:
1. Ruth Chebitok (KEN)   2.25.49
2. Belaynesh Tsegaye (ETH)   2.27.08
3. Worknesh Mola Alemu (ETH)   2.28.19
4. Alemitu Abera Begna (ETH)   2.30.55

Nagoya, 11-3-2018:

1.	Meskerem Assefa (ETH)	2.21.45
2.	Valary Jemeli (KEN)	2.22.48
3.	Hanami Sekine (JPN)	2.23.07
4.	Rea Iwade (JPN)	2.26.28
5.	Keiko Nogami (JPN)	2.26.33
6.	Hanae Tanaka (JPN)	2.27.40
7.	Merima Mohammed (BRN)	2.27.41
8.	Rei Ohara (JPN)	2.27.44
9.	Mao Kiyota (JPN)	2.28.58
10.	Misaki Kato (JPN)	2.29.22
11.	Yurie Doi (JPN)	2.29.49
12.	Michi Numata (JPN)	2.30.07
13.	Ayaka Inoue (JPN)	2.30.43
14.	Karolina Jarzynska (POL)	2.30.46
15.	Sairi Maeda (JPN)	2.30.54

Seoul, 18-3-2018:

1.	Hirut Tibebu (ETH)	2.24.08
2.	Margaret Agai (KEN)	2.24.30
3.	Monica Jepkoech (KEN)	2.24.31
4.	Mulu Seboka (ETH)	2.25.01
5.	Do-Yeon Kim (KOR)	2.25.41
6.	Mercy Kibarus (KEN)	2.27.06
7.	Gutemi Shone Imana (ETH)	2.27.53
8.	Jane Chelagat (KEN)	2.30.13
9.	Gong Lihua (CHN)	2.31.05
10.	Munkhzaya Bayartsogt (MGL)	2.31.12

Daegu, 1-4-2018:

1.	Janet Jelagat Rono (KEN)	2.28.01
2.	Seul-Ki Ahn (KOR)	2.28.17
3.	Pamela Rotich (KEN)	2.28.45
4.	Winny Jepkorir (KEN)	2.28.49
5.	Souad Kabouchia (MAR)	2.31.53

Rotterdam, 8-4-2018:

1.	Visiline Jepkesho (KEN)	2.23.47
2.	Biruktayit Eshetu (ETH)	2.26.56
3.	Sentayehu Lewetegn (ETH)	2.30.29
4.	Joan Jepchirchir (KEN)	2.30.33
5.	Sifan Melaku (ETH)	2.33.40

Paris, 8-4-2018:

1.	Betsy Saina (KEN)	2.22.56
2.	Ruth Chepngetich (KEN)	2.22.59
3.	Gulume Chala (ETH)	2.23.06
4.	Ashete Dido Bekele (ETH)	2.23.27
5.	Stella Barsosio (KEN)	2.23.43
6.	Marta Megra (ETH)	2.24.08
7.	Abebech Afework (ETH)	2.25.02
8.	Yuka Takashima (JPN)	2.26.13
9.	Desi Jisa Mokonin (BRN)	2.31.30
10.	Kasumi Yoshida (JPN)	2.38.15

Rome, 8-4-2018:

1.	Rahma Tusa (ETH)	2.23.46
2.	Dalila Abdulkadir (BRN)	2.26.46
3.	Alice Jepkemboi Kibor (KEN)	2.28.19
4.	Sharon Jemutai Cherop (KEN)	2.29.26
5.	Jemila Wortesa Shure (ETH)	2.32.00

Milano, 8-4-2018:

1.	Lucy Kabuu Wangui (KEN)	2.27.02
2.	Vivian Jerono Kiplagat (KEN)	2.27.08
3.	Sheila Chepkech (KEN)	2.29.25
4.	Dorist Chepkwemoi Changeywo (KEN) 2.29.49	

Pyongyang, 8-4-2018:

1.	Hye-Gyong Kim (PRK)	2.27.31
2.	Un-Ok Jo (PRK)	2.27.42
3.	Kwang-Ok Ri (PRK)	2.27.55
4.	Ran Jong (PRK)	2.31.22
5.	Biruk Konjit Tilahun (ETH)	2.31.39
6.	Son-Hui Kim (PRK)	2.31.41
7.	Kim-Ok Hyang (PRK)	2.31.56

Boston, 18-4-2018:

1.	Desiree Linden (USA)	2.39.54
2.	Sarah Sellers (USA)	2.44.04
3.	Krista Duchene (CAN)	2.44.20
4.	Rachel Hyland (USA)	2.44.29
5.	Jessica Chichester (USA)	2.45.23
6.	Nicole Dimercurio (USA)	2.45.52
7.	Shalane Flanagan (USA)	2.46.31
8.	Kimi Reed (USA)	2.46.47
9.	Edna Kiplagat (KEN)	2.47.14
10.	Hiroko Yoshitomi (JPN)	2.48.29

London, 22-4-2018:
1. Vivian Jepkemoi Cheruiyot (KEN) 2.18.31
2. Brigid Jepcheschir Kosgei (KEN) 2.20.13
3. Tadelech Bekele Alemu (ETH) 2.21.40
4. Gladys Cherono (KEN) 2.24.10
5. Mary Jepkosgei Keitany (KEN) 2.24.27
6. Rose Chelimo (BRN) 2.26.03
7. Mare Dibaba (ETH) 2.27.45
8. Lily Partridge (GBR) 2.29.24
9. Tracy Barlow (GBR) 2.32.09
10. Stephanie Bruce (USA) 2.32.28

Wien, 22-4-2018:
1. Nancy Jepkosgei Kiprop (KEN) 2.24.18
2. Tsegaye Melesech (ETH) 2.29.51
3. Celestine Jepchirchir (KEN) 2.30.39
4. Fatuma Sado (ETH) 2.32.18
5. Askale Alemayehu (ETH) 2.32.47

Warszawa, 22-4-2018:
1. Nastassia Ivanova (BLR) 2.28.03
2. Azmera Abreha (ETH) 2.28.07
3. Izabela Trzaskalska (POL) 2.32.26

Hamburg, 29-4-2018:
1. Shitaye Eshete (BRN) 2.24.51
2. Birke Debele (ETH) 2.25.28
3. Mimi Belete (BRN) 2.26.06
4. Sylvia Jebiwot Kibet (KEN) 2.30.27

Düsseldorf, 29-4-2018:
1. Volha Mazuronak (BLR) 2.25.25
2. Fabienne Amrhein (GER) 2.32.35

Dongying, 5-5-2018:
1. Letebrhan Haylay Gebreslasea (ETH) 2.24.47
2. Yebrgual Melese (ETH) 2.27.47
3. Peris Jerono (KEN) 2.28.27
4. Rael Nguriatukei Kinyara (KEN) 2.31.06
5. Caroline Cheptanui Kilel (KEN) 2.34.39

Praha, 6-5-2018:
1. Bornes Chepkirui (KEN) 2.24.19
2. Belaynesh Oljira (ETH) 2.25.13
3. Amane Gobena (ETH) 2.27.43
4. Risper Chebet (KEN) 2.29.32
5. Susan Kipsang Jeptoo (KEN) 2.30.50
6. Filomena Chepchirchir (KEN) 2.32.10

Ottawa, 27-5-2018:
1. Gelete Burka (ETH) 2.22.17
2. Hiwot Gebrekidan (ETH) 2.26.11
3. Sara Hall (USA) 2.26.20

Gold Coast, 1-7-2018:
1. Ruth Chebitok (KEN) 2.24.49
2. Jessica Trengova (AUS) 2.26.31
3. Agnes Jeruto Kiprotich (KEN) 2.27.46
   (= Barsosio)

Berlin, 16-9-2018:
1. Gladys Cherono Kiprono (KEN) 2.18.11
2. Ruti Aga (ETH) 2.18.34
3. Tirunesh Dibaba (ETH) 2.18.55
4. Edna Ngeringwony Kiplagat (KEN) 2.21.18
5. Mizuki Matsuda (JPN) 2.22.23
6. Helen Tola (ETH) 2.22.48
7. Honami Maeda (JPN) 2.25.23
8. Carla Salome Rocha (POR) 2.25.27
9. Miyuki Uehara (JPN) 2.25.46
10. Rei Ohara (JPN) 2.27.29
11. Rachel Cliff (CAN) 2.28.53
12. Lyndsay Tessier (CAN) 2.30.47
13. Inés Melchor (PER) 2.32.09
14. Andrea Deelstra (NED) 2.32.41

Beijing, 16-9-2018:
1. Valary Jemeli (KEN) 2.21.38
2. Eunice Chebichi Chumba (BRN) 2.26.56
3. Fatuma Sado (ETH) 2.27.41
4. Tejitu Daba (BRN) 2.28.50
5. He Yinli (CHN) 2.31.45
6. Li Zhixuan (CHN) 2.31.59

Buenos Aires, 23-9-2018:
1. Vivian Kiplagat Jerono (KEN)   2.29.03
2. Leah Jerotich (KEN)   2.32.58
3. Amelework Fekadu Bosho (ETH)   2.34.56

Cape Town, 23-9-2018:
1. Helalia Johannes (NAM)   2.29.28
2. Failuna Matanga (TAN)   2.30.00
3. Urge Diro Sokoka (ETH)   2.30.31
4. Ayantu Gemechu Abdi (ETH)   2.31.33
5. Askale Alemayehu Adula (ETH)   2.31.34
6. Ellie Pashley (AUS)   2.31.52

Hengshui, 29-9-2018:
1. Waganesh Mekasha (ETH)   2.25.57
2. Workenesh Edesa (ETH)   2.26.28
3. Gebeyanesh Ayele (ETH)   2.26.54
4. Maureen Chepkemoi (KEN)   2.27.12
5. Sichala Kumeshi (ETH)   2.30.28
6. Caroline Cheptanui Kilel (KEN)   2.31.29
7. Mirriam Wangari (KEN)   2.31.36

Chicago, 7-10-2018:
1. Brigid Jepcheschir Kosgei (KEN)   2.18.35
2. Roza Dereje Bekele (ETH)   2.21.18
3. Shure Demise Ware (ETH)   2.22.15
4. Florence Kiplagat (KEN)   2.26.08
5. Veronicah Nyaruai (KEN)   2.31.34
6. Sarah Crouch Porter (USA)   2.32.37
7. Taylor Ward (USA)   2.32.42
8. Kate Landau (USA)   2.33.26
9. Melanie Myrand (CAN)   2.34.08
10. Marci Klimek (USA)   2.34.53

Kosice, 7-10-2018:
1. Miliam Nakt Ebongon (KEN)   2.27.16
2. Sheila Jerotich (KEN)   2.29.40
3. Jemila Wortesa Shure (ETH)   2.32.32

Amsterdam, 21-10-2018:
1. Tadelech Bekele Alemu (ETH)   2.23.14
2. Shasho Insermu (ETH)   2.23.28
3. Azmera Gebru (ETH)   2.23.31
4. Desi Jisa Mokonin (BRN)   2.23.39
5. Linet Chepkwemoi Masai (KEN)   2.23.46
6. Jackline Chepngeno (KEN)   2.24.38
7. Zinash Mekonen (ETH)   2.25.55
8. Meseret Defar (ETH)   2.27.25
9. Miharu Shimokado (JPN)   2.34.11
10. Sisay Meseret Gola (ETH)   2.34.15

Toronto, 21-10-2018:
1. Mimi Belete (BRN)   2.22.29
2. Marta Megra (ETH)   2.22.35
3. Ruth Chebitok (KEN)   2.23.29
4. Jessica Trengove (AUS)   2.25.59
5. Celestine Chepchirchir (KEN)   2.26.58
6. Amane Beriso Shankule (ETH)   2.28.56
7. Kinsey Middleton (CAN)   2.32.09
8. Helen Davies-Decker (GBR)   2.35.12
9. Leslie Sexton (CAN)   2.36.03
10. Krista Duchene (CAN)   2.36.46

Frankfurt, 28-10-2018:
1. Meskerem Assefa Wondimagegn (ETH) 2.20.36
2. Haftamnesh Tesfaye Haylu (ETH)   2.20.47
3. Bedatu Hirpa Badane (ETH)   2.21.32
4. Belaynesh Oljira Jemama (ETH)   2.21.53
5. Dera Dida Yami (ETH)   2.22.39
6. Sentayehu Lewetegn Hailemichael (ETH) 2.22.45
7. Nancy Jepkosgei Kiprop (KEN)   2.22.46
8. Betsy Chepkemboi Saina (KEN)   2.24.35
9. Stellah Jepngetich Barsosio (KEN)   2.25.00
10. Abebech Afework Bekele (ETH)   2.25.17
11. Mare Dibaba Hurssa (ETH)   2.25.24
12. Worknesh Alemu Mola (ETH)   2.26.50
13. Lindsay Flanagan (USA)   2.29.25
14. Katharina Heinig (GER)   2.29.55
15. Valdilene dos Santos (BRA)   2.32.01

Ljubljana, 28-10-2018:
1. Visiline Jepkesho (KEN)   2.22.58
2. Selly Chepyego Kaptich (KEN)   2.23.15
3. Dibabe Kuma (ETH)   2.23.34
4. Sharon Jemutai Cherop (KEN)   2.25.02
5. Shuko Genemo Wote (ETH)   2.26.10
6. Lilia Fisikovici (MDA)   2.28.26
7. Sutume Asefa Kebede (ETH)   2.29.45

New York, 4-11-2018:
1. Mary Jepkosgei Keitany (KEN)   2.22.48
2. Vivian Jepkemoi Cheruiyot (KEN)   2.26.02
3. Shalane Flanagan (USA)   2.26.22
4. Molly Huddle (USA)   2.26.44
5. Rahma Tusa (ETH)   2.27.13
6. Desiree Davila-Linden (USA)   2.27.51
7. Allie Kiefer (USA)   2.28.12
8. Lisa Weightman (AUS)   2.29.11
9. Mamitu Daska (ETH)   2.30.31
10. Belaynesh Fikadu (ETH)   2.30.47
11. Stephanie Bruce (USA)   2.30.59
12. Roberta Groner (USA)   2.31.01
13. Gerda Steyn (RSA)   2.31.04
14. Carrie Dimoff (USA)   2.31.12
15. Samantha Bluske (USA)   2.32.04
16. Sydney Devore (USA)   2.32.43

Hangzhou, 4-11-2018:
1. Hirut Tibebu (ETH)   2.25.10
2. Yetsehay Desalegn (ETH)   2.27.35
3. Sifan Melaku (ETH)   2.31.47

Istanbul, 11-11-2018:
1. Ruth Chepngetich (KEN)   2.18.35
2. Margaret Agai (KEN)   2.25.04
3. Fatuma Sado (ETH)   2.31.05

Beirut, 11-11-2018:
1. Medina Deme Armino (ETH)   2.29.31
2. Nazret Weldu (ERI)   2.29.48
3. Selamawit Getnet Tsegaw (ETH)   2.31.42
4. Ednah Mukhwana (KEN)   2.31.53

Hefei, 11-11-2018:
1. Magdalene Masai (KEN)   2.28.22
2. Racheal Mutgaa (KEN)   2.28.39
3. Aberash Fayesa (ETH)   2.29.05

Shanghai, 18-11-2018:
1. Yebrgual Melese (ETH)   2.20.36
2. Azmera Abreha (ETH)   2.21.51
3. Betty Lembus (KEN)   2.23.40
4. Afera Godfay (ETH)   2.23.54
5. Muluhabt Tsega Chekol (ETH)   2.25.48
6. Alemu Megertu (ETH)   2.28.08

Firenze, 25-11-2018:
1. Loah Chemtai Salpeter (ISR)   2.24.17
2. Caroline Chepkwony (KEN)   2.30.46
3. Clemantine Mukandanga (RWA)   2.30.59

Valencia, 2-12-2018:
1. Ashete Bekere Dido (ETH)   2.21.14
2. Lydia Cheromei (KEN)   2.22.11
3. Tinbit Gidey Weldegebril (ETH)   2.23.37
4. Aberu Mekuria Zennebe (ETH)   2.24.35
5. Ana Dulce Felix (POR)   2.25.24
6. Pamela Jepkosgei Rotich (KEN)   2.29.47
7. Stephanie Twell (GBR)   2.30.14
8. Valeria Straneo (ITA)   2.30.26
9. Hanna Lindholm (SWE)   2.30.37
10. Demisei Fadisu Mulu (ETH)   2.34.23

Abu Dhabi, 7-12-2018: (course too short?):
1. Ababel Yeshaneh Birhane (ETH)   2.20.16
2. Eunice Chebichii Chumba (BRN)   2.20.54
3. Gelete Burka Bati (ETH)   2.24.07
4. Chaltu Tafa Waka (ETH)   2.25.09
5. Caroline Cheptonui Kiliel (KEN)   2.29.14
6. Genet Yalew Kassahun (ETH)   2.31.34

Guangzhou, 9-12-2018:
1. Tigist Girma (ETH)   2.26.44
2. Zinash Debebe (ETH)   2.27.15
3. Sviatlana Kudzelich (BLR) 2.32.04

Saitama, 9-12-2018:
1. Dalila Gosa Abdulkadir (BRN)   2.25.35
2. Shitaye Eshete (BRN)   2.25.39
3. Sylvia Jebiwot Kibet (KEN)   2.28.38
4. Marie Imada (JPN)   2.29.35
5. Mao Kiyota (JPN)   2.31.07
6. Saki Tokoro (JPN)   2.32.11

Shenzhen, 16-12-2018:
1. Mulu Seboka (ETH)   2.27.12
2. Flomena Chepchirchir (KEN)   2.32.05
3. Ashu Kasim (ETH)   2.38.35

OVERVIEW WORLD OUTDOOR CHAMPIONSHIP FINALISTS OF PAST 6 YEARS

	Wch 17	OG 16	Wch 15	Wch 13
Rose Chelimo (BRN)	2.27.11 (1)	2.27.36 (8)		
Edna Kiplagat (KEN)	2.27.18 (2)		2.28.18 (5)	2.25.44 (1)
Amy Cragg (USA)	2.27.18 (3)	2.28.25 (9)		
Flomena Daniel (KEN)	2.27.21 (4)			
Shure Demise (ETH)	2.27.58 (5)			
Eunice Kirwa (BRN)	2.28.17 (6)	2.24.13 (2)	2.27.39 (3)	
Helah Kiprop (KEN)	2.28.19 (7)		2.27.36 (2)	
Mare Dibaba (ETH)	2.28.49 (8)	2.24.30 (3)	2.27.35 (1)	
Jessica Trengove (AUS)	2.28.59 (9)			
Berhane Dibaba (ETH)	2.29.01 (10)			
Jemima Sumgong (KEN)		2.24.04 (1)	2.27.42 (4)	
Tirfi Tsegaye (ETH)		2.24.47 (4)	2.30.54 (8)	
Volha Mazuronak (BLR)		2.24.48 (5)		
Shalane Flanagan (USA)		2.25.26 (6)		
Desiree Linden (USA)		2.26.08 (7)		
Hye-Song Kim (PRK)		2.28.36 (10)	2.30.59 (9)	
Tigist Tufa (ETH)			2.29.12 (6)	
Mai Ito (JPN)			2.29.48 (7)	
Serena Burla (USA)			2.31.06 (10)	
Valeria Straneo (ITA)				2.25.58 (2)
Kayoko Fukushi (JPN)				2.27.45 (3)
Ryoko Kizaki (JPN)				2.31.28 (4)
Alessandra Aguilar (ESP)				2.32.38 (5)
Emma Quaglia (ITA)				2.34.16 (6)
Madaí Pérez (MEX)				2.34.23 (7)
Hye-Gyong Kim (PRK)				2.35.49 (8)
Deena Kastor (USA)				2.36.12 (9)
Susan Partridge (GBR)				2.36.24 (10)

OVERVIEW TOP 10 WORLD OUTDOOR RANKINGS OF PAST 5 YEARS

	2018	2017	2016	2015	2014
Gladys Cherono Kiprono (KEN)	2.18.11 (1)	2.20.23 (5)		2.19.25 (1)	
Vivian Jepkemoi Cheruiyot (KEN)	2.18.31 (2)				
Ruti Aga (ETH)	2.18.34 (3)	2.20.41 (6)			
Brigid Kosgei (KEN)	2.18.35 (4)	2.20.22 (4)			
Ruth Chepngetich (KEN)	2.18.35 (4)				
Tirunesh Dibaba (ETH)	2.18.55 (6)	2.17.56 (2)			2.20.35 (5)
Roza Dereje (ETH)	2.19.17 (7)				
Boru Feyse Tadese (ETH)	2.19.30 (8)				
Yebrgual Melese (ETH)	2.19.36 (9)				
Birhane Dibaba (ETH)	2.19.51 (10)				2.22.30 (10)
Mary Keitany (KEN)		2.17.01 (1)			
Sarah Chepchirchir (KEN)		2.19.47 (3)			
Valary Aiyabei (KEN)		2.20.53 (7)			
Purity Rionoripo (KEN)		2.20.55 (8)			
Jordan Hasay (USA)		2.20.57 (9)			
Agnes Barsosio (KEN)		2.20.59 (10)			
Tirfi Tsegaye (ETH)			2.19.41 (1)		2.20.18 (1)
Aberu Kebede (ETH)			2.20.45 (2)	2.20.48 (5)	2.22.21 (9)
Amane Beriso (ETH)			2.20.48 (3)		
Helah Kiprop (KEN)			2.21.27 (4)		
Florence Kiplagat (KEN)			2.21.32 (5)		2.20.24 (3)
Amane Gobena (ETH)			2.21.51 (6)		
Meselech Melkamu (ETH)			2.21.54 (7)		
Kayoko Fukushi (JPN)			2.22.17 (8)		
Edna Kiplagat (KEN)			2.22.36 (9)		2.20.21 (2)
Eunice Kirwa (BRN)			2.22.40 (10)	2.22.08 (8)	
Mare Dibaba (ETH)				2.19.52 (2)	2.21.36 (7)
Aselefech Mergia (ETH)				2.20.02 (3)	
Lucy Kabuu (KEN)				2.20.21 (4)	
Shure Demise (ETH)				2.20.59 (6)	
Mulu Seboka (ETH)				2.21.56 (7)	
Tetiana Shmyrko (UKR)				2.22.09 (9)	
Sairi Maeda (JPN)				2.22.48 (10)	
Feyse Tadese (ETH)					2.20.27 (4)
Shalane Flanagan (USA)					2.21.14 (6)
Tigist Tufa (ETH)					2.21.52 (8)

WORLD RANKING ALL TIME:

1.	Paula Radcliffe (GBR)	2.15.25 (2003)
2.	Mary Jepkosgei Keitany (KEN)	2.17.01 (2017)
3.	Tirunesh Dibaba (ETH)	2.17.56 (2017)
4.	Gladys Cherono Kiprono (KEN)	2.18.11 (2018)
5.	Vivian Jepkemoi Cheruiyot (KEN)	2.18.31 (2018)
6.	Ruti Aga (KEN)	2.18.34 (2018)
7.	Brigid Chepchirchir Kosgei (KEN)	2.18.35 (2018)
	Ruth Chepngetich (KEN)	2.18.35 (2018)
9.	Catherine Ndereba (KEN)	2.18.47 (2001)
10.	Erba Tiki Gelana (ETH)	2.18.58 (2012)
11.	Mizuki Noguchi (JPN)	2.19.12 (2005)
12.	Roza Dereje (ETH)	2.19.17 (2018)
13.	Irina Mikitenko (GER)	2.19.19 (2008)
14.	Boru Feyse Tadese (ETH)	2.19.30 (2018)
15.	Asselefech Medessa Mergia (ETH)	2.19.31 (2012)
16.	Lucy Kabuu Wangui (KEN)	2.19.34 (2012)
17.	Deena Kastor (USA)	2.19.36 (2006)
	Yebrgual Melese (ETH)	2.19.36 (2018)
19.	Sun Yingjie (CHN)	2.19.39 (2003)
20.	Yoko Shibui (JPN)	2.19.41 (2004)
	Tirfi Tsegaye (ETH)	2.19.41 (2016)
22.	Florence Kiplagat (KEN)	2.19.44 (2011)
23.	Naoko Takahashi (JPN)	2.19.46 (2001)
24.	Sarah Chepchirchir (KEN)	2.19.47 (2017)
25.	Edna Ngeringwony Kiplagat (KEN)	2.19.50 (2012)
26.	Zhou Chunxiu (CHN)	2.19.51 (2006)
	Birhane Dibaba (ETH)	2.19.51 (2018)
28.	Mare Dibaba (ETH)	2.19.52 (2012)
29.	Debele Degafa (ETH)	2.19.53 (2018)
30.	Rita Jeptoo Sitienei (KEN)	2.19.57 (2013)
31.	Haftamnesh Tesfaye (ETH)	2.20.13 (2018)
32.	Prisca Jeptoo (KEN)	2.20.14 (2012)
33.	Bezunesh Bekele (ETH)	2.20.30 (2012)
	Aberu Kebede (ETH)	2.20.30 (2012)
35.	Meskerem Assefa (ETH)	2.20.36 (2018)
36.	Berhane Adere (ETH)	2.20.42 (2006)
37.	Tegla Loroupe (KEN)	2.20.43 (1999)
38.	Gelete Burka (ETH)	2.20.45 (2018)
39.	Galina Bogomolova (RUS)	2.20.47 (2006)
40.	Jemima Jelagat Sumgong (KEN)	2.20.48 (2013)
	Amane Beriso Shankule (ETH)	2.20.48 (2016)
42.	Valary Jemeli Aiyabei (KEN)	2.20.53 (2017)
43.	Purity Cherotich Rionoripo (KEN)	2.20.55 (2017)
44.	Jordan Hasay (USA)	2.20.57 (2017)
45.	Shure Demise Ware (ETH)	2.20.59 (2015)
	Agnes Jeruto Barsosio (KEN)	2.20.59 (2017)

Colofon

Author: Ton van Vuuren

Title: Athletics Rankings and Results 2018 in historical perspective

Publisher: Ervala

Editor: Miriam Bondt

Copyright   © Ton van Vuuren, 2019

First Edition

Disclaimer

Printed in Great Britain
by Amazon